MANAGEMENT POLICY, STRATEGY, AND PLANS

MILTON LEONTIADES
Rutgers University

LITTLE, BROWN AND COMPANY
Boston
Toronto

To Susan, Lora, and J.R.

Library of Congress Catalog Card No. 80–85436

ISBN 0–316–521043

9 8 7 6 5 4 3 2 1

VB

Published simultaneously in Canada
by Little, Brown & Company (Canada) Limited

Printed in the United States of America

Preface

This book was written for both undergraduate and graduate courses. Business policy is considered here as planning for a firm's performance in three phases: policy (overview), strategy (strategic alternatives), and plans (tactical support). Within this framework of planning, several complicating elements interact: steady-state versus evolutionary management style, business-level versus corporate-level planning, and single-business versus multibusiness organizations. Discussing these factors illuminates yet complicates the total planning perspective. To help you guide the student through this rich texture, I include a simplified conceptual model of an integrated planning system. This multidimensional view of planning heightens the student's appreciation for the very great complexities in planning.

Although I cover here the basic concepts of the field, the subjects I emphasize in some areas are relatively unique. Unrelated acquisitions as a strategy for diversification, for example, are given more than typical coverage, because they have been an important means for restructuring American companies. A viable theory of business cannot ignore them. Financial analysis of companies also is stressed in a comprehensive appendix. This section is included because it has been my experience that students are often unprepared to interpret basic financial statements. Finally, managerial values and perceptions are viewed as critical in the ultimate choices of policy, strategy, and plans and therefore the ultimate success or failure of individual businesses. This view does not exclude other important factors like environmental change, strategies of competitors, and economic conditions, but I do pay more attention to the managerial elements than do authors of more traditional textbooks. The emphasis, in short, makes this textbook different from others, though the range of topics may be similar.

The book provides two main features: flexibility and an innovative approach, with its focus on special topics and its reality-based theme. For some students, combining questions and mini-exercises at the end of each chapter is a useful technique for elaborating on theory; for others, taking the supplemental readings together with the more difficult cases may be an appropriate combination.

Teaching methods for this course have less formal structure and permit greater latitude than do older, more traditional courses. Policy instructors who are specialists in one or more of the other business disciplines often approach the course with a unique orientation. To provide for diverse teaching methods, I include a number of "extra" features. Some or all of these may be used, depending on your approach, giving you greater flexibility in designing the course: (1) questions at the end of each chapter; (2) mini-exercises at the end of each chapter; (3) supplementary reading references at the end of each chapter; (4) an appendix on financial analysis for use in case evaluations; (5) a note on methods for evaluating cases; (6) a large and balanced mix of cases — the majority are published here for the first time; (7) four short cases integrated within the text in order to illustrate complex aspects of theory. Also, an instructor's manual is available. This supplement is more extensive than others in the way it covers the more difficult cases in the text. Several thoroughgoing student solutions to those cases are included.

If the theory of business policy is rooted in the practice of business firms, it follows that we should be able to find real situations that explain and illustrate theory. Throughout this text, theory is reinforced with practice. Whenever possible, connections are drawn between what is feasible and what is fact. And all through the text I have integrated references to companies whose situations illustrate the concepts of policy, strategy, and plans. A balanced selection of cases uses actual companies and industries. Finally, the perspective for the student is management of the entire enterprise, but the focus is on the chief planning officer, not the chief executive officer. This identity is more realistic for most students, yet it retains the broad corporate overview inherent in the business policy course.

In sum, this textbook is designed to innovate and create within established boundaries of the field, and yet provide students with a reality-based framework for analyzing management policy, strategy, and plans.

Contents

INTRODUCTION
A Conceptual Framework for Decision Making

The Decision Process: Policy, Strategy, and Plans

This is a book about decision making in business. More specifically, it covers three connected sequences in decision making: proceeding from the statement of overall management policy, to the development of strategy, and ultimately to the detailed plans that elaborate on strategy and policy. The emphasis is on the formulation of policies, strategies, and plans, although, as Exhibit I.1 implies, successful performance relies on implementation as well as formulation.

Before proceeding to in-depth coverage of each phase in this decision-making process, we shall need a clarifying set of definitions, because many definitions of the terms "policy" and "strategy" have been used by various authors.[1] For example, "policies" and "strategies" both refer to broad characterizations of long-range organizational aims. Depending on the context, meanings can overlap, with distinctions increasingly difficult to draw. One

THE DECISION PROCESS

FORMULATION   IMPLEMENTATION

EXHIBIT I.1
THE DECISION PROCESS

author has observed that such terms are "accordionlike," stretching to accommodate a wide range of the decision-making spectrum.[2]

A factor contributing to the semantic confusion is the fact that *the process* of setting overall policies, selecting appropriate strategies, and developing detailed plans may be conducted by more than one level, and by many units within the organization. As Exhibit I.2 illustrates, there can be a great many "Strategic Business Units" (SBUs) in a large, diversified corporation like General Electric. The SBU is a business unit "serving a clearly defined product-market segment with a clearly defined strategy."[3] For each SBU, a policy → strategy → plans process is undertaken, similar to the one conducted for the whole organization, but more limited in scope and shaped to the needs of the business unit. In a sense, each part of a business must conceive an overall policy, define its strategies, and develop detailed plans, although each level in an organization is constrained by the policies, strategies, and plans of a higher level. It would of course be confusing to attempt a full explanation of decision making at every organizational level and every SBU. Moreover, the business policy course, as established by the American Assembly of Collegiate Schools of Business, is oriented to "integrating analysis and policy determination at the overall management level."[4] For these reasons, we shall in this introductory chapter refer to the concept of decision making as it applies to the whole company rather than its component parts.

A first step in our explanation of the three-part decision-making process is a simple but comprehensive set of definitions for the three principal phases of decision making that I shall refer to throughout this text. These definitions are offered with the knowledge that they can conflict with interpretations by other authors. Part of the difficulty in writing a business policy book is the field's lack of uniform definitions or a universal model of the

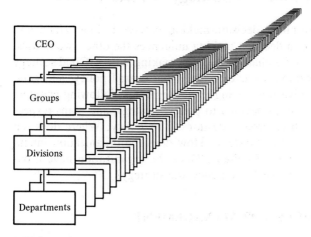

EXHIBIT I.2
ORGANIZATIONAL STRUCTURE AT GENERAL ELECTRIC
Source: "Strategic Management in GE," Corporate Planning and Development, General Electric, 1978.

decision-making process. Because the formulation of decisions is dynamic, complex, and ongoing, it defies simple analysis. But for classroom exposition, some simplification is necessary. Exhibit I.3 briefly defines policy (and objectives), strategy, and plans formulation. Brief introductions follow for each of these three phases of decision making — stressing the interrelationships among them — and providing illustrations of actual decisions in each area.

EXHIBIT I.3
DEFINITIONS

I. *Policy formulation:* Establishing broad purpose and direction for the total organization, as in answering the question "what type of company do we want to be?"

   Objectives: Quantifiable measures that complement the general statement of policy.

II. *Strategy formulation:* Developing strategy alternatives that will be consistent with, and optimize on, the company's policy.

III. *Plans formulation:* Identifying specific tactical programs and steps to fulfill the identified strategies.

Elaboration of the Policy → Strategy → Plans Process

Each part of the three-phase decision-making process is intertwined and reinforcing. Each phase in decision making influences the other two phases. If one link is weak, the entire chain of decision making suffers. Good strategy is an aimless pursuit without clear direction from overall policy; and good plans assist in the effective functioning of strategy. The following chapters are arranged in three sections devoted to policy, strategy, and plans respectively, each addressing three broad questions: (1) Policy: Where does top management want to go? (2) Strategy: How does the organization intend to get where it wants to go? (3) Plans: Does the organization have a detailed schedule of activities to achieve policy and strategy?

POLICY: WHERE DOES TOP MANAGEMENT WANT TO GO?

"Policy" refers to top management's overall direction of the firm. As one authority defined it: "Policy is distinguished by its concern with what is relevant and critical for the enterprise as a whole. It deals with the problems and processes of top management, which is the agency responsible for the short- as well as the long-run viability of the *total enterprise,* its relationship to the environment, and its effect in fulfilling its purpose." [5]

The careful structuring of policy sets the tone for organizational participation throughout the company. A weak or unclear statement of purpose at the corporate level creates a domino effect on other links in the management chain. In the absence of a clear idea of where to go, a company will go in the direction the collective pull of its businesses takes it. It would not be without direction but it would be without leadership.

Further, in pursuing a well-defined corporate policy, a company generally commits its resources to long-term courses of action, the consequences of which may not become clearly evident for many years. The longer the time span the more resources are required and the less reversible the commitment becomes. For United Fruit, once the dominant company in banana production, the critical effect of losing sight of the firm's primary purpose shows in this passage:

> United Fruit, now part of United Brands, is an example of a company failing to keep its long-term perspective. The company became so involved in running a fleet of ships, setting up company towns for the workers, building schools and churches, and carving out railroad spurs in the wilderness that it began to think of itself as a country instead of a company. It suffered from a sort of self-perpetuating megalomania. The firm's management began to believe that it had a mission in life to give

bananas to the hungry world. It lost sight of the fact that it was in business to make money.[6]

Finally, a company that chooses the correct policy stance eases the burden on strategy and plans to provide satisfactory total performance. It is axiomatic that it is easier to achieve satisfactory results in the right industry than to fight the unfavorable economics of a declining industry. In Alfred Chandler's famous work on *Strategy and Structure* he quoted the then top executive of Sears, Roebuck as saying that in the company's early years it "made every mistake in the book," yet the firm's continued success in retailing could be credited to the original concept: "Business is like war in one respect — if its grand [concept] is correct, any number of tactical errors can be made and yet the enterprise proves successful." [7]

Objectives. Objectives are used to complement and clarify policy by expressing the policy statement in quantitative terms. Without such accompanying detail, the policy statement can offer only limited explanation of top management's purpose.

Exhibit I.4 illustrates the reinforcing nature of policy and objectives. One without the other is less effective than the two combined. Quantitative measures provide the needed precision to refine the policy statement, yet

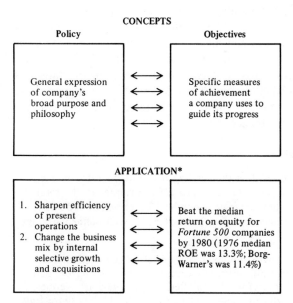

EXHIBIT I.4
COMPLEMENTARITY OF CORPORATE POLICY AND OBJECTIVES
* *Source:* Borg-Warner's Annual Report, 1976, p. 10.

they alone would not adequately indicate management's design for reaching the numerical targets.* Subsequently, "policy" and "objectives" will be used interchangeably to refer to the top-level orientation for the firm. But for references to quantifiable measures of direction, "objectives" will be used.

STRATEGY: HOW DOES THE ORGANIZATION INTEND TO GET WHERE IT WANTS TO GO?

Strategy depends on identifying the correct alternatives to pursue. In Exhibit I.4, for example, Borg-Warner's policy options suggest both external and internal strategies. Internal strategic options can be viewed as raising the *efficiency* of an organization, by improving the performance of current business operations, while external strategic options can raise the effectiveness of an organization, by changing the business areas in which a company operates.[8] Among external strategic alternatives are acquisitions, divestments, joint ventures, and licensing (discussed in Chapter 5); internal alternatives include a wide range of possibilities, which are classified under defensive, offensive, and breakthrough strategies in Chapter 6.

Strategy and policy are interdependent parts of effective decision making. Even if policy decisions place a company in the right industry, it must cope with a number of competing firms, all seeking to maximize their position within that industry. Thus, although good policy can position the company in the right business, good strategy is required for superior competitive performance within that business. Many real-life situations confirm the contention that the right strategy can make the difference. Firms within the same industries and starting with comparable opportunities for success are eventually separated on the basis of their choice and implementation of strategies (and the successful choice and execution of plans to support those strategies). A familiar case history shows how different strategies resulted in dramatically different performance.

K-Mart and W. T. Grant

K-Mart (formerly Kresge's) is the leading discount operator in the United States. In 1975 W. T. Grant, once a front-runner in the retail field, died of self-inflicted strategic wounds. The principal difference between the two companies was that K-Mart had a well-defined strategy

---

* A desired 10% earnings growth, for example, could be achieved through internal or external diversification, production improvement, or market extensions. Numbers alone could, therefore, be fulfilled through various avenues, including those contrary to what management had in mind. Unless more fully expressed, a strictly numerical objective would provide inadequate guidance for planning a company's performance.

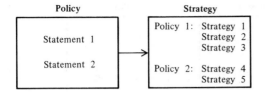

**EXHIBIT I.5
AN ILLUSTRATION OF THE POLICY AND STRATEGY
FORMULATION PHASES**

for growth while W. T. Grant did not. K-Mart went to considerable effort to evaluate the discount industry and determine the critical elements for a successful operation, and then built a strategy reflecting its strengths and the observable weaknesses of the competition. W. T. Grant, on the other hand, was never able to develop a coherent strategy to combat K-Mart's inroads or those of other competitors. It was indecisive on strategies for the optimum size of stores, merchandising mix, and pricing structure. It was in sum reacting, rather than planning its growth.

A number of strategies can be pursued, simultaneously, just as more than one policy aim may be appropriate. In early writings, Peter Drucker observed that the single-minded pursuit of a dominant strategy would tend to unbalance the total needs of an organization and lead to lower long-run performance.[9] It is not the number of strategies that is important, but that strategies build on, and extend, initial policy directions, as is graphically illustrated in Exhibit I.5.

PLANS: DOES THE ORGANIZATION HAVE
A DETAILED SCHEDULE OF ACTIVITIES
TO ACHIEVE POLICY AND STRATEGY?

Plans are the most systematically detailed phase of the decision-making process. Plans are tactical rather than strategic and focused on specific product/market areas of opportunity. Plans are not as dependent on conceptual insight as on careful attention to detail. Following the relatively broad mapping of policy and strategy, plans must extend the process by providing the final guideposts that enable the organization to get from where it is to where it wants to go. Even if good policy formulation places a company in the right business sectors, and optimum strategy alternatives would exploit the company's relative competitive advantage, it still remains for plans to provide the details, which can facilitate or frustrate successful fulfillment of expectations.

**EXHIBIT I.6
AN ILLUSTRATION OF THE POLICY, STRATEGY,
AND PLANS FORMULATION PHASES**

An example of success through carefully executed plans is provided by McDonald's Corporation. In a field crowded with competitors, McDonald's has managed to maintain a leadership position owing, in no small measure, to its detailed and explicit instructions for each store manager in such areas as quality control, customer service, and store cleanliness. By carefully monitoring the operations of each outlet, McDonald's assures customers of uniform consistency and quality throughout its nationwide chain of stores. By sending its managers for intensive training, it ensures their familiarity with McDonald's basic procedures and routine. Perhaps the highest testimony to McDonald's approach is the imitation of its practices by competitors. Burger King, one of McDonald's chief rivals, hired McDonald's third-ranking executive officer to revitalize its organization in 1977. One of his first moves was to replace eight of Burger King's top ten officers with McDonald's alumni. He also revamped Burger King's field operations to where "it is a direct copy of McDonald's. . . . The big difference at Burger King these days, Smith [the new chief executive] contends, is that things are done right more often. . . . At McDonald's, Smith learned the secrets to domination of the fast-food business: consistently providing speedy service, clean surroundings, and fresh food in every single outlet." [10] These expressions of intent are similar to what every fast-food chain would logically endorse. The difference comes in implementation, and that, in turn, requires a carefully planned blueprint for execution.

In sum, plans are the final stage in the continuum from developing overall policy, to selecting appropriate strategies, to, finally, sharpening the focus to specific programs and action steps in the formulation of plans. Exhibit I.6 shows the flow of decision making from policy to strategy to plans.

Refinement of the Policy → Strategy → Plans Process

It should now be apparent that the entire process of decision making is too complex to be encompassed by a one-dimensional view of policy, strategy, and plans. We have already referred to distinctions between strategy and plan formulations according to whether a firm was internally oriented (toward greater efficiency) or externally oriented (toward greater effectiveness).

This distinction influences the participation in the planning process by the corporate level (effectiveness oriented) and the business level (efficiency oriented). A natural separation between corporate and business levels exists in any organization and, for each level, a different perspective on, and approach to, strategy and plans is implied. For example, if a company decides to concentrate solely on the efficiency of current operations, then it clearly constrains the scope of analysis required for total decision making and emphasizes business-level decision making. If, on the other hand, management's policy is to also pursue external effectiveness options in order to improve overall performance, then the corporate level can play a significant role in the final decisions.

Second, the decision to follow an internal emphasis on efficiency or an external emphasis on effectiveness invariably reflects the philosophies of top management. Top management can elect to adopt what will be referred to in subsequent chapters as "steady-state" or "evolutionary" management styles. Basically, a steady-state management style reflects management's decision to concentrate on current operations (and improve efficiency) and an evolutionary management style indicates management's willingness to diversify beyond current operations (and improve effectiveness). The choice of a steady-state or evolutionary style of management is decided in the policy formulation phase. Depending on which direction is indicated by the policy phase, the scope of succeeding strategy and plans activities will be either narrowed or broadened.

In sum, then, companies with different management styles can influence the decision-making process, either narrowing or broadening its scope and the relative scope for policy, strategy, and plans. Also, participation in the planning process can differ by corporate and business levels in the firm. Basic assumptions and brief explanations in the rest of this chapter for these two fundamental dimensions of decision making will aid in understanding the structure of the rest of the book.

Two Types of Management Policy: Steady-State and Evolutionary

Two broad policy choices are open to top management: (1) a steady-state policy oriented internally to the management and development of current operations, and (2) an evolutionary policy that encompasses external as well as internal opportunities for development. The prevailing overall policy set by a company defines the effective boundaries within which decisions on strategy and plans will be made. These guidelines, for instance, determine which set of strategic alternatives a company will employ. If, for example, a company's management is interested in pursuing development through improvement of existing business lines alone, then it has proscribed such external growth possibilities as mergers and acquisitions. An illustration of such a policy and strategy orientation is provided by the chief executive officer of the Loctite Company, a leading manufacturer of specialty chemicals.

> Loctite is the brainchild of the late Vernon Krieble, a chemistry professor at Hartford, Conn.'s Trinity College. . . . His son Robert, a remarkable man himself, now heads the company and is its largest stockholder, controlling 37% of the 9.7 million shares. Explains Bob Krieble:
> "My father invented [the first practical anaerobic sealer; a metal-to-metal sealer that sets and grips in the absence of air] in Trinity's Lab. . . ."
> Loctite is now on its fourth generation of anaerobic patents, which won't run out until the 1990's. "If we can keep our resources focused on our strength, we will stay where we dominate," says Krieble. Meaning that he expects to resist the temptation to expand into other lines of business. Says he: "Maybe it's not as exciting to keep doing the same thing again and again and again — even though it's the most profitable." [11]

The Loctite Company in this case has built a profitable business out of a single-minded pursuit of the market for anaerobic sealers. There is no foreseeable need to change the policy that has been so successfully implemented. Perhaps more important, there is no apparent inclination by management to deviate from its formula. Management perceives continued growth opportunities from further exploitation of its current product line and, therefore, it will continue to pursue those strategies consistent with a policy focused on internal growth.

There are, however, a considerable number of companies that would find the Loctite policy too confining. An ever-increasing number of industrialized companies have opted to diversify into new businesses. Since the mid-1960s there has been a persistent, although fluctuating, trend to external development through acquisitions. The unrelated acquisition, where a company diversified into a completely unrelated field, has been a dominant theme of this acquisition movement. While we need not stop at this point to examine the evidence, the conclusion is abundantly clear: external options for growth, especially acquisitions of the conglomerate type into unrelated areas, is a policy accepted by a large and growing percentage of the nation's industrialized firms.*

---

* The evolution and diversification of organizations is discussed in detail in Chapter 4.

Thus, while Loctite's Bob Krieble is determined to stay within his area of specialization because of its past and potential performance, other companies are equally determined to diversify away from current businesses because of the limited opportunities management perceives. A number of organizations have switched to this latter policy over roughly the past two dozen years. One example of a large and conservatively managed company that has considered such a policy switch is Kraft.

> For Kraft, the food business accounted for all of last year's [1978's] sales of $5.6 billion and earnings of $184 million. Yet management is increasingly concerned about Kraft's huge exposure to ever more volatile commodity prices. More than 75% of Kraft's costs are attributable to such raw agricultural materials as milk, cheese, and vegetable oil. Government support prices for dairy products make costs unpredictable while other government policies at times make higher costs difficult to recoup in product prices. "With no way of fully protecting themselves from big price swings, Kraft needs to broaden its product line," asserts Donald J. Lupa, an analyst with Duff & Phelps, Inc.
>
> "We're not approaching it in a panicky way because we're an extremely strong company," Richman [Chief Executive Officer for Kraft] says, "but we are looking at a number of acquisition possibilities. It might be in the best interest of our stockholders to have another leg to stand on." [12] *

Both Loctite's and Kraft's policies are legitimate means for a common objective of improved performance. Neither choice is uniquely "right" or "wrong"; it all depends on the circumstances of the firm and the policy orientation of its senior management. Regulated firms — like utilities, airlines, railroads, and trucks — may have a more limited range of policy choices, and therefore limited strategy alternatives in support of policy. Other nonregulated firms governed by an aggressive management style seem to be in an almost continual state of evolution and change. Moreover, environmental shifts can induce changes in policy. In the case of Kraft, for example, increasing government influence on the price of its raw materials was an external factor causing the company to reexamine a policy of continued dependence on the food business.

This interaction of policies and strategies precludes a simplistic approach to decision making. In the chapters that follow, we have instead used the two principal options of a steady-state or evolutionary policy as a means for dealing separately with the different issues of strategy and plans associated with each major policy alternative.

---

* In 1980, Kraft and Dart Industries, a large diversified manufacturer, merged and formed a multibillion-dollar conglomerate.

Two Levels of Input to the Decision Process: Business and Corporate

A second dimension of decision making is organizational and involves the level primarily responsible for the development of strategy and plans. Here again there are two main branches: the corporate level and the business level.* "Business level" refers to the operating entities of an enterprise. "Corporate level" refers to the top-management structure of the corporation to which the various business entities report. In a large decentralized organization, there may be a number of business levels, including various divisions and product lines within divisions. In smaller firms, the business level may refer to only one product line or to several related product lines. These traditional distinctions between simple and complex organizational design are illustrated in simplified fashion in Exhibit I.7.

Whether the organization is large and complex or smaller and simply structured, a distinction between corporate and business levels is natural. At a business level, strategy and plan formulation must understandably emphasize the performance of existing operations. This is to be expected, since it is in a line manager's self-interest in terms of rewards and incentives to maximize the utilization of assets over which he or she has direct control. In an organization such as Loctite, where the principal strategies for performance revolve around its specialty line of chemicals, the corporate-level planning staff's main responsibility would be to aid and support the activities of the business-level managers responsible for the chemicals business.

In a company like Kraft, however, strategy and plans must reflect top management's decision to pursue a policy of diversification rather than containment. For the firm with an externally oriented view of future development, resources would no longer be reinvested automatically to build up existing operating units. Line managers would have to vie for available funds not only against each other but also against the potential claims from the new business investments that would be necessary to fulfill the company's broad corporate policy. Moreover, line managers could not provide the necessary objectivity in planning diversification away from their areas

---

* An additional functional level is also possible, which refers primarily to the "maximization of resource productivity. Synergy and the development of distinctive competence, therefore, become the key strategy components, while scope drops sharply in importance." [13] Although the functional level is a legitimate area of focus, particularly if one wishes to consider the most detailed aspects of decision making, it can be considered a subset of the business-level category and, for purposes of simplicity, is not accorded individual attention or analysis in our discussion.

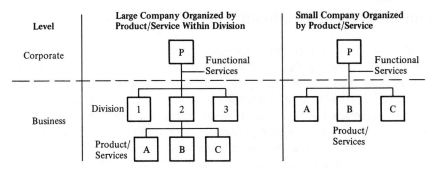

EXHIBIT I.7
PLANNING BY ORGANIZATIONAL LEVEL

of operation. In making such resource decisions, top management would have to rely on corporate-level staff analysis for the necessary studies of new business opportunities, and possibly the divestment of current under-performing business.

Obviously, varying degrees of influence can be assumed by each organizational level, depending on the leanings of top management toward a steady-state or evolutionary policy as a means for achieving desired performance objectives. In the case of Kraft, for example, the corporate executive office is just beginning to explore the possibility of diversification and thus the influence of the conservative Food divisions is probably still dominant.* On the other hand, in actively diversifying conglomerates like International Telephone & Telegraph, Gulf & Western, and Tenneco, which frequently reposition the business/market mix of the total enterprise, the corporate-level influence on strategy can be relatively high.

Since the middle of the 1960s the trend to corporate-level, externally oriented growth has altered a conventional emphasis on business-level, operations-focused strategy. The aim of operational strategy has been previously characterized as promoting efficiency. This translates into a steady-state policy of reinvesting resources into existing product lines. But with an evolutionary policy, the resource-allocation decision covers a wide range of possible external investments, such as acquisitions or joint ventures, which must be balanced against the advantages of reinvestment in current businesses. As corporations continue to diversify, a policy consistent only with reinvestment to further existing operations becomes increasingly limiting. It neglects the functioning of strategy at a second, corporatewide level.

---

* See footnote on page 11.

The Structure of This Book

In effect we have relaxed the simplifying assumptions with which we constructed the initial policy → strategy → plans model. Using the terms "steady-state" and "evolutionary" to depict differences in management policy, we have provided a framework for dealing separately with the different strategy and plans issues that arise when one or the other of these policy alternatives is indicated. Shown graphically in Exhibit I.8, the policy phase can lead to either external or internal development strategies, or to a combination of the two. In turn, internal strategies indicate primarily business-level plans, whereas external strategies rely more on corporate-level plans. As indicated in the diagram, the branches from the initial policy phase are not mutually exclusive paths but parts of an integrated pattern of decision making comprised of several possible combinations of strategy and plans. Also, because the parts of the decision process are interdependent, there is feedback among policy, strategy, and plans. Although further discussions will emphasize the dominant thrust from broad to narrow focus, or policy to strategy to plans, the interaction and coordination among the three phases is implicit, and is not underscored at every point merely to avoid unnecessary repetition. This expanded view of the decision-making process provides the basis for organizing the materials in the chapters that follow.

In Part I, policy formulation is developed. This is a common first step all firms must take. Once an overall management policy is determined, then attention turns to the next two steps: strategy and plans formulation. In Parts II and III, we deal with strategy and plans in dual environments,

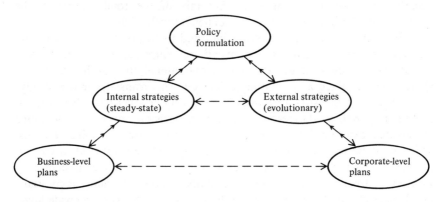

EXHIBIT I.8
EXPANDED VERSION OF THE DECISION-MAKING PROCESS

steady-state and evolutionary, which reflect the policy choices made by management in Part I.

Summary

Planning for a company's successful performance is a very demanding task. It is also a very complex process that is difficult to illustrate simply. In this chapter, two principal dimensions of such complexity are introduced: steady-state versus evolutionary management style, and corporate-level versus business-level activities. Exhibit I.8 shows how these two elements are interrelated with the three-phase decision process of policy, strategy, and plans. In succeeding chapters, more detailed discussions of each piece of the model in Exhibit I.8 will be undertaken. A number of practical examples and cases will be used to illustrate the underlying theory and bring it into sharper perspective. The result should be deeper understanding of, and appreciation for, the complexities of decision making in business organizations.

QUESTIONS

1. How are policy, strategy, and plans interconnected in support of specific decisions? Suppose, for example, that U.S. Steel acquired a large coal company. Trace that action backward in terms of a policy, strategy, and plans rationale.

2. Which of the three phases (policy, strategy, and plans) is most important?

3. What factors determine whether recommendations on strategy are made primarily by corporate-level or business-level personnel?

4. How might investment decisions be influenced by a company's management policy (steady-state or evolutionary) or by the organizational focus of decisions (business or corporate level)?

5. Identify the type of management policy and organizational focus for decisions you would associate with each of these: (a) state government; (b) electric utility; (c) conglomerate; (d) university; (e) small, high-technology firm.

6. Suggest two companies that illustrate steady-state and evolutionary policies. Support your answers.

MINI-EXERCISES

1. Assume you are made president of an ailing supermarket chain. Your election to this post was recommended by the board of directors, who felt that a strong, outside top manager was needed in order to restore profitability. You are given broad autonomy in your new position but it is made clear that significant improvements are expected within two years. What initial actions might you and your employees be expected to take in policy, strategy, and plans?

2. In the 1960s and 1970s, managers of electric utilities had to face changes in environment such as pollution requirements, siting restrictions (particularly for nuclear power plants), skyrocketing costs for fuel, and active protests by consumer groups. This has changed the demands on management in this industry. Comment on the types of changes that would be required in management policy and organizational levels of decision making.

   SUGGESTION: There are three sides to the utilities' dilemma: management, consumers, and the rate-making commission as the compromising body. The class can be divided into three groups representing each of the three sides; then research, evaluate, and defend a recent rate hike awarded to a local electric utility.

REFERENCES

1. George A. Steiner and John B. Miner, *Management Policy and Strategy* (New York: Macmillan, 1977), p. 19.

2. Kenneth R. Andrews, *The Concept of Corporate Strategy* (Homewood, Ill.: Dow Jones–Irwin, 1971).

3. William K. Hall, "SBU's: Hot, New Topic in the Management of Diversification," *Business Horizons,* February 1978.

4. American Assembly of Collegiate Schools of Business, "Policies, Procedures and Standards," 1969 and annually thereafter.

5. Ram Charan, "Business Policy: Goals, Pedagogy, Structure, Concepts," *Harvard Business School Bulletin,* July–August and November–December 1966.

6. *Forbes,* September 15, 1967, p. 150.

7. Alfred D. Chandler, *Strategy and Structure* (Cambridge, Mass.: MIT Press, 1962), p. 235.

8. Chester I. Barnard, *The Functions of the Executive* (Cambridge, Mass.: Harvard University Press, 1962).

9. Peter F. Drucker, *The Practice of Management* (New York: Harper & Row, 1954).

10. *Business Week,* October 8, 1979, p. 132.

11. *Forbes,* October 15, 1977, p. 136.

12. *Business Week,* February 19, 1979, p. 26.

13. Charles W. Hofer and Dan Schendel, *Strategy Formulation: Analytical Concepts* (New York: West, 1978), p. 29.

FURTHER READING

Fleming, John E. "Study of a Business Decision." *California Management Review,* Winter 1966.

Folsom, Marion B. *Executive Decision Making.* New York: McGraw-Hill, 1962.

Harrison, Frank. *The Managerial Decision-Making Process.* Boston: Houghton Mifflin, 1975.

Leontiades, Milton. *Strategies for Diversification and Change.* Boston: Little, Brown, 1980.

————. "Planning for Change in Stages of Corporate Development." *Long Range Planning,* December 1979.

MacCrimmons, Kenneth R. *Managerial Decision-Making.* In Joseph W. McGuire, ed., *Contemporary Management: Issues and Viewpoints.* Englewood Cliffs, N.J.: Prentice-Hall, 1974.

Shull, Fremont A., Andre L. Delbecq, and L. L. Cummings. *Organizational Decision Making.* New York: McGraw-Hill, 1970.

PART I

FORMULATING POLICY

CHAPTER 1

Policy Formulation and the Managerial Factor

Importance of Management Policy

The aim of business is to produce and sell goods and services in a competitive environment. Constraints on business operations include the external environment — such as government regulations, competition, consumer reaction, and social responsibilities — and an internally consistent approach on employee compensation, dividend payout, and reinvestment in the business. The business managers who most skillfully balance all these variables run the most successful enterprises.

This demand on business to manage trade-offs between internal factors and external forces has recently become extremely complex. A number of new trends, crises, and concerns have made management an ever-broadening skill. Cultural historians have described the current discontinuities as part of an "axial age"; that is, a pivotal time in history when institutions and values undergo major change. As a consequence, businessmen need to be more than technically competent in running their operations. They have to be increasingly attuned to environmental change. Managers need to widen their vision to encompass international, political, social, and economic trends and understand better their implications for business. In sum, to perform satisfactorily in this "axial age" managers must anticipate and react to change. "The essence of management," as one author puts it, "is the creation, adaptation, and coping with change." [1]

To deal with change, a company needs an overall philosophy of purpose. In order to express this philosophy, management must develop a clear understanding of where it wants to go. More specifically, it should develop appropriate policies and objectives to give its purpose explicit meaning and to provide its managers with clear direction. These policies, in turn, serve two functions: (1) to position the company for future growth; (2) to provide direction and cohesion for operations.

POSITIONING THE COMPANY FOR FUTURE GROWTH

If carefully thought out, corporate policy can be the most important determination that management will make. It is the conceptual blueprint for performance. In an observation that is now a cliché, Theodore Levitt said that management's first task is to correctly evaluate what business it is in or should be in.[2] Using the example of railroads, Levitt argued that the Penn Central should have considered itself in the transportation business, rather than limiting its horizons, and thus opportunities, to the railroad business.* With subsequent authors like Peter Drucker[3] refining this concept of "knowing your business," the importance of this type of evaluation is now widely acknowledged.

The consequences of ignoring this attunement of overall policy with an organization's environment can be severe. In extreme situations, entire industries may become obsolete because of changes they were not prepared to meet. An important but little discussed side effect of technological change, for example, is the potential havoc it wreaks among industries and companies wherever it is a significant competitive factor. Within this century we have witnessed jet airplanes replace propeller-driven airplanes, refrigeration displace the icebox, mass production overwhelm custom crafting, and television overshadow radio. More currently, electronic timepieces threaten to make obsolete the conventional wristwatch.

* Perhaps interpreting Levitt's suggestions too broadly, Penn Central diversified into a number of businesses that were only marginally, if at all, related to railroading, and eventually entered into bankruptcy proceedings.

A check of the top one hundred industrial companies ranked by size of assets over the last six decades shows the dangers of complacency and lack of purpose. Some companies managed to maintain their leadership positions. But of the top one hundred firms in 1917, only about forty remained in that position by 1977. Some companies were acquired, others disappeared entirely, and newcomers moved up.[4]

There are many reasons for corporate mortality or decline. Sometimes a company fails to anticipate new technology or new products. Or an outdated but unbending business philosophy of senior management may be at fault. Often it is traceable to an original visionary concept that was never subsequently reviewed or revised. Whatever the specific reason, it is ultimately the failure to maintain the guiding corporate policies in tune with the changing environment. The two cases which follow offer specific examples of success followed by failure. Although both businesses survive in one form or another, neither has been able to regain its former position of leadership in American industry.

United Drug (now part of Dart Industries)

Ironically, good fortune as well as bad can sometimes cause a company to fail: The immediate success of a good idea can so dazzle a man that he comes to look upon himself as almost infallible. That's what ruined Louis Liggett and his United Drug Co., once a great company. Liggett's original concept was to manufacture and package proprietary medicines for hundreds of independent druggists — who then received an exclusive franchise for their sale. A fine idea. But Liggett fell in love with size. Without thinking through the advantages — or lack of them — he began buying up other companies. In 1916 he pulled off what was then the largest merger in the history of the drug industry — with the Riker–Hegeman–Jaynes drug interests. In 1928 and 1929, at the height of the stock market boom, he acquired both Bristol-Myers *and* Sterling Drug. Had the mergers held together, United Drug today would be a mighty company.

The trouble was that Liggett wasn't sure whether he was a retailer or a manufacturer. He forgot or overlooked the precise combination of factors that had made his initial idea a good one. He went on an extravagant buying spree that exploded in the stock market crash and great depression.[5]

P. Lorillard (now part of Loews)

Another company that lost ground even though it was in a growth industry was P. Lorillard. It became so entranced by the profit from its Turkish cigarette business that it completely lost sight of the basic principle of any packaged-goods operation: change. You've got to be prepared to bet millions on an indication of a change in consumer taste. When returning World War I doughboys spread the blended cigarette habit in the United States, Lorillard stuck with its stronger Turkish cigarettes.

It was in 1926, almost eight years after, that Lorillard followed its competitors into the market with a blended cigarette, Old Gold, to compete with the by-then entrenched Lucky Strike, Chesterfield and Camels. Lorillard had waited so long that the effort was ruinously costly. Years later it almost killed its successful Kent cigarette by keeping the price too high.[6]

PROVIDING DIRECTION AND COHESION

By systematically evaluating the business a company happens to be in and what business it should be in, a company takes the first step in the formal process of controlling its performance. The establishment of policy guidelines provides the discipline within which strategy and plans will function. Without a clear policy of overall direction by top management, the various organizational units would act as independent entities and the organization as a whole would not operate as an integrated system.

If operational self-interests are allowed to dominate, then the company's policy becomes an arbitrary result of these diverse interests. Instead of monitoring the external environment impartially for opportunities and threats, for instance, a company's focus would turn inward and be guided by the narrower concerns of its operating units. The combination of various operational interests would be suboptimal in relation to a unified corporate-level perspective, which encompasses all units and weighs their relative contribution to the total organization. As succinctly phrased by Robert Katz, "What is best for the total enterprise is always sub-optimal from the point of view of an individual unit or function.... The operating performance of an enterprise is often at variance with the requirements of chosen strategic performance objectives."[7] Only by providing guidance from the top and toward common policies can an organization ensure internal cohesion and optimum use of its resources.

Scope of Policy

An important element of an effective policy statement is clarity. Does the statement convey management's intent? Is it actionable? In short, how detailed must the policy statement be? This is a question to make management pause. A broad statement of policy without objective, measurable guidelines provides no barometer to measure future success or failure. To be a "successful" company is redundant. To provide "an adequate return to shareholders" is implicit, and the operation of the company is not improved by making the obvious explicit. On the other hand, a too strong emphasis on details can sacrifice the flexibility needed to adapt to changing environmental conditions. Unfortunately, no answer can be so finely tailored to serve as the model for all companies. A balance is necessary between too general and too specific a definition. Below are actual statements of policy from two firms. The first is an example of too broad a statement and the second includes information more appropriate to a statement of substance: *

> ... to selectively position ourselves in worldwide markets, offering profitable financial and financially related services to meet the changing needs of consumers, businesses, governments and others in those markets.[8]

> [The company] will remain primarily a manufacturer, emphasizing internal growth, international as well as domestic, of distinctive wood and related products which require innovation, special aesthetic features or fabrication, and significant marketing skill.[9]

Once defined, a policy remains valid as long as a company's commitment to it is unshaken. The more changeable the environment, the greater the need to monitor closely and to reevaluate the company's position and the desirability of revisions. For companies in mature or stable environments, reevaluation of policy is relatively less important. Examples of ongoing and relatively stable policy guidelines are likely to be found in companies that remain within regulated industries like utilities, railroads, trucking, and airlines. Companies in these industries typically tend to be less diversified, with some significant exceptions. Also, legal constraints may prohibit the freewheeling diversification employed by some manufacturing conglomerates in the 1960s and 1970s.

Interaction of Policy, Strategy, and Plans

It is occasionally helpful to remember that the description of any phase in the decision process is incomplete without an awareness of its interaction

---

* In our suggested approach, quantitative measures (objectives) would have been used in conjunction with these statements of policy.

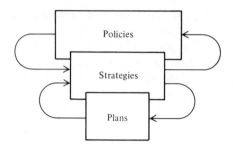

EXHIBIT 1.1
MULTILEVEL INTERACTIVE PROCESS

with other phases. As I mentioned in the Introduction, there is a feedback effect among policy, strategy, and plans. Also, each strategic business unit of the organization formulates policy, but such policies are subordinate to, and in conformity with, the master policy of the enterprise. An oil firm dedicated to remaining in the oil business would not permit one of its divisions to acquire an electronics company, for instance. Similarly, hierarchic relationships apply to strategy and plans, with upper organizational levels establishing the parameters for lower organizational levels. The master policy is designed with an appreciation for these interdependencies; in particular, the master policy should be consistent with the strategy and plan capabilities of the major organizational units. In effect, a "logical master [policy] must not only be consistent with environments but also the internal capabilities of the organization." [10] For instance, it is not unusual for initial policy objectives to be modified later as more information becomes available and strategic alternatives become clearer. This is because the formulation of policy is dependent on such tests as the realism of objectives, availability and amount of financial resources, and organizational competence. Since this information is typically developed in depth only in later stages of strategy and plans analyses, the eventual policy course may be influenced by feedback from findings in these areas (see Exhibit 1.1).

The following quotation gives an example of a potentially overambitious policy; of reaching beyond reasonable implementing capabilities of the organization:

> A strategy "to provide safe, low cost means of personalized air transport for personal and business use" appears consistent with the design, production, and marketing capabilities of Piper Aircraft. Conversely, a statement "to provide vehicles for above ground or sea transport" is a much broader statement that could imply military, space, and airline

transport products. Since the functional requirements of such vehicles are so different from the capabilities inherent in providing light aircraft, the master strategy for a company employing such a statement would appear rhetorical and pompous, rather than a realistic guide to the products and services that Piper could reasonably hope to offer.[11]

Developing a corporate policy is obviously complex, often subjective, and characterized by iterative checks throughout the process. It does not proceed lineally forward from one logical step to the next. Rather, management must begin by providing a tentative structure for the analyses that follow. The succeeding evaluations then either reinforce and support this concept or uncover reasons for modifying and reshaping the original assumptions. However, the difficulty of formulating the policy from partial knowledge should not obscure the importance of purpose before action. Implementation of specific strategies should flow from agreement on overall policy — even if tentatively defined — on what position the company should assume.

A common mistake of management is to assume that it can reserve its major participation in the policy, strategy, and plans process until the end, after staff and line managers' findings and recommendations are formally presented. This is clearly turning priorities upside down. At this stage management can react only to what is presented. It may find recommendations with which it agrees. It may even select the right formula for success. But the results would be fortuitous rather than planned. The odds are greatly improved if the parameters for the strategy and plans phases are sharply defined at the start.

Determinants of Policy

So far we have dealt with the importance, scope, and place of policy in the decision-making process. Now we're ready to deal with the process of formulating policy. To do so one must consider the major elements that influence policy. This is a complex task. No one force determines the shape of the policy statement. In undertaking the task of determining an organization's future direction, management must decide, among an almost unlimited number of possibilities, which are the most significant influences for the future performance of the organization. Management can decide to stress growth in revenues or earnings, balance among its various business areas or product lines, a reduced risk exposure, higher market shares, or a combination of these as well as other factors. Management can adopt either a steady-state or an evolutionary philosophy, remaining a single-industry

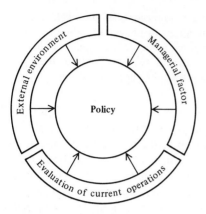

EXHIBIT 1.2
DETERMINANTS OF POLICY

organization or diversifying into related or unrelated fields. The ultimate policy decisions of management are influenced by a multiplicity of factors, which will be grouped and examined here under three separate headings: external environment, evaluation of operations, and managerial values (see Exhibit 1.2).

EXTERNAL ENVIRONMENT

One important element that affects management's perspective is uncertainty. Since external variables are generally outside the control of management, they pose increased uncertainty relative to internal considerations. Authors Katz and Kahn, for example, have made a case for external factors as the principal explanatory variables for organizational change.[12] In Chapter 2, an analysis of environments and their impact on policymaking is developed.

EVALUATION OF OPERATIONS

A second significant influence on policy is internal capability. Are the resources of the organization adequate for fulfilling the desired policy objectives? Total resource capability obviously influences the attainability of management's objectives. If an internal review of operations suggests a shortfall between policy objectives and current capabilities, management might then reevaluate its policy position. This important step of evaluating internal capabilities is the subject of Chapter 3.

MANAGERIAL VALUES

The third element in this three-factor view of policymaking is the managerial factor. For the rest of this chapter, we shall focus on this part of the policy equation.

The Managerial Factor

Management's subjective decisions are the "persuasive element that can affect all aspects of organizational behavior." [13] All decision factors, whether external or internal, are influenced by management's perception of them. This perception by top management in turn reflects management's collective values, backgrounds and experiences. Thus, the policy statement must invariably be affected by the personal traits of those who formulate it. To paraphrase Cyert and March, decisions are ultimately made by *individuals* who base these decisions on their *perceptions.*[14]

Many real-life situations support the view that management's perceptions can make the difference. Using comparable environments for firms within the same industry and at a similar stage of development, it is possible to demonstrate radically different patterns of organizational development. The IBM and Sperry Rand situation helps to make the point.

> A classic example of missed opportunity is Sperry Rand (then Univac) and computers. Although IBM's name is now almost synonymous with computers, Univac developed the first commercial computer. And though Univac is still in the computer business, it is a distant competitor to IBM. It has been estimated that in 1952 Univac had two thirds of the technical experts in computers; by 1955 the company had already sold three of its famous Univac Is to the government.

> However, the opportunities in this industry were seen more clearly by another company. That other company was, of course, IBM, which took advantage of the confused direction at Univac, and especially the lack of marketing strategy. There was no question in the early 1950s of Univac's superior technical talent, product, and early lead in computer technology. Yet Univac's management was incapable of developing marketing and organizational strategies around a unifying master policy in order to grasp this opportunity effectively.

The predilections of management can range from aggressive to conservative outlooks, encompassing vague or specific objectives, creative or technical orientation, broad or narrow vision, and weak or strong commitment to formal planning. Some companies are so strongly directed by, and identified with, a single chief executive that one person's values are synonymous with those of the company. Some examples of chief executives who have dominated the companies they have led include Charles Bluhdorn (G&W), Harold Geneen (ITT), George Scharffenberger (City Investing), John Seabrook (IU International), Dr. Henry Singleton (Teledyne), and Dr. Armand Hammer (Occidental Petroleum). These men have almost single-handedly accounted for the direction of their companies during their tenure at the top. Other companies are organizationally structured so that power is dispersed among a number of persons and exercised primarily through key committees. How many people can name the head of GM, or AT&T, or IBM? In these eminent blue-chip institutions the identity of the chief executive is secondary to the identity of the corporation, and responsibility for running the institution is spread among a top-management team and organized around key policymaking committees.

For many companies in the broad middle ground between a domineering central authority and an institutional structure, the emphasis a company's policy will take is influenced by the background of the top-management team. Although no hard-and-fast rules apply, functional expertise can deeply influence the emphasis and tone of a company's policy.[15] Exhibit 1.3, for instance, illustrates potential associations between managerial specializations and objective measures of performance used to define the company's policy.

In addition to a manager's functional expertise, personal values can influence how an individual manager interprets environmental signals. For example, the classic theory X versus theory Y type of leadership[16] — where managers differ according to the degree of personal concern for subordinates as individuals — can affect management's choice of decisions when faced with, say, declining profits and intensifying competition. One possibility could be to reduce costs sharply by laying off employees. Another approach might involve increased advertising and promotional outlays to increase sales and gain market share. A theory Y manager strongly motivated by concern for employee welfare might resist the first alternative and, guided by his particular set of values, be drawn toward the second alternative. A considerable amount of research is available that says personal values can influence the ultimate choice in a number of such multiple-option situations in decision making;[17] [18] and that substantial variations of style exist among chief executive officers.[19]

Mintzberg has developed a categorization of managerial work roles descriptive of different managerial styles associated with various positions and duties within an organization.[20] The chief executive officer who, for instance, is generally the spokesman for the organization on important external dealings with government and consumer groups as well as dealing with critical competitive crises should be oriented to handle the roles of "disturbance handler," "resource allocator," and "entrepreneur" (see Exhibit

EXHIBIT 1.3
MANAGERIAL VALUES

Functional speciality	Management focus	Values
Accounting	Costs	Cost reduction, minimizing of cost/sales ratios
Finance	Return on investment	Return on capital, measures of profitability
General management	Profits	Broad based, no specialization
Marketing	Sales	Higher volumes, market shares
Personnel	Organizational design	Staffing of company, reporting roles, line-staff relationships
Production	Operating efficiency	Scheduling and productivity; efficiency of facilities
Research and development	Product innovation	Product performance, superiority, and leadership

1.4). Conversely, the chief operating officer, the inside man responsible for day-to-day operating problems and communications with the operating units, requires greater mastery of such roles as "leader," "motivator" and "disseminator." There are obviously a number of managerial styles suitable for a number of different organizational work roles. The degree to which managers' styles are adapted to their work roles can significantly affect their ability to function effectively, with differences in "fit" among organizations explaining, in part, the variability in policy thrusts for similar types of corporations sharing similar environments.

Finally, personal traits not only influence how managements will *react* to stimuli, they also influence how managements will *plan* for the future. A decision to diversify into a new business area, for example, is a conscious management decision to move the organization into a new field of perceived opportunity. Similarly, a decision to remain concentrated within a current business is also a conscious decision and one that can be perceived to offer equal or better performance potential than the option of diversification. Here again, in many situations otherwise comparably situated companies have differed on the future direction a company should take. Such conflicts reflect management's best judgment of the future, which, in turn, invariably reflects management's values and attitudes. We have referred previously to

EXHIBIT 1.4
TEN MANAGERIAL WORK ROLES

Role	Description	Typical activities
Interpersonal roles		
Figurehead	Symbolic head; performs routine duties of a legal or social nature	Ceremony, status requests
Leader	Responsible for motivation of subordinates and for staffing and training	Almost all managerial activities involving subordinates
Liaison	Maintains network of outside contacts to obtain favors and information	Handling mail, external board work, telephone calls
Informational roles		
Monitor	Seeks and receives information to obtain thorough understanding of organization and environment	Reading periodicals, observational tours
Disseminator	Transmits information received from outsiders or insiders to other organization members	Forwarding mail, review sessions with subordinates
Spokesman	Transmits information to outsiders on organization plans, policies, actions	Board meetings, handling mail
Decisional roles		
Entrepreneur	Initiates and supervises design of organizational improvement projects as opportunities arise	Strategy and review sessions regarding change efforts
Disturbance handler	Responsible for corrective action when organization faces unexpected crises	Strategy and review sessions regarding disturbances
Resource allocator	Responsible for allocation of human, monetary, and material resources	Scheduling, requests for authorization, budgeting
Negotiator	Responsible for representing the organization in bargaining and negotiations	Collective bargaining, purchasing

Source: Adapted from Figure 8 in *The Nature of Managerial Work* by Henry Mintzberg. Copyright 1973 by Henry Mintzberg. Reprinted by permission of Harper & Row Publishers, Inc. This version from *Management Policy and Strategy* by George A. Steiner and John B. Miner (Copyright © 1977, Macmillan Publishing Co., Inc.).

two fundamental managerial choices: steady-state and evolutionary policies. To appreciate the judgmental nature of management's ultimate choices, we discuss below the merits of remaining a "single business" (a steady-state policy), as well as the merits in diversifying toward a "multibusiness" structure (an evolutionary policy).

The Managerial Factor: A Single-Business Policy

It is common for new or small businesses to operate within a single industry or with a single product line. Such a limited scope is natural owing to the demands of initiating and expanding a business. Companies in the early stages of development first optimize the use of resources in their current business. This means an initial period of accumulating resources in order to meet growing demand, then expansion of the product line into new geographic markets and customers, and finally rationalizing the position of the firm within its industry. Since the roster of corporations is continually regenerated, including a large number of new businesses, a significant fraction of firms is always logically "single business" because of their early stage in corporate development.

A second category of firms in the single-business category chooses to occupy a well-defined niche in the market. Many companies perform well by nestling in a part of a market the giant companies overlook or consider too small to serve. As long as they continue a "niche" strategy, such companies can prosper without assuming the greater risks of diversification or competing against the majors in their field.

Finally, a firm may elect to remain with its particular product because that product is still growing. There are literally thousands of companies unable to cope with all the opportunities their current business affords. Loctite is one of the most successful companies in the chemical industry even though it is small relative to the giants of the industry, and narrowly specialized in comparison to these leaders. Even IBM can be considered predominantly a one-industry company — the computer industry — although it is a giant enterprise. Thus firms classed as single business are not necessarily small or underperformers. They may in fact demonstrate exceptional growth because of their relatively small size or the favorable life-cycle characteristics of the industry they are in.

The Managerial Factor: A Multibusiness Policy

Not all businesses are growing, or growing fast enough, however. A company in a mature industry is faced with a difficult or impossible management task of overcoming the gravity effect of declining growth. Many of the dominant enterprises of today trace their beginnings to the era of emerging large business consolidations in the mid-to-late nineteenth century. Such organizations have grown dominant within their original line of business as well as having consolidated horizontally and vertically to the limits of the law. Today these firms are faced with the prospect of continuing along the less attractive phase of the life cycle for their industry or of taking opportunity, if afforded, of renewed growth through participation in new and fast-growing business sectors. Given such alternatives, it is not surprising that increasing numbers of large industrial organizations are diversifying into new business fields. For reasons documented elsewhere, acquisitions are often the preferred route to diversification.

There is, in short, a case to be made for either a narrow or a broad definition of corporate purpose — depending on management's perception of its opportunities. For this reason the remainder of this book takes into account steady-state policies of containment as well as evolutionary policies of diversification.

Summary

The interactive nature of decision making has been stressed continuously. For the policy-formulation phase we have identified three broad categories of factors that influence the final thrust of the policy statement — managerial, environmental, and evaluation of internal operations — and have dealt with the managerial factor in this chapter. Within each of these three areas are a great number of combinations of factors that can affect, and variously influence, the decision makers of an organization. Even more complex are the infinitely numerous combined factor-influences when we consider the interaction among the three areas of influence simultaneously. We cannot dwell at length on any area, or the combined force of the three areas, but it is important to recognize the underlying complexity of decision making and thus appreciate that only the tip of the process, or any of its parts, can be reflected in our analysis.

QUESTIONS

1. Assume that you have inherited the family's small retailing business specializing in young women's sports fashions. What type of overall policy would you establish? Outline initial steps you would take to develop your policy.

2. At what organizational level of a company would responsibility lie for developing the corporate policy? Why is it important to be thorough and precise in the wording of the policy?

3. Based on continuing rapid change in the external environment, what personal characteristics do you feel a chief executive officer should possess? What background experience do you feel would best prepare a chief executive officer to manage a railroad, an electronics company, a bank?

4. "Our company is dedicated to a fair return to our shareholders and a fair price for our customers." Is this an effective policy statement?

5. A company typically spends considerable time and effort in drafting its policy statement. How often should this corporate philosophy be revised? (You may illustrate this point with a particular company or industry, contrasting the 1960s with the 1970s.)

6. It is sometimes said that being in the right industry is as important as having the right management. Do you agree? Do you think the management of IBM could be just as successful in managing Gimbels, a major department-store chain?

MINI-EXERCISES

1. Find examples of two companies that have recently changed their corporate policy in a major way. (A few back issues of *Business Week, Forbes,* or *Fortune* magazines should produce several examples.) Evaluate the basis for the change, doing if necessary some further research on each company's situation. What recommendation would you have made regarding a change in policy?

2. The automobile industry has lost a significant market share over the years to foreign imports. Volkswagen was previously the only foreign car maker with any significant number of exports; now Toyota, Datsun, Honda, and others are exporting to the United States market. Was this intrusion into Detroit's home market avoidable? Do you believe Detroit might have taken more effective action to protect the small-car portion of its market?

    SUGGESTION: Break class into pro and con sides on Detroit's policy. Have each side research its respective position and defend it in class.

3. Oil companies are a dramatic case of an industry facing major changes and challenges. If forecasts of oil supply are accurate, the world will exhaust known reserves in a few decades. This is a scientifically demonstrable fact; only the timing is debatable. Facing the prospect of

loss of their major product, what steps should major oil companies be taking? What revisions in their policy do you believe to be appropriate?

SUGGESTION: Mobil, SOCAL, and Exxon have different approaches to meeting this future impact on their primary business. Study the differences in approach taken by each and try to rationalize these differences. Which approach do you believe has the most merit?

REFERENCES

1. Igor H. Ansoff, "The Changing Shape of the Strategic Problem," in Dan E. Schendel and Charles W. Hofer, eds., *Strategic Management* (Boston: Little, Brown, 1979).

2. Theodore Levitt, "Marketing Myopia," *Harvard Business Review,* July–August 1960.

3. Peter Drucker, "The Big Power of Little Ideas," *Harvard Business Review,* May–June 1964.

4. *Forbes,* September 15, 1967.

5. Ibid.

6. Ibid.

7. Robert L. Katz, *Cases and Concepts in Corporate Strategy* (Englewood Cliffs, N.J.: Prentice-Hall, 1970).

8. Rochelle O'Connor, "Corporate Guides to Long-Range Planning," The Conference Board, 1976.

9. Ibid.

10. Max D. Richards, *Organizational Goal Structures* (New York: West, 1978).

11. Ibid.

12. David Katz and Robert L. Kahn, *The Social Psychology of Organizations* (New York: John Wiley, 1966).

13. John Child, "What Determines Organizational Performance?" *Organizational Dynamics,* Summer 1974.

14. Ian C. MacMillan, commentary, pp. 166–72, in Dan E. Schendel and Charles W. Hofer, *Strategic Management* (Boston: Little, Brown, 1979).

15. Neville Osmond, "Top Management: Its Tasks, Roles, and Skills," *Journal of Business Policy* (now *Journal of General Management*), Winter 1971.

16. Douglas M. McGregor, *The Human Side of Enterprise* (New York: McGraw-Hill, 1960).

17. Jay Hall, Vincent O'Leary, and Martha Williams, "The Decision-Making Grid: A Model of Decision-Making Styles," *California Management Review,* Winter 1964.

18. John B. Miner, *The Management Process: Theory, Research, and Practice* (New York: Macmillan, 1973).

19. Chris Argyris, "The CEO's Behavior: Key to Organizational Development," *Harvard Business Review,* March–April 1973.

20. Henry Mintzberg, *The Nature of Managerial Work* (New York: Harper & Row, 1973).

FURTHER READING

Aguilar, Francis J. "Setting Corporate Objectives." In Richard F. Vancil, ed., *Formal Planning Systems — 1971.* Boston: Graduate School of Business Administration, Harvard University, 1971.

Ansoff, Igor H. "The Changing Manager." In Ansoff, Declerck, and Hayes, *From Strategic Planning to Strategic Management.* New York: John Wiley, 1976.

Bauer, Raymond A. "The Study of Policy Formulation: An Introduction." In Raymond Bauer and Kenneth Gergen, eds., *The Study of Policy Formulation.* New York: Free Press, 1968.

England, George W. "Personal Value Systems of American Managers." *Academy of Management Journal,* March 1967.

Kepner, Charles H., and Benjamin B. Tregoe. *The Rational Manager: A Systematic Approach to Problem Solving and Decision Making.* New York: McGraw-Hill, 1965.

Lundberg, Olof, and Max D. Richards. "A Relationship Between Cognitive Style and Complex Decision Making: Implications for Business Policy." *Academy of Management Proceedings,* August 1972.

Lusk, Edward J., and Bruck L. Oliver. "American Managers' Personal Value Systems — Revisited." *Academy of Management Journal,* September 1974.

Mintzberg, Henry. "The Manager's Job: Folklore and Fact." *Harvard Business Review,* July–August 1975.

Newman, William H. "Shaping the Master Strategy of Your Firm." *California Management Review,* Spring 1967.

Osmond, Neville. "Top Management: Its Tasks, Roles and Skills." *Journal of Business Policy,* Winter 1971.

CHAPTER 2

Scanning the Environment

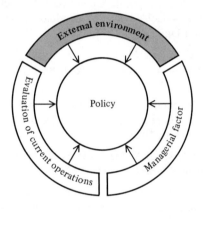

Business management today is in need of thoughtful, analytical, and creative academic research to guide its efforts in adapting to a world economy whose shape is, at present, only dimly seen. . . . Timely warning of trends and proposal of new patterns of organization, investment, and management could enable private enterprise to adapt in time not only to survive, but also to help build a new social and economic architecture structured around the needs and the liberties of the whole of humankind.[1]

One might expect these words from a university professor, or a government official, or the president of a national foundation. They are less expected from the chief executive of a major corporation. Yet this statement was made in 1977 by Reginald H. Jones, head of General Electric. It signifies businessmen's growing awareness of the changing external environment and its significance for business.

To survive and prosper, a corporation must increasingly pay attention to external forces — social, governmental, economic, and market — as well as traditional internal factors like finance, human resources, and research and development. An essential part of policy formulation, therefore, is environmental scanning and analysis: that is, the development of scenarios to identify those external forces important for a firm's continued performance and the means for taking account of such forces in the firm's determination of policy. Attesting to the rising importance of the environment is the increasing percentage of time spent on external affairs by chief executive officers (see Exhibit 2.1).

Predictably, a fast-changing external environment has had an impact on the managerial decision-making process. Businessmen's flexibility of action, while never unlimited, has been drawn much tighter in many areas. In addition, business has had to anticipate and plan more carefully for

EXHIBIT 2.1
TIME SPENT ON EXTERNAL RELATIONS BY CHIEF EXECUTIVE OFFICERS

A: How much of the chief executive's time is spent on external relations?

Percent of time	Number of CEOs
0 percent	0
1–25 percent	103
26–50 percent	72
51–75 percent	6
76–100 percent	0
Total	181

B: Is the chief executive spending more time on external relations now than three to five years ago?

	Number	Percent
More time	171	92%
Less time	2	1%
About the same	12	6%

Source: Managing Corporate External Relations, The Conference Board, Report No. 679, 1976.

EXHIBIT 2.2
CHANGING RELATIONSHIPS BETWEEN BUSINESS AND ITS
ENVIRONMENT

Industrial era (1900–1955)	Postindustrial era (1955–1975)	Future (1975–1990)
Emphasis on product/ market expansion to meet growth in demand.	Saturation of demand and growing environmental turbulence due to government, foreign, and technological turbulence.	Increasing vulnerability to external environment due to sociopolitical influence, constraints on growth, and strategic surprises.

Source: Adapted from Exhibit 1.1, Igor H. Ansoff, "The Changing Shape of the Strategic Problem," in *Strategic Management* (Boston: Little, Brown, 1979), p. 36.

potential external reactions to its decisions. This trend for external considerations to exert a mounting influence on corporate decision making has been visualized as an observable, cumulative process in Igor H. Ansoff's view:

> From the mid-1950's, accelerating and cumulating events began to change the boundaries, the structure, and the dynamics of the business environment. Firms were increasingly confronted with novel unexpected challenges which were so far-reaching that Peter Drucker called the new era an *Age of Discontinuity.*[2] Daniel Bell labeled it the Postindustrial Era.[3] . . . Today change continues at a pace which makes it safe to predict that the current escalation of turbulence will persist for at least another ten to fifteen years.[4]

Ansoff divided his conceptualization of change into a three-part view of industrial, postindustrial, and future environments, as presented in simplified fashion in Exhibit 2.2. Ansoff saw the trend from traditional production processes serving conventional markets and customers to an increasingly turbulent external environment posing new constraints, new rules, and unexpected situations. In essence, United States business would be shifting away from familiar supply-and-demand uncertainties to new and unfamiliar types of externally generated uncertainties. To illustrate only one dimension of this new turbulent environment, we can take a brief look back at the evolution of society's concern for protection of the ecology.

Development of a Postindustrial Society and Beyond

In the nineteenth and early part of the twentieth centuries, ecology evoked no emotional response. Companies poured waste into the waterways and discharged pollutants into the air because that was cheaper than processing the wastes. The public tolerated these practices because businesses were smaller then and the natural resources of the United States were considered almost limitless. Moreover, the alternative would have raised the costs of production and, ultimately, the prices paid by consumers. Thus, at an early developmental stage, the interests of the public and business could be considered mutually to favor this least-cost approach to production.

However, as corporations became large and their impact on the environment more noticeable, the interests of consumers and producers began to clash. Inevitably, the externalities of production — undesirable side-effects of dirty production methods on the environment — could be tolerated only so far. As the corporate impact on the environment increased, the cost of protecting the environment from further erosion had to be faced.

The need for change eventually became obvious to producers and consumers alike. But considerable disagreement arose over means and the burden of costs. Businessmen's former cost-free methods of handling waste products were suddenly to be curtailed or eliminated. Business would also be required to invest heavily in new antipollution equipment and clean production methods. Moreover, the time limits and compliance standards were thought to be overly restrictive by many businesses. Given the public demand for corrective measures and the inability of business to act in a unified fashion, government intervention was inevitable.

The resulting legislation has been impressive. Regulations now determine standards for maximum discharges into streams and lakes, smokestack emissions into the atmosphere, and exhaust emissions from automobiles, as well as general health and welfare guidelines that companies must follow. New federal agencies have been created to ensure compliance with the new regulations. In sum, a bureaucracy has been created to ensure that business adheres to higher minimum standards of social responsibility in terms of its abuse of the environment.

Moreover, the emphasis on ecological reforms has been duplicated in many other areas. As a result, over the past two decades or so, our societal expectations have been raised. Expectations from the business community by its external publics have escalated: "They associate with rising real income, cleaning up the environment, immediate rather than delayed gratifications, city rebuilding, an end to all poverty, and so on." [5]

Inevitably, these new demands on business have forced a reevaluation of profits as the sole motivator for top management. Although profits are still required for competitive survival, there is more to top management's responsibility than profits alone. In contemplating a new steel mill, U.S. Steel cannot calculate its return on investment considering only cost of construction and demand for the product. It must consider the costs of an environmentally "qualified" investment, including indirect costs of processing, reviewing, and approving all the required forms by many levels of government, as well as the direct costs of equipment to control the plant's impact on the environment. Similarly, nonferrous metal, paper, and chemical producers, and other manufacturers using historically "dirty" processes, would be constrained from a pure "profits" approach to new investment.

To the extent that society imposes additional environmental costs on business investment decisions, it increases management's decision variables. Such environmental costs were largely ignored in the profit equation in the past. They can no longer be ignored. They represent a first priority; those types of costs which cannot be avoided if an investment is to be made. As such, increasing attention to environmental factors will replace an earlier emphasis on internal product/market decisions designed solely to maximize profits.

Typology of the Environment

In positioning a company within its environment, one might choose a number of environmental factors for study. There are in fact an infinite number of external influences that comprise the environment for the entire business community. These external elements differ in their impact on various companies. They also fluctuate in intensity. In a well-known typology developed by Emery and Trist,[6] four types of environments were identified, ranging from placid and random (type 1) to turbulent field (type 4). Each type characterized greater and greater uncertainty for organizations. Correspondingly, for each type of environment a company would have to develop an appropriate policy, with a dynamic and complex environment requiring the most comprehensive yet flexible type of adaptation.

Corporate approaches to environmental scanning vary. For one company, a very broad perspective on a wide number of external forces may be desirable. For another, a selective focus on one or two principal areas of concern might suffice. Exhibit 2.3 shows a great number of external trends that are typically followed by the giant retailing firm of Sears, Roebuck. In contrast, a company specializing in infants' clothing may be primarily interested in trends in births and number of marriages.

A considerable amount of study has been undertaken in classifying typologies, notably Aguilar's general work on *Scanning the Business Environment*,[7] with later works by Newman[8] and Rhenman.[9] * Despite considerable progress in describing and classifying typologies, however, there has

---

* For a review of research on relationships between environments and organizations, see Miles, Snow, and Pfeffer.[10]

EXHIBIT 2.3
EXTERNAL TRENDS FOLLOWED BY SEARS, ROEBUCK AND CO.

Demographics

Population
Size & characteristics
  Size
  Growth rate
  Sex
  Age
  Marital status
    Singles
    Marriages/Divorces
    Remarriages
Births
  Birth expectations
  Birth/fertility rate
Location/mobility
  Regional
  Metro/non metro
  Farm
  Central cities
  Congressional districts
Households/families
  Age of head
  Average size
  One-person households
Minorities
  Illegal aliens
  Spanish Americans

Employment
Civilian labor force
  Growth rate
  Size & characteristics
    Full time/part time
    Sex
    Working wives
  Occupation
Regional distribution
Labor union membership
Hours
Benefits

Income
Distribution by
  Region
  Age

Earners per family
Education
Median income
  Household
  Family
  Individual
Personal income
  Components
Disposable personal
  income (DPI)

Spending
Personal consumption
  Expenditures (PCE)
Consumer price index
Consumer credit

Housing
Existing housing
  Units
  Type
  Region
Housing costs & sales
Housing starts
Incomes of purchasers

Values/lifestyles

Values
Work & leisure
Entitlement
Consumption vs. conservation
Consumer assertiveness

Lifestyles
Marriage/family structure
Homes/mobility
Shopping habits
Aging/retirement
Singles

Resources

Energy supply & demand
Coal
Electric power
  Backlog of appropriations

continued

EXHIBIT 2.3 *continued*

Natural gas
Petroleum

Mineral & chemical supply
Imported vs. domestic
metals

Agriculture
Food
Fertilizer
Agribusiness

Water availability
Supply, surface & underground
Delivery problem areas
Drought areas

Strategic depletion/shortage
Industrial capacity

Land

Technology

Expenditures for R & D
Federal
Total R & D expenditures
Defense
HEW

Alternate energy sources
Nuclear
Solar
Hydro, geothermal, &
photochemical, other

Plastics

Electric communications
Computers
Personal/small business
Network systems
Entertainment and games
Satellite communications

Transportation
People
Materials
Automobile
Electric auto

Manufacturing techniques
Durables/non-durables

Product development

Public attitudes

Consumer confidence/
Buying plans index

Public attitudes toward
Government regulations
Large companies
Corporate social responsibility
Industries & products
Energy situation
Environment

Public interest groups

Consumerism

Government

Operations
Government purchases
Government expenditures
Social welfare
Social security cost
Veterans benefits
Employes
Public debt
Rational economic planning

Government regulations agencies
Cost/criticism
Reform
Corporate crimes
Business lobby

Legislation
Anti-trust
Consumerism

Employment
Physical conditions
Equal opportunity
Benefits/security

Economic controls
Reporting/disclosure

Environment
Land use
Air, water, noise, waste disposal

Consumer credit	Energy
Physical distribution	Raw materials
Transportation	*Trade*
Warehousing	Trade/payments balance
Privacy	Exports/imports
Consumer	protectionism
Employe	Tariffs
	Cartels
Products	*Developing nations*
Safety	OPEC
Quality/life cycle	LDC's
Communication with customers	*Technology transfer*
Advertising/selling practices	
Complaint procedures/redress	*Economic indicators*
Warranties	
	Economics
Service	Gross national product
Repair quality/standards/licensing	Inflation rate
Postal service	Interest rate
Health care	Unemployment rate
Taxes	Productivity
Personal	AAA bond interest rate
Corporate	Capital investment requirements
Social security	Wage levels
International	Benefit cost levels
World population	Economic forecasts
Resources	Corporate profits and cash flow
Food	Capital formation/needs

Source: Reprinted by permission from "The Business of Issues: Coping with the Company's Environment," The Conference Board, Report No. 758, 1979, p. 11.

been limited integration of environmental analysis with the development of policy. One explanation is that each organization's situation tends to be unique. It is unlikely that a few isolated environmental factors are the sole external agents for change in all situations. As a general rule, the greater the degree of change the more likely it is that several forces will be involved. Thus, even if in some specific cases the important external pressures could be identified, these could not be generalized into a typological model that would capture the important causal factors for change that might exist for business as a whole. Therefore, despite progress on classifying typologies, the translation of such knowledge into effective business applications remains limited. As a rule, research has been "more descriptive and normative than predictive . . . with only a few exceptions . . . little has been done concerning the ways in which managers perceive the environment, in classifying these perceptions, or in explaining how different perceptions influence their decisions." [11]

A methodology for connecting external environments with the formulation of policy is beyond the scope of this survey. We shall, instead, develop a generalized typology of four broad external factors important to many companies without implying these particular factors are equally relevant for all companies. However, at various times and in various degrees, all companies will be exposed to one or more of these four external elements: government, consumers, economic conditions, and market conditions.

GOVERNMENT

The one influence perceived by chief executives as increasingly restrictive and unpredictable is government, and in particular the federal government (see Exhibit 2.4). As the private business sector expands, its operations tend to have an ever greater impact on society and the environment, with a correspondingly expanding regulatory role assumed by the federal govern-

EXHIBIT 2.4
THE ROLE OF THE CHIEF EXECUTIVE WITH
THE EXTERNAL PUBLICS

Public	Number of times cited by 185 chief executives[a]
Government relations	124
Investor relations	74
Relations with special interest groups (consumers, customers, minorities, etc.)	52
Media relations	25
Business and professional associations membership	21
Community and civic affairs	20

[a] Figures are not totaled because many chief executives mentioned more than one role.
Source: Reprinted by permission from *Managing Corporate External Relations,* The Conference Board, Report No. 679, 1976, p. 51.

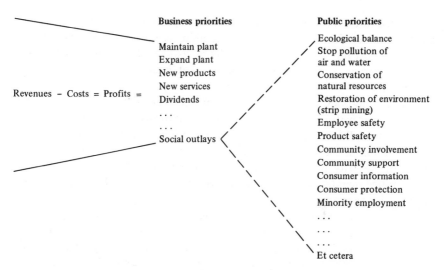

Business priorities

Maintain plant
Expand plant
New products
New services
Dividends
. . .
. . .
Social outlays

Public priorities

Ecological balance
Stop pollution of
air and water
Conservation of
natural resources
Restoration of environment
(strip mining)
Employee safety
Product safety
Community involvement
Community support
Consumer information
Consumer protection
Minority employment
. . .
. . .
. . .
Et cetera

Revenues − Costs = Profits =

EXHIBIT 2.5
A VIEW OF ALLOCATION BETWEEN BUSINESS PRIORITIES
AND PUBLIC PRIORITIES

ment. As a result, a number of legislative reforms have been enacted to restrict business practices. A look back through business history would reveal that, in general, business has been pushed into greater societal responsibilities by legislation rather than pulled there by a voluntary commitment to new environmental trends and social values. There is, one hopes, growing awareness and movement by business toward grasping the initiative for external responsibilities, as expressed in the epigraph at the head of this chapter.

However, some tension is probably inevitable, arising from differences in motivations and reward systems of business and government. Businessmen's most fundamental orientation must be the competitive survival of the organization. As such, they must carefully balance the consequences of spending for broad societal improvements against the costs of underinvesting in productive equipment and thus impairing the firm's future performance potential. The majority of companies lack the resources of an IBM or a Xerox and can ensure future survival only by carefully husbanding present resources. Whereas business resources are limited, potential environmental improvements are not. Consider the diagram in Exhibit 2.5.

Sales minus costs equals profits. Out of profits comes the ability to cover all corporate objectives including social objectives. Future ability depends on future profits, which will be sufficient only if certain private needs take priority over public objectives. The process won't work in reverse.

Public priorities can't be set with only the *hope* that there will be enough profits to meet them. The process diagrammed, for instance, can't begin with an almost limitless list of public demands to be forced within the considerably narrower range of possibilities that business can accommodate from profits.

In the end, although business has moved from a narrow emphasis on profits, profits will continue to be a prime motivator for most businesses. An important difference, however, is an increasing number of new external costs that will affect attainable profits. The government's role will be to increase the priority given by business to public considerations. In essence, the priorities mandated by government will become a cost of doing business. Since an increasingly active future role by government is anticipated, businessmen's costs, and ultimately prices paid by the public, will escalate. The government must "allow" higher prices in order to maintain the viability of business and thus continue to be able to fund social programs through revenues from private enterprises. Looking again at Exhibit 2.5, we can see that only by treating public priorities as costs can we assume that they will be covered by profits — and only by allowing prices to rise can profits be ensured to cover such costs.

As government increases its supervision, either indirectly through persuasion or directly through regulation, private decisions will increasingly tend to consider and reflect public interests. Profit accumulation will decline as a sole motivator to the extent that private interests no longer serve as the sole decision makers. In large firms profits may even be replaced as the prime motivators to the extent that government places a prior lien on profits to meet public goals.

Ultimately desirable would be a partnership whereby government could effectively monitor and control business practices without imposing so burdensome a bureaucracy as to vitiate the desirable initiatives and competitiveness of the business sector. Cooperation along the lines of Japan's business/government coordination of national objectives suggests a possible useful development. But to assume such a fortuitous result from today's tentative partnership would be speculative. On the other hand, it seems safe to predict that government will continue to assume an active role in reconciling relationships between businesses and their external publics whenever a basic conflict is involved.

CONSUMERS

The "consumer sector" could conceivably encompass the broad sweep of societal elements not included in the other three parts of the environment. Trends in cultural, legal, and political change, for example, are not specifically covered in our typology. But rather than try to be all-encompassing, we have deliberately focused on four broad environmental areas, and within the consumer area we shall be further selective by concentrating on two trends important for most businesses: demographics and consumer values.

Demographic Trends.   Relationships between consumer spending patterns and demographic factors like age and income are continually researched by business — for obvious reasons. A boom in the twenty-five- to thirty-four-year-old segment of the population in the 1970s, for instance, had significant marketing implications and will continue to be significant as these persons mature into more affluent consumers in the 1980s. At the same time, the number of births per family has consistently declined. The latter trend can be of utmost importance to a company like Gerber, which specializes in baby foods and products, whereas the former trend may be of greater relevance to companies like Avon and Revlon, for which young adults comprise a significant market for cosmetics and similar products.

Highlighted below are several major demographic trends that will be instrumental in determining future spending patterns and thus, indirectly, important in shaping the policy of firms who use them as inputs for decisions (see also Exhibit 2.6).

EXHIBIT 2.6
SELECTED DEMOGRAPHIC TRENDS

The past — and forecast
(*Dollar figures in 1978 prices*)

	1975	*1980*	*1985*	*1990*
Gross national product (billions)	$1,829	$2,298	$2,743	$3,213
Disposable personal income (billions)	$1,292	$1,569	$1,925	$2,305
Per capita disposable income	$6,048	$7,062	$8,264	$9,466
U.S. population (millions)	213.6	222.2	232.9	243.5
Persons by age	100.0%	100.0%	100.0%	100.0%
Under 18	31.0	27.9	26.7	26.6
18–24	12.9	13.3	12.0	10.3
25–34	14.5	16.3	17.1	16.9
35–44	10.7	11.6	13.5	15.0
45–54	11.1	10.2	9.7	10.4
55–64	9.3	9.5	9.3	8.5
65 and over	10.5	11.2	11.7	12.2

continued

EXHIBIT 2.6 *continued*

Births (millions)	3.2	3.4	3.9	4.0
Families (millions)	56.2	58.5	63.1	67.2
Households (millions)	72.9	79.7	88.5	96.8
Educational attainment	100.0%	100.0%	100.0%	100.0%
Elementary or less	21.9	18.3	14.4	11.3
Some high school	15.6	16.3	15.4	14.5
High school graduate	36.2	37.9	38.9	39.3
Some college	12.4	12.5	13.7	14.8
College graduate	13.9	15.0	17.5	20.1
Labor force participation rates				
Men	77.3	77.2	76.9	76.7
Women	45.7	47.8	49.7	51.4
Households by income class	100.0%	100.0%	100.0%	100.0%
Under $5,000	15.9	14.1	12.4	10.6
$5,000–$10,000	19.8	18.2	17.2	15.8
$10,000–$15,000	18.1	16.6	15.6	14.4
$15,000–$25,000	27.7	28.1	27.5	26.4
$25,000 and over	18.5	22.9	27.4	32.9

Source: Reprinted by permission from Fabian Linden, "Keys to the '80s," in *Across the Board,* Volume XVI, No. 12, The Conference Board, December 1979.

Trends for the 1980s

Overall population will expand around 10 percent, but the 25- to 44-year-old segment will grow 2½ times as fast. Thirty will be the key age — the age at which most families search for homes of their own.

In the coming decade it is expected that the average woman will have relatively few babies — but there will be many more children simply because there will be many more young women.

Educational levels will continue to rise. By 1990, 35 percent of the nation's adults will have had some college education compared to about 27 percent in 1980, resulting in a more sophisticated and demanding consumer.

Women will continue to increase their participation in the labor force. This will boost average family incomes and account for different types of spending preferences.

Real incomes will continue to rise. Over the past ten years households
with real annual incomes over $25,000 increased by about 80 percent,
and include 23 percent of all households. By 1990, roughly one-third of
the households will exceed this income level in real terms.[12]

Changing Values.   The changing demographic pattern of age has had and
will have a profound effect on changes in values. The "new morality," as
Daniel Yankelovich has called it,[13] was rooted in the surge of babies born
during and immediately after World War II. The sheer number of persons
born in this period has had an unparallelled effect on our society, unmatched
in our history. It is, according to one account, a unique one-time occurrence
that "will not ever happen again." [14]

Needless to say, this impact of new, youthful outlooks imposed on
traditional values caused severe strains and resistance. In the 1960s the
effects were reflected most noticeably in students' and young people's re-
bellions; moderating but continuing to shape society's total value structure
in the 1970s; and moving strongly to translate the effects of mass population
numbers/new values into major purchasing decisions in the 1980s. A number of attempts have been made to rationalize the development of emerging
values, particularly among the nation's youth,[15] as well as translating the
new values into meaningful market impacts for producers.[16] In Exhibit 2.7,
an example of five values representative of the "new morality" is con-
trasted with the corresponding traditional values most affected by them.

Although different interpretations of the "new morality" and its business implications can be drawn, there is little disagreement that value
changes are here to stay and that these changes will have substantial importance for business. A huge purchasing power "bloc" will be concentrated in
twenty-five- to forty-four-year-olds in the 1980s, with their buying impulses
influenced by the values this group will bring with them. As one observer
has noted:

> The more businessmen stand still as a new value system develops around
> them, the wider the gap, the lower their penetration of the market becomes,
> and the less able they are to provide satisfaction in return for any one
> dollar spent in an effort to do so. To sell them, one must know what
> they are thinking and feeling. Otherwise, product development, packaging,
> promotion, advertising, and sales begin to function at increasing levels of
> inefficiency until the business is no longer profitable.[17]

In brief, the 1980s should see a unique monetization of new tastes
and values; i.e., a wave of new consumers young enough to alter traditional
values and affluent enough as a group to translate these new values into
new patterns of consumption.

EXHIBIT 2.7
TRADITIONAL VALUES VERSUS NEW MORALITY VALUES

A. Life goals

Traditional morality	*New morality*
A. Social status B. Money	A. Social status B. Money *plus* C. New experiences, learning, creativity

B. Personal goals

Traditional morality	*New morality*
Economic	
A. Financial and personal security and stability (even at the price of boredom)	A. Financial and personal security and stability (but *not* at the price of boredom) *plus, therefore* B. Stimulation and excitement
Social	
A. Responsibility for making an economic contribution to family, community, and country	A. Responsibility for making an economic contribution to family, community, and country *plus* B. Social contribution to others: outside family, outside community, outside country

C. Work goals

Traditional morality	*New morality*
A. Making more money B. Increased power and authority	A. Making more money B. Increased power and authority *plus* C. Helping people D. Increased emotional gratification at work

D. Social goals

Traditional morality	*New morality*

Family relationships

A. Loyalty and support of spouse	A. Loyalty and support of spouse *plus* B. Good psychological communication C. Good mutual sex

Nonfamily relationships

A. Respect for authority	A. Respect for authority *plus* B. Respect for peers

E. Personal style

Traditional morality	*New morality*

A. Control of feeling and competitive behavior is how a man acts B. Display of feeling and deferential behavior is how a woman acts	A. Control of feeling and competitive behavior is how a man acts B. Display of feeling and deferential behavior is how a woman acts *plus* C. Each sex can develop the personal characteristics associated with the opposite sex

Source: Reprinted by permission from "Dr. Spock's Babies Take Charge," by Jeanne Binstock, from *Corporate Planning: Techniques and Applications,* Allio and Pennington, eds. © 1979 by AMACOM, a division of American Management Associations. All rights reserved.

ECONOMIC CONDITIONS

Uncertain economic conditions have always been with business, but the level and types of uncertainties had assumed new dimensions by the 1970s. In addition to the recurring problems of business cycles, contracting markets, and fluctuating profits, businessmen were faced with a host of new problems not amenable to old solutions. Most prominent of these was energy. Instead of plentiful oil supplies under the control of United States oil companies, the United States and the industrialized world had become subject to production limits and prices dictated by a new Mideast cartel of the Organization of Petroleum Exporting Countries (OPEC).

The result was sharply escalating prices for energy, which contributed to a related economic problem at home: inflation. The United States was unaccustomed to double-digit inflation, and no remedies reduced spiraling prices significantly. Moreover, inflation was only one area in which the "old" economics no longer seemed to apply. Much of the conventional wisdom of Keynesian economics — named after the famous British economist who wrote the so-called *General Theory*[18] — was developed in the environment of the Great Depression of the 1930s and was therefore oriented to solve different types of problems. Existing theory did not envision price inflation and low economic growth persisting concurrently; a new term, "stagflation," was coined to acknowledge this new phenomenon. Neither were higher prices and higher unemployment supposed to go in tandem. Also, little attention was paid historically to the supply side of the economist's supply/demand equation, so that disruptions in oil supplies as well as potential disruptions in availability of metals and other imported commodities could not be readily incorporated into current economic models. In addition, there was increasing criticism, from within and outside the economic community, that economics had failed to keep pace with the changing realities it is presumed to explain, as the following quotation illustrates:

> . . . we may have lost a generation or so of economists to a preoccupation with econometrics and mathematical "modeling" in the 1950's and 1960's. Such efforts have not been without their usefulness, but they diverted some of the best minds in the profession from examining the ways in which our economy has been changing and developing. For a good many years the economics profession was not really thinking about creating an analytical framework applicable to the world that had developed, but was preoccupied with perfecting techniques for projecting on the basis of past relationships.[19]

The declining ability of economics to explain much of America's problems has left a vacuum that as yet no authority has adequately filled. Thus, although economic uncertainty has always been a consideration for policy and strategy formulation, it currently presents even greater uncertainties and risks simply because traditional knowledge is not sufficient to furnish answers for many of the critical new economic problems that have arisen.

MARKET CONDITIONS

Market conditions are the last external factor in our typological model, and perhaps the easiest for businessmen to deal with in conventional fashion. This is not to imply stable or predictable market conditions. Technological change, for example, has been extremely rapid. Obsolescence has been a critical factor for many companies unable to stay abreast of fast-changing technological developments in such fields as computers, electronics, and telecommunications. Also, competition among companies is no less a threat merely because it is a familiar threat. Increased competition from foreign firms for shares of the United States market has, in particular, added to market pressures.

But difficult as these problems may be, they are the type of threats businessmen have been conditioned to expect. They can be countered by effective product/market policies and strategies based on traditional evaluations of market size, number of competitors and intensity of competition, and reactions to competitors' initiatives. It is an area of the environment over which business may not exert much control, but one in which, through long experience and practice, business has developed effective techniques for survival. In contrast, external pressures from the government and consumer sectors of the environment, as well as new aspects of the economic sector, create unfamiliar risks, which often catch businessmen unaware and preclude a routine approach to decision making.

An Example of Environmental Scanning

It is clear that integrating the multitude of externally important trends into the decision-making process of an organization is a complex and individualized procedure. Each company's perception of its environment is influenced by its corporate circumstances and its own priorities. A small business selling a single product, for example, may be interested in only one environmental factor that tends to influence sales of that particular item strongly. A manufacturer of specialized machinery for street and sewer construction may be primarily interested in contracts for new street and sewer construction in his territory. On the other hand, a large organization diversified into many businesses would naturally have a broader interest and thus monitor a greater number of external trends.

It may be helpful in explaining business' collective attempts to deal with environmental changes to refer to the approach of a specific company. General Electric's approach to environmental analysis has been made public[20] and is outlined below in three stages to demonstrate how one com-

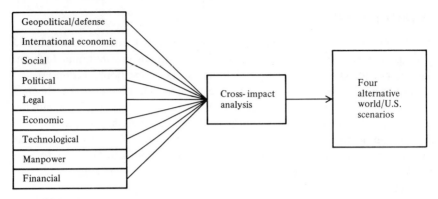

EXHIBIT 2.8
GENERAL ELECTRIC'S THREE-STAGE ENVIRONMENTAL FORECAST
Source: From Ian H. Wilson, William George, and P. J. Solomon, "Strategic Planning for Marketers," *Business Horizons,* December 1978, p. 70. Copyright, 1978, by the Foundation for the School of Business at Indiana University. Reprinted by permission.

pany has used environmental scanning for decision making (see Exhibit 2.8).

STAGE 1: SECTORAL FORECASTS

In this first stage, the basic identification and analysis of discrete future trends and developments are carried forward in nine sectors — two international (geopolitical/defense and economic) and seven domestic (social, political, legal, economic, technological, manpower, and financial). In each of these sectors the following elements were present:

(a) a brief historical review (1960–70) to give background and perspective, and to indicate the nature and momentum of then current trends;

(b) an analysis of the most probable forces for change, to provide a benchmark forecast (or, as Herman Kahn says, a "surprise-free" future) for 1971–80;

(c) identification and assessment of potential discontinuities — major inflection points in the probable trends — that might lead to "canonical variations" (to use another of Kahn's terms) of the surprise-free future;

(d) enumeration of the key strategic and policy implications of these trends for General Electric.

Collectively, these nine sectoral analyses supplied an extensive data base of forecasted trends, events, and discontinuities. However, they were segmented views — "tunnel visions," they might be called — of the future that took inadequate account of the possible interactions among sectors.

STAGE 2: CROSS-IMPACT ANALYSIS

To try to identify these intersectoral effects, cross-impact analysis was used. First, however, it was necessary to reduce the inventory of trends, events, and discontinuities (developed in Stage 1) to manageable proportions; the hundreds of discrete forecasts were simply too numerous to encompass in a cross-impact matrix. This reduction was achieved by rating the forecasts for (*a*) probability and (*b*) their importance to the company's planning, and then selecting the fifty or so trends or events with the highest combined rating of probability and importance. (This double-barreled rating is essential: Scenario development — and planning — must take note of future trends and events that, however low their probability, would have major impacts on the organization in question, *should they occur*. Conversely, it may be able to ignore, or lay to one side, highly probable events that are irrelevant to the organization.)

Working on the residual trends and events, the cross-impact analysis supplied the dynamic of interactive relationships essential to scenarios. In effect, this type of analysis traces domino effects, with one event triggering another, until it is possible to construct an internally consistent configuration of a possible future.

STAGE 3: SCENARIO WRITING

The final form taken by this environmental forecast was a set of four internally consistent scenarios, derived from varying combinations of discontinuities and the chain reactions revealed by the cross-impact matrix, and describing alternative views of the future for the United States and the world between 1971 and 1980. Included in this set were: a benchmark (for "surprise-free") scenario; a scenario of "more inward-looking" societies (essentially, a continuation of the trajectory current then); a scenario of "more integrated" societies (or what might be called a scenario of "more disarrayed" societies, or "the worst of all possible worlds").

Summary

Historically, decision making was much simpler for businessmen. Policy was what the president of the firm said it was. Reactions of government and consumers to business practices were usually a minor consideration in a firm's decision-making process. Motivated primarily by profit accumulation, firms could focus single-mindedly on this objective with relatively few external disturbances other than the ever-present ups and downs of the economy and the competition of the marketplace.

That has changed dramatically. It is now clear that business increasingly operates in an open environment. Not only must managers deal with internal problems of managing but they must devote ever more of their time to such external factors as government regulation, corporate image, consumer relations, and an accelerating rate of technological and economic change. Obviously, the panoply of actions and reactions that impact on a typical business can be only briefly touched on in a single chapter. Instead, an illustrative typology and a real but isolated corporate case have served as proxies; attempting to convey the sense of conflict and complex changes facing modern organizations, yet stopping short of a specific model integrating environmental factors with policy actions — a resolution that still depends on individual approaches and is influenced by differing corporate circumstances. The final area of analysis needed to complete our three-phase approach to policy formulation will be developed in Chapter 3.

QUESTIONS

1. Although reasonable people may agree on general social propositions such as the need for consumer safety, there can be disagreement over specific regulations. For example, safety belts in automobiles are a proven aid in reducing accidents. Yet some auto buyers object to their mandatory installation in cars and an accompanying buzzer that activates if they are not fastened. How far should government go in enforcing its standards for everyone? In the case of safety belts, would statistics on the reduction of accidental deaths and injuries from using belts be adequate, with the decision to install belts an option the auto buyer can choose to accept or to reject? Similarly, how far should government go in protecting consumers against potential health hazards of cigarettes and liquor?

2. The Food and Drug Administration has established numerous procedures to be complied with before a new drug is approved for sale. Over the years the procedures have proliferated and the length of time between discovery of a new drug and its final approval has been extended. As a consequence, drugs that might cure the critically ill have been held off the market. At least one research study concluded that the loss in lives from withholding new drugs outweighs the potential lives saved from a lengthier review period (which may prevent the

occasional disaster such as the use of the birth-deforming drug thalido-
mide in the 1960s). How would you weigh the pluses against the
minuses? What factors would influence your outlook as director of the
Food and Drug Administration; as president of a major drug company?

3. Demands for increased attention to social problems have induced
many companies to reorient their organizations to reflect this environmental force. Which personnel in the organizational structure of a
typical company would be likely to be affected? What would be their
change in title and responsibility?

4. Many large United States corporations have admitted to offering
bribes to officials in foreign countries. A partial defense offered is
that it is often necessary to pay bribes in other countries in order to
do business. It is also contended that it is unfair to apply United
States standards of morality to countries in which standards may vary
drastically from those in the United States. What is the government's
side of the issue? What factors has the government probably considered
in making its case?

5. During the early 1970s there was a lively debate over whether or not
the supersonic Concorde airplane developed by France and England
should be allowed to land in the United States. The arguments
against the Concorde were primarily environmental: noise pollution
and emissions. Eventually it was decided to allow the Concorde to
land at selected United States airports. What factors do you believe
swung the final decision in favor of the Concorde? Do you agree with
the decision? What are the international versus the environmental
implications?

6. Some companies have created the position of consumer ombudsman
within their organization; that is, an individual employed by the company who is to look at issues from the consumer's point of view and
report consumer complaints to management. What potential conflict
is built into this approach? Do you believe it can be effective? Individual students may be interested in finding an example of a corporate
ombudsman and then investigate effectiveness of this approach in
practice.

MINI-EXERCISES

1. From a recent issue of a business magazine (*Business Week, Forbes,*
or *Fortune*), prepare to present an example of corporate responsibility
being tested. In order to stimulate discussion, the class can be divided
into *A* and *B* groups. The *A* group can identify with the role of the

defendant (management) and present its case, and the *B* group can assume the societal role and argue its case.

2. When reading about corporate bribery, price fixing, or abuse of the environment, one may think that modern business personnel are uniquely corrupt. In order to gain perspective, review and comment on the activities of some businessmen from the past and relate their morality to their present-day counterparts. For example, Cornelius Vanderbilt, John Jacob Astor, John D. Rockefeller, and Jay Gould are good case studies to develop and present. Then contrast the morals of that period with those of today.

3. For one class session, a local businessman can be invited to present his company's viewpoint on environmental issues that have an impact for his organization. A good speaker might be a representative from the local utility serving the area, because of the many environmental issues that have developed for this industry. Another possibility would be a typical capital-goods company in the vicinity — such as a steel, cement, or paper producer — that has been subject to stringent anti-pollution standards. Prepare for this session by reviewing the background of the company and the environmental issues involved. This should lead to a stimulating debate and a better appreciation of points on both sides.

4. An alternative to Exercise 3 is to visit a plant site. Preferably, the company would be one that has been in the news or that is subject to close government supervision of water or air emissions, or safety standards. Meet with several representatives of the company and see the actual conditions under which the plant operates. After the visit, either develop a written report of the visit or use the visit as the basis for a classroom debate.

REFERENCES

1. Reginald H. Jones, "Meeting the Future Unsurprised"; presented to Beta Gamma Sigma National Honorees Luncheon at the Annual Meeting of the American Assembly of Collegiate Schools of Business, Toronto, Canada, April 14, 1977.

2. Peter Drucker, *The Age of Discontinuity: Guidelines to Our Changing Society* (New York: Harper & Row, 1969).

3. Daniel Bell, *The Coming of Post-Industrial Society* (New York: Basic Books, 1973).

4. Igor H. Ansoff, "The Changing Shape of the Strategic Problem," in Schendel and Hofer, eds., *Strategic Management* (Boston: Little, Brown, 1979).

5. George A. Steiner, *Business and Society* (New York: Random House, 1971).

6. F. E. Emery and E. L. Trist, "Causal Texture of Organizational Environments," *Human Relations,* February 1965.

7. Joseph F. Aguilar, *Scanning the Business Environment* (New York: Macmillan, 1967).

8. William H. Newman, "Strategy and Management Structure," *Academy of Management Proceedings,* August 1971.

9. Eric Rhenman, *Organization Theory for Long Range Planning* (New York: Wiley, 1973).

10. Raymond E. Miles, Charles C. Snow, and Jeffrey Pfeffer, "Organization-Environment: Concepts and Issues," *Industrial Relations,* October 1974.

11. George A. Steiner, *Management Policy and Strategy* (New York: Macmillan, 1977).

12. Fabian Linden, "Keys to the '80s — Youth and Affluence," in *Across the Board,* The Conference Board, December 1979.

13. Daniel Yankelovich, *The New Morality: A Profile of American Youth in the Seventies* (New York: McGraw-Hill, 1964).

14. Patrick D. Moynihan, "Peace — Some Thoughts on the 1960's and 1970's," *The Public Interest,* Summer 1973.

15. Robert Flack, *Youth and Social Change* (Chicago: Markham Press, 1971).

16. *The Yankelovich Monitor,* an annual published by Daniel Yankelovich, Inc.

17. Jeanne Binstock, "Dr. Spock's Babies Take Charge," in Allio and Pennington, eds., *Corporate Planning: Techniques and Applications* (New York: AMACOM, 1979).

18. John Maynard Keynes, *General Theory of Employment, Interest, and Money* (New York: Harcourt, Brace, 1935).

19. Guy E. Noyes, "An Economist Looks Back," *The Morgan Guaranty Survey,* March 1979.

20. Ian H. Wilson, William George, and P. J. Solomon, "Strategic Planning for Marketers," *Business Horizons,* December 1978.

FURTHER READING

Ansoff, Igor H. "Managing Strategic Surprise by Response to Weak Signals." *California Management Review*, Winter 1975.

Child, John. "Organizational Structure, Environment and Performance — The Role of Strategic Choice." *Sociology*, January 1972.

Duncan, Robert. "Characteristics of Organizational Environments and Perceived Environmental Uncertainty." *Administrative Science Quarterly*, September 1972.

Miles, Raymond E., Charles C. Snow, and Jeffrey Pfeffer. "Organization-Environment: Concepts and Issues." *Industrial Relations*, October 1974.

Organ, Dennis W. "Linking Pins Between Organizations and Environment." *Business Horizons*, December 1971.

CHAPTER 3

Evaluating the Potential of Current Operations

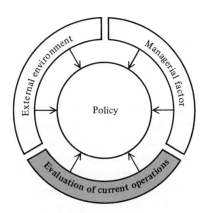

Once policy aims are established, management should test the capacity of present operations to fulfill them. Only after this internal evaluation is complete should management consider external opportunities and directions. It is axiomatic that familiar operations with known risks will be easier to manage than new and unfamiliar businesses. A fundamental rule for all companies should be to maximize advantage in present markets, products, or customers. A related but opposite corollary is to cut losses in areas that do not have the potential to meet minimum expectations. The philosophy of backing strong performers and cutting losers has been forcefully stated by Peter Drucker, who believes that "the areas of greatest potential should be given the fullest resource support — in quantity and quality — before the next promising area gets *anything.*" [1]

We are thus interested in an internal evaluation of present operations as the third part of overall policy formulation in order to determine the potential for achieving management's policy objectives with current operations before we consider alternate, external means.

EXHIBIT 3.1

Implementation of policy objectives

Policy objectives	From	To		By
1. Shift to consumer business areas	20%	40%	Consumer business	1985
2. Lower risks	50%	30%	In cyclical businesses	1985
3. Raise earnings per share (EPS)	6%	8%	Growth a year	All new
4. Raise return on investment (ROI)	9%	13%	After tax	1981 projects

As a precondition to an internal evaluation, we shall first provide an illustration of a possible set of policy objectives, which will serve as the background against which the results of an internal evaluation will be measured. Exhibit 3.1 refers to a hypothetical set of objectives and a timetable for a large and diversified company.

These objectives are detailed and clear, but in lieu of in-depth studies of the company's current operations, they must be considered tentative. They should reflect top management's considered ideas. They should also reflect its commitment to the general "type of company we want to be." As a practical matter, however, management's policy objectives may not all represent reasonable targets that the present business units can realistically hope to achieve. If the policy of the company is dramatically changed, for example, existing operations may not meet expectations no matter how efficient they become. For instance, we have used the illustration of a company basing its future course on four aims: (1) shift to consumer business areas, (2) lower risks, (3) raise earnings per share (EPS), and (4) raise return on investment (ROI) for new investments. Of these four criteria, only EPS and ROI could be improved by upgrading operations. The criteria of risk and consumer orientation depend not on how well present businesses perform but on whether or not they are inherently cyclical or consumer-oriented. To the extent that management wants to reorient the direction of the company away from existing cyclical areas or more into consumer lines, it has already made a decision that requires more than an internal tightening of operations could deliver. Thus internal evaluation would be only the first phase of a more extended analysis. And the efficiency of present operations would be measured only against the relevant parts of the corporate mission — EPS and ROI in this case.

It is further possible that businesses performing satisfactorily in non-cyclical consumer fields could still fall short of the desired objectives. As a general rule a business is judged by its competition. It rates "good" or "bad" marks relative to others in the same line. But satisfactory competitive marks will not necessarily satisfy overall corporate objectives. For example, a business in mature or declining stages of its life cycle may compete well with similarly situated businesses and still be unable to achieve ambitious performance targets in overall sales or earnings. Likewise, a conventional low-margin business like food retailing or wholesale distribution may not be able — owing to the characteristics of the industry — to raise profit margins sufficiently to match corporate objectives. The A&P cannot hope to attain the profit margin of IBM, even if A&P could cure its chronic operating problems, because of the fundamental differences between the two industries. Just as businesses can be cyclical and therefore judged inappropriate to the new mission, businesses can also be judged "good" in the traditional test of comparison to the competition and yet fall short of corporate objectives.

Generally, the more sharply a company's future course contrasts with its past, the more important will be external evaluation in fulfilling the new mission. But this does not diminish the value of internal evaluation and improvement. Companies seldom liquidate and rise anew. Even the most avid conglomerate companies have tended to diversify around a core business. And it is at least as important to maintain the thrust of the core business as it is to look for new opportunities. Determining the ability of the core business to meet corporate objectives — along with possible improvements in the core business — is the subject of this chapter. Subsequent chapters will deal with alternate options for improving corporate performance.

The Evaluation Process

Assuming top management has decided the company's broad policy objectives, it is time to consider if current operations can fulfill them. The following questions summarize the major points a company should address in evaluating the upward potential of existing operations: (1) Can policy objectives be met with present operations? (2) Can policy objectives be met if underperforming businesses are improved? (3) Can underperforming businesses be improved enough to meet the policy objectives?

PROJECTED OPERATIONS: THE BOTTOM-UP FORECAST

How will the company perform on a momentum basis with no change in the current mix of businesses? In order to answer this question, performance estimates from each business unit are required. The sum of these estimates will, theoretically, reflect expected total performance by the company.

However, business managers tend to be optimistic. On a historical basis, cumulative expectations of individual managers tend consistently to exceed results for the company as a whole. This tendency perpetually to forecast better results "next year" reflects pressures on business managers to demonstrate favorable results for their operations in competition with other managers, plus a reward system generally geared to performance measures. The resulting upward bias in estimates must be taken into account before one proceeds to evaluate the company's momentum against its established objectives.

PROJECTED OPERATIONS: THE DISCOUNTED FORECAST

Separate estimates from each business are reviewed at the corporate level and adjustments are made, based on past experience, to derive a composite projection. Some companies have developed fairly sophisticated techniques of adjustment. The following case uses actual review procedures undertaken by a large diversified company, although the figures used are hypothetical.

> Using 1976 as an example, the long-range forecasts of the various business units out to 1981 add up to about $1.2 million in earnings. Our estimating tools found a 10 percent overoptimism in the forecasts, giving the Discounted Long-Range Forecast (LRF) in Exhibit 3.1.

> Additionally, risks were not fully considered by the business units, including such risks as lower market growth than the business units expected, price competition and government regulatory restraints on pricing; foreign competition in our markets; product maturity and increased commoditization of products.

> These risks took an additional 18 percent off the original long-range forecast of the business units in order to be two-thirds sure we could achieve $900 thousand in earnings ($2.50 EPS) in 1981.... Thus we arrive at the momentum trajectory: what the company will earn on present strategies, all risks considered, on a two-thirds probability basis.[2]

PROJECTED OPERATIONS: CLOSING THE GAP

After deriving a discounted estimate of the combined business-level projections, the company is ready to compare continuing momentum growth with the desired performance objectives. In Exhibit 3.2, the adjusted momentum earnings of the corporation represent a compounded annual growth rate of 6 percent from 1976 to 1981. If this is not consistent with the desired growth objective for earnings for the period, the company would turn its attention to evaluating the possibility of closing the performance gap by improving current operations. In our prior example we indicated a policy

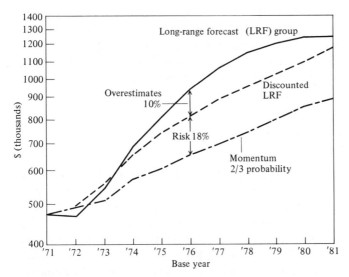

EXHIBIT 3.2
CORPORATE EARNINGS TRAJECTORY WITH ADJUSTMENTS

objective of raising the targeted earnings growth from 6 percent a year to 8 percent a year by 1981. In order to achieve the desired earnings objective internally, the performance of "momentum" earnings would have to increase by two percentage points, or roughly $100,000 in 1981 (see Exhibit 3.3).

Techniques of Evaluation

Companies have worked out various evaluative techniques for measuring the performance potential of operating units. But whatever methods are used, a manager must make three critical decisions: (1) performance cri-

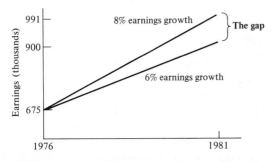

EXHIBIT 3.3
A PROJECTED EARNINGS GAP

teria to use in evaluating the businesses, (2) definition of types and amounts of resources required to upgrade underperforming businesses, and (3) which of the currently underperforming businesses are worth keeping. The final judgments on which criteria to use in reaching decisions are at least as important as the techniques employed. The three steps in the decision process are described below.

STEP 1: PERFORMANCE SCREEN TO RANK BUSINESS UNITS

Each business unit is measured against management's criteria for future expected performance. But in order to estimate a business unit's future, management must first evaluate past performance records. In effect, a profile is developed of each free-standing business. This profile provides background for management to evaluate the characteristics of the business; its past strategies, its actual performance, and its comparison to competition in its markets. Such an evaluation might include a review, for each business, of size and rate of revenue growth, profit and rate of earnings growth, return on investment and a risk/reward test, market share and trend, technical or product leadership, major new products or strategies, business unit and industry maturity, and competitive position assessment.

Profiling a business unit clearly involves considerable work and scope. However, the findings from the evaluation of past performance are important only as they enable management better to estimate a business unit's *future* ability to meet current corporate objectives. Each business unit will typically face three phases of evaluation: (1) profiling based on past performance, (2) testing against current objectives, and (3) ranking for relative attractiveness.

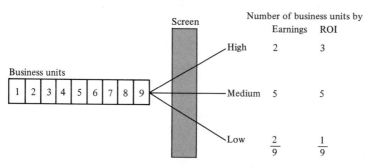

EXHIBIT 3.4
TEST OF BUSINESSES AGAINST CORPORATE OBJECTIVES

Exhibit 3.4 illustrates phases 2 and 3. The selection of ROI and earnings as management's performance screens carry forward the example of policy objectives used at the beginning of this chapter. In actuality, the screening process would generally involve a large number of tests and a more elaborate screening process. Yet the exhibit here is consistent with our earlier assumptions. Once management decides on the particular parameters for judging performance, the actual ranking of business units is a more or less mechanical — even if complicated and taxing — effort of collecting and evaluating data.

STEP 2: NEEDED RESOURCES TO UPGRADE UNDERPERFORMING BUSINESS UNITS

After ranking business units to isolate the underperformers, a decision to keep or sell must be made. This is a tough decision — and one that management often skimps. It requires an extra look at each underperforming business unit to determine if additional investment could bring it up to management's standards. Further, the investment must be specified by type of resource, and the commitment of these resources evaluated and compared with alternative investments the company might make. None of these is a simple decision. None can be totally answered by using scientific formulas or computer models. To complicate the analysis further, top management may have developed a strong personal commitment to, and identification with, businesses that make objective appraisals difficult.

Yet specific recommendations must be made. And a quantitative basis for conclusions is desirable if it is possible. Therefore, the chief planner must, with top management's direction, attempt to provide hard guidelines for some very difficult questions:

Even with its best effort, can the business unit be turned around?

If yes, how much investment is required and over what period?

What types of resources are indicated and can they be spared from the rest of the company?

What are the relative costs/benefits of such an investment?

What is the return from our best available deployment of funds were the business to be sold?

Again, the hard analysis required to answer such questions is submerged in the straightforward results shown in Exhibit 3.5. Here, business units have been measured against three types of needed resources: financial, managerial, and plant and equipment. In order to rank the business units,

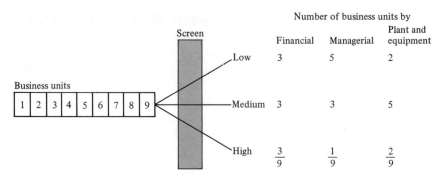

EXHIBIT 3.5
RESOURCE NEEDS FOR UNDERPERFORMING BUSINESS UNITS

these resources must be measured against a common denominator, such as the dollar equivalent of managerial and structural resources. Or a system of subjective weights may be used if a less precise determination will suffice and/or dollar equivalencies are difficult to compute.

STEP 3: DECIDING WHICH UNDERPERFORMING BUSINESS UNITS SHOULD BE KEPT

Finally, the findings from the first two steps can be used to decide which underperforming business units to sell and which to keep. The first step established the distance between management's targets and business units that were estimated to perform below these targets. The second step analyzed each underperforming business unit in terms of added investment needed to reach management's targets. Some of the decisions should now begin to come into focus.

For example, those business units which fall considerably below management's objectives and also require substantial investment can be tagged for disposition — or at best retention on a minimal investment basis with the cash generated by these businesses used to feed other parts of the company. The latter option describes management's decision at Standard Brands with relation to its Chase & Sanborn coffee.

> Standard Brands is [launching] . . . a series of new products that will concentrate on the consumer market. . . . Standard's consumer coffee business, represented by its Chase & Sanborn label, does not figure in those plans. Dropping from a 40% share of the market in the 1940's to less than 5% today, Chase & Sanborn will not get investment dollars. Instead, Johnson [chairman of Standard Brands] will continue to take profits from it, noting "It takes a long time to kill a brand." Adds Gutoff [president of Standard Brands], "If a market is in a decline and

your share is low, you almost have to be masochistic to try to grow that business." [3]

Another criterion management may use to make difficult keep/sell decisions is the fit of the business unit with the future plans and objectives of the company. That is, a business that is a satisfactory performer may not even be considered for further investment if it does not fit into management's future plans. This was the rationale of NL Industries (formerly National Lead) disposing of its familiar Dutch Boy Paints Division: "In 1976, to further improve our efficiency and to facilitate the pursuance of *our longer range goals,* we disposed of a number of operations. Late in the year we sold the Dutch Boy Paints Division, *our only consumer product business.*" [4]

Also, the size of the business can be important. A potentially satisfactorily performing business, but one that accounts for a small contribution to total operations, is more readily divested than a larger business unit. In disposing of Dutch Boy Paints, NL Industries was influenced by the fact that while it was "historically important to us, the operation accounted for less than 4% of Company sales." [5] Similarly, when Philip Morris decided in 1977 to dispose of its American Safety Razor Company, a determining factor was its modest $40 million in sales compared to more than $3 billion for the parent company. [6]

A framework such as that seen in Exhibit 3.6 provides a guide that can assist in marshaling the data for systematic analysis. In addition, mar-

EXHIBIT 3.6
FIVE-YEAR FINANCIAL PLAN FOR UNDERPERFORMING
BUSINESS UNITS (Dollars in Millions)

Underperforming business units	Business units to be retained (added spending)		Business units for divestment (added cash)
A	New plant	$45	
B	Working capital	5	
C	New equipment	12	
D	Management and staff	2	
E	Overhaul distribution system	10	
F	Modernizing of plant	8	
G	Divest		10
H	Divest		4
I	Divest		14
	Totals	$82	$28
	Net inflows (outflows)	($54)	

ginal cases can be influenced by management's current alternatives for deployment of funds. If ready opportunities exist for investment of divestment proceeds, then a decision to redeploy the funds is more likely to be made. Ultimately, decisions will reflect a mix of fact and judgment.

Revised Company Outlook

Management has now gone full circle in evaluating present operations. It has determined which business units conform to its corporate objectives and also meet its performance criteria. It has also decided which business units can be kept but need strengthening and which can be sold to provide funds to be redeployed throughout the company. With a now revised composite operation, management can once again test future performance of operations against corporate objectives. If the revitalized organization can meet the firm's objectives, future strategy will consist of internal improvements and investments. But if a gap between policy objectives and the momentum thrust of the organization persists, management must look to external means to fulfill its policy objectives or possibly revise its objectives. It can be said that "the essence of management is creation, adaptation, and coping with change. Seen from the viewpoint of general management, there are two basic types of change. One, is the fluctuations in the operating

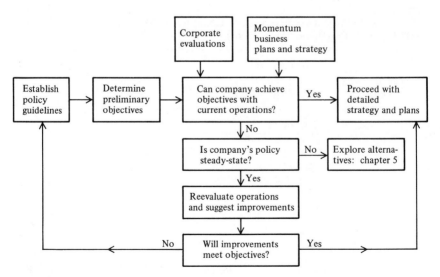

EXHIBIT 3.7
FORMULATION AND TESTING OF POLICY

levels and conditions: in sales, profits, inventory, labor force, budgets, productive capacities, etc. This kind of change expands and contracts the activities of the firm, but leaves the nature of the firm intact. The other type transforms the firm." [7]

The first kind of change in this quotation is considered in this text to require a steady-state management policy and the latter is viewed as an "evolutionary" management policy. In Chapters 4 and 5, we look first at the development of external options for measuring up to corporate policy objectives, assuming that internal upgrading of operations would by itself be insufficient to close the performance gap. This would be the path indicated if a company had an evolutionary policy. In Chapters 6–8 the improvement of current operations is considered. This chapter is oriented primarily to situations in which management has a steady-state philosophy, precluding any but an internal operations-based strategy for improvements. In Exhibit 3.7 the decision points that management has faced thus far are summarized.

Summary

In this chapter we have examined the third factor — evaluation of current operations — which influences policy formulation. Current operations are the logical place to test the feasibility of achieving management's desired policy objectives. As part of the evaluation process these three questions were addressed:

1. Can policy objectives be met with present operations?

2. Can policy objectives be met if underperforming businesses are improved?

3. Can underperforming businesses be improved enough to meet the policy objectives?

Assuming the capacities of existing operations are sufficient, or can be economically improved, to meet management's policy objectives, the development of strategy and plans will then center on existing businesses. Also, policy formulation will be oriented internally to development and improvement of current businesses.

QUESTIONS

1. In evaluating the total enterprise, why is it important first to support the areas of internal growth and promise before looking for external opportunities?

2. In what circumstances might an existing business unit be outper-forming its industry and still be deemed an unsatisfactory performer by top management?

3. Explain what is meant by a sales or earnings gap. What two primary alternatives are available to close the gap? How will management choose between alternatives?

4. In what ways does a performance screen help in evaluating current operations? What types of criteria might you establish when developing such a screen for (a) a food retailer, (b) an auto-parts distributor, and (c) an airline?

5. What steps are open to management when a business unit is initially defined as an underperformer? Is there a specific time within which actions must be taken?

6. In the text Standard Brands' Chase & Sanborn coffee was mentioned as a marginal product that was being "milked." What were the reasons? What other products can you name by brand that you believe are in a position similar to that of Chase & Sanborn coffee? Why are companies still sticking with these products?

MINI-EXERCISES

1. Propose a set of performance criteria for a specific company *before* you do any research on that company. Once your performance criteria are established, research the company and see how close it comes to your expectations. If there is a gap between your criteria and its performance capability (based on historical trends), to what do you ascribe it? Is the gap reconcilable? How?

2. Assume that you have been assigned the task of evaluating the potential of a medium-sized company in a competitive industry (e.g., retail trade; and an actual company like Macy's department store, with which most students are familiar, is desirable). How would you approach such an assignment?

   SUGGESTION: Identify the major areas for investigation, suggest sources of information for supplying answers, and develop a technique for assimilating data and arriving at a conclusion. The methodology rather than precise figures is the important thing.

REFERENCES

1. Peter F. Drucker, "Managing for Business Effectiveness," *Harvard Business Review*, May–June 1963, p. 59.

2. This is paraphrased from an executive planning session of a large diversified manufacturing company.

3. *Business Week,* May 16, 1977, p. 41.

4. *Annual Report 1976,* NL Industries, p. 2 (italics added).

5. Ibid.

6. *Wall Street Journal,* May 20, 1977, p. 3.

7. Igor H. Ansoff, "The Changing Shape of the Strategic Problem," in Schendel and Hofer, eds., *Strategic Management* (Boston: Little, Brown, 1979), p. 30.

FURTHER READING

Buchele, Robert B. "How to Evaluate a Firm." *California Management Review,* Fall 1962.

Gross, Alfred. "Meeting the Competition of Grants." *Harvard Business Review,* May–June 1967.

Rothschild, W. E. "Competition Analysis." *AMA Management Review,* July 1979.

Shank, John K., and Michael Burnell, "Smooth Your Earnings Growth Rate." *Harvard Business Review,* January–February 1974.

Wald, J. "What the Competition Is Doing." *Harvard Business Review,* November–December 1974.

PART II

FORMULATING STRATEGIES

CHAPTER 4

Strategies for Evolution and Change – Background: Evolution and Diversification of Business

Some companies stay in the same line of business, don't grow very large, and are successful. Many local businesses such as law firms, accounting firms, independent grocery stores, and retail shops are satisfied to stay within a limited geographical area and to accept an accompanying restraint on the growth of their operations. Such firms are generally small because there is only so much business to be had within any locality. The growth is seldom dynamic because the market is mature, meaning that demand is geared to growth in local population and incomes.

An alternative path to growth is to remain in a business but to expand it into a number of geographical areas. Ultimately, a company could become dominant within its selected product line nationally and even internationally. Large national firms that have achieved prominence in their industry include R. R. Donnelley in commercial printing, Wm. Wrigley in chewing gums, and Crown Cork and Seal in closures and containers. These companies are not only successful in their respective industries but are apparently satisfied to remain within their area of specialization. However, this strategy is fast becoming a minority tactic within the fraternity of large industrialized companies. By staying within an industry, growth is limited to the automatic growth of the market or to increases in a company's share of the market. As a market approaches maturity, the rate at which the total market expands will moderate. This means that a company wishing to sustain or improve on its past rate of growth must capture market share from a competitor — not an easy task in the highly competitive environment typical of a mature market.

Many large industrial corporations have chosen not to accept these limitations on growth. In order to sustain satisfactory rates of growth, many major companies have diversified into other fields. By 1968, 184 of the 200 largest industrialized firms in the United States had already diversified into more than five product categories (by 4-digit Standard Industrial Classification Codes).[1] The primary means of diversification was acquiring other companies, as the Federal Trade Commission has noticed:

> The increase in diversification may have been partly accounted for by internal entry, but it is likely that merger played the major role. This is illustrated by a recent study of diversified food manufacturers. The "Economic Report on the Structure of Food Manufacturing" showed that between 1950 and 1966, 30 large food manufacturers entered 186 new 5-digit product classes (and) acquisitions accounted for 150 of the 186 extensions.[2]

The surge of acquisitions after World War II, and particularly since the mid-1950s, has altered the organizational strategies and structures of American industry. In an evaluation of the major changes since World War II, the rate of change in the environment has been isolated as one of the two most significant factors. The second major force placing increased demands on the use of strategy has been

> the massive growth in the size and complexity of business organizations themselves. . . . The different businesses in such complex enterprises must . . . be integrated effectively, as must different cultures in the multinational enterprise, and all of these factors together must be integrated across time. Such integration has required an elaboration of the basic concept of strategy that is at the core of the policy and planning field today.[3]

Rumelt has provided the evidence that the majority of *Fortune* 500 industrialized firms developed from a single-business emphasis in 1949 to a multibusiness form of organization by 1970.[4] Increasingly, firms are deploying resources beyond the boundaries of current operations. Moreover, they are accomplishing such diversification by acquiring the assets of other companies rather than stressing internal diversification. This strategy is currently setting the evolutionary style for many dominant United States companies, although the strategy is not necessarily intended, or appropriate, for all companies. Many firms have grown and prospered by following a restrained scope of operations (see Exhibit 4.1). A majority of the 10,000 to 11,000 estimated private business organizations in the United States are undiversified and will probably elect to remain so. Nor is there any inherent advantage in diversification, and in particular extreme diversification of a conglomerate nature, over nondiversification or diversification into closely related activities. There are in fact studies that question whether or not unrelated diversification has improved the performance of acquiring companies.[5]

Nevertheless, diversification through external means is an important strategic concept worth discussing for two principal reasons: (1) it has played a significant role in the strategy of large, complex organizations, which play such an important part in our economy, and (2) it appears to be a strategy such firms seem determined to pursue and, therefore, to understand the field of business policy requires an appreciation for the motivation and rationale behind such a trend.

EXHIBIT 4.1
THE AMP CONNECTION

How do you diversify out of the one-product-line dilemma when you get to be around $1 billion in sales? Here's AMP's surprising — and successful — solution: Don't.

A portrait of the late Uncas A. Whitaker, founder of AMP, Inc., dominates the company's Harrisburg, Pa. headquarters lobby just as the executive offices upstairs are still steeped in his philosophy. "Whit always said the perfect recipe for a company was the 'magic 10s,'" says J. D. Brenner, president and chief executive officer. "Real growth of at least 10% a year, minimum 10% aftertax margins and at least twice 10% on equity." Brenner leans back cheerfully. "That's what we try to do."

No wonder he's cheerful; most of the time AMP does better than the "magic 10s." Last year it earned over $120 million aftertax on more than $1 billion in sales, for a return on equity of about 30%. It has been clicking off average growth rates of 15% or more practically forever, without a single acquisition. This darling of the institutions (Chemical Bank and J. P. Morgan between them hold some 4.8 million of the 36.2 million shares) traded recently at 40, a generous 12 times earnings.

AMP has achieved this impressive record with a most unprepossessing product line: electrical connecting devices. Whitaker led AMP, which began in 1941, in

continued

EXHIBIT 4.1 *continued*

pioneering a relatively simple "crimp" technique for connecting wires and terminals and a hand tool to do it that often replaced laborious hand soldering.

A nice business, that, but too easy to get into; there are limitless ways to connect one metal thing to another, many of them simple. So there were and are hundreds of U.S. competitors, including the likes of ITT, Amphenol, 3M and TRW. Overseas, where AMP gets nearly half its revenues, there are several hundred others. So, how to get an edge?

Fortunately, Whit also invented an enormously successful business formula. First, be on the leading edge with product improvements. This was Whitaker's forte, particularly when it came to the automated machinery for attaching connectors that proliferated in the 1950s. Second, broaden the line by logical extensions from existing items — today AMP offers over 60,000 different types and sizes of connectors, ranging from three-millimeter items to special cable splices that are six inches wide.

Beyond that, AMP's real secret weapon has been to build the product into a customer's plants so thoroughly he'd practically have to tear them down to get it out. AMP engineers design automated connector-fastening machines to fit into industrial assembly lines, sometimes even while the end product is still being designed. They install the machines, train the operators and maintenance men to service and repair the machines and, when technology advances, replace the machines. So AMP not only owns the machines, it also provides the only workable "razor blades" for its custom-made "razors." About two-thirds of AMP's $1 billion volume is in connectors, some at premium prices, some not, that feed all those cost-cutting machines.

To run this carefully planned company AMP likes to "overhire," as Brenner puts it — assign people initially to jobs that don't quite come up to their capabilities. Brenner himself has been with AMP for nearly 33 years, coming up through the ranks of engineering and manufacturing. He says, "Whit didn't treat management as a pure skill, like ITT does. Everybody here has to be steeped in the business. That's called 'knowing the territory.' "

But the sayings of Chairman Whit didn't cover everything. AMP was jolted shortly after its founder's death in 1975. Earnings, which never declined seriously in previous recessions, collapsed in 1975 from $1.23 a share to 73 cents. "Two things were wrong," says Brenner, still cheerful. "Primarily, our sales were off because customers were liquidating huge inventories, and our managers overseas were faced with inflexible labor costs during a slowdown."

So Brenner came up with some solutions of his own. Diversify the product? Not at all. Rather, diversify the markets. Now the recession-resistant computer industry accounts for almost 30% of domestic sales, while consumer products take just 10%. Overseas volume meanwhile has more than doubled.

How long can AMP continue these fugue-like variations on its central theme? Brenner, who soon must pass on Whit's baton (he is 62), is starting to go a little farther afield. Working backwards from connectors, AMP is increasingly developing electromagnetic filters important to computer makers, and specialized electrical cable among other products.

But Whit's formula still holds: Don't diversify; elaborate.

Source: From *Forbes*, January 21, 1980, p. 76. Reprinted by permission of Forbes Magazine.

Let us now distinguish between growth in mere size and growth by means of organizational change. General Motors is a vast industrial enterprise that has grown tremendously yet has not outgrown the basic organizational logic developed by Alfred Sloan and adopted in 1920. A company like ITT, on the other hand, has achieved its current giant size mainly by acquisitions, and it has had to develop a more complex and evolving organizational structure to manage a strategy of diversified growth.

Because this book is about the management of change, and because change, as opposed to mere growth, is represented at present primarily by the strategy of external diversification, let us review the empirical evidence for this trend. Also, merger* cycles and their influence on evolving corporate structures deserve more than the scant attention they have received in scholarly works. The inescapable fact is that diversification is a corporate way of life. Before anticipating future organizational structures and strategies one should have an understanding of major changes that have shaped the past.

Three Major Merger Movements

THE FIRST TWO MERGER WAVES[6]

The first great merger movement occurred from 1889 to 1902, with a peak in 1899. This first burst of activity represented a drive for monopoly power, primarily through horizontal and vertical mergers, which created some of the more formidable corporations in American business history. The most notable of these combinations resulted in the formation of the United States Steel Company in 1901. In total, 2,700 industrial and mining company mergers occurred during this initial merger period.

The second wave of activity occurred from 1925 to 1931 and involved more than 5,800 mergers. The focus of merger interest continued to be consolidation of industries through vertical integration of buyer-seller relationships and horizontal product and geographic extensions. Nearly 70 percent of the mergers from 1926 through 1930 involved the elimination of direct competitors.

Each of these merger movements was instrumental in altering the structure of corporate enterprise. During the first period, leading manufacturers consolidated their positions in such basic industries as steel, tin cans, farm machinery, tobacco, copper, chemicals, and typewriters. The second merger movement extended the market power of leading corporations and tended to increase market concentration in a number of American industries.

---

* "Merger" is used interchangeably with "acquisition" in a nontechnical reference to the combination of two firms.

The motivations for merger actions by powerful companies in these two periods are clear enough. In merging horizontally, companies forged a broad base of market power. Complementing this move were vertical extensions that achieved efficiencies in production and distribution, permitting lower unit costs and thus strengthening competitive positions. However, these stimuli to growth were severely curtailed after enactment of the Celler-Kefauver Amendment to Section 7 of the Clayton Act in 1950. Since then the antitrust agencies have actively enforced this amendment against hundreds of merger proposals that would have reduced or eliminated competition. This amendment has succeeded in dramatically reducing the number of horizontal and vertical combinations.

THE PRESENT MERGER MOVEMENT: THE RISE OF CONGLOMERATE MERGERS

The third and still continuing merger period began in the mid-1950s. During this movement the conglomerate merger — acquisition of a company in an unrelated business — became prominent. More than ever before, companies were diversifying beyond familiar industry boundaries. Many seemingly incompatible and, in the opinion of some, irrational combinations resulted. The emphasis was exactly opposite from the two prior merger waves: instead of striving for the economies offered by combining businesses in the same or related industries, companies expanded by entering the most promising fields, regardless of any relationship to the present business. Exhibit 4.2 illustrates the growing importance of this diversification strategy. From 1951/55 to 1975, the percentage of horizontal and vertical "large" * mergers declined from 47.3 percent to 11.9 percent of all mergers. In contrast, the "total conglomerate" category — the most unrelated of merger actions as defined by the Federal Trade Commission (FTC) series — rose consistently from 52.7 percent to 88.1 percent of all mergers.

Although the duration of the third movement is the longest in history, the magnitude of merger activity is not unique. Only during the peak years of 1967 and 1968 was the level of mergers able "to match *in relative terms,* the hectic pace of 1923 and 1928 to 1931." [7]

After the peak of conglomerate activity in the late 1960s, a number of ill-conceived mergers unraveled in the first half of the 1970s. Undoubtedly the acquisition fever of the late 1960s included many companies ill-prepared for the difficult task of managing a multi-industry operation. However, the

---

* Large mergers as defined by the Federal Trade Commission involve acquired companies with assets of $10 million or more.

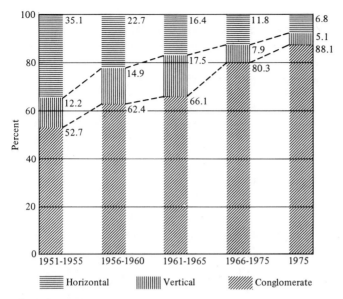

EXHIBIT 4.2
PERCENTAGE DISTRIBUTION OF LARGE* MERGERS BY TYPE AND PERIOD, 1951–55 TO 1975
Source: Bureau of Economics, Federal Trade Commission.

interest in unrelated mergers remains high. Indeed, although the frenzy of the late 1960s is gone, the interest in rational policies of diversification may be increasing.

Divestments, for example, have developed as an important part of an overall diversification strategy. A significant permanent trend in the number of divestments, beginning in 1970, is illustrated in Exhibit 4.3.

Part of the reason for the activity in divestitures can be attributed to abandonment of some mergers hastily conceived in the heyday of the 1960s, coupled with a financial bind from the recession in the early 1970s. A number of companies followed the expansion-contraction pattern of Fuqua Industries (see Exhibit 4.4). An ambitious period of expansion from 1966 to 1969 established Fuqua in a number of principal operating areas. By the end of the decade, however, Fuqua began to regret some of the acquisitions and found others incompatible with the company's long-range plans. Thus a retrenchment phase followed, with seven acquired businesses being divested from 1968 to 1973.

The breakup of large numbers of mergers in the early 1970s confirmed the suspicions with which many persons viewed the conglomerate movement. At the peak of merger activity in 1967–68, it was fashionable to

EXHIBIT 4.3
ANNUAL COUNTS OF ACQUISITIONS AND DIVESTMENTS

Year	Acquisitions Federal Trade Commission	W. T. Grimm	The Conference Board Acquisitions	Divestments
1960	1345			
1961	1724			
1962	1667			
1963	1479	1361		
1964	1797	1950		
1965	1893	2125		
1966	1746	2377	1797	
1967	2384	2975	2045	
1968	4003	4462	3220	
1969	4550	6132	3918	
1970	3089 [a]	5173	2312	393
1971	2633	4645	2043	598
1972	3006	4804	1786	464
1973	2826	4040	1527	422
1974	1762	2861	1050	364
1975	1228	2295	1010	432
1976	1441	2276	1158	455
1977		2224	1197	403
1978		2106	1342	424

[a] Revised from 2916.
Source: Reprinted by permission from data compiled by The Conference Board.

isolate the most unlikely combinations, such as an automotive parts distributor merging with a movie producer, as a temporary phenomenon and dismiss the entire conglomerate movement as a passing and ill-fated event. But the underlying strength of the movement proved greater than was imagined. Even if no further acquisitions are made, the great majority of large industrialized firms in the United States are already conglomerates. Even if strategies evolve no further, development that has *already occurred* implies major organizational changes and challenges for future managers.

However, the conglomerate movement is not likely to stop dead in its tracks. Mergers will continue to influence growth, although the character and intensity of the merger movement may change. A strong argument can be made, for example, that the movement has entered a period of increased "rationality" compared with the judgmental approach to unrelated mergers in the 1960s. To return to our example of Fuqua Industries, it is still a company diversifying and divesting — but with a difference. It is now pursuing defined "operational acquisitions"; namely, additions that will fill specific needs and add complementary strengths. In addition, Fuqua made a major acquisition in 1978 of National Industries, which was financed in part with a selective divestment program for 1975 and 1976. This respect for a structured diversification program is illustrated as phase II of Fuqua's development in Exhibit 4.4.

For those familiar with business and planning literature, Fuqua's strategy should strike a familiar note. It reflects a structured approach to acquisitions typical of a more mature and experienced generation of corporate managers. The mistakes of early conglomerateurs have not been lost on current managers. Moreover, the drive for corporate diversification is apparently a continuing strategy for many companies.

EXHIBIT 4.4
PHASE I: ACQUISITIONS, 1966–1969

Fuqua became established in many of its current principal operating areas in the period 1966–1969.

			$ Million sales	
Area	*Entry company*	*Year acq'd.*	*1970*	*1977*
Entertainment	Fuqua Communications (broadcasting) Martin Theatres	1966	26.4	56.8
Shelter	Stormor (agricultural buildings) Fuqua Homes (mobile homes)	1966 1968	34.1	80.9
Lawn and garden	McDonough (snapper)	1967	22.2	77.3
Photofinishing	Colorcraft	1967	17.9	64.4
Transportation	Interstate (motor freight)	1968	113.2	259.4
Sporting goods	Yarbrough (boat trailers)	1968	17.1	92.9
Others	(subsequently divested)		96.9	—
Total			327.8	631.7

continued

EXHIBIT 4.4 *continued*
PHASE II: DIVESTITURES

Year	Company (*products*)	*$ Million sales*	*Sold to*
1968	Natco (clay products)	10	Glen-Cery Corp.
1970	Ward (camper trailers)	11	Ward Interfinancial
1970	Varco-Pruden (steel build-ings)	19	Dombrico, Inc.
1971	Career (vocational schools)	9	Fortune Enterprises
1973	Trojan (seed corn)	17	Pfizer, Inc.
1973	Rome (farm implements)	10	Wyman, Gordon Co.
1973	Scorpion (snowmobiles)	8	Individuals
1975	Mountain Products (camping equipment)	3	Sportcaster, Inc.
1976	Thunderbird (power boats) (Sigma, Browning)	13	Porter, Inc.
1976	A&T Ski Co. (snow skis)	13	K&B Ski, Inc.
1976	Hendel Mfg. Co. (tennis apparel)	3	Pro-Group, Inc.
1976	Pacemaker Corp. (power yachts)	18	Mission Marine Assoc., Inc.

PHASE III: OPERATIONAL ACQUISITIONS, 1970–74

Year	Company	Products	*$ Million sales*
1970	A&T Ski Co.	Snow ski products	$ 8.8
1971	Hutch	Athletic equipment	4.8
1972	Ajay	Golf equipment	14.2
1972	Mountain Products	Camping equipment	.4
1973	Hendel Mfg. Co.	Tennis apparel	2.5
1973	Columbus Cycle Co.	Bicycles and accessories	18.6
1973	Wheelsport	Motorcycle parts	4.1
1974	Fox Distributing	Motorcycle parts	1.3
1974	Full House	Motorcycle parts	1.0
1974	Ebonite	Bowling balls	7.2
1974	ATI (Ebonite)	Billiard tables	8.9
1974	Western Skis	Water skis	2.8

Because unrelated acquisitions have been an important path to growth in the past, and promise to be a significant avenue for future growth, we turn now to the rationale behind such acquisitions.

Rationalizing the Unrelated Acquisition

Several reasons favor acquisitions as a means of entering new businesses: long lead times and associated risks of building a position from the ground up in an unfamiliar field, capital barriers that discourage new entrants in capital-intensive industries, and an existing distribution/customer network, which would be difficult to duplicate. These reasons, however, explain better why a company doesn't diversify through internal means than why a company chooses to diversify into new and unfamiliar fields in the first place. Among the possibilities for choosing to make an unrelated acquisition, the following four reasons commonly rank at the top.

DIVERSIFY TO IMPROVE OVERALL PROFITABILITY

A common attraction of a different business is the potential for raising overall corporate performance. For instance, a firm dependent on government business, where profit margins are closely controlled and where an individual firm may have little influence over the terms of a contract, may wish to reduce its reliance on this one powerful customer. Rohr is a company that for many years was a subcontractor to the aerospace and aircraft industries. To lessen its dependence on these markets, it diversified broadly into mass ground transportation. It was an important contractor for the Bay Area Transit system of San Francisco. Rohr even moved into the manufacture of city buses by acquiring Flexible Company of Loudonville, Ohio.

Another tack a company may take is to diversify away from manufacturing and into services. With services continuing to outpace manufacturing growth, industrial companies have sought acquisitions in the service sector of the economy. Specifically, a growing emphasis on recreation has in the past proved a powerful motivation for diversifying into leisure products and services. The American Machine and Foundry Company, for example, decided in the 1960s to change its image from that of a government contractor to a multi-industry company with an emphasis on leisure. A first step was a name change to AMF. More substantial actions included a number of acquisitions into the leisure field, including the manufacture of pleasure boats, motorcycles, skiing equipment, bicycles, and a variety of other sports equipment as well as sportswear.

DIVERSIFY TO REDUCE RISKS

Companies in a highly volatile business where earnings can fluctuate randomly and sharply, such as a ship chartering service, may wish to reduce exposure to the downside risks. In exchange, peaks in earnings would be moderated. This dampening of the risk cycle may be achieved, for instance, by acquiring a firm with relatively modest but predictable earnings growth. By nature, this type of risk spreading could be achieved only through an unrelated acquisition, where opposite risk characteristics would most likely be found.

Diversification of risk may also involve reduced dependence on the movements of a single economic variable, such as the impact of interest rates on housing starts. In this case, the ideal acquisition would be a business whose sales were directly, instead of inversely, related to interest rates, so that the opposing cycles of the separate businesses would smooth the trend in earnings for the whole enterprise.

Finally, there is a risk in staying in a declining or stodgy industry. This is similar to diversifying for profitability but with a stronger motivation. Textron, for example, was originally the American Woolen Co. The textile business by itself offered a limited future from Textron's viewpoint. Subsequently, Textron evolved into one of the most diversified firms with significant interests in office supplies, zippers, helicopters, electronics, and so forth. Textron obviously went much further than was needed to escape the restraints of the textile industry. Critics of conglomerate companies like Textron may consider them less advantageously positioned now than before they became conglomerates. Yet there are numerous examples of companies that have diversified away from the business in which they started because the future seemed limited or precarious.

TO MAKE USE OF THE LEVERAGE FROM A HIGH PRICE-EARNINGS RATIO

During the merger frenzy of the 1960s, one of the narrow financial reasons for acquisitions was the leverage advantage of a high price-earnings (P-E) multiple. Suppose companies A and B had the same earnings for each share of stock outstanding but company A's earnings were capitalized at two and one-half times the value of company B's earnings by the stock market. Then if company A acquired the shares of company B based on these relative values (in Exhibit 4.6 one share of company A would be exchanged for two and one-half shares of company B), and the P-E ratio of company A remained the same, company A would have increased the price of a share of common stock in the new company, and the total market value, by 25 percent (see Exhibit 4.5).

EXHIBIT 4.5
ILLUSTRATIVE IMPACT OF DIFFERENT P-E RATIOS
IN A MERGER

Before the merger	Shares	EPS	P-E	Common stock price	Total market value
Company A	10 million	$1.00	25 times	$25	$250 million
Company B	5 million	$1.00	10 times	$10	$50 million
After the merger					
Company A	12 million	$1.25	25 times	$31.25	$375 million

The appeal of such "instant wealth" tempted companies to continue looking for lower-capitalized shares to acquire. As long as company A's P-E multiple remained unchanged, other things being equal, the process could be repeated indefinitely. However, other things seldom are equal in such situations. A low value on earnings generally reflects a low quality of earnings. Short-term financial gains often crumbled as earnings of acquired companies deteriorated, or the acquiring company could no longer effectively manage all the firms it had acquired. Many companies that made acquisitions based on this narrow financial stratagem found that it provided a poor long-term rationale for building a sound operating company.

TO TAKE ADVANTAGE OF SPECIAL
TECHNICAL CONSIDERATIONS

A variety of special considerations may prompt the takeover of one firm by another. A common illustration is the tax-loss carryover. In a nontechnical explanation of what can be a very complicated maneuver, company A uses company B's tax losses to reduce the amount of company A's profits subject to tax. Company B in this instance is restrained from utilizing its tax losses because there are insufficient or no profits against which they might be used. Thus, merger with a profitable company offers benefits, and a bargaining position, for both parties.

A company seeking to obtain critical raw materials, or acquire management strengths, or increase its supply of other management resources may seek an acquisition with that specific purpose in mind. One company with a powerful but aging president, for example, decided to acquire a successor by acquiring a smaller competitor. Some years ago, another company was acquired primarily for its patent of a unique technology with wide application in the field of the acquiring company, thus increasing the acquiring company's position in the industry and blunting potential competition.

Do Unrelated Acquisitions Make Economic Sense?

Despite such varied reasons for making unrelated acquisitions, there has been scant theoretical support for conglomerate type mergers. The conglomerate movement was initiated and promoted within the business community. It is a concept unsanctioned by formal theory and thus far has been given little chance of ultimate success. Although the conglomerate trend has persisted over several decades, economic theory until now argues against any long-term benefits from such actions. Economists have found support for their position in the many conglomerate-like acquisitions that have come unstuck. Undoubtedly, the acquisition bandwagon of the 1960s included many companies ill-prepared for the difficult task of managing a multi-industry operation. However, all conglomerate companies have not failed. Some conglomerates came through the difficult down cycles of the 1970s in better fashion than the average industrial company. On reflection the wonder is not that some conglomerate mergers failed but that so many succeeded. In brief, there is a gap between the pragmatic approach of the businessman, who has relied on the unrelated acquisition as a means of growth and superior performance, and economic theory, which withholds justification for the long-term benefit of such action. The conglomerate acquisition is looked at from both the businessman's and the economist's points of view in the following sections.

Conglomerates, Economic Theory, and Business Practice

We can begin our economic analysis with Adam Smith, whose basic economic theorems survive surprisingly intact as the foundation for current merger theory. Adam Smith showed that productivity increases when labor performs simple, specialized tasks. Large-scale business permits greater specialization of labor and thus can achieve greater efficiencies. Large size also permits conservation of space, management, and equipment required per unit of production. Over the years, the justification for greater size has been anchored to the concept of lower unit labor and other production costs. The potential for economies in a merger can be summarized in two premises: (1) There is a product or market relationship between the firms. (2) There is integration of related activities after the merger.

The glue of economic logic is in *related* size. The more similarity, the more efficiencies are possible. The epitome of economy of scale would be Hertz merging with Avis. This could produce maximum cost reductions by integrating similar functions: management, advertising, sales force, marketing channels, and overhead. At the other extreme is the completely unrelated merger, such as an electronics firm acquiring a hotel chain. Here there are no apparent efficiencies from merging common activities. The completely unrelated merger is regarded by economists as an act of pure investment.[8] In effect, current theory tends to deny conglomerates or unrelated mergers an economic justification for existence. If the theory is absolute then conglomerate organizations are economic dinosaurs doomed to extinction.

Even if the theory is not absolute, and there are few absolutes in economics, economists have not dignified conglomerates with formal analysis. They are for the most part ignored. Where economics of scale are discussed in relation to conglomerate corporations, they are treated as of marginal importance. For example, Donald Turner, former chief of the antitrust division of the Justice Department, reviewed in some detail the potential for conglomerate types of economies in production, distribution, research, management, selling, and capital costs; he found little support for prosecuting conglomerates on the basis of inherent economic advantages or potential to achieve anticompetitive results:

> Tentative as our analysis has been, it indicates quite strongly that one cannot support an attack of much greater breadth on conglomerates without trenching on significant economic and other values, and therefore without an unprecedented reliance on judgments of an essentially political nature.[9]

Similarly, the professional economist who is prone to criticize conglomerates finds it frustrating that he is armed with no stronger theoretical weapon than his preconceptions.

> . . . when faced with a truly dangerous phenomenon, such as the conglomerate mergers of the 1960s, produced by financial manipulations making grist for their security mills, the professional antitrust economists were silent. Like other realities of a modern enterprise, this phenomenon, which will probably subvert management effectiveness and organizational rationale for generations, is outside their conceptual framework.[10]

The conglomerate movement has tended to emphasize and develop as a distinguishing characteristic a different organizational approach to the management of its parts. It departs dramatically from a traditional pyramid structure of centralized control from the top down; shifting from an emphasis on close operating control by top management to a decentralized structure with financial and planning controls at corporate headquarters and a large degree of autonomy to its operating divisions. This is a concept almost diametrically opposed to large-scale efficiency as envisioned in economics textbooks.

Instead of integrating functions, conglomerates leave acquired companies with a large degree of autonomy. Instead of acquisitions being evaluated by vertical and horizontal advantages of expanding into compatible fields, managements evaluate acquisitions by their performance potential, regardless of relation to present activities. While close operating controls give one type of efficiency, conglomerates find this impedes the planning and flexibility required in a widely diversified firm.

That a rationale for organizational change exists is strongly suggested by continued corporate interest in unrelated diversification, and by the dissatisfaction of top management with present limiting and inefficient organizational structures. The potential in the management style typified by today's so-called conglomerates may not be the final answer. But it is misleading to judge this potential by criteria designed to measure efficiency in vertical and horizontal diversification. On this basis we would expect that conglomerates with a wide diversity of interests would continually receive low marks from economists.

Whatever the "true" merits of unrelated acquisitions, the trend to diversification into new areas and away from reliance on a single industry is undeniable. Many hastily structured combinations have failed, but a great many more have survived. And the majority of the largest United States corporations can be classified as conglomerates in the sense of being diversified into a number of unrelated fields.

The Unrelated Acquisition in Perspective

Therefore, the burden of proof on conglomerate efficiency seems to rest with economic theory. The longer the conglomerate form persists, and performs satisfactorily, the more tenuous become the assumptions of economic theory. In essence, current theory is in conflict with the facts. If data continue to support the contention that the conglomerate organization is permanent and profitable, then the study of diversification into unrelated businesses through acquisition becomes an important if not central part of strategic management of the firm.

It might help in developing theory if economists would keep one eye turned to the outside world. It makes sense, after all, that if unrelated acquisitions are the preferred route to growth there must be some benefit to be realized. Royal Little, former chairman of Textron and one of the early proponents of the conglomerate logic, puts the case succinctly:

> It has been shown that through the combination of normal internal growth, plus growth through unrelated business acquisitions, you can get a better cumulative growth rate on capital than can be obtained in any normal, single-industry operation. That, I believe, is why unrelated diversification is here to stay, because you just can't beat it unless you're the one in a hundred thousand that comes up with a Xerox or Polaroid. Unrelated diversification will beat any normal single-industry company when it comes to return on net worth and cumulative growth rate of earnings per share of common stock. When we started, we set as a goal 20% after taxes on net worth. Last year Textron accomplished that.[11]

Summary

In the end a lasting justification for conglomerates must be based on more than criticisms of existing economic theory. Conglomerates are not inherently superior to vertically or horizontally structured firms, or even to small local entrepreneurship. They are different. Within these differences lies the explanation for their ability to grow and proliferate. These areas of difference should be the focus of investigations for economists as well as management theorists.

QUESTIONS

1. While there are "normative" stages of development that can be postulated for companies as a whole, each firm chooses its own development strategy. McDonald's fast-food chain, for instance, has developed far beyond its origins as a small roadside drive-in, but it is still basically in the fast-food business. Do you foresee any changes in McDonald's basic concepts over the next ten years? What might influence its choices?

2. One of the reasons given for the many acquisitions made in the 1970s was that company assets were priced, on stock-market valuation, at below replacement values. What does this mean? How did it encourage the large numbers of acquisitions? Which of the motives for diversification did this satisfy?

3. How does the formulation of policy affect a company's evolution and development? Suggest some policy guidelines for a local bank, a large regional bank, and a giant money-center bank.

4. A firm may grow large by concentrating in a single business or diversifying into many different businesses. There are many examples of both options. What are some factors influencing the choice of development paths? Why, for instance, is General Motors largely concentrated in the automobile industry, whereas General Electric has diversified into many businesses?

5. Do you believe unrelated acquisitions are the ultimate stage of corporate development? Should all companies strive to become conglomerates? Give specific reasons for your answer.

6. The first two great merger waves in America largely reflected vertical and horizontal combinations of firms. Yet the dominant merger trend since World War II has been toward unrelated, or conglomerate, combinations. Why this shift in merger emphasis? What are the relative advantages of vertical, horizontal, and conglomerate acquisitions?

7. How will the choice of merger strategy affect the organizational structure of a company?

MINI-EXERCISES

1. The Bendit Manufacturing Co. is a hypothetical medium-sized public company. The firm has been fairly successful in supplying bathroom fixtures to residential builders. Over the past ten years sales and earnings have averaged roughly 10 percent per annum growth. However, the pattern of growth has been erratic, reflecting the sharp ups and downs in housing starts over this period. Mr. Ronald, president of Bendit, has decided to reduce the dependence on the housing industry as part of an overall policy of smoothing out his sales and earnings trend. The company is financially healthy. Its stock price is $24 per share and it has a price-earnings multiple of 11. Mr. Ronald is undecided on strategies for implementing his policy. Assuming you were Mr. Ronald's chief corporate planner, what advice would you give? (Assume current economic, capital, and stock-market conditions.)

2. Contrast the structure of two similar organizations you have researched. Which of the organizations has developed the best approach to dealing with its environment? What are the major differences, and advantages, in the two approaches?

    SUGGESTION: You may elect to study your own educational institution and contrast it with one of similar size and orientation (e.g., liberal arts, technical, business). A standard presentation in both instances might include an overall organizational chart and information about the particular unit: What are the reporting relationships? How does the unit relate to the other units? Is it a flexible structure for making decisions?

3. Select a company and trace its evolution from its origin to the present. Identify important turning points and strategies in its development. With hindsight, rationalize its pattern of development.

REFERENCES

1. Federal Trade Commission, Bureau of Economics, "Economic Papers 1966–69, Summary of Economic Report on Corporate Mergers," *Hearings Before the Subcommittee on Antitrust and Monopoly,* 1969.

2. Ibid., p. 37.

3. Dan E. Schendel and Charles W. Hofer, *Strategic Management,* Introduction (Boston: Little, Brown, 1979), p. 7.

4. R. P. Rumlet, *Strategy, Structure, and Economic Performance* (Boston: Harvard Business School, Division of Research, 1970).

5. Darryl J. Ellis and Peter P. Pekar, Jr., "Is 50–50 Good Enough?" *Planning Review,* July 1978, Boston.

6. Alfred A. Chandler, Jr., *Strategy and Structure: Chapters in the History of the American Industrial Enterprise* (Cambridge, Mass.: MIT Press, 1962).

7. Samuel R. Reid, "Is the Merger the Best Way to Grow?" *Business Horizons,* February 1969; see also reference cited in n. 1.

8. Federal Trade Commission, "Economic Papers 1966–69."

9. George J. Stigler, Foreword to Michael Gort, *Diversification and Integration in American Industry* (Princeton: Princeton University Press, 1962).

10. Donald F. Turner, "Conglomerate Mergers and Section 7 of the Clayton Act," *Harvard Business Review,* May 1965.

11. Robert Solo, "New Myths and Old Sterilities," *Saturday Review,* January 22, 1972.

12. Royal Little, "Interview of Royal Little," *Dun's Review,* May 1968.

FURTHER READING

Alchian, Armen A. "Uncertainty, Evolution and Economic Theory." *Journal of Political Economy,* June 1950.

Franko, Lawrence. "The Move Toward a Multi-Divisional Structure in European Organizations." *Administrative Science Quarterly,* December 1974.

Greiner, Larry E. "Evolution and Revolution as Organizations Grow." *Harvard Business Review,* July–August 1972.

Jacoby, Neil. "The Conglomerate Corporation." *The Center Magazine,* Center for the Study of Democratic Institutions, July 1969.

Leontiades, Milton. *Strategies for Diversification and Change.* Boston: Little, Brown, 1980.

————. "What Kind of Corporate Planner Do You Need?" *Long Range Planning,* April 1977.

————, "Dimensions of Planning in Large, Industrialized Companies," *California Management Review,* Summer 1980.

————, "Unrelated Diversification: Theory and Practice," *Business Horizons,* October 1979.

Margulies, Newton, and John Wallace. *Organizational Change: Techniques and Applications.* Glenview, Ill.: Scott, Foresman, 1973.

Pitts, Robert A. "Strategies and Structures for Diversification." *Academy of Management Journal,* June 1977.

Rumelt, Richard P. *Strategy, Structure and Economic Performance.* Boston: Graduate School of Business Administration, Harvard University, 1974.

Starbuck, William. *Organizational Growth and Development.* Harmondsworth, England: Penguin, 1971.

Stopford, John. "Growth and Organizational Change in the Multinational Field." Doctoral dissertation, Harvard University, 1968.

Tennican, Michael L. "Diversification by Acquisition." In F. J. Aguilar, et al., *Formal Planning Systems — 1970.* Boston: Graduate School of Business Administration, Harvard University, 1970.

Terreberry, Shirley. "The Evolution of Organizational Environments." *Administrative Science Quarterly,* March 1968.

CHAPTER 5

Strategies for Evolution and Change – Evaluating External Alternatives

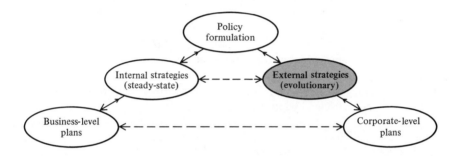

Having reviewed the evolutionary pattern of diversification through acquisitions, we shall now discuss this option, as well as the alternative external options, for meeting overall policy objectives. As indicated in our diagram of the policy → strategy → plans process, external means of improving corporate performance is part of an evolutionary style of management. During this phase of the total decision-making process, a number of external strategic actions are considered for closing a perceived performance gap. The purpose of this external search is to develop a set of strategy alternatives that will, in conjunction with contemplated internal improvements, permit the company to meet the targeted policy objectives; that will, in short, provide the thrust for getting from where the company is to where management wants it to be.

Of the four measures of sales, earnings, balance, and lowered risk that we have used previously in Chapter 3, we have discussed why the latter two objectives may fall outside the range of expectations from an internal im-

EXHIBIT 5.1
PERFORMANCE GAP AFTER INTERNAL IMPROVEMENTS

	Current Year	Plan (Years)				
		1	*2*	*3*	*4*	*5*
Sales (billions)						
Plan	$ 10	$ 11	$12.1	$13.3	$14.6	$16.1
Gap	—	—	(.1)	(.4)	(.8)	(1.2)
Earnings (millions)						
Plan	$100	$110	$121	$133	$146	$161
Gap	—	(1)	(3)	(7)	(11)	(18)
Balance[a]						
Plan	50/50%	50/50%	40/60%	40/60%	30/70%	30/70%
Gap	Not affected by internal improvements					
Risk[b]						
Plan	75/25%	70/30%	60/40%	50/50%	50/50%	50/50%
Gap	Not affected by internal improvements					

[a] Military/consumer businesses (measured by percentage of sales).
[b] High risk/low risk businesses (measured by cyclicality of earnings).

provement program alone. In Exhibit 5.1 we have used these four objectives again, along with a hypothetical five-year projection of improved performance anticipated from increased efficiency from internal operations.

The figures in Exhibit 5.1 assume a partial closing of the gap in sales and earnings from improving existing operations but that total dollars will fall short of objectives in these areas by $1.2 billion and $18 million respectively; the entire burden of meeting the objectives of a balanced mix of consumer/military businesses and a lowered risk exposure will depend on the search for external solutions.

Borg-Warner is a diversified industrial firm that conducted an internal evaluation like the one described in Chapter 3. Borg-Warner realized that internal improvements alone, *no matter how effective,* would not produce the desired superior performance objectives the company had set for itself. As outlined in its 1976 *Annual Report,* Borg-Warner made the following analysis of its situation.

[Sharpening the efficiency of present operations was] very promising. But when we ran five-year projections of where we would be if all our present businesses achieved *all* their efficiency goals, it still wasn't enough: If each became as good as the best in its business or industry, Borg-Warner as a whole would be lean, trim and more healthy financially — but *still* not the profitability star we want it to be.

Thus our second objective: to change our business mix, by concentrating our future investments in business areas likely to be more profitable than the corporate average. This part of our strategy would apply to *all* opportunities, whether in present business lines or new businesses.[1]

In the strategy process characterized in Exhibit 5.2, Borg-Warner was at the point of assessing five external strategies for growth: acquisitions, divestments, joint ventures, venture capital investments, and licensing. These five possibilities are major choices for inducing change from outside the company. More than one of these options may be followed simultaneously.

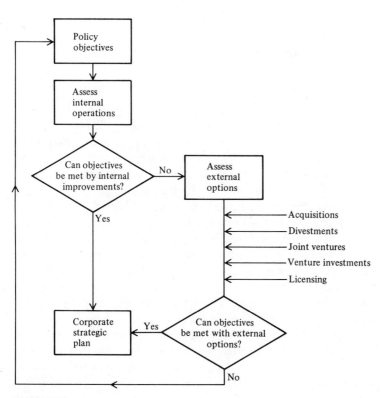

EXHIBIT 5.2
THE STRATEGIC PLANNING PROCESS

Moreover, because it is difficult to predict the degree of success from a single venture, companies may prefer to keep their options open rather than eliminating all but a single preferred way to close the performance gap.

McGraw-Hill, a diversified media company, outlined a multiple external offensive in its strategic plan for the company's growth to the 1980s and beyond. The company proclaimed a philosophy geared to growth, and a strategy of maintaining balanced growth by following a portfolio approach: "That is, we recognize that we can grow by several means simultaneously — by acquisition (particularly of embryonic and growth businesses); by internal development; through joint ventures; and, to a limited degree, through licensing. Thus we can be flexible in entering markets which we have determined to be attractive." [2]

Other companies may focus more closely on a single or a limited set of strategic possibilities. Following is a brief discussion of the five major external possibilities we have mentioned: acquisitions, divestments, joint ventures, venture capital investments, and licensing.

Major External Strategies

ACQUISITIONS [3]

There are a number of acquisition strategies a company can follow. The most venturesome and difficult strategy to implement effectively is the acquisition of an unrelated business. This requires integrating and controlling an operation that is dissimilar to management's experience and background. A safer choice from a strictly operational viewpoint is a horizontal acquisition with a company in a similar business, such as a food processor adding another food product. For example, Kellogg acquired Mrs. Smith's Pies in 1976. This was related to Kellogg's broad position in the cereal and food field. It is in contrast to the acquisition in 1977 of Avis (rent-a-car) by Norton Simon (a loosely linked company whose major businesses include Hunt's foods, Canada Dry beverages, Halston fashionwear, Max Factor cosmetics, and others).

Although no formula approach can guarantee success in an acquisition, the chance of a successful acquisition program is greatly enhanced if formal criteria guide the search. This enables a systematic screening of acquisition candidates against management's stated objectives. It also implies that management has thought sufficiently about the acquisition program to develop specific parameters for acquisitions rather than just endorsing the general notion of external growth and letting the corporate planning staff independently set criteria for the screening process.

Northwest Industries displays a carefully thought-out rationale for acquisitions. This conglomerate company explained its strategy in a series of full-page advertisements in the *Wall Street Journal*. These advertisements spelled out in detail the overall philosophy of the company and why it felt able to succeed where many conglomerates had failed. In particular it pointed to the following underlying criteria of its acquisition program that made it work: (1) The company must earn at least a 12 percent after-tax return on total capital. (2) Pretax return on sales should be at least 10 percent. (3) Management must be excellent and willing to stay on (no unfriendly acquisitions). (4) The company's earnings history should not reflect large cyclical swings (no interest in "turnarounds"). (5) Payment would be, preferably, in cash. (6) Before concluding an acquisition, a thorough audit of the company by qualified experts should be undertaken.*

DIVESTMENTS

Divestments have developed as an important part of an overall diversification strategy.[4] As indicated in Exhibit 5.2, the number of divestments since 1970 suggests a permanent trend in this aspect of diversification.

Part of the explanation for a greater emphasis on divestments is that managements are more systematically evaluating the types of businesses they are in and the types of businesses they would like to be in. Those business operations which don't fit into policymakers' perceptions of the type of company they want to be, or fail to meet established corporate financial objectives such as return on assets or earnings-per-share growth, are scrutinized closely for possible disposition. With the trend toward unrelated acquisitions spanning several decades, the level of sophisticated in making acquisitions and in disposing of ill-fitting corporate operations has increased.

Undoubtedly a number of speculative acquisitions made during the 1960s and 1970s constitute part of the increase in divestments. In the early phases of the movement toward unrelated acquisitions, a great number of combinations were made for impulsive reasons of short-term gain. As the diversification trend matured, however, the approaches to external diversification became more purposeful: adding businesses to fill specific product/market needs and disposing of businesses that fail to complement corporate strengths. Moreover, a number of relatively new analytical tools have been developed that allow a company to weigh the contribution of various business units against overall objectives (e.g., PIMS, portfolio management, and life-cycle analyses are three such techniques, discussed in Chapter 9).

---

* See Chapter 10 for an extended discussion of an acquisition program.

So far these techniques have been used to identify underperforming but isolated product lines. Divestments of *major* business operations have been few. The primary focus has been on acquiring new businesses rather than eliminating traditional ones. Acquisitions can be thought of as the first step of an ongoing process of rationalization. Acquisition is the intuitive first move once the concept of unrelated diversification is accepted. After companies have achieved a desired spread of operations into a number of new businesses, the next evaluation may turn inward. For example, are existing operations hampering the realization of growth that the entry into new businesses has provided? Does it make overall sense for General Electric, for instance, to acquire Utah International, a major new business for future growth, while retaining the major-appliance business, where growth prospects are limited? To a large extent, these types of hard internal decisions have been secondary to the thrust into new businesses. It is easier to graft a new business onto an organization than to perform major surgery on one of its parts.

There is evidence, however, that companies are ready to reevaluate major, traditional areas of operations as impartially as they seek out new fields of opportunity. Ashland Oil, for example, decided, after an extensive review of its operations, to get out of the oil-producing end of the business, for the following reason: "The company simply didn't think its energy reserves were producing adequate cash return, and it shifted its corporate sights. . . . The Ashland strategy is to maximize cash generation, getting rid of businesses that tie up huge amounts of capital in relation to cash return." [5]

Ashland is not an isolated instance. Even "mighty General Motors dumped the appliance business it pioneered by selling Frigidaire, once a synonym for refrigerator." [6] Thus, while diversification is still not an objective science, there appears to be a better "rationality" in management's approach to major divestments and acquisitions, and less emphasis on purely speculative or intuitive motivations.

JOINT VENTURES

Another path for external growth is through joint ventures. [7] Traditionally, joint ventures have been viewed in the United States as a means for penetrating foreign markets wherein the United States partner can accelerate entry into growing foreign markets while reducing his business risk. In the early rush of American firms into the European market, for example, joint ventures were a common way to gain access to an attractive market, with the United States partner furnishing the technology and product knowhow and the foreign partner providing production and distribution facilities. Many of these joint ventures, however, proved to be less than satisfactory.

The basis for the agreements often omitted details on respective responsibilities, financial obligations, and rights of minority owners. In addition, a common staffing approach to the joint venture — using United States personnel rather than foreign nationals — often caused friction and operational difficulties.

However, multinational United States companies have long since passed this initiation phase. The technique of joint ventures, if not mastered, has at least become a familiar and tested way of doing business abroad. A casual scanning of a few issues of the *Wall Street Journal* uncovered the following information:

> Pennwalt Corporation signed a contract with two Japanese companies to form a joint venture to manufacture a chemical used in making synthetic rubber. Pennwalt will own 40 percent of the joint venture, with Nippon Soda owning the rest.[8]

> Rockwell International and Creusot-Loire, a Paris-based steel and nuclear equipment builder, will establish a jointly owned subsidiary in France to produce industrial valves.[9]

> SmithKline Corp. agreed with Fujisawa Pharmaceutical Co., Osaka, Japan, to form a joint venture to market pharmaceutical products in Japan. Terms of the agreement call for the two companies to share equally in the expenses and earnings of the venture.[10]

Joint ventures need not be limited to foreign investment. Domestic companies often pool resources to gain advantages of complementary specialties, such as an industrial contracting firm joining a coal company on a pilot coal-gasification plant. Even giant industrial firms may combine to diversify their investments and limit their risks, as indicated by the following arrangements:

> Standard Oil Company (Indiana) and Gulf Oil authorized the spending of $93 million for a five-year oil-shale development program as equal partners on a 5,100 acre tract in Colorado.[11]

> DuPont Co. and Atlantic Richfield Co. said their Centennial Hydrocarbons Co. joint venture has taken an option on about 5,700 acres in Brazoria County, Texas, as a possible site for a previously announced $1 billion organic chemical plant. DuPont and Arco each owned 50 percent of the venture.[12]

VENTURE CAPITAL INVESTMENTS

Venture capital investments[13] are a way for companies to risk limited sums in new technologies, new products, or new applications in the hope of backing a successful venture that could develop into the next Xerox or Polaroid. Obviously, the probabilities are small for success on that scale. But the potential is sufficiently attractive to encourage venture investments as an alternative diversification strategy for companies.

In some cases, the synergy of the match between the investor and the venture firm is primarily financial: the investor has the money, and the venture firm has the idea but only limited capital. This is the common tack taken when the investing party is interested primarily in capital gains — but not in operating the company, or benefiting directly from the product innovations it produces. In another case, the investing company has a more direct stake in the venture business and how it might eventually fit into the plans of the parent company. One reason for large companies investing in venture situations is the desire to diversify technologically by backing entrepreneurial efforts of others rather than enlarging internal research and development operations. Also, large industrial companies deterred from acquisitions because of potential antitrust violations may see venture investments as a noncontroversial way to diversify externally. Such giant corporations as General Electric (GE) and Exxon have long sponsored venture investment programs. Exxon in particular desires to develop options for what it sees as an uncertain political and economic future for the oil industry.

> Exxon Enterprises, Inc., officially known as the "new business development arm" of Exxon, has so far plowed $276 million into disparate companies. Most of that, about $200 million, has been spent on two wholly owned subsidiaries: a gasoline-pump company and Exxon Nuclear, which is getting involved in all stages of nuclear fuel production. But over the past eight years, Exxon Enterprises has quietly invested the remaining $76 million in more than two dozen small new ventures, either by joining other investors in traditional venture-capital deals or by funding new in-house businesss created and run by its own employees.[14]

LICENSING

Licensing,[15] like joint ventures, has commonly been associated with doing business in foreign markets. As in joint ventures, it originally provided a number of advantages for United States companies that wanted to avoid the risks of direct investment abroad yet wished to tap the populous and increasingly affluent foreign markets. From the licensee's point of view, a United States partner offered a relatively quick and easy means to broaden products and markets — and acquire the then undisputed United States leadership in technology. From that early perspective the use of licensing has developed considerably, including a range of applications well beyond conventional licensing of technology for industrial products, as the following agreement indicates:

> Great Western United Corp. said its Shakey's Inc. unit agreed to license a unit of Collins Foods International Inc., Los Angeles, exclusively to develop Shakey's pizza restaurants in Australia.
>
> Collins, which operates Kentucky Fried Chicken franchises in the U.S., already has franchised fried chicken operations in Australia, Great Western said. It added that the two companies have agreed on a goal of 60 pizza restaurant openings by 1986.
>
> In addition, Great Western said Shakey's joint venture with Mitsubishi Corp. and Kirin Brewery Corp. in Japan plans to open 44 Shakey's restaurants there by 1982 and 48 more by 1988. It said there are currently 20 such restaurants in Japan, being operated by Shakey's of Japan Ltd., the joint venture, or by its licensees.[16]

In addition to foreign opportunities, licensing agreements offer an attractive way to diversify domestically. A company with strong marketing and distribution resources, for instance, may hedge its operations by licensing products from others rather than depending solely on internal product development. In the pharmaceutical industry, where new product introduction has escalated tremendously in cost, time, and uncertainty, the alternative of licensing has proved an attractive supplement to the traditional in-house development of new drugs.

Choosing an External Strategy

In choosing among the several external options for growth, there are a great number of possible combinations. In order to concentrate on a manageably small number of high-priority options, a company must define the limits of its search. As aids in this process, one can rely on three criteria: (1) objective performance measures, (2) management values, and (3) corporate resources.

OBJECTIVE MEASURES OF PERFORMANCE

An obvious first screen is to establish performance measures that restrict the search to those companies or businesses able to meet the criteria management has established. Northwest Industries' acquisition criteria of a 12 percent return on total capital and a 10 percent pretax return on sales are such measures. A company that falls short of meeting these objective tests would be eliminated from the list of potential candidates in the search process. However, this type of screening — based primarily on past financial performance — could by itself still leave a wide number of possible areas to screen. Moreover, while financial performance can be a useful means of evaluating acquisitions, it is not so relevant a measure for judging other external search options like joint ventures, venture investments, and licensing.

VALUES OF MANAGEMENT

An added determinant to guide the external search is management's values. In deciding the direction of the search, the corporate staff should be sure to choose a course management is inclined to follow. For example, managements of companies vary in their attitudes (or biases) toward certain external options that might appeal to, say, the corporate planning staff, when judged by strict economic criteria, but which nevertheless don't appeal to top management. This tends to exclude certain options from practical consideration, such as the three types of constraints that follow.

Methods of Financing.   A conservative management may voluntarily exclude from external opportunities those projects which require stock financing, thus avoiding an increase in the number of common shares and potential dilution of shareholder equity. Northwest Industries has a preference for cash in payments for acquisitions, for example. A bias against borrowing may also exist. A former president of a major television-set manufacturer firmly steered his company away from long-term debt and thus restricted expansion to internally generated funds, no matter how potentially profitable a forecasted situation might be. By 1965 one-third of the largest United States industrial corporations had not raised a single dollar of long-term debt through a bond issue since the end of World War II.[17] Exhibit 5.3 suggests that a number of companies still had an apparent preference for cash in 1977.

Blind Spots.   Joint ventures, licensing and venture investments may not be viewed objectively. Because of bad past experiences, management may avoid future joint ventures or licensing arrangements. Venture investments may be regarded by management as having an unfavorable risk/reward ratio even though companies like Exxon, W. R. Grace, GE, and General Telephone and Electronics have all adopted this strategy at one time or another.

Scope of Business.   Limiting the types of businesses in which management is interested is a common way to limit the external search. This can be done

EXHIBIT 5.3
CASH-RICH COMPANIES: 1977

	Cash and equivalents	Cash, as % of current liabilities
	(mil)	
Tampax	$62	402%
Petrie Stores	99	392
Simplicity Patterns	57	379
Howard Johnson	80	276
Skyline Corp.	49	268
Ideal Basic Ind.	52	199
Freeport Minerals	95	180
Diebold	36	167
Maytag	30	156
Cannon Mills	44	134

Source: From *Forbes,* April 15, 1977, p. 116. Reprinted by permission of Forbes Magazine.

indirectly by performance criteria. A direct approach begins by defining the limits of the search. For instance, management can restrict the search to expansion into only closely related industries Carrier Corporation, a major air-conditioning firm, outlined a carefully defined three-pronged approach to new businesses which included (1) existing products and businesses, (2) related operations in environmental building controls and high technology products, and (3) services in energy and process industries.[18] Such explicit business boundaries immediately focus the search and make the work of the corporate planning staff immeasurably easier.*

CORPORATE RESOURCES

A final limit to external alternatives is dictated by available corporate resources. A small company is unlikely to acquire a larger company, although exceptions occur. Investments require adequate financial resources, particularly if the size of the initial commitment is large or the time before payback begins is long. In short, one important corporate resource is money (or borrowing power). The more financial resources, the wider the scope of external possibilities that generally exist.

---

* In total contradiction to this carefully expressed strategy, Carrier soon after acquired a large diversified manufacturer of industrial paints, Inmont Corp. And soon after that Carrier itself was acquired by a large conglomerate, United Technologies. Although the merger movement has its haphazard side, this ranks as one of the most unlikely scenarios.

A second critical resource is management. Companies lean in management depth may seek alignments only with businesses where management transfers are not required. Referring back to Northwest Industries, one of its acquisition requirements is good management that is willing to stay put after the merger. The reverse is also possible. Companies with management-in-depth may seek to leverage this resource by looking for situations that could be improved with an infusion of good management.

Technical resources comprise a third category that can help define a company's areas of interest. High technology can act as an effective barrier to mass entry into markets by less sophisticated companies. Therefore, high-technology companies wishing to maintain this edge will expand externally only if the situations involve high-technology products, high-technology companies, or combinations with other firms where high technology is a necessary ingredient.

Reconciliation of Objectives, Values, and Resources

Performance objectives, management values, and corporate resources thus all play a part in narrowing the scope of the search. But they work in parallel. One factor cannot be used in isolation from the others. Also, the balancing of the three criteria is part art, part science. How much weight to put on objective performance measures versus management values is in the end itself a value judgment. Exhibit 5.4 illustrates the containment of the possible external options within the restraints of performance, values,

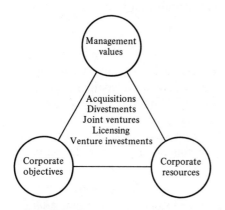

EXHIBIT 5.4
RECONCILIATION OF OBJECTIVES, VALUES, AND RESOURCES IN SEARCH FOR EXTERNAL OPTIONS

and resource. If balanced properly, these restraints will (*a*) enable the identification of the alternatives best suited for the strategic aims of the company, and (*b*) win the solid endorsement and backing of top management.

Role of Long-Range Forecasting

One element missing from this discussion of long-range strategy is a long-range forecast of economic and business conditions. The omission is deliberate. Although forecasting is an unavoidable part of long-range strategy, it does not play the central role. As Peter Drucker wisely observed, "We must plan because we cannot forecast." [19]

Economists have not demonstrated an ability to forecast with any degree of accuracy. While econometric models used to predict the economy have become increasingly sophisticated, their ability to foresee dips and turns has not noticeably improved. In the final analysis, events have often proved as difficult to forecast with an econometric model as without one. As the Federal Reserve Board of Boston pointed out, "forecasts not based on formal econometric models appeared to be generally as accurate or more accurate." [20]

This is not to downgrade the importance of econometric modeling or the very capable economists who develop such models. But a company's future is too important to be left to a model. Corporations that have attempted to forecast events and then position themselves in the right place at the right time have more often than not been wrong. In the early 1960s sophisticated companies like Xerox, IBM, and GE foresaw a big market for teaching machines based on computers. But the educational market resisted the best marketing efforts of such companies, and is still resisting. Computer-based teaching may eventually come, but it is not in sight. Real estate also beckoned companies in the 1960s; many a company invested huge sums of capital before admitting that there again was a market where appeal was more apparent than real.

Forecasting can aid strategy, but is no substitute for it. The task of strategy begins with a set of policy objectives. These policy objectives guide the strategy analysis that follows. This analysis proceeds in the knowledge of what type of business you want to be in; it does not necessarily include a forecast of which business will be the most profitable. Some examples from the oil industry make this important point.

In 1966 Continental Oil acquired Consolidation Coal. This acquisition transformed Continental Oil into a broad-based energy company. This was years before the oil embargo (1973), the emergence of the OPEC bloc, and the current enhanced outlook for coal. Indeed, for many years the outlook for coal was as modestly dim as when Continental Oil made its acquisition. Yet the initial strategy proved sound; not because Continental Oil foresaw the oil embargo, obviously, but because it positioned itself to benefit from a switch to alternative sources of energy. Companies like Shell and Exxon have increased their investments in shale, geothermal, and solar energy in similar strategy moves.

Another large oil company, Mobil, has taken a different tack. Based on a less than optimistic view of the future of oil, and desiring to diversify away from dependence on foreign earnings, Mobil has acquired Marcor, a merchandising and paper products enterprise; failed in an attempt to acquire Irvine, a large real estate concern; and continues to seek other investments in order to meet its diversification objectives.

Numerous alternative rationales exist for strategic change: a lower-risk profile, lessened dependence on a single business cycle, lessened dependence on a single product, a better balance among mature and emerging businesses. None of these strategies depends explicitly on the accuracy of long-range forecasts. It is not necessary to know the future in order to be prepared for it. By diversifying into different businesses or different markets, for example, a company can minimize risks. It can, in effect, reduce future shock *without having to forecast the exact nature of change to take place.*

Interestingly, forecasting assumes greater relevance as the time frame of planning decreases. Annual forecasts are usually an integral part of the annual planning cycle discussed in Chapter 12. The reasons are twofold. First, it is much easier to estimate near-term developments. As long as forecasts are within a range of six months to a year, they are influenced to a large degree by the momentum of existing trends, and these can be adequately captured by econometric models. Second, forecasts are a necessary ingredient in a uniform budgeting system. Corporate-level econometric forecasts, even if not precisely accurate, are preferable to each business manager using his or her own assumptions as the basis for sales, earnings, and production estimates.

Although many companies also include five-year economic forecasts as part of the annual planning cycle, these forecasts are reviewed and revised annually. They provide only a conditional target for the operating groups to work with. They should not be mistaken for long-term strategic planning based on long-term economic forecasts.

Summary

We have reviewed the major external strategies available to managements to close a perceived performance gap between desired policy objectives and the capabilities of current operations to reach these objectives. The assumption here is that external alternatives would be consistent with an evolutionary style of management. In addition, management can review internal operations with a view to raising performance levels above the historic norm. This approach would be consistent with a steady-state type of management. The possibilities for such operational improvements are the subject of Chapter 6.

QUESTIONS

1. How does the evaluation of external alternatives differ from the evaluation of internal operations? Is it possible for a selected external strategy to fail even if the methodology for evaluation was correct?

2. Value judgments are important in developing a company's strategy. How do value judgments combine with technical skills, for example, in determining whether to invest in a new product or in deciding the size and siting of a new plant?

3. Based on total evaluation of a company's opportunities — both internal and external — how is the allocation of monies to be determined; that is, how many dollars should go to improving internal operations, and how much to pursuing external opportunities?

4. Some parts of an external strategy, such as acquisitions or divestitures, cannot be precisely planned because they depend on the availability of sellers or buyers. Thus, what value does a timetable serve that indicates when future profits or losses are to be realized, including acquisitions and divestitures?

5. Many factors that ultimately shape strategic decisions are outside management's control (e.g., economic conditions, government regulations). How are these factors taken into account in management's strategy exercises?

MINI-EXERCISES

1. Two companies in the same industry often follow completely different strategies. For example, McDonald's and Wendy's are two major fast-food chains specializing in hamburgers, and have to date enjoyed considerable success. Yet their management philosophy differs. McDonald's emphasizes low prices and pre-prepared orders. Wendy's has higher prices and a wide variety of made-to-order hamburgers. Investigate the relative success of each of these chains by analyzing past growth in key areas. Explain how both companies can be successful while following divergent strategies. Which seems better positioned for future growth?

2. There are defensive as well as offensive strategies. Some companies have become successful only after severe adversity. Mattel, for example, was on the brink of insolvency but has become a successful toy company once again. How do strategies for turnaround situations differ from strategies for ongoing businesses?

   SUGGESTION: Select a company like Mattel, Singer, or Addressograph and study the steps taken to effect a turnaround. Discuss these situations in comparison to strategic development of a successful company.

3. One of the most important determinants in the success of a strategy is the individual or individuals in an organization who make it work. Take a company in the turnaround situation discussed in Exercise 2. Discuss what percentage of the success of the effort you believe was due to personal strength of top management and what percentage to proper techniques or systems analysis. Develop a systematic basis for weighing both sets of factors to support your conclusion.

REFERENCES

1. Borg-Warner *Annual Report,* 1976.

2. McGraw-Hill *Report* to shareholders, Fourth Quarter, October–December 1976.

3. See Norman A. Berg, "Strategic Planning in Conglomerate Companies," *Harvard Business Review,* May–June 1965, on how conglomerates differ.

4. For more information on divestments, see S. C. Gilmour, "The Divestment Decision Process," unpublished doctoral dissertation, Harvard Business School, 1973.

5. *Wall Street Journal,* January 15, 1980.

6. Ibid.

7. For more information on joint ventures, see S. Gullander, "Joint Ventures and Corporate Strategy," *Columbia Journal of World Business,* Spring 1976.

8. *Wall Street Journal,* June 16, 1977.

9. Ibid., June 14, 1977.

10. Ibid., June 8, 1977.

11. Ibid., June 17, 1977.

12. Ibid., June 20, 1977.

13. For more information on venture capital investments, see S. R. Osgood and W. E. Wetzel, Jr., "A Systems Approach to Venture Initiation," *Business Horizons,* October 1977.

14. *Fortune,* April 1977.

15. For more information in licensing, see P. R. Budak and J. C. Susbauer, "International Expansion Through Licensing," *Journal of Small Business Management,* January 1977.

16. *Wall Street Journal,* May 14, 1977.

17. Milton Leontiades, "Use of Capital Markets by Large Manufacturing Corporations," *Financial Analyst's Journal,* March–April 1967.

18. *Wall Street Journal,* June 16, 1977.

19. Peter F. Drucker, "Long-Range Planning: Challenge to Management Science," *Management Science,* April 1959.

20. Federal Reserve Board of Boston, December 1976.

FURTHER READING

Bettauer, Arthur. "Strategies for Divestments." *Harvard Business Review,* April–May 1967.

Davis, James V. "The Strategic Divestment Decision." *Long Range Planning,* February 1974.

Leontiades, Milton. *Strategies for Diversification and Change.* Boston: Little, Brown, 1980.

Arthur D. Little, Inc. *A System for Managing Diversity.* Cambridge, Mass., 1974.

Lorsch, Jay W., and Stephen A. Allen III. *Managing Diversity and Interdependence: An Organizational Study of Multidivisional Firms.* Boston: Graduate School of Business Administration, Harvard University, 1973.

Moose, Sandra O., and Alan J. Zakon. "Divestment — Cleaning Up Your Corporate Portfolio." *European Business,* Autumn 1971.

Parker, Treadway C. *The Formation and Management of New Business Ventures.* New York: The Presidents' Association of the American Management Association, 1973.

Peterson, Russell W. "New Venture Management in a Large Company," *Harvard Business Review,* May–June 1967.

CHAPTER 6

Strategies for Current Operations – Evaluating Internal Alternatives

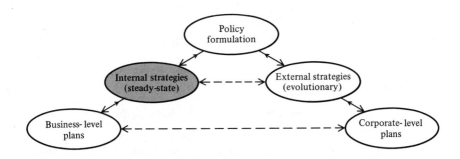

Strategy Formulation at the Business Level

Improving current operations is primarily a business-level responsibility. The corporate staff can assist and coordinate the effort but the major strategy initiatives rest with the managers responsible for each business unit. If the overall policy of the organization is oriented to current operations it is axiomatic that "a strong chief executive will most likely sacrifice his staff advisors rather than disrupt reporting relationships with those responsible for operations." [1]

The focus of business-level strategy in this chapter is on (1) industry evaluation, (2) competitor evaluation, and (3) evaluation of the firm's relative strengths and weaknesses. Based on an integrated view of the results from these three types of evaluation, a firm can formulate strategies consistent with its overall objectives.

INDUSTRY EVALUATION

Measures of Industry Attractiveness. A number of traditional measures are used to gauge the attractiveness of an industry. These would normally include indices of trends in the market, the competition, measures of profitability, and rates of technological innovation. In Exhibit 6.1 a set of hypo-

EXHIBIT 6.1
INDUSTRY ATTRACTIVENESS

Market

Size — 1979 — $2.5 billion

Growth ($ in thousands)	Volume	Price	Total
1974–79 $	$450	$560	$1010
Rate/year	3.6%	3.5%	7.1%
1969–74 $	$350	$230	$ 580
Rate/year	6.2%	4.1%	10.3%

Market stabilizing, competition increasing, price increases lagging behind cost increases.

Competition

Concentration high within major products	Top 4 firms
Product X	76%
Product Y	52%
Product Z	61%

Recent Changes
    Competition Z (foreign) acquired competitor E (domestic).
    Competitor B's market share down 3 points in 2 years.
    Competitor A has increased rate of product introduction; heavy promotion campaign.

Profitability

Modest: Leader A (4% ROS, 10% ROI).

Marginal profits if not in top three market share positions.

Technical

Technology change moderate, but many product extensions.

New product opportunities exist.

Other

No "dominant" industry giant.

High labor input — contract settlements critical.

---

thetical figures is used to define each of these subheadings. For example, as a measure of the market, Exhibit 6.1 lists its absolute size, growth over the most recent five-year periods for which statistics are available in dollars and percentage terms, plus comments on current events in the market. Additional data are also often included as a means of further elaborating on the attractiveness of the industry.

This is an obvious beginning point of industry analysis. It provides a data framework necessary for subsequent, deeper evaluation of the industry. Although such broad parameters of the industry may be instinctive for the manager of a business, they are nevertheless essential in developing a formal strategy that will be understood and accepted at higher organizational levels. Once this aggregate level of detail is provided, the manager can proceed to develop additional, more insightful industry perspectives as part of his overall strategy analysis.

Life-Cycle Patterns.   In evaluating its industry a firm needs tools of analysis. One of the more helpful aids for both corporate- and business-level evaluations is the product life cycle. The concept rests on documented observations of how product performance tends to vary with the evolution and maturity of the product. At the corporate level the perspective is on evaluation of different product lines or even businesses; at the business level the same device can be used as a measure of individual products within a product line.

As an example, we can take the major home appliance industry. Companies like White Consolidated Industries, Magic Chef, and the major appliance business of General Electric have products in most parts of this product line. But not all the products are at the same point of maturity, and therefore different products can have different growth and profit potential. In a conventional life-cycle example, three stages are often depicted that illustrate early growth, maturity, and decline. In Exhibit 6.2 we have used levels of market saturation as a proxy to indicate these three stages. In this illustration, refrigerators and clothes washers are in the ultimate stage of evolution and market saturation, with both appliances found in practically all homes wired for electricity. Clothes dryers and ranges are in an advanced stage of maturity, with only microwave ovens in the "takeoff" stage of early growth. By contrast with other major appliances, microwave ovens account for only a modest share of the total potential market, but the rate of market penetration is increasing rapidly. Associated with each of these three ranges of market saturation are correspondingly attractive or pessimistic outlooks for sales and earnings growth and other indicators of financial performance. By way of illustration some hypothetical figures on sales and earnings have been used in Exhibit 6.2.

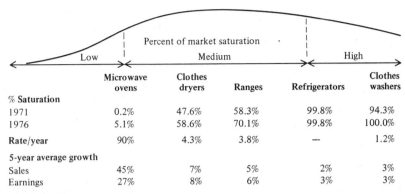

	Microwave ovens	Clothes dryers	Ranges	Refrigerators	Clothes washers
% Saturation					
1971	0.2%	47.6%	58.3%	99.8%	94.3%
1976	5.1%	58.6%	70.1%	99.8%	100.0%
Rate/year	90%	4.3%	3.8%	—	1.2%
5-year average growth					
Sales	45%	7%	5%	2%	3%
Earnings	27%	8%	6%	3%	3%

EXHIBIT 6.2
PRODUCT MATURITIES
(Major Home Appliances)

Source: Saturation statistics from *Merchandising: 55th Statistical Issue and Marketing Report,* March 1977. Sales and earnings data are hypothetical.

In brief, the picture is one of an industry well beyond middle age. Although some segmentation is evident, particularly for the fast-growing new microwave appliance, the bulk of the products are past the optimum point in their life cycle. Thus the industry can be characterized as nearly fully developed and opportunities restricted mainly to strategies of outperforming the competition, rather than riding the wave of a fast-growing, minimally saturated market. Consequently the performance goals of individual firms must reflect modest industry growth, with added growth supported by strategies designed to improve a firm's position within its industry. White Consolidated Industries, for instance, has become an industry power in major home appliances "thanks to a strategy that is disarmingly simple in concept, if not in execution. The company has merely elevated the doctrine of cost control to a corporate religion, one it pursues with messianic fervor, using an incredible array of cost-cutting techniques. . . . White Consolidated has achieved a drastic increase in the efficiency of plants, people, and equipment that were cast off in despair by much bigger corporations." [2]

Industry Structure. A variety of specific questions can be asked in order to profile the industry, but they will all lead to the ultimate question: "How can our firm maximize its position in this industry?" An answer requires complete understanding not only of a company's segment of the market but of all the related and interconnected segments that comprise the whole. Every organization should undertake this type of evaluation in order to answer the now familiar and fundamental point of strategy: "What type of business are we in?" If a trucking firm has too narrowly defined itself as a freight carrier, it can overlook such potentially attractive segments of the industry as truck leasing, financing, and intermodal systems of transportation that interface with the trucking industry. Unless a firm is positioned in the best part of its industry, its performance will not be optimal. And the best position may require occupying a different niche in the market, or adding a new product, or expanding existing services. In short, serving the most profitable parts of the market.

Fundamental to successful positioning, however, is a clear understanding of the "critical" elements for success. In case after case, firms have occupied what appeared on the surface to be a logically related piece of the industry, only to realize, after the investment was made, that they misunderstood the "critical" elements for success. In one actual situation a large plumbing-equipment manufacturer decided to integrate forward into the distribution of plumbing hardware on the basis of being able to sell at lower average prices than existing wholesalers. After considerable investment in building several wholesale centers, the manufacturer discovered that this industry was fragmented and localized, and customers continued to buy from local wholesalers because of long-standing relationships and a stress on personal service. The basic strategy of lower prices was, in other words, an oversimplification of what was needed to succeed. After losing a sizable sum of money, the much larger manufacturing company decided to abandon this venture. Companies in other fields that have invested before investigating have discovered too late that most businesses have "critical" characteristics, which must be understood and evaluated prior to making a successful strategic action.

In addition to maximizing opportunity through repositioning, a firm will repeatedly be faced with conventional decisions of resource allocation among various products in its product line. Here again an understanding of the industry is helpful. This time the focus may be on deeper understanding of the external factors that influence the demand for different products. Such understanding generally requires estimates of demand for the various products and, particularly if the company is international, the elements of demand can be difficult to estimate without a structured model of the industry. As an example, Exhibit 6.3 shows a model of demand that might be used by a large automobile-tire manufacturer to predict demand for (a) replacement tires and (b) original equipment (OEM) tires. This total-demand model could then be adapted to the manufacturer's product line to indicate expected growth for its segment of the market and, second, the relative product emphasis on replacement tires versus OEM tires.

A sophisticated model of demand is obviously not within the capabilities of every firm. However, every organization regardless of size makes estimates of demand, whether intuitively or through systematic analysis. In

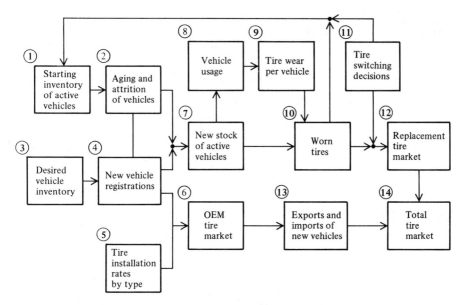

EXHIBIT 6.3
DEMAND ANALYSIS MODEL FOR A TIRE MANUFACTURER
Source: S. Ranji, "A New Route to the Bottom Line," *Planning Review,* May 1978, p. 23.

the process, the characteristics of the industry are considered in arriving at conclusions. In using a formal model such as the one in Exhibit 6.3, a firm can define the structure of the industry in systematic detail and, as a result, improve the accuracy of its estimates compared to naïve models or purely subjective judgment.

COMPETITOR EVALUATION

Once the industry is evaluated, the next step is to assess the firm's competitive position within the industry. This requires rating the firm against major competitors on a number of basic factors. For example, Exhibit 6.4 provides a generalized illustration of how a company could rate four competitors on six competitive factors. This type of matrix allows a company to identify and exploit potentially weak positions of its competition as well as appraise its own competitive strengths and weaknesses. The level of detail in the matrix can be expanded and the ratings can be converted into objective weights. For comparative purposes the type of format used in the industry analysis can also be extended to include competitor evaluations. However, the fundamental point of such illustrations, whatever their specific design, is simply to

EXHIBIT 6.4
COMPETITOR ANALYSIS

Competition indicators	Major competitors			
	A	B	C	D
Market position	Vulnerable	Prevalent	Strong	Vulnerable
Profitability	Low	Average	Average	Average
Financial strength	Low	High	Unknown	Low
Product mix	Narrow	Broad	Narrow	Narrow
Technological capability	Average	Strong	Average	Weak
Product quality	Minimum	Good	Satisfactory	Minimum

bring the level of analysis one step further: from an industry overview to a perspective on different competitors within the industry.

One of the valuable benefits from a factor analysis of major competitors is the insight it provides of their strategies and thus an ability to develop effective counterstrategies. Also, such strategic insights can be sharpened if they are combined with a knowledge of the firm's stage of development. Strategies of firms with a single product line, for example, can be easier to anticipate than a firm that is part of a conglomerate's diversified mix of businesses. After Philip Morris purchased Miller Brewing, the resulting success of Miller shook the rest of the industry. Part of the surprise came from successful application of market segmentation to brewing, a technique Philip Morris had used with good results in its cigarette business. Supplementing this basic strategy were financial strength and marketing expertise beyond Miller Brewing's former abilities as an independent, seventh-ranked producer. Also, the initial low returns on investment that Philip Morris was willing to accept in order to build Miller Brewing into an industry leader might have been an unacceptable strategy had Miller Brewing remained a single-product-line firm. In sum, the strategy for Miller Brewing as part of Philip Morris's diversified organization was different from the strategy Miller had pursued prior to being acquired, and the strategy of Philip Morris was not successfully anticipated by other brewing firms after Miller Brewing was acquired.

For a single-product or product-line firm, the range of strategic moves is less complex, even if the moves are not always predictable. A firm concentrated in one industry is likely to be aggressive along a historically consistent strategic pattern. White Consolidated Industries, as previously noted, emphasizes cost effectiveness as a dominant strategy. It is known throughout the industry for its "commitment to cost controls." In an industry noted for extreme price competitiveness, the lowest-cost producer is obviously in a position to stay in the game longer at a profit than the rest of the players. Although this knowledge may not permit a firm to beat White Consolidated Industries at its particular strategy, it would be extremely pertinent information in developing an alternative strategy for another manufacturer of major home appliances.

RESOURCE EVALUATION (STRENGTHS AND WEAKNESSES)

The third part of a firm's total evaluation process is to conduct an internal audit of its strengths and weaknesses. This internal evaluation produces what is sometimes termed the firm's "distinctive competence." This refers to a firm's points of leverage, i.e., areas of resource strength and competitive advantage. The profile of resource capabilities is then combined with the previously developed profiles of the industry, and profiles of the competition to aid in formulating an integrated strategy from these three perspectives. There are three basic reasons why an inventory of strengths and weaknesses is important in this three-phase strategic exercise: (1) capitalizing on a competitor's weaknesses implies knowledge and effectual use of a firm's own strengths; (2) protecting one's firm from a competitor's moves requires knowledge of weaknesses as well as strengths in order to build an effective defense; (3) few if any companies excel in all respects. Thus, strategies ultimately are a compromise between offense and defense with the optimum balance dependent on awareness of external conditions and skillful utilization of internal resources.

There are numerous examples of companies with superior records of performance, but which are neither dominant in their industries nor necessarily the best in any particular resource area. Such organizations have achieved their distinctive competence through strategies that combined a sensing of market opportunity with a leveraging of specific but limited resources. A couple of case histories make the point here.

Perrier. France's Perrier mineral water had long been identified with a limited appeal, snob-effect market. In 1976 Perrier's share of the United States soft-drink market was "so small that it had to be expressed in a five-digit decimal." [3] Convinced that America's growing health consciousness offered a new and increasing segment of the consumer market, Perrier was launched in the United States in mid-1977 with a modest $2 million advertising budget. In two years, "U.S. sales rose thirtyfold and could reach $120 million this year [1978]" from about $1 million in 1976. Obviously soft-drink giants like Coca-Cola and PepsiCo, as well as many other United States beverage firms, had better United States marketing resources in almost all respects than Perrier. But their greater relative strengths were effectively countered by an opportunistic strategy.

Xomox. This company's success was based on "spotting the potential in someone else's product and exploiting it to the full." [4] The founders of the company had spotted a new valve design in a trade show. "The valve was an ordinary plug valve, one of the oldest types of valve in existence. . . . [The] innovation was to insert a Teflon sleeve into the body before inserting the plug into the sleeve." [5] This new twist on an old product allowed complex internal configurations and eventually developed into a very profitable line of products. Again this was an instance where success depended almost wholly on a strategic concept rather than a specific resource or skill.

These examples demonstrate that individual companies can succeed in spite of limited resources or limited size. However, the underdog position is not normally a virtue. It is obviously easier to succeed with superior resources than to have to overcome the advantages of others. In the establishment of a company's distinctive competence, we can focus on four types of resources found in most firms.

Perhaps the most obvious of these resource traits is *financial strength,* since it is a critical element in almost all aspects of a firm's development. Another critical resource, but one that is more difficult to measure and compare among companies, is *managerial expertise.* Quality of management is frequently mentioned by professional money managers and investment advisers as the most important factor in appraising a firm. A third important factor is *technical capability.* Does the firm have the R & D resources required to develop new products, as demanded in competitive consumer businesses, or to leapfrog the technological status quo as is often required to stay viable in a still developing field like computer software or computer peripheral equipment? Finally, a company can look to its *physical assets,* to such items as age and efficiency of plants and equipment, inventories and distribution facilities, as a source of potential relative advantage.

An Integrated View of Strategy Formulation at the Business Level

Evaluating strengths and weaknesses provides one of the foundations for effective strategy formulation. The other two supports are industry evaluation and competitor evaluation. From the results of evaluations of these three areas a company can begin to construct the outlines of its strategy.

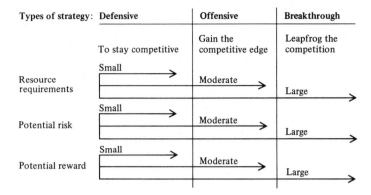

EXHIBIT 6.5
STRATEGIC OPTIONS

Depending on its relative industry position, and the evaluation of internal strengths and weaknesses, a number of alternative strategies are possible. These options can be classified under three broad strategies: defensive, offensive, and breakthrough. As illustrated in Exhibit 6.5, each of the three fundamental strategies is divisible into a number of more specific strategic actions. Certain levels of resource commitment, risk, and payoff are also associated with each major strategy. For instance, a defensive strategic posture is designed primarily to maintain current momentum, with correspondingly low risk and modest rewards. A breakthrough strategy, on the other hand, should leapfrog the company ahead of its competition, based on development of a new product, a new market, or a new technology, to a "new position of dominance."

In terms of specific strategic actions, we can list several typical projects that would implement each of the three principal strategies.

Defensive strategy	Offensive strategy	Breakthrough strategy
Cost reduction	Extension of existing product	New product
Product pruning	New domestic market for old product	New venture
Normal investment in plant and equipment	International expansion Promotional and advertising campaigns	New technology

For the most part each of the projects listed is familiar and self-explanatory. The optimum strategy may dictate two or more projects to be undertaken simultaneously. Thus a company may actively pursue a cost-reduction program in the face of deteriorating economic conditions (a defensive strategy), at the same time planning a major new-product development program (a breakthrough strategy). This would be consistent with an overall policy of making current operations as cost efficient as possible while looking for a logical new product market to exploit.

Summary

In summation, Exhibit 6.6 provides a graphic representation of this chapter: from the perception of a performance gap, to the three internal strategies, to, finally, the specific types of projects available to implement major strategies. Although examples of each type of project could readily be supplied to illustrate the different strategic options, this would not provide as illuminating an insight as going into one or two actual business histories in depth.

In Chapters 7 and 8 two projects in two companies are used to demonstrate the types of problems and decisions that arise in more or less typical cases of strategy formulation. The first case refers to R. J. Reynolds Industries' introduction of a new cigarette brand, which we view as an offensive strategy of "product extension." The second case began as a conventional defensive strategy of normal investment in plant and equipment based on A. H. Robins's decision to build a new $6 million chemical facility. Although a $6 million investment in a chemical facility would appear to be a straightforward project for this big pharmaceutical firm, it offers, as the story unfolds, an intriguing insight into "intracompany warfare and of unexpected economic and business developments — as well as how real

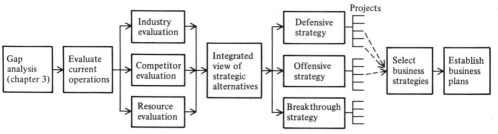

EXHIBIT 6.6
STRATEGY FORMULATION AT THE BUSINESS LEVEL

people make real decisions in the real world." [6] As such, it captures a side of the strategic process that a two-dimensional diagram is unable ever to fully convey.

QUESTIONS

1. Why is a strategy for improving current operations seen as uniquely a business-level responsibility?

2. In 1979 Chrysler faced a precarious financial situation. It had large backlogs of cars in dealer showrooms — mostly large, low-mileage models. It was almost time for new models but Chrysler couldn't introduce its new models until it first worked down the excess current inventory. The company was also pressed financially for funds to meet operating expenses and to invest in facilities in its smaller, gas-efficient models, which were selling well. Chrysler was, in short, in desperate financial straits with a near-term infusion of cash imperative. What short-term strategies might Chrysler consider? What longer-term strategies would you suggest?

3. As manager of the Chevrolet Division of General Motors you are responsible for submitting a competitor evaluation of new car models just introduced by two other automobile manufacturers. What information would you want? How would you go about getting it? What would you do with it?

4. How would the process of internal evaluation differ in a small one-product company from an international multi-industry firm?

MINI-EXERCISES

1. In a broad sense each individual makes internal evaluations and develops strategy for future development. Like corporations, individuals may take different career paths and choose different strategies. Make a personal inventory of your strengths and weaknesses and attempt a ten-year "strategy" for your development. Then identify the factors that will make this a "successful strategy" for you. What outside factors might ultimately influence its pattern? Are you planning your development or letting it happen?

2. Select two companies of roughly comparable size in the same industry. Develop a competitor analysis of each along the lines of Exhibit 6.4. Which of the two is the sounder company in your estimation? If you

were the chief planner of the other company, what steps would you take to close this "gap"?

REFERENCES

1. Hugo R. Uyterhoeven, R. W. Ackerman, and J. W. Rosenblum, *Strategy and Organization: Text and Cases,* rev. ed. (Homewood, Ill.: Richard D. Irwin, 1977).

2. *Business Week,* May 7, 1979.

3. Ibid., January 22, 1979.

4. *Forbes,* April 30, 1979.

5. Ibid.

6. *Wall Street Journal,* October 22, 1975.

FURTHER READING

Day, George S. "A Straight Perspective on Product Planning." *Journal of Contemporary Business,* Winter 1975.

Leontiades, Milton, "Evaluating a Firm's Performance Potential," *Business Horizons,* August 1980.

Moose, Sandra O., and Alan J. Zakon. "Frontier Curve Analysis: As a Resource Allocation Guide." *Journal of Business Policy,* Spring 1972.

Schendel, Dan E., and Richard Patton. "Corporate Stagnation and Turnaround." *Journal of Economics and Business,* Spring–Summer 1976.

Shames, William H. *Venture Management.* New York: Free Press, 1974.

CHAPTER 7

Strategies for Current Operations – Product Extension: R. J. Reynolds Industries

In almost all marketing departments there are two approaches to planning — the clairvoyant approach and the systematic one.

The clairvoyant planner believes he can cut to the heart of the problem with creativity and experience. He often rushes to conclusions based on his intuitive "feel" for the marketplace.*

The systematic marketing planner, on the other hand, knows how to use a disciplined, deliberate approach of examining the facts, considering the alternatives, and determining the best strategy. This planner's approach is based not only on experience and an innovative mind, but also on thorough understanding of data and alternatives.

The following is a case study that used this more deliberate approach successfully. It demonstrates the use of long-range planning in developing strategies for consumer marketing.

---

* Reprinted from James F. Hind, "Making MORE from Planning: R. J. Reynolds' Approach to Marketing Strategies," *Planning Review,* November 1978.

In this instance, the planning process guided the new products development group of our marketing department by identifying consumer needs and matching them with company needs, forming the basis for a new product concept.

The Planning Process

In order to follow our planning process through the case study, I will briefly describe the six steps in the process.

Our first step is to conduct environmental analyses. Here we identify major trends, issues, events outside the company. We want to project the environment or marketplace in which we will be operating for five years.

The sources are varied, including both formal analyses by our marketing research department or outside firms and a survey of the literature or personal interviews with individuals and organizations outside the company. An additional valuable source is line management's own qualitative judgments.

The second step is development of an external forecast from these environmental analyses. This forecast "paints the scene" down the road. It identifies the implications of the major trends or events, their timing, and the extent of their impact on our company. It thus uncovers critical problems and opportunities.

The third step in our long-range marketing planning is identification of the internal strengths and weaknesses of each of our brands and our company cigarette line in total.

Fourth, we extrapolate key marketing issues based on our external forecasts and our analyses of our product line. We define key issues as significant problems or opportunities that could greatly affect our marketing department's ability to accomplish corporate goals.

At this point, the fifth step, we develop objectives and strategies that correspond to these key issues.

Objectives are specific results to be achieved. A strategy qualitatively describes what must be done to accomplish the objective. Emphasis is on the course of action, timing, and the direction in which we are allocating resources — not the specific tactics used to implement the strategy.

The last step in our marketing planning process involves tactics, or specific action programs, used to implement the strategy.

In examining the case study, we will cover only the points relevant to this example.

External Forecast

The first step, the environmental analyses, began nearly five years ago and covered four areas: Economic Factors, Cigarette Categories, Consumer Values/Lifestyles, and Demographics.

Forecasted economic factors which were felt to have a future major influence were increasing retail cigarette prices and decreasing consumer purchasing power.

In the area of cigarette categories, we saw three growth segments — menthol cigarettes, low tar cigarettes, and extra-long (100 millimeter) cigarettes.

In consumer values and lifestyles, we saw two trends. First, there was a continued increase in the number of working women — which meant a different set of values and aspirations for women, revolving around a career and a strong desire for independence.

Second, there was a significant trend toward new values in both sexes. These new values focused strongly on self-realization and physical enhancement — individualism, if you will, as opposed to the more traditional values centered on the family, community, and nation. These new values had a direct bearing on the consumer's product needs and preferences. The physical enhancement trend among men had already resulted in several new products and market segments.

Increased fashion consciousness in men led to a market for less conservative business clothing. For example, the John Weitz Palm Beach line combines style with function, offering more alternatives in sportswear. This fashion awareness also carried over to accessories, and men's jewelry, watches, and scents have blossomed into lucrative businesses. Who would ever have thought there would be a Chanel for men? Markets for products and services ranging from hairpieces and hair transplants to physical fitness apparatus and clubs have grown tremendously as a direct result of this physical awareness.

Consumer values, then, have a most important influence on consumer needs and preferences which, in turn, indicate directions for the marketing planner. This area must be an important part of external forecasting for any consumer product, because the key to defining real opportunity in the marketplace is seeing people's needs through *their* own eyes.

Another important area in our external forecast was demographics. Here, we noted that the 18–34 population "bubble" — a result of the postwar baby boom — was moving through the marketplace. Additionally, our survey data showed quite clearly that more women were smoking more cigarettes.

Internal Strengths and Weaknesses

Our next step was to identify the internal strengths and weaknesses of our total cigarette line. We found that our product line, relative to the population, was:

> Strongest in the over-35 age group, weakest under 35, particularly among males.

> Strongest among smokers having the older or more traditional values, weakest among those with newer or more contemporary values.

> Strongest in low tar and menthols, weakest in the growing, extra-long cigarette category — the 100 millimeters.

> Strongest in the South and in middle-to-small population cities, weakest in the Northeast, the West and large metropolitan areas (such as New York, Los Angeles, San Francisco, Detroit, etc.).

Key Issues

Key issues, based on the external forecast and our product line evaluation, were divided into problems and opportunities.

> *Problems were company line weaknesses in:*

> The growing, extra-long cigarette category (i.e., the 100 mm);

> Smokers having the "new values";

> The under-35 age group, particularly among males; and

> Large urban markets.

> *Our opportunities were:*

> A strong trend toward increasing retail cigarette prices and decreasing consumer purchasing power, which suggested that extra value (more puffs per cigarette) could be a meaningful benefit.

> A strong trend among men toward new values — individualism and physical self-enhancement — suggesting that fashion and style in a cigarette targeted at men would be a meaningful benefit heretofore limited mainly to women.

Additionally, the strong desire of women for independence suggested a new, bolder receptivity on their part to new, adventurous lifestyles and products.

These key issues gave direction to a new cigarette concept at R. J. Reynolds. Through a thorough consumer testing program, a strong new brand concept evolved.

Objectives and Strategies

Our objectives for this new brand were: (1) to achieve an incremental 0.8 percent share of the market in one year; and (2) to help overcome existing product line demographic and geographic weaknesses.

The result was MORE, a cigarette longer than the extra-longs and unique in appearance by virtue of both its length (120 millimeters) and its brown cover. Advertising was aimed at positioning MORE in a niche, as yet unoccupied by other cigarette companies, with appeals to style, value (more puffs per cigarette) and self-enhancement.

MORE's advertising is simple and direct, built around the brand name in clever, easy to remember headlines noting the benefits it gives to the consumer. For example: "What's MORE. It's longer. It's leaner. It's slower. It's easy drawing. It's a cigarette."

Closing copy points out MORE's value: "Over 50% more puffs than a 100 mm cigarette, yet MORE doesn't cost more."

Word play off the name MORE, in fact, was the basis for all the new cigarette's advertising. The value story was pointed out at the point-of-sale in window posters and counter displays.

MORE quickly achieved close to a 1 percent share of the market, worth $72 million annually in sales to R. J. Reynolds. In its third year, it has continued to grow in sales at a rate approaching 10 percent, versus a 1 percent growth rate for the cigarette industry as a whole.

"Cannibalization" is estimated at 20–25% of our company line, and geographic and demographic targets were met.

Summary

The concept of a new experience in smoking, built around the unique physical properties and appearance of the cigarette, played successfully to the value trends. Adding the value story of "extra puffs" was timely in an inflationary period. Targeting it to demographic and geographic weaknesses in the company line meant incremental business.

The accelerating pace of change in our society — in consumers and their values, in industry and in the total environment — makes development of new products increasingly difficult. The days of the clairvoyant planner are over. Power in the marketplace, better resources, and smarter people no longer make the difference in the cigarette industry. The critical factor has become a practical, systematic, and meticulous planning process.

QUESTIONS

1. On hindsight, MORE cigarettes proved only a marginally satisfactory new product for R. J. Reynolds. What might have gone wrong? Merit cigarettes, introduced by Philip Morris around the same period, on the other hand, was a huge success. What might have gone right?

2. Assume you are in charge of introducing a new brand of bathroom soap for Proctor & Gamble. Outline in brief the major steps you would take to ensure its success.

3. Although many marketing-oriented companies have attempted to associate demand for new products with emerging consumer trends (e.g., swinging singles, smaller families, working wives), it has proved an elusive objective. What are some important qualifications to this approach?

CHAPTER 8

Strategies for Current Operations – New Investment: A. H. Robins

The story of how A. H. Robins came to make its $6 million investment is worth telling. It's a tale of more than a year of intensive planning, of intra-company warfare, and of unexpected economic and business developments — as well as of how real people make real decisions in the real world "that you'd never learn about at Harvard Business School," as one Robins insider puts it. Among other things, Robins started out planning to build or buy a plant of its own; it wound up, almost at the last minute, in a joint venture with a big West German pharmaceutical concern, Boehringer Ingelheim Associated Cos.*

---

* From "How A. H. Robins Co. Made Decision to Build a Chemical Facility," *Wall Street Journal*, October 22, 1975. Reprinted by permission of The Wall Street Journal, © Dow Jones & Company, Inc., 1975. All Rights Reserved.

Important Decisions

The story is also important for what it tells of the problems that business-men face these days in trying to decide whether to commit funds to capital projects, whatever their size. The level of capital spending this year and next is likely to be a key factor in determining whether and how fast the Ameri-can economy recovers from its worst recession in decades. Last month, the Commerce Department projected that 1975 capital spending would plum-met 11.5% below last year's, and most economists are cautious about next year's outlook.

The story of the A. H. Robins project actually begins in 1958, when company chemists first synthesized a white powdery chemical called metho-carbomal. A muscle relaxant, methocarbomal was patented and sold in pill form under the name Robaxyn after receiving government clearance. Con-tracts were given to several chemical makers to supply Robins with raw methocarbomal, since the company only made finished pharmaceuticals.

Robaxyn was a big success. By 1967, Robins believed it was buying enough methocarbomal to consider making the chemical for itself. The com-pany was also purchasing large volumes of glyceryl guaiacolate (GG) for its Robitussin cough medicine, and since methocarbomal was a derivative of GG, manufacture of the two petrochemicals seemed desirable, according to William L. Zimmer III, Robins' 63-year-old president.

Delayed by FDA Study

But the idea hit a snag and was shelved in 1970 when the Food and Drug Administration's Drug Efficacy Study, an industry-wide review of pharma-ceuticals, gave methocarbomal a "questionable" rating. Although the FDA eventually cleared the chemical in 1974, the review kept methocarbomal, along with Mr. Zimmer's idea of manufacturing it and GG, under a cloud for four years.

The idea was revived by the 1973–74 oil crisis and the resulting short-ages of petroleum-based chemicals. "Skyrocketing chemical prices were cut-ting into our profit margins," Mr. Zimmer says, noting that the price of methocarbomal shot up more than 40% in 1974 alone. Even worse, at times methocarbomal and GG were unavailable at any price; the costly pro-duction closedowns that ensued "were cutting into the lifeblood of our busi-ness," Mr. Zimmer says. He says he decided in April 1974 that Robins "would no longer be a pawn of the market."

On May 16, 1974, Robert G. Watts, senior vice president, sent a memo to the heads of seven corporate divisions. "Mr. Zimmer has requested that immediate attention be given to the feasibility of the manufacture of selected chemicals," the memo stated. It announced creation of a secret, high-level task force to "be responsible for providing recommendations for compounds to be considered, acquisition possibilities, site selection and facilities, as well as financial justification for same."

Two Teams Set Up

The task force met June 1, 1974, and was quickly broken down into two subgroups, one to study the acquisition of a chemical plant and the other to look into building one from scratch.

The "build" unit, headed by Mr. Watts, a tough 42-year-old ex-Navy officer, sought out six process engineering firms and was approached by dozens more. "These engineers have a grapevine that's incredible," Mr. Watts says. "You talk to one and they all come along." In early October the group settled on Lockwood–Greene Engineering Co., Atlanta.

In March 1975, Lockwood–Greene delivered to Robins an inch-thick, $16,000 volume that detailed design criteria, the chemical-making process, an equipment list, environmental impact statement, project schedule, drawings and, most important, a preliminary cost estimate. The engineering firm calculated that a plant making 200,000 pounds of GG and 500,000 pounds of methocarbomal annually, Robins' projected 1978 needs, would cost $6 million, plus 30% or minus 20%.

Robins' officers calculated that the same amounts of chemicals would cost $6,050,000 if purchased on the open market, but that it could be manufactured for only $3.5 million. Based on a $6.2 million capital outlay ($6 million for the plant and $200,000 for the land), the pretax return on investment (compared with continued outside purchases) would exceed 40%, and the investment would pay for itself in less than three years.

Meanwhile, consultants for the "buy" team identified over 100 existing plants that seemed to meet Robins' needs. Of these, about 20 were actually contacted by the company and three strong candidates ultimately emerged. One was Hexagon Laboratories Inc., New York, which later was acquired by the West German concern that eventually became Robins' partner in the joint venture in Petersburg.

Hexagon was up for sale and it was already a big supplier of methocarbomal to Robins. Little plant modification would have been necessary. "But Hexagon was in the Bronx and there was no room for possible expansion," Ernest L. Bender, Jr., senior vice president of Robins, says. Also, a Robins spokesman notes, "Hexagon's plant was unionized, and we've always tried to steer clear of unions." The buy group finally settled on a plant in Sheboygan, Wis.

The "build" and "buy" units developed a keen rivalry, with personal reputations and egos becoming involved in the outcome. "The acquisitions people were desperate for something big," Mr. Watts asserts. "They really wanted another feather in their cap." One member of the acquisition team retorts that Mr. Watts wanted to build a plant "so that he could have another picture hanging on his wall." (Mr. Watts' office wall bears architectural renderings of plants he has been responsible for in Puerto Rico and Richmond.)

Mr. Zimmer minimizes the effect of the rivalry; he says he had hoped for just such "creative tension." But in the meantime, more serious questions were being raised — including doubts about whether Robins should get into the chemical business at all.

A Case of Cold Feet

Carl Lunsford, vice president in charge of chemical research—and one of the discoverers of methocarbomal in 1958 — had begun to develop cold feet about the project. He suggested that the proposed plant be scaled down by about half.

"You don't just go out and build a chemical plant," he recalls saying. "It takes expertise and technical knowhow. Since this was our first move into a new area, I thought it would be well to leave room for a third party to supply us. There's always the possibility for a plant going down because of fire or some other catastrophe."

Mr. Lunsford's hesitation came on the heels of a study commissioned by Robins from Chase Manhattan Bank. The Chase analysts argued that Robins shouldn't go through with the project because of the cyclical nature of the chemical business. By prudent hedging operations — buying supplies when prices were low — Robins could assure itself of the necessary raw materials, they said.

Mr. Zimmer, still vividly remembering the 1973 oil embargo, rejected the Chase argument out of hand. "Any savings we'd obtain would quickly be lost if supplies were interrupted," he says. Of Mr. Lunsford's objections, Mr. Watts says dryly: "I think our suppliers convinced him."

Ironically, however, it was Mr. Lunsford's vision of the course Robins should take that came closest to what actually happened — although not necessarily for the reasons he cited.

Economic Ills Noted

Planning for the project was coming to a head in the midst of a precipitous decline in the economy. "Some of our meetings were pretty strained," one insider recalls. "Inflation was rushing along and the recession just kept getting worse. Some of us felt we were just spinning wheels, that the state of the economy — the sheer uncertainty of it all — would preclude a big commitment of capital."

G. E. R. Stiles, vice president and treasurer, says those who were worried about the recession were overruled because a company can't look at short-term fluctuations in determining capital spending policies. "This is long-term planning," he says. A recession, he adds, "is a one-to-three-year thing. When you're talking about a new plant, you're talking 10 to 20 years." Besides, Robins was able to minimize the recession's impact because a strong balance sheet allowed the company to finance the project internally rather than compete for funds on the capital markets.

By last March [1975], the management team had studied its "build" and "buy" options for about 10 months, and a showdown was slated. The proponents of purchasing the Sheboygan plant made a persuasive presentation. The next day, the "build" forces counterattacked with an equally persuasive proposal, aided by an artist's sketch, for a custom-built facility in Virginia. The costs were about equal.

The decision, by Mr. Zimmer in consultation with Chairman E. Claiborne Robins, Sr., went in favor of the "build" team. "We really wanted that damned plant in Virginia," Mr. Zimmer says. "That way we can run down and touch it just to make sure it's there every once in a while." Virginia industrial development officials were asked to help choose the site; they assigned the project the code name "Operation Dogwood" and soon narrowed the search to nine possible locations.

But no sooner had the decision seemingly been made between "buy" and "build" than a third possibility arose. Hexagon Laboratories, the Bronx concern considered as a potential purchase possibility, had been acquired in February for $4 million by Boehringer Ingelheim, a big pharmaceutical and chemical concern based in Ingelheim, West Germany. Subsequently, Hexagon officials had gotten wind of Robins' plans for a captive source of methocarbomal and GG, and two Hexagon representatives were dispatched to Richmond in April in an effort to keep the Robins' business.

Hexagon offered to build a plant in Virginia and negotiate a long-term sales agreement with Robins. Robins, which had gone this far down the road, demurred. Hexagon offered Robins an equity interest in the plant as a sweetener. Mr. Zimmer struck: "I said 50% or nothing at all. Take it or leave it."

A Surprised Executive

"I almost dropped my teeth," recalls Mr. Lunsford, who was at the meeting and saw a joint venture with an experienced chemical concern as the solution to his fears about building a chemical plant. Mr. Lunsford worried that Mr. Zimmer's insistence on a half interest might be unacceptable to Boehringer.

But Boehringer eventually agreed to the transaction. Most of the plant's output would be sold to Robins, profits would be divided equally and Robins would have an option to buy Hexagon's share after an unspecified period of time. The package neatly disposed of nearly all the objections that various Robins factions had about the build or buy options. Among other things, for example, it will allow Robins to hold capital spending next year to about $7 million, the same as this year, because Robins' share of the project will result in an outlay of only about $1.5 million to $2 million next year, with the remainder in 1977. The plant is slated to open in early 1978.

"We'd have probably gone ahead alone and built a new plant," Mr. Zimmer says, "but the joint venture sure makes us feel more confident about this project."

QUESTIONS

1. Contrast the financial approach to investment by A. H. Robins with the traditional approach to financial decision making contained in textbooks. Discuss the differences.

2. Critique the approach used by A. H. Robins. Do you agree with the methodology? Do you agree with the solution?

3. In arriving at its final decision, A. H. Robins had to take a number of factors into consideration. In a simplified diagram, illustrate the decision-making process, including the major variables that influenced the outcome. Which variables, in your estimation, were the most influential in arriving at the final decision?

PART III
FORMULATING PLANS

CHAPTER 9

Planning for Evolution and Change – Three Valuable Planning Techniques

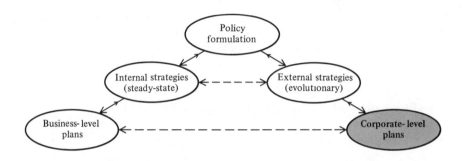

Any well-managed firm employs techniques to determine the allocation of resources among the parts of the organization. The criteria used to determine such allocations will naturally vary with the circumstances. A chemical firm, for example, may view the supply and price of oil-based feedstock in an energy-short era as crucial, while a consumer-oriented retailer may be preoccupied with increasing market share. In either case, however, similar techniques of analysis could be used to increase allocations for some business units and determine where reductions in allocations may be made among other business units.

In developing a corporate strategic plan, a first step is to isolate the business units to be analyzed. In a single-product firm this may seem redundant. But for a diversified organization the number of business units that plan may number over one hundred. Even firms with a single product line may have several distinct products within that line. Any business unit with profit-center responsibility could qualify for analysis. Moreover, such business units (sometimes called strategic business units or SBUs) can usually be defined in terms of a product sector with well-defined boundaries and competition.

In illustrating the use of various techniques of evaluation, a diversified organization with many business units is assumed to be the model. Such an organization can illustrate the maximum flexibility of the various approaches. However, the techniques are versatile. They can be used to contrast as few as two different business units or as many units as might apply. They can accommodate an almost infinite number of criteria to arrive at final decisions, although only a few criteria can be comfortably managed simultaneously. Finally, these methods lend themselves to rating a firm's competitors as well as rating a firm's own operations.

Among the most commonly used methods of analysis, three stand out. These techniques are primarily the product of experimentation and innovation by management consultants and practitioners: (1) profit impact of marketing strategy (PIMS); (2) portfolio management; (3) strategy centers (life-cycle patterns).

Profit Impact of Marketing Strategies (PIMS)

The PIMS method grew out of an approach developed at General Electric to explain the success and failure of its various business units in terms of return on investment (ROI) and cash flow. Eventually the methodology was extended beyond GE to businesses generally through cooperation by General Electric with the Management Science Institute and Harvard University in establishing the PIMS project.

The PIMS program is now the product of the autonomous nonprofit Strategic Planning Institute. There were fifty-seven participating companies in 1978 with assets ranging from $200 million to $10 billion and with 620 separate businesses that contribute information to PIMS's "experience" pool.[1]

The aim of PIMS is simple, if ambitious. On the basis of information on hundreds of diverse businesses, PIMS hopes to isolate the key factors that determine the success or failure of an individual business. The primary measure used to define success is ROI, because this measure is most often used in strategic planning.

Among the many factors analyzed for their impact on ROI are market share, marketing expenditures, product quality, research and development, size, and degree of diversification. One of the most important influences on ROI, according to the PIMS findings, is market share, as discussed in the following research findings.

ROI (%)

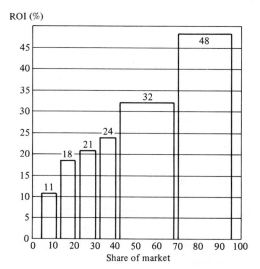

EXHIBIT 9.1
MARKET SHARE HELPS PROFITABILITY
Source: Bradley T. Gale, "Planning for Profit," *Planning Review*, March 1978. Reprinted by permission of Planning Review, a bi-monthly journal published by the North American Society for Corporate Planning, 1406 Third National Building, Dayton, Ohio 45402.

SOME RESEARCH FINDINGS

The PIMS staff has built a number of empirical models to explain why profitability and cash flow differ from business to business. These models contain factors that affect financial performance. Some representative findings are summarized in Exhibits 9.1 and 9.2. PIMS participants find these

Market share growth rate

	-1%	4.4%	
13%	1	0	-8
28%	-2	2	0
	11	7	0

Market share

EXHIBIT 9.2
CASH FLOW AS A PERCENTAGE OF INVESTMENT
(Determined by Market Share and Market Share Growth)
Source: Bradley T. Gale, "Planning for Profit," *Planning Review*, January 1978. Reprinted with permission from Planning Review.

exhibits especially interesting when they imagine the position of their business, or a portfolio of businesses, within the context of the exhibits.

Market Share Helps Profitability.   It is now widely recognized that one of the main determinants of business profitability is market share. Under most circumstances, businesses that have achieved a high share of the markets they serve are considerably more profitable than their small-share competitors. Exhibit 9.1 shows average ROI (pretax) for groups or businesses in the PIMS program, highlighting their profit enhancement from successively larger shares of their markets.

There are several reasons why a high share of the market causes high profitability. First, large-share businesses usually enjoy scale economies in working capital, marketing, research and development, and certain other cost components. Second, they also enjoy economies of cumulative volume, which reduce unit costs via the experience-curve effect and by spreading setup costs over a longer production run. Third, customers eager to minimize the risk of making a wrong choice may favor a large-share business. This customer behavior gives dominant suppliers a share-based product-differentiation advantage. Finally, large-share businesses often have greater bargaining power over customers and suppliers, and frequently they are able to take the initiative over their competitors.

Gaining Market Share Drains Cash.   High-share businesses generate more cash than low-share businesses, but the process of building market share absorbs cash. In Exhibit 9.2, the number of businesses in PIMS's sample is divided into three approximately equal groups on the basis of two factors: market-share growth rate and market share. The figures in each of the nine boxes represent the joint effect of market-share growth and market share on the ratio of cash flow to investment. For example, the companies represented in the upper-right-hand box of Exhibit 9.2 have high growth rate but low market share, which creates a negative cash flow relative to investment. This is because small-share businesses that are rapidly gaining share absorb a good deal of cash; they tend to have low profitability combined with large additions to productive capacity needed to meet growing market demand. In contrast, large-share businesses where growth in share is declining or is low, as in the lower-left-hand box of Exhibit 9.2, tend to generate large amounts of cash — as reflected in the relatively high (11%) ratio of cash flow to investment.

Cash flow in a particular year is defined as cash generated by after-tax earnings minus cash absorbed by an increase in working capital or by an increase in net investment in plant and equipment. The ratio shown in Exhibit 9.2 is average cash flow for a four-year period expressed as a percentage of the average level of investment tied up in the business during this four-year time period. Investment is defined as the level of net book value of plant and equipment plus working capital. Cash flow is before dividends.

In summary, the PIMS program has developed a strategic planning service designed to satisfy many of management's needs. Information on strategic actions, market and industry situations, and results achieved has been compiled and organized into a multipurpose data base. The analysis of this data base has shown which business characteristics are the important determinants of profitability and other success measures. Executives of the participating companies are using the findings, reports, and services in a variety of ways to develop and appraise strategic plans for individual business units and to balance their portfolios of product-line businesses.

The PIMS method is a welcome addition to the store of information businesses can use to make informed decisions. It is particularly valuable because the data are collected from actual businesses and designed for practical applications. There are, however, qualifications to the PIMS approach. It does not, for instance, differentiate its results by industries. It assumes a sufficient commonality among industries to give the findings universal application, regardless of the industry a company happens to be in. This is assumed despite the fact that "different businesses have different market demand relationships, different production technologies and different accounting and financial structures," [2] all of which would intuitively question a holistic approach. Other criticisms concern the use of ROI as the sole criterion of performance, use of cross-sectional as opposed to time-series data, the reliance on a single linear-regression equation to explain ROI, and so forth. In listing a number of such qualifications, one source summarized the various types of reservations by stating: "The most critical fault with PIMS approach is its supposition of causal relationships with little theoretical or statistical basis." [3] Even in this instance of underlining why PIMS is not a perfect predictor or a guarantor of successful performance, there was no attempt to deny the real contribution that such a tool can provide to decision makers.

Portfolio Management

A simple portfolio management approach is typified in Exhibit 9.3 by a four-square matrix into which each of a company's businesses can be classified according to market growth and market share. Developed by the Boston Consulting Group, this technique has become a familiar device for analyzing business prospects. It suggests a broad strategy for each of the four categories of businesses below.

```
High ┌─────────────┬─────────────┐
     │ Star        │ Speculation │
     │             │             │
     │ High growth │ New venture │
  ┌──┤             │             │
  M  │ Expanding   │ Tomorrow's  │
  a  │ bus-        │ star        │
  r  │ iness       │ (it is      │
  k  │             │ hoped)      │
  e  ├─────────────┼─────────────┤
  t  │             │             │
     │ Cash cow    │ Dog         │
  g  │             │             │
  r  │ Low growth  │ No growth   │
  o  │             │             │
  w  │ Mature      │ Potential   │
  t  │ business    │ sale        │
  h  │             │             │
 Low └─────────────┴─────────────┘
      High                   Low
          Market share
```

EXHIBIT 9.3
PORTFOLIO MANAGEMENT MATRIX

Cash-Cow Businesses (*Low Growth, High Market Share*).   Businesses in this category are often called cash cows. They throw off large amounts of cash but the prospects for future growth in the field are limited. These businesses should be milked in order to support more promising opportunities. New investment is therefore limited to a maintenance level.

Star Performers (*High Growth, High Market Share*).   A star business represents a fast-growing operation with a dominant market share. This is an enviable position. The successful new ventures of companies will, it is hoped, turn out to be stars — although many more generally fail than succeed. A star business generates large amounts of cash that may exceed its reinvestment needs, depending on the rate of growth in the market and the capital intensity of the business. From this optimum point of high market share and market growth, a business will eventually develop into a cash cow as its market matures and growth declines.

Speculations (*High Growth, Low Market Share*).   A speculative business is by definition one that entails high risks. Therefore, a typical company can afford to back only a limited number of such speculative ventures. The strategy is based on probabilities of one or more carefully selected ventures developing into a star performer, and thus balancing the failures or modest successes of other speculative ventures. A firm in this category must pursue aggressive strategies designed to gain market share. Texas Instruments' aggressive price strategies in pocket calculators and electronic watches were such examples. If the strategies succeed, the company will establish a dominant market share position, and move to the star performer category.

Dogs (*Low Growth, Low Market Share*).   In many large diversified companies there are usually a few businesses that can be described as dogs. There is little to recommend their retention or further investment by the company. They are typically the businesses tagged for divestment at an early opportunity. However, the classification of, or admission to, dogs in the company is not always straightforward. Management may spend considerable resources attempting to turn around a business that in the end defies all treatment. Top managers can lose their objectivity in taking necessary action on investments they have recommended and with which they are still closely identified.

Portfolio management has obvious implications for corporate strategy. It provides a basis for balancing the mix of businesses among cows, dogs, stars, and high risks. This in turn provides a basis for resource allocation to each business. As an overall strategy, the company should optimize the value of its portfolio in terms of those objectives management has defined as primary. Portfolio management can also be useful in diversification strategy by identifying areas in which a company may wish to acquire new products or services as well as areas where it wishes to reduce its exposure.

The version of portfolio management we have described was deliberately simple in order to illustrate the concept. In practice larger matrices with a variety of different criteria could be employed. As an example, we can refer to a matrix employed by Shell in what it calls its Directional Policy Matrix (DPM). The results of a hypothetical situation used by Shell have been plotted on the matrix in Exhibit 9.4. In explaining the three competitor positions on the matrix, Shell has made the following distinctions among the so-called "leader," "try harder," and "double or quit" designations.[4]

Leader.   Competitor A, the largest producer with the lowest unit costs and a commanding technical situation, is in the highly desirable position of leader in a business sector with attractive prospects. His indicated strategy is to give absolute priority to the product with all the resources necessary to hold his market position. This being a fast-growing sector he will, before long, need to install extra capacity. Although in all probability he is already earning satisfactory profits from product X, his current cash flow from this source may not be sufficient to finance a high rate of new investment. In that case the cash must be found from another sector of his business. Later, as the growth rate slows down, product X should be able to finance its own growth and eventually become a net generator of cash.

Try Harder.   Competitor B is in this position. It implies that products located in this zone can be moved down toward at least an equality position by the right allocation of resources. However, competitor B does not appear

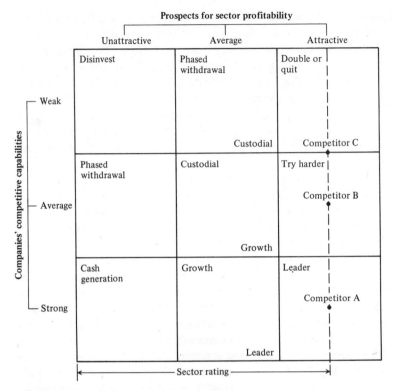

EXHIBIT 9.4
DIRECTIONAL POLICY MATRIX — PRODUCT X
(Used by Shell)
Source: Derek F. Channon. "Strategic Planning Portfolio Models: Practical Progress and Problems in Practice," Manchester Business School, draft, 1976. Reprinted by permission.

to have any special advantages in this sector and unless he can strengthen his position by, for example, licensing one of the new processes, he may be condemned to remain No. 2. This is not necessarily an unacceptable position in the short term but is likely to become increasingly vulnerable with the passage of time.

Double or Quit.   This is the zone of the matrix from which products that are destined to become the future high fliers should be selected. A company should not normally seek to diversify into any new sector unless the prospects for it are judged to be "attractive." Only a small number of the most promising should be picked for "doubling"; the rest should be abandoned. Competitor C, on the strength of his successful feedstock process development and his licensing relationships with Eastern Europe for the X process, has already decided to "double," that is, invest in a commercial plant. He is therefore on the borderline of the "double or quit" and "try harder" zones: his production capability and product R & D ratings are both higher than his present market rating. Competitor C faces a more uncertain prospect of reaching a viable position in this sector than if he had been first in the field like competitor A.

This describes the application of the DPM analysis of three of the different sectors in a diversified business of a particular company and ranking these sectors for priority in allocation of resources. As such it can be extended to other sectors and provide a valuable aid to planning and management decision making in a highly competitive environment.

Here again, however, the portfolio-management approach has its critics. The gist of the criticism is aimed not so much at the technique itself but at the tendency to claim more for this approach than it was designed to deliver. One major area for caution is a simplified approach to market segmentation. Since a major application of this device has been in differentiating among business units of large diversified companies, it is important that these business units be properly defined. It is often possible, for instance, for an underperforming total business unit to mask several superior and separable product/market pieces. Exhibit 9.5(a) shows a music recording company in a favorable market position. In Exhibit 9.5(b) the company has been broken into identifiable smaller product/market segments, which

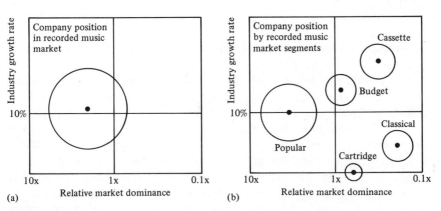

EXHIBIT 9.5
IMPORTANCE OF MARKET SEGMENT IDENTIFICATION
FOR BUSINESS ANALYSIS
Source: From Derek F. Channon, "Commentary" (on "Strategy Formulation: Analytical and Normative Models" by John H. Grant and William R. King) in Dan E. Schendel and Charles E. Hofer, eds., *Strategic Management: A New View of Business and Policy Planning,* Ex. 3.14, p. 130. Copyright © 1979 by Little, Brown and Company (Inc.). Reprinted by permission.

vary significantly in attractiveness/unattractiveness. There may also be difficulty in making cross-comparisons between PIMS and the portfolio-management approach. It is possible "that a low market share business in a low growth market could be extremely attractive in cash flow terms if it was also low in capital intensity, while such a 'dog' business in [portfolio management] terms could well be a candidate for divestment." [5]

These types of qualifications for both PIMS and now the portfolio-management approach suggest that decision making benefits when more than one technique is used and that no technique yet devised can replace the individual manager's judgment in interpreting and weighing the impact of various factors.

Strategy Centers (Life-Cycle Patterns)

The final technique is the so-called strategy-centers approach. This method was devised by the consulting firm Arthur D. Little, Inc. It uses stages of development in a typical life-cycle pattern as a measure for classifying businesses and developing strategies. Based on growth in volume, a business can be classified in one of the following four stages of development: *embryonic* — a highly competitive market situation where market shares are typically small and available volume is spread among many participants; *growth* — market shares of surviving firms have increased and the industry is more stable; the market continues to have growth potential; *maturity* — a relatively small number of firms command a majority of the market, but growth of the market has declined; *decline* — very little or no growth potential exists and the firms, although commanding high market shares, are situated in an industry with dim prospects.

The strategy-centers approach is similar in many respects to portfolio management. One might, in fact, substitute the terms "risk," "star," "cow," and "dog" for the stages of development shown in Exhibit 9.6 and approximate a classification system, with comparable financial attributes, as was described in portfolio management. In the strategy centers, as with portfolio management, individual business units may or may not fit neatly into a single classification. For example, a business may include products in more than one of the strategic growth phases. Also, a business that is mature in the United States may be a growth business in Europe and an embryonic business in less developed countries. It is therefore necessary to treat strategy centers as a tool that can aid management in the development of strategy, like PIMS and portfolio management, but one whose simplicity disguises the hard analysis required to define each business properly and to develop separate strategies for each consistent with overall resource limits of the firm.

Category	Characteristics			
Market	High growth-low share	High growth-high share	Low growth-high share	Low growth-low share
Financial	Cash hungry Low reported earnings Good P/E High debt level	Self-financing, cash hungry Good to low reported earnings High P/E Low-moderate debt level	Cash rich High earnings Fair P/E No debt-high debt capacity	Fair cash flow Low earnings Low P/E Low debt capacity
Stage	Embryonic	Growth	Maturity	Decline

EXHIBIT 9.6
STRATEGY CENTERS APPROACH
(Life-Cycle Patterns)

Summary

With the growing sophistication in planning concepts have come a number of technical aids in handling the information for making planning decisions. Among the most useful of these management aids are PIMS, portfolio management, and strategy centers. The necessity for such decision-making tools has sharply increased since the mid-1950s because of the trend to diversification away from a single or primary product line. In a multi-industry enterprise, management must make difficult allocation decisions, determining which businesses to expand and which to liquidate. In an earlier period when companies were concentrated in a single industry, management's actions were to a large extent dictated by the economic cycles of that industry. Now, with greater latitude to vary the direction and intensity of its investments among businesses in several industries, management is taking advantage of new analytical tools to sharpen its judgments.

QUESTIONS

1. Contrast the relative merits and objectives of PIMS, portfolio management, and strategy centers. Which of these methods would be most

appropriate for a multidivisional company that has losses and wishes to evaluate its total operations for possible divestment of losing businesses?

2. Suppose you were responsible for developing the criteria to be used in evaluating a major retail chain like Radio Shack. Which method would you use? How would you apply it?

3. The methods of evaluation suggested in the text are useful, although by themselves they do not comprise the whole of the evaluation process. What factors other than the ones used in these methods would you want to consider? What factors would top management have to consider, for instance, before divesting a major division of a company?

4. Assuming a division of a company has been identified as an under-performer, management still must decide whether to sell it or invest additional dollars in the hope of a turnaround. What steps would you take to assist in arriving at a decision in such a situation?

5. A company's evaluation of its operations is in large part based on past performance. Since a company's strategy is future-oriented, of what value are exercises that evaluate a company's past record?

6. Despite the progress made in the use of advanced analytical tools, and the application of computers to decision making, business failures and mistakes appear as persistent as ever. How do you reconcile these two apparently contradictory trends? In what situation would you envision the scientific approach working optimally?

7. Return on invested capital for the Saturna Co. has tended to decline systematically over the past three years. The adverse trend coincides with Saturna's purchase of a promising but speculative company that prospects for oil and gas. It has been only modestly successful until now, when a test well indicated "significant" quantities of oil and gas. However, the investment needed to develop this opportunity fully would require Saturna to borrow substantial sums and raise its debt-to-equity ratio from 20 percent to over 60 percent. What would you recommend to the president of Saturna (a conservative manager)? Could you use any of the three analytical tools to bolster your arguments?

8. As a recently hired planner for a medium-sized company in the drapery hardware business, you are forced to make several strategic investment decisions for inclusion in next year's plan. As a former executive in a life insurance company, you have little intimate knowledge of your new business. Suggest a way PIMS could assist you in

making initial strategy determinations. What questions might you
want to ask of the PIMS consultant to your company?

MINI-EXERCISES

1. Select a well-known diversified company. Break it down into its major
    parts (the different businesses it is in). Select one of the three methods
    of evaluation mentioned in the text and use it to measure the past
    performances of each of the individual businesses of the company.
    Which are the company's strongest businesses? Which are its weakest?
    What strategy would you suggest for this company based on your
    evaluation? Might a rationale exist for the company's retaining busi-
    nesses that you have objectively measured as underperformers?

2. Based on the materials presented in this chapter, how would you
    proceed to evaluate the future prospects for the domestic steel indus-
    try? What do you believe should be the key factors used to measure
    the future potential, or lack of it, for the industry?

3. Illustrations in this chapter have emphasized large companies or large
    industries. Yet proper evaluation is just as important for the small
    company. Choose a local enterprise. Gather information on it from
    public records, estimates based on competitors or creative research;
    for example, its degree of competition, growth in sales and earnings,
    and so forth. Based on your research, and use of one or more of the
    evaluative techniques, develop a judgment on this company's prospects
    for success or failure. What steps might be taken to improve current
    operations?

4. Select a single-industry company that has a number of product lines
    (e.g., a large paper company) and use the strategy-centers approach
    to evaluate each product line. How will such an evaluation influence
    your resource-allocation decisions for next year's budget?

REFERENCES

1. Bradley T. Gale, "Planning for Profit," *Planning Review,* January 1978.

2. Thomas Naylor, "PIMS: Through a Different Looking Glass," *Planning
    Review,* March 1978.

3. Frank Paine and Carl Anderson, "PIMS: A Reexamination," *Academy
    of Management Review,* July 1978.

4. Derek F. Channon, "Strategic Planning Portfolio Models: Practical
    Progress and Problems in Practice," Manchester Business School, un-
    published draft, 1976.

5. Derek F. Channon, commentary in Dan E. Schendel and Charles W. Hofer, eds., *Strategic Management* (Boston: Little, Brown, 1979).

FURTHER READING

Buzzell, Robert D., Bradley T. Gale, and Ralph G. M. Sulton. "Market Share–Key to Profitability." *Harvard Business Review,* January–February 1975.

Fruhan, William E., Jr. "Pyrrhic Victories in Fights for Market Share." *Harvard Business Review,* September–October 1972.

James, Barrie G. "The Theory of the Corporate Life Cycle." *Long Range Planning,* June 1973.

Levitt, Theodore. "Exploit the Product Life Cycle." *Harvard Business Review,* November–December 1965.

O'Connor, Rochelle. *Corporate Guides to Long-Range Planning.* New York: The Conference Board, 1976.

Polli, Rolando, and Victor Cook. "Validity of the Product Life Cycle." *Journal of Business,* October 1969.

Porter, Michael E. *Competitive Strategy: Techniques for Analyzing Industries and Competitors.* New York: Free Press, 1980.

Rue, Leslie W. "Tools and Techniques of Long Range Planners." *Long Range Planning,* October 1974.

Wasson, Chester. *Product Management: Product Life Cycles and Competitive Marketing Strategy.* St. Charles, Ill.: Challenge Books, 1971.

CHAPTER 10

Planning for Evolution and Change – An Acquisition Analysis

As we saw, acquisitions have been and continue to be a prominent means for diversifying and restructuring American business. As such, they are worthy of study in some detail, and a pragmatic method for learning about acquisitions is to choose an actual situation to study. In this chapter an acquiring company and a potential company to be acquired, both real companies, are used as our case example. A systematic method of evaluating the principal financial aspects of the acquisition is provided in the following sections. The emphasis is on financial analysis of the acquisition although a number of other factors — including marketing position, channels of distribution, product/market compatibility, and so forth — can clearly be important. However, the financial aspects have been chosen because (1) financial analysis is invariably a major consideration in making an acquisition and (2) focusing on this aspect allows us to consider it in some depth rather than presenting a summary evaluation of a number of factors.

Annual reports and standard reference sources have been used to generate data required to complete the necessary financial workups. The next sections follow the five-step procedure below.

Step 1: Determining of Diversification Strategy

Diversification strategy depends on corporate policy. There are three basic options: (1) vertical diversification: acquisitions that extend the present industry position backward toward raw material sources or forward to the consumer; (2) horizontal diversification: acquisitions that strengthen the present industry position through related acquisitions; (3) unrelated diversification: acquisitions to position the company in fields unrelated to its present business.

The corporate philosophy or statement of policy will determine which of these options apply. For example, a large oil-company policy might "focus on the discovery and development of major deposits of oil and gas, and the related activities of production and distribution, needed for the advancement of industrial society." This policy statement clearly implies an intention to stay with the primary business of oil and gas; therefore acquisitions of this company, if any, would be vertical diversification. A broader sense of mission by another large oil company might include, in addition to the business of oil and gas, an interest in becoming "a factor in the chemical business." Such a policy would allow a more open approach to acquisitions, including related acquisitions in chemicals as well as possibilities within the oil and gas business (horizontal diversification). Finally, the conglomerate approach is completely open, guided solely by the opportunity for meeting its objectives regardless of industry (unrelated diversification). On this last basis, the identification and acquisition of optimum candidate companies is extremely challenging.

Establishing the policy of a company is obviously a preliminary step to conducting an acquisition search (see Chapter 1 for discussion of policy formulation). Here we make an arbitrary selection of Anheuser-Busch as the company to study; a related, or horizontal, acquisition strategy will be assumed.

Once these determinations are made, a suitable list of possible firms for acquisition can be generated. For example, based on the strategy assumption of a horizontal type of acquisition we can confine our search to industries related to the brewing industry. A helpful tool in this procedure is the Standard Industrial Classification (SIC) manual. This government publication provides us with a system (SIC codes) by which we can identify firms in the brewing industry as well as two closely related industries that would initially fit our strategy, namely, malt liquors (SIC code 2082), wines (SIC code 2084), and distilled liquors (SIC code 2085). Companies that fall into these industry classifications comprise our Master List and may be compiled from a number of public sources. Exhibit 10.2 presents such a list by the three major SIC categories.

Step 2: Preliminary Evaluation of Eligible Companies

After a suitable list of companies is generated, the task of evaluating these companies and eliminating the less promising candidates can begin. The first step is designing a rough screen to eliminate companies for fairly obvious reasons. Companies larger than the acquiring corporation, for example, would be unlikely merger possibilities. Companies that fall below a minimum earnings level may be considered too small to contribute significantly to overall corporate goals. An illustrative set of criteria that Anheuser-Busch could use as a screen is shown in Exhibit 10.1, with the results of how the companies on the Master List would fare shown in Exhibit 10.2.

At this juncture, feedback from top management would be essential. Because Anheuser-Busch is America's largest brewer, management may decide that potential antitrust action by the Justice Department would preclude acquisitions of other brewers. In addition, it may be management's judgment to remain in industries it could dominate, which would eliminate the liquor industry where, at best, it would become one of several giant firms

EXHIBIT 10.1
CRITERIA FOR FIRST SCREEN

Type of firm	Minimum	Desirable
Size		
Sales	$50 million	$100–500 million
Earnings	2 million	5 million
Growth (5-year trend)		
Sales	5% per year	10% per year
Earnings per share	positive	8% per year
Profitability (5-year averages)		
Return on equity	8%	12%
Return on total capital	6%	10%
Risk		
Debt-to-equity ratio	.40	.20

EXHIBIT 10.2
MASTER LIST OF POSSIBILITIES TESTED AGAINST MINIMUM CRITERIA FOR ACQUIREES

	Size (1975)		Growth (5-year trend)		Profitability (5-year averages)		Risk
	Sales	Earnings	Sales	Earnings	ROE	ROTC	D/E ratio
Brewers (SIC 2082)							
1. Coors (Adolph)	$ 525	$56.6	16.4%	12.2%	14.6%	14.6%	Nil
2. Falstaff	182	(6.3)	4.8	NMF	def.	def.	44%
3. Heileman (G)	165	5.9	14.5	2.2	15.9	11.9	40
4. Pabst	495	20.8	12.9	NMF	10.8	10.8	Nil
5. Schaefer (F&M)	248	(1.2)	6.5	NMF	NMF	2.6	208
6. Schlitz	935	33.5	15.1	2.1	15.7	12.6	73
Distillers (SIC 2085)							
7. American Distilling	141	(5.5)	NMF	NMF	4.0 [a]	3.7 [a]	16
8. Brown Forman	360	20.0	10.1	6.5	11.2	9.4	32
9. Heublein	1500	61.5	20.5	28.5	18.2	12.4	63
10. National Distillers	1300	58.0	4.7	12.2	9.8	7.7	33
11. Publicker Industries	215	1.6	4.3	NMF	3.4 [b]	3.4 [b]	Nil
12. Seagram	1930	74.1	6.1	5.5	8.7	7.2	52
13. Walker (Hiram) — Gooderham & Worts	864	50.7	3.9	0.8	12.0	12.0	Nil
Wineries (SIC 2084) [c]							
14. Almaden Vineyards	69	5.0	19.7	11.5	11.3	10.6	27
15. Taylor Wine	67	5.4	9.2	5.2	13.0	12.4	Nil

Note: Dollars in thousands   NMF = No meaningful figure
[a] 1971–74   [b] 1973–75
[c] Ernest & Julio Gallo is a big winery that might be considered, but since it is a private company data are insufficient for a detailed analysis and comparison with other companies.

in the industry. Thus a checkpoint with management could save considerable effort in the acquisition program. In this case the wine industry alone would remain of the three possible industries identified for investigation.

Assuming a long list of possibilities to investigate within the wine industry, a fact sheet on each company may be developed to reflect its relative performance within the industry. This additional step would establish another checkpoint where top management could again review the possibilities and, by eliminating some prospects from further consideration, allow more efficient direction of the research effort. Since only two companies, Taylor Wine and Almaden Vineyards, remain as possibilities, this step would be unnecessary. Moreover, since only Taylor Wine is truly independent (roughly 80 percent of Almaden Vineyards being owned by National Distillers), we can focus on Taylor Wine to illustrate the succeeding steps of analysis.*

Step 3: Detailed Financial Evaluation of Most Likely Companies

Here candidates that have survived would be subject to detailed financial evaluation. These evaluations would answer how each potential acquisition would rank in terms of fit with the acquiring company. In actuality, a total evaluation of possible acquisitions would include investigation of non-financial areas like the number of products and market shares, marketing and distribution systems, physical facilities, employee benefits, and so forth. For our analysis, we have limited our focus to preliminary, and often determining, financial aspects of the acquisition analysis. One of these financial considerations is the effect on earnings per share (EPS) of the acquiring company before and after the potential acquisition. Because EPS is one of the most important measures for judging the quality of management, it is an indicator that management views with particular sensitivity. An acquisition that would significantly dilute a firm's EPS would be severely questioned. Further, if the EPS were to show a year-to-year decline immediately after the acquisition, management might abandon that target acquisition regardless of its other features.

Probably second to EPS as a financial consideration is the return on investment (ROI). In addition to return on its initial investment, an acqui-

---

* Our candidate, Taylor Wine, was subsequently acquired by Coca-Cola. Since this does not affect the lesson of our analysis, Taylor Wine has been retained for our acquisition analysis.

sition can generate funds above those needed to maintain the ongoing business. These funds would flow to the acquirer, reduce its initial investment, and raise its financial returns. For example, a mature company may generate more cash than it needs. A fast-growth acquiree, on the other hand, may consume cash faster than it can be generated from internal sources. From the acquirer's point of view, the most desirable candidate is that company whose cash needs complement those of the acquirer. For this type of evaluation the portfolio management matrix illustrated in Chapter 9 would be a useful guide. A growing conglomerate, for example, may be on the lookout for companies that throw off excess cash, which can be utilized to expand other, fast-growing divisions. For such a conglomerate, an ideal candidate would be a firm with cash flow exceeding its investment needs.

A final financial judgment to be made in our analysis is a combined view of EPS and ROI. It is possible for an acquisition to dilute EPS, yet show attractive returns on investment. In such cases it is necessary to weigh the drawback of a dilution in earnings versus a high cash flow on the monies invested in the new business.

To use a practical case to demonstrate these concepts, Taylor Wine has been selected as an acquisition candidate and it will be "worked-through" Exhibits 10.3 to 10.6. These exhibits provide the information necessary to answer questions of financial compatibility with the acquirer in terms of EPS and ROI. Actual data have been used from the annual reports of Anheuser-Busch and Taylor Wine in order to approximate a real situation. This enables you to check each step of the procedure.

FIVE-YEAR PROJECTIONS

Exhibit 10.3 — Sales and Income (both companies)

Exhibit 10.4 — Balance Sheet — Taylor Wine

Exhibit 10.5 — Sources and Uses of Funds Statement — Taylor Wine

Exhibit 10.6 — Analysis of the Companies Combined

A step-by-step explanation follows each of these exhibits. The concepts used to derive the data can be readily understood and applied to a company selected by students for their own project. A few of the calculations rely on one of a wide number of available computer packages, primarily for regression analyses. If computer facilities are not available, simple time-series trends or even annual-growth averages may be used and the calculations performed by hand.

Step 4: Interpretation of the Financial Evaluations

What insights do these exhibits provide? The information developed in the final Exhibit, 10.6, indicates the impact on earnings per share (EPS) and return on investment (ROI) from acquiring Taylor Wine. First, EPS from acquiring Taylor Wine are not as high as EPS without making the acquisition ($2.28 vs. $2.31 in 1976); moreover, the trend continues in an unfavorable direction. However, ROI by 1980 is a respectable 17¼ percent and it is rising annually. The reason for the favorable trend in ROI is due to the relatively static level of investment (projected sources and uses of funds are nearly in balance) combined with a rising trend in net income. Thus Taylor Wine presents a marginally favorable investment *based on these two financial measures.* In a real situation one would clearly wish to look at important nonfinancial possibilities: for example, can Anheuser-Busch improve Taylor Wine's profitability by employing its greater marketing and financial leverage? Would the modest dilution in EPS be worth the addition of a wider product line and access to different segments of the "drinking" market? Would benefits from a consolidated operation produce economies not captured by a linear projection of historical trends based on two separate organizations?

To sum up, is Taylor a good acquisition for Anheuser-Busch? That depends. The facts are now available for an initial appraisal. The decision may be left for the class to resolve, from the viewpoint of senior managers of Anheuser-Busch and with the benefit of information developed thus far.

Step 5: Test Feasibility of Acquiring the Best Candidate

When sufficient progress has been made in narrowing the list of candidates and the acquirer is ready to begin negotiations, then the brunt of the acquisition effort may be shifted to outside specialists. Sources often used to suggest names of potential acquirees in the beginning of the evaluation process may be helpful in making the initial contacts; for example, investment bankers, brokerage firms, and outside directors. During this stage, the balance of success or failure may rely as much on personal chemistry and subjective reaction to the acquirer's proposal as the factual presentation of the case.

Until companies are "tried on for size," there is no assurance of the ultimate practicality of acquiring the ideal first, second, or subsequent choice pinpointed by an objective investigation. It is an iterative and sometimes fortuitous process that brings forth the candidate who is finally selected, as opposed to the one a company may have initially identified as most desirable.

There is, however, considerable merit in developing a faculty for the mechanical aspects of the acquisition process. Studying the way an acquisition is pieced together gives us an understanding of the critical factors that determine a Yes or a No decision. After evaluating a number of situations through financial evaluations similar to those just described, pinpointing which parts of the analysis will develop the most insight in the least time and with the least effort becomes instinctive. This mastery of fundamentals is a valuable attribute for the beginning analyst, since important decisions often require quick yet informed judgments.

Moreover, a more simplified analysis, such as dividing projected earnings of the acquiree by the number of shares given up, may have provided an off-the-cuff reaction; the trade-offs among EPS and ROI suggest a more complex decision process. Real acquisition decisions are seldom simple. By developing the information in these five exhibits, and tracking through the various accounts on the balance sheet and sources and uses of funds statement, key assumptions that go toward making a financially satisfactory acquisition are revealed. Once understood, assumptions can be changed and a number of "What if?" questions raised to further test the desirability of making an acquisition under different conditions. The facts on Taylor Wine, for example, are not one-way. The management of Anheuser-Busch may, and probably would, wish additional computations to be made using varying assumptions.

EXHIBITS 10.3–10.6
A Practice Illustration: Anheuser-Busch and Taylor Wine

EXHIBIT 10.3
SALES AND INCOME
(Dollars in Millions)

	Anheuser-Busch Acquirer			Taylor Wine Acquiree		
	(1)	*(2)* Profit margin %	*(3)*	*(4)*	*(5)* Profit margin %	*(6)*
	Sales	*margin %*	*Income*	*Sales*	*margin %*	*Income*
1965	422	6.1	25.8	20.8	11.0	2.4
1966	485	6.9	33.6	23.2	11.7	3.2
1967	555	6.5	36.2	26.0	13.9	3.6
1968	653	6.8	44.6	27.2	13.7	3.6
1969	667	6.8	45.3	32.1	13.2	4.1
1970	793	7.9	62.6	34.7	12.8	4.2
1971	902	7.9	71.6	40.8	12.3	5.0
1972	978	7.8	76.4	43.2	12.7	5.5
1973	1110	5.9	65.6	51.0	13.4	6.8
1974	1413	4.5	64.0	56.4	12.2	6.9
1975(e)	1486	6.0	89.2	62.8	12.4	7.8
1976(p)	1735	6.0	104.1	72.1	12.4	9.0
1977(p)	2026	6.0	121.6	84.8	12.4	10.5
1978(p)	2359	6.0	141.5	97.9	12.4	12.1
1979(p)	2655	6.0	159.3	109.2	12.4	13.6
1980(p)	2944	6.0	176.6	119.9	12.4	14.9

Note: (e) = estimated for current year
      (p) = projected

EXPLANATION OF EXHIBIT 10.3

Historical data, 1965–1974
   Columns 1–6. Data are taken from the annual reports of Anheuser-Busch
         and Taylor Wine.

Projected Data, 1975–80
   Column 1. Sales of Anheuser-Busch (A-B) were forecast using a common
         "Statpack" computer program for multiple regression. As it
         turned out, a simple correlation of A-B's sales with disposable
         personal income gave a very high coefficient of correlation

(.99) and low standard error of the estimate (.38). The fore-casting equation was: A-B's sales = −470.7 + 1.85 (disposable personal income in billions of current dollars).

If computer facilities are not available, calculate a simple annual average growth rate in sales; in this case, an average of 14.35% per year between 1965 and 1974.

Column 2. Future profit margins of Anheuser-Busch are based on a rough simple average of the past profit margins from 1965 to 1974.

Column 3. Column 2 × column 3.

Column 4. The approach is similar to that used for Anheuser-Busch. The forecasting formula was: Taylor's Sales = −15.2 + .082 (personal consumption expenditures in billions of current dollars).

Column 5. Repeat column 2.

Column 6. Repeat column 3.

EXHIBIT 10.4
BALANCE SHEET — TAYLOR WINE
(Dollars in Millions)

			PLAN				
	Prior year	Current year	1	2	3	4	5
Assets							
1 Current assets	33.6	39.6	46.0	54.8	63.9	71.8	79.8
2 Net property, plant, and equipment	23.3	27.2	31.6	38.1	44.4	49.1	52.3
3 Other assets	1.3	1.3	1.3	1.3	1.3	1.3	1.3
4 Total	58.1 a	68.1	78.9	94.2	109.6	122.2	133.4
Liabilities and Shareholders' Equity							
5 Current liabilities	3.4	4.3	4.4	4.6	4.8	4.9	5.0
6 Other liabilities	.8	.8	.8	.8	.8	.8	.8
7 Long-term debt	.1	.1	.1	.1	.1	.1	.1
8 Shareholders' equity	53.8	62.9	73.6	88.7	103.9	116.4	127.5
9 Total	58.1 a	68.1	78.9	94.2	109.6	122.2	133.4

a Actual data; these totals do not coincide with subtotals owing to rounding of figures.

EXPLANATION OF EXHIBIT 10.4

Column 1. All data were taken from the annual report of Taylor Wine.

Columns 2–6. Projections for the year of acquisition and five years hence.

Line 1. Current assets (CA) were obtained by correlating past CA to past sales. The equation was: CA = −4.08 + .695 (sales). Substituting the forecasts of sales from column 4, Exhibit 10.3 in the equation gave the figures for CA. A simple ratio average of CA to sales may also be used.

Line 2. Three items of information are needed:

A means to forecast gross property (GP), derived by correlating GP to sales; see explanation for line 5, Exhibit 10.5.

The percentage rate of depreciation to apply to GP to get annual depreciation; see explanation for line 2, Exhibit 10.5.

Annual retirements; an estimated yearly amount. Net property, plant, and equipment (P P & E) are then calculated:

Beginning balance	(from preceding year)
+ Additions to GP	(from formula)
Total	
− Depreciation	(depreciation rate × GP)
Ending balance	
− Retirements	(estimated yearly amount)
Net P P & E	

Line 3. Carried as a constant amount in this simplified pro forma.

Line 4. Total of lines 1 through 3.

Line 5. Current liabilities (CL) were obtained by correlating past CL to past sales. The equation was: CL = 3.49 + .012 (sales). Substituting the forecasts of sales from column 4, Exhibit 10.3 in the equation gave the figures for CL.

Line 6. Carried as a constant amount in this simplified pro forma.

Line 7. Adjusted only for scheduled retirements; in this simplified pro forma no adjustments were necessary.

Line 8. A residual figure based on the difference between line 4 and the total of lines 5 through 7.

Line 9. Same as line 4.

EXHIBIT 10.5
SOURCES AND USES OF FUNDS STATEMENT — TAYLOR WINE
(Dollars in Millions)

			PLAN				
	Prior year	Current year	1	2	3	4	5
Internal sources							
1 Net income	6.9	7.8	9.0	10.5	12.2	13.6	14.9
2 Depreciation	2.0	2.3	2.7	3.1	3.6	4.0	4.4
3 Other sources	—	—	—	—	—	—	—
4 Total	8.9	10.1	11.7	13.6	15.8	17.6	19.3
Uses of Funds							
5 Gross additions to P P & E	4.5	5.0	5.8	6.8	7.8	8.7	9.6
6 Reduction in long-term debt	—	—	—	—	—	—	—
7 Other uses	—	—	—	—	—	—	—
8 Increase (decrease) in working capital (Exhibit 10.4)	4.4	5.1	6.3	8.6	8.9	7.8	7.9
9 Funds to (from) acquirer	n.a.	—	(.4)	(1.8)	(.9)	1.1	1.8
10 Total	8.9	10.1	11.7	13.6	15.8	17.6	19.3

EXPLANATION OF EXHIBIT 10.5

Line 1. From column 6, Exhibit 10.3.
Line 2. Depreciation rate times gross property. The depreciation rate is the average ratio of depreciation to gross property from 1965 to 1974. For calculation of gross property see line 5.
Line 3. Carried as a constant zero amount in this simplified pro forma.
Line 4. Total of lines 1 through 3.
Line 5. Gross property (GP) was obtained by correlating past GP to past sales. The equation was: $GP = -3.77 + 7.60$ (sales).
   Substituting the forecasts of sales from column 4, Exhibit 10.3 in the equation gave the figures for GP. Changes in GP were then calculated for each year.
Line 6. From line 7, Exhibit 10.4.
Line 7. Carried as a constant zero amount in this simplified pro forma.
Line 8. From Exhibit 10.4: changes in line 1 minus changes in line 5.
Line 9. A residual figure based on the difference between line 4 and the total of lines 5 through 8.
Line 10. Same as line 4.

EXHIBIT 10.6
ANALYSIS OF THE COMPANIES COMBINED

	(1) *Net income* *(acquiree)*	*(2)* *Net* *investment* *(see "Assumptions")*	*(3)* *Funds to* *(from) acquirer* *(line 9, Exhibit 10.5)*
1975 (est.)	7.8	——	——
1976	9.0	84.36	(.4)
1977	10.5	84.76	(1.8)
1978	12.1	86.56	(.9)
1979	13.6	87.46	1.1
1980	14.9	86.36	1.8

	(4) *Return on investment* *(column 1 ÷ column 2)*	*(5)* *Net income* *(acquirer)*	*(6)* *EPS of acquirer* *(without acquisition)*
1975 (est.)	——	89.2	1.98
1976	10.67	104.1	2.31
1977	12.39	121.6	2.70
1978	13.98	141.5	3.14
1979	15.55	159.3	3.53
1980	17.25	176.6	3.92

	(7) *EPS of combined companies*	*(8)* *Difference in EPS* *gain or (loss)*
1975 (est.)	——	——
1976	2.28	(.03)
1977	2.66	(.04)
1978	3.10	(.04)
1979	3.48	(.05)
1980	3.86	(.06)

Assumptions: Acquisition by pooling; 25% premium over market price of common stock paid by acquirer.

Information at time of acquisition:

Stock price of acquirer: $18½ per share.
Stock price of acquiree: $15½ per share (before 25% premium).
Acquiree's shares outstanding: 4.534 million.
Acquirer's shares outstanding: 45.068 million.
Additional shares needed for acquisition: 4.56 million.

Total initial investment: $84.36 million.

EXPLANATION OF EXHIBIT 10.6

Column 1. From column 6, Exhibit 10.3.

Column 2. From Exhibit 10.6 (Assumptions) for initial investment, with subsequent years adjusted based on fund flows indicated in column 3 in Exhibit 10.6.

Column 3. From line 9, Exhibit 10.5.

Column 4. Column 1 divided by column 2 in Exhibit 10.6.

Column 5. From column 3, Exhibit 10.3.

Column 6. Column 5 divided by the number of shares outstanding in Exhibit 10.6 (Assumption).

Column 7. Totals of columns 3 and 6, Exhibit 10.3 divided by total number shares outstanding after the acquisition in Exhibit 10.6 (Assumptions).

Column 8. Difference between column 6 and column 7 in Exhibit 10.6.

Summary

This chapter gives an example of a brewer acquiring a winery. The financial aspects of this hypothetical merger are stressed. This deliberate choice is made to provide a detailed financial analysis rather than a more general discussion of mergers and acquisitions. By working through the exhibits, and possibly applying the procedure to other acquisitions, real or prospective, one can learn a great deal about basic financial relationships that often determine the success or failure of actual merger proposals.

QUESTIONS

1. Some mergers are "unfriendly," that is, the acquired company is taken over against its wishes. Proponents of this tactic claim that such acquisitions keep management on its toes; in effect, stodgy managements doing a poor job for their shareowners should be taken over. The unfriendly merger also purportedly stimulates competition in industries that could effectively exclude outsiders from entering in any other fashion. What arguments would you make against unfriendly mergers?

2. An important aspect of mergers is how to finance them. Assuming you were a majority owner of a small firm being acquired by a conglomerate, what type of financial package would you want? If you were the president of the conglomerate, what might you offer?

3. The federal government has long been studying the possible breakup of many large companies dominant in their industries (AT&T to divest Western Electric, General Motors to break up into Chevrolet and other

auto divisions, oil companies to divest all but a single area of the oil business). What is the rationale behind the government's studies? Do you agree?

4. "Synergy" was a term frequently used to justify companies' making of unrelated acquisitions during the 1960s. In effect, the combination of two firms was expected to produce better results than the sum of what each company could do separately. Since the unrelated merger did not combine companies with similar products and resources, on what bases did managements rest their case?

5. Mergers have often come unglued because the acquisition was less than what the acquiring company had been led to believe, as a result of deceptive or "creative" accounting practices. How can a company protect itself against such major postacquisition surprises? What are some of the areas the company should be looking at?

MINI-EXERCISES

1. Find a recent acquisition or proposed acquisition reported in the news. Examine the terms of the acquisition from the viewpoint of the criteria covered in the practice illustration (Anheuser-Busch). Does it seem to be a logical and profitable acquisition from the viewpoint of *both* the acquirer and the acquiree? How would the evaluation process described in the practice illustration apply in this case?

   For an example, see *Business Week,* September 20, 1976, p. 32, for details on the acquisition of Rucker by NL Industries. Excerpts of the terms of the agreement, below, should serve as a jumping-off point for a critique of the merger:

   The deal will give New York-based NL, whose mix of chemical, pigment, castings, and metal operations generated sales of $1.3 billion last year, a broad position in the oil tool and services business. Rucker, which had sales of $161 million last year, gets a financially well-muscled parent, and its stockholders get a sweet deal. NL proposes a stock swap, valued at $164 million, which would give owners of Rucker common stock a 53% premium on their shares and a more than fivefold increase in their dividend.

2. Divide the class into two groups. Designate a company to be the parent company in a proposed merger. Each group will have the task of independently evaluating a company to be acquired by the parent company, using the procedures outlined in the practice illustration for the

selection process. Each group will then present its choice of the potential candidates and justify the company picked. The remainder of the class, or the instructor, may assume the role of president of the parent company, who must choose between the two possible acquisitions and who will be judging the groups on the merits of their respective presentations.

3. Repeat the procedures in Exercise 2, but both groups will study the same acquisition candidate. Let one side represent the buyers (the parent company) and the other side the prospective sellers (the acquisition candidate). Each side should develop its most persuasive arguments for the best deal as seen from its particular self-interest. Again the rest of the class, or the instructor, may judge the effectiveness of the respective positions.

4. Select a parent company for study, as in Exercise 2. This time focus on choosing the best acquisition for the parent company within an industry designated by the instructor. You will have to develop a systematic routine for evaluating similar companies. Criteria may include objective as well as subjective factors; for example, sales and earnings growth rates plus organizational structure and management strengths. The procedure may follow primarily a descriptive analysis, using standard reference sources for information. Or, if facilities are available, a simple computer routine may be developed in order to test each potential acquisition mechanically against criteria established for the parent company; for example, minimum size of acquired company, minimum level of earnings, five-year growth trends in sales and earnings, and so on.

5. Divide the class into groups according to specializations, each group taking one aspect of the acquisition process to deal with in depth. For example, one group may be good in quantitative analysis; its job would be to select a company and develop a sales forecasting model for that company. Since forecasting techniques range from simple judgmental models to complicated econometric forecasting models, the company to be forecast will determine the difficulty of the problem.

    Another topic that could be developed is the sources and uses of funds statement. Although a simple sources and uses of funds example was used in the practice illustration, a more difficult and realistic assignment may be appropriate for a group of accounting majors. Using a company's annual report as the basis for this project, a pro forma statement of sources and uses of funds may be projected forward.

FURTHER READING

Ansoff, Igor H., J. A. Anderson, F. Norton, and J. Fred Weston. "Planning for Diversification Through Merger," *California Management Review,* Summer 1959.

Boulden, James B. "Merger Negotiations: A Decision Model," *Business Horizon,* February 1969.

Cash, W. H., and J. M. Revie. "The Long-Range Planner and Acquisition Planning," in Richard F. Vancil, ed., *Formal Planning Systems — 1971.* Boston: Graduate School of Business Administration, Harvard University, 1971.

Leontiades, Milton. "Planning for Change in Stages of Corporate Development," *Long Range Planning,* December 1979.

———. *Strategies for Diversification and Change.* Boston: Little, Brown, 1980.

Mace, Myles L., and George G. Montgomery. *Management Problems of Corporate Acquisition.* Boston: Graduate School of Business Administration, Harvard University, 1962.

Rappaport, Alfred. "Strategic Analysis for More Profitable Acquisitions," *Harvard Business Review,* July–August 1979.

Slater, Malcolm S., and Wolf A. Weinhold. *Diversification Through Acquisition.* New York: Macmillan, 1979.

Steiner, George A. "Why and How to Diversify," *California Management Review,* Summer 1964.

CHAPTER 11

Planning for Evolution and Change—New Venture: Fast-Food Chain

In addition to diversification by acquisition, a number of other external options for growth are available (see Chapter 5). One of these possibilities is the new venture, and one of the popular ways to participate quickly and on a broad geographical basis in the new ventures is through franchising. The following discussion is an elaboration of the mechanics of this device for corporate diversification.*

There are several advantages offered by a franchise distribution system. The four main attributes are: (1) rapid access to markets; (2) reduced investment by the franchisor; (3) risk-sharing between franchisors and franchisees; and (4) highly motivated owner/operators. Other advantages include: managerial work-sharing between franchisor and franchisee, protection from antitrust action, ability to service marginal locations, promotion of

---

* Reprinted from Darryl J. Ellis and P. P. Pekar, Jr., "Franchising: Friend or Foe?" *Planning Review,* January 1979.

independently owned business reduction in economic concentration, and protection against unionization. If the concept to be franchised is new, or rapid entry into the market is needed, franchising can minimize the risks of the venture.

However, managers must recognize that as a franchise operation gains in maturity, numerous problems develop. Primary among these are: problems of flexibility with new techniques; overexpectations of franchisees; reduced profitability of franchise units versus company-owned units; a growing militancy among franchise operators, which leads to class-action suits; and lack of control — particularly in the area of quality.

As the franchise approaches maturity in the business development cycle, franchisors usually find it beneficial to move toward company-owned and controlled operations, and thus seek to repurchase those operations not under their direct control.

The Nature of Franchising in the United States

McDonald's hamburger stands and Kentucky Fried Chicken units are so commonplace today that a discussion of franchising could center on them as illustrations. However, there are many kinds of franchises in fields other than fast foods — all with different types of contractual arrangements. Establishments that are often franchised include laundry and drycleaning, campgrounds, gasoline service stations, automobile dealerships, motels, soft-drink bottlers, real estate agencies, income tax services, and other kinds of rental services and business aids. Exhibit 11.1 shows the frequency of various kinds of franchises.

History of Franchising

In its modern form, franchising originated with the Singer Sewing Machine Company, which developed an elaborate franchising system in the United States during the period following the Civil War. Despite Singer's success, this system gradually declined, and it was not until the automobile and soft-drink industries surfaced that franchising became an integral part of the distribution system. By 1910 the basic pattern found in modern franchising had been established.

In the automotive industry the franchise relationship became one between manufacturer and retailer. In the soft-drink field, the association became one between syrup manufacturer and bottle-wholesaler. Another line of manufacturer-retailer franchising began around 1930, with manu-

EXHIBIT 11.1
TYPES OF FRANCHISES AND NUMBER OF UNITS

Kinds of franchised business	Establishments (number)			Sales ($000)		
	Total	Company-owned	Franchisee-owned	Total	Company-owned	Franchisee-owned
TOTAL — ALL FRANCHISING	457,693	82,999	374,694	194,587,109	31,526,069	163,061,040
Automobile and truck dealers	32,327	300	32,027	94,289,000	6,009,000	88,280,000
Automotive products and services	52,430	5,128	47,302	5,288,203	2,001,053	3,287,150
Business aids and services	26,218	4,723	21,495	1,615,382	339,576	1,275,806
Accounting, credit, collection agencies, and general business systems	3,863	55	3,808	162,761	6,202	156,559
Employment services	3,154	559	2,595	592,162	203,190	388,972
Printing and copying services	1,524	108	1,416	106,680	7,710	98,970
Tax preparation services	8,177	3,861	4,316	171,499	94,920	76,579
Miscellaneous business services	9,500	140	9,360	582,280	27,554	554,726
Construction, home improvements, maintenance and cleaning services	13,480	258	13,222	761,833	42,819	719,014
Convenience stores	14,997	9,300	5,697	4,375,954	2,526,770	1,849,184
Educational products and services	1,579	283	1,296	189,481	34,808	154,673
Fast-food restaurants (all types)	47,311	12,258	35,053	12,923,173	4,412,331	8,510,842
Gasoline service stations	189,000	37,800	151,200	48,150,000	9,630,000	38,520,000

Hotels and motels	6,133	1,191	4,942	5,154,431	1,578,936	3,575,495
Campgrounds	1,163	27	1,136	70,841	4,036	66,805
Laundry and drycleaning services	3,710	108	3,602	240,671	10,765	229,906
Recreation, entertainment, and travel	3,275	79	3,196	161,100	23,960	137,140
Rental services (auto/truck)	6,667	1,426	5,241	1,447,220	903,651	543,569
Rental services (equipment)	1,515	131	1,384	132,270	47,204	85,066
Retailing (non-food)	39,784	8,994	30,790	9,930,125	3,211,598	6,718,527
Retailing (food other than convenience stores)	13,102	696	12,406	1,605,210	385,927	1,219,283
Soft-drink bottlers	2,200	85	2,115	7,766,000	287,000	7,479,000
Miscellaneous	2,802	212	2,590	486,215	76,635	409,580

facturers licensing in-store departments. This method of franchising single departments in stores has been used successfully in the appliance, radio, and television fields. In the 1930s another type of franchise system developed in which a wholesaler served as a franchisor of retail outlets. Walgreen's and Ace Hardware are good examples of wholesaler-retailer franchise systems. Oil companies also found franchising a good means to be competitive in local areas. Oil producers found that stations were unprofitable to a large extent because of local price wars. Without modern communication devices, it was all but impossible for central management to make appropriate price decisions — thus the decision was made to franchise outlets.

Diverse factors contributed to the speed and success of franchising at various times. The deep economic depression of the thirties, which created professional unemployment, appears to have provided talent for the first franchise attempts.

Early franchise agreements were quite restrictive. The pre-World War II agreements between franchisors and franchisees, especially with large petroleum marketers, allowed cancellation with as little as ten days' notice for minor offenses. In 1949 inclusive representation, territorial security, and antibootlegging provisions were dropped from many franchise agreements.[1]

Franchising Today

The "franchise boom" of the past 20 years has been in trade-name (service sponsor) retailer systems. McDonald's, Dunkin' Donuts, Howard Johnson's, Holiday Inns, and Hertz are examples. Formation of new franchise chains from 1955 to 1960 was double that in the previous five years, and growth continued at a fast pace until 1968, when probably more fast-food companies were formed than in all previous history. During the 1974–75 period, high interest rates and scarce capital apparently inhibited company-owned expansion. Expansion via the franchise route became more attractive to corporations.

In 1976 retail franchising accounted for about 28 percent of all retail sales in the United States, and for about 30 percent of total receipts in eating places. It was estimated that total retail sales of all franchise firms would reach $218 billion in 1977.

Significant funds were channeled into franchise activities despite the difficult economic times of the 1970s. Many investment analysts, including specialists at the United States Department of Commerce, have formulated the hypothesis that the less buoyant economy made available individuals who had been forced out of previous careers, but who, nevertheless, had funds available for investment (similar to the experience of the 1930s). If

EXHIBIT 11.2
TOTAL INVESTMENT AND START-UP PER UNIT
CASH REQUIRED — 1974

	Total investment — per unit		
Franchised business	*Company-owned*	*Franchised-owned*	*Start-up cash franchisee*
Automotive services	$ 50,000	$ 35,000	$10,000
Home improvement	90,000	22,000	10,000
Convenience stores	70,000	65,000	10,000
Fast-food restaurants	135,000	80,000	20,000
Campgrounds	480,000	250,000	50,000
Rental services (auto/truck)	390,000	100,000	30,000

Source: Franchising in the Economy — 1974–76, U.S. Department of Commerce, U.S. Government Printing Office, Washington, D.C., p. 44.

such is the case, it would be prudent to embark on franchise ventures during periods of economic uncertainty. During these periods, investors with available funds, and, more important, some degree of management talent, enter the market.

Probably interest is aroused because of the lower initial investment. A study by the United States Department of Commerce (Exhibit 11.2) demonstrated that not only is the initial investment hurdle relatively low for the franchisee, but also, despite the franchisor's investment in the franchisee's outlets, the combined total investment is lower than in new company-owned operations.

Managerial Assessment of Franchising

In 1974 senior executives from many well-known franchise companies spoke at an East Coast conference covering the advantages and disadvantages of franchising. The range of companies represented included General Motors, McDonald's, Sheraton, and Hardee's. These executives agreed that franchising offers these benefits:

> *Capital.* Less capital is required by the franchisor; hence the franchisor can employ capital for other purposes.

> *Motivation.* Through the binding nature of the investment, the franchise system instills into the local manager the profit incentive.

Economy.   Economies of scale arise in the areas of purchasing and advertising.

Local awareness.   As a local citizen, the franchisee is apt to handle local authorities with greater sensitivity.

Central management.   Franchising alleviates the pressure on central management to develop a sizable management structure during the early, and usually rapid, expansion phase.

Labor relations.   The franchise system handles employees individually, by unit, making it difficult for unions to organize workers on a company-wide scale; and thereby enabling the franchisee to benefit from local labor conditions. In addition, international franchised operations can profit from variations in foreign labor rates in nondomestic units.

Market share.   Franchising allows a company to penetrate and capture market share with less capital ventured, since most financial obligations of franchisees are not guaranteed by the franchisors.

However, as one would expect, there are some drawbacks. Some executives felt that although market penetration through company-owned operations was significantly slower, the long-range benefits outweighed the advantage of quick market penetration. The advantages of company-owned operations are:

Profitability.   Company-owned units, on average, appear to be more profitable than franchised units. Although it is difficult to quantify, we believe the reduced profitability of franchises is a result of two key components — the lower initial investment and the choice of site.

Control.   Company-owned operations allow for better control, especially quality and accounting control.

Flexibility.   Company-owned operations allow greater flexibility in the introduction and testing of new products, and in the development of alternate business techniques.

Communications.   The vertically integrated chain has better feedback and cumulative experience, which can be exploited. This feedback aids development of management personnel.

Managerial profile.   Since the initial investment for a franchise unit is an entry barrier, it acts as a screen for applicants. As a result, only those with funding apply; and these applicants tend to be older. On the other hand, company-owned stores can recruit younger and more aggressive managers, thus building a management pool for expansion.

Expectations.   Franchisees, after a year or two, begin to lean more heavily on the franchisor's ability to solve major problems. Additionally, the early rewards, although good, do not satisfy the franchisees, particularly because returns of early entrants to the system are sometimes exorbitant. Some franchisees recover the initial investment in three to four years.

Business services.   The operating cost of a franchised operation appears to be greater than a company-owned one. It was pointed out that all services required in the company-owned chain are also needed in the franchised one — services such as consumer advertising, market research, computerized credit accounting, franchise sales department, and real estate purchase group.

Legal.   The integrated chains did not so often come under franchise antitrust fire, class action suits, and various legal attacks.

Current Trends

Having discovered that there can be more profit in owning an operation than in franchising it, many of the largest fast-food chains, most of which owe their present size to franchising, are finding ways to increase the number of company-owned units. Consider the following example.

McDonald's is usually cited as the most successful, if not the largest, franchisor. In 1976 the company-owned share of 4,178 stores was 29 percent, while in 1967 it was only 24 percent. Even though McDonald's has maintained nearly a 30–70 percent split between company-owned and franchised units, it is interesting to note the respective percentage contribution of each category to consolidated income. It appears that with less than a third of the outlets, the company-owned operations contribute nearly 50 percent of McDonald's income (see Exhibit 11.3).

Despite McDonald's claim to being a franchised business operation, it has deftly pursued ownership of a different nature. McDonald's views ownership in terms of land and facilities, not just business operations.

While McDonald's attempts to maintain a 30 percent direct ownership, it is actively purchasing new sites which are then leased by McDonald's and operated by a franchisee. Consequently, McDonald's is becoming a major landlord, charging a minimum fixed rental for land and buildings, plus royalty fees and special assessments against revenue (see Exhibit 11.3).

EXHIBIT 11.3
McDONALD'S CORPORATION

	1976	1975	1974	1973	1972
Contribution to consolidated income from—					
Licensed restaurants	50%	49%	48%	48%	44%
Company-owned restaurants	45%	46%	47%	48%	51%
Other income	5%	5%	5%	4%	5%
	100%	100%	100%	100%	100%
% Company-owned units	29%	30%	31%	33%	35%

McDONALD'S CORPORATION OWNERSHIP STATUS OF LOCATIONS

Period ending	Total units	Own land and buildings	Own land only	Own building only	No interest
1975	3,706	50%	34%	15%	1%
1974	3,232	47%	37%	14%	2%
1973	2,717	39%	45%	14%	2%
1972	2,272	34%	51%	13%	3%

Moreover, the company feels that ownership of real estate will yield long-term benefits such as continued appreciation in land values and controlled expansion of its food service operations.

Summary

Franchising can afford numerous rewards. The most important is rapid market entry or expansion. The short-run nature of full-scale franchising might be predicted. As markets mature, franchisors, operating under increasingly favorable conditions, appear to want to reduce the number of franchise outlets in favor of more easily controlled, owned stores.

A recent study undertaken by Lillis, Narayana, and Gilman[2] supports this contention. For fast foods, the conclusion was that the advantages of rapid market penetration and franchise motivation are perceived as sufficiently important in the early life-cycle stages; and franchising becomes an attractive entry distribution system. But once the franchise matures, franchising becomes less desirable than a fully integrated direct distribution system with direct control. This would be especially true with overseas operations.

Depending upon a company's position in the marketplace and its financial position, the choices quickly become apparent. If the competition has established market position, franchising is a quick method of entry with reduced capital commitment. If the company is introducing a new concept, it faces a choice between slow and deliberate market growth through company-owned operations or more rapid broad-based market growth through franchising. However, success in the early stages often can lead to serious difficulties in the market maturity stage. Therefore, if sufficient financing is available to preclude the need for franchising, and rapid market penetration is neither necessary nor desirable, franchising may not be worth the anguish which may arise later.

QUESTIONS

1. Of the many fields in which a franchise might be obtained, how would you make a decision on the best franchise opportunity for you (based on $10,000 available for investment and your immediate market area)? What factors did you take into consideration in your conclusion?

2. From a franchisor's point of view, what might influence whether you followed a strategy of company-owned or franchised units? Would the maturity and type of franchise operation make a difference?

3. From a franchisee's point of view, would you rather own or lease your operation?

4. McDonald's apparently is counting on ownership of real estate and facilities, which are then leased to operators, to optimize its long-term returns. What elements do you believe contribute to McDonald's strategy? Can you think of a situation in which this might not be a preferred strategy?

5. It is relatively easy in retrospect to envy the wealth accumulated by many of McDonald's original franchisees. But, like most important decisions, it appeared riskier at the time. In today's environment, which franchise areas, if any, do you visualize as the next "success" stories? Support your answer.

REFERENCES

1. For an in-depth analysis, refer to Charles Mason Hewitt, Jr., *Automobile Franchising Agreements,* Indiana University School of Business, Bureau of Business Research Study No. 39.

2. Charles M. Lillis, Chem L. Narayana, and John L. Gilman, "Competitive Advantage Variation over the Life Cycle of a Franchise," *Journal of Marketing,* No. 4 (October 1976): 40, 77–80.

CHAPTER 12

Planning for Operations – Operational Planning and the Annual Planning Cycle

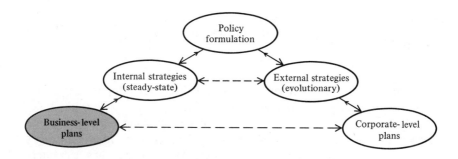

The basic element in planning for operations is the annual budget. Development of an annual budget for existing businesses is done through the mechanics of an annual planning cycle. There are established forms to be completed, deadlines to be met, and reviews to be conducted — all the coordinating mechanisms necessary to move the process through the organization within the allotted twelve months. The immediate result of this cyclic procedure is development of next year's budget and programs.

In addition, the typical planning document looks forward an added number of years; a five-year plan is a common planning horizon. The short- and long-range plans are locked together in the annual cycle, with the initial year's budget representing the first stage of the conventional five-year planning document. As the cyclic procedure is repeated, a new fifth year is added and the first year of the prior plan is dropped. This linkage ensures a continuity and consistency of planning. Whereas next year's budget is clearly a decision that must be made final at the end of each planning year, there is

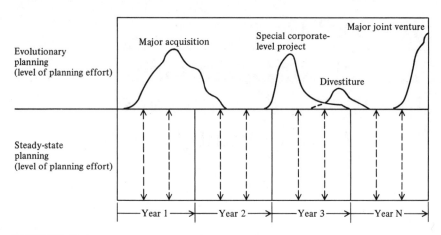

EXHIBIT 12.1
AN ILLUSTRATIVE CONCEPT OF EVOLUTIONARY VS.
STEADY-STATE PLANNING

also opportunity for a longer view of business threats and opportunities, and a tentative five-year perspective of performance.

However, neither one-year nor five-year planning perspectives are designed to accommodate fundamental external changes in a company's strategy, such as acquisitions or divestitures. As one expert has accurately observed, "formal [business-level] planning procedures are *not* intended to facilitate strategic decisions such as this — if only because a [business-level] manager rarely recommends the [restructuring] of his operation. Rather, formal planning has the more modest, if no less crucial, purpose of seeking to optimize the collective thrust of the continuing businesses."[1]

Because external strategic planning that entails major restructuring of the organization has an obvious and dramatic impact, it often draws the lion's share of attention. Yet operational planning is the bedrock on which strategic planning of this sort must rest. If a company lacks the planning discipline to manage what it has, it is unlikely to be able to plan effectively for, or to manage, businesses it has yet to enter. Moreover, planning for operations is planning that every company undertakes. It is also the only planning some companies need to undertake; for instance, firms committed to a steady-state policy implemented through an internal, operations-based strategy.

Implicit in the separation of steady-state planning of current operations from evolutionary change involving restructuring of the existing organization are (1) an internal orientation, (2) initiative and responsibility at the business level, and (3) a structured and precise timetable for decisions. Exhibit 12.1 shows graphically the distinction between the two types of planning: steady-state planning applied to operations as the stable component, representing a fixed and predictable planning effort, if you will, and evolutionary change as the variable component, or fluctuating planning effort. In this chapter we shall discuss the major steps in the steady-state planning of current operations.

Planning and the Planning Cycle

The annual planning cycle is, in essence, a tightly organized, continuous-flow routine with interaction among organizational levels, and with respect by all parties for critical progress points built into the schedule. There are many possible variations on the annual planning cycle. Firms tailor the format to suit their needs and circumstances. However, a normative model that captures the essential elements of most plans would comprise the following four steps, which are expanded in Exhibit 12.2 to include related activities.

Step	Level of effort	Output
1	Corporate level	Corporate assumptions
2	Business level	Business plans
3	Corporate and business levels	Review and reconciliation of plans
4	Corporate and business presentations for executive review	Budget approvals and capital allocations

The first step in the planning cycle — inputs by corporate headquarters — sets the tone and provides the planning assumptions that will guide the operating units in developing their plans. Corporate headquarters also stipulates the mechanics of the planning process, namely, the format and timing of planning inputs. It further conveys the overall policy and strategy

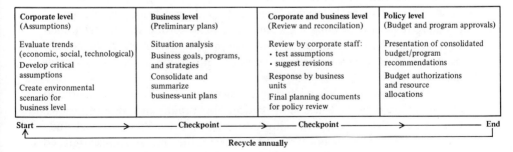

Corporate level (Assumptions)	Business level (Preliminary plans)	Corporate and business level (Review and reconcilation)	Policy level (Budget and program approvals)
Evaluate trends (economic, social, technological)	Situation analysis	Review by corporate staff:	Presentation of consolidated budget/program recommendations
Develop critical assumptions	Business goals, programs, and strategies	• test assumptions	
		• suggest revisions	
Create environmental scenario for business level	Consolidate and summarize business-unit plans	Response by business units	Budget authorizations and resource allocations
		Final planning documents for policy review	

Start ——————————————→——— Checkpoint ———————→——— Checkpoint ——————————→—————————— End

Recycle annually

EXHIBIT 12.2
A TYPICAL ANNUAL PLANNING CYCLE

of the total enterprise (as developed in prior chapters). However, once these initial "enterprise guidelines" are developed, they do not have to be repeated every time the plan is recycled. Assuming constant overall policy and strategy, a recurring reminder of such guidelines is unnecessary. In the section below the focus is on corporate- and business-level inputs that are permanent and continuing parts of a typical *operational* plan conducted by every "strategic business unit."

Corporate-Level Inputs

The corporate planning staff will develop a scenario for next year and generally the next five years. The scenario will be developed from a set of critical factors or issues deemed most likely to impinge on the businesses within the relevant time-frame of the plan. The scenario's conclusions will be disseminated to the operating units and form the assumptions underlying their business plans. A typical list of factors a company might evaluate could include economic conditions, social change, technological change, and special unforeseen trends or events.

Each factor will be analyzed by the corporate planning staff. Where circumstances warrant, and where time permits, a special task force may be assigned to provide an in-depth report on especially critical trends. But the corporate planning staff's input *must* be completed within its allotted time in the planning cycle. This means review of all factors and integration into a corporate-level scenario in time for the operating units to begin their phase of the planning cycle.

LIMITS TO CORPORATE PLANNING STAFF'S ASSUMPTIONS

One of the most difficult tasks of the corporate planning staff is to limit its role in the annual plan to the ongoing businesses. From its headquarters perspective, it can often perceive threats to present operations, which suggest external strategies of redeployment of assets or reorganization of operations. As valid as such insights may be, they do not belong in the annual planning review. Operating units cannot respond to directives outside their control, and top management cannot give major external issues of strategy the attention they deserve within the strict time-frame of the annual planning review.

The annual plan has a rhythm and urgency of its own. It is geared to ongoing operations and near-term budget and capital allocation decisions. Longer-term shifts in corporate direction and strategy deserve detailed study outside the annual planning cycle. To the extent the annual plan is stretched to accommodate suggestions for basic repositioning, neither corporate-level nor business-level management of the firm will be well served. The hallmark of a good planning system is to address operating issues within the annual plan, "change" issues outside the annual plan, and to maintain the self-discipline to keep the two separated within the overall planning system.

SELECTION OF CRITICAL ISSUES TO EVALUATE

Deciding which issues are critical is as important as dealing with the issues themselves. Certain inputs, like a forecast of general economic conditions, have a permanent place in the corporate scenario. Other inputs assume a critical dimension because of unforeseen circumstances. In the early 1970s, for example, the oil embargo, shortages of raw materials, and spiraling food and energy prices demanded the attention of corporate planners. None of these factors was a significant business issue in the preceding decade. Some of them have already receded in importance and may not appear soon again in corporate-level planning assumptions. It is the purpose of the initial phase of developing corporate assumptions to determine which issues among a numerous set of possibilities will be the most critical for the company within the time-frame and scope of the annual planning cycle.

DISSEMINATION OF INFORMATION
TO OPERATING UNITS

After careful consideration of the critical issues, the corporate assumptions and their implications are issued to operations. These assumptions will follow from the evaluation of each area of study. For instance, let's assume that a large diversified manufacturing company defined four critical areas for analysis in the initial phase of the planning cycle as follows: (1) weak economic conditions forecast for three of its five major businesses (70 percent of sales); (2) slower growth in electric consumption affecting electrical systems and parts sold to utilities (31 percent of sales); (3) strong import competition in electrical parts and assemblies sold to radio and television industries (24 percent of sales); (4) cost acceleration in raw-materials-intensive businesses (55 percent of sales).

Based on a study of each area, the appropriate corporate directives may be given to business units as indicated in Exhibit 12.3. This brief summary would of course be supported by many man-hours or work by the headquarters planning group. These corporate assumptions should then be reflected in the plans submitted by the operating units. In the subsequent dialogue between corporate and business levels, the corporate staff will be measuring the operating plans against these assumptions, as well as testing the internal logic and consistency of the operating plans with respect to projected shares of market, sales and earnings figures, and other information relevant to the plans of the various business units.

EXHIBIT 12.3
SUMMARY OF CORPORATE DIRECTIVES
(diversified electrical manufacturer)

Risk factors	Percentage of company sales	Key options to evaluate
1. Weakening economic conditions	70	Impact of "most likely" and "pessimistic" economic scenario on sales and earnings Standby cost reductions
2. Slowing growth in electric consumption	31	Reevaluation of investments based on "old" consumption estimates Study of alternate energy possibilities
3. Strengthening import competition	24	Strategies to moderate impact on earnings
4. Inflation in raw materials	55	Long-term contracts to protect against price escalation Suggest acquisitions to meet most "critical" raw materials needs

Business-Level Inputs

Each business unit responsible for planning formulates a strategy based on an overall evaluation of its situation. As such, parts of the analysis are similar to earlier discussions of formulating of corporate-level strategy. At the business level, however, planning is more specific and pragmatic. Business units are concerned with individual products, specific competitors' actions, industry growth, market segmentation, and pricing — all familiar points of analysis — but the scope is limited to issues having a direct impact on a closely defined business unit. These variables are evaluated within a limited framework that leads to logical strategies relevant to the particular business unit.

A typical approach is to use a three-part method of analysis (see Exhibit 12.2): (1) situation analysis; (2) business goals, programs, and strategies; (3) consolidation of business plans. These three phases constitute a building process. Each phase leads to the next and, in total, the combined data supply the complete documentation for a comprehensive business-unit plan. The content of each phase is discussed below.

SITUATION ANALYSIS

Before planning its strategy, each business unit must assess its present position. This suggests a review of the external environment as well as an internal analysis. In fact, many companies adopt the following two-pronged approach to development of their situation analysis: external analysis and internal analysis.

External Analysis. External reviews focus on the industry and the competition. Data are intended to provide an overview of certain major industry characteristics: size, rate of growth in sales and earnings, strength of competitors, relative position of competitive products, pricing flexibility, and technical change and innovation.

A considerable amount of time and effort is required for a reliable industry analysis. Competitive data are particularly difficult to develop and generally require a composite of data from informal contacts, unpublished price lists, government data, and a variety of trade statistics. It is important to focus on the changes in this analysis from the preceding period; that is, new product development, a shift in marketing emphasis, innovative strategy from a major competitor, or unusual financial expenditures to promote and position products.

Exhibit 12.4 defines one method of collecting information on the external environment. Such a format should focus on those areas of the industry which the planning unit wishes to monitor closely because of their potential for exploitation or because of potential threats from other firms in the industry.

EXHIBIT 12.4
EXTERNAL ANALYSIS

Competitors	A	B	C	D
Most serious competition Now 5 years hence				
Sales volume Rate of growth				
Market share Change from 5 years ago				
Technology				
Major strength				
Major weakness				

Internal Analysis.   A planning unit's internal emphasis is on its strengths and weaknesses. Strengths identify those areas in which a distinctive competitive competence or edge is enjoyed. Such strengths represent opportunities for maximizing the unit's relative position in the market. A list of such strengths might include management skills, superior R&D capabilities, low-cost production processes, and abundant financial resources.

Weaknesses are points where the unit feels exposed. These areas represent blind spots that the competition could possibly exploit. They are shortcomings that the unit is aware of but has not yet been able to reverse. Strategies suggested in the final plan should include means to eliminate or modify these shortcomings. Exhibit 12.5 gives a shortened version of an internal analysis.

A unit's external and internal analyses should bring to light threats as well as opportunities. Indeed, the successful isolation of potential new areas of growth, or successfully blunting a competitor's strategy, is the ultimate benefit from this planning exercise. If carefully conducted, the situation

EXHIBIT 12.5
INTERNAL ANALYSIS

	Opportunities	*Problems*
Rapidly growing division	Greater profit and revenue opportunities.	Large working capital requirements.
		Hard pressed to keep plant capacity expansion programs up with sales.
		Dealer and distributor growth hampered by their working capital limitations.
Division ranks third in size in industry	Can better attract new and larger share of business from major national accounts.	Acquisition candidates hard to qualify due to division's dominant market position.
	Manufacturing and engineering strengths and efficiencies bring products to market competitively priced.	Present plants at maximum capacity.

Source: Reprinted by permission from The Conference Board, *Corporate Guides to Long-Range Planning,* 1976, p. 54.

analysis is a critical evaluation that will suggest how the present year's posture can be improved upon. In order to highlight areas for improvements, some companies prefer to condense the situation analysis onto a single page. Such a shortened form is also preferable for executive-level presentation, where the time available to review a single business unit is limited and thus important points must be reduced to their simplest, yet understandable, form.

BUSINESS GOALS, PROGRAMS, AND STRATEGIES

Once opportunities and threats are identified, goals* must be forthcoming. Goals should flow consistently from an observed strength or weakness in the situation analysis. Goals should be specific and quantified, if possible. Goals should also be developed on a priority basis and framed within the financial, managerial, and other resource capabilities of the firm.

Requiring unit managers to develop written statements in support of each goal often helps to refine a unit's goal-setting process. These statements should address specific points: (1) What are the criteria for the goals selected (for example, to counter a competive threat, exploit a market niche, or maximize on the firm's financial strength)? (2) What alternative goals were considered? (3) Is this a new goal or a restatement or refinement of a prior goal? (4) Rank the goals in order of their importance and their contribution to the unit's performance.

A second approach is to outline in a one-page summary the basic goals (with supporting documentation submitted only if requested). This approach provides top management with the essentials of business-unit thinking. Although some companies demand that full analyses accompany the planning document, it is rare that the executive review of business-level plans probes each unit's plan in depth. The manager who presents his plan should be prepared to support his position verbally; if additional documentation is required, he can then supply the details for a full evaluation. (The evaluations will have been prepared in advance as part of the programs and strategies phase of the planning process.)

Programs and Strategies. Programs and strategies contain the necessary details to implement goals. The support may sometimes be demanded at other stages of the planning process, as noted, but in general the detailed information is important at the operations level of the business. It provides the data necessary to develop strategies and monitor their implementation. Each program is based on answers to specific issues, although the issues that are considered important vary among firms. Exhibit 12.6, for example,

---

* "Goal" is used here to refer to a business-level target as distinguished from "objective," which has been used to designate a corporate-level target.

EXHIBIT 12.6
ACTION PROGRAM SUMMARY FORM, WITH ILLUSTRATIONS — A PAPER MANUFACTURER

Program title: *Earnings improvement of the Y–Supplies Business*
Program purpose: *Strengthen the profitability and defensibility of our position in the Y–Supplies market*

Goals	Strategies	Tactical goals	Tactical actions	Resources required	Target dates Begin	Target dates End	Responsibility
1. Profitably commercialize new product YZ and achieve an annual sales rate of 1.5 million units by the end of 1978.	1. Introduce product YZ with a concentrated promotion campaign into the Southeastern region at a premium price.	Annual sales rate of 400,000 units in Southeastern region at a minimum price of $5 each by end of 1975.	Launch a 4-month, direct-mail campaign at city engineers of all cities with population of 5,000 or more.	$25,000 and 2 man-months	June 1, 1975	Sept. 30, 1975	Marketing Manager of Southeastern region
			Launch personal sales contact campaign at city engineers of all cities with 50,000 or more population.	$40,000 and 8 man-months	August 1, 1975	Nov. 1, 1975	Same
			Develop indirect sales channel by adding one distributor in Alabama and Georgia and two in South Carolina. etc. other tactical actions, etc.	$100,000 cash investment for capital and 2 man-months	April, 1975	Aug. 1975	Same

Objective	Program	Strategy	Budget	Date		Responsibility
2. Build a small initial plant in Birmingham with 1 million-unit capacity which can be doubled in capacity to 2 million units in 1977 if the market sustains a growth rate of 10% or more through 1976.	Construct original 1 million-unit plant within total cost budget of $1.3 million.	Use turnkey contract for speedy design and construction of the plant. Specify the X-11 vacuum molding process in the design of equipment.	$1,300,000 and 20 man-months	January 1, 1975	Aug. 15, 1975	Project Manager
	Start up initial new plant and achieve a direct unit cost under continuous operation of $1.50 per unit by the end of September, 1975.	Complete training program of key personnel prior to completion of construction.	$50,000 and 15 man-months	May 1, 1975	Aug. 1, 1975	Plant Manager
		Other tactical actions, . . . etc., . . .				
2. Upgrade quality of products Y9 through Y15 and their acceptance in the market while increasing our average Y gross margin to 35% by the end of 1976.	1. Reorganize the purchasing department . . . and so forth. . . .	Reduce spoilage in raw material . . . and so forth. . . .				
		Use national account purchasing as leverage for . . . and so forth. . . .				

Source: Reprinted by permission of The Conference Board, *Corporate Guides to Long-Range Planning,* 1976, p. 81.

expands on a basic list of goals by providing additional information on strategies, goals, action steps, resources, timing, and responsibilities.

CONSOLIDATION OF BUSINESS PLANS

For a firm with only one product there may be only a single business plan. For a more diversified company operating in several distinct businesses with many different products, a consolidated picture of planning goals, programs, and strategies is necessary. This requires a combination of individual business-level plans and a review of these plans at the corporate level. A principal criterion in the review process is consistency with the company's overall policy and strategies. More specifically, each plan must also reflect the planning assumptions made at the beginning of the planning cycle by the corporate planning staff. Tests for consistency are performed by the corporate planning staff. These evaluations can be extensive and technical.

Exhibit 12.7 summarizes checks against several performance measures. Such an abbreviated format permits a quick review of each new thrust of a business unit. It not only provides a test of each business unit's new programs against established corporate criteria, it also allows a comparative view of the total proposed commitments of the company.

The report shown in Exhibit 12.7 is a form of "exception reporting." It isolates for corporate attention those projects or products that represent new strategies. In addition, there are forms for ongoing programs and

EXHIBIT 12.7
NEW PROGRAM EVALUATION

	Program 1				*Program 2*				*Program 3*			
Year:	*C.Y.*	*1*	*2*	*3*	*C.Y.*	*1*	*2*	*3*	*C.Y.*	*1*	*2*	*3*
Investment												
Market share												
Market size												
Performance measures												
Return on sales (%)												
Return on assets (%)												
Asset turnover												

Note: C.Y. = current year.

strategies, which include information on targeted goals, progress to date, and variances from targets. The documentation in support of business-level plans can be voluminous. Each planning unit accumulates its own "proofs." Depending on the number of units, the total volume of paper can be overwhelming to the point where it would defy analysis if passed on to each level of review. Thus what emerges from the planning units, and is forwarded for review at the corporate levels, is only a fraction of the total work effort by the business units.

Corporate- and Business-Level Interactions

At this point in the planning process, a dialogue ensues between corporate- and business-level planning staffs. The nature of the dialogue depends on the types of strategies proposed by the business units and the quality of the supporting materials.

At one extreme is the perfunctory review. The firm may be an old-line company in a mature industry with a management that is not inclined to explore new strategies and does not anticipate any significant threats. In such a situation, a planning review is a formality. Indeed, if such a placid company actually exists, a corporate planning staff would be redundant.

At the other extreme is the growth-oriented firm in a business with a fast-changing technology and subject to fierce competitive pressures. This scenario is not too different from the true situation for many firms in electronics-related businesses — computers, calculators, semiconductors, circuitry, and communications. In these situations, strategies may be obsolete before the time for the next planning cycle. Thus the quality of the planning process is extremely important. On the other hand, the quick-change environment suggests a less formal planning apparatus. The layers of review and the thickness of documentation may not be so deep as that of the average firm. A more continuous interaction between planning levels may occur throughout the planning cycle. The typical company is somewhere between these two extremes. A certain formality of planning exists, and some routine is customary.

Budget and Capital Appropriations

The final stage of the planning cycle is the approval of budgets and the funding of programs. This is the acid test for business-level planning. Were the plans ultimately persuasive in selling the desired programs and strategies to top management?

In most companies, the amount of funds needed to implement programs desired by all the business units exceeds the funds management is willing to commit. Compromises are almost inevitable. Programs may be reduced or eliminated; strategies may have to be revised or abandoned. The final decisions are not easy. Every program and strategy has at least a surface attractiveness or it wouldn't have traveled that far. In the end the decisions to fund or not to fund depend on the persuasiveness of the arguments in the business plan. Therefore it is critical for line managers to perfect the art of planning if for no higher reason than to support their own operation and thus indirectly to promote their own chances for advancement.

There is no single approach to capital-allocation decisions. Although methods for selecting one program or strategy over another are generally systematic, there is no scientific tool of management to guarantee that the right choices will prevail. In spite of numerous advances in management techniques, coupled with the aid of computers in consolidating budgets and data from a number of competing business units, there is stubborn consistency in the uncertainty of future events. For many companies, conventional returns on investment techniques still suffice; that is, funding requests are funneled up by way of the various business plans and ranked according to prospective returns on investment. Financial criteria are important in deciding on individual proposals with staff and line supporting arguments aiding the decision process. Large, financially strong organizations generally are able to devote greater resources and more sophisticated management techniques to the process; but even so, capital allocation remains a top-executive decision dependent on a measure of judgment and conviction.

Contingency Plans

Planning is predicated on the best current estimates of future events. But as environmental uncertainties increase, companies have found it desirable to develop contingency plans for second or third most likely occurrences. For instance, inflation is much more prevalent and unpredictable an influence than companies have been accustomed to deal with. Energy shortages are another potentially disruptive new element. These and other relatively unfamiliar external influences over which companies have little control have made initial "best estimates" more subject to reevaluation.

The purpose of contingency plans is to anticipate likely discontinuities in the major planning assumptions and minimize their impact on planning performance. This requires alternative assumptions and even alternate sets of plans. Understandably business managers are reluctant to devote a great deal of effort for contingencies rating only a second order of probability at

EXHIBIT 12.8
VARIANCES FROM PLAN
(for major product line A)

	Net sales ($000)	Earnings ($000)
Optimistic case		
Most likely case		
Pessimistic case		

best. Planning is a rigorous and demanding process. To undergo supplemental planning requires a sense of commitment by top management and a feeling of urgency by line managers. A compromise between a full-blown duplicate planning exercise for contingencies is to highlight certain important variables by programs under "optimistic," "most likely," and "pessimistic" assumptions, as in Exhibit 12.8.

Summary

The annual planning cycle is fundamentally a process for consolidating and coordinating the budgets and programs of the various operating units of an organization in order to determine the most efficient allocation of resources among each of these units. It is a traditional practice of fostering performance internally by allocation among the various product lines of the organization. Growth is internal because strategy is based on current operations. Diversity by external means and major organizational change are not alternatives because they are not functions of business-level plans. While in appearance the planning process resembles aspects of strategy formulation and objective-setting for the total enterprise, the annual planning cycle is an ill-suited vehicle for "effectiveness" planning at the corporate level. The standardized routine of the annual planning review fits only the steady-state, or operational, part of enterprise management.

QUESTIONS

1. The annual planning cycle is primarily geared to existing business units rather than planning for new external business opportunities. Explain.

2. One of the initial steps in the annual planning cycle is for the corporate level to determine important environmental issues that the business level should address. Based on current environmental conditions, which factors would you include for business-level analysis, assuming you were the chief corporate planner for (*a*) a bank, (*b*) an oil company, (*c*) a coal company, (*d*) a cosmetics firm?

3. What planning horizon would you recommend for the operations plan of (*a*) a computer firm, (*b*) a utility, and (*c*) an engineering and construction company?

4. How would a one-year budgetary plan for organizations in Question 3 integrate with the longer-term perspective?

5. Can the elements of the annual planning cycle be applied to the public sector? What differences, if any, might you make in the planning routine if it were to be used by your state government?

6. The ultimate goal of a manager is to design a plan sufficiently persuasive to justify all of his requests. Toward this end some managers consistently inflate their estimates, hoping for a final decision close to their real needs. As a business-level manager, is this a tactic you would consider? As a top executive, how can you control unrealistic estimates by business-level managers?

MINI-EXERCISES

1. Select a small company or a division of a large company to research. Develop an external analysis for this firm along the lines of Exhibit 12.4. Also develop a set of programs designed to counter any major external threats you perceive.

2. Repeat Exercise 1 but focus on an internal analysis such as occurs in Exhibit 12.5.

3. Assume you are the new planning officer, a newly created position, for a division of a large company. The firm has recently made three acquisitions in unrelated fields. It now feels the need for systematic planning. As the top planner for one of the newly acquired firms, your job is to design a formal planning document for next year. The corporate planning staff will set guidelines for completion of certain stages of the plan, and will suggest a minimal amount of standardization. However, for this start-up year, each individual business-unit planner is required to develop his own analysis of his situation. What initial steps would you take in formulating your plan?

CHAPTER 13

Planning for Operations – Planning at IBM

A planning and control system pervades the entire organizational structure at IBM. It serves as a primary communication link between corporate and operating-unit management for establishing unit objectives and strategic direction, negotiating plan commitments, and measuring performance against plan.

The bulk of the planning done within IBM is not only decentralized into the several operating units; within any given unit, planning is further decentralized to the plant and laboratory levels. To place planning in perspective, it is necessary to examine the nature of IBM business, its organizational philosophy, and its structure.*

---

* Pages 201–211 are from Abraham Katz, "There's No Room for Guesswork at IBM," *Planning Review*, November 1977. Reprinted by permission.

   IBM illustrates the difficulty of defining a "standard" case. IBM focuses on a three-year planning horizon and lower functional levels rather than on the conventional one- and five-year plans with corporate- and business-level interfaces.

The Nature of IBM Business

The IBM corporation develops, manufactures, markets, and services a wide variety of information-handling products. Most of these products fall into three business areas: data processing (DP), the products making up the larger-scale data-processing systems such as the System 370; general systems (GS), those for the smaller-scale data-processing system such as the System 3, as well as sensor-based systems such as the System 7; and office products (OP), including typewriters, copiers, and other products used in the office. The remaining IBM activities deal with advanced technology and special systems to meet the needs of the United States Government; with disk packs, data modules, and supplies used in information-handling systems; and with educational materials and services for schools and industry.

IBM does about half of its business outside the United States. The scale of our operations worldwide is reflected in these 1976 data:

Gross income from sales, rentals, and services	$16.3 billion
Total assets	17.1 billion
Number of employees	292,000

ORGANIZATIONAL PHILOSOPHY

Insofar as planning is concerned, IBM's philosophy of organization is implemented as follows:

> IBM activities are grouped into a number of operating units which, where feasible, have profit/loss responsibility. These units are differentiated by business area and geographic region, and have the range of functions needed to conduct their assigned missions as autonomously as practical.

> Operating unit management is responsible for development and implementation of its plans. Prior to implementation, plans are reviewed and approved by corporate management. Performance against plan is measured and controlled by operating unit management, and monitored by the corporate staff. Periodically, the results of operations are reviewed with corporate management. Plan changes, as necessary, are also reviewed and approved by corporate management.

> Business policies are controlled at the corporate level, and provide the broad framework within which all operating units function.

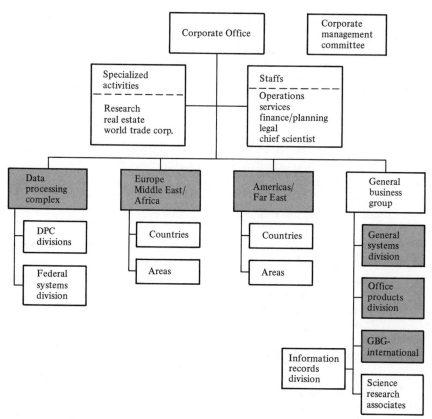

EXHIBIT 13.1
STRUCTURE OF IBM

In its review and assessment of the operating units' plans and performance, corporate management is assisted by the corporate staff which provides counsel and performs certain centralized services.

IBM STRUCTURE

The organizational structure of IBM is depicted in Exhibit 13.1. Shown in shaded form, six operating units involved in the three major business areas have been assigned missions as follows:

Data Processing Complex (DPC) — For the DP business area, DPC has responsibility for coordination of market requirements and development of products worldwide, and for manufacturing, marketing, and service within the United States.

General Systems Division (GSD) and Office Products Division (OPD) — For the GS and OP business areas respectively, GSD and OPD have responsibilities worldwide and within the U.S. which are analogous to those of the DPC.

Europe/Middle East/Africa (EMEA) and Americas/Far East (AFE) — For the DP business area, EMEA and AFE have responsibility for manufacturing, marketing, and service within their respective geographic regions. For the GS and OP business areas, they have responsibility for marketing and service within the larger countries outside the U.S.

There are strong dependencies among these six units and some degree of overlap among the three business areas. Consistent with our philosophy of decentralized management of operations, the planning and control system requires the designated units to develop and implement their separate but coordinated plans within an integrated corporate framework.

The Basic Planning Process

Information-handling products are used across the entire spectrum of human activity and in every part of the world. The number and scope of product applications are expanding rapidly, being limited only by the creativity which the users and firms like our own bring to bear on solving information problems.

DEALING WITH CHANGE

Continuing and rapid change is, therefore, inherent in our business. Technology is advancing rapidly; competition is intense; the world economy is in flux; governmental actions often affect the business environment; and societies everywhere are moving through an "age of discontinuity." Expecting change and recognizing that it may take many forms, IBM scans the environment through two organizational mechanisms — one being the operating units affected and the second, the corporate staff.

Operating unit management maintains an awareness of emerging problems or opportunities which may affect its business. Concurrently, within their respective areas of functional expertise, the various corporate staffs are also monitoring change. When an event or trend of potential significance is detected (e.g., slackening of economic conditions in a country we serve), the operating unit affected will alert corporate management as to the magnitude and timing of the expected effects. In some cases, the unit is joined by the corporate staff in developing and recommending a course of action. Once accepted, these recommendations are then built into the unit's plan by its management. Where a problem is of major and continuing importance (e.g., energy), a joint council involving affected units and staffs will be created to monitor and recommend action on a regular basis.

ORGANIZING FOR PLANNING

As indicated at the outset, planning and implementation are line management responsibilities. However, planning staffs to support line management exist at the corporate, operating unit (and where these are large, at the divisional or country), and plant/laboratory levels. The size and functional mix of these staffs depend on the specific responsibilities of the line managers they support. At the operating unit level, the executive will normally have finance and planning, as well as functional skills needed to develop a properly balanced profit plan. For example, his technical staff will review and assist in integrating the various product plans into the unit plan. The unit executive makes the final judgments as to business volumes to be achieved, resources required, and risks to be accepted.

At the corporate level, the line executives also have finance, planning, and other functional staffs to assist them. For example, among the responsibilities of the Corporate Business Plans staff are design of the IBM planning system, establishing the plan guidance and data requirements, managing the plan schedule, recommending profit targets for the various operating units, and reviewing and assessing their strategies and plans.

PROGRAM AND PERIOD PLANNING

There are two distinct but interactive kinds of planning within the IBM system, as shown from Exhibit 13.2 (light outline for program planning; bold, for period planning):

> Program planning (e.g., a program to develop a product or improve the productivity of a function) is characterized by the following: The program plan generally has a single objective, but may involve several functional elements. Its time horizon is determined by the nature of the specific program objective and the work processes required to achieve it; its cycle for review and decisionmaking, by the inherent dynamics of the program.

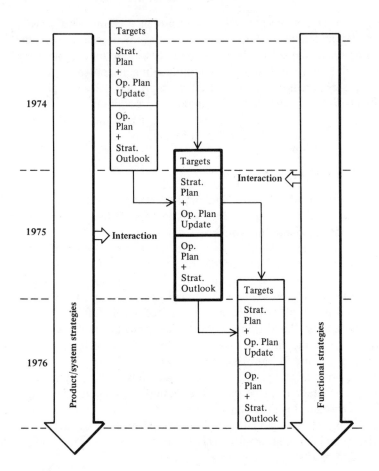

EXHIBIT 13.2
PERIOD AND PROGRAM PLANNING AT IBM

At any point in time, each operating unit has a large portfolio of product and functional programs in various stages of planning and implementation.

Period planning complements program planning and is characterized by the following: The period plans balance among multiple-program and other objectives to achieve the profit targets assigned. Its time horizons are fixed by corporate management, being two years for the operating plan and five years for the strategic plan. The cycle for review and decisionmaking is tied to the calendar to assure the availability of an operating budget for each unit at the beginning of each year.

Clearly, decisions made as part of the period planning process affect the program plans — accelerating some, terminating others, and so on. The converse is also true — some program decisions require changes in the period plan of an operating unit. It is the responsibility of operating unit management to establish and maintain the proper balance among its objectives and resources.

Program Planning

PRODUCT MANAGEMENT

Program planning may be directed toward a system product, industry (i.e., a specific class of customers), or functional objective. To illustrate the process, consider the planning associated with a product program. Such planning generally proceeds in two distinct stages: defining the market requirements and, once the requirements have been accepted, translating them into products.

In most cases, the market requirements relate to an existing IBM product, one for which there has been a continuing need. As part of his normal activities, the manager within an operating unit having responsibility for a certain product will periodically measure the performance program vs. program plan for the product he currently has in the field. Concurrently, he will be proceeding with the development of advanced techniques and devices for the next generation product. Depending on the sales performance of the current product and the availability of new technology, he will recommend to his management whether and how to enhance or replace it. Since many of our products work together within a data-processing system, the product manager's recommendations must always be considered within the total system's framework, since system integrity must be maintained.

In some cases, a customer's needs may be basically new, lying beyond IBM's current skills and experience. Product planners will then work with the marketing force on case studies, interviews, and questionnaires to determine the user's requirements, the functional characteristics needed in the new product, and its expected mode of use. Depending on the prospects for an economically sound program, the product manager will make his recommendations as to proceeding with it.

At its discretion, operating-unit management initiates programs which fall within the assigned missions, approved strategies, and negotiated organizational budgets of the unit. Once a program is initiated, management periodically reviews performance against plan. These reviews typically occur as the product program moves from one phase into the next (e.g., from study into design). The product manager reviews all aspects of the program (forecasts of business volumes, cost estimates, technical problems, schedules, etc.) with the operating-unit management and with all functions and operating units having an interest in the program. Prior to product announcement, there must be agreement as to its economic soundness, and commitment from each organization to do its part. After announcement, there are periodic reviews of performance against plan, with corrective action taken as necessary.

FORECASTING

IBM relies on in-house econometric models to forecast both the U.S. economy and the demand for certain of the company's products. The same techniques are now being used for international forecasts. Economists in the major countries work with the Corporate Economics Department to assure proper reflection of the local situations.

The company uses two national income and expenditure models in its forecasts of the U.S. economic picture. The quarterly model produces forecasts for use with the company's two-year operating plan; the annual model produces forecasts for use with the strategic plan. IBM also uses an input/output model to project industry supply and demand patterns. The first two models each contain about fifty behavior equations, each one relating to some economic variable such as the consumption function of durables. The programs are written mainly in Fortran and run on 370/155s and a 360/91.

Product forecasters in each operating unit use a wide range of forecasting methods, including analyses of growth and replacement patterns for new product or systems; extrapolation from a sample of case studies selected to represent industry, size, or application distribution; interviews or questionnaires for new products; and projections based on sales or backlog analyses for products already announced. Through the use of typical system configuration ratios, systems forecasts are decomposed into forecasts of the individual products they comprise.

Period Planning

An overall planning system is necessary to meet the business needs of the corporation and its operating units. In this system, each IBM operating unit annually performs both strategic and operating planning. The purpose of strategic planning by a unit is to establish its business direction; that of operating planning, to implement the direction within budgeting requirements and to commit the unit to achieving planned results.

STRATEGIC PLANNING

Key elements in strategic planning are corporate targets, operating unit goals, product/system and functional strategies, and a strategic plan. The five-year time horizon for strategic planning lies sufficiently beyond the two-year operating period so that sound and timely decisions on business direction can be made. The strategic process is as follows:

Corporate Targets and Operating Unit Goals.   Corporate management assigns targets (profit and profit margin) to each operating unit. In response, each operating unit management develops and assigns goals to its product/system and functional management to guide their strategy development.

Strategies.   Operating units with development responsibilities prepare and maintain product/system strategies to serve as the foundation for their marketplace offerings. All units prepare functional strategies to assure that the most effective organization and business approaches are used to achieve increasing productivity of resources. As part of its marketing strategy, a unit may assign industry goals and develop strategies to meet the needs unique to specific customers' sets.

Strategic Plan.   The strategic plan integrates the several product/system and functional strategies of the units, presents the financial results over the plan period, and compares planned results against corporate targets. This plan (and selected strategies) is submitted to the Corporate Management Committee (CMC) by the operating unit executive. The plans are reviewed by the corporate staff and, prior to CMC review, their assessments are forwarded to the CMC and the operating unit. Among the bases for these assessments are:

Consistency with approved strategic direction

Balance between objectives sought and resources required

Relationships to plans of other operating units

Excellence in each functional area

Certain staffs also write short critiques as to the strengths, weaknesses, or risks associated with the individual plans. On the basis of these staff inputs and the operating unit presentation, the CMC approves the unit's proposed business direction, resolves nonconcurrences, reevaluates its targets and reassigns them.

To support this planning work, the operating units with product development responsibility generate product assumptions; Corporate Economic provides the economic and environmental assumptions; and the various corporate staffs issue functional guidance as necessary. Other factors and trends are monitored and analyzed to determine their possible implications (e.g., environmental issues, consumerism, privacy and data security, and international political and economic relationship).

Using the product and economic assumptions, the forecasting department of each operating unit produces an overall set of business volumes by integrating the individual product forecasts previously developed with the results of the supply-demand balancing against the order backlog. These volumes provide management with a projection based on explicitly defined and quantifiable factors. Management then applies judgment to take into consideration the unquantifiable considerations previously mentioned, and the adjusted business volumes are distributed to the various functions as the basis for their plans. Based on historical experience, each function then uses its own planning factors and models to translate these volumes into workload, resources, and cost/expense. Computer models are widely used at both the operating unit and corporate levels. For example, all manufacturing activities use computers extensively for balancing supply against demand and determining plant loading; engineering, for design automation; Marketing and Service, for territory analysis and proposal preparation. The unit staff then integrates the several functional inputs into a properly balanced plan, which the unit executive approves and submits to corporate management.

As one approach for dealing with the problems of uncertainty, corporate management may request contingency analyses to test, for example, the effect of a more extreme set of economic assumptions on unit plans. Corporate Economics will then issue two outlooks — one for the base plan and a second for the contingency plan. Operating units will then develop two plans and review them with corporate management. This approach has proven useful in improving the speed and flexibility of our response to unanticipated conditions.

Operating Plan

Based on the business direction in the approved strategic plans and including changes as necessary, the unit then develops an operating plan which focuses on implementation over the current year plus two. This plan contains detailed business volumes and workload forecasts, as well as functional resources and financial plan commitments. These data are developed through planning processes similar to those for the strategic plan described above. The operating plan is used to establish budgets and other objectives for the next year. Certain units provide selected revenue and resource items in a long-range outlook at the time of the plan submission to show the probable extended effects, risks, and exposures of the proposed plan. After approval by the operating unit executive, the plan is submitted for corporate review and assessment (as for the strategic plan). The CMC resolves nonconcurrences and approves the unit plan.

When significant deviations occur in actual results vs. plan, a unit may request approval for changes in its operating plan. All requests are coordinated by the IBM Director of Budgets (and, indeed, may be initiated by him); those requiring CMC approval are reviewed and assessed by appropriate corporate staffs.

QUESTIONS

1. IBM is a uniquely successful company. How has its approach to planning contributed to this success?

2. Two other large and successful companies with sophisticated planning systems are GE and RCA. Yet each of these two abandoned its investment in computers because of an inability to compete profitably in the computer industry. Do you believe their failure was attributable to bad planning? What other factors might have been involved?

3. IBM stresses the importance of anticipating and dealing with change and, indeed, technological obsolescence is an ever-present threat in the computer field. How is this type of one-industry change different from the changes encountered by a very diversified firm, or one in a cyclical but mature industry (e.g., cement)?

CHAPTER 14

Basics
of Financial Analysis*

Section 1: The Income Statement

The income statement is a record of a company's revenues, its expenses and taxes, and its earnings over a period of time — usually a year or a quarter. It is closely related to other financial statements — which we'll be reviewing before long — including the balance sheet.

The best way to understand an income statement is to look at one. So, let's do just that. Exhibit 14.1 is a replica of General Foods' 1978 income as reported to stockholders in its annual report. It's actually more than just an income statement: it's the *Consolidated Statement of Earnings & Retained Earnings.*

---

* This material was prepared by Steven Lewins, Research Director and Editor of the Value Line Investment Survey, a service of Arnold Bernhard & Co., Inc. in New York. Reprinted by permission.

EXHIBIT 14.1
**GENERAL FOODS CONSOLIDATED STATEMENT OF EARNINGS
& RETAINED EARNINGS**

(All dollar amounts are expressed in thousands, except figures given on
a share basis)

| | For the 52 weeks ended | |
	April 1, 1978	April 2, 1977
REVENUES		
Net Sales	$5,376,204	$4,909,737
Other Income	13,294	16,543
	5,389,498	4,926,280
COSTS AND EXPENSES		
Cost of Sales	3,545,516	3,165,942
Marketing, General and Administrative Expenses	1,475,676	1,364,824
Interest Expense	37,700	27,676
	5,058,892	4,558,442
EARNINGS BEFORE INCOME TAXES	330,606	367,838
INCOME TAXES	161,100	190,500
NET EARNINGS	169,506	177,338
RETAINED EARNINGS — BEGINNING OF PERIOD	924,244	823,396
	1,093,750	1,000,734
CASH DIVIDENDS	81,798	76,490
RETAINED EARNINGS — END OF PERIOD	$1,011,952	$ 924,244
NET EARNINGS PER SHARE	$3.40	$3,56
DIVIDENDS PER SHARE	$1.64	$1.53½

Consolidated means General Foods is combining in one place all the information for the headquarters company and its subsidiaries, both stateside and abroad. *Statement of Earnings* is synonymous with income statement. *Statement of Retained Earnings* is an addendum to the income statement that ties it to the balance sheet. Don't worry about it right now; we'll come back to it.

The income statement happens to be the financial report most frequently looked at by investors, even though it may not be the most important one. The balance sheet may be more important but because the income statement is easier to comprehend, we're starting with a review of it.

LET'S LOOK AT SALES

The first caption on General Foods' income statement is *Revenues,* which are made up of *Net Sales* and *Other Income.* Total revenues for General Foods in 1978, which you may have noticed ended on April 1, 1978, not at the end of a calendar year, were $5,389.5 million. (We rounded $5,389,498 to $5,389.5 million in order to make it easier to handle and remember the figure.) Of this sum just about all of it, $5,376.2 million, is represented by net sales.

Net sales are not the same as *sales.* What a company sells may be returned. *Net sales* are the dollar sales of the company less all discounts and returns; they are *net* of illusory sales. The net sales figure should be a rock bottom number representing what the company sold over the 52-week period that began April 3, 1977 and ended April 1, 1978.

Other Income, which is included in revenues by General Foods, is often shown elsewhere on the income statement — usually alongside other expenses, or miscellaneous items. General Foods chose to combine sales and other income into one figure, namely revenues. That's perfectly all right, although from an analytical standpoint we prefer to examine net sales — which stem from the company's basic operations — independent of other income that can come from a variety of sources. Dividends received on investments or royalty payments are examples of revenues that can be derived from sources other than sales.

The next major income statement classification is *Costs and Expenses.* These include *Cost of Sales* (mainly wage and salary disbursements, raw materials outlays, various production expenses, and an allowance for the depreciation of plant). *Marketing, General and Administrative Expenses* (which are just what they appear to be) and *Interest Expense.* Interest expense is usually shown *net* of interest income but this may not always be the case. Sometimes interest income is included by a company as part of other income. It doesn't matter as long as the company is consistent from year to year in the way it reports.

The interest figure represents the total interest expense of the company, including interest on long-term debt as well as on short-term debt. The difference between long- and short-term debt is simple: Long-term debt is an obligation of the company that matures in more than a year; short-term debt is payable within 12 months. Companies usually opt for short-term debt to finance current operations; they use long-term funds to pay for long-lived assets — like a factory.

WHAT'S THE BOTTOM LINE?

The next figure shown in the financial statement is pretax income. General Foods sold over $5 billion of products, about 40% of which was represented by coffee. It earned $330.6 million before paying Uncle Sam and other income-taxing authorities $161.1 million of income taxes. (Other taxes — like real estate or payroll taxes are included in operating costs.) That may sound like a lot of profit, but it really isn't relative to the sales base. If we take $330.6 million and divide it by $5,376.2 million of net sales, we end up getting a pretax return on sales of 6.1%. The company, in other words, earned about 6¢ on every dollar of sales — *before* payment of income taxes. It earned $169.5 million after taxes — or 3.2% of sales. How does that compare to the amount earned in 1977? Look to the right. You'll see the number $177.3 million. That is how much the company made the previous year. It earned more then! There was a decline of $7.8 million (or 4.4%) from one year to the next.

Why did this happen? It's possible that labor costs got out of hand; taxes may have risen sharply; the company could have experienced plant startup expenses; or perhaps the price of coffee beans simply rose sharply. Or maybe sales declined.

We see — by way of a quick glance at the top line — that net sales increased from $4,909.7 million to $5,376.2 million, or 9.5%, in fiscal 1978. We come to that 9.5% growth rate by dividing 5,376.2 by 4,909.7 and getting 1.095. We then subtract 1.0 and multiply the remainder (.095) by 100 to arrive at 9.5%. This is the easy way to compute percentage change. . . . How well does the 9.5% growth compare to overall change in the U.S. economy? GNP (gross national product, which is the nation's total production of goods and services) expanded from $1807 billion in the first quarter of calendar 1977 to $1992 billion in the first three months of calendar 1978 — or 10.2%. General Foods didn't increase its business quite as fast as the economy grew. (The GNP figures are available from a variety of government and private sources. . . .)

EXAMINE COSTS

Now, let's take a look at how rapidly cost of sales rose from year to year. If we divide $3,545.5 million of 1978 costs by $3,165.9 million in 1977, we get 1.120 — which translates into a 12.0% increase. There it is! One problem General Foods faced during the course of 1978 was a 12% increase in its production costs at a time when net sales rose only 9.5%.

Did any other expense items increase more rapidly than sales? You do the computations. How fast did marketing, general and administrative outlays rise? Did interest expenses increase faster than sales? (If they did,

do you think it was because interest rates rose during the year? They did.)
How about tax payments?

General Foods is helpful in explaining why its production costs rose
more rapidly than its dollar sales. We show in Exhibit 14.2 the fourth page
of the annual report where the company shows a graph of spot green coffee
prices. What is a spot green coffee price? It is the price of green coffee at
any point in time in the open market. And, as you can see, green coffee
prices peaked around April 1, 1977 — which is precisely when General
Foods' 1978 fiscal year began! If you take a pencil and sketch in an average
price for green coffee prices in the fiscal year of '78 (about $2.35) and com-
pare a similar line with fiscal '77 (something like $1.80), you will find that
on average green coffee prices were about 30% greater in fiscal '78 than in
fiscal '77. When one of a company's major raw materials costs rises that
rapidly and sales are besieged by heavy competition (which is precisely
what General Foods tells us was the case in the description it gives us in
Exhibit 14.2 of its 1978 operations), one can expect a profit margin squeeze
of one sort or another. The heavy competition, as an aside, helps explain
why net sales did not grow as fast as the economy that year while expenses
did.

We've just used the words "profit margin." A profit margin is any income figure divided by sales. We computed the pretax margin previously
when we divided earnings before income taxes by sales and arrived at 6%;
we also computed the net income margin: 3%. Now, let's calculate the
operating profit margin, which is the return on sales before deductions are
made for depreciation, interest and taxes. It's arrived at by dividing operating
profits by sales. Where in the income statement does one find operating
profits? Nowhere. That figure must be computed.

WORK UP OPERATING EARNINGS

Calculation of operating profits is a little bit more difficult than it may appear on the surface; that is because operating profits — which are the

EXHIBIT 14.2
GENERAL FOODS. DOMESTIC GROCERY OPERATIONS

On balance, GF's grocery operations in the United States had another good
year in fiscal 1978. Some brands of packaged convenience foods performed
exceptionally well, adding significantly to sales volumes and earnings. Franchises
and margins were successfully maintained on others, especially those in markets which showed slower than expected growth. However, grocery coffee

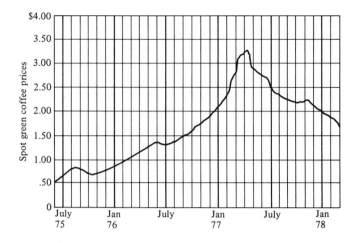

products in the U.S. posed problems throughout the year, as was the case worldwide.

After continuing increases during fiscal 1977 in the cost of green coffee, which were necessarily reflected in the price of coffee on grocery shelves, the early months of fiscal 1978 found GF's grocery coffee products in the U.S. facing both consumer resistance to high prices and a sharp decline in the green coffee market, as the chart on this page shows. Nearly $4 for a pound of ground coffee proved to be a point beyond which many consumers would not go and consumption declined.

When a drop-off in green coffee prices started, many Americans decided to wait for lower prices and began consuming the coffee they had purchased earlier when prices were going up. As a result, our grocery trade customers cut their inventories.

GF's sales volumes on grocery coffee — both inside and outside the United States — fell off dramatically during the first half of fiscal 1978, and the extent of this volume decline caused GF's worldwide coffee inventories to become temporarily out of balance with needs. Also, the company felt pressure on margins because of the lag between the purchase of green coffee beans and their appearance on grocery shelves in processed form. However, the final six months of fiscal 1978 saw some firming of green coffee prices, with sales improved over the first half-year.

Although fiscal 1978 was a rough year for GF's coffee business and one characterized by even more intense competition than formerly, coffee remains an important part of General Foods' business. Coffee also remains an area where innovation continues to pay off. GF's coffees specially developed for automatic coffee makers, now available in Sanka and Yuban brands in addition to the Maxwell House brand which initiated this special blend two years ago, are proving very successful. Mellow Roast, a coffee and grain beverage introduced to consumers at the close of fiscal 1977, went into national distribution at mid-year. This new product combines quality coffee beans with cereal grain to produce a smooth, mild coffee beverage.

earnings that stem from the company's basic operations before any charge is made for interest and other miscellaneous items — *exclude* depreciation.

General Foods' 1978 operating profit is arrived at by subtracting all operating costs *except* depreciation and amortization from sales. Thus: deduct $3,545.5 million of cost of sales and $1,475.7 million of marketing, general and administrative expenses from net sales of $5,376.2 million. The remainder, $355.0 million, is operating income *after* depreciation and amortization charges. How do we know that? It's simple: General Foods doesn't break out depreciation and amortization on its income statement. The depreciation charge is embedded in some other expense item, namely cost of sales. We must therefore add depreciation back to the $355 million in order to come up with operating profits *before* depreciation. (Confused by *before* and *after*? All *before* means is before subtracting depreciation and amortization from profits; likewise *after* means after the subtraction.)

. . . General Foods' 1978 depreciation and amortization charge was $69.5 million vs. a higher $71.3 million the year before.

Depreciation and amortization charges usually rise from year to year. Why did General Foods' charges decline? That answer is found in a footnote to the financials. . . . General Foods explains in the footnotes to its financials that the depreciation provision (i.e., charge) was $67.3 million in fiscal 1978, up from $60.9 million in 1977. Therefore we can determine amortization by subtracting depreciation ($67.3 million and $60.9 million) from depreciation and amortization ($69.5 million and $71.3 million respectively):

	1978	1977
Depreciation	$67.3 mill.	$60.9 mill.
Amortization	2.2	10.4
Depreciation and Amortization	69.5	71.3

The 10.5% increase in depreciation charges is pretty much in line with sales gains. But note the steep slide in amortization charges.

WHAT'S AMORTIZATION?

Amortization is akin to depreciation. Companies depreciate away fixed assets like plants. Less tangible assets — like the value of a patent or trademark — are depreciated away too, but that's called amortization. Every profession has its jargon; so does accounting. When an asset is depreciated or amortized, that means a *non-cash* charge is taken against income.

Did we lose you by referring to *non-cash* charges? That's a tough concept for the layman. Most expenses taken by a corporation represent genuine cash outlays. Some do not: Depreciation and amortization, for example.

The cash outlay for a factory or machine tool comes at the time of its purchase. The plant and equipment purchase is not charged against income all at once; it's spread out over, say, twenty years. In other words, if a coffee-roasting company buys a new coffee roaster for $10 million every ten years, it doesn't expense (i.e., charge off against income) $10 million once every ten years. Rather it expenses $1 million annually. But it's already spent the $10 million of cash. Therefore the $1 million is a non-cash charge representing the wasting away of the roaster over time. . . .

It's important to recognize that earnings are arrived at after the subtraction of all cash *expenses* and non-cash *charges*. The true cash flow of the company is different from earnings. The cash flow is the sum of earnings plus all those non-cash charges. Simply stated, cash flow equals profits plus depreciation and amortization. There are other non-cash charges (and even some non-cash credits) but let's not cover that just now.

Let's return briefly to the steep decline in General Foods' amortization charges and explain it away by saying the company found less need in 1978 than in 1977 to reduce intangible assets (as opposed to tangible ones like plant and equipment). Perhaps it fully amortized away some intangibles in 1977, thereby reducing the overall annual amortization requirement.

GETTING BACK TO OPERATING PROFITS

Now we can get back to calculating operating profits. But before we wrap up the computation, may we ask a question? Can you see why we want to calculate operating profits *before* deducting depreciation, etc.? We want to pin down the profit level before we get to all those odd non-cash charges and other expenses. Reason: we want to measure how healthy the company's basic operating business is.

We previously computed earnings *after* cost of sales and *after* marketing, general and administrative expenses. Remember the figure? It is $355.0 million. If we add back depreciation, etc. of $69.5 million, we find that 1978 operating profits came in at $424.5 million. The operating profit margin (operating profits divided by sales) comes to 7.9%. What was it the year before? Work out the number. Answer: 9.2%!

General Foods' operating profitability fell sharply from year to year — because of all that competition and soaring green coffee prices.

CHECK OUT PROFITABILITY

Various profit margins usually move in the same direction from one year to the next. When they don't, we should find out why. Let's take a quick look at General Foods' key profit margins. We've already identified most of them; so all we have to do is tabulate them:

	1978	1977
Operating Margin	7.9%	9.2%
Pretax Margin	6.1%	7.5%
Net Margin	3.2%	3.6%

Notice that all three profit rates slipped in 1978. . . .

There is a concept that's the reverse of the profit margin. It's the expense ratio. An expense ratio is computed by dividing expenses (rather than profits) by sales. Expense ratios are used most commonly by utility analysts but are applicable to all types of security analysis.

The 1978 operating expense ratio is simply $3,545.5 million of sales costs plus $1,475.7 million of general expenses less $69.5 million of depreciation divided by sales of $5,376.2 million — or 92.1%. Notice that the operating margin (7.9%) plus the expense ratio (92.1%) *always* equals 100%.

THE RETAINED EARNINGS STATEMENT

Let's return to General Foods' consolidated statement of earnings and retained earnings for a moment. There are a number of items that we have not examined and really ought to before going on to the balance sheet. Below the net earnings line we have a new item, *Retained Earnings — Beginning of Period.* That is the sum of all the earnings of General Foods in all years less all the dividends paid out in all years. In other words, at the beginning of fiscal 1978 General Foods' total retained earnings were a shade under a billion dollars ($924.2 million to be exact). The company then earned $169.5 million in 1978 and paid out cash dividends of $81.8 million. At the end of the year the total amount of retained earnings was just a little bit over a billion dollars: $1,012.0 million. This is an interesting number. Reason: In all of General Foods' history it has retained a sum equal to only about one-fifth of its sales in its most recent fiscal year! Those retained earnings represent investment over time by the company in its own business.

THE PAYOUT RATIO

The last two items on the statement are the ones that most investors scrutinize most of the time: earnings per share and dividends per share. The company declared dividends of $1.64 a share in 1978 and earnings per share were $3.40. If we divide the dividends per share by the earnings per share we get a payout ratio: $1.64 divided by $3.40 equals 48%. We should get a similar ratio if we take the total cash dividends and divide by the net earnings: $81.8 million divided by $169.5 million equals 48%. We do.

This will not be the case with all corporations. It is true of General Foods because its financial statements are relatively simple. . . .

HERE'S AN EXERCISE

The consolidated statement of earnings and retained earnings is really two financial statements in one. The income statement begins with revenues and ends with net earnings. The retained earnings statement begins with retained earnings — beginning of period — and ends with retained earnings — end of period. General Foods chooses to combine the two reports into one statement for simplicity. We have no difficulty with that. We hope you won't.

Retained earnings, by the way, is a balance sheet item. The subsequent chapters will explain how to read a balance sheet. But before we start a new topic, please do a short exercise. Take General Foods' income statement and recast it into a standard format. Which format? We show it in Exhibit 14.3. We've done the figure work for fiscal 1977. You enter the numbers for fiscal 1978.

Can you define gross income and gross margin yourself? Can you guess (or explain) why General Foods' 1977 tax rate is so high? The first question is easy to answer. The second is easy when you know it: General Foods is based in tax-burdened New York. The average stockholder-reported income tax rate for U.S. industrial companies was 49.9% in 1977. . . . You'll find, when you work through your exercise, that the tax rate fell sharply in 1978. That's not due to excessive generosity on the part of New York but because General Foods included some non-taxable *inventory* gains related to foreign

EXHIBIT 14.3

	1978	1977
Sales ($mill.)	_____	4909.7
Cost of Sales ($mill.)	_____	3094.6
Gross Income ($mill.)	_____	1815.1
Gross Margin (%)	_____	37.0%
M, G & A Expense ($mill.)	_____	1364.8
Operating Expense ($mill.)	_____	4459.4
Operating Income ($mill.)	_____	450.3
Operating Margin (%)	_____	9.2%
Depreciation Charge ($mill.)	_____	71.3
Interest Expense ($mill.)	_____	27.7
Other Income ($mill.)	_____	16.5
Pretax Income ($mill.)	_____	367.8
Pretax Margin (%)	_____	7.5%
Income Taxes ($mill.)	_____	190.5
Income Tax Rate (%)	_____	51.8%
Net Profit ($mill.)	_____	177.3
Net Margin (%)	_____	3.6%

currency fluctuations in its pretax earnings. It had losses the year before. Inclusion of non-taxable gains always serves to reduce the effective tax rate. We're told all about this in the company's footnotes.

Section 2: The Balance Sheet — Current Accounts

Have you completed the exercise at the end of Section 1? If not, please do it and check your answers against the figures shown below. If you have completed it and you understand the answers, then let's go on to a discussion of the balance sheet.

Answers to Section 1 Quiz

	1978
Sales	5,376.2
Cost of Sales	3,476.0
Gross Income	1,900.2
Gross Margin	35.3%
M, G & A Expense	1,475.7
Operating Expense	4,951.7
Operating Income	424.5
Operating Margin	7.9%
Depreciation Charge	69.5
Interest Expense	37.7
Other Income	13.3
Pretax Income	330.6
Pretax Margin	6.2%
Income Taxes	161.1
Income Tax Rate	48.7%
Net Profit	169.5
Net Margin	3.2%

Exhibit 14.4 presents General Foods' *Consolidated Balance Sheets* as of April 1, 1978 and April 2, 1977. A balance sheet is simply a ledger page on which the assets of the company balance out against the liabilities and ownership of the company. Take a look at General Foods' balance sheet. You will see that total assets at the end of 1978 were equal to $2,433 million. Likewise the sum of stockholders' equity and all liabilities was $2,433 million. That total assets equal the sum of total liabilities and stockholders' equity is the essence of the balance sheet.

The balance sheet is a "snapshot" of a company's financial position at a point in time. A balance sheet theoretically can be constructed for each day of the year. The income statement is different; it is a description of the changes that occurred during a specific time period, a quarter or a year, that's framed at each end by a balance sheet. The income statement is dynamic; the balance sheet is static.

CURRENT VS. NON-CURRENT

There are two types of assets, namely current assets and long-term assets. *Current Assets* are either in the form of cash, securities that may easily be converted into cash, or items that will be turned into cash or consumed

EXHIBIT 14.4
GENERAL FOODS CONSOLIDATED BALANCE SHEET

(All dollar amounts are expressed in thousands)

ASSETS

	April 1, 1978	April 2, 1977
CURRENT ASSETS		
Cash	$ 29,240	$ 28,420
Temporary Investments, at cost, which approximates market	103,246	100,983
Receivables, less allowances of $10,803 in 1978 and $10,029 in 1977	572,613	459,920
Inventories		
Finished Product	473,707	456,765
Raw Materials and Supplies	344,068	433,162
	817,775	889,927
Deferred Income Tax Benefits	68,660	70,614
Prepaid Expenses	26,225	18,679
Current Assets	1,617,759	1,568,543
LAND, BUILDINGS, EQUIPMENT, at cost, less accumulated depreciation	762,227	728,525
LONG-TERM RECEIVABLES AND SUNDRY ASSETS	26,739	32,574
GOODWILL, less accumulated amortization of $17,732 in 1978 and $15,746 in 1977	26,299	28,990
Total	$2,433,024	$2,358,632

LIABILITIES AND STOCKHOLDERS' EQUITY

CURRENT LIABILITIES		
Notes Payable	$ 119,726	$ 105,320
Current Portion of Long-Term Debt	15,728	17,353
Accounts and Drafts Payable	310,192	294,551
Accrued Liabilities	329,013	307,071
Accrued Income Taxes	85,059	127,121
Current Liabilities	859,718	851,416
LONG-TERM DEBT	259,802	270,177
OTHER NON-CURRENT LIABILITIES	19,740	21,030
PROVISION FOR DISCONTINUED FAST-FOOD OPERATIONS	18,321	20,268
DEFERRED INCOME TAXES	101,679	110,779
STOCKHOLDERS' EQUITY		
Common Stock Issued	50,910	50,865
Additional Paid-In Capital	146,579	145,530
Retained Earnings	1,011,952	924,244
Common Stock Held in Treasury, at cost	(35,677)	(35,677)
Stockholders' Equity	1,173,764	1,084,962
Total	$2,433,024	$2,358,632

within a year or less. All other assets (including land, buildings, long-term investments and miscellaneous long-term assets) are not likely to be converted into cash over the next 12 months and, as a result, are classified as non-current.

The liabilities and stockholders' equity section of the balance sheet, which is frequently known as the right-hand side of the balance sheet (although in the case of General Foods, it happens to be the bottom half), breaks down into current liabilities, long-term liabilities and the stockholders' ownership in the company.

Current Liabilities, like current assets, apply to the next 12 months. A current liability is one that comes due (i.e., must be paid off or refinanced) within the next year. A long-term liability, such as long-term debt, is just what it sounds like — an obligation of the company that must be met but *not* in the immediate future.

Excessive current liabilities can strangle a company. That's because they must be paid down in the very near future. Therefore, it is essential for most companies that current assets exceed current liabilities by a comfortable margin. Current assets exceeded current liabilities by a shade over 80% for the average industrial company at the end of 1977. In other words, the so-called *Current Ratio,* which is simply current assets divided by current liabilities, for industrial companies in the aggregate was 1.8 (i.e., 1.8:1 or 180%) at the end of 1977. This compares with a ratio of 1.9 ($1,618 million of current assets divided by $860 million of current liabilities) for General Foods as of April 1, 1978. (Note: 9 months of General Foods' 1978 fiscal year actually fell in calendar 1977.) General Foods' current position, as measured by the relationship of current assets to current liabilities, was superior by 0.1 (or 10 percentage points) to the current ratio for the average industrial company. Where did we dig up the typical industrial company ratio? We referred to Exhibit 14.5, The Value Line Industrial Composite of 900 companies that's published periodically in The Value Line Investment Survey.

Current assets need not exceed current liabilities for all companies. That they do not is most common in the case of electric utilities — where current liabilities usually exceed current assets. The prompt payment of electric bills by utility customers makes it possible for the utilities to pay off their obligations on time even though the near-term assets they possess do not equal their obligations. This is another way of saying that utility current assets get converted into usable cash far more quickly than current obligations must be met. Other companies, say machine tool manufacturers, would go bust under similar circumstances.

The relationship of current assets to current liabilities is known as the "current ratio." If, rather than dividing one by the other, we subtract current liabilities from current assets — we get working capital. In the case of

General Foods: $1,618 million of current assets less $860 million of current liabilities yields $758 million of working capital.

WORKING CAPITAL IS ESSENTIAL

Working Capital is the surplus of current liabilities and represents the amount of financial buffer a company has to withstand adversity — and to pay dividends and build plants. Just about all companies, with the exception of a few capital-intensive corporations like the utilities, require working capital. A company may be losing money and showing a deficit on the income statement, but, so long as it has a sound working capital cushion, probably won't go belly up.

How much working capital is needed? This depends on the level of revenues and unique company characteristics — from internal financial controls to types of markets served. The average industrial company needed about 15½¢ of working capital for every dollar of sales in 1977. (That's the same as saying the working capital-to-sales ratio was 15.5%.) Some required more; others less. We know from General Foods' income statement that the company generated $5,376 million of net sales in the year ended April 1, 1978. If we divide this figure into the $758 million of working capital, a working capital-to-sales ratio of 14% is attained. This is less than the average ratio of an industrial company — by 1½ percentage points. The question then is, "Does General Foods need additional capital in order to support future sales growth, or does the company usually run with a lower-than-average level of working capital relative to sales?" It is difficult to fully answer that question right off the bat. Let's see how much we can answer.

Let's compute the ratio for the year ended April 2, 1977. Subtract current liabilities of $851 million from current assets of $1,569 million and divide the resulting figure, $718 million, by net sales for that year of $4,910 million; the resulting working capital-to-sales ratio is 14.6%. Observation: In the fiscal year that ended in April 1977, General Foods did in fact operate with more working capital relative to revenues than it did in '78. But that does not mean it had too little capital in 1978. We really require a more extensive history of General Foods' relationship of working capital to sales in order to be able to answer the critical question, "Is the company shy of cash?"

CASH IS THE FIRST CURRENT ASSET

Now let's examine the components of General Foods' current asset account. The first item shown is *Cash*: $29.2 million. That $29.2 million was cash in hand, or at least in the company's bank accounts. It was readily available to meet bills coming due.

A very commonly constructed ratio — known as the *Acid Test Ratio* — is the cash the company has on hand plus its marketable securities, all divided by current liabilities. The value of the *Marketable Securities* owned by General Foods is shown on the next line: *Temporary Investments, At Cost, Which Approximates Market*. All that descriptive material means one thing — that the company reports it purchased $103.2 million of short-term securities and that those securities, as of April 1, 1978, were still worth *approximately* $103.2 million. Most short-term securities that approximate market value are in fact government securities like 90-day Treasury bills. Such securities are the equivalent of cash because they can be readily sold. That is why many companies, rather than simply breaking out cash and temporary investments in two separate lines, present a single figure: *Cash and Equivalents*.

The *Cash and Equivalents* total for General Foods is the sum of $103.2 million and $29.2 million or $132.4 million. Cash and equivalents the year before equaled $129.4 million. They increased about 2.3% during the course of the year, which is significantly less than the increase in net sales (9.5%).

Cash and equivalents may grow slower than sales in any particular year but over time they should trend up somewhat in line with revenue growth, although because of the extensive use of computers the ratio of cash to sales for most companies has declined during the postwar period. Sometimes it is difficult to tell whether a downward drift in the ratio is the result of better cash management or financial trouble. But a detailed analysis of the overall balance sheet, which we are working up to doing, can help in making that very important determination.

CARRYING RECEIVABLES CAN BE COSTLY

The next item the company reports is its *Short-Term Receivables*. Receivables are paper the company holds on items that have been shipped to others. A receivable on General Foods' books means another company or individual owes General Foods a specific amount of money. General Foods was owed $572.6 million at the end of 1978; this compares with $459.9 million at the end of 1977. How much of an increase is this? Just divide $572.6 million by $459.9 million, subtract 1.0 and multiply by 100 to get your answer: 24.5%. That is an astonishingly large increase in receivables given that sales gained only 9.5% (see Exhibit 14.1: $5,376 million divided by $4,910 million, etc.). So sharp an increase in receivables relative to the sales improvement suggests that General Foods bankrolled its customers in 1978. By this we simply mean that General Foods probably was slow in collecting its bills for, say, Sanka coffee, and, as a result, lost interest income that might have been earned had the company been paid promptly. General

Foods, of course, believes it will receive payment on most of its outstanding receivables.

Are any of the bills doubtful and perhaps uncollectible? That's easy to answer. The receivables the company reported are less *Allowances for Doubtful Accounts*. A doubtful account is one the company does not think it will be able to collect. Allowances for doubtful accounts on April 1, 1978 totaled, as you see, $10.8 million — up only 8% (a shade less than sales) from $10 million in 1977. So while overall receivables increased sharply, General Foods apparently believed that most of those receivables were owed it by credit-worthy customers who would pay off. General Foods is a high-quality company itself. A less creditable company might leave one feeling somewhat insecure about the "quality" of the receivables number given that allowances had not increased as fast as the total. A reduction in the "quality" of receivables would simply mean a lesser portion of the receivables reported by a company and expected to be converted into the cash over the coming months will in fact be converted. If such were the case some write-offs against sales (in other words a penalty against profits and a narrower operating profit margin) would be likely as the bum receivables surfaced.

The sharp rise in receivables from 1977 to 1978 must have been costly to General Foods because it meant that the company did not have as much cash in hand as it might have to invest profitably. Its customers had the cash! They invested the cash while General Foods held the paper. General Foods, a giant company, may have consciously decided to finance its receivables as a way to preserve market share. Or perhaps some financial controls weren't as effective as they could have been. But in any event, the sharp rise in receivables relative to sales helps explain the deterioration in the operating profit margin we discussed in the first section.

WATCH THOSE INVENTORIES

Inventories represent another current asset. The inventory account typically breaks down into three categories: *Raw Materials and Supplies, Products in Intermediate Stages of Production, and Finished Products.*

General Foods did not have a significant number of products in the *Intermediate Stages of Production* at the end of fiscal 1978. How do we know? Take a look at the inventory account. No figure is given for that category; it isn't even shown. If there were any products not yet completed, they represented a very small proportion of the inventory account.

General Foods reports its *Finished Product Inventory* and its *Raw Materials and Supplies Inventories*. The finished product inventory was $473.7 million at the end of 1978. The stock of raw materials and supplies totaled $344.1 million. Total inventories came to $817.8 million, a *decline* of $72.1 million from 1977 to 1978. The decline in inventories during a period of revenue growth suggests that the company was more efficiently using its inventory base and as a result, was more productive. This increased efficiency tended to offset the higher costs of carrying receivables.

Take another look at the inventory account. Where did General Foods cut back on its inventories? Was it in the finished products area or in raw materials and supplies? Finished goods actually rose 3.7% to $473.7 million. Raw materials, on the other hand, fell $89.1 million or 20.6%.

It looks on the surface like General Foods very wisely increased the level of its finished goods in order to be able to support demand from the field while cutting back on unnecessary raw materials. That's one conclusion. Another is that it's entirely possible General Foods was unable to get hold of enough raw materials. There's a third: All of the amounts shown on the balance sheet are in dollars, not units, and it's quite plausible that there was a decline in the price of the company's raw materials during the year — which resulted in a falloff in the booked value of the inventories.

Let's go back to Exhibit 14.2 and take a look at the chart of spot green coffee prices once again. You will immediately notice that coffee prices peaked during fiscal '77 and declined steadily through fiscal 1978. The decline was very steep — from something over $3.25 a pound to well under $2.00 a pound. A comparison of the raw materials and supplies accounts with that chart of coffee prices provided by General Foods in its annual report suggests that a major reason the inventory of raw materials declined, including green coffee beans of course, was that prices fell for raw beans. Actual unit volume of coffee beans may well have been stable or have increased from year to year. We have no way of telling with any degree of certainty from the financial statement. But there is one conclusion we can come to, namely that the decline in the price of green coffee augurs well for overall company profitability in the future — at least as long as there's adequate consumer demand for the beverage.

The difference between finished products (like coffee that is ready to be shipped to the grocer) and raw materials (like those green coffee beans) is the value added by General Foods in converting raw coffee beans into consumable items. The value added includes labor costs involved in processing the coffee beans as well as overhead costs, advertising outlays, and plant and equipment expenses. It is only as goods are sold that expenses associated with processing a raw material into a finished product are charged off against sales. Until an actual sale is made, the production costs are *deferred* and carried in the inventory account. The accumulation of deferred charges in inventories is very important. Had General Foods' stash of finished products grown far more rapidly than sales, a hefty portion of the company's operating expenses could have been embedded in inventory and not charged against revenues. That would have masked some of the inventory carrying costs.

It is not uncommon for companies to manage earnings by tinkering with their inventory accounts, especially in unaudited quarterly reports. It's more difficult to fool around with audited year-end accounts. And a company of General Foods' stature would not even consider such a ploy.

The last two items shown as current assets by General Foods, *Deferred Income Tax Benefits* and *Prepaid Expenses,* are miscellaneous current items. *Deferred Income Tax Benefits* are benefits of one sort or another due General Foods from the federal government and payable over the next 12 months. Possibly the company paid some taxes ahead of time; maybe some were in dispute and the company won its argument. . . . *Prepaid Expenses* include any of a number of items that the company decided to pay ahead of time. There are many examples of prepaid expenses such as prepaid royalties, commissions, insurance premiums, supplies for the office and the like. These two items are small in the aggregate, accounting as they do for only 5.9% of current assets.

CHECK THE CURRENT LIABILITIES

Now let's turn to current liabilities. The company has a certain amount of debt that comes due over the next year. This is classified in two places, as either *Notes Payable* or the *Current Portion of Long-Term Debt.* Notes payable, $119.7 million, probably represent bank obligations that must be paid in the months to come. The current portion of long-term debt, $15.7 million, is that portion of the company's outstanding funded (i.e., long-term) debt that is due in the near future.

The sum of notes payable and the current portion of long-term debt, $135.4 million, is the *Debt Due in the Current Year.* It's a pretty hefty chunk of money, equal to 80% of the company's reported net earnings of $169.5 million. But don't get nervous. The company's "cash flow" in 1978 was $239 million ($169.5 million plus depreciation and amortization of $69.5 million). Debt due as a percentage of the "cash flow" was significantly less: 56.6%; and relative to working capital, it came to an even less worrisome 17.9%. (The relationship of current debt to working capital was *also* 17.9% at the time for most companies.) Relative to both its "cash flow" and working capital, General Foods has it made when it comes to paying off near-term debt obligations.

Has General Foods' short-term indebtedness grown too fast? The sum of notes payable plus the current portion of long-term debt in 1978 was $135.4 million compared with $122.7 million a year before, which represents an increase of 10.4% — just a little bit more than the overall boost in sales. There seem to be no problems of any sort in the short-term debt accounts.

Now let's take a look at accounts and drafts payable. *Accounts Payable* are on the other side of the coin from receivables. Receivables represent what others owe General Foods; the accounts payable, on the other hand, indicate what General Foods owes others. You may recall that the company's receivables account increased 24.5%, year over year. In contrast, General Foods had been an excellent customer: Its accounts and drafts payable increased only about 5.3%, from $294.6 million in 1977 to $310.2 million the following year.

The sharp increase in receivables relative to the 9½% boost in sales and compared with the 5% gain in accounts payable indicates that General Foods not only was prepared to finance its customers but was also quite ready to support its suppliers. Why do we say this? Because it let its receivables grow faster than sales while it allowed its accounts payable to increase at only half the pace of sales. When a company does that it penalizes its own earning while assisting both its customers and suppliers. (Industry leaders often provide such a "banking" or support function.)

Management, in the new fiscal year, may move to slow receivables' growth and allow the accounts payable to build up somewhat more rapidly. This would permit the company to finance fewer receivables relative to sales while letting suppliers pick up the tab to some extent for its payables account. Such an action would tend to bolster the profit margin.

The next liabilities item presented, *Accrued Liabilities,* is a big number: $329 million compared with $307 million the year before, up 7% in a year. Accrued liabilities in the current liabilities section are akin to prepaid expenses on the asset side. Accrued liabilities may include wages of employees (on either biweekly or monthly payrolls) who have yet to be paid; interest that has accrued on debt but which has not as yet been forwarded to the bank; or other expenses a company recognizes as having been incurred and which will be paid in the future.

The last current liability reported by the company is *Accrued Income Taxes.* These are taxes owed and payable to Uncle Sam or the state governments. You can bet they will be paid in the near future.

SPOT THE LIGHT ON KEY RATIOS

There are a number of important ratios at which one should take a look when examining the current accounts of an industrial company. Some of the most important of these are: *the Ratio of Cash to Liabilities, the Current Ratio, the Working Capital-to-Sales Ratio, the Inventory-to-Sales Ratio, the*

Accounts Receivable-to-Sales Ratio, and the Accounts Payable-to-Sales Ratio.

We show below these ratios for General Foods' 1977 fiscal year. Before proceeding to the next section, please compare the information in Exhibit 14.4 with the sales data in Exhibit 14.1 (in Section 1) and calculate the related ratios for fiscal year 1978.

Compare the ratios you have come up with for 1978 with those that we computed for 1977. As you do this keep in mind that when a current or working capital-to-sales ratio is too low a company risks running aground

EXHIBIT 14.5
THE VALUE LINE INDUSTRIAL COMPOSITE; FINANCIAL RESULTS, 1973–1977

Assets ($ bill)	*1973*	*1974*	*1975*	*1976*	*1977*
Cash & Equivalents	55.24	58.19	69.27	86.29	87.98
Accounts Receivable	121.20	144.30	144.85	159.14	179.29
Inventories	132.53	171.76	169.55	184.45	204.01
Other	15.06	17.36	17.89	19.16	23.34
Current Assets	324.03	391.61	401.56	449.04	494.62
L. T. Investments	49.97	53.78	63.99	67.94	75.39
Gross Plant	520.44	576.20	619.04	672.95	748.49
Accum Depreciation	235.63	256.11	270.86	291.91	320.32
Net Plant	284.81	320.09	348.18	381.04	428.17
Deferred Charges	5.33	5.83	6.36	6.93	7.87
Intangible Assets	12.23	13.17	13.00	12.81	13.50
Other	10.46	11.03	12.01	13.00	13.96
Total Assets	686.83	795.51	845.10	930.76	1033.51

Liabilities, equity ($ bill)	*1973*	*1974*	*1975*	*1976*	*1977*
Notes Payable	27.46	38.95	28.81	27.58	29.79
Current L. T. Debt	7.04	8.43	9.48	9.56	9.93
Accounts Payable	84.04	108.07	110.48	123.23	140.03
Taxes Payable	22.71	28.57	25.34	31.52	31.97
Other	31.03	37.93	44.28	52.66	61.60
Current Liabilities	172.28	221.95	218.39	244.55	273.32
Deferred Taxes	20.81	25.21	29.95	35.09	40.59
Minority Interest	6.85	8.12	8.67	8.88	9.94
Other Liabilities	20.54	23.61	29.61	33.07	39.14
Total L. T. Debt	126.00	141.65	159.86	170.02	185.77
Conv L. T. Debt	12.12	12.26	12.43	12.20	10.80
Total Pref Equity	17.03	16.59	16.17	16.02	16.36
Conv Pref Equity	14.89	14.32	13.60	13.24	12.22
Common Equity	323.32	358.38	382.45	423.13	468.39
Total Equity	340.35	374.97	398.62	439.16	484.75
Total Capital	466.35	516.62	558.48	609.18	670.52
Total Liab & Equity	686.83	795.51	845.10	930.76	1033.51
L. T. Debt Due, 5 Yr	43.72	53.24	55.11	56.26	59.81

Ratios, return rates	1973	1974	1975	1976	1977
% Cash/Curr Liab	32.1%	26.2%	31.7%	35.3%	32.2%
% Current Ratio	188.1%	176.4%	183.9%	183.6%	181.0%
% Inventory/Sales	15.6%	16.1%	15.3%	14.7%	14.4%
% Acct Rec/Sales	14.3%	13.6%	13.0%	12.7%	12.7%
% Wkg Capl/Sales	17.8%	15.9%	16.5%	16.3%	15.7%
% Gross Plant/Sales	61.2%	54.1%	55.7%	53.8%	53.0%
% Total Capl/Sales	54.8%	48.5%	50.3%	48.7%	47.5%
% L. T. Debt/Capl	27.0%	27.4%	28.6%	27.9%	27.7%
% Common Eq/Capital	69.3%	69.4%	68.5%	69.5%	69.9%
% Equity/Capital	73.0%	72.6%	71.4%	72.1%	72.3%
% L. T. Debt Due/Eq	12.8%	14.2%	13.8%	12.8%	12.3%
% Earned Totl Capl	10.8%	11.1%	9.2%	10.7%	10.8%
% Earned Equity	13.6%	14.0%	11.5%	13.4%	13.5%
% Earned Comm Equity	14.1%	14.4%	11.7%	13.7%	13.8%
% Earned Net Plant	16.2%	16.4%	13.1%	15.4%	15.3%

Share data	1973	1974	1975	1976	1977
Shares, Outstanding (bill)	17.28	17.37	17.55	17.83	18.10
Shares, Diluted (bill)	18.19	18.30	18.49	18.79	18.88
Sales Per Share	49.23	61.26	63.29	70.16	78.04
Cash Flow Per Share	4.36	4.86	4.59	5.40	5.90
Primary E.P.S	2.63	2.98	2.56	3.25	3.56
Dividends Per Share	0.95	1.04	1.05	1.19	1.38
Book Value Per Share	18.71	20.63	21.79	23.73	25.88
Tangible B.V.P.S	17.70	19.54	20.68	22.62	24.70
Avg Annual Price	36.03	27.42	28.35	33.86	32.31
Avg P/E (primary)	13.70	9.21	11.09	10.42	9.07
Avg Annl Divd Yield	2.6%	3.8%	3.7%	3.5%	4.3%

Income statement ($ bill)	1973	1974	1975	1976	1977
Sales or Revenues	850.49	1064.32	1111.10	1251.31	1412.39
Cost of Goods Sold	606.62	778.50	819.26	923.42	1044.86
Gross Income	243.87	285.82	291.84	327.89	367.53
Gross Margin	28.7%	26.9%	26.3%	26.2%	26.0%
Sls. Gen & Adm Exp	122.47	134.94	148.76	166.56	186.20
Operating Income	121.40	150.88	143.08	161.32	181.33
Operating Margin	14.3%	14.2%	12.9%	12.9%	12.8%
Depreciation, etc.	29.54	32.55	35.42	37.71	42.25
Depreciation Rate	5.7%	5.6%	5.7%	5.6%	5.6%
Income After Deprec	91.86	118.34	107.66	123.61	139.08
Margin After Deprec	10.8%	11.1%	9.7%	9.9%	9.8%
Short-term Interest	3.16	5.34	5.01	3.82	4.44
Long-term Interest	8.34	9.87	11.32	12.66	14.27
L. T. Int Coverage	11.6X	12.5X	9.9X	10.4X	10.3X
Other Income	7.75	10.29	10.23	12.18	13.30
Other Expense	1.71	2.52	2.81	2.88	3.32
Equity, Subs Earn'gs	2.39	2.62	2.34	2.97	4.24
Pretax Minority Int	−0.08	−0.07	−0.11	−0.12	−0.11
Unusual Items	−0.04	−0.32	−0.26	−0.12	−1.03

continued

EXHIBIT 14.5 *continued*

Income statement ($ bill)	1973	1974	1975	1976	1977
Pretax Income	88.67	113.12	100.72	119.16	133.45
Pretax Margin	10.4%	10.6%	9.1%	9.5%	9.4%
Cash Taxes	38.26	55.11	48.33	52.93	60.02
Cash Tax Rate	43.1%	48.7%	48.0%	44.4%	45.0%
Deferred Taxes	3.16	4.00	4.74	6.05	6.52
Total Taxes	41.42	59.11	53.07	58.99	66.54
Income Tax Rate	46.7%	52.3%	52.7%	49.5%	49.9%
After Tax Income	47.25	54.01	47.65	60.17	66.91
Minority Interest	−0.84	−1.24	−0.94	−1.07	−1.23
Special Items	−0.16	−0.30	−1.03	−0.36	−0.37
Extraordinary Items	0.38	0.22	0.27	0.72	0.02
Net Income	46.61	52.70	45.94	59.47	65.33
Net Income Margin	5.5%	5.0%	4.1%	4.8%	4.6%
Preferred Dividends	0.81	0.79	0.80	0.80	0.87
Net for Comm Margin	5.4%	4.9%	4.1%	4.7%	4.6%
Net for Common	45.81	51.91	45.14	58.67	64.46

Flow of funds ($ bill)	1973	1974	1975	1976	1977
Beginning Wkg Capl	135.01	151.75	169.66	183.17	204.49
Net Income	46.61	52.70	45.94	59.47	65.33
Depreciation, etc	29.54	32.55	35.42	37.71	42.25
Net Income & Deprec	76.15	85.25	81.36	97.18	107.58
Property Sales	5.09	5.95	6.46	5.88	5.94
Long-term Debt Fin	19.72	28.96	36.93	31.50	29.37
Common Financing	1.89	1.73	3.23	4.08	2.80
Preferred Financing	0.24	0.33	0.68	0.95	1.85
Options	0.39	0.40	0.43	0.70	0.48
Other	7.28	10.00	4.09	10.92	15.16
Total Sources	110.75	132.62	133.18	151.21	163.18
Common Dividends	16.34	17.99	18.48	21.20	24.93
Preferred Dividends	0.80	0.78	0.78	0.78	0.83
Total Dividends	17.14	18.77	19.27	21.98	25.76
Plant Spending	55.00	73.59	74.49	76.14	87.02
Other Investments	6.11	7.39	6.22	8.47	10.19
L. T. Debt Retired	13.23	13.67	19.05	22.13	20.60
Common Retired	2.36	1.10	0.42	1.00	2.43
Preferred Retired	0.17	0.19	0.23	0.17	0.37
Total Uses	94.01	114.71	119.67	129.89	146.37
Ending Working Capl	151.75	169.66	183.17	204.49	221.30
% Cash Flow Payout	22.5%	22.0%	23.7%	22.6%	23.9%
% Net Income Payout	36.8%	35.6%	41.9%	37.0%	39.4%
% Working Capl/Sales	17.8%	15.9%	16.5%	16.3%	15.7%

due to inadequate cash. On the other hand, when the current or working capital-to-sales ratio is too high, the company may not be efficiently using its capital base. Likewise when the inventory-to-sales ratio is too low, the company may not be in a position to satisfy its customers when orders are placed. But when the inventory-to-sales ratio is too high, the company may get stuck with surplus inventory that might have to be liquidated at distress prices. Inventory liquidation occurs when a company shuts down factories and lays off workers in order to sell goods off the shelf (rather than out of production) until the relationship of inventory to sales returns to an optimum level. Remember that when a company slashes inventories due to adverse market conditions, it generally ends up substantially penalizing profitability.

	1978	1977
Cash and Equivalents to Current Liabilities	_____	15.2%
Current Ratio	_____	1.8
Working Capital to Sales	_____	14.6%
Inventories to Sales	_____	18.1%
Accounts Receivable to Sales	_____	9.4%
Accounts Payable to Sales	_____	6.0%

The cash-to-current liabilities ratio is a measure of immediate coverage of obligations coming due shortly. Too low a ratio, *even if* the working capital-to-sales ratio is wide, could mean trouble.

The accounts receivable-to-sales ratio is also a two-edged sword. A runup in accounts receivable indicates that the company is not collecting its bills fast enough and that it is unnecessarily penalizing its profits. An exceptionally low accounts receivable-to-sales ratio could mean the company is actually offending its customers by being overly demanding and losing some market share as a result.

A bulging accounts payable-to-sales ratio may mean the company is offending its suppliers by not paying bills on time and may have trouble purchasing supplies in the future. But, by the same token, it is earning interest on the cash that would have been used to pay bills — or perhaps sidestepping the need to borrow to cover them. Companies will frequently stretch out bills payments when interest rates are high, because it becomes profitable for them to do this despite possible adverse supplier reactions. At such times suppliers, of course, step up their collection efforts and may actually try to charge interest on outstanding bills. A low accounts payable-to-sales ratio suggests that the company is paying its bills and assisting suppliers while giving up the opportunity to earn some interest. It passes that opportunity along to others.

NOW COMPARE THE COMPANY WITH ALL INDUSTRY

We show below related ratios for The Value Line Industrial Composite of 900 companies. Compare the ratios for General Foods in 1977 and 1978 with those for the Value Line Industrial Composite and come to your own conclusions as to what the various current account ratios mean for General Foods. (You may in good conscience compare General Foods' 1978 ratios with the 1977 figures for the Composite because 75% of the company's 1978 fiscal year fell in calendar 1977, the period covered by the Composite.) But in doing so, don't go off the deep end. General Foods in 1978 was an excellent company, one that was financially sound. There are no surprises in the financial ratios, and, quite frankly, two interpretations are possible for every comparison.

	1/1/78	1/1/77
Cash to Current Liabilities	32.2%	35.3%
Current Ratio	1.8	1.8
Working Capital to Sales	15.7%	16.3%
Inventory to Sales	14.4%	14.7%
Accounts Receivable to Sales	12.7%	12.7%
Accounts Payable to Sales	9.9%	9.8%

Section 3: The Balance Sheet — Long-Term Accounts

This section will cover the part of the balance sheet not reviewed in Section 2, namely, Long-Term Assets, Long-Term Liabilities and Stockholders' Equity. Before we proceed with the discussion, please be sure you have completed the short exercise at the end of Section 2 relating to the calculation of some key short-term account ratios. The answers are tabulated below:

ANSWERS TO SECTION 2 QUIZ

	1978	1977
Cash to Current Liabilities	15.4%	15.2%
Current Ratio	1.9	1.8
Working Capital to Sales	14.1%	14.6%
Inventory to Sales	15.2%	18.1%
Accounts Receivable to Sales	10.7%	9.4%
Accounts Payable to Sales	5.8%	6.0%

General Foods, in its balance sheet — which appears in Exhibit 14.4 (Section 2) — identifies three major categories of long-term assets: *Land, Buildings, Equipment; Long-Term Receivables and Sundry Assets; and Goodwill.*

Land, Buildings and Equipment comprise what is known as "net plant." *Net Plant* is the gross value of the company's property, plants, and equipment *less* all accumulated depreciation charges. It is stated at *original cost* less accumulated depreciation of the *original cost* (i.e., it is not shown at *today's* prices). *Gross Plant,* which equals accumulated depreciation *plus* net plant — in other words the original purchase price, is not shown on General Foods' balance sheet but does appear in one of the footnotes. *Accumulated Depreciation* is the sum of the annual depreciation charges for all years — taken against plant and equipment that have not as yet been fully depreciated. Once a plant is entirely depreciated, it is removed from the balance sheet *even though* it may still be in use. . . . Companies have the alternative of showing a complete plant account on the balance sheet (one that presents gross plant, accumulated depreciation and net plant) or just the depreciated original cost value: net plant. In Exhibit 14.6, we show Footnote 3 of the 1978 General Foods' financial report, which displays the detailed breakdown of the gross plant account.

Gross plant of $1,388.5 million consisted of $407.0 million of bricks and mortar (i.e., buildings), $889.2 million of machinery and other equipment, $44.1 million of land, and $48.2 million of construction work in progress.

The current land value is surely significantly higher than $44.1 million. General Foods is a big company and it has been around for a long time; it probably purchased its land years ago at much lower prices than

EXHIBIT 14.6
GENERAL FOODS PLANT ACCOUNT

Land, buildings, equipment	1978	1977
Land	$ 44,141,000	$ 40,097,000
Buildings	407,014,000	395,155,000
Machinery and Equipment	889,184,000	837,659,000
Construction Work in Progress	48,160,000	33,686,000
	1,388,499,000	1,306,597,000
Less Accumulated Depreciation	626,272,000	578,072,000
	$ 762,227,000	$ 728,525,000

now prevail in the marketplace. Also, it may have cost $407 million to erect the buildings the company owns but to replace them at this juncture doubtlessly would cost far more than $407 million. The same is true for the $889.2 million of machinery and equipment.

Construction Work in Progress or *CWIP* represents plant that is in the process of being erected but is not yet on-stream. It is, as a result, not currently being depreciated. About 3.5% of General Foods' gross plant was not being depreciated in 1978, but will be as soon as the facilities are up and running. The proportion of CWIP to gross plant in 1977 was somewhat lower: 2.6%. The sharp 43% increase in CWIP from $33.7 million in 1977 to $48.2 million in 1978 suggests the company is engaging in a big expansion program that will increase its earnings base in the future.

How old are General Foods' facilities? A rough estimate can be made of the youngest they can be on average. *Here's how:* Divide the 1978 depreciation accrual ($67.3 million; see Section 1) into accumulated depreciation ($626.3 million); the resultant — 9.3 years — is the estimated youngest average plant age. Many plants and pieces of equipment have been fully written off over the years and consequently are not included in the depreciation figures. This means General Foods' plants on average are probably over ten years old. The comparable figure for most industrial companies is about eight to nine years. (We figured that out using the data in Exhibit 14.5 in Section 2.) Relatively old standing facilities may explain the 1978 surge in General Foods' CWIP. Management could be trying to catch up! Which means the company may for a while have to contend with start-up costs, significantly higher depreciation charges, and pressure on the pretax and net profit margins.

THERE ARE OTHER NON-CURRENT ACCOUNTS TO EXAMINE

Long-Term Receivables and Sundry Assets of $26.7 million represent the second long-term General Foods' asset. A long-term receivable may be likened to a short-term receivable except that it is due in more than a year. One type of long-term receivable is an installment account stretched out over several years. Sundry assets are miscellaneous ones.

The last asset shown is *Goodwill.* This is an *intangible* asset in contrast to a piece of equipment, which is a *tangible* one. Goodwill arises when one corporation purchases another for more than the value of the acquired company's stockholders' equity. In other words, the net assets received (total liabilities) are less than the buyout price. In a loose sense, goodwill may be considered the value of an acquired company's trademarks, customer contacts, or anything else that might make the company worth more than the value of its assets alone.

You will recall that the asset side of a balance sheet must add up to equal the sum of liabilities and equity on the other side. If you pay more for a company than it is worth on its books, you need a fudge factor when you include its assets on your own books to represent the difference between the net assets received and the purchase price. This fudge factor is known as "goodwill" or the *excess* of purchase price *over* net assets received in a purchase acquisition. (A "purchase" acquisition involves buying assets for cash. A merger involving an exchange of stock is another acquisition technique known as "pooling of interests," but it does not create a goodwill account. Both types of merger accounting are too complex to be covered here.)

The value of goodwill, which in the case of General Foods was $26.3 million in 1978, must be amortized over a period of time — either about 40 years or the useful life of the asset associated with the goodwill. Amortization of goodwill explains why General Foods reports goodwill *less* accumulated amortization. It had amortized a total of $17.7 million of goodwill through April 1, 1978, but has an additional $26.3 million to go. If the food giant acquires another company for cash in the near future and does so at a higher price than the net asset value of the company purchased, its goodwill account will increase and the amount of yearly amortization will rise.

DEFERRED CHARGES ARE IMPORTANT
INTANGIBLE ASSETS TOO

Goodwill is an intangible asset. *Deferred Charges* are another garden variety intangible asset. General Foods does not report any deferred charges on its balance sheet but if it did, we would want to subtract both deferred items and goodwill from stockholders' equity in determining rock-bottom *tangible* equity.

A *Deferred Charge* is a cash outlay the company has made, but — rather than flowing it through the income statement as an expense against sales or burying it in the inventory account — it shows the cost as a long-term asset on its balance sheet and then amortizes it away. (In other words it takes the expense in small doses rather than all at once.) Many deferred charges are legitimate. For example, a company may be involved in a major long-term development program and defer charges until the program begins generating profits. But other deferred charges are not so legitimate. One company we came across some years ago, for example, included a portion of the company president's salary in the deferred charge account. (It ultimately went under.) To be on the safe side — since any deferred charge can result in an immediate write-off should the program or product with which it's associated flop — we suggest that you subtract *all* deferred charges and *all* goodwill from stockholders' equity in determining tangible (i.e., excluding intangible assets) book value.

We'll compute General Foods' 1978 tangible book value momentarily. But first let's answer a question that may have come up while you read through the last paragraph: "When may long-term deferred charges legitimately be included in the inventory account? When not?"

A deferred expense associated with a reasonably assured long-term contract on which the company is receiving progress payments from the customer may be added to the inventory account. Deferred costs on a development project — say a new form of transmission — may not. The most conservative company won't ever show such outlays as non-current assets; it will expense them as incurred. The more conservative a company, the lower its profit margin but the superior the quality of earnings. The reverse is true for corporations that employ liberal bookkeeping methods. In theory at least, the stocks of companies with high-quality earnings command premium P/E ratios.

There's an easy way to measure earnings quality. We won't take the time right now to explain why, but the closer the income tax rate reported to stockholders is to 45%–50%, the greater the income quality — as a general rule.

General Foods' stockholders equity totaled $1,173.8 million at the end of fiscal 1978. Less goodwill of $26.3 million leaves tangible stockholders' equity of $1,147.5 million. The computation of tangible equity is designed to allow one to arrive at an equity or ownership number that is as solid and as "fluffless" as possible.

SPOTTING THE LIGHT ON LIABILITIES

The balance sheet includes, in addition to stockholders' equity and assets, both short- and long-term liabilities. We covered current liabilities in Section 2. The long-term liabilities are our next topic.

Long-Term Debt ($259.8 million) consists of the debt obligations of General Foods coming due in more than 12 months. If you are interested in total company debt outstanding, you must add together long-term debt, notes payable and the current portion of long-term debt. That total was $395.2 million on April 1, 1978. Long-term debt of $259.8 million as a percentage of the total debt stood at 65.7% or about two-thirds at the end of fiscal '78.

A greater proportion of all debt is made up of non-current obligations for the average company: 82.4% (see Exhibit 14.5 in Section 2). This means General Foods may be able to run with less funded debt proportionately than other companies because it is big and a blue chip, or that it really has too much short-term debt and will soon issue a new bond or seek out long-term funds of another sort (perhaps an insurance company loan). Both explanations may of course be valid. If, however, management opts for, say, a debenture issue and rolls short-term debt into long-term debt, then current liabilities will be pared. Working capital (remember: current assets less current liabilities), as a result, would be beefed up — thereby improving the working capital-to-sales ratio; you'll recall from last section's discussion that the working capital-to-sales ratio was a shade on the low side relative to other industrials and had declined modestly from 1977 to 1978.

RESERVES ARE IMPORTANT

General Foods had some miscellaneous long-term liabilities in 1978, just as it did a number of sundry assets: *Other Non-Current Liabilities.*

The third long-term liabilities classification is *Provision for Discontinued Fast Food Operations:* $18.3 million. This is a reserve. A reserve shown on the liabilities side of the balance sheet is an account that represents a previous charge made against income to cover cash outlays that are *anticipated in the future.* (Future charges against income that represent cash outlays *already made* are displayed on the asset side.)

General Foods decided to discontinue some of its fast-food operations. Certain costs will be associated with that discontinuation. At the time it made the decision to shutter part of the fast-food business, General Foods charged tens of millions of dollars against earnings. But it did not spend any money at that time! Instead it established the reserve account. When actual termination expenses are incurred, the company will not need to penalize current income. It will merely reduce the balance sheet provision for discontinued fast-food operations. And you can see that there was a decline from 1977 to 1978 of about $2 million in this reserve account — which means the company spent $2 million in 1978 shutting down fast-food businesses but did not make a charge against income because it had already banked the needed funds. Had General Foods not established the reserve, its stockholders' equity would have been greater by the amount of the reserve: $18.3 million. But earnings then would be directly penalized each year for the continuing drag of winding down these operations. Establishment of the reserve improved the solidity of book value by removing "water" from it.

It is considered conservative and proper acounting for a company to establish a reserve in anticipation of a future loss, when that potential red ink can be identified. General Foods has obviously followed good accounting practices. In addition, by creating the reserve, it has cleared the slate and moved to insure (i.e., buffer or support) future reported earnings.

The last liabilities line is *Deferred Income Taxes.* This account, like the previous one, is a reserve to cover potential future expenses. Most companies, including General Foods, employ *straight-line* depreciation in their stockholder reports but use some form of *accelerated* depreciation methodology in filing income tax returns. The difference between these two accounting methods results in higher depreciation accruals being reported to the Internal Revenue Service than to stockholders. This results in income reported to the taxman being *less* than what's reported to the stockholders. *But the company uses the same tax rate to determine its tax liability in each case!* The difference between greater taxes shown on the stockholder income statement and taxes actually paid represents an extra non-cash charge taken by the company. This non-cash charge goes into a reserve bank: the deferred tax account.

Companies *sometimes* slow down capital expansion programs for a number of years and, as a result, the depreciation reported to the tax collector on an accelerated basis ends up being *less than* the straight-line figure reported to stockholders. (Straight-line depreciation accounting calls for equal charges to be made each year; under accelerated accounting, more is charged off in the early years and less in the later ones.) If that happens to a company that's built up a deferred tax reserve, it will be able to draw down upon the reserve rather than increasing the level of taxes reported to stockholders. In other words, actual cash outlays can in part be offset by non-cash benefits resulting from making withdrawals from the deferred tax account. This process serves to bolster profitability reported to stockholders. The reason a company can do this is that it made the charge for the taxes in the first place. In the case of a growing company like General Foods, it's not likely that depreciation determined on a straight-line basis will ever fall below depreciation computed using the accelerated technique. Therefore the deferred tax account should continue to grow over time.

Whoa! General Foods' deferred tax account dropped $9.1 million during fiscal 1978. Meanwhile the gross plant account swelled $81.9 million. The decline in the deferred account means General Foods bolstered profitability in 1978 by drawing down on its banked reserves — at the same time as it spent heavily on new facilities. Doesn't this contradict the rule that "the deferred tax account should continue to grow over time?" Answer. "yes" and "no."

The company has more than one deferred tax account (see Exhibit 14.7). The depreciation-related account rose — just as it should have according to the thumb rule. Thumb rules, however, are often dumb rules —

EXHIBIT 14.7
GENERAL FOODS INCOME TAX FOOTNOTE

INCOME TAXES
The provision for income taxes consists of the following:

Currently payable:	1978	1977
Federal	$127,386,000	$142,024,000
State and city	20,185,000	20,558,000
Foreign	20,567,000	21,876,000
	168,138,000	184,458,000
Deferred Taxes	(7,038,000)	6,042,000
Income Taxes on Earnings	$161,100,000	$190,500,000

Deferred taxes result from differences between the time that certain revenue and expense items are recognized in computing tax expense for financial statement purposes and when these items are reported for income tax purposes. The following items are components of deferred taxes which are added to (deducted from) income taxes currently payable in determining income taxes on earnings:

	1978	1977
Depreciation	$ 9,254,000	$ 7,713,000
Foreign inventory tax allowances	(15,207,000)	9,530,000
Marketing expenses	2,352,000	(9,342,000)
Other items, net	(3,437,000)	(1,859,000)
	$(7,038,000)	$ 6,042,000

Investment tax credits earned in fiscal 1978 and 1977 were applied as a reduction of income taxes and amounted to approximately $5,100,000 and $6,800,000, respectively.

Income taxes as reported reflect effective tax rates of 48.7% and 51.8% for fiscal 1978 and 1977, respectively, compared to the United States statutory tax rate of 48%. The higher effective tax rates reflect principally state income taxes and non-taxable foreign currency translation effects, offset by items such as differences between United States and foreign tax rates and investment tax credit.

No provision has been made for future U.S. income taxes on the undistributed earnings of international operations since they have been, for the most part, indefinitely reinvested in these operations. At the end of fiscal 1978, such earnings aggregated $149,565,000. If those earnings were distributed, the related U.S. income taxes would be substantially offset by available tax credits.

---

because they aren't all-encompassing. A total of two deferred tax accounts increased in 1978 and two shriveled. The *net* swing in one year was $13 million, from a tax-increasing $6 million figure to a tax-reducing $7 million number. 1978 earnings would have been $156.5 million — or only 2.9% of net sales — had the swing from a deferred tax charge ($6 million in '77) to a deferred tax credit ($7 million in '78) not occurred. Reread the last sentence and take a second look at Exhibit 14.1 in Section 1. Note how important amortization of a reserve can be to income — when it's on the right side of the balance sheet (i.e., the liabilities side).

Have you noticed a pattern that involves all deferred accounts? There's a very important one: Establishment of deferred accounts on the asset side involves actual money already spent but not expensed; *amortization of these accounts will penalize earnings over time.* A buildup of reserve banks on the liabilities side arises from non-cash charges made to income in anticipation of future dollar outlays; *their amortization bolsters income.*

THEN THERE'S THE EQUITY ACCOUNT

We have not yet covered the components of *Stockholders' Equity.* Although some companies have complex equity accounts including preferred stocks, preference stocks, convertible preferred issues and possibly multiple classes of common stock, General Foods' stockholders' equity account consists entirely of one type of common stock. The par value (i.e., the nominal or face value) of the *Common Stock When It Was Issued* to the public was $50.9 million in the aggregate. But that common issue was sold for far more than $50.9 million in the marketplace. The public actually paid $197.5 million. The difference between common stock issued, which is its par value, and the price paid by the public is known as *Additional Paid-In Capital.* General Foods gives us that figure: $146.6 million.

Retained Earnings are the sum of all the earnings of a company in all the years of its existence less all of its dividends in all years. That figure was $1,012 million at the end of General Foods' fiscal '78. It is identical to the retained earnings reported in its statement of retained earnings in Exhibit 14.1 (Section 1).

General Foods has repurchased some of its common stock and as of April 1978 held these shares in its treasury. It may use treasury stock to allow officers to exercise options or for sales to employees; the shares may also be issued in the case of a merger. The cost of buying up the treasury stock in the open market was $35.7 million at the time it occurred. This sum must be subtracted from the total of common stock issued, additional paid-in capital, and retained earnings in the calculation of total stockholders' equity. Reason: The treasury shares are not in the public's hands.

You will frequently find that companies with high capital turnover ratios also have hefty debt-to-equity ratios. Utilities, oils, steels, and railroads are all examples. Some — like electric utilities — can get away with lots of leverage; they're regulated monopolies. Others cannot, and have been hurt, like the steels and railroads.

Compare General Foods to The Value Line Composite of 900 companies (Exhibit 14.5 in Section 2). How does the company stack up? Does it work its plant base as hard as industry in general? How leveraged is it relative to other industrials? How much would its long-term debt-to-equity ratio rise if the company increased its long-term debt-to-total debt ratio from 65.7% to the industry norm: 82.4%? What would happen to the working capital-to-sales ratio? This time, answers to the exercise and to the following questions are not provided.

THE SCHEMATIC BALANCE SHEET

The balance sheet can be graphically depicted. The left-hand side is comprised of current assets and long-term assets. The right-hand half consists primarily of current liabilities, long-term liabilities and stockholders' equity. This conceptual framework can be simplified by subtracting current liabilities from current assets. Result: working capital, which is also known as "net current assets." If we do this, then the asset side of the balance sheet consists primarily of working capital and net plant while the liabilities and equity side is made up mostly of long-term debt and equity. It looks, in other words, very much like the picture in Exhibit 14.8.

Remember this equation: Working capital plus net plant equals long-term debt plus equity. Or working capital plus net plant equals total capital. (Total capital in its simplest form consists of long-term debt and stockholders' equity; for a utility that hasn't any working capital, net plant tends to approximate total capital.) . . .

Current assets	Current liabilities							
	Long-term debt	=	Working capital	Long-term debt	=	Total capital		
Net plant	Stockholders' equity		Net plant	Stockholders' equity				

EXHIBIT 14.8
A SCHEMATIC BALANCE SHEET

IT'S EXERCISE TIME AGAIN

We'll wrap up with another short General Foods exercise. The first three ratios represent various capital turnover ratios. (A capital turnover ratio is any major long-term asset or liability related to sales.) The last two are measures of leverage, which is the degree to which a company borrows rather than issues stock to finance growth. A company that can regularly earn more on borrowed funds than it pays out in interest charges has successfully leveraged itself.

The lower the various turnover ratios, the more efficiently a company probably is working its plant or equity base. A low ratio means fewer investment cents are required to generate a dollar of sales. (General Foods, for example, required about 26½ cents of gross plant to come up with one sales dollar is fiscal 1977.) But if, say, the gross plant-to-sales ratios gets too low, it may mean the company has run out of capacity and can't meet customer orders; also, if it's too low, marginal fully depreciated plants may have to be fired up. A low ratio may also stem from a runup in dollar sales resulting from a price explosion; old plants — stated at "old" historical prices — can also wear down the ratio. Which means the company will have to invest to expand its capacity. A high ratio relative to the past means factories are probably standing idle; carrying poorly utilized equipment is very expensive and can result in plant shutdowns, write-offs, or divestitures. But sometimes a marketplace crisis can occur that'll require use of idle facilities. Coal mines, for examples, had oodles of surplus capacity until the dawn of the energy crisis.

Gross plant-to-sales ratios vary from company to company and across industry lines. They're really most meaningful when studied over time for one company and against its industry. Industry-to-industry comparisons can also be meaningful. Capital-intensive utilities may require a couple of dollars of invested plant or capital to generate a buck of business. An industrial company may require only 50¢. A service company, even less. General Foods is an industrial company. Why do you think its gross plant-to-sales ratio was low? Do you think the high price of coffee may have been a factor? Or that its plants appear to be older than the average and, as a result, stated in cheaper dollars than the average?

Leverage is an important concept. The more a company amplifies its equity base by borrowings, the wider profits will be — so long as pretax earnings cover interest costs. The more leverage, the fatter profits can be in good times. Leverage, however, cuts both ways. Too much debt relative to capital — which is the same as saying too little equity supporting capital — can in bad times throw companies into the red, and even force them to go belly up. (Note: The sum of the debt-to-capital and the equity-to-capital ratios is always 100%.)

	1978	1977
Gross Plant to Sales	—————————	26.6%
Total Capital to Sales	—————————	24.6%
Equity to Sales	—————————	22.1%
Equity to Total Capital	—————————	80.1%
Long Term Debt to Total Capital	—————————	19.9%

PART IV

CASES ON POLICY, STRATEGY, AND PLANS

Introduction:
A Guide
to Case Analysis

Although it has become customary in policy textbooks to provide a guide to case analysis, all that is possible are some guidelines to introduce you to basic elements of casework and to help you avoid the more common mistakes in preparing cases. Casework is perfected through practice.

One thing we soon notice about cases is that they require an approach different from that of problem solving in familiar management disciplines like accounting, finance, marketing, personnel. The bases for differences are twofold.

1. Answers are not absolute. Cases cannot be solved in the same sense as an accounting problem. Two students may have completely different solutions to the same case yet both receive the same grade. This is because the emphasis is on the process of decision making rather than its product. Because real complex decisions depend on future conditions — and since different interpretations of future conditions are possible — problem solving relies on developing a solid case from imperfect information subject to

varying degrees of uncertainty. This in turn requires a disciplined method for assembling and interpreting the available information, and then drawing reasonable conclusions. The more incomplete or uncertain the information, the more emphasis is placed on the rigor of the analysis.

2. Answers generally require a multidisciplinary approach. A typical solution to a case situation may demand inputs from such disciplines as accounting, finance, and organizational behavior. This departure from the formal structure of a single discipline often confuses beginners. Accustomed to learning a more or less standard approach to decision making within the parameters of a particular discipline, one must now learn to broaden his or her scope in order to deal with many variables associated with several disciplines. Integration of information becomes more relevant than depth of knowledge in one area. This in turn requires a structured framework for analyzing a great amount of unstructured information.

Students may decide to develop a personal approach to casework or to rely on one of the so-called scientific methods. The five steps below are typical of the scientific method. They do not go much beyond what seems intuitively obvious, but they help in establishing at least a minimum framework for analyzing cases. With experience, we develop our own instincts for problem solving. For now, this is a convenient device for breaking any problem into a logical sequence of steps for systematic analysis.

1. Clearly define the central problem(s) or objective(s).

2. Assemble available information to address each major element of the problem.

3. Analyze these elements through a systematic means of evaluation.

4. Develop logical alternatives.

5. Support your recommended solution(s).

Each case may differ in important respects from every other case. Each solution therefore tends to follow a different pattern. That is sufficient reason to avoid giving a packaged answer to a sample case. Such a tactic gives the appearance of conveying more information than it does. It also can give a false sense of assurance. Although the suggested solution is designed to fit tightly the illustration used, students generally find such examples serve poorly as a standard approach for the many types of cases they confront. Thus the emphasis here is on supplying a few general guidelines instead of offering a specific solution to a sample case. Keep the following points in mind.

1. Be specific. Where possible, use factual evidence to support arguments. For instance, "improve cash position" is too general. "Reduce inventory by 20 percent in order to increase cash by $1,000" is better.

2. Include your own research, exhibits, graphs, tables, and extending details where applicable. Most cases furnish sufficient rather than exhaustive information. Students are in competition with each other on cases. Those best prepared will supplement the facts of the case with relevant outside details when possible.

3. Develop a coherent story. Use assumptions where necessary. The ultimate test of a good case is its ability to convince the audience of its logic (in this case your policy professor or fellow students). A tightly structured case analysis should lead a person from one point to the next, building to the final solution or recommendation.

4. Participate in class. Personal involvement is most important. It is usually a factor in the grading process. It is also the only way students can maximize their learning experience. It is clearly preferable to learn to articulate a point of view in the classroom than be embarrassed when asked for an opinion in a business environment.

5. Read your completed case. Is it convincing? What grade do you objectively think it deserves? Have you developed your arguments in a logical sequential manner, always keeping in mind the overall problem or objective? Would you be comfortable presenting this report orally before your professor and fellow students?

Aldo, Inc.*

Background

Aldo, Inc. is a high-technology company started by two graduates of the Massachusetts Institute of Technology. It is not too different from the many "brain" factories around the suburbs of Boston. Its original product had been sold to the government, which supplied the first contract to start Aldo in business and subsequently ordered a number of carry-on contracts to help the company grow from a standing start to over $4 million in sales by 1980.

The sole product of the company was an advanced, specially designed computer for estimating trajectories, speed, and reentry characteristics of NASA's various space projects. Although the space program had gone through a number of budget crises, the Aldo company had thus far managed to escape major project cancellations. They were in fact now working on an advanced version of their original design, with greatly improved performance characteristics and with only a moderately higher price tag.

Problem

At this juncture the two founders, Jack Harder and Bill Tripp, felt it was a good time to evaluate the future for Aldo, Inc. Both of them were still young, in their early thirties. A staff of fifteen engineers worked for them in an informal "family" style of management; many of the employees were former students recruited from neighboring universities and not much younger than Jack or Bill. All operations were carried on in a two-story

---

* Prepared by Milton Leontiades.

EXHIBIT 1

Income statement
(000s omitted)

	1980	1979
Sales	$4179	$3960
Cost of goods sold	2758	2613
Gross profit	$1421	$1347
General and administrative expenses	878	832
Operating profit	$ 543	$ 515
Provision for income taxes	270	253
Net profit	$ 273	$ 262

Operating results

Year	Shipments (#)	Sales (000s)	Net profits (000s)
1980	42	$4179	$273
1979	40	3960	262
1978	34	3230	305
1977	22	2090	160
1976	19	1805	110
1975	12	1020	70
1974	4	300	nil

modern brick building (leased), of which Aldo used a floor and a half and rented out the rest of the space.

A minimum marketing effort was required because each computer was designed to exacting specifications, and each model could vary slightly from every other one to meet the customer's unique requirements. The "salesmen" were highly qualified engineers who spent only a portion of their time with customers, most of whom are equally qualified NASA personnel.

Over the years the company has managed to show respectable profits, as shown in Exhibit 1. Aldo is in fairly liquid position (see Exhibit 2) with a comfortable ratio of cash to current liabilities. Thus far growth has been financed internally and Jack and Bill would prefer not to borrow long term, and to keep any bond financing to a minimum. But they would not be afraid to borrow if they felt the opportunity was right.

EXHIBIT 2
ALDO, INC. BALANCE SHEET
(000s omitted)

Assets	1980	1979
Current assets		
Cash	$ 405	$ 345
Accounts receivable	442	377
Inventory	103	88
Total current assets	$ 950	$ 810
Fixed assets		
Plant and equipment	$ 510	$ 490
Less accumulated depreciation	102	98
Net plant and equipment	$ 408	$ 392
Total assets	$1358	$1202

Liabilities and equity		
Current liabilities		
Accounts payable	$ 130	$ 158
Notes payable	105	101
Accrued payroll	98	63
Accrued taxes	159	151
Total current liabilities	$ 492	$ 473
Equity		
Common stock	$ 100	$ 100
Retained earnings	766	629
Total equity	$ 866	$ 729
Total liabilities and equity	$1358	$1202

Strategic Alternatives

In a brainstorming session with three other senior people, Jack and Bill decided on an overall policy of lessening the company's dependence on NASA. In recent years variations in NASA's budgets, and subsequent cancellations and postponements of contracts, have convinced them that they should not keep all their eggs in this basket. Among the alternatives they have considered are the following:

1. *Develop a small computer for the home consumer market.* The concept is for a simple computer that consumers could learn to operate at

home. Jack and Bill have been aware of a growing trend for computers to have simplified programming and operating characteristics so that the average person, with a few hours of instruction, could perform a number of routine operations at home. A number of practical applications that the computer could perform are calculation of interest terms on a mortgage or consumer loan; simple forecast formulas used to project sales or earnings — for personal investments or business purposes — as well as tie-ins with a number of computer data banks where specialized information could be accessed, for a fee, for a variety of consumer purposes. Jack and Bill were particularly intrigued by an article describing the success a national consumer electronics chain was having with a simple computer model of the type they envisioned.

Jack and Bill figured that the technology demands of a switchover to a simple, small consumer-oriented computer would be easy for their engineering staff. Ed Blaski, one of their best engineers, could be appointed to handle the development of the new model. From rough calculations, Bill, Jack, and Ed estimated that they could develop a product far superior to any on the market, and priced at the "top of the line" segment of the market.

The initial outlay for equipment, design work, and parts would be about $150,000. An additional $55,000 to hire three engineers to work on the project was anticipated. In order to achieve breakeven, an estimated 300 models would have to be sold annually at approximately $1,600 each. Breakeven would be expected to occur around the middle of the third year.

2. *Be acquired by another company.* A number of larger companies had been interested in acquiring Aldo in the past. Jack and Bill were sure they could find a suitable company to merge with if that was the direction in which they wanted to go.

Both Jack and Bill had mixed feelings on being acquired. On the one hand, they wouldn't have to worry as much about financing the things they felt could be done to expand and diversify the business. The responsibilities and workload had been extremely heavy in the past few years and both partners would welcome sharing the burdens with a larger, better-resourced parent.

However, Bill and Jack enjoyed the freedom to make their own decisions. They started their business by identifying an opportunity and moving quickly to capitalize on it. They were afraid that in a bureaucratic organization they would lose personal freedom and flexibility in decision making.

In all, both of them could find pro and con arguments on a merger. If the terms were right, they would not preclude the possibility.

3. *Buy their building.* When Bill and Jack started Aldo, they negotiated a ten-year lease on a building in good condition, well located and with more space than they needed. They anticipated their future expansion

would require additional space and, in the meantime, they were renting out the extra space to help defray expenses.

In the original lease agreement, Bill and Jack had retained an option to purchase the building at any time during the term of the lease for $600,000. Due to inflation, the market value of the building was roughly 50 percent above this figure. Although the lease had three more years to run, if Aldo exercised its option to purchase now it could realize a sizable capital gain while still enjoying future appreciation on the building. A mortgage could be obtained for 75 percent of the purchase price. Interest and other carrying charges would be partially offset by the rental income from the quarter of the space that would remain rented. The net effect would be to increase Aldo annual pretax income by $8,000.

4. *Pay dividends*. Aldo, Inc. had never paid any dividends. As majority shareholders, Jack and Bill preferred to plow earnings back into the business. They were also concerned with the irregularity of contracts with NASA and preferred to avoid a dividend policy they might not be able to maintain.

However, Bill and Jack have also considered the possibility of going public. Both of them feel that a modest dividend policy might help the sale of shares to the public and make ownership in the company more attractive. "We've been so busy building the business we haven't paid much attention to such matters," said Bill, "but it may be a worthwhile move at this time." "I agree," said Jack, "it could also help us in raising future capital if we adopted a policy of steady dividend payments."

Conclusion

All members of the ad hoc executive committee agreed to make these four items the central issue for the next board of directors meeting. They felt confident that the board's input would be useful in helping them decide the appropriate strategic direction for the company.

Assignment

1. Evaluate each of Aldo's indicated alternatives; conclude with the comments you would make if you were a member of the board of directors.

Richmond Brick Company*

Dick Wood, director of industrial relations, and Sam Verney, controller of the Richmond Brick Company, met in the dusty, noisy courtyard encircled by the company's one-story office building, the shipping dock, a warehouse and the railroad track. It was a hot August morning in 1976. Stopping at the Coke machine, Dick offered Sam a Coke.

"Sam," he said, "I'm getting concerned that our Policy Committee hasn't met for over a month. I've got my job evaluation program and EEOC audit report and some other items that need discussing. And we haven't made progress on our critical issues list."

Sam scuffed some dust over the courtyard bricks and replied thoughtfully, "Well, we'll be ready to discuss the preliminary budget numbers with

---

* This case was prepared by Robert N. White, Babcock Graduate School of Management, Wake Forest University.

the president in a few days. But budget numbers are one thing — and specific department plans for achieving them are something else. Why can't we get down to cases on our action plans?"

They were joined by Vance McGee, vice-president for manufacturing. "Hey, guys," Vince said in his bluff manner, "Why don't we just call our own management meeting here and now, and set some corporate objectives? Then I can get some decisions on the new plant project." The three men looked at each other unhappily, finished their Cokes and moved on to their offices.

Background of the Company

Richmond Brick Company, founded in 1935 by Simon Todd, began with a small, one-kiln plant in Richmond, Virginia, site of the present executive offices. The company grew steadily, adding brick plants, expanding facilities and moving into concrete block as well.

In 1976, Richmond operated six brick plants and four concrete block facilities with a total annual capacity of 305 million bricks and 8.4 million 8-inch concrete block equivalents.

It was the largest brick manufacturer in the Virginia/North Carolina region. This region produces about 16.2 percent of all this country's brick. In 1976, Richmond shipped 186 million, or 19 percent of the regional market.

All of the company's plants were located near major population centers and along interstate highways which go through the middle of the Southeast, the fastest growing area of the United States. Due to freight and transportation costs, plant location is a very important factor to every brick manufacturer. However, since U. S. brick production is concentrated in only a few clay soil regions, there is considerable rail shipment into non-producing areas.

The regional market accounted for 78 percent of Richmond's sales; the remaining 22 percent of sales were distributed throughout the eastern half of the United States. Richmond marketed its brick and block through its own direct sales force of 12 salesmen and 3 sales managers, who work on commission. In 1976, the average age of the sales force was 48 years old.

Five major customers accounted for a total of 9 percent of sales. No other customer account represented more than 1 percent of total sales. Home builders and contractors represented 80 percent of Richmond's sales, while 20 percent was sold through distributors and dealers. The mix of residential vs. nonresidential sales has been shifting in recent years and was roughly 50–50 in 1976.

The company owned a substantial acreage of clay and shale land in Virginia and North Carolina, sufficient to supply its forecasted needs for a half century in the future. This provided a significant competitive advantage in raw material cost (they have owned the land for many years); and in quality of their clay resources.

The company used natural gas to fire its kilns. While costly, this fuel was still available in early 1976. The company could convert to oil without interrupting production, but fuel costs would rise about 8–10 percent.

The Industry

The brick and concrete block industry was dominated by numerous regional and local companies. In 1976, of an industry total of 8.1 billion bricks produced nationally, 2.1 billion (value $90 million) were produced in Richmond's regional major market. Because the product is an undifferentiated one, meeting price competition, service and personal contacts were all important marketing issues. This market had the highest forecast of growth of all regional brick markets.

A perceptible trend was evident in that large companies, both those already in the industry and from outside, were acquiring regional brick and block companies. General Shale, Justin Industries and Boren Clay Products Company were examples of acquiring companies which have employed this route to growth.

Richmond's comparative ratios placed it right at the upper range of the better-run companies in the industry.

Starting with the business downturn in 1973, the construction industry in this region suffered through its worst period in many decades. Richmond, like its competitors, laid off workers (but no management people); they cut costs in every conceivable way; price-cutting was used to try to keep the kilns operating.

Exhibit 1 provides more detail on the industry and factors significant to its future.

EXHIBIT 1
INDUSTRY TRENDS: EXCERPTS FROM RICHMOND MARKETING DEPARTMENT, MARCH 1976

The economic outlook facing the industry was summarized by an industry economist in these terms:

> The 1976–77 period reflects the most difficult recovery (from 1974–75 recession) that housing has undertaken in the postwar era. The money market squeeze could tighten uncomfortably as the Federal Reserve continues the fight on inflation. Mortgage rates should hover a little below historic heights.

continued

EXHIBIT 1 *continued*

> New housing will remain disconcertingly expensive. And the consumer will still be trying to get over the worst scare he had since the '30's. The housing industry will have to live with some of these problems for a long time to come. The home building climate has changed, perhaps forever. Two million starts a year may prove the peak, not the norm.

The forecasts indicated that the Southeast would be the most favored section of the country with respect to housing growth. Richmond's brick shipments had traditionally paralleled closely with national private housing starts. A trend toward more emphasis on the industrial and commercial sector of the construction market was identified by industry researchers. Richmond's sales emphasis was still heavily oriented toward residential and the institutional (education, municipal, church) sector.

The economic analysis also pointed out that brick usage over the long term was declining in relation to the trends of housing starts and per square foot of wall and floor. It was believed that two factors significant to these trends were periodic brick capacity shortages in times of high demand, and skillful promotion of competing materials.

The industry economists pointed out these favorable indicators:

1. Family incomes are rising faster than construction costs of one family homes.
2. Brick prices have not increased as much as the price of other building materials.
3. Wage rates for bricklayers are not increasing faster than other building trades.

Richmond's own survey through its sales force reflected the following factors of changes in marketing in its region.

1. More and better media advertising and promotion from competition.
2. Expansion of direct sales forces by competitors.
3. Continued emphasis on new brick colors and new block surface designs.

The Industry
Brick and block companies have historically offered products of those materials only. The main efforts at product development were in textures, sizes and colors of brick; and in surface design of block. Richmond had a fairly wide range of these product offerings. However, some competitors had achieved limited market acceptance with brick and block prefab panels.

Expansion and diversification by industry companies took the form of either geographic expansion to compensate for business decline in a regional area; adding ready-mix to block operations; centralizing brick and block manufacturing, and combining this with marketing of other "hard materials" (frames, doors, glass, non-wood panels, roofing, etc.). This latter type of diversification had been discussed on several occasions by Phil Todd with his management group; but no study of costs or marketing implications had been made.

Competitive strategies to improve position focused on deviations from price levels, more effective selling and service, limited use of advertising and promotion.

Presidency of Mr. Simon Todd

Mr. Simon Todd was a dominant, driving force in the development from a one-kiln plant to leadership in the Virginia/North Carolina brick industry. A tough, abrasive individual, he kept on top of even the smallest details of company operations. Several times a day he would sally forth into the center courtyard to reprimand a worker or collar a passing salesman. He had no truck with new-fangled ideas such as organization charts, salary administration programs, computer controls and the like. His managers were trained to bring him the problems and implement his decisions — right away. The company grew and prospered under his leadership.

Mr. Todd's son, Phil Todd, started with the company directly out of college. He showed an aptitude for both manufacturing and sales. Under his father's tutelage, Phil learned the business from the ground up. However, he was treated like all the other managers; and accorded Mr. Todd the same respect and obedience that was demanded of all company managers.

In 1974, Mr. Todd elevated Phil to president and chief executive officer. He gave Phil his paneled office overlooking the courtyard in which a picture of the stern-faced founder hangs behind the president's chair. Mr. Todd continued as chairman of the Board.

Profiles of the key management people as of 1976 are shown in Exhibit 2. The organization chart is in Exhibit 3.

EXHIBIT 2
PROFILES OF TOP MANAGEMENT PERSONNEL

Phil Todd
President   He was 46 years old with over 24 years of service to the company. He went to work for the company after graduating from college, and had worked in every major operation of the company. Phil Todd was quite active in the industry groups. He was also a director of several companies and a bank.

George Semlow
Treasurer   He joined the company as an accountant in 1950 and served as assistant secretary, assistant treasurer and controller prior to becoming treasurer in 1964. George had a B.S. degree in accounting from the University of Virginia, and was a Certified Public Accountant. He was also a graduate of the Executive Program at the University of Virginia. He was 58 years old.

Elwood "Teddy" Shanaberger
Vice President-Sales   Joined Sampson Brick & Tile Company (Division of Richmond Brick Company) as sales manager in 1964. In 1966, he became regional sales manager. He became general sales manager in 1969. From 1950 to 1964, Teddy was a district sales manager for Merry Brothers Brick & Tile in Georgia. He had an A.B. degree from Clemson University and had done graduate work at Washington and Lee. He was 56 years old with 13 years of service.

continued

EXHIBIT 2 *continued*

Vance McGee
Vice President-Manufacturing   He joined the company in 1961 as an industrial engineer and moved up through manufacturing supervision. He was made vice-president in 1974. He attended South Carolina University and the Executive Program at the University of Virginia. He visited European plants in 1965 and had played an extensive role in bringing automation to the company.

Richard "Dick" Wood
Vice-President of Industrial Relations   Dick was employed by Richmond in 1967 as director of industrial relations and was promoted to vice-president in 1970. For several years he also served as division manager of the Richmond plant. Previously he worked as director of industrial relations for Hanes Hosiery Company. He was a graduate of Hamilton College. He was 50 years old with 7 years of service.

Sam Verney, Jr.
Controller   Sam joined Richmond Brick Company as controller in November 1975. Prior to this move, he had held senior accounting positions at Warner & Swazey Company and White Motor Company. He started in public accounting with Arthur Anderson. Sam was 44 years old.

Harry Cannon
Vice President-Raleigh Division   Harry had been employed by the Company since 1938. He had worked as a salesman, shipping and payroll clerk, loading foreman, burning superintendent and plant superintendent before becoming plant manager in 1966. He had a degree in business administration from Clemson University. He was 60 years old.

The Outside Group Moves In

Early in 1974, Phil Todd was surprised to receive a phone call from a Harold Ornstein. Mr. Ornstein introduced himself as vice president-corporate development of General Time Corporation, a conglomerate company headquartered in New York City. He explained that his company was interested in investing in Richmond Brick Company.

Phil Todd, who had only nominal stock in his own name, relayed the inquiry to his father; and was somewhat taken aback at the extent of the interest shown. Family estate concerns were the motivating factor.

Within two months, the discussions moved into an active stage and in July 1974, a deal was consummated under which General Time took over voting control of Richmond and paid off the Todd family. Exhibit 4 details the financing program. This reflects a pattern employed by General Time

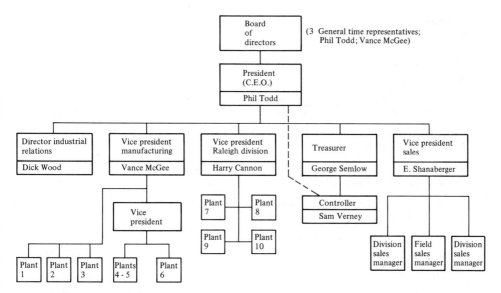

EXHIBIT 3
RICHMOND BRICK COMPANY ORGANIZATION CHART
AS OF JULY 1, 1975
Source: Chart drawn from discussions by Stanley Rutledge, June 1975.

in previous acquisitions. Phil Todd and six other members of Richmond management were offered (and accepted) the opportunity to buy stock in Richmond.

General Time did not seek any changes in Richmond's management and stated they considered their purchase to be an investment. However, they indicated they expected to "actively monitor and participate in the future development of the company." By this, they meant: receiving informal and formal reports on progress; requiring long- and short-term plans and budgets; and providing financial advice. General Time had stated to Phil Todd that they believed in supporting their acquisitions with capital where the new funds invested could return an ROI higher than the present return on total capital employed in that acquired company. Also, that they expected growth in revenue and profit over the long term from all their acquisitions.

EXHIBIT 4
FINANCING PROGRAM

The $26,815,000 required to finance the acquisition to be raised through the issuance of the following securities:

7-Year Senior Bank Notes repayable in equal installments from 1975–1981 @ 1% over prime	$ 9,000,000
16-Year Senior Notes repayable in equal installments from 1981–1990 @ 10%	9,600,000
16-Year Senior Subordinated Notes repayable in equal installments from 1981–1990 @ 10%	5,550,000
6½% Non-Cumulative Convertible Preferred Stock convertible into 300,000 shares @ $4 per share	1,200,000
Common Equity from the sale of 505,000 shares @ $3 per share	1,515,000
Total Raised	$26,865,000

Present shareholders to be paid off from corporate cash in amount of approximately $1,700,000.

General Time arranged the following sequence of steps in order to place the debt incurred by the above financing on the books of Richmond Brick Company:

1. General Time established a new subsidiary corporation called RBC Corp., which issued the convertible preferred and common stock (above) and received payment for this stock.
2. RBC Corp. borrowed from financial institutions on the notes (above).
3. RBC Corp. purchased the assets of Richmond Brick Company.
4. RBC Corp. changed its name to Richmond Brick Company; and the old Richmond Brick Company changed its name to Richmond Liquidating Company.
5. Richmond Liquidating Company paid off the stockholders in the old Richmond Brick Company; and, a year later, went out of existence.

Developments in Management Starting in Mid-1975

In May 1975, Dick Wood, director of industrial relations, received his MBA degree from the graduate school of management at a nearby university. Dick concluded that the concepts he had been studying could, if properly applied, help Phil Todd and the Richmond Brick Company return to its former prosperous condition and grow over the longer term. He brought Stan Rutledge, his professor in corporate planning and business policy at the school, and Phil Todd together for discussions. These led to Stan Rutledge becoming a consultant to the company.

The consultant's initial step in this arrangement was to conduct a two-day retreat in planning concepts attended by Phil Todd and six of his top men. This session brought out a number of points:

1. The only formal planning going on was one-year budgeting, initiated the year before.
2. The management group evidenced a strong desire to get on with the job of improving the company; but was not at all sure what should be done first.
3. The management members were hesitant to be critical of company policies and even to take a stand on future directions of the company. Many side-long glances were cast at Phil Todd during the discussions. He spoke very little.
4. A strong need for a management development program was voiced.
5. There were no organization charts or management job descriptions available.

The group agreed to undertake steps proposed by Stan Rutledge in order to institute a planning system in the company. These were summarized as follows:

1. Develop data on market and competitive trends, advances in processing technology, fuel availability and other pertinent factors in the external environment.
2. Identify, in specifics, the company's abilities and deficiencies in marketing, production, controls and other functional areas.
3. Assessing internal capabilities in the light of developing external trends to identify strengths and weaknesses; and provide the basis for establishing realistic objectives and strategies for the long-term.
4. Developing the annual business plan and conforming the budget to the business plan.

Each of these, and their requirements for information development and analysis, were discussed in some depth at the retreat. Phil Todd spoke briefly on the importance of pushing forward with the tasks outlined.

During this same period (mid-1975) Phil Todd was taking other steps to strengthen the management team. First was a series of seminars in management concepts conducted by the university faculty and attended by 26 members of Richmond management. The seminars, conducted in late 1975 and early 1976, generated considerable enthusiasm both because of the pertinence of the concepts to Richmond's problems; and because of the evidence they seemed to signify of top management's interest in these concepts.

Phil Todd was advised by the faculty members that his management people would, in all likelihood, as a result of the seminars, be putting pressure on him for changes in company policies and operational methods. However, in discussion with Stan Rutledge about this issue, Phil repeated an earlier-voiced concern, "When Simon Todd was running things, none of these fellows had a chance to make their own decisions. Now I'm trying my best to get them to make decisions — and they won't do it. They just wait for me to tell them what to do. I hope they'll start now to do their jobs without asking me. However, I'm not sure they all can change. Mr. Todd left a strong imprint on a couple of them."

Phil also created a Policy Committee of the executives reporting to him, which was to meet monthly. Phil did not put himself on this committee, offering this comment, "I'll come in when they invite me." He also set up a Management Advisory Committee, composed of 30 members of management, to meet monthly. This was conceived of as primarily a sounding board and communications agency.

Late in the fall of 1975 a new member of senior management was added, Sam Verney, as controller. Sam, age 44, had had considerable professional experience in other companies, both larger and smaller. His enthusiasm and evident good judgment soon developed respect for his opinions among the management group. Early on, Sam encountered a disturbing situation. He had understood that his boss would be Phil Todd. Upon joining the company, he found that the treasurer believed that he was Sam's boss. Six months later, this question of who was his boss was still not entirely clear despite two discussions with Phil Todd on the topic.

Sam Verney quickly moved to develop and push through the Policy Committee a series of accounting policies to replace the outmoded, informal practices that were causing confusion and inefficiency. These moves established some needed groundwork; but Sam had his sights set on a couple of major targets — a modern inventory control program; and a computer-based accounting system. Both of these, in his opinion, were badly needed. Sam was an enthusiastic supporter of the long-range planning concept.

During the winter/spring of 1976, business was picking up but not reaching the company's budgeted levels. A salary and wage freeze which Phil Todd imposed in September 1975, was continued into the spring. Top management pressured for increased selling effort. A sales incentive program was developed in the fall and applied in December and January 1975. This program was dropped when two salesmen achieved compensation levels above that of the top marketing executive.

Progress on Long-Range Planning

The long-range planning activity, initiated with enthusiasm at the management retreat, was lagging. Completion of the 1975 budget had tied up the management group generally. Then Stan Rutledge had difficulty mustering staff help to assemble external analysis data on markets, competition, economics, technological developments, etc. This effort was finally launched in late December 1975 and targets for its completion were moved back several times (see Exhibit 5, the planning calendar). It was finished in March 1976.

Since Rutledge had set with Phil Todd a revised target of completing objectives and strategies by mid-April 1976, he launched the internal analysis step while the external analysis effort was still in progress. Members of the management group were asked to submit their views on key issues in the functional areas of the company (manufacturing, sales, personnel, etc.); and on organization and general management. The results of this survey highlighted the major problems of the company. A list of the major problem areas is shown in Exhibit 6.

Setting Corporate Objectives

The stage had finally been set by May 1976 for establishing corporate objectives. Before meeting with the Policy Committee, Stan Rutledge had several informal discussions with Phil Todd to clarify his views on the future of the company. Phil's concept of the company's future emphasized these issues:

1. Growth in sales volume. But, more important, profitability.

2. Changes in marketing methods to match trends in the construction industry. For example, the full-line building supply houses were gaining position rapidly.

3. Streamlining the organization and freeing him of detail.

Stan Rutledge felt that these informal discussions had been helpful in getting Phil to voice his opinions on where the company should be heading. But he was concerned that Phil didn't seem to base his views on the external environment data that had been prepared by the Marketing Department, nor on the weaknesses brought out by the internal analyses. In fact, some of Phil's views seemed to ignore the realities of the problems identified by his own management group in the internal analysis survey.

A meeting with the Policy Committee to define company objectives and strategy was tentatively scheduled by Phil Todd for late June. But further delays developed due to an EEOC audit; loss of a plant manager; and announcement that the company, a major user of fuel, would get no natural gas after September 1976.

EXHIBIT 5
RICHMOND BRICK COMPANY PLANNING CALENDAR (FISCAL YEAR IS SEPT. 1–AUG. 31)

1975 Sept.	Oct.	Nov.	Dec.	1976 Jan.	Feb.	Mar.	April	May	June	July	Aug.
1	2			3	4	5		6			7

Steps in planning process

1. Explain planning to managers
2. Develop external environment data
3. Analyze internal capabilities
4. Assessment
5. Develop objectives and strategies (long range)
6. Develop action plans (1-year plan)
7. Finalize budget

Source: Presented at management retreat, June 1975, by Stanley Rutledge.

EXHIBIT 6
CORPORATE POLICY COMMITTEE REPORT ON MAJOR PROBLEM
AREAS DERIVED FROM THE SUMMARY OF STRENGTHS
AND WEAKNESSES (JUNE 8, 1976)

1. The organizational structure of the company needs to be defined and communicated. Responsibilities and corresponding authority also need to be defined and communicated.

2. Programs in management development, training, and management recruitment are needed to insure proper utilization of manpower.

3. Corporate goals and objectives should be defined, and assignment of responsibilities for short- and long-range planning is needed to attain these goals.

4. Development of a purchasing policy is needed to achieve maximum savings at the local and corporate level.

5. Establish policy and procedures for production planning, scheduling, and inventory control.

6. Establish an incentive compensation plan for salaried employees using the Management by Objectives concept.

7. Develop policy and procedures for the control and coordination of trucking and transportation.

8. Establishment of a corporate preventive maintenance program.

9. Develop a quality control policy giving this department new and stronger positions.

10. Establish methods and responsibility for product pricing to achieve maximum profits.

11. Establish better and more effective procedures for communications.

Present Situation — Early August 1976

Sam Rutledge, the consultant, was puzzled about his progress in introducing planning. It had taken a full year since June 1975 to move through the ground-laying stages of the company's first planning cycle. The management meeting on objectives and strategies was still not firmly scheduled.

The budgeting process, under Sam Verney's direction, was moving steadily forward. September 1 was the target date for finalizing the budget. Shortly thereafter, a meeting was planned with the bankers on the loan repayment schedule. Operations were at 85 percent of capacity, a level that would normally be producing reasonable profits, but the debt service requirements were draining the cash flow. Exhibit 7 provides the financial data as of this time.

EXHIBIT 7
COMPARATIVE BALANCE SHEETS, RICHMOND BRICK COMPANY
(amounts in thousands — 000s omitted)

	Period ended									
	7/31 1976	*9/30 1975*	*9/30 1974*	*7/31 1974*	*12/31 1973*	*12/31 1972*	*12/31 1971*	*2/28 1971*	*2/28 1970*	*2/28 1969*
Current assets										
Cash or equivalents[a]	$ 843	$ 915	$ 795	$ 2,786	$ 4,854	$ 6,481	$ 6,021	$ 4,092	$ 3,381	$ 4,220
Receivables — net	3,311	2,471	2,661	3,558	2,355	2,571	2,607	1,931	2,133	2,364
Inventories	3,777	4,334	4,689	3,873	2,645	1,857	2,151	2,835	2,698	1,932
Prepaids and other	102	101	84	81	48	8	29	6	29	39
Total current assets	8,033	7,821	8,229	10,298	9,902	10,917	10,808	8,864	8,241	8,555
Fixed assets — net	18,833	20,175	21,156	12,830	11,657	8,180	7,899	7,577	7,914	7,838
Other assets	567	615	806	547	766	564	405	331	329	338
Total	$27,432	$28,611	$30,191	$23,675	$22,325	$19,661	$19,112	$16,772	$16,484	$16,731
Current liabilities	$ 4,050	$ 3,855	$ 5,418	$ 3,050	$ 2,237	$ 1,694	$ 2,420	$ 1,472	$ 1,661	$ 2,355
Long-term notes	22,760	24,638	23,303	168	120	321	521	723	819	1,055
Stockholders' equity	622	118	1,470	20,457	19,968	17,646	16,171	14,577	14,004	13,321
Total	$27,432	$28,611	$30,191	$23,675	$22,325	$19,661	$19,112	$16,772	$16,484	$16,731

[a] Represents cash in checking accounts, savings accounts, certificates of deposits and marketable securities.

EXHIBIT 7 *continued*
STATEMENTS OF INCOME, RICHMOND BRICK COMPANY
(amounts in thousands — 000s omitted)

	Period ended									
	7/31 1976a	9/30 1975	9/30 1974b	7/31 1974c	12/31 1973	12/31 1972	12/31 1971a	2/28 1971	2/28 1970	2/28 1969
Net sales d	$19,824	$18,423	$ 3,395	$13,271	$24,519	$22,277	$17,778	$14,910	$15,114	$14,981
Cost of sales	15,481	13,915	3,129	9,824	15,922	14,643	11,322	10,494	10,359	9,930
Gross profit	4,343	4,508	266	3,447	8,597	7,634	6,456	4,416	4,755	5,051
Selling, general and administrative expenses	2,081	3,339	701	2,134	3,915	3,270	2,638	2,887	2,791	2,529
Operating income (loss)	2,262	1,169	(435)	1,313	4,682	4,364	3,818	1,529	1,964	2,522
Interest expense	1,995	2,593	475	11	29	35	44	57	83	98
Other income (expense)	237	72	(11)	146	441	287	152	227	155	203
Income (loss) before taxes	504	(1,352)	(921)	1,448	5,094	4,616	3,926	1,699	2,036	2,627
Income taxes	—	—	—	597	2,031	2,169	1,805	800	962	1,274
Net income (loss)	$ 504	$(1,352)	$ (921)	$ 851	$ 3,063	$ 2,447	$ 2,121	$ 899	$ 1,074	$ 1,353

a Ten months
b Two months
c Seven months
d Net of discounts, allowances, and delivery costs

EXHIBIT 7 *continued*
**STATEMENTS OF CHANGES IN FINANCIAL POSITION,
RICHMOND BRICK COMPANY**
(amounts in thousands — 000s omitted)

	Period ended									
	7/31 1976	9/30 1975	9/30 1974	7/31 1974	12/31 1973	12/31 1972	12/31 1971	2/28 1971	2/28 1970	2/28 1969
Source of funds										
Net income	$ 504	$ —	$ —	$ 851	$ 3,063	$ 2,447	$ 2,121	$ 899	$ 1,074	$ 1,353
Initial capitalization			2,438							
Depreciation, depletion and amortization	1,112	1,341	312	717	1,665	1,317	1,022	1,251	1,373	1,423
Deferred taxes and other	311	402	159	219	(6)	66	234	—	24	71
Decrease in working capital			3,972	417	1,560					
Increase in long-term debt	44	1,395	24,300a	171	—	—	—	—	—	—
Total	$ 1,971	$ 3,138	$31,179	$ 2,375	$ 6,282	$ 3,830	$ 3,377	$ 2,150	$ 2,471	$ 2,847
Application of funds										
Net loss	$ —	$ 1,352	$ 921							
Increase in working capital	1,781	1,155				837	998	809	381	1,203
Capital expenditures	137	473	28,445	1,890	5,172	1,608	1,697	915	990	1,067
Dividends			1,291	363	743	572	392	326	392	392
Payment of long-term debt	53	60		122	200	200	200	94	237	158
Purchase of treasury stock						398				
Other	—	98	522	—	167	215	90	6	471	27
Total	$ 1,971	$ 3,138	$31,179	$ 2,375	$ 6,282	$ 3,830	$ 3,377	$ 2,150	$ 2,471	$ 2,847

a Could be included in "Initial capitalization" of new company.

Explanatory Notes, Richmond Brick Company for Various Periods Ended As Shown

1. The company was on a fiscal year ending February 28 through February 28, 1971. The periods ended February 28, 1969, February 28, 1970, and February 28, 1971, are for full fiscal years (twelve months).

2. A change to a calendar year was made in 1971. The period ended December 31, 1971, is for ten months. Periods ended December 31, 1972, and December 31, 1973, are for full fiscal years.

3. Sale of the company was consummated on July 31, 1974, and the transaction represented a sales/purchase of assets. The period ended July 31, 1974, is for seven months.

4. The new company adopted a fiscal year ending September 30 and the period ended September 30, 1974, is for two months. A full fiscal year is represented for the period ended September 30, 1975.

5. The ten months ended July 31, 1976, is the most recent data available for the current fiscal year which will end September 30, 1976.

For the second year, the budgets were not being backed up with either marketing or manufacturing plans since action plans were not scheduled for development until after the objectives and strategies had been outlined. Thus, attainment of budget targets for revenue and costs were based on commitments by the respective division heads, but not supported by specific plans. The Policy Committee had not met for over a month. Their top priority issue — the need for clarification of organization responsibilities and authorities — was resting with the president. Phil Todd had requested job descriptions from his top people in May and was to review these, and feedback changes and clarifications to the incumbents. He had not provided this feedback.

In discussing with Stan Rutledge the potential for cost reduction in the company, Sam Verney commented on the performance of a competitor, Triangle Brick Co. "Triangle," Sam said, "just reported year-end figures reflecting a 30 percent increase in sales, and significant improvement in gross margins." Stan responded, "How does that compare with Richmond?" "Well," Sam said, "our sales and gross margins were flat, with a 4 percent price increase during the year. Triangle had an 8 percent price increase. They also had a new highly-automated brick facility they haven't put on stream yet — and still they increased sales and margins! We seem to be pricing low and falling behind on manufacturing costs. What's even worse, the latest industry figures show our market share has dropped 3 percentage points in two years — from 22 percent to 19 percent. We're still #1 in market share by several percentage points but the competition is moving up."

Stan and Phil Todd had confined their discussions primarily to long-range planning steps. On the infrequent occasions when the discussion got into management effectiveness, Phil spoke rather harshly about the ineffectiveness of several of his key people. When Stan asked him what action he planned to take, Phil turned the discussion to other matters.

Phil was meeting every two months with Harry Crowder, the General Time executive assigned to monitor Richmond. These meetings focused on financial review and outlook; but little advice was offered. So far there was no indication of pressure for changes in Richmond's management approach.

Several members of top management had recently contacted Stan Rutledge hoping he could help in generating needed decisions on organization and long-term direction of the company. Those who had invested in stock at the time of the takeover were particularly concerned.

A Phone Call

On August 22, Phil Todd had a phone call from Harry Crowder's secretary. She said Mr. Crowder wanted an appointment to meet at Phil's office on

August 24. She also passed the message that the subject for discussion was to be "company strategy."

Questions and Assignments

1. Discuss policy and strategy formulation undertaken by Richmond Brick Company since its acquisition by General Time. If you were to chair the forthcoming meeting on "company strategy," what would be the major items on your agenda? (Assume the role of Stan Rutledge.)
2. Evaluate, and make recommendations, on the agenda items identified in Question 1.

Winter Wonderland*

In September 1963, Philip Scott, a sophomore in college, found himself in a position to acquire the assets and manage the operations of Winter Wonderland — a public ice skating rink. Although Scott had little experience in business, he believed through hard work and enthusiasm he could make a success of this enterprise.

History

The ice skating rink was built in 1957 as part of the Deauville Hotel — then, the newest and largest (670 rooms) luxury resort hotel on Miami Beach — in its desire to create a unique tourist appeal. Located in the lower lobby of the Deauville, covering over 6,000 square feet, including 60 feet of glassed frontage, Winter Wonderland was the first commercial ice skating rink, not only in Miami Beach, but the entire state of Florida.

Since its inception in 1957, through 1963, the ice skating rink, while providing a promotional advantage to the Deauville Hotel, was a constant source of problems. It was a leased concession with the lessee providing the equipment and accessories necessary for skaters and the Hotel providing the refrigeration necessary for maintenance of the ice. The cost of keeping the ice frozen, at temperatures ranging from $-6°$ to $11°$ F., were approximately $12,000 a year. This cost was absorbed by the Hotel, as the raison d'être for the rink was free ice skating for hotel guests. Income was, therefore, entirely dependent upon local residents and tourists of other hotels.

---

* This case was prepared by Eric H. Shaw as the basis for class discussion rather than to illustrate either effective or ineffective handling of an administrative situation.

Copyright © 1973 by Eric H. Shaw. Reprinted by permission.

The low level of revenues provided by these markets was reflected in seven changes of leases between 1957 and 1963. Further, there were frequent periods of time when no rent or only partial payment of rent was provided to the Hotel.

In mid-1963, Philip Scott became acquainted with Andre Taussig, the current operator of Winter Wonderland. Mr. Taussig was at this time also producing Frolics on Ice, an ice skating show, and had arranged for a South American tour. He wished to divest himself of responsibility for the skating rink and the debts he had incurred in its operations in order to devote full time to his tour. The rental fee for the privilege of operating the skating rink had gradually dropped from an original $500 per month to $200 per month under Taussig's lease. At this time rent was $400 in arrears.

Initial Arrangements

The Deauville Hotel was concerned with continued operations and partial recovery of their ice maintenance costs. Due to the unsatisfactory rental payments and the casualness with which leases were broken in the past, the Hotel welcomed a change of management, but they were not anxious to grant Scott an immediate lease. Rather, the Hotel required continuous monthly payments of $200 rental and receipts to be recorded daily by their internal auditing staff. The purpose of this was to determine the feasibility of ever obtaining satisfactory payment of rent and the maximum amount, or of the possibility of placing the skating rink under direct hotel management.

For a no-cash down payment, Scott agreed to repay Taussig, on a monthly basis, for the balance of cost on 150 pairs of rental ice skates. Further, Scott agreed to repay various miscellaneous bills incurred by Taussig. The total of these payments were about $1,500. The furniture owned by Taussig was retained by him; and the hotel provided 100 chairs and twenty-five occasional tables for the convenience of skaters and onlookers.

In summary the arrangements were:

1. Rent to be paid the Deauville at $200 per month and receipts to be monitored. Furnishings and linen service to be provided by the Hotel free of charge.

2. Taussig to receive monthly payments of $75 over a period of one year. In addition, approximately $200 of outstanding debts were to be paid as they came due.

3. The $400 back rent to be paid on a feasibility basis by Scott, with the implicit understanding that repayment and satisfactory performance would result in reinstatement of a leasing contract.

At the time of these negotiations the unique appeal of ice skating in Miami Beach had vanished. In 1961, the Fountainbleu Hotel was completed

— surpassing the Deauville as the largest hotel (1,000 rooms) in the city — featuring its own ice skating rink. Further competition was developing across Biscayne Bay in Miami, where a much larger commercial ice skating rink was nearing completion. There was even an ice skating show being performed in nearby Dania as a dinner attraction.

When Scott took over operations in September, the following schedule had been in effect: Daily sessions from 3:00–5:00 P.M., and 7:00–9:00 P.M.; and weekends included an additional 9:00–11:00 A.M. session. Rates were $2.00 for skating. As this was the beginning of the tourist season, there were mostly hotel guests using the facilities — free.

Marketing

To stimulate local interest and attract more business, Scott made many changes over the next few months. First, there was a separation of the $2.00 skating charge into an admission fee and a skate rental fee. Admission would continue to be free for hotel guests; however, skate rental fees would be charged. This was done after considerable discussion with, and approval by the Hotel management. Second, reduced rates were given to local students, and shorter, more numerous sessions were initiated. This resulted in the schedule shown in Exhibit 1.

Additional promotional efforts included a discount book of ten admissions for the price of six, family discounts, mothers' and fathers' days, and reduced group rates for parties of ten or more.

Private ice skating instruction, which had been offered at $5.00 to $7.50 per half-hour previously, was continued with the acquisition of a professional skating instructor from the dinner show in Dania. Group instruction was introduced at $2.00 an hour per student for ten to fifteen students per class.

Advertising was undertaken in the "What to Do on the Weekend" sections of local newspapers; and Scott obtained a discount on radio spots from an FM station broadcasting from the Deauville Hotel. Additional publicity was gained through the use of free admission passes to television telethons, charities, and hospitals.

A small crisis arose when Scott had vending machines delivered to the rink. The independently leased restaurants, also located in the lower lobby, and the hotel dining room complained this would affect their businesses. In an amiable discussion with the Hotel management, Scott was allowed to keep the popcorn, candy, and hot drink machines, but the cigarette and sandwich machines were removed.

Scott also renovated the "pro shop" to include sales of skates, skating apparel, and accessories, all obtained on consignment. He believed these

EXHIBIT 1

Daily: Monday thru Friday

1:00 P.M.	to	3:00 P.M.
3:30 P.M.	to	5:30 P.M.
7:00 P.M.	to	9:00 P.M.

Saturday, Sunday, and holidays

10:00 A.M.	to	11:30 A.M.
12:00 noon	to	1:30 P.M.
2:00 P.M.	to	3:30 P.M.
4:00 P.M.	to	5:30 P.M.
7:00 P.M.	to	9:00 P.M.
10:00 P.M.	to	12:00 midnight

Fees

Admission		Skate rental
$ .75	children	$1.00
.75	students	1.00
1.50	adults	2.00

sales, as with the other programs he initiated — aside from revenue considerations — would promote local interest, as the purchasers would have a commitment to the use of the merchandise. Furthermore, only admissions and skate rentals were monitored receipts.

In February 1964, the rock singing group the "Beatles" were making their United States debut on the Ed Sullivan Show being broadcast live from the Deauville Hotel. Scott wanted to cash in on the publicity windfall this would generate. While hundreds of teenagers were awaiting the arrival of the Beatles at Miami International Airport, Deauville Hotel was being cordoned-off to restrain the thousands of teenagers wishing to glimpse their recording idols' arrival at the hotel.

Scott took advantage of the situation by assuring that local police would admit anyone wishing to use the ice skating rink's facilities. This allowed hundreds of teenagers access to the hotel, and two sold-out sessions for Scott. Gross receipts for the day exceeded $1,000. On the following day, the Beatles were invited to a doors-locked private ice skating session. While they were being filmed by national television, hundreds of people strained to see them through the 60 feet of glass partitioning. From this publicity, Scott estimated revenues increased by 100 percent over the next several months.

Many repairs became necessary after the new year. The guard railing made of wood was deteriorating and new rubber mats were needed for the floors. The Hotel would not make these repairs and Scott refused to undertake them without a lease.

In May 1964, after eight months of satisfactory rental payments — including Scott's repayment of Taussig's $400 back rent — the Deauville Hotel and Scott agreed to a one-year lease at an annual rental of $4,800. This was higher than the Hotel's average return for the past six years; although it still represented a loss of $600 per month on ice maintenance costs. Scott was confident that increased profits could be maintained, enabling him to justify the doubling of rent.

Current Operations

Admissions and skate rentals had increased dramatically. Sales of ice skates and accessories, as well as instruction were increasing steadily. Vending machines were adding a small, but constant revenue; and Scott had two new ideas he was planning to implement.

Since the reduced group rate to parties of ten or more was attracting many birthday parties to the rink, Scott began to provide food and have these parties catered. Again, an altercation between the Hotel's dining services and Scott arose. This was resolved by the Hotel doing the catering, although at substantially higher rates than could be obtained privately.

Scott also introduced a package arrangement with other hotels and motels whereby their guests would be provided with free admission. This was done through discounted blocks of 100 to 500 admission passes at 50 to 60 percent of the regular price. This allowed other hotels to advertise free ice skating for their guests. Although the Deauville had no legal recourse to this action, and was faced with a fait accompli, they were nevertheless bitter — leading to strained relations between Hotel management and Scott.

New Opportunity

In late March 1965, a guest of the Deauville, Burton Littenhouse, President of Stubber and Burton, Ltd., of Bristol, England, a manufacturer of ice skates, approached Scott with the possibility of importing and distributing their ice skates in the United States. This venture was appealing because Stubber and Burton had no outlets in the U.S., had a fine product which could be obtained at a low cost, and had the potential for large profits.

Scott readily agreed to consider the feasibility of this venture and to further correspond with Mr. Littenhouse after Littenhouse's return to England.

Looking further into the Stubber and Burton offer, Scott learned that import duties would be minimal if the skates and blades were shipped separately and assembled in the United States. He realized these ice skates could be attractively priced with skates of comparable quality. Stubber and Burton had agreed, if Scott undertook the wholesale distribution, to initially provide the skates on a consignment basis. This would reduce Scott's investment to shipping charges, import duties, and assembly costs.

Crisis Situation

On April 2, 1965, the Deauville Hotel informed Scott that the lease would be renewed, but at an increased rental of $1,000 per month, or 250 percent. The lease's expiration on April 30 left Scott little time to negotiate this decision.

In a meeting with the Hotel management on April 12, the Deauville manager stated his position. The rink was no longer a unique proposition and could sustain its own operations. This was due in part to competing ice skating rinks, but mostly because of the availability of free skating for the guests of other hotels through the medium of free admission passes.

Scott took the position that the increased popularity of the rink, particularly the use of it by other hotel guests, benefited the Deauville. Also, his use of advertising always mentioned the Deauville Hotel by name. This, he emphasized, gave the Hotel a considerable promotional advantage. He also stated his outside activities, which were expected to generate new sources of revenue, made necessary the hiring of additional employees, raising operational costs.

While the meeting failed to reconcile the conflict and no compromise was reached, both parties resolved to consider the rental structure at a subsequent meeting.

As he considered the situation, Scott reasoned he was dealing from a position of strength. First, he didn't believe the Hotel would close the rink because of its use in the Deauville's promotional program. However, some uncertainty did exist as Scott had learned of a former feasibility study utilizing the rink's 6,000 square feet for convention rooms; but this did not seem likely to him.

Second, Scott didn't believe the Hotel could find a suitable replacement in the event they retained the rink without him. A new lessee would incur initial costs of at least $2,500 (150 pairs of rental skates at $15.00 per pair) which would probably be prohibitive, not to mention the one thousand a month rent. Furthermore, the Hotel had been receiving regular

EXHIBIT 2
INCOME STATEMENT FOR THE YEAR ENDED APRIL 15

	1965	(Projected) 1966
Admission revenue		
General public	$ 9,810	$11,480
Private parties	1,090	2,350
	$10,900	$13,830
Skate rental		
General public	9,675	10,400
Hotel guests	3,140	3,990
Private parties	2,535	3,500
	$15,350	$17,890
Other revenue (instructions, vending machines, etc.)	5,800	6,900
Total operating revenue	$32,050	$38,620
Operating expenses		
Utilities	$ 3,600	$ 4,000
Payroll expenses (no payments to Scott)	7,500	10,000
Insurance expenses	945	1,000
Advertising expenses	450	1,000
Maintenance & repair	1,315	2,000
Administrative expense	1,100	1,500
Rental expense	4,800	12,000
Payments to Taussig	600	—
Miscellaneous expense	400	500
Total operating expense	$20,710	$32,000
Net income (before payments to Scott)	$11,340	$ 6,620

rental payments and would not chance the situation which existed with prior operators.

Using pro forma income statements and balance sheet data (see Exhibits 2 and 3), Scott attempted to determine maximum affordable rental fees under existing operations. He also considered the effects of reducing costs, particularly wages to employees; and the cost-benefit aspects of developing other sources of revenue.

EXHIBIT 3
BALANCE SHEET FOR THE YEAR ENDED APRIL 15

	1965	(Projected) 1966
Current assets		
Cash	$ 1,225	$ 1,000
Inventory	200	200
Accounts receivable	200	250
Prepaid advertising	85	150
Prepaid insurance	445	450
Prepaid rent	200	1,000
Total current assets	$ 2,355	$ 3,050
Fixed assets		
Skates	$ 900	$ 900
Accumulated depreciation	(300)	(540)
Sound equipment	500	500
Accumulated depreciation	(167)	(300)
Sundry equipment and furnishings	225	250
Total fixed assets	$ 1,158	$ 810
Total assets	$ 3,513	$ 3,860
Liabilities		
Accounts payable	$ 454	$ 600
State sales taxes	321	290
Prepaid ticket subscriptions	225	600
Wages payable	144	—
Total liabilities	$ 1,144	$ 1,590
Payments to proprietor		
Previous retained earnings	$ 2,369	$ 2,369
Net income	11,340	6,620
Adjusted balance	13,709	8,989
Withdrawals by Scott	(11,340)	(6,719)
Balance retained earnings	$ 2,369	$ 2,270
Total liabilities and retained earnings	$ 3,513	$ 3,860

Facing internal problems with the Hotel and external problems with competition, Scott wondered if he should continue operating the ice skating rink or independently pursue the Stubber and Burton offer.

Assignment

1. What would be your advice to Scott? Support your recommendations as
   fully and factually as you can.

The Consumer Magazine Industry*

Introduction

The consumer magazine industry has survived periods of gloom and doom and very bleak times. A few heralded "deaths" of popular magazines in the late 1960s and early 1970s punctuated the severe crunch of the industry, caught between spiraling costs and increased competition from television for advertising dollars. The business recession of 1974 further squeezed advertising and circulation. However, since 1975 the picture for the industry has considerably brightened. Readers apparently hadn't deserted magazines, but their interests had changed. So did the approach of a number of successful new magazine ventures that replaced those which had failed. Their focus shifted to special rather than general interests; they were tailored to carefully defined market segments rather than mass circulation. It is by no means sure that the magazine industry is on a permanent new uptrend of prosperity, but it was definitely a much different, and healthier, industry in the late 1970s than it was in the preceding decade.

Rise and Fall of Individual Magazines

LOOK, LIFE AND THE SATURDAY EVENING POST

Not too long ago top magazines like *Life, Look,* and the *Saturday Evening Post* were folding; seemingly nobody could make money publishing magazines. The *Saturday Evening Post* was the first of these three to go under, in 1969. Readership had dropped off dramatically. Aimed at an older

---

* Prepared by Milton Leontiades. Based in part on materials from the *Morgan Guaranty Survey* (November 1977 and February 1979), a publication of the Morgan Guaranty Trust Company of New York. By permission.

generation, the *Post* failed to keep up with the changing times. Attempts to change the *Post*'s image were too late, and management too torn by dissension. Soon afterward *Life* and *Look* experienced a downturn in circulation and advertising revenues, and they also went under. *Look* stopped publication in 1971 and *Life* at the end of 1972. The reasons in both cases were similar.

Preparation, printing, and circulation expenses of the magazines escalated, forcing sharp increases in the newsstand prices. The higher prices in turn led to buyer resistance. With accompanying drops in newsstand sales and subscription renewals, advertising revenues fell off. By the early 1970s, competition from television had also eaten into the magazine's revenue base. Plunged into debt in the final year of publication and with even bleaker predictions for the next year, the managements decided to discontinue operations.

Paradoxically, *Look* and *Life* are also illustrative of the new vitality in the magazine industry. The "new" *Look* and *Life,* that is. The new *Life* magazine features big pages, big pictures, high-quality paper, and superb color. This time the magazine is attempting to target a smaller, more affluent audience willing to pay top prices. *Look* began its new edition in early 1979 with an issue published every other week.

NEW MAGAZINES

Although *Look* and *Life* have been rejuvenated, the theme of the new magazine trend is best captured by the special-interest, defined-market formula designed to appeal to specialized audiences as diverse as joggers and pot smokers. Specialized magazines keyed to leisure or personal interests have existed for many years, of course. But with the demise of one mass-circulation magazine after another, specialization became synonymous with survival. Rather than a circulation numbers game, specialized magazines offered advertisers a select, identifiable audience — one that commanded higher advertising rates. The rush was on. One statistic tells the story: more than one hundred new consumer magazines have been started every year since 1973. And each one has sought a special audience.

If you are a surfer there's *Surfing.* If you like to play paddle tennis you can subscribe to *Paddle World.* If you like dogs but love German shepherds you can get your own magazine: *German Shepherd Dog Review.* Are you a fireman or merely interested in firehouse activities? Pick up *Firehouse Magazine. Retirement Living* had an obvious but vague market, so the name was changed to *50 Plus,* a specific market of 56 million people. And so it goes, almost endlessly, with a magazine for nearly every interest.

General Health of the Industry

As previously indicated, the dire predictions for the consumer-magazine industry of just a few years back have been shown to be false. Magazines are now gaining ground on the other media in the competition for advertising dollars. Circulation figures are also increasing strongly and there have been numerous startups in this revitalized industry.

Part of the cause of this new vitality in the industry is the same factor that helped to cause the slump, namely, television. Television emerged in the 1950s as an advertising competitor, and the competition proved too great for many magazines over the years. Recently, however, the cost of television advertisements has risen so much that many companies have shifted a good deal of their advertising to other media, with magazines receiving a good portion of the rerouted advertising dollars.

On a cost-per-thousand of audience reached, only radio can show a slightly lower increase in prices during the 1960–78 period (see Exhibit 1). In terms of unit price trends, magazines have demonstrated the most modest increases over the same period (see Exhibit 2). Meanwhile, the major competitor, television, jumped its cost-per-thousand advertising rates dramatically in 1977 and 1978. It had reached the point in 1977 where a 60-second commercial on prime-time television — measured in cost-per-thousand — was only a bit cheaper than the cost-per-thousand for a full-page, four-color advertisement in many magazines. As recently as 1972,

EXHIBIT 1
MEDIA COST-PER-THOUSAND TRENDS
(1967 = 100 for all media)

	1960	1970	1972	1973	1974	1975	1976	1977	1978a
Magazines	93	106	112	109	113	120	125	132	143
Newspapers	88	115	122	126	135	154	169	183	197
Network tv	86	108	105	114	120	126	149	174	194
Spot tv	79	99	104	109	112	119	147	157	166
Network radio	110	96	96	95	94	98	111	127	141
Spot radio	81	102	102	106	108	114	122	130	136
Outdoor	81	117	130	136	142	151	161	173	183
Composite	87	109	111	118	124	136	152	166	178
National	87	107	108	114	119	127	144	159	173
Local	86	112	118	122	129	146	161	173	185

a Estimated

Source: Advertising Age, September 25, 1978, from data developed by McCann-Erickson, Inc. Reprinted by permission.

EXHIBIT 2
MEDIA UNIT PRICE TRENDS
(1967 = 100 for all media)

	1960	1970	1972	1973	1974	1975	1976	1977	1978a
Magazines	73	109	110	110	115	122	127	136	150
Newspapers	83	115	123	128	140	160	176	192	209
Network tv	74	113	125	140	151	160	189	223	250
Spot tv	69	105	117	127	135	145	181	195	207
Network radio	100	101	105	105	106	112	128	147	165
Spot radio	82	107	109	114	119	125	135	146	155
Outdoor	64	125	145	155	166	178	192	207	221
Composite	78	111	120	126	136	149	168	185	202
National	75	110	119	126	135	145	166	185	202
Local	82	113	121	126	137	154	171	186	202

a Estimated

Source: Advertising Age, September 25, 1978, from data developed by McCann-Erickson, Inc. Reprinted by permission.

television's cost-per-thousand compared with magazines' cost-per-thousand was much lower (less than $4 for a 60-second spot as against $6 for one four-color page in magazines). Predictably, advertisers began showing new interest in other media. Funds began to be diverted into print and radio, with magazines getting most of the benefit from shifts in the media mix.

Beyond the fortuitous lift from higher television pricing, the magazine industry has taken some positive steps of its own to strengthen its competitive status in the media world. Three major conceptual changes stand out:

1. *Editorial specialization.* This approach has enabled magazines to sell advertisers a select consumer group. As a consequence, advertising rates have been freed from any direct correlation with overall audience growth, and many magazines have been removed from direct competition with television.

2. *More aggressive pricing.* Specialized magazines of editorial quality have bred reader loyalty, which has enabled the publications to make substantial boosts in prices charged to newsstand buyers and home subscribers. Circulation revenues are no longer merely an addendum to advertising revenues.

3. *Opening up of local advertising.* The market for local advertisements, traditionally the domain of newspapers, has been successfully penetrated by metropolitan and regional publications. Among many examples: *New York Magazine, Texas Monthly,* and *Washingtonian.* While such inroads are unlikely to make any serious dent in newspaper advertising dollars, the trend does represent a new market for magazines.

Readership Demographics

One of the basic strategies for a successful new magazine is to target its audience. As mentioned earlier, the shift from general to special-interest magazines has been a major trend in the latter part of the 1970s. As part of such a strategy it is obviously important to segment the market to which you wish to appeal. The increase in health-consciousness, and in particular in jogging as a means of healthy exercise, for example, has developed a natural market for new "jogging" magazines, of which there are now several titles.

Although the bare statistics of readership demographics on income, age, sex, and so forth seldom provide the necessary insights by themselves for a successful magazine venture, defining the market is a critical initial step in a successful strategy. As an aid there are abundant data with which to work. Indeed, the problem is not the lack of data but the ability to develop relevant insights from the great mass of data available.

For instance, a now familiar observation is how the age composition of the population is changing. Exhibit 3 shows the overall shifts by age groups for three decades ending in 1990. It shows the swollen numbers of twenty-five- to thirty-four-years-olds in the decade of the 1970s moving progressively through the population pipeline in the 1980s, with a predictable influence for each successive decade. This population bulge is a unique occurrence.

If you go from 1890 to 1960, you find the size of this subgroup, 14–24 years of age (the 25–34 age group in the 70s and the 35–44 age group in

EXHIBIT 3
THE POPULATION'S CHANGING AGE COMPOSITION
(in millions)

Age groups (years)	1970	1980	1990	% change 1970–80	% change 1980–90
Under 18	69.7	62.0	64.8	(11%)	5%
18–24	24.7	29.5	25.1	19	(15)
25–34	25.3	36.2	41.1	43	14
35–44	23.1	25.7	36.6	11	42
45–54	23.3	22.7	25.3	(3)	11
55 and over	38.8	46.1	50.6	19	10
Total	204.9	222.2	243.5	8%	10%

Source: United States Department of Commerce.

the 80s), growing a little each succeeding decade: 10 percent, 8 percent, sometimes not at all, but usually growing a little bit. In the whole of the 70 years from 1890 to 1960, the total increase of the "cohort" as we say, was 12.5 million persons. Then, in the 1960s it grew by 13.8 million persons, an increase of 52 percent in one decade, five times the average rate of the preceding 70 years. *It grew by 13.8 million persons: it will grow by 600,000 in the 1970s: it will decline in the 1980s.* It's all over; it happened once; it will not ever happen again.[1]

Along with the change in age distribution is a corresponding change in consumer spending patterns. A strong growth in the thirty-five- to forty-four-year age group in the 1980s will mean a corresponding shift toward more affluent consumers. This could mean a boost for producers of items bought from discretionary income as well as top-of-the-price-line items generally.

However, the age and income relationships, as strong as they are, are a composite picture that masks a multitude of diverse trends, many of which would be more important for the potential producer of a special-interest magazine. Among the most familiar of these that we shall briefly mention are (1) the rising percentage of working women, (2) the higher proportion of senior citizens, and (3) the changing character of the family.

First, the rising participation of women in the work force (46% of women of working age were in the work force in mid-1978, compared with only 35% in 1960) is expected to continue in the decade of the 1980s. That uptrend, particularly among married women with families, will significantly influence spending patterns. Two-income families will be better able to afford costly items ranging from second homes to exotic vacations. Already, working women, short on time to browse through stores, are giving a big lift to the mail-order business: in 1977 mail-order sales reached more than $36 billion, up nearly 100 percent over the amount only five years earlier. Total retail sales in that same five-year period rose only 58 percent. Clearly this shift in consumption patterns can be translated into advertising revenues for the right media.

Second, the "graying" of America is a potent population force second only to the unique population bulge mentioned earlier in its marketing implications. In the decades ahead, a huge group of older Americans will contrast with a shrinking base of younger workers and taxpayers. In 1940 there were about nine active workers for every retired person. Today the ratio is closer to six to one. Some analysts predict that within fifty years there will be only three workers to support each retired person. This trend reflects a substantial "aging" of the population averages. It also signifies a massive market, growing in size and influence. Moreover, as opposed to a population bulge that moves from one age group to another over time, this age group will grow monotonically larger from period to period.

Third, the symbol of the American family has drastically changed. One major statistic for the 1970s reveals one important dimension of the change. The divorce rate has doubled over the past decade, rising from 2.5 per 1,000 of the population in 1966 to 5.0 in 1976. The rise in divorces and separations is pronounced among young adults. For example, the number of divorced persons under age thirty-five, per 1,000 married persons under age thirty-five, was forty in 1970. By 1975 the number had risen to 79. The Census Bureau estimates that, if recent trends continue, one in every three married persons between twenty-five and thirty-five years of age may end their first marriage in divorce, and that a higher proportion (four in ten) of those in their second marriage may end that one in divorce.

Submerged within all these demographic shifts, and perhaps most important of all, is a change in lifestyles. As the 1970s wore on, earlier fads and fashions faded only to be replaced by new vogues. Jeans seem to have taken over as the majority costume. "Jonesism" — emulating the neighbor's lifestyle and material possessions — declined among many Americans. The preference shifted to leading a quieter, simpler life. The dominant themes in clothing, food, and hairstyles became simplicity, naturalness, and individuality.

Merchants feel the effects of changing moods, tastes, and needs. For example, with young people having fewer children — and having them later — expectations of the 1960s and early 1970s for various product lines, from infants' wear to toys, are having to be revised. As a consequence, merchants' marketing tactics may need to be changed: As more and more youths move into their adult years — the postwar generation coming of age — more accent is being placed on quality, durability, and function when one makes buying decisions. And the merchants' concerns and messages rely on an effective advertising media to reach their customers.

The radically changed profile of America is both a challenge and an opportunity for the opportunistic marketer — whether it is of merchandise or of magazines. It provides new markets for new products as old loyalties and customs become obsolete. It is not an easy path toward success. There are a great number of interpretations possible from different readings of the same data. Moreover, the data themselves are based on forecasts that have often proved to be far off the mark in the past. It is, in short, a place to begin but a difficult equation to solve.

New Magazine Ventures: Two Successful and One Potential

Representative of new magazine strategies, and the dollar appeal for those that succeed, are two publications of the diversified publisher Time Inc.: *People* and *Money*.

Since *People* started in 1974, the weekly magazine's advertising rate base has jumped from 1 million to 2.3 million by January 1979. Also impressive are 1978 advertising revenues of more than $66 million. The publisher of *People,* Richard Burell, claimed that the magazine was now "the fastest growing weekly magazine in the country."

People is aimed toward the reader between the ages of eighteen and thirty-five who wants "fun" reading. The magazine is designed to be read quickly, within forty minutes. The articles are at most 1,800 words, or by issue 20,000 words. The individual who reads this magazine wants enjoyment and a bit of gossip about personalities.

Since the huge success of *People,* newspapers and other publishers are starting to copy Time Inc.'s idea. Newspapers in many parts of the country have "people" sections now with short articles on celebrities. *Us* magazine came out in 1977 as a direct competitor and imitator of *People.*

Money is another successful venture of Time Inc. Begun in 1972 it had achieved an advertising rate base of 800,000 by 1979. Beginning in 1977, *Money* began offering regional editions to advertisers. It has also been promoted extensively on television, thereby using a traditional competitor to advantage.

There is no mystery to the attraction of the magazine's topic, but *Money*'s editorial staff was able to develop a magazine more lively, entertaining, and current than the many "how-to-get-rich" type of imitators. It covers a broad range of subjects for a variety of ages and income levels. However, the primary target audience seems to be the upwardly mobile young individual or couple reading for entertainment as well as information.

A third potential new entry in the magazine field is *Inside Sports.* This would be a monthly magazine launched by *Newsweek,* a unit of the Washington Post Co. As described in the *Wall Street Journal* (July 5, 1979):

> *Newsweek* will offer about 120,000 copies of *Inside Sports* for sale in the Northeast this September. The magazine, which will be printed on heavy, glossy paper and have a cover price of $1.50, will specialize in coverage of football, baseball, basketball and hockey. . . . *Inside Sports* will contain profiles of sports figures, memoirs of ex-players, sports columnists, "long and arduously researched stories" and "lavish picture spreads."
>
> The test edition of 136 pages will cost *Newsweek* $500,000 to $1 million and will help determine to what extent editorial content should be varied by geographical regions. . . . *Inside Sports* may evolve as "four distinctly editorially different magazines by regions."
>
> The new sports magazine, if the market test is successful, will enter a field already served by *Sports Illustrated,* which is owned by Time Inc., *Sport* magazine, owned by Charter Co., and the Times Mirror Co.'s

Sporting News. In addition, CBS Inc. has tested a sports magazine, but hasn't announced whether it will proceed with the magazine.

Revenue and Cost Factors

Revenue sources for the consumer magazine industry are sale of advertising space plus circulation income, which includes subscriptions and newsstand sales. The primary source of revenues for the average magazine publisher has been advertising, and this is still true in general although publishers of certain magazines emphasize revenues coming from circulation income. Growth of newsstand sales is outstripping subscription sales due partly to increasing postal rates. In recent years supermarkets have become the main distribution centers, accounting for approximately 60 percent of all single-copy sales of consumer magazines.

The consumer magazines remain sensitive to television demand, benefiting from a spillover of television advertising dollars when television's rates are at a peak and television advertising schedules are heavily booked; and suffering from an ebb of dollars into television when television advertising rates are soft. Overall, specialization appears to have stabilized consumer magazines' share of the total advertising dollar, with a figure of 5.3 percent in 1976 ending a five-year decline (see Exhibit 4). The magazine share of national advertising revenues has also climbed, gaining relative advantage over other major competing media in 1977 and 1978 (see Exhibit 5). Moreover, the major gains in the magazine share were due to volume increases in advertising pages, compared to higher prices. While network television relied almost exclusively on price increases for greater

EXHIBIT 4
ADVERTISING EXPENDITURES
(in percentages)

Media	1971	1972	1973	1974	1975	1976	1977	1978(p)
Newspapers	29.9	30.1	30.2	29.9	29.9	29.5	29.2	29.0
Television	17.0	17.6	17.8	18.2	18.6	20.0	20.0	20.2
Radio	7.0	6.9	6.9	6.9	7.0	6.8	6.9	6.8
Magazines	6.6	6.2	5.8	5.6	5.2	5.3	5.7	5.9
All other	39.5	39.2	39.3	39.4	39.3	38.4	38.2	38.1
Total	100.0	100.0	100.0	100.0	100.0	100.0	100.0	100.0

Source: Standard and Poor's Industry Surveys.

(p) = preliminary

EXHIBIT 5
MAJOR MEDIA SHARE OF NATIONAL AD REVENUES

	1975	1976	1977	1978
Network tv	34.9	34.4	36.4	35.8
Spot tv	24.5	25.9	23.2	23.8
Subtotal	59.4	60.3	59.6	59.6
Magazines	22.1	21.6	22.7	23.4
Newspapers	18.5	18.1	17.7	17.0
Total	100%	100%	100%	100%

Source: Exhibits 5 and 6 reprinted from *Advertising Age,* September 25, 1978, from data developed by the McCann-Erickson advertising agency.

advertising revenues from 1976 to 1978, magazines had a healthy 12 percent average growth each year in real terms (see Exhibit 6).

Over the past three decades, advertising spending in America appears to have gone through two distinct phases. It may now be poised for a third phase.

Phase one stretched from 1945 through the late 1950s. Generally, it was a boom period for advertising. Consumer demand, pent up during the war, exploded into buying of houses, appliances, and furnishings. Advertisements, of course, played a major role in the distribution and marketing system. Additionally, a new advertising medium — television — opened its

EXHIBIT 6
UNIT PRICE CHANGES COMPARED TO VOLUME CHANGES

	1976	1977	1978
Network tv			
Prices	+18%	+18%	+12%
Volume	+ 5	+ 2	0
Spot tv			
Prices	+25	+ 8	+ 6
Volume	+ 6	− 5	+10
Magazines			
Prices	+ 4	+ 7	+10
Volume	+17	+13	+ 6

screens for sellers of goods and services. Advertising growth, overall, marched upward in line with expanding gross national product (GNP).

Phase two took over in 1960 and stretched into 1975 — a fifteen-year period marked by the Vietnam War, a speedup in inflation, recessions, and most recently, a continuing energy crisis. Midway in this second phase, along about 1967, total advertising expenditure growth began to trail that of the GNP. Result: a gradual decline in the advertising expenditure component of GNP from the historic 2.2 percent to a low of 1.86 percent in 1975. In 1976 a turnabout occurred; advertising expenditures began moving up at a rate above the growth in GNP and continued a favorable trend into 1977 and 1978.

The improved outlook for advertising expenditures has cheered publishers, but there is a perennial concern over mounting costs. Paper prices have been climbing at a 10 percent annual rate since 1970, with printing and binding costs climbing approximately 7 to 8 percent per year. Postal fees — another major cost — have soared fivefold since 1970, and there is no end in sight.

These cost pressures have forced changes in the industry. Magazines have shifted to lighter-weight paper, and magazine size has been trimmed. Moreover, many publishers have been testing private mail systems, which may provide a feasible alternative in the 1980s, when the average private delivery cost per magazine should equal the United States Post Office rate.

The impact of such costs is heightened by the almost total lack of vertical integration in the industry; the paper is purchased, but the printing and frequently the distribution are contracted. This has the effect of lowering capital investment, and so enabling easy entry into the industry, but increases the proportion of variable costs. Postage, paper, distribution, and printing are all variable costs, varying with the size of circulation. Low subscription prices make these variable costs even more important. It is possible for a magazine to lose more money with increased circulation unless advertising revenues are high enough to offset losses on subscriptions. Costs that are relatively fixed (with respect to circulation) include editorial expense, promotion of new subscriptions, company overhead, and circulation record-keeping.

Another important financial factor is the large cost outlay needed to develop and promote a new magazine. This outlay is generally not fully recovered in the initial "test" period of increasing market penetration, with the magazine going into the black only after pages of advertising and advertising rates increase. The uncertainty of selling into an untested market is particularly a burden for the small, financially thin publisher. "A larger company can put out a one-shot, or test, issue and see how it goes on the stands before making a long-term commitment to it. Those who can't —

who just put out their magazine with 2,000 others competing for the reader's attention — are in for a tough time," to quote from *Business Week* of January 15, 1979.

Looking Ahead

The magazine industry, overall, is in better shape today than it has been for several years. Readers are more loyal. Many advertisers have lost some of their earlier single-minded enchantment with television as specialized publications have pinpointed consumer groups. Leading magazine advertisers are large, financially strong firms with consistently high advertising

EXHIBIT 7

Top ten advertisers	1978	1977	% change
Seagram Co.	$10,503,619	$ 924,127	+999
R. J. Reynolds Industries	7,069,519	5,604,476	+ 26
Chrysler Corp.	5,040,849	788,284	+539
Sears, Roebuck & Co.	4,433,798	2,580,628	+ 72
Philip Morris	4,235,289	3,643,350	+ 16
General Foods	2,798,144	2,081,073	+ 34
Procter & Gamble	2,725,084	1,483,108	+ 84
General Motors	2,252,554	2,607,064	− 14
American Brands	2,158,928	2,165,591	
Loews Corp.	2,071,394	1,892,601	+ 9

Top ten product categories	1978	1977	% change
Beer, wine and liquor	$18,584,387	$ 7,206,298	+158
Cigarettes and tobacco	18,017,524	16,988,485	+ 6
Automotive	17,757,447	10,629,162	+ 67
Food and food products	12,471,617	9,253,939	+ 35
Business and consumer services	10,946,737	6,805,594	+ 61
Toiletries and cosmetics	9,589,529	8,957,975	+ 7
Publishing and media	7,443,983	5,445,123	+ 37
Retail and/or direct-by-mail	5,081,310	4,279,505	+ 19
Household equipment and supplies	4,919,921	2,909,225	+ 69
Travel, hotels and resorts	4,665,934	3,698,664	+ 26

Source: Compiled and published for Publishers Information Bureau by Leading National Advertisers, Inc. Reprinted by permission.

budgets. In two dominant product categories — cigarettes and liquor — advertising on television is prohibited and therefore increases in these areas of advertising expenditures tend to benefit the magazine industry directly (see Exhibit 7).

Rising costs continue to be a problem, as everywhere else in American industry. Moreover, many magazine managements have yet to modernize their operations. A slow evolution in developing sophisticated marketing information systems has begun, but it is far from pervasive in the industry. And magazine publishing, what with the unpredictability of audience tastes, has a special dimension of riskiness — especially in light of the spate of magazine startups. Many have failed and many more, inevitably, will fail to click and will be quietly interred.

As most magazine publishers do not own printing facilities, capital requirements are relatively low, with costs concentrated in editing, production, and promotion. The low cost of entry and the high operating leverage have attracted many entrepreneurs, fragmenting the industry and intensifying competition. Such intraindustry competition, as well as that of other media, increases the probability of failure of many of these publishing ventures.

Marginal publications — especially at times of economic downturn — will be vulnerable. Among these will be some general-interest publications and publications ranking fifth or lower in a specialty group.

Question and Assignment

1. Assuming you were to begin a new magazine, on what subject area or target audience would you focus? Support your answer.

2. Develop a systematic approach to introduction of a new magazine, indicating in a logical sequence the steps you would take, along with data, resource, and financial considerations. You need not supply actual figures. Instead, the purpose is to formulate a structured method for integrating relevant information as it is developed.

REFERENCE

1. Patrick D. Moynihan, "Peace — Some Thoughts on the 1960s and 1970s," *The Public Interest,* no. 32, Summer 1973.

The Motorcycle Industry*

Introduction and Background: The United States

PAST GROWTH PERFORMANCE

North America has led the world in the development of what may be described as secondary uses of motorcycles. The primary use of the motorcycle has been as a basic means of transportation at speeds comparable to those of an automobile, but at costs that are substantially lower. For lower-income consumers a motorcycle therefore becomes a feasible and desirable vehicle to own at a time when a car still remains beyond their budget. As incomes rise, however, consumers tend to replace their motorcycles with cars, since for basic transportation the automobile offers levels of convenience and comfort that the motorcycle cannot match. Consequently motorcycle usage falls, and during the 1950s was at very low levels in the United States, with only about 0.3 percent of the population owning motorcycles. Since the late 1960s, Americans have "discovered" the motorcycle, and ownership had risen to 2.4 percent of the American population by 1974. This rapid growth of motorcycle usage has been among riders who have chosen a motorcycle not because they could not afford a car but because they *preferred* a motorcycle to a car or, more frequently, wanted one in addition to a car. For this kind of purchaser, motorcycles provide a source of enjoyment and a leisure activity rather than a basic means of transport; we here describe these uses of motorcycles as secondary.

The general growth in secondary usage of motorcycles led to a rapid increase in sales throughout the United States and Canada. In 1960 less

---

* Adapted by Milton Leontiades from a study of the British motorcycle industry by the Boston Consulting Group Ltd for the United Kingdom's Department of Industry in 1975.

EXHIBIT 1
SALES OF BIG BIKES IN THE USA

	1968 sales (000 units)	1974 sales (000 units)	1968–1974 growth (%/yr.)	1968–1974 volume increment (000 units)
450–749 cc	57	139	16	82
>750 cc	17	168	47	151

Source: R. L. Polk.

than eighty thousand units were sold in the United States, whereas in 1974 total sales were over a million units, a compound growth rate of around 20 percent annually in units sold. Through this period riders became more sophisticated, and although the sales boom in the early 1960s was mainly in the lightweight, low-displacement, street machines, the market evolved by the 1970s to include substantial sales of larger street machines, competition bikes, and on/off road combination motorcycles.

Exhibit 1 shows United States sales in 1968 and 1974, annual average compound growth rates, and the total volume increments for large street machines.

These are extremely rapid rates of growth, well in excess of those achieved by the total market, which grew at 15 percent/yr. in overall units during the same period. The reasons for this unusual growth were as follows:

1. There was a period of very rapid growth for motorcycles of less than 450 cubic centimeters (cc) beginning in the mid-60s and ending in 1971, and it is this wave of purchasers which is now moving on to bigger machines.

2. Before 1970 there were few machines on the market in these displacement classes but now many more big bikes have become available, and are being actively marketed by all the major competitors.

3. There has been a tendency for riders who want a big bike to look for larger and larger displacements over time. Over time demand has increased for the over 750 cc class relative to the 750 cc class, and for the 750 cc class itself relative to the 450–749 cc class.

FUTURE GROWTH PROSPECTS

Prospects for future growth of the total market depend mainly upon increased usage of motorcycles, because the total United States population will be growing only very slowly. Increased usage follows from increasing levels of affluence and, as disposable income rises, we can expect usage of motorcycles to rise too. However, the rate of growth of total ownership has been decelerating since 1967. The energy crisis, which appeared briefly to offer the opportunity to expand the market, now appears to have had little impact on the underlying demand for the types of use of motorcycles that characterize the North American market. Extrapolating past trends of ownership in the light of future forecasts of income levels and car usage, it was projected that between 2¾ and 3 percent of the United States population would own a motorcycle in 1980.

Exhibit 2 shows the growth of the total market broken down into individual displacement classes. It can be seen that the growth of the cc classes less than 500 cc has been flat since 1971; therefore only limited growth can be expected from trade-ups in the pipeline.

Specific forecasts of demand for the United States market are set out in Exhibit 3. It should be noted that in any market the growth rate for motorcycles will be affected by cyclical macroeconomic factors, so that growth will oscillate about the forecast trend. However, for purposes of

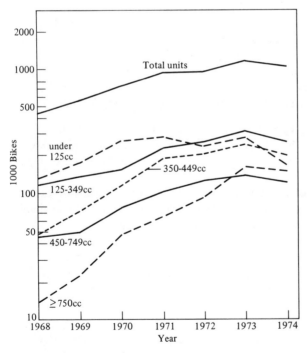

EXHIBIT 2
THE U.S. MOTORCYCLE MARKET 1968–1974 — GROWTH IN TOTAL UNITS AND BY CC SIZE CLASS
Source: R. L. Polk.

EXHIBIT 3
SALES OF MOTORCYCLES IN THE USA

	1974 sales (000 units)	1980 sales (000 units)	1974–1980 growth (%/yr.)	1974–1980 volume increment (000 units)
Total market	1011	1205	3	194
450–749 cc	139	169	3	30
750 cc	91	133	7	42
>750 cc	77	108	6	31

Source: R. L. Polk, BCG Forecasts.

long-term strategic planning we should focus on the underlying trend in growth rates.

Marketing and Market Share

PRODUCTS

Market share in each cc class is clearly a function of sales of particular models, and the sales potential of each model will depend upon its attractiveness relative to competition. It is hard to be precise about the features that are necessary for a product to sell well, because other considerations such as price and selling and distribution systems, which we shall discuss below, vitiate any direct comparisons between models, and because the appeal of the features built into particular models is in any case largely subjective. However, it can be observed that new models typically register substantial sales advances. In fact the life cycle of a successful model normally involves two to three years of rapid sales growth after which sales level out leading to an eventual decline or phasing out of the model. The Honda CB 750 is a good example of this. It was launched and extremely well received in the early 1970s, but has now begun to decline in sales in Europe, and has ceased growing in North America.

This life cycle is easily explained. In its early years a new model will be attractive both because it is new, and hence appealing to the fashion element of the market, and because it will incorporate the most up-to-date technology and design concepts available to its manufacturer. In later years it can be kept alive through modifications — and the Honda 750 has received a facelift — but over time it becomes increasingly hard to update a model in ways that make it truly comparable with the newer models introduced by competitors.

The pace of new-model introduction in a cc class is largely determined by the growth rate of the class with rapid rates of growth associated with numerous new-model introductions. The superbike class, which has grown at 47 percent annually in the United States since 1968, has attracted many new entrants, and most of the major manufacturers are planning new models in this class during the next few years. In a fast-growth market, the growth is therefore taken up by new models, which are being introduced with high frequency, whereas in a slow-growth market fewer new models appear. Older models tend to maintain or slightly reduce their volumes in both cases, but in terms of market share, they are losing at a much more rapid rate in fast- than slow-growth situations.

PRICE

Just as it is hard to separate out and assess the effect of the various product features on market share, so it is difficult to isolate the relationship between price and market share.

There are, in fact, few examples of a price cut leading to significant volume increments. The Japanese competitors' practice is to introduce new models at highly competitive prices, and to tend to reduce prices in constant money terms thereafter.

SELLING AND DISTRIBUTION SYSTEMS

We have so far discussed market share as a function of the product features and prices of particular models. Market share across all cc classes is also influenced by what we shall call the selling and distribution system (s and d system). Within the s and d system we include the following activities of the marketing companies:

Sales representation at the dealer level
Physical distribution of parts and machines
Warranty and service support
Dealer support
Advertising and promotion
Market planning and control

We also include the effects of the dealer network established by the marketing companies:

Numbers and quality of dealers
Floorspace devoted to the manufacturers' products
Sales support by dealers

The s and d system supports sales of the manufacturer across the whole model range, and its quality affects market shares in each cc class where the manufacturer is represented. Exhibit 4 compares the s and d sys-

EXHIBIT 4
THE SELLING AND DISTRIBUTION SYSTEMS OF JAPANESE COMPANIES IN THE USA

	Estimated total s and d expenditure by sales company 1974 ($m)	Advertising expenditure 1972 ($m)	Dealers 1974 Numbers	Units sold per dealer	1974 % Share of total market (units)	Lowest % share of any cc class	Highest % share of any cc class
Honda	90–100	8.1	1974	220	43	34	61
Yamaha	40–45	4.2	1515	135	20	4	34
Kawasaki	30–35	2.2	1018	127	13	9	19
Suzuki	25–30	3.0	1103	98	11	5	16

Sources: R. L. Polk, *Motorcycle Dealer News.* Ziff-Davis Market Research Dept., BCG Estimates.

EXHIBIT 5
ESTIMATED U.S. SALES PER DEALER IN 1980

	Estimated market share	Estimated no. of dealers	Estimated sales of superbikes (>750 cc)	Estimated sales per dealer
Honda	30–35%	2000	80,000	40
Yamaha	12–15%	1600	35,000	22
Kawasaki	12–15%	1200	35,000	29
Suzuki	8–10%	1200	24,000	20
Harley-Davidson	15–20%	500	48,000	96

tems of the four full-line Japanese manufacturers in the United States, and shows that high market shares both overall *and* in each cc class go with high levels of expenditure on s and d and with extensive dealer networks.

In particular cc categories, each manufacturer's position is substantially influenced by its specific product offerings. For example, Kawasaki is strong in the 750 cc and over class due to the Z-1 model, and Yamaha has been weak due to its poor 750 cc model. Outstanding products obtain market shares that are unusually high for a manufacturer, and weak products lead to atypically low market shares. For products of average attraction, however, market shares seem to move toward some equilibrium level. For each manufacturer this level in 1980 for the USA is estimated in Exhibit 5.

In the United States the fact that dealers are typically exclusive adds to the influence of the s and d system. In an exclusive dealership the dealer has a strong interest in selling his manufacturer's model in each cc range whatever its attraction to the rider, while in shared dealerships good products can be allocated more showroom space, consistent with their sales potential. Individual models can thus be pushed or held back according to the dealer's perception of their merits. For each manufacturer an exclusive dealership system will lead to more market share stability and a shared dealership system will lead to more volatility. In Exhibit 5 the estimated sales and dealership positions for 1980 of the major motorcycle manufacturers are compared.

Competition

The common theme running through our discussion of the various influences on market share is the essential dependence of each company's market position on its strength *relative to competition.* An understanding of the capabilities and intentions of the major world competitors is therefore important in assessing market prospects.

HONDA MOTOR COMPANY

Honda is the world's largest producer of motorcycles (1974 output of 2.1 million units), and holds leading market positions in nearly every market where it competes.

The company's market success has been built upon a range of products that have met the requirements of the vast majority of riders, and at prices that they could afford. It is often said that Honda created the market — in the United States and elsewhere — for what we have called secondary uses of motorcycles, through their extensive advertising and promotion activities; and it is true that Honda presented the attractions of motorcycling as a "fun" activity in a new way, and with a level of media support not previously attempted by motorcycle manufacturers. However, the success of this campaign depended in the last resort on the fact that the lightweight machines that were then the company's primary product *were* fun and easy to ride, did not give the mechanical problems that had traditionally been associated with motorcycles, and were cheap to purchase. In the same way, Honda's successful move into superbikes in 1969 received heavy advertising support, but was made possible by a product, the CB 750, which was technically ahead of its competitors, and offered features that were at that time unique. Honda's basic strength in product design stems from an extremely heavy commitment to R & D that ensures that its products can be produced to meet the needs of any segment of the market, and that these products remain in the forefront of technical development.

Honda's pricing policy aims to introduce new products at prices which are below those of comparable competitive models, and which are designed to develop substantial sales volumes. In the infrequent instances where Honda has found itself selling a model at a price disadvantage that threatened to impact on its sales volumes, it has been prepared to introduce special price cuts to ensure that its competitors did not gain on Honda. An example of this behavior was a $200 special discount maintained throughout a season on a 250 cc off-road bike in order to match — and in fact undercut — Yamaha's model in this range. Honda appears prepared to sustain losses in the marketing channel for as long as necessary to establish the kind of system they require.

Exhibit 6 shows Honda's market share, overall and in big bikes, in five major European countries, as against the United States.

EXHIBIT 6
HONDA MARKET SHARES (%) 1974

	Total market	Superbikes
USA	43	36
UK	54	4
France	37	27
Germany	39	22
Italy	17	17
Holland	41	32

YAMAHA

Yamaha has grown more rapidly than Honda since 1962 and occupies second position in world production of motorcycles. Their particular strength has been in off-road machines, and they have supported their sporting image with numerous racing successes.

They have a similar volume orientation to Honda, which is illustrated by the fact that they have added capacity three times in their low cc machines, despite the fact that Boston Consulting Group Ltd. understands that they lose $20 on each one they sell in Japan. They evidently regard the preservation of their market share in this class as sufficiently important in its impact on their overall position to justify this decision.

Yamaha has been the last of the Japanese firms to enter the bigger bike field. It now has machines of 500 cc and 650 cc (the latter a close copy of British products) that sell well.

KAWASAKI

Kawasaki was the last of the big four Japanese companies to enter the industry in a serious way and is now fighting for third place with Suzuki. Motorcycles in fact form only a small part of the total group and the decision to enter this business area in the early 1960s appears to have been a classic diversification move. Kawasaki had been for many years in heavy industrial products, and it decided it should begin to participate in a market closer to the final consumer. Its two-stroke three-cylinder machines (500 and 750 cc) are fast, but only the more recent four-stroke 900 cc Z-1 model combines performance with handling, styling, and other features. The Z-1 is very well regarded in the industry, and represents the eventual success of Kawasaki's R & D department in putting together a motorcycle with real "class."

The Kawasaki story is an interesting illustration of the difficulty of breaking into and gaining market share in the world motorcycle industry. It is only because Kawasaki has been prepared to undergo a long period of losses, to redesign and refine its products in a constant attempt to improve their appeal, and to focus on *long-term* market share and profitability goals, that it has achieved its present position. Kawasaki remains small relative to Honda but is now becoming a real threat to the market leaders. It has been the fastest growing of the Japanese companies, and with strong corporate backing, without which it could never have financed the many years of losses, it is now formidable competition.

SUZUKI

Suzuki has been gaining share of world markets since 1972 and has expanded its production a great deal during this time. To maintain volume in the depressed US market it has had to offer a rebate scheme of $50 off each 380 cc, $75 off each 550 cc, and $100 off each 750 cc. Their latest model, into which considerable development effort has been put, is the Rotary RE-5, a model that has not so far been well received by the market.

Suzuki, like Yamaha, has tended to be stronger in off-road than on-road machines, has concentrated even more exclusively on two-stroke machines, and has also done well in competition racing. But their image is less clearly defined as sporting, since the performance of their production machines has not been particularly good.

THE JAPANESE MARKETING PHILOSOPHY

The market approach of these Japanese companies has certain common features which, taken together, may be described as a "marketing philosophy." The fundamental feature of this philosophy is the emphasis it places on market share and sales volume. Objectives set in these terms are regarded as critical, and defended at all costs.

The whole thrust of the marketing program in each country where the Japanese operate is toward maintaining or improving market-share position.

A number of more specific policies follow from this general philosophy, and our descriptions of each of the Japanese competitors provide ample examples of these polices:

1. Products are updated or redesigned whenever a market threat or opportunity is perceived.
2. Prices are set at levels designed to achieve market-share targets, and will be cut if necessary.

EXHIBIT 7
GROWTH OF JAPANESE PRODUCTION

	Production in 1959 (000 units)	Production in 1974 (000 units)	Average annual growth rate (%/yr.)
Honda	285	2133	14
Yamaha	64	1165	21
Kawasaki	10	355	27
Suzuki	96	840	16

Source: Japan Automobile Industry Association.

3. Effective marketing systems are set up in all markets where serious competition is intended, regardless of short-term cost.
4. Plans and objectives look to long-term payoff.

These policies have, of course, been spectacularly successful for the Japanese competitors. The rates of growth of the four major Japanese companies from 1959 to 1974 were as shown in Exhibit 7.

Japanese producers have come to dominate the world motorcycle industry, and Exhibit 8 summarizes the degree to which they have penetrated the major markets of the world. The Japanese challenge from 1959 to 1974 in fact led to the elimination of many of the smaller and more marginal competitors. However, in the larger displacement machines in particular there do remain some other significant competitors, often with bases in their own national home markets.

EXHIBIT 8
PERCENT MARKET SHARES OF TOTAL UNITS SOLD: 1974

	USA	Canada	UK	France	Germany	Italy[a]
Honda	43	41	54	37	39	17
Yamaha	20	18	19	19	20	1
Kawasaki	13	17	5	5	5	8
Suzuki	11	12	13	13	6	4
Total	87	88	74	74	70	30

[a] Japanese competitors are not allowed to import machines of less than 380 cc.

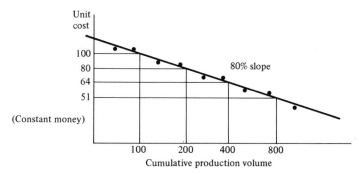

Note: Each point plotted represents the data for a particular year in the product history.

EXHIBIT 9
THE EXPERIENCE CURVE
(SCHEMATIC)

Economics of the Motorcycle Business

It has long been recognized that the labor input required to manufacture a product tends to decline systematically with increases in accumulated production. The type of relationship involved — originally called the "learning curve" — has been frequently found empirically to apply also to the *total cost* involved in manufacturing, distributing and selling a product. The relationship can be expressed simply as follows (see also Exhibit 9):

> Each time the accumulated experience of manufacturing a particular product doubles, the total unit cost in real terms (i.e., in "constant money," net of inflation) can be made to decline by a characteristic percentage, normally in the region of 20 to 30 percent.

APPLICATION TO THE MOTORCYCLE INDUSTRY

As overall market leaders, the Japanese have dominated pricing in the motorcycle industry. It is therefore appropriate to begin this analysis by examining the extent to which the experience curve concept appears to explain the performance of the Japanese.

Japanese Price Performance. Price experience curves for the Japanese motorcycle industry as a whole show price reduction performance of a consistent nature for each of the size ranges of motorcycle considered, the rate of price reduction being most rapid of all in the largest range, 126–250 cc, which is following an experience curve slope of 76 percent. The other slopes are more shallow, at 81 and 88 percent, but there is no mistaking the fact that real prices are descending smoothly over time. These experience-based price reductions clearly go a long way toward explaining the historical competitive effectiveness of the Japanese in the marketplace in small and medium motorcycles.

Price performance in the large bikes has been consistent with that in small: real prices have declined along experience curve slopes in the region of 85–87 percent. This has also been true of the price in the United States, when converted into yen terms.

An interesting feature of the curves is that the prices in the United States are so much higher than that of the same products in Japan. The premiums are high across almost the entire range of bikes and are far larger than seems necessary, even allowing for the extra costs incurred for duty, freight, and packing in shipping bikes from Japan to the United States.

COMPETITIVE STRATEGY IMPLICATIONS

As discussed, failure to achieve a cost competitive position — and hence cost reductions over time — equivalent to that of the competition will result in commercial vulnerability. At some point competitors will start setting prices that cannot be matched profitably, and losses will ensue. The strategic importance of the experience curve is that it explains clearly the two possible long-term causes of uncompetitive costs: (1) Relative growth: failure to grow as rapidly as competitors, thereby progressing more slowly than they along the experience curve. (2) Relative slopes: failure to bring costs down the characteristic experience curve slope achieved by competitors.

Summary

Japanese manufacturing policy is based on the concept that high volume per model provides the potential for high productivity. This potential is realized in practice by using capital-intensive and highly automated techniques. The Japanese now have large factories specialized by model, component and/or function. Their focus on volume-based cost reduction results in extensive use being made of advanced techniques such as automated high pressure die casting of large engine components; forging and sintering to reduce machining and material waste; rotary index and in-line transfer machines, largely made in-house; and conveyorized assembly lines.

The full extent of the present disparity in productivity is reflected by comparisons of value added per employee. Honda has achieved the highest value-added figure. As one would expect, given their lower volumes, the smaller Japanese producers achieve lower levels of value added per man than Honda. Honda's advantage is of the order of four to five times; in the case of Yamaha and Suzuki, the advantage drops to a factor of two to three times.

The cost advantage of the Japanese is securely based on this higher productivity. It does not arise from lower labor costs. The overall result of the Japanese strategy is that the productivity improvements resulting from their growth and scale have been sufficient both to allow rapidly advancing rates of pay for their employees, and to bring down the real costs and prices of their products in the marketplace.

It can therefore be seen that the Japanese emphasis on market-share objectives has led in the longer term not only to high output volumes, but also to improved productivity, lower costs and higher profitability.

Questions and Assignments

1. Describe the basic Japanese "marketing philosophy" and the elements that comprise it.

2. Does this approach by the Japanese differ in a significant respect from the marketing philosophy of the typical United States manufacturer as you know it?

3. What specific policy and strategy decisions do you believe were primarily responsible for the Japanese being able to invade and dominate the United States motorcycle market successfully? What counterstrategies might United States producers have tried? (Suggestion: you may want to develop an explanation of the "economics of the industry" as part of your answer.)

Harley-Davidson*

AMF Corporation

Harley-Davidson is part of AMF, a large multinational corporation that began in 1900 in New Jersey as a wholly owned subsidiary of American Tobacco Company. Originally founded for the purpose of cigarette machine manufacturing, AMF has grown to its present size with seven basic divisions. The orientation has changed to that of a leisure products company, although the company still is involved in industrial products.

AMF's divisions are separated into two product groups. The leisure product group is composed of (1) Marine and sports products; (2) Motorcycle and other travel vehicles (including Harley-Davidson); (3) Wheel goods and lawn and garden products; (4) Bowling products. The industrial group consists of (1) Electronic/electrical components; (2) Automated machinery; (3) Industrial and government products.

Background Information on Harley-Davidson

Harley-Davidson comprises the bulk of the Motorcycles and Other Travel Vehicles Division of AMF and is a significant contributor to AMF's overall revenues. Harley-Davidson is the only United States manufacturer of motorcycles of any size left. Before World War II there were a number of motorcycle producers in the United States, but a shrinking of the market in the 1940s and 1950s, and in particular the intense competition from the Japanese in the 1960s, drove almost all domestic producers out of the motorcycle business.

Harley-Davidson has been in business for over three-quarters of a century and its name is synonymous with heavyweight motorcycles. It is in fact the world's leading producer of heavyweight machines. It specializes in

---

* Prepared by Milton Leontiades.

machines of 900 cc displacement and over, and its record line of heavy-weight machines include the 1000 cc Sportster and the XLS; 1200 cc Low Rider and Super Glide; and 1340 cc Electra Glide Classic.

Harley-Davidson enjoys 40 percent of the domestic market in heavy-weight motorcycles. However, this is only a fraction (less than 10%) of the entire domestic market, with the Japanese dominating the lightweight category of machines. Overall, the Japanese control approximately 85 percent of the United States motorcycle market. The Japanese are intense price competitors, and Harley-Davidson filed a petition with the U.S. Treasury in 1977 claiming unfair price competition. In essence, the argument was that the Japanese were "dumping" their machines in the United States at prices lower than those charged in Japan or Western Europe. In 1978 the U.S. Treasury ruled that (1) there was "dumping" but (2) Harley-Davidson wasn't injured by the practice. Although largely a symbolic victory, the decision may contribute to more cautious and equitable future pricing practices by Japanese manufacturers.

Significant improvement in Harley-Davidson's position, however, will depend on improved market conditions and its own competitive strengths. In the former case, demographic statistics seem to weigh against the future growth of the industry. Teenagers and young adults are the prime purchasers of motorcycles. It is estimated that roughly one out of four United States motorcycles are purchased by persons aged fifteen to twenty-five. Further, it is projected that this age group will shrink by about 2 million persons by 1985.

Another potentially complicating factor for all motorcycle manufacturers — but especially Harley-Davidson — is antinoise regulations. The Environmental Protection Agency (EPA) has proposed minimum standards of noise tolerance. Since Harley-Davidson produces only "hogs" — the largest machines — with appeal and image based at least in part on the deep-throated roar they make, the noise regulations would be aimed at a critical aspect of Harley-Davidson's machines.

Major Developments at Harley-Davidson, 1974 to 1978

Significant developments by Harley-Davidson in competing with the Japanese threat and maintaining its competitive position are reviewed here (based on the annual reports of the parent, AMF):

1974

14-week strike at Harley-Davidson's Milwaukee plant.

But sales are up, and there is difficulty meeting demand.

$9.4 million is invested in plant and equipment: over one half for engines and transmissions at Milwaukee plant; new lightweight motorcycle line for United States market added in plant at Varese, Italy.

Two lightweight motorcycles — SX-175 and SX-250, in the 175 cc and 250 cc classes — went into full production.

1975

Total motorcycle registrations off about 25 percent from 1974.

Harley-Davidson suffered less than rest of market; due largely to comparisons with the strike year of 1974.

Japanese introduced heavyweight motorcycles for the first time in the United States.

Demand for lightweight motorcycles fell sharply.

Harley-Davidson introduced new versions of lightweight 125 cc, 175 cc, and 250 cc combination street/trail motorcycles.

1976

Sales of both heavy and lightweight motorcycles below 1975 levels.

1976 unit sales for industry only 5 percent over 1975.

Fierce competition from Japanese; heavily overstocked inventories with price discounting by dealers.

Harley-Davidson introduced a new heavyweight machine: the Cape Racer. It also introduced new touring version of the Sportster and new sport model of the Electra Glide.

Harley-Davidson International, established in 1975 to build dealer network in Europe, opened a distribution and service center at Gross Gerau, West Germany.

SST 250, special street model of SS 250 equipped with disc brakes, was introduced in spring and contributed to a 25 percent increase in international sales of lightweight cycles.

Major expansion of engineering operations nearly doubled staff by 1976 over 1975, with further expansion planned for 1977.

New dealer support programs, including financing, announced.

1977

Harley-Davidson filed petition of unfair price competition with the U.S. Treasury against four major Japanese producers.

Total United States registrations rose 7 percent; with large machines (900 cc and over) also increasing 7 percent.

Harley-Davidson continues as leader in the heavyweight segment with 40 percent of the market.

Low Rider heavyweight motorcycle introduced in 1977; also introduced MX 250, a professional motocross bike.

Completed major expansion of engineering facilities at Milwaukee.

1978

U.S. Treasury ruled top three Japanese makers were "dumping" but that no injury resulted to Harley-Davidson.

Harley-Davidson completed over 300 percent increase in engineering expenditures over past two years to develop higher quality products.

Production of lightweight motorcycles ceased (made unprofitable by drastic price-cutting by Japanese). This segment accounted for less than 10 percent of Harley-Davidson's revenues.

Other Developments

The current trend seems to be turning in Harley-Davidson's favor. Although motorcycle registrations dropped off nearly 30 percent from 1976 to 1978, the demand for heavyweight machines in the 900 cc class and above nearly doubled. Many of the younger generation of motorcyclists have matured and are trading up to heavier machines.

In addition, Harley-Davidson is benefiting from a favorable turn in the foreign exchange markets. With the value of the United States dollar declining relative to the Japanese yen, Harley's products are increasingly price competitive. In 1978, for example, Harley's big machines averaged about $500 more than comparable Japanese motorcycles. A year earlier, the gap was twice that. Furthermore, Harley enjoys a trade-in advantage because of the Harley's durability. While a five-year-old Harley motorcycle may command close to its original price when new, a Japanese heavyweight model may be worth half its original cost. For machines that cost $5,000 and more, this can be an important consideration.

A final difference between Harley and Japanese models is in the engines. Harley-Davidson is committed to an older, two-cylinder engine for its motorcycles. This design gives a vibration and throaty noise; and not incidentally provides a merchandising difference that Harley's dealers use to advantage. The Japanese have opted for four-cylinder engines, which are generally quieter and smoother than Harley's. Because of EPA's proposed standards — which could, if implemented, reduce noise levels 50 percent by 1985 — Harley-Davidson could require substantial modifications to bring its models into compliance. However, Harley is not inclined to depart from the macho image and selling advantage provided by the two-cylinder engine.

Financial Condition

Since Harley-Davidson is a part of the larger AMF corporation, separate balance sheet and income statements are not available. However, financial details illustrated in Exhibits 1 and 2 give a good indication of important

EXHIBIT 1
AMF INCORPORATED FIVE-YEAR FINANCIAL STATISTICS
(in thousands of dollars)

Summary of operations	1978	1977a	1976a	1975a	1974a
Revenue by product category					
Marine and sports products	$ 322,270	$ 273,766	$ 230,271	$ 189,032	$ 177,681
Motorcycle and other travel vehicles	227,770	203,639	189,081	190,794	152,578
Wheel goods and lawn and garden products	193,826	174,258	158,167	144,961	224,934
Bowling products	133,850	137,829	125,840	109,518	101,952
Total leisure time products	877,716	789,492	703,359	634,305	657,145
Electronic/electrical products	233,485	209,036	180,973	142,229	157,869
Automated machinery	102,283	125,971	146,449	140,467	115,410
Other industrial and government products	102,898	90,766	82,932	88,719	93,531
Total industrial products and services	438,666	425,773	410,354	371,415	366,810
Total revenue	1,316,382	1,215,265	1,113,713	1,005,720	1,023,955
Cost of sales and expenses	1,230,145	1,131,676	1,035,528	932,563	969,315
Income from operations	86,237	83,589	78,185	73,157	54,640
Other income (principally interest)	16,283	15,859	17,438	15,773	15,350
Net foreign exchange losses	(878)	(1,985)	(3,983)	(1,716)	(1,880)
Interest expense	(21,828)	(23,213)	(21,370)	(25,946)	(30,224)
Income before income taxes	79,814	74,250	70,270	61,268	37,886
Income taxes	34,866	34,884	32,518	29,811	20,295
Net income	$ 44,948	$ 39,366	$ 37,752	$ 31,457	$ 17,591
Weighted average common shares	19,894,344	19,782,712	19,689,689	19,658,082	19,645,741

Per share statistics

Earnings	$ 2.26	$ 1.99	$ 1.91	$ 1.60	$ .89
Earnings assuming full dilution	2.21	1.95	1.88	1.58	.89
Dividends paid	1.24	1.24	1.24	1.24	1.24
Stockholders' equity	19.10	18.08	17.30	16.60	16.19

Balance sheet data at December 31

Current assets	$ 603,485	$ 575,714	$ 589,604	$ 547,407	$ 604,447
Current liabilities	307,109	261,941	278,259	244,324	339,342
Working capital	296,376	313,773	311,345	303,083	265,105
Working capital ratio	2.0	2.2	2.1	2.2	1.8
Machines leased to customers (net)	19,149	17,789	17,551	15,680	15,030
Property, plant and equipment (net)	246,449	230,466	227,641	211,563	189,056
Total assets	907,725	865,396	875,041	827,759	862,672
Long term debt/capital lease obligations	186,183	218,385	233,728	235,962	188,013
Stockholders' equity	382,668	360,441	343,074	328,124	319,832

a Restated for change in accounting for leases in accordance with FASB Accounting Standard No. 13.

Source: 1978 Annual Report of AMF.

EXHIBIT 2
REVENUE AND OPERATING PROFIT

	Revenue		Operating profit	
	1978	1977[a]	1978	1977
Marine and sports products	$ 322,321	$ 273,806	$ 21,465	$ 24,331
Motorcycle and other travel vehicles	227,775	203,639	1,258[a]	1,476[a]
Wheel goods and lawn and garden products	198,330	177,002	10,448	7,890
Bowling products	133,850	137,829	40,497	46,476
Electronic/electrical products	234,007	209,973	24,573	17,941
Automated machinery	102,567	126,021	14,536	20,077
Other industrial and government products	102,912	90,833	23,301	13,295
Product category totals	1,321,762	1,219,103	136,078	131,486
Eliminations	(5,380)	(3,838)	(1,180)	(894)
Consolidated totals	$1,316,382	$1,215,265	134,898	130,592
Corporate expenses, interest, and foreign exchange losses			(55,084)	(56,342)
Income before income taxes			$ 79,814	$ 74,250

[a] Includes losses associated with the lightweight motorcycle and recreation vehicle businesses sold in 1978.

EXHIBIT 2 *continued*

ASSETS, DEPRECIATION, AND CAPITAL EXPENDITURES

	Identifiable assets[b]		Depreciation and amortization expense		Capital expenditures[b]	
	1978	1977[a]	1978	1977[a]	1978	1977[a]
Marine and sports products	$203,421	$183,596	$ 6,159	$ 5,310	$ 9,495	$ 5,982
Motorcycle and other travel vehicles	99,637	114,345	6,348	6,157	9,000	7,259
Wheel goods and lawn and garden products	69,490	76,074	4,379	3,669	4,747	4,338
Bowling products	183,985	180,386	4,580	4,873	9,004	6,685
Electronic/electrical products	128,619	117,751	8,373	8,733	14,325	11,526
Automated machinery	56,978	59,531	2,997	4,149	4,764	5,029
Other industrial and government products	83,320	74,817	3,520	2,350	8,136	8,973
Product category totals	825,450	806,500	36,356	35,241	59,471	49,792
Corporate amounts	82,275	58,896	1,530	852	6,509	488
Consolidated totals	$907,725	$865,396	$37,886	$36,093	$65,980	$50,280

[b] Identifiable assets by product category include approximately $207,000 in foreign countries in 1978 and $188,000 in 1977.
[c] Includes additions to machines leased to customers.

Source: The Brewers Almanac. Reprinted by permission of the U.S. Brewers Association, Inc.

financial characteristics of Harley-Davidson within the category of Motorcycle and Other Travel Vehicles, of which Harley-Davidson is by far the dominant product line.

Assignments

1. Evaluate AMF's past strategic moves.
2. Develop future strategy alternatives for AMF and support your choice of the most appropriate strategies to follow.

The Brewing Industry*

Brewing beer was once a conservatively managed business. Established practices were followed. Major brewers set the pace for the industry and certain markets were the recognized "turf" of individual brewers. Contributing to this constrained competitive environment was the family ownership and outlook of many local and regional brewers. Even today such giant public corporations in the industry as Anheuser-Busch, Schlitz, and Coors are family controlled.

However, the equilibrium of the industry was upset when Miller Brewing, a newcomer backed by the massive resources of its parent, Philip Morris, became a participant. Acquired in 1970, Philip Morris transformed this lackluster seventh-place performer into a second-place contender in seven short years. By 1977 Miller had displaced Schlitz as number two in the industry and was publicly targeting for Anheuser-Busch's number one position. Not since Anheuser-Busch had performed this feat in the late 1950s — moving Schlitz from number one to number two — had the industry been so dramatically altered by a single brewing company.

Not only was Miller threatening the market shares of the major brewers, it was forcing the other companies to adopt new strategies and attitudes toward brewing. In the 1960s, when Anheuser-Busch was competing with Schlitz, the basic strategies were price competition and lower costs of production. Now Miller has shifted the emphasis toward its own strategies of advertising, promotion, and market segmentation. Also, the cost of competing on a national basis has been escalated, with only the financially well heeled predicted to keep the pace necessary to maintain or improve market position.

---

* Prepared by Milton Leontiades.

EXHIBIT 1
CONCENTRATION IN THE BREWING INDUSTRY: 1968–1976

Year	Number of breweries[a]	Year	Number of breweries[a]
1976	97	1971	148
1975	102	1970	154
1974	111	1969	158
1973	122	1968	163
1972	147		

[a] Maximum number licensed to operate at any time during the fiscal year ending June 30.
Source: The Brewers Almanac. Reprinted by permission of the U.S. Brewers Association, Inc.

Competition and Concentration

Increasingly the brewing business is only for large national companies. Small local or regional firms drop from the list of breweries every year. Among the exceptions that are expected to stay in the competition are Heileman, a consistently profitable firm that resembles a conglomeration of several regional breweries, and Coors, which is a strong regional brewer with potential for national distribution. However, the prevailing trend is toward a shrinking number of breweries, as indicated by Exhibit 1, and dominance of the industry by a few large firms as shown by Exhibit 2B. Exhibit 2B reveals a

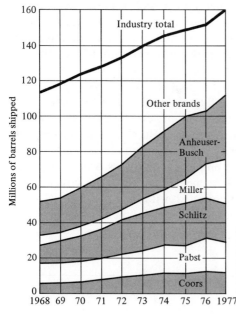

Changes in market shares reflect a new competitive climate in the U.S. beer Industry. Until the past couple of years, big brewers were able to grow handily, mainly at the expense of smaller brewers. But those easy pickings are just about gone, and recently the growth of Miller and Anheuser-Busch has come at the expense of sales from others of the "Big Five" — Schlitz in particular.

EXHIBIT 2B
MARKET SHARES BY MAJOR BREWERS
(barrels in millions)

Year	Anheuser-Busch (bbls)	(%)	Miller (bbls)	(%)	Schlitz (bbls)	(%)	Pabst (bbls)	(%)	Coors (bbls)	(%)	Other (bbls)	(%)
1977	36.6	23.3	24.2	15.4	22.1	14.1	17.0	10.8	12.8	8.2	44.2	28.2
1976	29.1a	19.3	18.4	12.2	24.2	16.1	16.3	10.8	13.7	9.1	48.7	32.4
1975	35.2	23.8	12.8	8.6	12.2	15.7	15.6	10.5	11.9	8.0	49.3	33.3
1974	34.1	23.4	9.1	6.3	22.7	15.6	14.3	9.8	12.3	8.5	53.0	36.4
1973	29.9	21.6	6.9	5.0	21.3	15.4	13.1	9.5	11.0	7.9	56.3	40.6
1972	26.5	20.1	5.4	4.1	18.9	14.3	12.5	9.5	9.8	7.4	58.7	44.5
1971	24.3	19.3	5.2	4.1	16.7	13.3	11.8	9.4	8.5	6.7	59.5	47.2
1970	22.2	18.3	5.2	4.3	15.1	12.4	10.5	8.6	7.3	6.0	61.1	50.3
1969	18.7	16.0	5.1	4.4	13.7	11.7	10.2	8.7	6.4	5.5	62.6	53.6
1968	18.4	16.5	4.8	4.3	11.6	10.4	10.9	9.8	5.3	4.8	60.4	54.2

a Affected by 96-day strike in spring of 1976.
Source: Beverage Industry Annual Manual, 1976–1977, Modern Beverage Age and Annual Reports.

steadily increasing share for the top five breweries and a diminishing share for the rest. The trend is expected to continue. Projections are for even fewer breweries in the future and a growing portion of total sales accounted for by the top few producers.

One of the forces pressuring the smaller breweries is economy of large size. With large breweries vertical integration of production and modern technology have helped lower costs of production. When the situation is reversed for the typically smaller local or regional brewery, with reduced production capabilities per plant and less efficient technology, their costs per barrel of beer can be twice as much, or more, as the leading national producers.

In the mid-1960s the majors began a construction spree of superlarge breweries, more than double the size of previous facilities, which sharply raised capacity levels for the industry. This increased capacity created further pressures to raise market shares. Caught between lagging efficiency in production and heightened competition by the majors to sell their increases in capacity, many of the smaller breweries were unable to survive.

Among the giant brewers the competition is also keen, although the basis is not primarily on costs of production. More and more, the key to success is shifting to marketing and finance. Marketing is the tool for creating brand preference for one beer over another and thus gaining market share, while finances are necessary because of the very expensive costs of national advertising and promotion. In addition, massive capital spending plans have been outlined by the leading firms. Both Anheuser-Busch and Miller, for example, planned to spend more than $1 billion for expansion between the late 1970s and 1982. Most of those dollars will go to further increase capacity which, in turn, will continue the pressure to capture market share. Since the "rest" of the industry's shares have been squeezed so severely, the most likely place for the majors to seek the necessary volume in the 1980s will be from each other.

Market Growth and Consumer Characteristics

Overall unit growth for the brewing industry has been tailing off since 1974 (see Exhibit 3). Projections of 3 to 4 percent growth for the next several years contrasts with average gains of 4 to 5 percent for the first half of the 1970s. Among the top five brewers, only Miller managed to outpace the averages with a fantastic 266 percent gain in unit volume from 1974 to 1977. During the same period, Schlitz and Coors's output remained essentially flat, and Pabst and Anheuser-Busch recorded only modest increases.

A near-term factor for beer consumption is the anticipated decline in the population aged eighteen to thirty-four, traditionally the heaviest beer-drinking segment, accounting for half of total sales. Exhibit 4 shows this age

EXHIBIT 3
TOTAL PRODUCTION (TAX-PAID WITHDRAWALS)

Projected	Millions of bbl	Percentage change (from prior year)
1990	214	—
1985	194	—
1979	166	3.1
1978	161	2.6
Actual		
1977	156.9	4.3
1976	150.4	1.2
1975	148.6	2.1
1974	145.5	5.1
1973	138.5	5.1
1972	131.8	3.5
1971	127.4	4.5
1970	121.9	4.8
1969	116.3	4.4
1968	111.4	—

Source: Past data, U.S. Brewers Association, Inc., and forecasts, *Predicasts.*

EXHIBIT 4
POPULATION CHARACTERISTICS

Year	Population (mil.)	18- to 34-year-olds Number (mil.)	Percentage
1990	243.5	66.2	27.2
1985	232.9	67.8	29.1
1980	222.2	65.7	29.6
1979	220.2	64.3	29.2
1978	218.4	62.9	28.8
1977	216.7	61.8	28.5
1976	215.1	60.2	28.0
1975	213.5	58.5	27.4
1974	211.9	56.7	26.8
1973	210.9	55.0	26.1
1972	208.8	53.3	25.5
1971	207.1	51.6	24.9
1970	204.9	50.0	24.4

Source: United States Department of Commerce.

group increasing its share of the total population until 1980 (actually 1981 is the peak year for growth and then the trend turns downward). As the post-World War II babies mature, growth in this favorable portion of the age distribution will then decline. By 1990 Census projections show the share of eighteen- to thirty-four-year-olds will have retreated to roughly the position held in 1975. This could escalate competition in the industry, because huge capital spending programs being planned in 1978 and 1979 will be coming into production at about the same time as the population demographics become unfavorable.

Offsetting the forecast for fewer persons of drinking age eighteen to thirty-four is an expectation of continued gains in per-capita beer consumption. By 1990 an estimated 27.2 gallons of beer a year will be consumed on a per-capita basis, compared to 22.5 in 1977 (see Exhibit 5). This forecast tends to extrapolate the steady gains shown throughout the 1970s. It further reflects confidence that brewers can continue to introduce new products to broaden their markets and also increase the average amount consumed by the traditional beer drinker. One reason for such confidence is the success of new products such as low-calorie, light beers. In just this one product category, beginning from a standing start in 1975 with the intro-

EXHIBIT 5
BEER PRODUCTION AND CONSUMPTION

Projected	Production[a] (millions of bbl)	Per capita consumption (gals.)
1990	214	27.2
1985	194	25.8
1979	166	23.4
1978	161	22.9
Actual		
1977	156.9	22.5
1976	150.4	21.7
1975	148.6	21.6
1974	145.5	20.9
1973	138.5	19.8
1972	131.8	19.5
1971	127.4	18.6
1970	121.9	18.7
1969	116.3	17.2
1968	111.4	16.7

[a] Tax-paid withdrawals.

Source: Past data, U.S. Brewers Association, Inc., forecasts, and U.S. Department of Commerce.

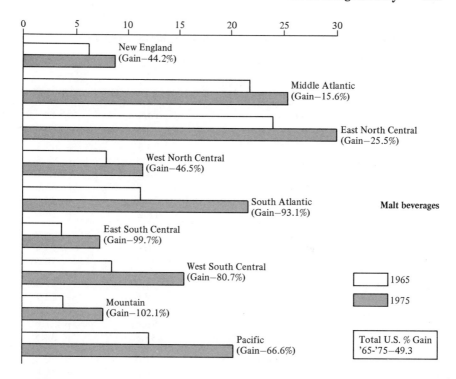

EXHIBIT 6
MALT-BEVERAGE SALES BY GEOGRAPHICAL REGIONS,
1965 VS. 1975
(millions of 31 gal. bbl)

Source: The Brewers Almanac. Reprinted by permission of the U.S. Brewers Association, Inc.

duction of Miller's Lite beer, low-calorie beers rose to about 8 percent of the market in 1977. A new consumer market segment was in effect developed, which consisted of persons who previously didn't drink beer, or very much beer, because of the high calorie content. Also, improving the taste of low-calorie beer contributed to its success among the traditional steady beer drinkers.

A final consideration in beer marketing is awareness of the different trends in consumption patterns by regions and by states. From 1965 to 1975, for example, the mountain states (Montana, Idaho, Wyoming, Colorado, New Mexico, Arizona, Utah, and Nevada) led all other regions with a 102.1 percent gain in malt beverage sales (see Exhibit 6). In contrast, the national average was only 49.3 percent, while the Middle Atlantic Region was able to show only a modest increase of 15.6 percent.

EXHIBIT 7
MALT-BEVERAGE SALES CHANGES, 1965–1975, BY MARKETS
(with listings of 1975 per capita-gallons)

	Markets by regions		
Region	Market	Per capita	% change '65 vs. '75
New England:	Maine	24.5	+ 65.3
	New Hampshire	32.8	+ 87.3
	Vermont	24.0	+ 53.1
	Massachusetts	22.8	+ 45.6
	Rhode Island	24.5	+ 24.3
	Connecticut	18.2	+ 26.6
Middle Atlantic:	New York	20.0	+ 6.7
	New Jersey	20.0	+ 15.4
	Pennsylvania	23.2	+ 30.0
East North Central:	Ohio	21.0	+ 21.4
	Indiana	17.6	+ 22.7
	Illinois	22.3	+ 22.4
	Michigan	23.8	+ 27.6
	Wisconsin	31.8	+ 34.5
West North Central:	Minnesota	22.0	+ 50.2
	Iowa	21.8	+ 46.9
	Missouri	21.0	+ 29.8
	North Dakota	23.4	+ 43.7
	South Dakota	18.5	+ 56.4
	Nebraska	23.6	+ 42.7
	Kansas	19.6	+ 95.1
South Atlantic:	Delaware	21.1	+ 41.9
	Maryland	23.1	+ 38.0
	D.C.	23.8	− 7.4
	Virginia	19.5	+ 61.7
	West Virginia	16.0	+ 42.7
	North Carolina	16.2	+172.2
	South Carolina	18.1	+152.5
	Georgia	16.1	+145.3
	Florida	24.0	+134.4
East South Central:	Kentucky	17.7	+ 50.0
	Tennessee	18.6	+109.5
	Alabama	14.7	+145.0
	Mississippi	16.6	+139.8
West South Central:	Arkansas	15.0	+112.5
	Louisiana	21.5	+ 51.7
	Texas	26.3	+ 83.8
	Oklahoma	16.9	+104.9

| Markets by regions | | | |
Region	Market	Per capita	% change '65 vs. '75
Mountain:	Montana	29.5	+ 45.3
	Idaho	24.5	+101.3
	Wyoming	31.1	+131.5
	Colorado	24.5	+114.3
	New Mexico	24.4	+ 95.8
	Arizona	26.8	+124.3
	Utah	14.1	+ 92.6
	Nevada	33.6	+ 93.2
Pacific:	Washington	23.2	+ 74.5
	Oregon	22.1	+ 61.7
	California	22.0	+ 60.7
	Alaska	25.2	+164.3
	Hawaii	25.2	+253.3

Per capita 1975: U.S. total +21.6

Source: The Brewers Almanac. Reprinted by permission of the U.S. Brewers Association, Inc.

On a per-capita basis, Texas, New Hampshire, Wisconsin, and Wyoming all showed an average of more than 31 gallons consumed in 1975 (see Exhibit 7). Percentage gains in per-capita consumption were highest in Hawaii — an exceptional 253 percent increase from 1965 to 1975 — with strong gains in North Carolina (172%), Alaska (164%), South Carolina (152%), Georgia (145%), and Alabama (145%).

Shifts in Brand Marketing

Behind Philip Morris's success in raising Miller to second place in the beer industry was an advertising strategy that recognized the fallacy in an "average" drinker image. While Anheuser-Busch had targeted its advertising on a basic profile of a blue-collar six-pack type, Philip Morris recognized, from its success in the tobacco business, that beer drinkers, like tobacco smokers, were not a single market but a number of differentiated market segments. Also, the rest of the brewing industry's advertising did not sufficiently reflect the fact that persons had shifted their drinking from the neighborhood bar to the home. While the traditional 1960s advertisements focused on a workingman's barroom drinking environment, the fact was that over half of all beer drinking was in the home. By 1978 roughly two-thirds of all beer was consumed in homes, with the shift away from bars expected to continue.

Miller capitalized on these trends by tailoring heavy advertising campaigns to appeal to new market segments and producing new products to sell in them. Introduction of a new seven-ounce "pony" bottle in 1972 was the first such marketing innovation, appealing to a particular market — mainly women and older people — who did not want to drink as much as the standard twelve-ounce bottle. But this success was only a modest introduction to the enormous popularity of Miller's Lite beer, the first volume low-calorie beer. Although there were a number of predecessor low-calorie beers, most notably Gablingers, these had previously been conceived and promoted for diet-conscious drinkers — a limited market. But Miller rightfully reckoned that low-calorie beer could be mass-marketed to the traditional heavier drinkers who didn't want to get filled up too fast.

Following the pattern of Miller, the rest of the industry has been busily introducing new products to catch up. Behind the new strategies is an implicit, if belated, realization that different beers can be promoted to appeal to different types of consumers. As demonstrated by Exhibit 8, consumers can be classified according to certain dominant lifestyle patterns, with accompanying concepts associated with each consumer category, including certain brands of beers to go with each consumer segment. The information

EXHIBIT 8
BEER PREFERENCES BY CONSUMER LIFESTYLE PATTERNS

	Tradition-alist	Achiever	Hedonist	New values
Product form	Popular	Premium	Super-premium and import	Light
Principal benefit	Price	Taste	Status	Health and new experience
Product life-cycle stage	Mature	Mature	Growth	Growth
Marketing focus	Price	Product/ promotion	Product/ promotion	Product/ promotion
Typical brands (company)	Old Milwaukee (Schlitz)	Coors (Coors)	Michelob (Anheuser-Busch)	Lite (Miller)

in Exhibit 8 is meant to be illustrative. It does not imply any proven associations but serves, rather, as an example of the types of marketing relationships that might be developed given the appropriate market research. There are, obviously, different consumer characteristics that could be used to develop brand differentiation. In studies led by Dr. Fred E. Emery,* for instance, three distinctive drinking types were identified and described:

1. *Reparative:* A controlled middle-aged, light drinker. Drinks at end of day or on weekends.

2. *Social:* Young adult who drinks heaviest on weekends, holidays, and vacations. Drinks more heavily than reparative drinker; but generally in control.

3. *Indulgent:* Heavy drinker of no particular age. Drinks heaviest when under pressure; may frequently drink out of control.

In moves to catch the fastest-growing segments of the market, brewers have introduced a number of new super-premiums and light beer. For years Anheuser-Busch's Michelob had the super-premium market pretty much to itself. Now Miller is planning a domestic version of Lowenbrau, Schlitz is contemplating introduction of a brew called Erlanger, and Coors is also planning a super-premium beer. As shown in Exhibit 9 the emphasis of new-product introductions is in the super-premium and light beers. In addition some tentative moves have been made to market imported foreign beers. Although at present imported beer is only 2 percent of the market, it is a fast-growing segment and one in which premium prices can be commanded.

Advertising Expenditures

Because of the power of advertising to influence consumers' brand and product choices, advertising has understandably attracted increasing attention. Part of this attention is translated into large advertising outlays. It is a very expensive contest. The three leading firms in 1977 each devoted over $30 million for advertising. On average, advertising expenditures run about 2 percent of net sales for the industry.

Perhaps more insightful, on a per-barrel basis, the top three advertisers each devoted well over a dollar per barrel to advertising. Just among the

---

* In studies performed at the Human Resources Centre of the Tavistock Institute in London, as reported by Ackoff and Emshoff, "Advertising Research," *The Sloan Management Review,* Spring 1975.

EXHIBIT 9
MAJOR BEERS BY PRODUCT AND COMPANY

Category:	Popular	Premium	Super-premium	Import	Low calorie
Company					
Anheuser-Busch		Budweiser	Michelob	Würzberger (n)	Michelob Light (n)
Miller		Miller High Life	Lowenbrau[a] (n)		Lite
Schlitz	Old Milwaukee	Schlitz	Erlanger (n)		Schlitz Light
Coors		Coors	Coors Super-premium (n)		Coors Light (n)

(n) = new or planned.
[a] Domestic version to be produced under license.

top five producers, the difference between the highest per-barrel expenditure ($1.85 for Schlitz) and the lowest (.31 for Coors) is roughly six times (see Exhibit 10). Moreover, except for Miller, whose per-barrel costs peaked in 1975, the other top producers have steadily and sharply increased their ante.

With the number of barrels of sales reducing advertising costs per barrel, it is obviously a game the major producers are best equipped to play. For example, assuming the fifth-ranked brewer, Coors, were to match Anheuser-Busch's $48+ million outlay, it would, for Coors, represent a $3.77 per-barrel advertising expense; a prohibitive cost disadvantage when compared with Anheuser-Busch's $1.32 per barrel.

Manufacturing Costs and Processes

Three types of costs associated with brewing relate to raw materials, containers, and manufacturing efficiency. The first category of cost is largely out of the manufacturer's control with commodity prices set by the marketplace. Malt is the most important ingredient and it tends to follow the price of barley, its major source. Corn and rice are the other two principal raw materials. Prices of these commodities have fluctuated, with corn showing the greatest volatility — particularly from 1973 to 1975.

EXHIBIT 10

	Advertising expenditures (000s of dollars)			
	1977	1976	1975	1974
Anheuser-Busch	48,287	28,470	20,457	12,901
Schlitz	40,832	33,756	23,254	18,256
Miller	30,846	27,378	20,852	11,648
Pabst	10,843	9,112	9,007	7,706
Coors	3,963	1,626	1,093	802

	Advertising expenditures per barrel			
	1977	1976	1975	1974
Anheuser-Busch	1.32	.98[a]	.58	.38
Schlitz	1.85	1.40	1.00	.81
Miller	1.27	1.49	1.63	1.27
Pabst	.64	.56	.58	.54
Coors	.31	.12	.09	.065

[a] Strike-affected year.

Source: Leading National Advertisers, Inc. Reprinted by permission.

A second type of cost is for containers, which cost more than the liquid they contain. Here producers have established some control over costs by vertically integrating backward. Coors produces all its can requirements, to lead the majors, while Schlitz meets about 80 percent of its needs and Anheuser-Busch 40 percent (as of 1979).

A final cost is the efficiency of the manufacturing process itself. Traditionally, Schlitz has been the industry's low-cost producer. With huge new and efficient plant expansion planned by Miller and Anheuser-Busch, however, the spread in operating efficiency should narrow. Among the majors most of the production is already from highly automated, low unit-labor-cost facilities. Direct unit labor costs should decline even further as planned facilities begin operations in the early 1980s.

Comparative Industry Data

Composite industry statistics, projections, and financial ratios developed by Value Line are provided in Exhibit 11.

EXHIBIT 11
COMPOSITE STATISTICS: BREWING INDUSTRY

1975	1976	1977	1978	1979	1980	© Arnold Bernhard & Co., Inc.	82–84E
4749.8	4909.0	5071.2	5567.6	**5500**	**7500**	Sales ($mill)	**11.180**
12.3%	13.8%	13.1%	11.4%	**12.5%**	**12.5%**	Operating margin	**12.5%**
152.9	174.5	199.3	218.8	**240**	**260**	Depreciation ($mill)	**360**
162.0	241.1	224.5	209.5	**257**	**310**	Net profit ($mill)	**555**
53.9%	47.2%	44.8%	45.5%	**44.0%**	**46.5%**	Income tax rate	**45.0%**
3.4%	4.9%	4.4%	3.8%	**4.0%**	**4.1%**	Net profit margin	**5.0%**
504.4	476.0	550.3	580.4	**655**	**635**	Working cap'l ($mill)	**940**
717.2	708.2	701.9	733.8	**805**	**936**	Long-term debt ($mill)	**1210**
1870.7	2068.0	2203.0	2278.6	**2485**	**2700**	Net worth ($mill)	**3770**
7.2%	9.7%	8.6%	7.9%	**9.0%**	**9.5%**	% Earned total cap'l	**12.0%**
8.7%	11.7%	10.2%	9.2%	**10.5%**	**11.6%**	% Earned net worth	**14.5%**
5.3%	8.5%	7.0%	5.8%	**7.5%**	**9.0%**	% Retained to comm eq	**11.5%**
40%	29%	33%	38%	**28%**	**25%**	% All div'ds to net prof	**24%**
22.3	13.3	11.1	11.2	Bold figures		Avg ann'l P/E ratio	**16.0**
1.8%	2.1%	2.9%	3.4%	are VL estimates		Avg ann'l div'd yield	**1.5%**

Source: The Value Line Investment Survey. Reprinted by permission.

Assignment

1. Philip Morris's Miller subsidiary is a classic example of the impact new, successfully implemented policies and strategies can make in an industry. Examine and evaluate the theory of proper policy and strategy formulation with the actions of the top four beer producers: Miller, Anheuser-Busch, Schlitz, and Coors.

Anheuser-Busch and Miller*

The brewing industry has been revolutionized since Philip Morris bought Miller Brewing in 1971. And no brewer was more surprised by the new and successful tactics of Miller than Anheuser-Busch. Accustomed to leading the industry, Anheuser-Busch was thrust unfamiliarly on the defensive. Even though Anheuser-Busch retains a comfortably larger market share, Miller has far outpaced every brewer in growth, and managed to rewrite the strategies for performance in the brewery business. A few short years ago no one would give credibility to Miller's bid for the top spot, but now few totally discount the possibility.

History and Management of Anheuser-Busch

Budweiser, the world's most popular beer, was created in 1876. After more than one hundred years, Budweiser continues to be brewed in exactly the same manner. This type of tradition is maintained by family control of the business (which owns about 25% of the stock). August Busch III is the fourth generation to head the company. Trained in Chicago's Siebel Institute of Technology to become a brewmaster, he worked in all operations of the firm before becoming president in 1974 and chairman in 1977.

Anheuser-Busch had unquestioned dominance of the beer industry until about 1975, when Miller introduced its low-calorie Lite beer. Since then events have tended to center around Miller rather than Anheuser-Busch. Using aggressive marketing and promotion tactics borrowed from the parent's tobacco business, Miller swiftly overtook competitors until only Anheuser-Busch was left. Too late, Anheuser-Busch realized that Miller had stolen a march on it. But once awakened, August Busch III was ready to

---

* Prepared by Milton Leontiades.

fight. Determined to stay on top, Anheuser-Busch geared up to meet and beat Miller. "Tell Miller to come right along, but tell them to bring lots of money," challenged August Busch III.

Miller also reflects the strong personality of its chief executive, John Murphy. Named to head the small brewery in 1971, after Philip Morris had purchased it from a discouraged W. R. Grace, Murphy spent some time analyzing the situation. What he saw was an operation with essentially static sales when other producers were showing gains of 5 to 10 percent. Once he was convinced the basic strategies successfully employed in the tobacco business were applicable to beer, Murphy moved quickly. In essence, he applied concepts that were common in consumer product areas but had been largely ignored in brewing; such classic marketing techniques as market segmentation, for example: identify separate consumer segments, produce new products with new packaging for these segments, and spend lavishly to promote them. So successful was Murphy's strategy that Miller jumped from 5 million barrels and a market share of 4 percent in 1972 to over 24 million barrels and a 15+ percent of the market in 1977.

Having succeeded thus far, Murphy was apparently not through. "You never start out to be number two," he has said. But the terrain may be a little more rugged from here on. At the beginning Miller was successful in filling voids in brand offerings, and developing new products for new market segments. Now Miller is challenging Anheuser-Busch head-on. For example, Miller has unveiled plans for a domestically brewed version of Lowenbrau beer — aimed squarely at Anheuser-Busch's most profitable beer: Michelob.

Product Strategy

The most familiar aspect of the war within the industry has been the novel marketing approach of Miller. Previously noted in the industry analysis was Miller's introduction of the seven-ounce bottle plus the tremendous popularity of the Lite beer campaign. Preceding these maneuvers, however, was Miller's initial success with Miller High Life, the "champagne of beers," and the only competitive brand the company produced. However, as Murphy diagnosed the situation, Miller High Life had an image problem: it was appealing to the wrong market segment. Attracting a disproportionate number of women and affluent occasional drinkers, it was missing the big money market of heavier, steady drinkers. Murphy saw it as a question of repositioning the product. Without changing the name or even the familiar "champagne of beer" slogan, Murphy hired a new advertising agency and developed a sequence of commercials around the theme of workingmen relaxing at the end of a hard day with Miller High Life. In the words of one of the advertising executives the strategy was to "Take Miller High Life out of the champagne bucket and put it into the lunch bucket without spilling a drop."

And it certainly worked. With advertising expenditures of between $10 to $13 million a year, the new Miller High Life theme was virtually unchanged for seven years and made Miller High Life one of the three top-selling beers.

Anheuser-Busch, on the other hand, had introduced only one new product — Busch Bavarian in 1955. Busch Bavarian was a popularly priced beer introduced mainly to improve capacity utilization. It was low profit and grabbed a significant market share in only a few states. It was aimed at the slow-growth end of the consumer market; it gained Anheuser-Busch few new consumers and missed the growing markets for super-premium and light beers.

When the threat of Miller became apparent, the strategies of Anheuser-Busch shifted accordingly. Busch Bavarian, for example, was reformulated in 1978 to attract younger drinkers. As the new Busch Premium it grabbed an initial 8 percent of the market in six New England states where it was initially introduced.

In 1977 Anheuser Natural Light was developed to compete with Miller's Lite beer. Anheuser-Busch followed in 1978 with a light version of Michelob called, appropriately, Michelob Light. It now is the only company with two brands positioned in this fast-growing market area.

Further, Anheuser-Busch announced plans to unveil still another super-premium beer. Recognizing that premiums, super-premiums, and light beers are not only growing faster than popular brands but are also about twice as profitable, Anheuser-Busch is developing a strategy of its own to bracket other brewers with two products in each of these high-profit markets. Also, Anheuser-Busch is experimenting with an imported beer called Würzburger. Although a small-volume market at present, imported beers have been growing at a 30 percent rate and could signal a significant new future market. Caught unaware once, Anheuser-Busch seems determined not be be a follower a second time.

Advertising

In 1977 the five largest brewers raised advertising outlays by 34 percent, with Anheuser-Busch raising its ante by a dramatic 70 percent. Advertising costs of $48+ million by Anheuser-Busch were in fact greater than the net sales of F & M Schaefer, the eighth-ranked domestic producer. For 1979, Anheuser-Busch had budgeted $115 million — a 134 percent increase. Just to introduce a new brand a company may spend up to $15 a barrel on advertising.

EXHIBIT 1
ADVERTISING EXPENSES
(first 9 months — 1978)

	Million
Anheuser-Busch Natural Light	$11.5
Budweiser	16.2
Busch	3.9
Michelob	9.1
Michelob Light	4.6

Source: Reprinted by permission from the Feb. 5, 1979, issue of *Advertising Age.* Copyright 1979 by Crain Communications, Inc.

Intimidating as these figures are, so far the major producers have justified them in order to retain or improve market position. Some of it is probably catch-up stimulated by Miller's grab of over 15 percent of the market by 1977. Miller is in fact the only one of the top five brewers whose advertising expenditures per barrel declined in 1976 and 1977.

There is undoubtedly some point at which the heat-up in advertising costs should moderate. With volume increases lagging significantly behind the jump in advertising costs, there is a question of returns on the advertising dollars. In Exhibit 1 are advertising figures for certain Anheuser-Busch brands for the first nine months of 1978. In addition Exhibit 2 provides expenditures by type of media for selected brands for the two leading companies. Finally, for Anheuser-Busch, data are available for distribution of its advertising dollars by brand and media from 1972 to 1977 (see Exhibit 3).

Costs, however, are only one-half of the advertising equation. Equally important is creating and promoting the right image on the right media. In the past, Miller had been the clear champion in this area. With Anheuser-Busch concentrating on its old rival Schlitz and traditional tactics of price and process efficiency, Miller was able to take advantage of the relative neglect of marketing strategy. Nowhere was this made more apparent than in the campaign for Lite beer. Miller virtually locked up all the top TV network sports shows in 1974, including *Monday Night Football* and *College Football Game of the Week.* Anheuser-Busch contends it was aware of Miller's strategy — it simply didn't believe it would succeed. Said August Busch III, "We were perfectly aware of when they bought the *Monday Night Football* package. Perfectly aware. We looked at the cost of that on a total dollars basis, but not on a cost-per-thousand-beer drinkers' basis. That's where we missed the boat. We were simply unsmarted." [1]

EXHIBIT 2
1976 MEDIA EXPENDITURES FOR SELECTED BEER BRANDS

Brand	Total	Magazines	Network TV	Spot TV	Net radio	Spot radio	Newspapers
Budweiser	$17,718,700	$1,072,700	$ 9,167,800	$2,184,800	$1,487,700	$3,436,600	$369,800
Michelob	$ 8,258,200	$ 891,600	$ 4,273,700	$1,638,700	$ 494,900	$ 776,900	$192,900
Miller High Life	$13,464,500	$ 68,700	$ 9,655,100	$2,727,900	—	$ 950,400	$ 62,400
Miller Lite	$14,785,900	—	$12,440,600	$2,345,300	—	—	—

Source: From an article titled "Brand Report 22: Beer," from *Media Decisions,* September 1977.

EXHIBIT 3
ANHEUSER-BUSCH MEDIA EXPENDITURES 1972 TO 1977
(in dollars)

Year	Brand	Total	Magazines	Network TV	Spot TV	Net radio	Spot radio	Outdoor
1977	Natural	10,658,000		6,659,900	1,249,600	386,100	1,746,100	616,300
	Budweiser	26,976,200	610,000	17,461,300	3,325,700	1,136,400	4,194,700	248,100
	Busch	5,114,200			2,998,500		2,110,400	5,300
	Michelob	10,259,200	1,625,700	7,789,200	221,900	329,500	289,800	3,100
1976	Budweiser	16,611,100	1,072,700	9,176,800	2,184,800	1,487,800	2,436,600	252,400
	Busch	5,842,700			2,735,400		2,747,300	
	Michelob	8,293,400	891,600	4,273,700	1,683,700	494,900	766,900	182,600
1975	Budweiser	12,802,800	907,600	5,846,300	2,008,700	755,700	3,238,500	46,000
	Busch	5,487,200			2,428,800		3,058,400	
	Michelob	7,296,400	910,200	3,622,100	1,706,900	489,300	537,600	30,300
1974	Budweiser	9,420,800	478,800	4,487,700	1,023,500	675,900	2,664,300	90,600
	Busch	3,949,400		120,000	1,540,900		2,287,200	1,300
	Michelob	4,193,500	416,400	2,446,300	1,024,900		302,100	3,800
1973	Budweiser	12,105,700	185,100	4,639,100	2,300,100		4,878,800	102,600
	Busch	4,002,200		1,913,000	2,076,100		1,917,000	9,100
	Michelob	3,306,000	61,800		1,158,100		173,100	
1972	Budweiser	13,699,700	887,900	3,496,400	3,029,500		6,255,400	30,500
	Busch	4,624,900			1,541,100		2,989,400	94,400
	Michelob	4,618,600	478,500	1,832,800	1,297,300	236,900	772,100	1,000

Source: From "Busch's Beer Battle" in *Media Decisions,* September 1978.

Not wishing to be "unsmarted" again Anheuser-Busch has since pumped tens of millions of incremental dollars into its advertising budgets. However, Miller is hardly backing off.

"NBC offered key spots to Anheuser-Busch during the Moscow Olympic Games on each of eighteen days for $18 million. When Busch turned the network down, Miller bought the package for an undisclosed sum. Next spring Anheuser-Busch will pay $654,000 for 150 seconds of commercials on ABC's Roots II. Blacks, not incidentally, consume some 22 million barrels of beer annually, representing 15 percent of the market." [2]

Some observers have raised the question of Miller's ultimate staying power. Backed by the resources of tobacco-rich Philip Morris, Miller is not about to run out of funds. But at some point it will have to justify Philip Morris's commitment to it. Philip Morris reportedly spent close to $1 billion for plant expansion in 1978, not counting the $227 million it paid to purchase Miller. Philip Morris is unlikely to have yet recovered sufficient profits to justify past expenditures although it has been amply rewarded in terms of sales growth. If and when Miller stands on its own feet, some observers wonder if it will follow the pattern of a similar purchase by Canada's Carling O'Keefe, Ltd.

"Carling O'Keefe, Ltd. bought tiny Carling Brewing Co. in the mid-1940's and poured huge sums of money into expanding the Carling Black Label brand in the U.S. Subsidized by a very profitable Canadian Brewing operation, Carling vaulted from 53rd place in the U.S. beer market to fourth by 1960. But after deducting interest on the money its parent was providing, Carling was not making a profit in those years of growth. Now Carling languishes in 11th place after losing $9 million last year (1975)." [3]

Expansion

Both Anheuser-Busch and Miller could have sold more beer in 1978 if extra capacity were available. Both companies were also expected to have difficulty meeting demand in 1979 because of insufficient capacity. And both announced ambitious expansion programs to raise capacity by 1982.

Miller's plans are for a $1 billion outlay to raise productive capacity to 55 million barrels. Anheuser-Busch plans to spend $1.5 billion and raise capacity to about 60 million barrels. Compared with 1977, each firm will increase capacity by 275% and 38% respectively (see Exhibit 4).

Manufacturing Processes

A major reason Anheuser-Busch's capacity per barrel is projected to be so much more expensive than Miller's is the pride and the cost in maintaining

EXHIBIT 4
CAPACITY AND EXPANSION
(millions of bbl)

	Anheuser-Busch	*Miller*
1982	60	55
1977(e)	43.5	20.0
1976(e)	39.5	16.8
1975(e)	38.5	13.5

(e) = estimates
Source: John C. Maxwell of Wheat First Securities and company statements.

a long tradition. Anheuser-Busch unquestionably could reduce its operating costs if it were to reduce its standards:

> By resorting to chemical additives, by using corn instead of rice in its top-of-the-line brands, by using domestic rather than imported hops, by applying every facet of newfangled technology that others take for granted, Anheuser-Busch could cut its cost significantly. Where most others require some twenty days to turn out a barrel of beer, Anheuser-Busch won't release its beer for a month or more. That seems a sacrifice to outsiders, but it is a commandment issued from St. Louis to its ten breweries. Were Anheuser-Busch to step in line with others in the industry, it could increase its profits measurably. Moreover, it could greatly increase the production in its ten breweries from the 41 million barrels it made and sold in 1978.[4]

But Anheuser-Busch is adamant. It will not stoop to the quicker brewing cycle and to anything less than the natural ingredients it has always used in its beers. Miller, on the other hand, is counting on the relative efficiencies of its methods. It does not deny using various artificial ingredients or a shorter brewing cycle. But it maintains its methods meet all federal regulations and are also common industry practices. In discussing manufacturing methods, John Murphy's response is, "After all, we're not in the brain-surgery business."

Financial Condition

Both companies are very strong financially. As a division of Philip Morris, Miller has tremendous resources behind it. Because it is consolidated as part of Philip Morris, however, it is difficult to get as complete financial information for Miller as for Anheuser-Busch. Exhibits 5 to 7 provide relevant available financial data for the two firms.

EXHIBIT 5
PHILIP MORRIS

	1978	1977	1976	1975	1974
Operating companies revenues (in thousands)					
Philip Morris U.S.A.	$2,437,465	$2,160,362	$1,963,144	$1,721,549	$1,502,267
Philip Morris International	1,810,861	1,349,280	1,083,970	1,040,002	887,077
Miller Brewing Company	1,834,526	1,327,619	982,810	658,268	403,551
The Seven-Up Company	186,494				
Philip Morris Industrial	237,165	216,699	169,096	151,960	155,390
Mission Viejo Company	125,952	148,017	94,762	70,635	62,676
Consolidated operating revenues	$6,632,463	$5,201,977	$4,293,782	$3,642,414	$3,010,961
Operating companies income (in thousands)					
Philip Morris U.S.A.	$ 568,145	$ 474,400	$ 401,426	$ 337,314	$ 286,225
Philip Morris International	188,561	153,791	130,104	112,975	94,017
Miller Brewing Company	150,300	106,456	76,056	28,628	6,291
The Seven-Up Company	26,291				
Philip Morris Industrial	15,024	14,860	10,620	8,052	12,280
Mission Viejo Company	19,761	33,225	16,333	5,875	4,772
Consolidated operating income	$ 968,082	$ 782,732	$ 634,539	$ 492,844	$ 403,585
Identifiable assets (in millions)					
Tobacco	$3,066	$2,510	$2,242	$2,047	$1,796
Beer	1,245	819	646	497	338
Other products	979	407	336	285	271
	$5,290	$3,736	$3,224	$2,829	$2,405
Depreciation expense (in millions)					
Tobacco	$ 52	$ 42	$ 39	$ 32	$ 25
Beer	41	27	18	10	6
Capital additions (in millions)					
Tobacco	$ 174	$ 78	$ 61	$ 86	$ 127
Beer	358	183	147	146	77

EXHIBIT 6
ANHEUSER-BUSCH, INC., AND SUBSIDIARIES
TEN-YEAR FINANCIAL SUMMARY
(in thousands, except per share and statistical data)

	1978	1977	1976
Consolidated summary of operations			
Barrels sold	41,610	36,640	29,051
Sales	$2,701,611	$2,231,230	$1,752,998
Federal and state beer taxes	441,978	393,182	311,852
Net sales	2,259,633	1,838,048	1,441,146
Cost of products sold	1,762,410	1,462,801	1,175,055
Gross profit	497,223	375,247	266,091
Marketing, administrative and research expenses	274,961	190,470	137,797
Operating income	222,262	184,777	128,294
Interest income	11,693	7,724	10,304
Interest expense	(28,894)	(26,708)	(26,941)
Other income net	751	4,193	1,748
Loss on partial closing of Los Angeles Busch Gardens			(10,020)
Income before income taxes	205,812	169,986	103,385
Income taxes	94,772	78,041	47,952
Income before extraordinary item	111,040	91,945	55,433
Extraordinary item			
Net income	111,040	91,945	55,433
Per share			
Income before extraordinary item	2.46	2.04	1.23
Net income	2.46	2.04	1.23
Cash dividends paid	37,013	32,036	30,646
Per share	.82	.71	.68
Dividend payout ratio	33.3%	34.8%	55.3%
Average number of shares outstanding	45,138	45,115	45,068
Book value per share	16.71	15.07	13.72
Balance sheet information			
Working capital	236,396	188,069	194,814
Current ratio	1.9	1.9	2.2
Plant and equipment, net	1,109,243	951,965	857,073
Long-term debt	427,250	337,492	340,737
Debt to debt plus total equity	34.5%	31.7%	34.0%
Deferred income taxes	153,080	125,221	99,119
Deferred investment tax credit	58,053	48,371	43,174
Shareholders equity	754,423	680,396	618,429
Return on shareholders equity	15.1%	14.2%	9.2%
Other information			
Capital expenditures	228,727	156,745	198,735
Depreciation	66,032	61,163	53,105
Total payroll cost	421,806	338,933	271,403
Effective tax rate	46.0%	45.9%	46.4%

Source: 1978 Annual Report of Anheuser-Busch.

EXHIBIT 6 *continued*

1975	1974	1973	1972	1971	1970	1969
35,196	34,097	29,887	26,522	24,309	22,202	18,712
$2,036,687	$1,791,863	$1,442,720	$1,273,093	$1,173,476	$1,036,272	$871,904
391,708	378,772	333,013	295,593	271,023	243,495	205,295
1,644,979	1,413,091	1,109,707	977,500	902,453	792,777	666,609
1,343,784	1,187,816	875,361	724,718	658,886	579,372	490,932
301,195	225,275	234,346	252,782	243,567	213,405	175,677
126,053	106,653	112,928	108,008	108,087	92,660	84,113
175,142	118,622	121,418	144,774	135,480	120,745	91,564
10,944	9,925	4,818	3,299	3,102	3,715	3,604
(22,602)	(11,851)	(5,288)	(6,041)	(6,597)	(7,104)	(7,401)
1,816	4,840	5,287	4,855	4,065	3,420	5,171
165,300	121,536	126,235	146,887	136,050	120,776	92,938
80,577	57,517	60,658	70,487	64,412	58,227	47,627
84,723	64,019	65,577	76,400	71,638	62,549	45,311
			4,093			
84,723	64,019	65,577	72,307	71,638	62,549	45,311
1.88	1.42	1.46	1.70	1.60	1.40	1.02
1.88	1.42	1.46	1.61	1.60	1.40	1.02
28,843	27,041	27,037	26,109	23,784	18,991	17,843
.64	.60	.60	.58	.53	.425	.40
34.0%	42.3%	41.1%	36.0%	33.1%	30.4%	39.2%
45,068	45,068	45,063	45,020	44,887	44,686	44,616
13.17	11.93	11.11	10.25	9.20	8.02	7.03
268,099	145,107	82,352	88,711	92,447	85,102	80,963
2.7	2.3	1.8	2.1	2.2	2.1	2.3
724,914	622,876	541,236	491,671	453,647	416,660	387,422
342,167	193,240	93,414	99,107	116,571	128,080	134,925
35.6%	25.7%	15.3%	17.2%	21.4%	25.6%	29.2%
80,748	66,264	54,281	41,456	34,103	27,274	23,212
24,293	21,157	17,225	14,370	14,276	13,563	12,577
593,642	537,762	500,784	461,980	413,974	358,476	314,121
15.0%	12.3%	13.6%	16.5%	18.6%	18.6%	15.1%
155,436	126,463	91,801	84,217	73,214	65,069	66,396
51,089	45,042	41,059	38,970	34,948	33,795	30,063
268,306	244,437	221,049	190,517	176,196	156,576	133,872
48.7%	47.3%	48.1%	48.0%	47.3%	48.2%	51.2%

EXHIBIT 7
ANHEUSER-BUSCH, INC., AND SUBSIDIARIES
CONSOLIDATED STATEMENT OF CHANGES
IN FINANCIAL POSITION

	Year ended December 31	
	1978	1977
	(in thousands)	
Financial resources were provided by:		
Operations —		
Net income for the year	$111,040	$ 91,945
Charges to income not involving working capital —		
Depreciation	66,032	61,163
Deferred income taxes	27,859	26,102
Deferred investment tax credit	9,682	5,197
Other, net	6,519	4,594
Working capital provided by operations	221,132	189,001
Proceeds from sale of 8.55% debentures	100,000	—
Decreased investment in and advances to unconsolidated subsidiaries	6,822	—
	327,954	189,001
Financial resources were used for:		
Capital expenditures	228,727	156,745
Cash dividends paid	37,013	32,036
Reduction in long-term debt	10,242	3,245
Increased investment in and advances to unconsolidated subsidiaries	—	3,430
Other, net	3,645	290
	279,627	195,746
Increase (decrease) in working capital	$ 48,327	$ (6,745)

ANALYSIS OF CHANGES IN WORKING CAPITAL

Increase (decrease) in current assets:		
Cash	$ 53,667	$ 7,630
Marketable securities	(11,399)	10,924
Accounts and notes receivable	17,169	6,683
Inventories	21,470	8,953
Other current assets	10,224	4,779
	91,131	38,969

continued

EXHIBIT 7 *continued*

	Year ended December 31	
	1978	*1977*
	(in thousands)	
Decrease (increase) in current liabilities:		
Accounts payable	(37,802)	(1,068)
Accrued salaries and wages	(5,996)	(4,400)
Accrued taxes, other than income taxes	(1,597)	(4,883)
Estimated federal and state income taxes	18,952	(38,201)
Other current liabilities	(16,361)	2,838
	(42,804)	(45,714)
Increase (decrease) in working capital	$ 48,327	$ (6,745)

Source: 1978 Annual Report of Anheuser-Busch.

Other Enterprises

Anheuser-Busch has on occasion expressed interest in diversifying from beer. It experimented with a soft drink called Chelsea with about .5 percent alcohol. Although unsuccessful with this venture, Anheuser-Busch remains interested in the soft-drink business. It is also interested in areas compatible with the beer business. At present roughly 10 percent of sales are accounted for by its entertainment division (Busch Gardens), the St. Louis Cardinals, and a miscellany of small industrial operations. While acquisitions are a possibility, the primary concern of August Busch III and his company at this juncture seems to be in keeping the "King of Beers" title.

Assignment

1.   Both Anheuser-Busch and Miller are in an obvious, determined battle for top spot in the beer industry. Develop strategies to achieve this position for Miller, and to maintain top position for Anheuser-Busch.

REFERENCES

1.   "We Missed the Boat . . . We Were Unsmarted," *Forbes,* August 7, 1978, p. 37.
2.   "August Busch Brews Up a New Spirit in St. Louis," *Fortune,* January 15, 1979, p. 97.
3.   "Miller's Fast Growth Upsets the Beer Industry," *Business Week,* November 8, 1976, p. 61.
4.   "August Busch Brews Up a New Spirit . . . ," p. 92.

Schlitz and Coors*

Schlitz and Coors, both previously very successful companies in the beer industry, share a common problem. They have lost their momentum. They are caught in an increasingly competitive fight between Miller Brewing and Anheuser-Busch for the top industry spot. Too big to serve a small, protected niche in the market, both firms must develop strategies to turn around their currently deteriorating market positions. In the following sections, the major problem areas of both companies are discussed.

Schlitz

Management is not all that went wrong with Schlitz but it is a good place to start. One of the biggest domestic corporations still under family control, the Uihleins own about 75 percent of Schlitz's stock. Along with control came active family management of the company from 1875 to 1975. Robert Uihlein, who had effectively run the company from 1962 to 1975, died in 1976 of leukemia. A number two man not having been groomed, Schlitz began a period of executive reshuffling. Included were departures of some talented top executives, aided, it was implied, by the omnipresent Uihlein influence on decision making.

In 1977 Daniel F. McKeithan was made chief executive officer, and he led a major shakeup of the top ranks. Many of the new appointments were from outside the company. A new president, for example, was a former top executive at Anheuser-Busch. A new executive vice-president for marketing joined the company from Coca-Cola; a senior vice-president for operations came from G. Heileman Brewing, and a vice-president for public relations formerly worked at Quaker Oats. It will take some time to feel the

---

* Prepared by Milton Leontiades.

effect of these management changes. But their mission is the heroic one of an almost complete revamping of Schlitz's past practices.

The year 1977 marked a turning point for Schlitz in other ways. It was the year Schlitz lost its number two position in the industry to Miller Brewing while experiencing a significant drop in volume. Its top-selling Schlitz brand beer suffered through an embarrassingly flat television campaign, which had to be hastily canceled. There were reported taste problems associated with a shortening of Schlitz's brewing cycle. Even Schlitz's officials had to admit the company had "image" problems. But many of the major deficiencies were more than image-deep.

CAPACITY UTILIZATION

From 1968 to 1976 Schlitz's volume more than doubled, for an annual growth rate of around 13 percent. Reflecting this favorable trend, Schlitz's capacity increased dramatically. Locked in a battle with Anheuser-Busch for top position, Schlitz relied on dual strategies of low-cost, efficient plants coupled with price competition to gain advantage. Striving to achieve dominance by lowering costs, Schlitz shortened its brewing cycle — whereas Anheuser-Busch retained a thirty-day brewing period — and substituted corn for more expensive rice products.

The experiment failed. The shorter-brewed beer reportedly lost flavor if it remained on the shelf too long. Forced to return to the lengthier brewing process, Schlitz not only lost the battle with its principal opponent, Anheuser-Busch, but failed completely to see the oncoming of Miller. In combination, the losing battle with Anheuser-Busch plus the loss of market share to Miller left Schlitz with large overcapacity by 1977. Operating at about 75 percent of its potential, Schlitz was by far the most inefficient utilizer of capacity among the industry's top five in 1977.

ADVERTISING

Once known for its advertising campaigns, Schlitz suffered a number of reversals. Among these was the failure of its "gusto" commercials, featuring a number of intimidating physical specimens who peered menacingly at the television viewer and said, "You want to take away my gusto?" This play on the "fight rather than switch" message evidently carried too threatening a tone for many beer drinkers. In the industry it became known as the "drink Schlitz or I'll kill you" commercial and ultimately Schlitz yanked it off the air. Therefore, while Schlitz had the highest advertising expenditures per barrel of the big five brewers in 1977, it got a lot less for its money. Media expenditures by brand are shown for 1976 in Exhibit 1.

EXHIBIT 1
1976 MEDIA EXPENDITURES (000s)

	Total	Maga-zines	Network TV	Spot TV	Net radio	Spot radio	News-papers
Schlitz	$17,887	—	$15,480	$1,029	—	$855	$523
Schlitz Light	9,530	—	7,781	1,563	—	6	—
Old Milwaukee	5,599	—	4,825	585	—	173	16

Source: From an article entitled "Brand Report 22: Beer," in *Media Decisions,* September 1978.

Some of Schlitz's advertising problems may be traceable to the departure of Fred R. Haviland, brought in from Anheuser-Busch to head marketing and advertising strategies in 1973. Haviland spent generously to support his approach. He also developed good relations with Schlitz's wholesalers. After his departure wholesaler relationships deteriorated and vital communications between the marketplace and top management broke down. According to one of Schlitz's more successful distributors in New Orleans, for example, he tried to get Schlitz to respond when Miller introduced its seven-ounce bottle. "But trying to talk to anybody there was like trying to force spaghetti through a keyhole. . . . It took more than two years [for Schlitz to come up with its own seven-ounce containers]. Miller was selling 100,000 cases a month before I got my first one, and they just gobbled us up." [1] Miller took over first place in New Orleans, and Schlitz dropped to second.

In another example, Schlitz Light — the first light beer on the market after Miller's Lite beer — was soon eclipsed after Anheuser-Busch introduced its light beer product. In an attempt to reverse such disastrous tactical mistakes, Schlitz steadily increased its advertising outlays. During 1978 Schlitz hired a new executive vice-president for marketing, revamped its marketing department, and hired new advertising agencies for its two major brands: Schlitz and Schlitz Light. Schlitz Light was also reformulated, along with a new packaging approach. Distributor communications were improved. Finally, in January 1979, a new super-premium beer called Erlanger was test-marketed, with development work in progress on other products as well.

LEGAL DEVELOPMENTS

A number of detracting legal developments occupied Schlitz's management in the late 1970s. One of these events concerned a Securities and Exchange

Commission allegation of illegal payments to distributors. Although some of the charges were similar to those aimed at other brewers — for example, Anheuser-Busch — and indeed were common practices by many producers, Schlitz seemed to make a large issue out of a commonplace finding. "It told the SEC it did not know how much, if anything, had been spent illegally, or how long the practices had been in effect. It then conducted an internal investigation that led to the suspensions of . . . top sales and marketing officers." [2]

In March 1978 a federal grand jury in Milwaukee also hit the company with a number of charges of marketing violations, after a three-year investigation. These included serious accusations of falsifying and destroying

EXHIBIT 2
CONSOLIDATED BALANCE SHEETS
DECEMBER 31, 1978 AND 1977

Assets	1978	1977
Current assets:		
Cash	$ 8,472,000	$ 8,348,000
Marketable securities, at lower of cost or market	18,173,000	13,756,000
Accounts receivable, less reserves of $805,000 in 1978 and $678,000 in 1977	27,161,000	30,441,000
Refundable income taxes	16,516,000	12,770,000
Inventories, at lower of cost or market	58,126,000	58,404,000
Prepaid expenses	7,403,000	10,620,000
Total current assets	135,851,000	134,339,000
Investments and other assets:		
Notes receivable and other noncurrent assets	5,474,000	5,166,000
Investments	16,522,000	16,871,000
Land and equipment held for sale, less reserve	7,492,000	5,766,000
	29,488,000	27,803,000
Plant and equipment at cost	839,693,000	855,279,000
Less — Accumulated depreciation and unamortized investment tax credit	313,097,000	290,659,000
	526,596,000	564,620,000
	$691,935,000	$726,762,000

Liabilities	1978	1977
Current liabilities:		
Notes payable	$ 5,614,000	$ 768,000
Accounts payable	45,725,000	44,229,000
Dividend payable	2,906,000	4,941,000
Accrued liabilities	38,563,000	32,712,000
Federal and state income taxes	2,789,000	3,995,000
Total current liabilities	95,597,000	86,645,000
Long-term debt	140,362,000	196,506,000
Deferred income taxes	100,970,000	86,906,000
Shareholders' investment:		
Common stock, par value $2.50 per share, authorized 30,000,000 shares, issued 29,373,654 shares	73,434,000	73,434,000
Capital in excess of par value	2,921,000	2,921,000
Retained earnings	285,279,000	286,978,000
	361,634,000	363,333,000
Less — Cost of 310,672 shares of treasury stock	6,628,000	6,628,000
Total shareholders' investment	355,006,000	356,705,000
	$691,935,000	$726,762,000

Source: From Schlitz Annual Report, 1978.

business records and income tax evasions. According to the company's 1978 annual report, however, "the most significant of these [major legal problems] were resolved during 1978."

FINANCIAL CONDITION

Schlitz's financial condition is reported in Exhibits 2 to 5. Schlitz has few demands for heavy capital spending in the foreseeable future. Schlitz's breweries are still among the most efficient in the industry. Also, Schlitz is second only to Coors in its captive can-making capabilities. Its relatively new and efficient can plants provide about 80 percent of Schlitz's needs.

EXHIBIT 3
STATEMENTS OF CONSOLIDATED EARNINGS
FOR THE YEARS ENDED DECEMBER 31, 1978 AND 1977

	1978	1977
Sales	$1,083,272,000	$1,134,079,000
Less — excise taxes	172,431,000	196,655,000
Net sales	910,841,000	937,424,000
Cost and expenses:		
Cost of goods sold	723,199,000	726,445,000
Marketing, administrative, and general expenses	151,594,000	150,124,000
	874,793,000	876,569,000
Earnings from operations	36,048,000	60,855,000
Other income (expense):		
Interest and dividend income	3,311,000	1,861,000
Interest expense	(15,359,000)	(16,724,000)
Loss on disposal of assets	(3,045,000)	(8,325,000)
Miscellaneous, net	(185,000)	(2,653,000)
	(15,278,000)	(25,841,000)
Earnings before income taxes	20,770,000	35,014,000
Provision for income taxes	8,809,000	15,249,000
Net earnings	$ 11,961,000	$ 19,765,000
Net earnings per share	$ .41	$ .68

Source: From Schlitz Annual Report, 1978.

EXHIBIT 4
STATEMENTS OF CHANGES IN CONSOLIDATED FINANCIAL POSITION
FOR THE YEARS ENDED DECEMBER 31, 1978 AND 1977

	1978	*1977*
Working capital was provided from:		
Operations:		
Net earnings for the year	$11,961,000	$19,765,000
Add — expenses not requiring outlay of working capital in current period —		
Depreciation of plant and equipment	45,946,000	41,127,000
Amortization of investment tax credit	(4,842,000)	(4,743,000)
Deferred income taxes	14,064,000	20,949,000
Loss on disposal of assets	1,050,000	8,325,000
Working capital provided from operations	68,179,000	85,423,000
Issuance of long-term debt	14,630,000	—
Retirement of plant and equipment	3,931,000	2,877,000
Investment tax credit	—	3,483,000
Decrease in other noncurrent assets	4,715,000	1,963,000
Total working capital provided	91,455,000	93,746,000
Working capital was used for:		
Additions to plant and equipment	14,461,000	35,670,000
Cash dividends declared	13,660,000	19,763,000
Reduction in long-term debt	70,774,000	26,689,000
Total working capital used	98,895,000	82,122,000
Increase (decrease) in working capital	$(7,440,000)	$11,624,000
Changes in components of working capital:		
Increase (decrease) in current assets:		
Cash	$ 124,000	$(6,805,000)
Marketable securities	4,417,000	(658,000)
Accounts receivable	(3,280,000)	5,001,000
Refundable income taxes	3,746,000	7,010,000
Inventories	(278,000)	(3,788,000)
Prepaid expenses	(3,217,000)	5,521,000
Increase in current assets	1,512,000	6,281,000
Increase (decrease) in current liabilities:		
Notes payable	4,846,000	(5,605,000)
Accounts payable	1,496,000	3,063,000
Dividends payable	(2,035,000)	—
Accrued liabilities	5,851,000	2,139,000
Federal and state income taxes	(1,206,000)	(4,940,000)
Increase (decrease) in current liabilities	8,952,000	(5,343,000)
Increase (decrease) in working capital	$(7,440,000)	$11,624,000

Source: From Schlitz Annual Report, 1978.

EXHIBIT 5
TEN-YEAR FINANCIAL SUMMARY

	1978	1977	1976	1975
Statements of consolidated earnings (000 omitted):				
Sales	$1,083,272	$1,134,079	$1,214,662	$1,130,439
Less — excise taxes	172,431	196,655	214,666	207,452
Net sales	910,841	937,424	999,996	922,987
Cost and expenses:				
Cost of goods sold	723,199	726,445	755,712	728,861
Marketing, administrative, and general expenses	151,594	150,124	131,639	110,641
	874,793	876,569	887,351	839,502
Earnings from operations	36,048	60,855	112,645	83,485
Interest expense	(15,359)	(16,724)	(17,220)	(14,526)
Other income (expense), net	81	(9,117)	1,299	(8,044)
Earnings from continuing operations before income taxes and extraordinary items	20,770	35,014	96,724	60,915
Provision for income taxes	8,809	15,249	46,777	30,019
Earnings from continuing operations before extraordinary items	11,961	19,765	49,947	30,896
Operating losses of former subsidiaries	—	—	—	—
Earnings before extraordinary items	11,961	19,765	49,947	30,896
Extraordinary items	—	—	—	—
Net earnings	$ 11,961	$ 19,765	$ 49,947	$ 30,896
Per common share:[a]				
Earnings before extraordinary items	$ .41	$ .68	$1.72	$1.06
Extraordinary items	—	—	—	—
Net earnings	$ .41	$ .68	$1.72	$1.06
Dividends	$ .47	$ .68	$ .68	$ .68
Balance sheet statistics (000 omitted):				
Net working capital	$ 40,254	$ 47,694	$ 36,070	$ 32,975
Current ratio	1.4 to 1	1.6 to 1	1.4 to 1	1.4 to 1
Plant and equipment, net	$ 526,596	$ 564,620	$ 585,785	$ 523,283
Long-term debt	140,362	196,506	223,195	212,717
Shareholders' investment per	355,006	356,705	356,703	326,519
share[a]	12.22	12.27	12.27	11.24
Other statistics (000 omitted):				
Depreciation of plant and equipment	45,946	41,127	35,685	27,697
Amortization of investment tax credit	(4,842)	(4,743)	(3,765)	(2,396)
Working capital provided from operations	68,179	85,423	101,178	73,884
Cash dividends declared	13,660	19,763	19,763	19,760
Capital expenditures	14,461	35,670	111,234	165,417
Brewery capacity in barrels	31,400	29,500	27,000	25,300
Barrels of beer sold	19,580	22,130	24,162	23,279

[a] Based on average number of shares outstanding during the year.

Source: From Schlitz Annual Report, 1978.

1974	1973	1972	1971	1970	1969
$1,015,978	$892,745	$779,359	$669,178	$594,437	$537,185
201,454	189,703	168,082	147,084	132,072	118,399
814,524	703,042	611,277	522,094	462,365	418,786
619,949	498,901	422,490	360,819	312,430	278,653
100,932	94,371	95,462	86,570	83,028	82,226
720,881	593,272	517,952	447,389	395,458	360,879
93,643	109,770	93,325	74,705	66,907	57,907
(7,857)	(6,071)	(5,747)	(5,910)	(4,066)	(1,341)
8,013	5,752	2,179	1,252	1,246	1,507
93,799	109,451	89,757	70,047	64,087	58,073
44,817	54,241	43,918	34,798	32,636	31,252
48,982	55,210	45,839	35,249	31,451	26,821
—	—	—	—	(1,300)	(1,947)
48,982	55,210	45,839	35,249	30,151	24,874
—	(1,535)	(8,300)	—	(1,100)	(4,000)
$ 48,982	$ 53,675	$ 37,539	$ 35,249	$ 29,051	$ 20,874
$1.69	$1.90	$1.58	$1.22	$1.04	$ .86
—	(.05)	(.29)	—	(.03)	(.14)
$1.69	$1.85	$1.29	$1.22	$1.01	$ .72
$ .67	$ .60⅖	$ .55⅓	$ .51⅔	$ .46⅔	$ .45
$ 57,296	$ 66,355	$ 68,638	$ 48,549	$ 40,797	$ 38,751
1.8 to 1	1.8 to 1	1.8 to 1	1.9 to 1	1.7 to 1	1.7 to 1
$ 400,363	$276,976	$240,015	$236,361	$207,948	$159,132
143,828	62,026	64,800	70,879	63,386	31,032
315,260	285,478	252,500	229,213	206,920	193,454
10.85	9.82	8.71	7.93	7.16	6.69
23,361	20,027	17,855	14,392	11,684	9,954
(1,669)	(1,391)	(1,201)	(896)	(619)	(444)
76,124	79,080	65,858	54,857	48,811	41,040
19,466	17,677	16,056	14,940	13,484	13,016
150,500	64,105	28,923	48,223	62,930	56,333
24,000	21,700	20,500	18,000	16,600	14,250
22,661	21,343	18,906	16,708	15,129	13,709

Coors

Coors is a family-run business. It prides itself on its 100 percent natural beer and the brewing excellence provided by its carefully monitored facility in Golden, Colorado. Traditionally ranked a top beer in its markets, the company had successfully fought to limit sales to its supervised territory. Indeed Coors developed its strategy on a single brewery, a single brand, and limited territorial coverage. Only recently have these concepts begun to give way under the increased competitive pressures of the industry. The decision in 1977 to market a light beer, for instance, broke a twenty-year tradition of brewing only a single product. Along with this product change, a number of other alterations may be necessary in the way Coors does business in the future.

MANAGEMENT

With phenomenal past success in its markets, Coors had little reason to question or change its basic strategies. It was not until 1977 that a series of misfortunes caused Coors to reevaluate its approach.

The primary concern was the drop in sales volume and the loss in market share in 1977. These events translated into a decline in earnings per share to $1.92 from $2.16 in 1976. This was an unaccustomed setback for Coors.

Some of the reasons appeared to be due to chance convergence of several incidents. Among the most disturbing of these incidents was a union-led boycott of Coors. When the Coors plant was struck in 1977 the company took a hard line. Although Coors was successful in attracting many of the workers back to their jobs and replacing those who refused — and continuing to operate effectively — George Meany, head of the AFL–CIO, called a boycott against Coors beer. In continuing controversy, employees of certain divisions in Coors voted to decertify their union in one case and to create an open shop in another. Wherever the merits lay in those instances, the fact is that Coors over the years has managed to outrage most minority groups, including Mexican-Americans, women, blacks, and gays; so much so that Coors finally created a task force in order to tell its side of the story.

Another unfortunate occurrence for Coors was the failure of a push-tab opener for its beer. Designed to be pushed into the container and thus avoid litter, it had the unfortunate side effect of catching consumers' fingers in the process. Faced with rising consumer complaints, Coors reverted to a conventional ring-pull lid.

Painful as these incidents were, however, the main damage was largely self-inflicted. While Miller successfully introduced its Lite beer and other brewers were hastily introducing their own version of light beer, Coors steadfastly retained its single product. Only in 1978, after the declines in volume, market share, and earnings per share, did Coors decide to market Coors Light and participate in this growth market. Even so, it was a reluctant decision. Bill Coors, head of the company, stated: "We're not very excited about the taste of light beer. And neither are the people who are drinking it."

ADVERTISING AND PROMOTION

Coors never had to rely much on advertising and promotion. Over the years the company built a loyal following in its western United States markets and a certain mystique beyond them: for example, people in the east would pay twice as much for a six-pack of Coors, stimulating a bootleg trade in the beer. Since Coors had established its position with minimal advertising outlays, it did not have a strong marketing and advertising staff. Among the top five brewers, Coors spent the least by far — in total or per barrel of sales — on advertising (see Exhibit 10 in The Brewing Industry case). It totally lacked the sophistication to emulate Philip Morris's market-segmentation policy, even if it had occurred to Coors to do so.

While Coors's low-profile policy served it well in the past, the future seemed destined to change it. Changes were almost forced on the company when it lost its leadership position in the three key markets of California, Utah, and Idaho — all to Anheuser-Busch. California in particular was a signal for new directions. Coors sold almost half its beer in California. But when Anheuser-Busch's second brewery opened in 1977, combined with a concerted advertising campaign, Coors's market share was cut in half. Meanwhile, Miller had captured 10 percent of the California market. Coors countered this sales erosion by moving into new markets. But as a longer-term strategy, Coors sharply increased its advertising budget, planned the introduction of a light beer, and began development of a super-premium beer. In essence Coors revamped its approach to product development, marketing, and promotion.

TERRITORY

Coors is steadily expanding its markets. In the mid-1970s Coors made its first territorial expansion in twenty years by moving into the southern two-thirds of Texas. In 1976 it moved into Montana, and in 1977 the company

EXHIBIT 6
ADOLPH COORS COMPANY AND SUBSIDIARIES OPERATIONS AND FACILITIES

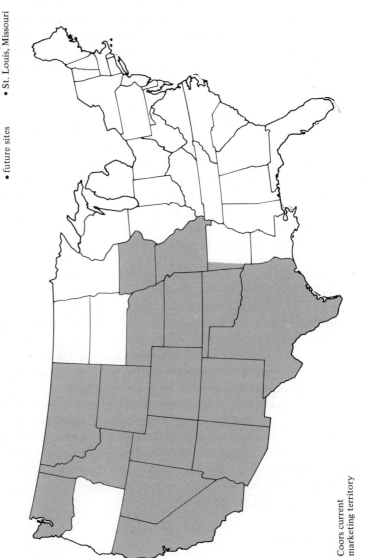

Main offices
Golden, Colorado
Largest single brewery and aluminum can manufacturing plant in the United States

Company-owned distributorships
Boise, Idaho
Denver, Colorado
Lakewood, Colorado
Omaha, Nebraska
Spokane, Washington
Tustin, California
• Cedar Rapids, Iowa
• St. Louis, Missouri

• future sites

Coors current marketing territory

EXHIBIT 7
ADOLPH COORS COMPANY AND SUBSIDIARIES
CONSOLIDATED STATEMENTS OF INCOME
AND RETAINED EARNINGS

	For the years ended	
	December 31, 1978	*December 25, 1977*
	(in thousands)	
Sales	$746,756	$716,609
Less — federal and state beer excise taxes	121,952	123,489
	624,804	593,120
Costs and expenses:		
Cost of goods sold	450,439	413,884
Marketing, general and administrative	79,369	49,842
Research and development	9,444	13,280
	539,252	477,006
Operating income	85,552	116,114
Other expense (income):		
Interest and dividend income	(7,067)	(3,876)
Interest expense	1,728	1,651
Gain on exchange of stock	(2,359)	(3,770)
Miscellaneous — net	(277)	2,547
	(7,975)	(3,448)
Income before income taxes	93,527	119,562
Income taxes		
Current:		
Federal	27,697	39,435
State	3,149	5,452
	30,846	44,887
Deferred — net	7,907	6,975
	38,753	51,862
Net income	54,774	67,700
Retained earnings at beginning of year	563,278	500,870
	618,052	568,570
Cash dividends — $0.25 per share in 1978 and $0.15 per share in 1977	8,802	5,292
Retained earnings at end of year	$609,250	$563,278
Net income per share of common stock	$1.56	$1.92

Source: From Coors Annual Report, 1978.

EXHIBIT 8
ADOLPH COORS COMPANY AND SUBSIDIARIES
CONSOLIDATED BALANCE SHEETS

	December 31, 1978	December 25, 1977
	(in thousands)	
Current assets:		
Cash, including short-term interest bearing investments of $75,830,000 in 1978 and $42,096,000 in 1977	$ 88,550	$ 72,001
Accounts and notes receivable	40,292	34,293
Inventories		
Finished	4,190	3,734
In process	27,471	23,552
Raw materials	61,407	69,930
Packaging materials	22,015	22,344
	115,083	119,560
Prepaid expenses and other assets	19,547	15,226
Accumulated income tax prepayments	7,214	7,135
Total current assets	270,686	248,215
Properties, at cost, less accumulated depreciation and depletion of $240,104,000 in 1978 and $201,372,000 in 1977	475,780	435,673
Excess of cost over net assets of businesses acquired, less amortization	2,808	2,893
Other assets	2,336	4,787
	$751,610	$691,568
Liabilities and Shareholders' Equity		
Current liabilities:		
Accounts payable	$ 37,413	$ 34,439
Accrued salaries and vacations	18,236	14,675
Taxes, other than income taxes	15,256	16,840
Federal and state income taxes	16,853	17,008
Accrued interest	5,988	4,989
Accrued expenses and other liabilities	13,874	11,087
Total current liabilities	107,620	99,038
Accumulated deferred income taxes	41,237	33,251
Other long-term liabilities	5,237	5,256
Shareholders' equity		
Capital stock:		
Class A common stock, voting, $1 par value, authorized and issued 1,260,000 shares	1,260	1,260
Class B common stock, non-voting, no par value, authorized and issued 46,200,000 shares	11,000	11,000
	12,260	12,260

	December 31, 1978	December 25, 1977
	(in thousands)	
Paid-in capital	2,011	2,011
Retained earnings	609,250	563,278
	623,521	577,549
Less — treasury stock, at cost, non-voting shares, 12,418,376 in 1978 and 12,250,295 in 1977	26,005	23,526
Total shareholders' equity	597,516	554,023
Commitments and contingencies		
	$751,610	$691,568

Source: From Coors Annual Report, 1978.

announced plans to add Nebraska, Iowa, Missouri, and the part of Washington not already served. Thus, Coors's expansion from fourteen to seventeen states (see Exhibit 6) has disguised the extent of loss in sales in other areas.

Coors has in fact depended on territorial expansion as a strategy to offset eroding market shares in its traditional strongholds. However, the territorial strategy has some limitations. Because Coors beer is not pasteurized — this is part of the family tradition that is unyielding — it must travel by refrigerated truck or insulated railcars. A too-long trip, say to the east coast, would threaten its quality, contends Coors, and it has in fact based a successful lawsuit to restrict sales to certain western states on this issue of perishability. Thus, although Coors can continue to push its markets outward, there must at some point arise a conflict with its policy on restricted marketing. If management remains firm, this would effectively keep much of the populated northeast out of its reach.

PRODUCTION PROCESS

Coors could of course build a plant to serve the eastern half of the United States. Here again, however, a potential strategy is frustrated by tradition. Because pure Rocky Mountain spring water is symbolic of Coors's pure taste and natural ingredients, a move eastward would upset traditions — or at least prove costly to maintain them.

A fundamental part of Coors's approach to date has been reliance on a single efficient facility to produce its carefully monitored brew. It is by

EXHIBIT 9
ADOLPH COORS COMPANY AND SUBSIDIARIES
CONSOLIDATED STATEMENTS OF CHANGES IN FINANCIAL POSITION

	For the years ended	
	December 31, 1978	December 25, 1977
	(in thousands)	
Financial resources were provided by:		
Net income	$ 54,774	$ 67,700
Add income charges (credits) not affecting working capital:		
Depreciation and depletion	41,968	38,215
Increase in accumulated deferred income taxes	7,986	7,840
Gain on exchange of stock	(2,359)	(3,770)
Retirements of properties	4,328	5,666
Working capital provided by operations	106,697	115,651
Fair market value of investment in common stock exchanged for treasury stock	2,479	3,975
	109,176	119,626
Financial resources were used for:		
Additions to properties	86,403	77,197
Cash dividends	8,802	5,292
Acquisition of treasury stock	2,479	3,975
Other — net	(2,397)	(3,036)
	95,287	83,428
Increase in working capital	$ 13,889	$ 36,198
Analysis of changes in working capital Increase (decrease) in current assets:		
Cash and short-term investments	$ 16,549	$ 17,398
Accounts and notes receivable	5,999	4,098
Inventories	(4,477)	5,572
Prepaid expenses and other assets	4,321	384
Accumulated income tax prepayments	79	865
	22,471	28,317
(Increase) decrease in current liabilities:		
Accounts payable	(2,974)	(8,217)
Accrued salaries and vacations	(3,561)	(1,100)
Taxes, other than income taxes	1,584	359
Federal and state income taxes	155	19,664
Accrued interest	(999)	2,222
Accrued expenses and other liabilities	(2,787)	(5,047)
	(8,582)	7,881
Increase in working capital	$ 13,889	$ 36,198

Source: From Coors Annual Report, 1978.

far the most vertically integrated firm in the industry. It produces all its own cans. It owns its own truck fleet. It has its own waste treatment facility and it designs and constructs nearly all its machinery and equipment. Although a second location is always possible, it would obviously represent a significant break with long-standing policy.

FINANCIAL CONDITION

The financial condition of Coors is contained in Exhibits 7 to 9.

Assignment

1. Schlitz and Coors are, in different degrees, fighting to regain lost momentum and prominence in the beer industry. Develop appropriate strategies for each firm.

REFERENCES

1. *Fortune,* "Getting Schlitz Back on the Track," April 24, 1978, p. 50.
2. Ibid., p. 51.

Mirco Games*

Mirco Games, a division of Mirco, Inc., designs, develops, and markets table soccer, electronic video, and pinball games for the coin-operated and home entertainment industries. Located in Phoenix, Arizona, the firm has experienced rapid growth in the sales of its games. Although Mirco Games was enjoying an increase in demand for its product lines, John Walsh, chairman of the board of Mirco, Inc., was concerned about what strategies the Games Division should employ over the next few years.

History of Mirco, Inc.

Mirco, Inc. (the company) was incorporated in Arizona on November 11, 1971, to succeed and to acquire the assets of a partnership known as John L. Walsh & Associates, which was composed of Messrs. John L. Walsh, Bruce E. Kinkner, and Robert M. Kessler, who are the founders of the company. As of January 1, 1976, the company consisted of the parent company, Mirco, Inc., and five divisions: (1) Mirco Electronic Distributors, (2) Mirco Systems, (3) Mirco Games, (4) Mirco Games Australia Pty., Ltd., and (5) Mirco Games of Europe.

At its founding, the company's business was to design, develop, and market computer software for automatic testing systems used in high-volume production maintenance, depot, and field testing facilities for electronic equipment. The Mirco Electronic Distributors division was established on December 15, 1972, to engage in business as a distributor of component

---

* This case was written by Robert B. Kaiser, Director of Marketing, Mirco Games, Lonnie L. Ostrom, Professor of Marketing, Arizona State University, and William E. Rief, Professor of Management, Arizona State University. Used with permission.

parts to electronic equipment manufacturers. On December 18, 1973, another division, Mirco Systems, was formed to carry on the electronic test business through the continued design and marketing of the company's software and to design and market test equipment. On December 26, 1973, the company acquired the assets and business of Arizona Automation, Inc., which was merged into another division called Mirco Games. The business of Mirco Games is to design, manufacture, and market table soccer, pinball, and electronic video games. Each segment of the company's business is more fully described below.

Generally, the parent company provides planning, accounting, legal, and financial services to each of the divisions. As of March 1976, corporate headquarters had 35 employees: the chairman of the board, president, vice president — operations, vice president — controller, an accountant, an office manager, 4 bookkeepers, 2 secretaries, 1 personnel specialist, and 22 purchasing, maintenance, quality control, and warehouse personnel.

In fiscal year 1976, ending January 31, 1976, the company achieved sales of more than $9 million, which represented an outstanding record of growth. Exhibit 1 contains consolidated income statements for the years 1973–76, and Exhibit 2 consolidated balance sheets for 1975 and 1976.

THE DISTRIBUTION BUSINESS

Mirco Electronic Distributors supplies component parts such as semiconductors, capacitors, connectors, and resistors to (1) manufacturers of electronic equipment and (2) users of the equipment for modification, replacement, or spare parts. This division performs an economic role by purchasing components from manufacturers (and sometimes from other distributors), maintaining an inventory, filling orders on demand, and providing quick delivery. In addition, it complements the other Mirco divisions by providing them with accurate information about the status of parts and equipment in the industry and supplying them with component parts and equipment at a reduced cost.

The distribution business is highly competitive. To meet competition, one must be able to obtain representation of lines of components, anticipate customers' future needs, and maintain inventories accordingly. If Mirco Electronic Distributors stocks components for which demand fails to develop, it will tie up working capital in unprofitable inventories that may have to be disposed of at or below cost.

Mirco Electronic Distributors is a regional distributor. Its market area includes Arizona; the Albuquerque, Las Cruces, and Roswell areas of New Mexico; the Denver and Henderson areas of Colorado; Los Angeles, California; Las Vegas, Nevada; and Salt Lake City, Utah.

EXHIBIT 1
MIRCO, INC. AND SUBSIDIARIES
CONSOLIDATED STATEMENT OF INCOME,
FOR THE YEARS ENDED JANUARY 31, 1973–1976

	1976	1975	1974	1973 (unaudited)
Net sales	$9,394,397	$5,033,717	$2,078,266	$1,156,319
Cost of sales	6,045,170	3,286,400	1,383,670	601,782
Gross profit	$3,349,227	$1,747,317	$ 694,596	$ 554,537
Operating expenses:				
Engineering	$ 897,407	$ 268,207	$ 255,130	$ 85,924
Selling	1,218,905	775,188	164,411	54,934
General and administrative	891,822	525,256	327,723	293,988
	$3,008,134	$1,568,651	$ 747,264	$ 434,846
Income from operations	$ 341,093	$ 178,666	$ (52,668)	$ 119,691
Interest expense	84,995	68,390	17,648	4,168
Income before income taxes and extraordinary item	$ 256,098	$ 110,276	$ (70,316)	$ 115,523
Provision for income taxes	123,000	48,625	31,048	55,145
Income before extraordinary item	$ 133,098	$ 61,651	$ (101,364)	$ 60,378
Extraordinary item — income tax reduction resulting from loss carry-forward benefits	—	48,625	—	15,708
Net income	$ 133,098	$ 110,276	$ (101,364)	$ 76,086
Income per capital and equivalent share:				
Before extraordinary item	$ 0.08	$ 0.04	$ (0.08)	$ 0.05
Extraordinary item	—	0.04	—	0.02
	$ 0.08	$ 0.08	$ (0.08)	$ 0.07
Average number of capital and equivalent shares outstanding during the year	$1,575,939	$1,450,112	$1,232,623	$1,114,173

EXHIBIT 2
MIRCO, INC. AND SUBSIDIARIES
CONSOLIDATED BALANCE SHEET
FOR THE YEARS ENDED JANUARY 31, 1976 AND 1975

Assets	1976	1975
Current assets:		
Cash and certificates of deposit	$ 129,556	$ 17,700
Accounts receivable, less allowance of $45,000 at January 31, 1976, and $181,500 at January 31, 1975, for doubtful accounts	839,730	813,473

EXHIBIT 2 *continued*

	1976	*1975*
Account receivable from Membrain, Inc. (a stockholder)	27,148	—
Notes receivable	14,586	—
Inventories	1,573,684	1,233,169
Prepaid expenses and other assets	27,497	5,986
Total current assets	$2,612,201	$2,060,328
Leasehold improvements	$ 47,812	$ 38,117
Machinery and equipment	300,197	178,902
Automobiles	13,028	14,324
Furniture and fixtures	56,627	26,579
Total leasehold improvements and equipment	$ 417,664	$ 257,922
Less: accumulated depreciation	112,782	53,603
	$ 304,882	$ 204,319
	$2,917,083	$2,264,647

Liabilities and stockholders' investment

Current liabilities:		
Notes payable	$ 610,000	$ 445,503
Current portion of long-term debt	15,213	12,923
Accounts payable	709,032	713,102
Accrued payroll	37,570	6,221
Accrued interest	6,702	8,727
Other accrued expenses	73,113	23,790
Income taxes currently payable	104,000	—
Total current liabilities	$1,555,630	$1,210,266
Long-term debt, less current portion	$ 33,838	$ 49,051
Stockholders' investment:		
Capital stock; no par value; 5,000,000 shares authorized; 1,607,423 shares outstanding at January 31, 1976, and 1,391,880 shares outstanding at January 31, 1975	$1,270,037	$ 947,863
Note receivable taken as consideration on sale of capital stock	(132,987)	—
Retained earnings	190,565	57,467
	$1,327,615	$1,005,330
	$2,917,083	$2,264,647

THE TEST BUSINESS

Mirco Systems designs, develops, manufactures, and markets hardware and computer software for the automatic testing of commercial and military digital electronic equipment. "Software" is a term generally used to describe computer programs; that is, a set of instructions which cause a computer to perform desired operations. The term "hardware" is used to describe the actual equipment.

Electronic equipment generally consists of numerous integrated circuit boards. Each circuit board contains approximately 10 to 300 components. These boards are tested for defects by the manufacturer at the completion of the manufacturing and assembly process. Boards also are tested after the equipment has been put into use as part of preventive or remedial maintenance programs.

Recent advances in technology have led to the development of computer systems to perform such testing automatically. These automatic test systems determine and identify faulty components in circuit boards. Automatic test systems are used primarily in high-volume production and maintenance testing facilities. The users of such systems include both the manufacturers and the owners of equipment using semiconductor components. It is possible to test circuit boards manually but it is becoming increasingly more difficult and costly to do so because of advanced technology and the time required to test the more complex boards.

At present, Mirco Systems markets its proprietary Fault Logic and Simulation Hybrid (FLASH) program. The FLASH program aids in the development of software for logic card testers, including the simulation of complex test patterns and the generation of a fault directory for logic components on printed circuit boards. It also is used to develop testing programs for specific circuit boards.

Mirco Systems also manufactures and markets automatic test equipment (hardware). In addition, it purchases test equipment from Membrain Limited, a United Kingdom corporation, for sale in the United States. Such equipment is usually sold in conjunction with the sale of software products generated by Mirco Systems. Although FLASH is considered a proprietary product, in reality the program has little protection from competition. Because there is a constant risk of obsolescence in the test business, the firm's long-run success may ultimately depend on the success of its research and development program.

Test Programming Services is a group that creates software and specific test programs for customers. It functions primarily in support of hardware sales. This capability is considered to be critical to the test business as it enables Mirco Systems to offer complete test systems. Mirco Systems has had no difficulty in recruiting suitable people to write test programs and expects to have no difficulty in the future.

Management believes that competition in the test business is based on quality, product performance, price, and postdelivery support. There are several other companies in the test business, most of whom are larger, well-financed, diversified electronics firms. Each competitor has its own systems.

THE GAMES BUSINESS

On December 26, 1973, Mirco, Inc., acquired the business of Arizona Automation, Inc., which had existed since 1970. The company issued 174,000 shares of its capital stock, without par value, to Richard N. Raymond and Virginia A. Raymond, his wife, who were the sole shareholders of Arizona Automation. The shares were valued, for the purposes of that transaction, at $3.50 per share. Arizona Automation was merged into Mirco, Inc. and became Mirco Games. Of the 174,000 shares, 30,000 shares were escrowed for a period of one year. The escrowed shares were to be available to the company in case any claims were to arise against the former shareholders in Arizona Automation on account of any breach of warranty made in connection with the transaction. The purpose of the acquisition was to acquire an existing marketing organization for the distribution of electronic games and to acquire the "know-how" in the games business possessed by Mr. Raymond.

Of approximately 150 employees in Mirco, Inc., about half of them are in the Games Division. The company has two main product lines: (1) table soccer, marketed under the name "Champion Soccer," which comes in a variety of models, and (2) video games, which consist of two versions of electronic Ping-Pong and come in either an upright cabinet or a cocktail table cabinet.

Of the $9.4 million total sales in fiscal year 1976, about $7.3 million were from the Games Division. Of the $7.3 million games sales, $1.2 million were from table soccer and $6.1 million from video games. The breakdown geographically was: $6.5 million in U.S. game sales, $200,000 in German and $600,000 in Australian games sales. This compares with games sales of just under $1 million in both fiscal years 1973 and 1974.

The company believed that competition in the games business was based upon playability, price, and quality. Contrary to soccer games, which have been marketed in Europe for over 50 years and have more recently established a strong market in the United States, it is difficult to predict whether electronic games will continue over time to have consumer appeal.

Mirco Games has several competitors in soccer and video games. The major competitors in soccer are Dynamo, Tournament Soccer, Garlando, and Deutsch Meister, while in video games they are Atari and Ramtek. There is also a risk that a major, well-financed firm will enter the video games market in which case the industry would be faced with much stiffer competition.

Australia and Europe were perceived to be good potential markets for video games. In order to avoid high import duties, Mirco began to assemble video games in Australia in April 1975 and in Germany in September 1975.

Amusement Games Industry

The term "coin-industry" is often applied to the manufacturers and distributors of coin-operated equipment for consumer use. The two main segments in this industry are vending machines (food, drink, cigarettes, and so on) and amusement machines.

Amusement machines consist of coin-operated phonographs (juke boxes) and amusement games, such as pool tables, pinball machines, table soccer, and video games. The principal manufacturers of pinball machines were Gottlieb, Balley, Chicago Coin, and Williams. Coin-operated phonographs are manufactured by Seeburg, Rock-ola, and Rowe. The newest

A. Conventional distribution network for coin-operated equipment

Manufacturer	--->	Distributor	--->	Operator	--->	Location owner

Functions	Functions	Functions
1. New equipment sales	1. Owns the equipment	1. Provides location (retains 50% of earnings)
2. Used equipment returns and resale	2. Provides routine servicing and maintenance	
3. Operator financing	3. Performs collection	
4. Replacement parts		

B. Primary distribution network for the home market

Manufacturer	--->	Large retail chains, sporting goods stores, and department stores	--->	Consumer

EXHIBIT 3
CHANNELS OF DISTRIBUTION FOR THE
AMUSEMENT GAMES INDUSTRY

development, video games, has been spawned by new companies outside of the traditional industry network.

Sales are seasonal in nature. New products are introduced in the fall and generally available in the following first quarter (February, March, and April). New product introductions are geared to the Music Operators of America trade show which is held annually in late October or early November.

The present structure of the amusement games industry was developed in the 1930s. At that time, the need for the distributor came into being with the introduction of coin-operated phonograph and pinball machines. The primary purpose of the distributor was to provide electrical and mechanical servicing. Distributors were either owned by the manufacturers or were independent. They, in turn, helped set up the operator, who was responsible for locating the game equipment and sharing revenues with the location owner. This distribution network remains virtually intact today.

The operator is the owner of the equipment. In addition to seeking out new locations, he is responsible for routine servicing. The operator typically has a route which he maintains, making periodic collections from the cash boxes attached to the equipment and dividing the earnings with the location owner (typically 50–50). The specific functions associated with each member of the conventional channel are identified in Exhibit 3.

Table Soccer

Table soccer appears to have originated in Germany in the late 1920s or early 1930s. Soccer is known as football in many European countries, and the German word for football, fussball, is the alternative name used for table soccer in the United States (under a variety of spellings). Presently, European versions of the game are manufactured in West Germany, France, and Italy.

The first soccer games that were exported to the United States in the mid-1950s were not readily accepted. In 1962, L. T. Patterson Distributors of Cincinnati made the first major commitment to distribute a German-produced table called "Foosball." Because it was a relatively unknown sport in America and required a high skill level, the acceptance was slow for many years and it was not until the late 1960s that table soccer became a significant factor in the games industry. One of the contributing factors to its growth in popularity in the United States was the demand created by servicemen who had been introduced to the game while stationed in Europe.

In 1967, Dick Raymond and John Walsh, while working for General Electric in Germany, became interested in table soccer. Soccer tables were found in many of the bars and taverns of France, Germany, and Italy and were avidly played by Europeans as well as by American servicemen and businessmen. Raymond and Walsh saw the potential for such a game and made plans to export tables to the United States.

When Raymond and Walsh returned to Phoenix in 1970, they formed Arizona Automation. Within a year following incorporation, Raymond purchased Walsh's share and became sole owner of Arizona Automation. In 1971, Arizona Automation began building a soccer table known as Champion Soccer. In four years, annual sales climbed from $15,000 to approximately $1 million.

MANUFACTURING

The component parts for Champion Soccer are purchased from outside vendors and the game is assembled by Mirco Games. There are presently alternate sources for all of the components except the figurines. Should that source fail, it is estimated that production would be delayed for approximately two months while a new source was found.

PATENTS, TRADEMARKS, AND LICENSING

The company has registered Champion Soccer as a trademark in the United States and in Canada. An application for trademark registration has been filed with respect to the design of figurines for the soccer game, and a patent has been granted for the "two point ball control" figurine. There are no other patents or other protection for the table soccer products.

COMPETITION

Due to the high quality of its soccer tables, Mirco has been a dominant force in the United States market with about $1.2 million in sales out of an industry total of $12 million. Recently, however, Mirco has experienced increased competition from a number of firms that have entered the market, especially Dynamo and Tournament Soccer. In order to maintain its leadership in the soccer table market, Mirco was forced to significantly redesign its soccer tables to improve their appearance, playability, and durability. Dynamo's approach to the market is similar to Mirco's in that they cultivate a high-quality image and have introduced several technical innovations into their product; among them are the textured tempered glass playfield, the massive table to prevent table movement during play, the balanced figurine, and precision ground steel rods. Mirco subsequently incorporated some of these innovations to maintain their market position. Tournament Soccer has pursued the market through an active and expensive program utilizing table soccer tournaments throughout the United States. Their current tournament program offers prize money in excess of $250,000 per year.

MARKETING

Mirco markets its coin-operated soccer games through approximately 50 distributors that are located for the most part in the United States and Canada (see Exhibit 3). As is typical of the industry, there are no binding contractual arrangements with any of these distributors. They are free to deal in competitive products or to discontinue to distribute Mirco's products at any time. Home table soccer games are distributed through major retail chains, sporting goods and department stores, and the American Express catalog. In addition, a small amount of government business is handled via the Government Services Administration.

Pricing. Pricing is consistent with Mirco's image as a quality producer of soccer games. There is only one distributor price regardless of quantity. A typical selling price to the operator for a high quality coin-operated table soccer game is around $675. The channel markup is approximately 35 percent.

Promotion. Mirco Games advertises in the coin-operated equipment trade journals, such as *Cashbox, Playmeter, Replay,* and in sporting goods magazines. It also promotes its products at trade shows like the National Sporting Goods Association and the Music Operators of America. Bob Seagren, Olympic gold medal winner and superstar champion, is used extensively in advertisements and trade show displays.

Mirco also has engaged in a series of promotional events, mainly in the form of statewide tournaments in key metropolitan cities. In 1973 and 1974, they sponsored the Louisiana State Soccer Tournaments, both of which were $2,000 events. In 1975, Mirco tournaments were held in Detroit, Minneapolis, Omaha, and Kansas City, with total prize money exceeding $16,000. The 1976 schedule includes St. Louis, Rochester, and Detroit.

Market Research. Market information is obtained from three principal sources: the distributors, operators, and location owners. At times, games are "test marketed" by placing them in selected locations and analyzing their earning power over a given period of time.

Electronic (Video and Pinball) Games

Atari was the first company to successfully market a video game. It was called "Pong" and was a two-player tennis-type game operated with electronic paddles and a ball. The acceptance of this product was phenomenal and before long more than 30 producers of video games were in the market, from the large established companies to the newly formed "garage-type" operations. Although it is relatively easy for a new company to enter the video games market, the failure rate of new entrants is extremely high, due primarily to a lack of adequate testing capability, poor service, high operating costs, limited financing, and little marketing expertise. According to one financial analyst who observed 24 games companies during 1974, 20 went out of business, 2 were marginal in nature, and the remaining 2 were Mirco and Atari.

Mirco Games entered the market in 1973 with its two-player video game, Champion Ping Pong, at a time when competitors were introducing a great variety of more sophisticated games. It was felt that the company's expertise in the area of electronic testing equipment would provide them with two immediate advantages over their major competitors: quick turnaround in servicing (24 hours) and a more reliable product. Unfortunately, these two advantages were not sufficient to offset Champion Ping Pong's lack of playability, which is the primary competitive factor in video games. The urgent need to develop new products was recognized by Mirco at that time; however, an extremely tight cash-flow position prevented major R&D expenditures for video games. In 1973, the Mirco Systems Division had invested heavily in R&D to develop its computer-controlled test equipment, which was not yet ready for production, and it had severely drained the company's finances.

In March 1974, Mirco Games introduced the Challenge upright four-player video game which featured one free game in the event that one or two players beat the machine in the player versus machine mode. Unfortunately, this innovative feature was not sufficient to offset the fact that competition had introduced four-player games 12 months earlier and the market was now saturated. In July 1974, the "Challenge" cocktail table version was introduced. The major advantage of this game was its appeal to sophisticated locations, such as Holiday Inns, Playboy Clubs, and country clubs, which previously had not been a viable market for video games. Unfortunately, the conventional distribution network was ill-equipped to implement a marketing strategy to take advantage of this new and rapidly expanding market.

Distributor. In order to exploit this new market for cocktail table models, Bob Kaiser, marketing manager, decided to set up an entirely new channel of distribution, which became known as the nonconventional distribution network (see Exhibit 4). He sought out individual entrepreneurs, such as real estate people and stocks and bonds salespersons, who, due to the recession, were without a product to market but had sufficient capital to invest in a new venture. This strategy proved to be very successful and, in fact, helped stimulate sales of the tabletop video game through conventional dis-

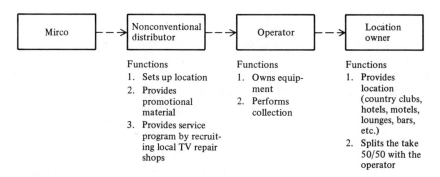

EXHIBIT 4
NONCONVENTIONAL DISTRIBUTION NETWORK FOR VIDEO GAMES

tributors and operators. One major advantage of the nonconventional channel is that terms are cash, whereas in the conventional channel they are net
30 and the manufacturer is frequently forced to extend credit for 60 to 90
days.

Innovation.   Innovation is a requirement for survival in the games industry.
Mirco's achievements in this area have not been spectacular. However, a
Mirco processor pinball machine, which was a first in the industry, was
introduced in late 1975. Management felt that this product would successfully lead Mirco into a new segment of the coin-operated market.

Pricing.   Two pricing constraints are active in the marketplace. In the segment of the market dominated by innovative games, particularly video,
pricing is determined primarily by the earning power of the machine, that
is, its ability to sit in a location and, without being promoted, attract players.
(The location life of a video game is less than 90 days as a rule.) In that
segment of the market where the products are stable and have a long life in
a specific location, such as pool tables and table soccer, pricing is solely a
function of competition.

MANUFACTURING

With respect to electronic games, Mirco purchases all components, such as
television monitors and subassemblies, from outside vendors and assembles
the games itself. At the present time, the sole source for television monitors
is Motorola. Although no difficulties are anticipated in obtaining sufficient
quantities of monitors from Motorola, significant production delays and
expenses probably would be encountered in changing to another vendor.

HOME VIDEO GAMES MARKET

Along with coin-operated electronic games, video and pinball games for the home promise to have a great future: projections go as high as $1 billion by 1980. In 1972, Magnavox brought out the first home video game, "Odyssey," for the price of over $100. Several new entrants are now active in this area, including Atari which introduced their home model version of "Pong" in 1975. One of the obstacles in this new market is that FCC approval is required for any games that hook up to a TV antenna.

Brisk sales were reported by both Magnavox and Atari during the 1975 Christmas season. Atari's version of "Pong" was sold by Sears, which stated that it could sell all it could get. Magnavox, which had introduced an improved version of Odyssey a few months earlier, marketed its products through its vast network of approximately 2,500 dealers throughout the United States.

It is anticipated that home video games will soon be available for $30–$40 retail. Most products will include multiple games, color, sound, and remote controls. On-screen score display and variable difficulty are possible features.

In January 1976, Mirco entered into an agreement with Fairchild Camera and Instrument to jointly develop and produce home video games. Christmas of 1976 was targeted for a major promotional effort for creating a new consumer mass market.

COMPUTERIZED PINBALL

In 1975, Mirco was the first on the market with a micro-computer pinball machine in which one printed circuit board handles all electronic functions. The game featured an electronic semiconductor memory, LED (digital display) readouts, and a self-diagnostic capability for quick troubleshooting. Although it was the hit of the annual Music Operators of America trade show, it was too early to tell what impact it will have on the traditional coin-operated pinball market. One concern is that because of Mirco's lack of expertise in backglass and playfield design, both strong competitive features in pinball machines because of their association with playability in the minds of players, it may not be able to take full advantage of being first in the microcomputer pinball market.

The Future of the Games Business

In 1976, the electronic games market was still in its infancy. Atari was the leader in video sales, with about $18 million in 1975, and "close to $30 million" projected for 1976. Although sales information is difficult to obtain about other firms in this industry, it was believed that Mirco Games was number two. Whereas Atari produces many different types of video games, Mirco has concentrated its efforts in producing a few models of one basic game. During the period in which Mirco successfully marketed the "Challenge" table top video game, Atari introduced 50 new game designs.

It is expected that semiconductor companies will play a major role in the games business. In early 1976, research was under way at General Instrument, Texas Instruments, and National Semiconductor to develop video products. With the possibility of many companies invading the territory of the traditional manufacturer of coin-operated games, the long-run outcome is somewhat uncertain. The traditional companies are likely to react strongly to protect their existing markets.

Table soccer appears to have a good 15 to 20 percent per year growth potential. In contrast to the video market, this market appears to be extremely stable.

Another uncertainty is the extent to which the expanding home game market will affect the sales of coin-operated games. The traditional companies feel that home games will stimulate rather than take away from their business, and they predict a steady growth in the next few years.

HOME GAMES MARKET

Strategies in the home games market are difficult to determine because of rapid technological changes. Games with their own video displays are likely to evolve and they may be tied in with the computer terminal that one day will be installed in most homes. One definite advantage for new companies entering this market is that because home electronics games (video and pinball) are so new, no strong brand loyalty currently exists.

Assignment

1. Based on Mirco's position in this industry and its relative strengths and weaknesses, what basic strategy or strategies would you recommend?

Light Whiskeys*

An important aspect of marketing — and this can be an attractive feature for some persons — is that it involves decision making under conditions of uncertainty. Consequences of decisions and actions cannot be predicted with certainty; there are risks involved that consumer acceptance will not be sufficient, or that competitors will thwart well-laid plans. Such a situation makes for heroes and failures.

Some marketing mistakes have been monumental, such as the Edsel and Corfam which cost well-heeled companies some hundred million dollars. In most mistakes with the benefit of hindsight we can detect crucial flaws in the decision and strategy used. In the light whiskey fiasco, the mistakes are less obvious.

In the late 1960s an ailing whiskey industry needed a product innovation. Consumers were demanding lighter flavored drinks; sales of vodka and imported Scotch and Canadian whiskeys were relentlessly moving upward, while sales of the stronger flavored domestic blended and straight whiskeys were steadily declining. What could be more reasonable in the face of this changing demand than to introduce new lighter flavored whiskeys to the market? The technology was there, most distillers had ample promotional budgets, and the federal government had bent enough to the demands of the industry to remove restrictions so that this innovation was possible.

The natural innovation was not supported by consumers. Somehow there was a faulty translation and interpretation of the trend in sales of vodka and scotch and other light flavored products. Perhaps the wrong promotional approach was used or the timing was wrong. Or was the product thought to be innovative and compatible with changing consumer demand

---

* Reprinted with permission from Hartley, *Marketing Mistakes,* Grid, Inc., Columbus, Ohio, 1976.

really not positioned right to tap this demand? Draw your own conclusions as you read further into the case. But first, let us look at the history of modern marketing in the liquor industry.

Background of Modern Liquor Marketing

Times were chaotic in 1934. Prohibition had just been repealed. Whiskey was being sold like a commodity with no distinguishable brands, and prices fluctuated wildly. Traditionally in the whiskey industry there had been no national brands; almost everything was sold through local or at the most, regional brands.

Sam Bronfman was the head of a small Canadian liquor company. In his judgment there was a need and an opportunity to develop a national brand. Such a product would have to have a flavor with wide appeal and be uniform so that a person could be assured of the same taste with every bottle. In addition a strong national distribution network would have to be established, one that would be loyal and supportive.

Prevalent at the time were straight, strong-tasting whiskeys. Bronfman decided to make his national brand candidate a considerably milder-tasting blended whiskey. Actually he introduced two whiskeys, 5 Crown and 7 Crown.

Back in 1934, Bronfman was fearful of selling to large dealers since he thought these would be too dictatorial. So he made the decision to use smaller stores to establish the reputation for his brands. He wanted to maintain the price at a level high enough to give his products a quality image, and he wanted his dealers to make enough profit so that they would push his brands. He gave liquor franchises to wholesalers who would guarantee that prices would be maintained as a fair-trade policy, or as Seagram termed it, a "fair-price policy." A lawsuit was brought against Seagram in 1935 contending that it was price fixing, but the Supreme Court upheld the right of Seagram to do so. This assured the loyalty of small retailers who were deadly afraid of the price cutting of larger firms.

In a matter of months, Seagram's two whiskeys outsold all others in the country. While 5 Crown has been dropped, 7 Crown remains still today the number one selling brand in the United States with 7,200,000 cases sold in 1974. A vast network of distributorships was built up numbering over 470 and using more than 8,000 salesmen. In addition, 1,800 "missionary men" were used, who, while taking no orders themselves, promoted Seagram's brands with dealers and distributors.

Most of its distributors have been with Seagram since the repeal of Prohibition; many have become millionaires many times over as the profit margins are some of the best in U.S. industry. The decisions of Sam Bronfman turned the small Canadian liquor company into the world's largest distiller in less than two decades. And the liquor industry became the sophisticated marketing entity that it is today.

Innovation in the Liquor Industry: Light Whiskeys

During most of the 1960s, liquor consumption increased five to six percent a year. Liquor executives looking at this solid growth rate confidently predicted its continuation through the 1970s. However, demand was shifting drastically away from domestic bourbons and blends as Exhibit 1 shows. Moreover, this change in preference was chiefly among young drinkers. Unless their preferences would change as they became older, the prognosis for the continued dominance of conventional whiskeys was not particularly promising.

A domestically produced, lighter-tasting whiskey seemed the answer. Prevented by federal regulation from the distilling and storing required for

EXHIBIT 1
MARKET SHARE TRENDS OF THE LIQUOR INDUSTRY 1959–1970

	Percentage of market		
	1959	1969	1970
Whiskey types:			
Straights	25.9	22.2	21.2
Spirit blends	32.1	21.2	19.6
Scotch	7.7	12.0	13.4
Canadian	5.0	8.8	8.5
Bonds	4.6	1.8	1.6
Other	.3	.3	.3
Total whiskey	75.6	66.3	64.6
Vodka	7.3	11.5	12.7
Gin	9.2	10.0	10.0
Cordials	3.5	4.6	4.9
Brandy	2.4	3.4	3.5
Rum	1.5	2.8	3.5
Other	.5	1.4	1.3
Total non-whiskey	24.4	33.7	35.4
Total consumption (millions of gallons)	228.2	363.9	367.0

Source: *Business Week* Survey and Estimates, as reported in "The Distillers Serve Up New Brands." *Business Week,* March 6, 1971, pp. 80, 81.

such lighter flavored whiskeys, American Distilling Company petitioned the Alcohol and Tobacco Tax Division of the Treasury Department to remove the restrictions. The Tax Division agreed to alter its regulations so that U.S. distillers could better compete with Scotch and Canadian imported whiskeys. New regulations specified that the industry could begin storing the new whiskey in 1968, could advertise it on April 1, 1972, and sell it beginning July 1, 1972. As a consequence, various distillers stored more than 190 million gallons of light whiskey in preparation for the July 1972 marketing date.

What is a light whiskey? As the name implies, it is light in color and also lighter in taste than traditional whiskey. How is this achieved? All American whiskey is made from a mixture or mash of corn, rye, and barley malt which is put in a still and heated. With heating the alcohol rises and carries off some of the water and flavoring. The longer distilled, the higher is the alcoholic content, and the less the taste. Federal regulations previously had prescribed that whiskeys had to be under 160 proof, which meant a rather short distillation period and a consequently strong taste. Now to achieve the "light" whiskeys, distillers were permitted to process from 160 to 190 proof. If a whiskey is heated until it reaches 190 proof, there will be no taste at all.

Federal regulations also required that whiskey be aged only in new charred casks, which removed the more unpleasant tastes resulting from the relatively low-proof distillation. Since the new higher-proof whiskey had already lost the unpleasant flavor, there was no need for charred casks. Distillers of light whiskey consequently were permitted to age their products four years or more in used barrels, which Scotch and Canadian producers had long been doing. These, of course, were less expensive than new barrels. (The higher proof at distillation of the light whiskeys did not necessarily mean that they were bottled stronger than lower proof whiskeys. After the distillation process, distilled water is added to produce the final proof which is comparable with other products on the market.)

SUCCESSFUL INNOVATION OF SMIRNOFF VODKA

There was precedent for a highly successful product innovation in the liquor industry. In 1946 a Hollywood, California, restaurant operator found himself with an oversupply of ginger beer. He teamed with Heublein, Inc., producer of Smirnoff, the sole domestic vodka available in the United States at the time, to promote a new drink called the Moscow Mule. The idea caught on quickly and Smirnoff, with sales of 6,000 cases annually, faced a burgeoning demand.

With the success of this "recipe" drink, other drink ideas were rapidly introduced with catchy names — the Bloody Mary, Vodka Martini, Screwdriver, and others. As sales increased, the ad budget kept pace, and Smirnoff was positioned as a "class" product, building an image of quality which permitted charging higher prices than competitive brands. New drink ideas are continually being introduced, one of the latest being a Bloodhound: a Bloody Mary with a dash of sherry.

Smirnoff has become the nation's second favorite alcoholic brand (after Seagram's 7 Crown, leader for 27 years), and is moving fast to overtake 7 Crown, with sales of 5,325,000 cases in 1974, up 13.3 percent from 1973, while 7 Crown barely held on to 7,200,000 cases.[1]

The Introduction of the Light Whiskeys

As the July 1972 introduction date approached, fifty brand names of light whiskeys had been registered with the government. Six companies or divisions earmarked multi-million dollar introductory advertising pushes:

Seagram's Four Roses Distillers Company
Seagram's Hunter-Wilson Distillers Company
Schenley Industries
Barton Brands
National Distillers Products Company
Brown-Forman

We will discuss each of these in turn.

Seagram's Four Roses Distillers Company.   Four Roses was an important brand for Seagram. Although sales had been slipping for several years, still over 1.1 million cases were sold in 1970, yielding some fifty million dollars annually at wholesale. Seagram replaced this long-time favorite with Four Roses Premium, hoping not to lose too many of its old customers, while adding many new ones with a different taste, look, and slightly higher price than the old Four Roses. This was introduced with a two million dollar promotion with the theme, "Lighter than Scotch, smoother than Canadian."

Revitalizing a slipping old brand was not new to Seagram. In 1963 it had reformulated a slipping Calvert Reserve into Calvert Extra, which had a lighter taste. The new brand became an outstanding success, reaching the top ten of all brands in sales. So the prognosis for the reformulation of Four Roses was pleasantly optimistic.

Seagram's Hunter-Wilson Distillers Company.   A new Galaxy brand light whiskey was introduced backed with a 500,000 dollar promotional push and priced below Four Roses Premium.

Schenley Industries. The company took six of its established brands and moved them into the light whiskey area. Promotional expenditures were stepped up, but no massive introductory campaign was used.

Barton Brands. In 1972 the company planned to spend $4,000,000 to promote Barton's QT light whiskey (QT standing for "Quiet Time"), with the theme "similar in character to other popular American whiskeys, but lighter and milder . . . "

National Distillers Products Company. Several million dollars were budgeted for the introduction of Crow Light, "a rate higer than any introduction in the company's history." [2] The name was derived from Old Crow bourbon, one of the company's most successful brands. The rationale for the similarity was that distributors and dealers were more likely to stock a well-known brand than an unknown one. In an attempt to reach the 21 to 35 age bracket, ads featured a "young guy who never goes anywhere without his gal and a crow perched on his shoulder." Ads stressed that Crow Light is "not a pale imitation of anything." [3]

Brown-Forman. The company bought from Publicker Industries, Inc., a Philadelphia distiller, a quantity of whiskey that had been stored in used barrels for about six years. Brown-Forman then triple-filtered the light color and much of the taste out of the whiskey so the result was an absolutely clear 80-proof whiskey. Thus the company jumped the gun on the July 1972 restriction (as did several other distillers including Seagram with its Four Roses Premium) since the Frost 8/80 was not technically a light whiskey.

So the battle lines were drawn. Most of the industry was optimistic. After all, a Leo Burnett Company survey in 1969 showed that women, who buy half the liquor sold, are more inclined than men to try new products. And women liked the idea of "light whiskey." [4]

Now let us follow more closely the efforts of the first firm to bring its new product to market, Brown-Forman, and its Frost 8/80.

RESEARCH AND PROMOTIONAL EFFORTS OF FROST 8/80

The major brands of Brown-Forman were Early Times and Old Forester bourbons, and Jack Daniels whiskey. However, these brands were facing the sliding industry demand for bourbons and blended whiskeys. Brown-Forman urgently needed to catch up with the changes taking place in American drinking habits.

In an effort to determine how to enter the light whiskey market, a concept study was taken involving some 2,400 persons. Glossy full-color photographs were made up to illustrate four kinds of possible new whiskeys, labeled "light," "clear," "separate" and "dry, white." Also included in the test was a photo of an amber Canadian whiskey. Some people were polled by mail and others by interviews. They were asked to rate the five photos on a number of criteria, including whether they would like to try each of the products pictured, whether they thought the products would be "fun" to drink, to give as gifts, and serve to guests. They were also asked how they thought the products should be priced in relation to existing brands.

The surveys showed "dry, white" whiskey to be an "almost universal winner on every measure of desirability." The people polled also thought that a "dry, white" whiskey should be priced among the "upper medium" brands now on the market. "They wanted something that smacked of quality," Joseph Simmons, manager of special projects heading the group that developed Frost 8/80, told *Wall Street Journal* reporters.[5] Simmons pointed out that what led to the decision to develop a dry, white whiskey was its showing on several key parts of the surveys. "It ranked first in uniqueness, which meant that people were curious to try it. This is vital to a new product . . . The group that responded best to dry, white were affluent, well-educated people in the 25 to 35 age group, the fun-oriented party-going types. This is a large and very desirable market. If the product had been picked mostly by 60-year-old men, we probably wouldn't have gone ahead . . . [as to price] we might have backed off if the surveys showed that people thought of it as low priced." [6] (See Exhibit 2.)

EXHIBIT 2
PRICING IN THE LIQUOR INDUSTRY

The price of a liquor is determined more by how it is packaged and advertised than by what is in it. A Brown-Forman executive notes that the whiskey in a fifth costs only 25 to 30 cents to make, and "there isn't a hell of a lot of difference" between the low-priced and high-priced brands in that respect. The "price of a product, after all, is the image that people have of its value — what they are willing to pay for it," said Joseph Simmons, Brown-Forman's manager of special projects.[7]

Much of the credit for the placement of "higher quality" products on the market is due to advertising, since in the liquor industry, executives readily admit that actual differences between many products are small and that tests have shown that a goodly number of drinkers have trouble distinguishing brands. Since all whiskeys cost about the same to make, pricing is largely a function of packaging and advertising: the dignity of the advertising, the style of a bottle and its label — these can impart "quality" and "dignity" to a brand, and enables a higher price to be charged.

The liquor industry is an example of a perception that many consumers have: the higher the price, the higher the quality.

The name "Frost" was picked from some 700 names which were first given a trademark search and then tested with consumers. Frost was seen as "upbeat, modern, clean, and psychologically right," Mr. Simmons noted. Among names seriously considered were "Verv" ("too modern"), "Ultra" ("too common"), and "Master's Choice" ("not upbeat enough"). The 8/80 in the name stands for the eight steps in its distilling process and the fact that it is 80 proof, and "numbers give a product's title more impact with young people today." [8]

A "quality look" was conveyed by packaging in a sleek bottle with a black and silver label. Attached to each bottle were small booklets containing recipes using Frost 8/80, such as a "Diamond Lil" which was a Bloody Mary using Frost 8/80 instead of vodka; a "Moby Dick" was a martini using Frost 8/80 instead of gin.

Distributors were given plastic display stands to make Frost 8/80 stand out from competing displays which were mostly cardboard. Dealers were also urged to place Frost 8/80 with the whiskeys instead of with gins and vodkas.

When competitors heard rumors that Brown-Forman intended to jump the gun in entering the light whiskey market, three competing distillers filed suit in a United States District court to get an injunction halting sale of the product. However, the injunction request was denied, and Brown-Forman received the go-ahead to put Frost 8/80 on the market as planned. This was done in February 1971.

Consumer advertising was launched with full-color spreads in *Esquire, Newsweek, Time, Redbook, Cosmopolitan, Sports Illustrated,* and *American Home* magazines, all of which had large audiences of young adults. Copy ran like this:

> The color is white. The taste is dry. The possibilities are endless.
>
> You've never seen a whiskey like this. Because there's never been one like it.
>
> It's hard to make. But it's easy to enjoy.
>
> And here's why.
>
> The mellowing is done in carefully seasoned oak barrels.
>
> And that's just the beginning. It goes through 8 full steps on the way to terrific. And it's filtered 3 extra times through:
>
> Hard wood, Soft wood.
>
> And nutshell charcoals.
>
> The result is the first whiskey that looks white, tastes dry, and mixes with just about anything. Orange juice. Tomato juice. Tonic. Ginger ale. Soda. Or you can drink it on the rocks. It's that good.

Frost 8/80 is easy to enjoy.

The color is white.

The taste is dry.

The possibilities endless.

Mr. Simmons and Brown-Forman spared little expense in the planning and introduction of their new product. Some two million dollars was spent for first-year advertising, another two million dollars was budgeted for the second year; two million dollars was spent to build an inventory of the product, $500,000 for new bottling and production equipment, some $250,000 for the salaries of executives and others who devoted nearly two years to the project; marketing research cost another $500,000 as eight outside research or packaging firms were employed to make Frost 8/80 a success. The breakeven point, at which time the product would be profitable, was calculated at 200,000 cases, a sales figure expected to be achieved by the third year. First year sales estimates were 100,000 cases and second year estimates, 150,000.

Results of the Light Whiskey Innovation

THE FAILURE OF FROST 8/80

A vice president at Brown-Forman told *Forbes'* reporters in July 1972: "We're gaining experience. In the first three years we don't expect to make any money with it." [9] That summer the ad approach was changed, and Brown-Forman moved Frost 8/80 to a new advertising agency, Richard K. Manoff Inc. Manoff invented a drink called the Sigmund Frost, made with Frost 8/80, and grapefruit, and pineapple, and advertising was geared around this. The Sigmund Frost was called "the crazy, mixed-up drink" and "the drink that defied analysis." Then in December 1972, 23 months after its introduction, Brown-Forman halted production of Frost 8/80. Volume had totaled just 100,000 cases, only one-third of the company's projections.

The company spent about 6.5 million dollars on the brand and lost about two million dollars of that. As with most business failures, individual casualties resulted. Joseph Simmons, who headed the task force that launched Frost 8/80, left the company. The account executives for Frost 8/80 at the first advertising agency, Gardner Advertising, moved on, as did the account executive at Richard K. Manoff. "That's the way it is in our business," said the general manager of Gardner Advertising's New York office.[10]

LACK OF SUCCESS OF OTHER LIGHT WHISKEYS

By the fall of 1972 other distillers were worried about the acceptance of the light whiskeys. The president of Seagram's Four Roses Distillers Company viewed the situation optimistically: "I'm strongly of the opinion that it is ultimately going to be the performance of a major brand which will draw attention to light whiskeys." And he pointed to the examples of Chivas Regal as gaining consumer recognition of premium scotch, Bacardi's impact on rum consumption, and Smirnoff's creation of the vodka market.[11]

The Four Roses Premium of Seagram had been able to beat the July 1972 date for introduction of light whiskeys, as had Frost 8/80. This was a lighter reformulation of the slipping Four Roses brand. However, despite a two million dollar introductory promotion in 1971, sales dropped twenty percent, from 1,125,000 cases to 900,000 cases. By 1972, sales had dropped drastically again, to 700,000 cases. For 1973 there was another sizable drop to 600,000 cases. Apparently, Four Roses Premium was not the brand to lead the light whiskeys into popularity.

Another contender for leader of the light whiskey innovation was Crow Light of National Distillers Products Company. But the company found that a major problem was to convince their dealers that they had something that would sell:

> After the introduction of the clear whiskeys and the gun-jumping "lights" that were not actually light whiskeys, there was a lot of misunderstanding among public and trade alike. We had a dealer in Louisiana, for instance, who ran an ad on our regular Old Crow along with the new Crow Light, and his headline said: "Buy Old Crow — Light or Dark." He did not understand that there are two entirely different products of different tastes, and we are not just putting a different color Old Crow on sale.[12]

National Distillers undertook major efforts to clear up the perception of the light whiskeys. For example, weekly sales bulletins were sent to the sales force of Crow Light explaining that tests had shown that consumers liked the product, but that retailers still had to be convinced to stock and display it. Salesmen showed Crow Light films to retailers, let them sample the product, put up point-of-sale displays, and talked up the ad campaign. One salesman even conceived the idea of placing a bottle of Crow Light on a retailer's counter and covering it with a paper bag lettered "What's New?" Curious customers then would lift it and discover the new brand for themselves.[13]

But the downtrend in bourbons and blends continued: the innovation of the "lights" hardly slowed the trend. After eighteen months on the market, only one brand, National Distillers' Crow Light, still had a sizable advertising and promotion budget. And sales had not crept up to the 500,000 case level, a point that serves to differentiate the thirty-five to fifty most popular brands of liquors. Only Four Roses Premium of Seagram could place in this 500,000+ category, and this brand had been so steadily fading from the 1,175,000 cases of 1969 that its viability was in jeopardy. Exhibit

EXHIBIT 3
MARKET SHARES IN THE LIQUOR INDUSTRY 1970–1974

	Percentage of market	
	1970	*1974*
Whiskey types:		
Straight bourbons	21.2	16.3
Blends	19.6	13.8
Scotch	13.4	13.7
Canadian	8.5	11.4
Bonded bourbons	1.6	1.0
Other	.3	.3
Total whiskey	64.6	56.5
Vodka	12.7	16.9
Gin	10.0	10.0
Cordials	4.9	6.2
Brandy	3.5	4.0
Rum	3.5	3.7
Other	1.3	2.7
Total non-whiskey	35.4	43.5
Total consumption (millions of gallons)	367.0	416.0

Source: Business Week Survey and Estimates, as reported in "Liquor Men Feel Like the
Morning After," *Business Week,* March 17, 1975, p. 88; and "The Distillers Serve Up New
Brands," *Business Week,* March 6, 1971, pp. 80, 81.

3 compares 1974 market shares of liquor categories with 1970. As can be
seen, the trend toward lighter liquor, but not the light whiskeys, continued
during this period.

The innovation that seemingly could not fail, that was in complete
harmony with changing consumer tastes, somehow faded from the scene,
despite millions of dollars of promotional efforts devoted to putting it across.
Not a single firm, but an entire industry had bit the dust in the attempt
to establish a product innovation.

By 1975, Four Roses Premium was no longer being sold as a "light,"
National Distillers was concentrating its efforts on Old Crow rather than
Crow Light, and only Barton's QT remained as a feeble vestige of the
country's great expectation of stemming the imports.

Post Mortem

. . . certain exogenous factors acted to impede success. In the liquor industry, which had been growing at a comfortable five to six percent rate

throughout the 1960s, consumption slowed drastically by the 1970s. U. S. liquor consumption rose only 2.3 percent in 1970, 2.9 percent in 1971, 2.6 percent in 1972, and 2.7 percent in 1973.[14]

Partly accounting for this was a sliding economy, which dispelled an old maxim that this business was recession-proof: "When people have money, they drink; when they don't have money, they drink." [15]

At first the liquor industry was worried that the turning of American youth to drugs would have an adverse effect on liquor sales. But most executives discredited this as a significant factor. What was significant, however, was a growing interest in wine by drinkers of all ages. In August 1972, for example, the United States imported 86 percent more wine than in the same month two years earlier, and twenty percent more wine was produced by domestic firms. The year-to-year growth rate of wine was around one percent in the 1950s, rose to five percent in the 1960s, and then leaped to ten to fifteen percent in the early 1970s. Undoubtedly this affected hard liquor consumption. Some distillers, encouraged by the success of Schenley with Portuguese wine — Schenley imported 1.1 million cases in 1972, compared with 25 cases in 1954 — began moving into the wine market.[16]

The coming of Frost 8/80 and several other brands of clear and light-colored whiskeys onto the market a year ahead of the official entry of light whiskey from other makers may have hurt the entire industry. For four years there had been widespread publicity about the flood of new products that would be introduced on July 1, 1972. But by then the official entry of light whiskeys was rather anticlimactic. This may have diluted the effective impact of this product innovation. Furthermore, retailers remained skeptical of all the new brands, especially since the early entrants such as Frost 8/80, Four Roses Premium, and Barton's QT all had unspectacular sales in 1971. Accordingly, the true light whiskeys had difficulty gaining market entry in 1972.

ANALYSIS OF THE FAILURE OF FROST 8/80

The withdrawal of Frost 8/80 from the market in December 1972, despite heavy promotional efforts, was bound to cast a pall over the optimism of the rest of the industry with other light whiskeys waiting to be introduced. Undoubtedly promotional budgets were cut back while a wait-and-see attitude prevailed on the part of some distillers. Regarding the demise of Frost 8/80, Carl Varga, vice president of Brown-Forman, said: "Thorough and reliable research told us everything was right: the product, the packaging, the advertising, the versatility — the possibilities were truly endless. The platform was further fortified by the overwhelming wholesaler reception, retailer reception, and the ensuing publicity in prestigious business publications. In the final analysis, everything had to be measured by how the consumer responded. The response has not been satisfactory." [17]

However, more specific faults could be attributed to the marketing efforts. William Carroll, who directed the sales of Frost 8/80, believed that "the research we had done probably was all right, but we misread it. The brand came off high on 'uniqueness,' and we interpreted this to mean that people would be anxious to try it. As it turned out, uniqueness was our biggest problem. The product looked like vodka but tasted like whiskey. It upset people." [18]

Brown-Forman could be criticized for not test marketing the new product in a few cities before distributing it broadly. However, to have done so would have given competition a chance to monitor the test and to possibly come out with competitive products. Perhaps in this case there was good justification to go national without a test market, although the risks of product failure were certainly increased.

The company's advertising also was subject to heavy criticism:

> They should have run more educational ads explaining what the product was and they should have started them before the product came out.

> The switch of ads in midstream wasn't too good either. They should have stuck with one approach or the other.

> I don't think anyone understood it (the second advertising approach). It confused people more.[19]

While the criticisms have some justification, the basic flaw was that the colorless whiskey simply lacked consumer acceptance, and this was not detected in time.

The Failure of Light Whiskeys

The liquor industry had come to believe that American consumers were not turning to imported whiskeys so much for their "snob appeal" as that "they have found a taste characteristic not present in the domestic whiskeys — they have found lightness, and they like it." [20] But the failure of the domestic light whiskeys suggests that the prestige of imported whiskeys was a large factor in attracting demand, that consumer needs for light whiskeys were being adequately satisfied, and there was no particular reason to change. Consequently, the market potential for light tasting domestic whiskeys — offered at about the same prices as the imported ones — was not nearly as great as the industry had estimated.

In refuting the idea that consumer preferences could be quickly changed, the president of the firm that imports Beefeater, the fastest climbing gin, noted shortly after the white and light whiskeys were introduced: "One of the distillers marketing a clear whiskey claims it can be used in mixed drinks — to make a kind of Bloody Mary, Orange Blossom, or even a martini. Well, we think martini drinkers will settle for nothing less than gin or vodka — not for something that may look the same, but tastes different." [21]

A vice president of Schenley agreed. He did not expect bourbon drinkers to give up their preference for a heavier taste, or other drinkers to give up the status of Scotch or Canadian. And he saw no effect on sales of rum, brandy, cordials, and other distinctive liquors.[22]

One of the problems of distribution which hurt the new brands was in cracking the market in the eighteen states where liquor is sold only through state-controlled stores. These stores buy only fast-moving brands. For any new product and brand just getting started, U. S. distribution is limited until such a time as a new product has proven itself. In 1971, Brown-Forman concentrated their efforts on fifteen population centers with high income and heavy liquor consumption. In these markets the company hoped to prove the popularity of Frost 8/80 sufficiently to enter the controlled states. But this never happened.

Part of the problem with the light whiskeys may have been the word "light" used to describe them. This adjective perhaps has been overused in promoting a host of products so it has little impact anymore on many people. Sales may also have been hurt by confusion and indecision on the part of some distillers as to whether to introduce all-new brands, or reformulate existing products and add the word "light" to a familiar brand name.

Finally, perhaps Frost 8/80 and the other white and light whiskey write-offs were abandoned too soon. Time is needed to build a brand and to induce the consumer to develop new taste habits. With a substantially modified product category, a slow buildup of preferences is all that can be reasonably expected, not the massive swing that some distillers had expected (based on consumer preferences for the lighter tasting imported whiskeys). For example, vodka required about ten years to really gain a foothold, so why should not light whiskeys take as long? But William Lucas, president of Brown-Forman, rejects this charge of pulling out too soon: ". . . we don't believe in perpetuating our failures. A lot of companies won't recognize a mistake and just let it go ahead, draining their resources and demoralizing their people. We took a risk, and we lost. That's the way it is in business." [23]

This is an argument that can hardly be settled: when is the right time to call quits? In the history of marketing, probably more firms have made the mistake of staying too long with poorly performing products than of cutting their losers promptly and turning to potentially more profitable undertakings.

What Can Be Learned?

The problems of the light whiskey innovation illustrate several important marketing caveats. First of all, regarding marketing research: even massive expenditures for marketing research do not guarantee correct decisions;

they improve the batting average of decision making, and this is important, but mistakes are still made despite such expenditures. Furthermore, research findings still have to be interpreted. Translating consumer expressed opinions into sales (as the makers of Frost 8/80 tried to do) is difficult.

Heavy advertising cannot force a questionable product onto the market. Perhaps a different advertising approach would have helped Frost 8/80; most likely it would have not. Advertising is most effective when it can apprise consumers of a clearly defined need and of the means to satisfy it.

And this brings us to the biggest lesson to be learned, and that is the difficulty of breaking into the market with a new product aimed at satisfying a need already being well satisfied by existing products. In this case, consumer desires for light flavored liquors were being met by vodka, rum, Scotch, and Canadian whiskeys. Why should consumers shift to domestically produced light whiskeys that cost about the same, tasted about the same, and had less status?

There are still risks in marketing; they cannot be escaped. Furthermore, they cannot always be predicted. But that is what makes marketing a never-ending challenge and a source of great opportunity for those who can best assess the market.

Assignment

1.   Evaluate the marketing strategies employed for Frost 8/80.

REFERENCES

1.   "Liquor Men Feel Like the Morning After," *Business Week,* March 17, 1975, pp. 88, 89.
2.   *Advertising Age,* July 3, 1972, p. 47.
3.   Ibid.
4.   "Light Whiskey Comes at Maybe the Wrong Time," *Business Week,* March 11, 1972, p. 100.
5.   "Taking the Plunge: Putting Out New Product Is Costly and Risky," *Wall Street Journal,* February 18, 1971, pp. 1, 14.
6.   Ibid.
7.   Ibid.
8.   Ibid.
9.   "Light Whiskies," *Forbes,* July 15, 1972, p. 40.
10.   "How a New Product Was Brought to Market Only to Flop Miserably," *Wall Street Journal,* January 5, 1973, pp. 1, 11.
11.   *Advertising Age,* November 27, 1972, p. 2.
12.   "A Barrel of Trouble for the Whiskey Makers," *Business Week,* March 10, 1973, p. 112.
13.   Ibid., pp. 113, 114.

14. "Why Wine Is Cutting into Liquor Sales," *Business Week,* March 9, 1974, p. 120.
15. "The Distillers Serve Up New Brands," *Business Week,* March 6, 1971, p. 80.
16. "Why Wine Is Cutting . . ."
17. "Brown-Forman Quits on Earthbound Frost 8/80," *Advertising Age,* December 18, 1972, p. 2.
18. "How a New Product Was Brought to Market . . . ," p. 11.
19. Ibid.
20. "Light Whiskey Comes at Maybe the Wrong Time," p. 100.
21. Ibid.
22. Ibid.
23. "How a New Product Was Brought to Market . . . ," p. 11.

Modern Office Supply, Inc.*

In July 1954, two experienced retail managers in their early thirties pooled their resources and purchased Greentree Stationery and Supply, Inc. This retail firm was a specialty-type store carrying high-quality lines of office supplies. The store was located on the main street in the downtown shopping area of Greentree, Ohio, an industrial community of 40,000 people located twenty miles east of Columbus.

Under its previous owner, the company had enjoyed 23 years of successful growth and profitability. Although it was small for its type, the company was financially sound and was well established as a reputable business.

Immediately after the purchase, the new owner-managers, Martin Hersh and Paul Dixon, ceased operations for a ten-week period in order to renovate and redecorate the store. Then, on January 10, 1955, under the new name of Modern Office Supply, Inc., the firm reopened to the public.

In its abbreviated first year of operations, Modern Office Supply had a sales volume of $37,080, a decrease of $5,315 from the previous year. This downturn was quickly reversed, however, and in the next 18 years of operation, the firm never again suffered a decrease in sales, as is shown in Exhibit 1.

The growth of the business necessitated an increase in inventory storage space and a larger sales area. Thus, in 1967, Modern Office Supply relocated across the street in a newly remodeled building which offered double the square footage of their first store.

There was also a steady need for additional employees. By 1972 the managers were supervising twelve full-time salesclerks. All the clerks were women, although men were also actively sought when positions were avail-

---

* Prepared by Professor John A. Pearce II, University of South Carolina. Used by permission.

EXHIBIT 1
MODERN OFFICE SUPPLY, INC. SALES
AND INCOME FIGURES 1955–1973

Year	Sales volume[a]	Percentage change for the year	Taxable income
1955	$ 37,080	−13	−$ 1,820
1956	55,620	+50	1,670
1957	63,960	+15	2,620
1958	71,680	+12	3,010
1959	81,730	+14	3,100
1960	90,730	+11	2,990
1961	98,890	+ 9	2,570
1962	107,800	+ 9	3,450
1963	115,340	+ 7	2,650
1964	129,200	+12	5,680
1965	143,410	+11	6,450
1966	159,180	+11	5,570
1967	173,510	+ 9	5,380
1968	194,330	+12	10,300
1969	221,530	+14	10,850
1970	243,700	+10	8,530
1971	265,620	+ 9	6,910
1972	281,160	+ 6	5,340
1973	287,190	+ 2	1,730

[a] All figures have been rounded.

able. Ten of the twelve were married, and, in 1973 they averaged 45.2 years of age, with a range of 32 to 62 years. Modern Office Supply also regularly employed four high-school students on a part-time basis to perform stockroom, janitorial, and delivery duties.

That Modern Office Supply had experienced an exceptionally low turnover rate throughout its history is shown by the fact that in 1973 seven full-time employees had been with the firm for over ten years. To a large degree, the appeal of the company as an employer was due to a fringe benefit program which was far superior to those offered by other local businesses. The Modern Office Supply plan included the following features:

1. Six paid holidays were given to all full-time employees.[1]

2. A Christmas bonus of $10 for every year of full-time employment and $5 for every year of part-time employment was paid on an individual basis to employees at the annual company-sponsored Christmas party.

3. Five paid but noncumulative sick days were available to full-time employees each year.

4. Paid vacations were given to full-time employees according to the following schedule: one week after one year, two weeks after five years, and three weeks after ten years or more with the firm.

In addition to the attractive benefit program, Modern Office Supply paid a wage which was competitive for the industry and the locale. Further, merit raises, based on the employee's individual performance, were awarded annually to deserving full-time saleswomen.[2] The hourly wages were also updated each year by an automatic raise of 2 cents. This minimum adjustment was seen by the managers as a protection for the employees against either economic inflation or unfair bias affecting the individual manager's decision on merit raises. Exhibit 2 illustrates the effect of raises on the wage payroll for the full and part-time sales personnel as of December, 1973.

Throughout Modern Office Supply's history, the management philosophy had been to maintain an image as merchandisers of high-quality products. This philosophy was an important factor in the rapid growth of Modern Office Supply, primarily because sales to industrial firms in the area, which constituted over half the company's business, were mainly of high-quality materials and equipment. In late 1971, however, a change in the industrial segment's purchasing behavior became evident, as an increasing inflationary trend and predicted recession in the economy caused business firms to begin cutting back on expenses. Companies were forgoing the purchase of new, expensive, high-quality equipment and materials and tended toward the purchase of medium-quality items. However, due to inventory and space limitations, and the management philosophy of offering quality products at a moderate price, Modern Office Supply chose not to compete on medium-quality lines. Perhaps as a result, the company experienced a leveling off in its yearly sales volume in 1972.

Recent Difficulties

In 1973 Modern Office Supply was confronted with a difficult situation. The firm's yearly sales had bettered those of the previous 12 months by a scant 2 percent, with sales in the industrial market most adversely affected. Area businesses had initiated harsh expense-cutting policies, and many had shifted a significant percentage of their purchases to low-priced, low-quality items, such as those carried by discount and department stores. The problem was amplified by the opening of a shopping mall in a location three miles from the Modern Office Supply facility. In addition to 23 other stores, this new shopping center housed a Murphy Mart, a Sears department store, and

EXHIBIT 2
MODERN OFFICE SUPPLY, INC. CURRENT WAGE STRUCTURE

Employee	Date hired	Years of employment	Base rate	Accumulated automatic raises (2¢/yr.)	Accumulated merit raises	Hourly rate before May 1, 1974
Full time[a]						
Gardner	01/09/55	19	$1.60	38¢	40¢	$2.38
Ulrich	04/09/58	16	1.60	32¢	22¢	2.14
Mockin	07/07/59	15	1.60	30¢	20¢	2.10
Gould	02/10/60	14	1.60	28¢	20¢	2.08
Butler	04/05/63	11	1.60	22¢	15¢	1.97
Bliss	05/20/63	11	1.60	22¢	12¢	1.94
Schoaf	07/14/63	11	1.60	22¢	12¢	1.94
Meyers	01/04/65	9	1.60	18¢	18¢	1.96
Liston	02/18/66	8	1.60	16¢	8¢	1.84
Freeman	03/15/68	6	1.60	12¢	5¢	1.77
Cline	03/15/68	6	1.60	12¢	5¢	1.77
Alloway	09/01/69	5	1.60	10¢	5¢	1.75
Part time[b]						
Fenton	10/22/69	5	1.36			1.61
Barbour	04/30/70	4	1.36			1.56
Kyle	09/01/70	4	1.36			1.56
Hinning	05/02/72	2	1.36			1.46

[a] Thirty hours a week or more.
[b] Less than thirty hours a week.

a locally owned and operated Cut-Rite outlet. These three stores in particular posed competitive challenges to Modern Office Supply sales in both the consumer and business markets. Items such as typewriters, office furniture, paper, and writing instruments could be purchased at a somewhat lower price from the mall stores, and thus they increasingly appealed to budget-constrained purchasers in spite of the fact that the apparent quality of these items was inferior.

The demand of furniture customers for the interior design service offered by Modern Office Supply dropped precipitously. Consumers considered this service expendable since, to the degree it was needed, this service could be performed by the purchaser. By so doing, the consumer saved the cost of the interior decorator and was spared any feeling of obligation to buy the high-priced furniture supplied by Modern Office Supply.

Faced with these conditions, Hersh and Dixon found it essential to cut back on their own expenses. This objective was accomplished by reducing the store's weekly hours. After a thorough analysis of the store's sales patterns, the managers decided to eliminate Modern Office Supply's Thursday night store hours from 5:00 P.M. to 9:00 P.M.[3] The reason for this step was twofold. First, it cut back on various operating overhead expenses. Second, it reduced the weekly hourly payroll by 36 hours, since nine full-time clerks were kept on the floor during these four evening business hours. Consequently, the average full-time week was reduced from 37.5 hours to 34.5 hours.

The new minimum wage law of 1974 presented Hersh and Dixon with an additional dilemma. This legislation had the effect of offsetting the decrease in expenses achieved by the reduction in store hours. The law required companies the size of Modern Office Supply to increase their minimum wage in progressive steps from the current level of $1.60 an hour to $2.30 an hour by 1977. Workers were to begin earning $1.90 an hour on May 1, 1974, $2.00 an hour on January 1, 1975, $2.20 an hour on January 1, 1976, and $2.30 an hour on January 1, 1977. The effect of these hourly wage changes is shown in Exhibit 3.[4]

The owners of Modern Office Supply saw this new law as potentially devastating to their profitable operations. The recent economic downturn, coupled with new competition from the mall stores, had caused such a significant decrease in the firm's sales volume that Mr. Hersh and Mr. Dixon had recently been finding it difficult to justify objectively even the current hourly payroll. Since the new wage legislation would force the amount of the payroll to rise if the total employee hours remained unchanged, the managers decided that they would have to reduce the payroll hours in order to stabilize the payroll. However, rather than cut back on individual weekly hours, the managers decided to lay off the full-time employees with the least

EXHIBIT 3
MODERN OFFICE SUPPLY, INC. PLANNED WAGES

Employee	1974 ($1.90 base)	1975 ($2.00 base)	1976 ($2.20 base)	1977 ($2.30 base)
Full time				
Gardner	$2.68	$2.78	$2.98	$3.08
Ulrich	2.44	2.54	2.74	2.84
Mockin	2.40	2.50	2.70	2.80
Gould	2.38	2.48	2.68	2.78
Butler	2.27	2.37	2.57	2.67
Bliss	2.24	2.34	2.54	2.64
Schoaf	2.24	2.34	2.54	2.64
Meyers	2.26	2.36	2.56	2.66
Liston	2.14	2.24	2.44	2.54
Freeman	2.07	2.17	2.37	2.47
Cline	2.07	2.17	2.37	2.47
Alloway	2.05	2.15	2.35	2.45
Part time				
Fenton	1.92	2.05	2.27	2.41
Barbour	1.87	2.00	2.22	2.36
Kyle	1.87	2.00	2.22	2.36
Hinning	1.77	1.90	2.12	2.26

seniority. They reasoned that it was better to provide 11 workers with the opportunity to earn a respectable income than it was to place 12 full-time employees at an income level approaching unemployment compensation.

Although this approach was not appealing, no other viable alternatives seemed available under the prevailing conditions. Before this action was initiated, however, several employees approached the managers with a proposal to avoid the layoff of their co-worker. The clerks had held a private meeting at which they had unanimously agreed to take whatever cuts were necessary in their individual weekly hours in order to maintain the present sales force. The managers were pleased and readily accepted the proposal, for it allowed them to achieve their goal of reduced payroll hours while also enabling them to retain a valued saleswoman.

One major issue still required resolution. The minimum wage legislation mandated a rate of pay substantially greater than that which would normally be paid at Modern Office Supply. When the new wage adjustments were added to the fringe benefit program currently offered by the firm, the payment to employees in real dollar terms far exceeded both the individual and local averages and the level which Mr. Hersh and Mr. Dixon felt was reasonable. Therefore, the managers decided to try to offset the future wage increases in other areas of the employees' total compensation package. This goal was achieved through modifications of the fringe benefit program which were made effective April 29, 1974:

1. The Christmas bonus plan was eliminated for all employees.

2. The number of paid holidays was reduced to three; namely, Christmas, Thanksgiving, and New Year's Day.

Two further changes pertained only to the fringes provided for employees hired after April 29, 1974:

3. The sick pay allowance was discontinued.

4. Paid vacations were given to full-time employees according to the following schedule: one week after one year and two weeks after five or more years with the firm.

Although these four modifications substantially decreased the worth of fringe benefits, the managers believed the benefits had only been reduced to the level that was considered average for local retail stores.

   The more difficult problem, however, from the perspective of the Modern Office Supply managers, was the proper means by which to administer the new wage legislation. A quick analysis of the net changes in the em-

EXHIBIT 4
MODERN OFFICE SUPPLY, INC.
INCOME STATEMENT FOR THE
YEAR ENDED DECEMBER 31, 1973

Net sales	$287,190
Cost of goods sold	159,100
Gross margin on sales	$128,090
Managers' salaries	50,000
Depreciation	3,250
Other general/administrative expenses	70,140
Operating income	4,700
Interest expenses	1,240
Income before bonus and taxes	3,460
Managers' bonus	1,730
Taxable income	1,730

EXHIBIT 5
MODERN OFFICE SUPPLY, INC. STATEMENT
OF FINANCIAL POSITION AS OF DECEMBER 31, 1973

Assets		
Current assets		
Cash	$10,101.06	
Accounts receivable	18,231.42	
Inventories	48,058.04	
Fixed assets		
Equipment	11,338.94	
Total assets		$87,729.46
Liabilities		
Current liabilities		
Accounts payable/trade	5,724.05	
Other current debt	2,948.73	
Long-term debt		
Long-term bank loans	12,092.18	
Total liabilities	$20,764.96	
Stockholders' equity		
Capital stock	32,500.00	
Retained earnings	34,464.50	
Total stockholders' equity	$66,964.50	
Total liabilities and stockholders' equity		$87,729.46

ployees' compensation package for 1974 disclosed that if the present work-week remained the same, and the hourly rates for all full-time employees were raised by 30 cent increments, the net change in the employee payroll would result in an increase of $5,619.08 (11 percent) over 1973.[5] Again, excluding the traditional merit and automatic raises, these same calculations extrapolated to 1977 showed an expected $16,869.43 increase in the yearly payroll. This amount constituted a percentage increase of 33 percent over 1973.

A careful study of their firm's financial statements, shown in Exhibits 4 and 5, convinced Mr. Hersh and Mr. Dixon that the net dollar impact of the new wage legislation must be further blunted. In formulating their strategy to accomplish this objective, the managers stressed consideration of five key elements of the total compensation package: (1) the fringe benefit program, (2) the minimum wage law changes in the hourly base,

(3) the automatic yearly 2 cent an hour raise, (4) the annual merit wage adjustments, and (5) the current status of several employees who were paid substantially above the minimum wage as a result of length of service.

The fringe benefit program, which was about to be severely cut, and the wage law changes were considered unalterable. However, Mr. Hersh and Mr. Dixon believed that, in effect, the new wage law required them to increase Modern Office Supply's annual 2 cents an hour automatic raises by a total of 62 cents an hour over the next four years. Thus, they decided to eliminate the traditional automatic raises.

The issue of whether or not to continue the policy of annual merit wage adjustments posed a more difficult dilemma. The managers thought that, because of the required increases in the wage base, any merit raises would be unaffordable. On the other hand, the perceived motivational benefits of the merit system would be lost if the plan were discontinued.

Closely related to the merit wage issue was the case of several senior employees who might be considered overpaid as a result of their long years of service. Although the $1.90 figure was intended by law as the lowest amount to be paid to clerks, it could also be viewed as the level at which clerks were to be paid. Because of this provision of the law, the Modern Office Supply owner-managers were compelled to increase the hourly rate of the four full-time employees who were paid less than $1.90 an hour. This strategy would greatly reduce the financial burden of the minimum wage legislation. However, the managers feared that such action might eliminate much of the motivational impact of previous merit and automatic raises. In addition, the higher hourly rates of the senior salesclerks often reflected their greater-than-average contributions to the operation of the firm. Senior clerks were often given responsibilities far in excess of those assigned to new, less experienced personnel. Therefore, their overpayment really represented fair compensation for services rendered. Thus, by narrowing the wage gap between the higher and lower paid employees, the managers believed that they would be taking the risk of alienating clerks who performed special functions for the organization.

Having carefully considered several different alternatives, the managers decided that in the years 1974 through 1977, the amount of the legislatively mandated wage base increases would be added to all full-time employees' rates across the board. Essentially then, in 1974, all full-time employees received a 30 cents an hour wage increase. In 1975 their wages were to be increased by 10 cents, in 1976 by 20 cents, and in 1977 by 10 cents. Part-time workers also received upward adjustments based on the governmentally legislated minimum of 85 percent of the base pay of full-time employees. Thus, in 1974, part-time employees' minimum wage jumped from $1.36 to $1.62 an hour, while their average workweek remained at 25.5 hours.

Dear

Recently President Nixon signed into a law a bill raising the minimum wage for workers in our size business in stages from $1.60 an hour to $2.30 an hour by 1977.

The wage scale provides that the workers in our category are to begin earning $1.90 an hour on May 1, $2.00 in January, 1975, $2.20 in January, 1976, and $2.30 in January, 1977.

It also provides that not more than four students may be employed at 85 percent of the regular full-time rate.

We are in agreement with this law as a protection of workers. Unfortunately it has not been designed to take into consideration the side benefits of any job, and therefore we now find it necessary to revise some of the company programs into "direct-pay" dollars which you are assured of receiving pay by pay.

For new employees hired *after* May 1, 1974, paid vacation earned after one full year of full-time employment will be one week until five years full-time employment, when paid vacation will be two weeks annually thereafter. *Present employees are not affected.*

Our company sick-pay policy will remain in force until attainment of sixty-fifth birthday for full-time employees hired *prior* to May 1, 1974. For persons hired *after* May 1, 1974, sick-pay benefits will go into effect on the anniversary of five years' employment.

The following will be paid holidays effective May 1, 1974: New Year's Day, Thanksgiving, and Christmas.

Although the monetary Christmas gift has been a happy tradition for many years, with the newly imposed hourly direct-pay regulations, this tradition must, regretfully, be discontinued.

On Monday, April 29, 1974, your hourly rate has been increased by $ to $ per hour and is $ above the $1.90 wage-law.

We have always tried to offer better than average hourly rates to our experienced employees and hope you will be pleased with this arrangement.

Sincerely,

EXHIBIT 6

On the morning of April 29, 1974, at a weekly Monday morning sales meeting, both full-time and part-time employees were informed of general changes in the company's wage-compensation program. That afternoon copies of a carefully prepared announcement letter (Exhibit 6) were mailed to each of Modern Office Supply's 16 sales personnel, detailing how their wages, in specific, would be affected by the minimum wage law and the changes in the firm's fringe benefit program.

Questions and Assignments

1. What were the principal external problems for Modern Office Supply in the years 1971–1973? What negative consequences were associated with these problems?

2. How do you characterize and evaluate the approach of Mr. Hersh and Mr. Dixon to environmental pressures?

3. If you were hired by Modern Office Supply as a consultant in July, 1974, what actions would you recommend?

NOTES

1. Holiday pay was calculated by dividing the average workweek by five and then multiplying this number by the individual's hourly wage rate.
2. *Full-time* was defined as thirty hours a week even though the average workweek of full-time employees had always exceeded this number of hours.
3. The remaining business hours were Monday through Friday from 9:00 to 5:00 P.M., Monday night from 5:00 to 9:00 P.M., and Saturday from 9:00 A.M. to 12:00 noon. With the exception of the Thursday night hours, these remaining hours were identical to those kept by the majority of retail stores located in downtown Greentree.
4. The reported profit figures of Modern Office Supply, Inc. (Exhibit 1) are misleading due to the impact of a bonus system which was designed to keep the firm's yearly taxable income below $25,000. Under this plan, both Mr. Hersh and Mr. Dixon received a yearly bonus of 25 percent of the company's pretax income.
5. Remember that the new wage law was in effect for only eight months (34 weeks) of 1974.

White Consolidated*

The major appliance industry has humbled some of the biggest names in the corporate lexicon. During the past dozen years, Westinghouse Electric, Ford, American Motors, and, most recently, General Motors have given up on making refrigerators, ranges, washers, and dryers.

Each of these giants suffered a strikingly similar fate. Their appliances sported widely recognized brand names such as Westinghouse, Kelvinator, Philco, and Frigidaire and were bankrolled by corporate treasuries much larger than most of their competitors. Yet none was efficient enough to withstand the brutal price competition that has long ruled the appliance trade. So after years of dismal financial returns, and sometimes huge losses, all of these operations were sold to a relatively little-known company that, until 1967, was not in the major appliance business at all — White Consolidated Industries Inc.

Although it is now clearly a big-league manufacturer of major household appliances, White Consolidated is anything but a household word. The company's headquarters — an anonymous brick office building wedged between a cluster of old factories and warehouses on the west side of Cleveland — befits a company that has scored big in a consumer business by relying on a 19th century devotion to cost-cutting that equals the passion most other consumer companies give to 20th century corporate imagery and marketing magic. "From a consumer standpoint, we aren't all that concerned about selling the name White Consolidated," explains Executive Vice-President Joseph L. McGowan.

Yet in the appliance industry, the name White Consolidated has come to stand for an awesome competitor. It has earned that reputation by repeatedly taking over the troubled appliance operations of once-larger rivals and transforming them into money-makers. After seven appliance acquisitions in a dozen years, the Cleveland company, too, has been transformed — from a $400 million-a-year purveyor of industrial equipment and sewing machines into a company that last year garnered 64% of its $1.7 billion in revenues from appliance operations. It is now the industry's third largest producer, after General Electric Co. and Whirlpool Corp.

The company is ready to apply its successful formula once again, having just made another big acquisition, one that brings into its fold a legendary name in appliances. When White Consolidated announced . . . that it planned to buy General Motors Corp.'s Frigidaire Div., which reportedly lost almost $40 million last year [1978] on sales of $450 million, it soon became apparent that the company's growing clout in appliances was at last drawing attention. Casting a wary eye on the effect that the Frigidaire acquisition would have on competition in the refrigerator market, the Justice Dept. reviewed the deal. But earlier this month, Justice put its imprimatur on the acquisition, and the stock market immediately displayed confidence in White Consolidated's ability to turn losers into winners: In the two days after the antitrust hurdle was cleared, the company's stock leaped 16%. (See Exhibit 2.)

Cost Control with a Vengeance

The Frigidaire move will cost White Consolidated an estimated $120 million, a figure that includes the purchase price along with the cost of readying the company's existing plants to manufacture the Frigidaire lines. And the acquisition will lift White's dependence on appliances to nearly 75%. But it also will boost the company's share in refrigerators, the largest single product category of the appliance business, from about 16% to almost 25% — putting it within striking range of the leaders in the market, GE with 30% and Whirlpool with 27%. According to 1978 market-share figures recently published by *Appliance Manufacturer* magazine, the Frigidaire acquisition could boost White's share of total dollar sales in the electric range market by six percentage points to 18%. The move may well lift the company's market share in electric clothes dryers by five percentage points to 15%, in gas dryers by five points to 14%, and in clothes washers by six to 14%.

White Consolidated has become an industry power thanks to a strategy that is disarmingly simple in concept, if not in execution. The company has merely elevated the doctrine of cost control to a corporate religion, one it pursues with messianic fervor, using an incredible array of cost-cutting techniques. At a time when executives, economists, and policymakers are deeply concerned about the long-term leveling of productivity in the U.S., White Consolidated has achieved a drastic increase in the efficiency of plants, people, and equipment that were cast off in despair by much bigger corporations.

Moreover, this feat is all the more striking because it has been accomplished not by dint of huge capital investments or by new technology — the classic productivity boosters of the modern era — but primarily through a Scrooge-like obsession with more prosaic measures. After each acquisition, White typically makes massive cuts in the work force, sometimes by as much as 40%. It also takes a hard line with unions. While its wage rates meet the industry average, the company has a reputation for its willingness to withstand strikes to get its way on other cost-cutting measures. "Without some strikes," stresses Chairman Roy H. Holdt, "we might not have been able to compete in the marketplace."

Every product line and model of a newly acquired appliance business is scrutinized, and many of the low-volume offerings are jettisoned. White has nonetheless decided to retain all of the dozen brand names it has purchased. The company's executives have figured that the various brand franchises and dealer networks were often the most valuable parts of the businesses it picked up. Instead of consolidating brands, White has concentrated on streamlining operations, which is its forte. But frequently, the manufacture of a given line is moved to one plant, making for longer, more economic production runs.

The company then installs its vaunted system of decentralized management. Each of the company's 15 appliance plants is run as a separate profit center, but that concept takes on much more meaning at White Consolidated than at most other companies that employ it. Each plant is run by a so-called president, and while he ultimately can be overruled by headquarters, he has substantial control over the design, engineering, and pricing of the products made at his plant, as well as the manufacturing process itself. He even supervises a plant-level sales force, which independently negotiates all sales to mass merchandisers. White does have national sales forces for 4 of its 12 appliance brands, but they handle only name brands. Still, the operating structure essentially gives White 15 competing companies. "It puts more pressure on the plant president to succeed as an individual business," explains McGowan, "and he can't blame success or failure on something else."

But when it comes to financial matters, plant autonomy comes to an abrupt end. For one thing, the plant presidents must deal with a corporate staff that forms a veritable Maginot line around the company treasury. Even some expenditures as small as $5,000 must be approved by the corporate office. As one former executive of the company puts it: "It's like a game of 'Simon Says.' You have to wait for the word from the headquarters Simon before you can make any capital appropriation, any budget commitment, or any expenditure." White's plant presidents also must adhere to an airtight financial reporting system that is a great deal more detailed than the reporting requirements imposed by the plants' previous owners. Expense, manufacturing, and profit statements are collected each day from every department. Every month, Cleveland headquarters receives two detailed operating statements from each plant — one from the plant president and another from the plant's controller, who reports independently. The controller "is not a spy," explains White President Ward Smith, "but he is there to provide an independent view of the operation."

The key to White Consolidated's success, however, is as much an attitude as a system. The emphasis on pennypinching is preached and practiced at every level of management. "When we bought a company," recalls one of White's recently departed corporate executives, "I reviewed every expenditure, right down to asking whether a particular desk needed a telephone and whether the phone should have two buttons instead of four. Even the purchase of pencils was examined." (See Exhibit 1.)

This approach has been applied to each of the company's seven appliance acquisitions. In many cases it has bought a losing property at well below book value, and, within a year or so, the operation has been made profitable. The pattern began in 1967, when the company bought Hupp Corp. for about $53 million, thus picking up Gibson brand refrigerators and air conditioners. Later that year it bought Studebaker Corp.'s Franklin Appliance Div. for $19 million.

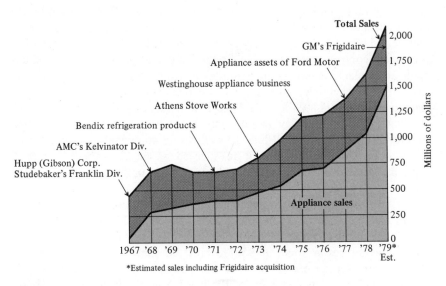

*Estimated sales including Frigidaire acquisition

EXHIBIT 1
HOW APPLIANCE ACQUISITIONS ARE FUELING GROWTH AT WHITE CONSOLIDATED

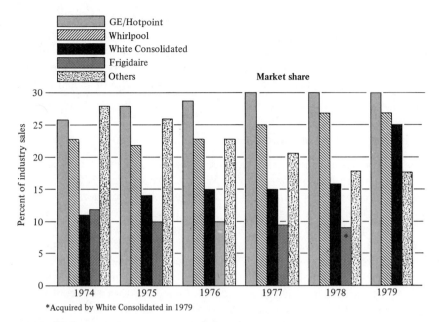

Market share

GE/Hotpoint
Whirlpool
White Consolidated
Frigidaire
Others

Percent of industry sales

*Acquired by White Consolidated in 1979

EXHIBIT 2
HOW FRIGIDAIRE WIDENS WHITE'S POSITION
IN REFRIGERATORS

In 1968, White acquired American Motors Corp.'s Kelvinator unit for $24 million and three years afterward picked up a Bendix Corp. plant that makes cooling compressors. Next, in 1973, it acquired a small Tennessee manufacturer of gas ranges, Athens Stove Works Inc. The biggest single move came in 1975, when Westinghouse sold its $376 million appliance business to White for $61 million. In 1977 the company bought from Ford certain remnants of Philco.

Because White Consolidated collects sick appliance makers, it often gets them at fire sale prices. The Westinghouse operation, for instance, was purchased at a 42% discount from its book value. "The undertaking business is a good business," one analyst notes wryly. After buying cheap, the company goes in swinging a hatchet. For example, half of the 510-member headquarters staff at Kelvinator was axed.

At White Consolidated's Mansfield (Ohio) facility, which was acquired from Westinghouse, William H. Eutzy, the local plant president, recalls that company officials "visited so frequently after the acquisition I could hardly stand them." After the troubleshooters sized things up, 39% of the salaried staff at Mansfield was fired, a move that was duplicated at two other big Westinghouse plants.

Says Charles C. Rieger, Jr., former president of White's Kelvinator unit and now a vice-president of Insilco Corp.: "As an outsider, White can make much more objective decisions than the guy running the operation, who is eminently inclined toward keeping 'old Joe,' who has been there 30 years and should have been fired 20 years ago." One upshot of personnel cuts, Eutzy notes, is that "the people who are left have to work harder."

Production-Line Economies

To boost production runs, White also weeds out any marginal product lines that come with an acquisition. Prior to White's takeover in 1975, Westinghouse manufactured more than 40 different models of refrigerators at its Columbus (Ohio) plant, making each model in production runs of about 500. White quickly cut the number of White-Westinghouse refrigerator models to 30 that represented 85% of sales. This allowed the company to double the production runs on each model. The move lessened the need for costly downtime previously required in the middle of a shift to change over production to a new model. "Even today," observes a former executive of the company, "White Consolidated has fewer models than anyone else in the business. But it has picked the models where the volume is and competitively priced them."

To achieve further economies, White's individual plants also focus on a limited number of products. At the huge Columbus plant acquired from Westinghouse, the company restricted production only to refrigerators, compressors, and dishwashers. Production of air conditioners, dehumidifiers, and water coolers, which had accounted for roughly 10% of the plant's output, was either totally eliminated or transferred to other White plants that make those products. "We think we have better control than if we had six or seven product lines there," explains Holdt.

Of course, such consolidation of acquired appliance operations is likely to produce only short-term gains, and White is mindful of the need for long-term productivity improvements. Thus, even the company's research work is decidedly slanted in favor of production economies instead of marketing innovations. The company spent $8.2 million on appliance research and development last year, and nearly all of it went to make money-saving changes in existing products rather than to develop new ones. White has no corporate R&D staff, preferring to cluster its research teams at the plants, where they are closer to the production operations that they are trying to improve.

Just completed is a five-year, $30 million project to redesign the entire refrigerator line at the company's plant in Greenville, Mich., formerly a Gibson facility. The objective was to replace the old fiber-glass-insulated models with ones using polyurethane foam. The foam not only insulates but, because of its heft, serves as a structural support for the metal covering, allowing the company to use thinner, prepainted steel. Thanks to the change, plant officials claim substantial savings in production costs.

Its commitment to cost controls has not exactly made White a financial standout in the appliance business. The company's operating profit as a percentage of appliance sales last year was 6.2%, no greater than the industry average. However, it achieved that level by acquiring properties that previously were coming nowhere near the industry standard. Westinghouse, for example, was losing $2 million a month on appliances, but after acquiring that operation it took White only three months to bring it to the break-even point. And the White-Westinghouse line has been consistently profitable ever since. "The thing that made the immediate difference in the bottom line was that we just ran a hell of a lot tighter ship," President Smith says.

In selecting an arena for its kind of cost and price consciousness, White hardly could have picked a better industry than major appliances. With the exception of a few smaller, specialty companies, such as Maytag Co. and Raytheon Co.'s Amana Refrigeration Inc., it is sharp pricing, not sophisticated consumer marketing, that is the industry's chief competitive tool. Production costs alone will make or break an appliance company.

Prodded by its market, the industry has posted much bigger productivity gains than those scored by most other businesses. Between 1958 and 1977, the average output per hour for each employee in the major appliance industry climbed 5% annually, almost twice the rate for all manufacturing.

In addition, most appliances last well over a decade, and the industry has been singularly unsuccessful in convincing consumers that they should trade in a functional refrigerator, washer, or dryer after a few years for a supposedly more fashionable model. Consumers generally remain unconvinced that there is any appreciable difference between the appliances of different manufacturers.

The lack of any genuine product differentiation makes pricing paramount. The wholesale price index bears testimony to that. From 1957 to 1977, the index for all commodities rose from 99 to 206, while the figure for major appliances increased from 101 to only 131. "The practice of selling on price," says White Consolidated alumnus Rieger, "is the cancer of the appliance industry. It sucked those people down that couldn't stay with it."

This competitive environment is well suited for a company with White's cost-cutting strengths. And the Cleveland manufacturer has also structured its appliance operation to respond to other trends that make the appliance business production-oriented. For example, the company has avoided advertising and marketing battles by selling about half of its appliances as private-label brands through such mass merchandisers as Sears, J. C. Penney, Montgomery Ward, Gambles, and Western Auto. As a result, White Consolidated, which did no national advertising until two years ago, spends less than 2% of appliance sales on advertising and promotion, compared with at least twice that level for most of its major rivals.

Selling to the big retailers has proved to be an astute move in terms of the public's buying habits. Today, as much as a third of all major appliances is sold by mass merchandisers, representing a significant increase over the past two decades. This shift has occurred because smaller appliance dealers, as well as department stores, have been unable to compete effectively in the pricing game against the mass merchants.

White's frugal bent predates the company's entry into the appliance trade. Its thrifty traits are the legacy of the late Edward S. Reddig, who died [in 1979]. Reddig stepped down as chief executive in 1976 at the age of 71, having ruled White's roost for 11 years. Holdt and Smith have abandoned Reddig's autocratic ways, delegating much more authority to other corporate officers. Now, too, the company is far more open to financial reporters and Wall Street analysts. Even the personal manners of the low-key Holdt are a striking contrast to the fiery, sharp-tongued Reddig.

Tough on Labor

Matters of personal style aside, however, the basic Reddig tenets still hold sway at White Consolidated. "Ed Reddig would have cut off his mother's leg if he thought that would increase the efficiency of the operation," says one close observer. Even today, executives well-remember Reddig's dictum: "There are no fixed costs, only variable costs." Nowhere is that attitude more evident than at company headquarters. The setting is Spartan, with few amenities or special privileges for top officers; Holdt lines up with everyone else for lunch in White Consolidated's gymnasium-like cafeteria.

For a corporation expected to pass the $2 billion mark in sales this year, the headquarters staff of 118 is remarkably lean. Yet White does not scrimp on the salaries of top executives: Holdt was paid $449,000 last year in salary and bonuses. Whirlpool Chairman John H. Platts received $277,000.

The company has not shown the same generosity toward labor. White has taken tough stands with unions to keep costs in line, and union officials acknowledge that this has curbed wage and benefit increases. Not surprisingly, labor leaders have mostly harsh words for the company. "White is red," one union organizer fumes, "White is bloody."

Still, the company's intransigence does not always yield the desired result. Recently, for instance, White tried to use the Frigidaire move as a bargaining wedge. The proposition: If the International Union of Electrical

Workers (IUE) at the Mansfield plant would accept lower rates for new employees, White promised to make Frigidaire electric ranges there, thus increasing the work force. But the union spurned that offer, so White moved the range production to its Grand Rapids plant.

One block to reducing labor costs further is White's national contract with the IUE covering six former Westinghouse operations, which had traditionally followed a pattern set by General Electric. White has fought to eliminate national bargaining, which gives the unions more clout, and negotiate on a plant-by-plant basis. On that issue, the union struck six of the company's facilities in 1976. A federal court upheld the IUE's national bargaining rights, but White is appealing the decision.

Still, its willingness to take strikes makes White Consolidated a tough negotiator. Because it has several plants producing the same types of products, White is capable of making up for a walkout at one plant with increased production at another.

Typical was the recent three-month strike at one former Kelvinator plant in Grand Rapids. According to Robert L. Hulsebus, a regional representative of the United Auto Workers, some production equipment was shipped to another compressor plant in Alabama so that facility could pick up the slack. "Companies are all tough at the negotiating table," observes Hulsebus. "But some are like an eggshell — you hit them hard and they crush. White doesn't."

Now, White Consolidated will put its cost-shrinking knowhow to work on Frigidaire. Even before the Justice Dept. approved the deal, the company's troubleshooters were at Frigidaire's plant complex in Dayton, looking over its tooling and equipment. Those will now belong to White, as will Frigidaire's famous trademark, its inventories, and a distribution and sales network that includes some 5,000 outlets. GM, however, will keep the two big Dayton factories, converting them to truck and diesel-engine production.

Despite its loss-ridden past, most industry executives and analysts predict that Frigidaire will be contributing earnings to its new corporate parent within months. Most of all, they say, White will be simply walking away from Frigidaire's bugbear — high labor costs. Although union officials deny it, salaries and fringe benefits wound up being roughly 25% above the appliance industry standard because they were fashioned after settlements at GM's auto plants.

White is also alone among the big appliance makers in having a wealth of idle capacity to absorb Frigidaire production. Its plants are now running at no better than 60% of capacity, enabling the company to handle Frigidaire lines by simply making greater use of its existing operations.

Simply having the spare capacity, however, is no guarantee that White can, or will want to, hold on to all of Frigidaire's market. Some Frigidaire dealers, fearing the worst, are already switching to competing appliance manufacturers. But others suggest that White's penchant for cutting costs and prices might be just what its newest acquisition really needs. "We always had quality, but the customer is going to pay the price," says William Figueroa, owner of Crest Appliance Service, a Frigidaire dealer in Merchantville, N.J.

Frigidaire may also benefit since appliances are the biggest part of its new parent's business. Appliance executives generally believe that GM, as well as the other auto companies that entered the industry, never gave their relatively minuscule appliance units enough attention. "I firmly feel that Frigidaire has been a byproduct for GM," says one top appliance man, "and they let the thing get away from them."

The auto companies began moving into the business well before World War II, when the market was big and growing rapidly and the production principles for heavy appliances were much the same as for autos.

For a while, the scenario was played out just as the auto companies had hoped. But by the late 1960s it had become clear to them that appliances were low-margin products that moved slowly no matter what marketing or promotional ploys were used — a big difference from the fast-moving auto market. Thus, they got out when they could. William V. Luneburg, former president of AMC, explains: "I don't think automotive management is attuned to the white goods business . . . In our case, we were automobile men. We didn't have much interest in anything else."

Valuable Talents

At White Consolidated, though, appliances are now the centerpiece of the company, even though White has in the last two decades acquired nearly 20 companies in such other fields as metal castings, machine tools, and asphalt paving equipment. "Appliances are important to us," Holdt stresses, "because they're the major part of our business."

With Frigidaire, of course, White Consolidated becomes even more an appliance company. To some corporate strategists, such a move toward one industry — particularly one that is so vulnerable during recessions — is not prudent. And if the widely forecast recession does occur later this year, White executives may wish that they were less dependent on white goods.

Yet, White's cost-cutting and aggressive pricing talents become all the more valuable during recessions. In past downturns, White Consolidated has suffered less than others because of the company's ability to whittle costs. As a result, the company emerges from recessions as an even stronger competitor. Recalling how the freezer market itself entered a very deep freeze during the last appliance slump in 1975, Holdt says that White "cut back to one shift at our freezer plants, but we still remained quite profitable."

Adds Smith, "it certainly helps if you don't carve out some chunk of expense and say, 'Gee, we can't touch that.' "

Questions and Assignments

1. What are the basic elements of White Consolidated's strategy?

2. Is White Consolidated's strategy transferable to companies in other industries? Can you think of an example?

3. What external and internal factors might be critical for White Consolidated's future in the appliance industry?

The March Machine Co.*

Rudi March's father had invented a machine to produce corrugated boxes in 1960. From a modest beginning with one machine built in his garage, the senior March had developed his company into a significant northeastern United States producer of machines that could manufacture corrugated boxes in a variety of shapes, strengths, and sizes. In 1972 the elder March passed on the presidency of the firm to his thirty-two-year-old son, Rudi. Rudi was an engineering graduate of Northeast Technical University. Upon graduation he spent several years in the family firm, progressing from rather menial, routine tasks to vice-president in charge of operations. Within three years of joining the firm, Rudi had invented two very successful modifications of the basic model for corrugating cardboard and had a number of patents to his credit.

The March Machine Co. was headquartered in a town of only 30,000 residents. The company was the town's largest employer, except for the state university, located in the same town, which had grown from 8,000 to 22,000 full-time and part-time students in the past two decades. Except for the university's facilities, the town had only two movie theaters, no museums, and few recreational or park facilities.

Rudi was a gregarious and public-spirited individual. As head of the town's largest private employer, he was asked to become a trustee of the university. He was flattered and eagerly joined, becoming the youngest member of the Board of Trustees. Rudi soon became closely involved with the affairs of the university. He at first participated primarily by devoting his time to various fundraising campaigns and committees. Eventually, however, Rudi began to involve both himself and his company more directly in the affairs of the university. He had received a sizable amount of cash

* Prepared by Milton Leontiades.

from his father upon graduation from college and, through sound investments and luck, he had built this initial sum into a very "comfortable" amount. He also was aware that he would eventually inherit a sizable fortune from his father. From this position of financial security, Rudi was able to indulge his personal and charitable interests. Increasingly this outlet began to revolve around projects for the university. He felt a certain personal obligation to serve the university owing to his position with the March Machine Co. But over and above his personal contributions, he came to believe that the company should also be involved in supporting the university.

Rudi's first significant personal contribution was a $250,000 gift in 1977 for the construction of a new library wing. About a year later, he chaired the committee to raise funds for a new sports stadium, one of the largest such facilities to be built in the region. In addition to his own personal contribution of $100,000, Rudi pledged $1 million in the name of the March Machine Co. On the heels of these two actions, Rudi and the March Machine Co. received a considerable amount of local attention and publicity. In addition, a national newsmagazine had picked up the story and used it as an example of corporate involvement and social responsibility, prominently featuring Rudi March in the article as the guiding hand behind these actions. Following the first two projects, Rudi March had decided to pledge $2 million toward the construction of a new engineering building, which would be called March Hall. Of the $2 million, Rudi would personally contribute $100,000 and the rest would be donated by the March Machine Co. This news was of course enthusiastically received by the university and resulted in even more attention for the philanthropic actions of Rudi March and the March Machine Co.

As Rudi March devoted a greater percentage of his time to his role as university trustee, his involvement with the March Machine Co.'s day-to-day affairs lessened. He began to delegate more of the operating tasks to his subordinates. As a result, it was often difficult to reach Rudi for important strategic decisions. Since Rudi remained the chief executive officer, decision making in his absence became diffused among several officers, none of whom felt he could authoritatively lead where the others didn't want to follow, and all of whom were hesitant to take significant steps that Rudi might later countermand.

Since the firm was in a very competitive business, the March Machine Co. soon began to reflect this neglect in declining sales and earnings. Distributors for the March Machine Co. began to complain about late deliveries and customers' complaints about inadequate servicing of the machines they had bought. During the time Rudi was distracted by external obligations, the company had dropped from second- to fourth-largest regional manu-

facturer of corrugated box machinery, and its marketing system had deteriorated to the point where three of the most successful distributors for
the firm's products had signed on with competitors. Also the firm's major
competitors had introduced several new models and refinements while the
March Machine Co. had been selling basically the same models for the past
five years.

In 1972 the company's sales were $15 million and profits were a very
respectable 30 percent of sales before taxes. The March Machine Co. had
not failed to earn a profit since its beginning in 1960. Sales and earnings had
progressed on a more or less steady trend under the elder March. When
Rudi assumed the presidency in 1972, the March Machine Co. boosted its
sales an average of 15 percent a year from 1972 to 1976 and even raised
before-tax earnings to a high of 36 percent of sales in 1976. However, in
the five years since 1976, sales growth averaged only 5 percent annually,
whereas the industry continued to grow 15 percent per year. Earnings meanwhile had consistently declined to where the March Machine Co. was facing
the prospect of its first loss in the current year. Dividends were cut in half
in 1979 and were eliminated entirely beginning with the last quarter of 1980.

The net result was that the March Machine Co. was facing a financial
crisis. Cash flow was down to a dangerous level and the company was barely
able to cover the interest costs on outstanding bank loans. In an effort to
conserve funds, the company had reduced employment for the first time
since its founding. Even though the workforce had been reduced by 10 percent, the prospect was for further reductions unless things improved.

The Board of Directors of the company had understandably become
restless. At first they had applauded Rudi's involvement with the university
and the resulting publicity. Most of the members were long-time friends and
acquaintances of the Marches. They were reluctant to criticize Rudi openly
out of regard for his father. However, the deteriorating situation, and in
particular the prospect of the company's first loss year, brought a change
of opinion. Pressures had also come from disgruntled shareholders, who
had seen first dividends and then earnings disappear. Some of the fired
workers were also complaining openly of the company's mismanagement as
the cause for their unemployment.

A few of the board members questioned the March Machine Co.'s
ability to solve its problems and were discussing the possibility of bankruptcy. Others, however, still retained faith in the inventiveness and managerial ability of Rudi, if he could only be persuaded to address the company's problems immediately and forcefully. At the same time, there were
those in the university who continued to praise the public-spirited attitude
of Rudi and the March Machine Co. and were supporting his nomination
for chairman of the Board of Trustees.

Although Rudi March was aware of the rising discontent among the various factions in his company and the Board of Directors, he was confident, as majority shareholder, of beating back any serious rebellion against his authority. While he mentally promised himself to devote more time to the business, he was adamant against reducing his commitment to the university. He felt that the company was going through a temporary down cycle. With a better industry climate, and some closer attention to details by his top officers, Rudi was confident that the company would solve its financial problems.

Stimulated by Rudi's unwillingness to see the situation as seriously as they, three members of the Board of Directors decided to hire an outside consultant to conduct an independent appraisal of the company and give them recommendations for change. Rudi did not oppose the move, but indicated to the board that he would not feel bound by whatever recommendations were forthcoming.

Assignment

1. Assume you are the outside consultant, and make your evaluation of the March Machine Co. Present effective recommendations for the major problems you perceive.

A Social Strategy Aimed at Profits*

Within the next few weeks, a major redevelopment of the rundown Warren-Sherman neighborhood in Toledo will begin. Leading the way with a $5 million investment is not the federal or local government but Control Data Corp. (CDC), the computer maker in Minneapolis. The obvious question is: What is a computer company doing rebuilding Toledo? It perplexes financial analysts and even insiders at the company.

CDC's Toledo project is at the heart of a controversial and risky strategy that its equally controversial chairman and founder, William C. Norris, has charted. In part, it is a continuation of Norris' past strategy — to avoid banging heads with International Business Machines Corp. in its major markets. But Norris also believes in the intrinsic value of CDC's thrust. "Technology exists to solve society's major problems," he says. "The company that can do that will be the company of the future."

While that may sound like lip service to social responsibility, that is not the case at CDC. Norris already has bet at least $300 million in trying to position Control Data for leadership in a wide range of socially oriented markets, especially education and training, although the investments have yet to return a dime in profits. That has upset even some CDC managers, who would much rather see CDC's money invested in its large scientific computers, data-processing services, and peripherals.

Vulnerability. CDC's socially oriented projects do make sense to some financial analysts, including John J. McManus, vice-president of Shearson Hayden Stone Inc., who feels that they will reduce the company's long-term vulnerability to IBM. McManus believes that today's social projects will lead into tomorrow's product niches. But Harry Edelson, vice-president of Drexel Burnham Lambert Inc., while he approves of Norris' diversification into

---

such niches as services and peripherals, believes that CDC's social orientation far exceeds its business orientation.

Whatever their merits, the programs in CDC's social flower garden continue to multiply. City Venture Corp., which will rehabilitate slum buildings and train disadvantaged youths in the Toledo project, is scheduled to do similar work in Minneapolis, and other cities will follow, according to Norbert R. Berg, the company's senior vice-president and social architect. In St. Paul, CDC has opened the first of 15 business and technology centers devoted to the care and feeding of fledgling entrepreneurs. The centers will provide utilities and other building services, as well as access to specialized CDC services that assist in the financing of small businesses and teach how to start and run one.

"Social problems," Norris contends, "provide profit-making opportunities." In recent years, his vision has been focused on CDC's sophisticated, high-priced, computer-based education system called Plato, and the company's entire social strategy has revolved around it. As a result, CDC sees its social projects as hatcheries for new applications of the Plato system.

Learning Centers.   Plato offers basic English and mathematics training, as well as more advanced courses, through 50 CDC learning centers linked to a central computer. The system is being expanded to 80 centers this year. In addition, some companies, such as American Airlines Inc. and United Airlines Inc., lease Plato terminals; the two airlines use them as a low-cost source of preliminary flight-simulator training for their cockpit crews.

Norris also sees hundreds of millions of dollars of untapped business in selling low-cost, computer-based training to small companies such as MCP Machining Co. in Dallas, which has sales of less than $1 million and about 20 employees. Houston W. Higgins, the company's president, says Plato was used at a CDC learning center to train two secretaries to become accomplished bookkeepers having "a basic knowledge of accounting." Yet Plato cost only half as much as college courses in bookkeeping and did not lock his employees into an inflexible class schedule. Says Higgins: "A small businessman looks at training as something for a large corporation and not for him. Plato is a way around that."

Losses.   But Plato has been expensive for Control Data. It reportedly lost about $15 million on sales of only $48.6 million last year, a heavy setback for the Computer Group, whose total earnings in 1978 were only $41.3 million. (Those earnings, however, do not include the contribution of CDC's money-lending subsidiary, Commercial Credit Co., which has been a steady $40 to $50 million per year for the past five years.)

Over the last six years, Plato has lost some $38 million as the company has struggled to expand the system. Its true costs may be even greater than stated, as former employees say Norris has ordered CDC units other than the education operation to bear part of Plato's launching costs.

This causes analysts to doubt the wisdom of Norris' persistence with Plato. It is "just too far ahead of its time and something you'd not want to put a lot of money into," says Drexel Burnham's Edelson. And Ulric Weil, vice-president of Morgan Stanley & Co., while acknowledging that "education is one of the really huge markets left," adds: "The problem is being cost-effective."

Indeed, the monthly rental of a Plato terminal runs as high as $1,100. That has opened the door to microcomputer manufacturers such as Apple Inc. and Tandy Corp., which are racing to add education and training courses to their libraries, for an assault on this market. CDC recently responded with a 16% discount on a package of eight Plato terminals. "Plato is not cost-effective yet in basic education skills, but no one has developed the computer software, that CDC has," says John E. Haugo, executive director of the Minnesota Educational Computing Consortium, which uses 42 Plato terminals and is buying 400 Apple microcomputers.

Privately, one Plato user describes it as "the Cadillac in a market where a Chevy will do." And some former CDC employees fault Norris for rushing headlong into the education industry without a solid marketing plan. Says one former vice-president, who also spent time at IBM: "At IBM you'd be darn sure the project had a chance at paying back within two years and that there was a clearly defined market."

"The Market Is There."   But Norris believes that the technology will sell itself, as long as the need exists. "You don't need any fancy market research," he says acidly. "You know the market is there."

Intuition aside, a key element at CDC is Norris' insistent orientation toward long-term profits, rather than the shorter view typical of most companies. Norris espouses "patient capital" — the idea that investors should not judge programs such as Plato on the basis of short-term benchmarks, because they stand to reap enormous returns further out. Plato, for example, is targeted to turn a profit in the mid-1980s, more than a decade after its introduction.

Whether or not Wall Street likes it, Norris has embedded part of his philosophy in CDC's corporate structure. To block corporate suitors who might not agree with his long-term objectives, Norris lobbied for, and won, an "anti-takeover" clause for CDC's bylaws. The change, adopted at the 1978 annual meeting, requires the directors to consider factors such as the community impact, in deciding whether to accept an acquisition proposal.

Perhaps because of the zeal with which Norris has pursued the social strategy, some see Control Data entering a troubled transition as it prepares for his eventual retirement. Norris, who will be 68 in July, has dominated CDC since he founded it in 1957, and insiders expect him to stay at the helm until he is ready to leave. They say that this strong-willed approach has led to the departure of many top-flight managers. "It's the kind of place you either fit into immediately, loyally following the path Norris has chosen, or you leave quickly," says one of these former managers.

Control Data's course after Norris is likely to be set by Robert M. Price, the president of the Computer Group and a confidant of Norris. While Norris has devoted himself to Plato recently, Price has been putting CDC's computer business back together from its difficulties of five years ago — a role that brings him frequent mention as Norris' logical successor.

The lingering troubles stem from CDC's old approach to winning contracts from customers as diverse as the U.S. Air Force, Union Bank of Switzerland, and the Washington (D.C.) subway system. CDC rushed in with rock-bottom prices and incomplete plans, but a $35 million aftertax loss for the Computer Group in 1974 was the result. To rebuild from that floor, Price has increased annual research and development expenditures by 47% to $107 million this year. In addition, he has set an 18% annual growth target for CDC's $697 million annual business in data processing and other services.

Confidence. Price's reconstruction of the Computer Group — a 2.2% return on sales last year, compared with 1.3% in 1977 — has won the confidence of analysts who had been severely shaken by the losses. McManus believes CDC now is run by "a much broader cadre of professional managers."

Price — and other top executives as well — proclaim their devotion to Norris' philosophy, but conservative financial analysts hope that a post-Norris management will back out of Plato and other social projects fast unless they show profits quickly. To such speculation, Norris' answer is a resounding "No!" CDC's investment in Plato will increase, he says, and by the 1990s education will be the largest contributor to the company's sales. "I've stayed around to nurse this along, and we won't back away from it," he says. "For Control Data, Plato is a way of life."

Questions and Assignments

1. In a unique experiment, Control Data Corporation is attempting to do well by doing good. What would be your position with regard to Control Data's efforts if you were (*a*) a stockholder in Control Data, (*b*) a consumer advocate on Ralph Nader's staff, or (*c*) an average consumer?

2. Can Control Data's philosophy be applied by other corporations to other areas of social need?

Chelsea, the Adult Soft Drink: A Case Study of Corporate Social Responsibility*

A corporation can regulate itself on social matters if it establishes a meaningful two-way dialogue with consumers.

Editor's note — Anheuser-Busch Company officials found themselves in the center of an unexpected controversy over a company product called Chelsea. Although called a soft drink, the product contained a small amount of alcohol and as a company spokesman said, "Chelsea conflicted with the social concerns of several individuals and groups." The company halted marketing and production and set up a social screening process to "help eliminate the conflict between corporate activity and larger social goals." A company spokesman discusses the experience.

Following World War II, the pent-up needs of American consumers were unleashed in the domestic marketplace. An unending stream of new consumer products resulted, and the marketing concept was born. Simply put, the marketing concept argued that products existed solely to fill consumer needs. Products were not purchased for their intrinsic value, but rather to satisfy a consumer need. The simple logic of the marketing concept was irresistible, so manufacturers began marketing their products instead of simply producing them.

Limits of the Marketing Concept

As the marketing concept flowered and consumer need research rivaled the aerospace program in detail, competition among manufacturers extended far beyond the characteristics of the product itself. Products were enlarged

---

* By Keith M. Jones, Anheuser-Busch, Inc. Reprinted by permission from the *Journal of Contemporary Business,* Vol. 7, No. 4, 1979.

to become the "augmented product" of Theodore Levitt. The "augmented product" was articulated by Professor Levitt in his mid-60's best seller, *The Marketing Mode* as:

> ... a new kind of competition that is in galloping ascendance in the world today. This is the competition of product augmentation: not competition between what companies produce in their factories, but between what they add to their factory output in the form of packaging, services, advertising, customer advice, financing, delivery arrangements, warehousing, and other things that people value.

As the augmented product achieved full dimensions, consumer needs to be fulfilled became increasingly complex: ego needs, status needs, and needs for conspicuous display of affluence. Ordering just a "scotch" whiskey for example was insufficient. Brand name scotch was required, and certain brands such as Johnnie Walker Black Label filled social needs that Johnnie Walker himself could never have imagined.

Product augmentation stretched the marketing concept to its furthest limits, and conflicts began to appear. Conflicts occurred between augmented products satisfying social needs and the larger role of the corporation in society. The need for convenient aerosol cosmetics conflicted with preservation of the environment. The stress and tension release provided by tobacco products conflicted with human longevity. The need for social lubricants conflicted with the social costs of alcohol abuse.

Marketing Concept versus Social Responsibility

What happened to corporations whose pursuit of the marketing concept conflicted with their larger role as a responsible social citizen? Historically there were three consequences:

> The product in question was publicly screened for social negatives.
>
> The federal government was the screening agent.
>
> The press had a field day at company expense.

There can be no doubt that the marketplace demands and deserves products free of social negatives. However, there is an alternative to coercive and often punitive governmental intervention. A corporation *can* self-screen its products by directly involving consumer opinion leaders. A case in point is the social screening of Chelsea, a controversial soft drink test-marketed by Anheuser-Busch. Rather than wait for governmental direction, Anheuser-

Busch employed a unique approach to resolve a conflict situation — consumer participation.

The following discussion of the Chelsea experience consists of two segments. *First,* the Chelsea product and the controversy is briefly reviewed. *Second,* a step-by-step description of the social screening process is detailed.

Chelsea, the Controversial Product

Chelsea was the culmination of more than two years of consumer needs research which indicated that adults wanted a soft beverage with three characteristics:

Less sweet, drier taste

All natural ingredients

Social acceptability as an alternative to alcoholic beverages

The resulting product was a light blend of all natural apple, lemon, lime, and ginger flavors. Since Chelsea was pasteurized, no artificial preservatives were needed and it had no caffeine or saccharin either. Because Chelsea contained one-third less sugar than regular soft drinks, there were one-third fewer calories. To compensate for the body of sugar, a malt product was added which contained about one-half of one percent of alcohol fermented naturally. Like apple cider, ginger ale, and beer, Chelsea was a golden color with a frothy head.

AN ADULT SOFT DRINK

The product was reviewed by the Federal Bureau of Alcohol, Tobacco and Firearms (BATF) and the alcohol control boards of five test market states and was found to fit the FDA and state definitions of a soft drink. In summary, Chelsea was a natural, less sweet, adult soft drink.

CHELSEA, THE AUGMENTED PRODUCT

To fulfill the adult need for a socially acceptable alcohol substitute, augmentation was required. *First,* a sophisticated package was selected with the sleek, thin shape and distinctive foil labeling an adult would expect. Next, Chelsea was priced higher than regular soft drinks to reinforce the "Cadillac" image of a natural, adult product. Finally, an advertising campaign was developed to communicate Chelsea as an extraordinary soft drink for extraordinary people aged 25 or older. Because Chelsea was "Not-So" sweet, "Not-So" heavy, "Not-So" artificial and "Not-So" ordinary as other soft drinks, the advertising slogan was the "Not-So" Soft Drink. Thus natural, less sweet Chelsea, was its packaging, pricing, and advertising augmentation entered into market test.

Chelsea, the Controversy

In Virginia test markets, Chelsea conflicted with the social concerns of several individuals and organizations. The Virginia Nurses' Association voted to boycott Chelsea. Seventh-Day Adventists condemned Chelsea as a contributor to the problem of alcohol abuse. Local educators, church groups and PTA councils even pressured store managers to remove Chelsea from their shelves. Press coverage of the Virginia controversy led to network television exposure and Chelsea became a national issue. Finally, respected national figures such as Senator Orrin Hatch (Chairman, Senate Sub-Committee on Alcoholism and Alcohol Abuse) and H.E.W. Secretary Joseph Califano publicly denounced the product and its manufacturer.

HOW COULD A NATURAL SOFT DRINK BE SO CONTROVERSIAL?

How could the first natural soft drink with less sugar and no chemicals or preservatives become so controversial? The problem was that although Chelsea was targeted for adults, it was by definition a soft drink, and therefore purchasable by children. Chelsea critics argued that children did not need a socially acceptable alcohol substitute because they could not consume alcohol in the first place. Reasonable people suggested that however unintended, the augmented product Chelsea was in conflict with the social responsibility of a major corporation.

The Management Decision to Act

Corporations interpreting social responsibility as simple profit maximization may have done nothing at this point. It would have been easy to argue "tough-it-out" or "let the marketplace decide." Anheuser-Busch management, however, realized that action was required, and the process of social screening was initiated. Because the screening process had to be conducted objectively, without the pressure of time, and would intimately involve Chelsea critics, the first step was to defuse the controversy. Therefore all Chelsea manufacture, advertising and promotion was suspended on October 21, five weeks after test market start-up. The suspension was a signal to Chelsea critics that the company valued its social responsibility more than Chelsea profits.

Dynamics of the Social Screening Process

The screening process is much easier to describe than to conduct. In essence the purpose of the process was to eliminate the conflict between corporate activity and larger social goals. At Anheuser-Busch the social screening process consisted of four steps:

Step I: Visible corporate commitment to social responsibility

Step II: Identification of the social issue

Step III: Active participation of consumer opinion leaders

Step IV: Public communication of screening results.

While the following discussion explores each step in detail, it should be pointed out that all four steps are intertwined in a continuous process and should not be considered as independent actions.

Visible Corporate Commitment

Effective social screening is impossible without commitment to social responsiveness at the highest levels of the corporation. Such commitment is not easy to demonstrate. It's not a matter of subsidizing the local symphony or of generosity during United Fund drives. It *is* a matter of ordering priorities. Corporate economic ends must clearly become subordinate to larger social objectives. Importantly, this ranking of priorities must be performed by top management. In the case of Chelsea, August A. Busch, III, chief executive officer and board chairman, made it perfectly clear that corporate responsiveness was a higher than profit and loss contribution.

Not only was this commitment made clear *inside* the corporation, but visible commitment was also communicated *outside* the corporation. For Anheuser-Busch, the October 21 public suspension of Chelsea manufacture, advertising and promotion conveyed this commitment.

IDENTIFICATION OF THE SOCIAL ISSUE

The best intentions are in vain if the corporate social screening process misidentifies or fails to identify the source of the conflict in question. With Chelsea, the basic social issue was not easy to pinpoint, and there were a few red herrings. The issue, for example, was not that children could purchase Chelsea. Restricting sales to minors would not have solved the problem. Nor was intoxication the issue (about 17 ten ounce bottles consumed in an hour would have been required for intoxication — more than a child's stomach capacity). The social issue in the Chelsea case was much more complex. The issue was one of social conditioning. Critics claimed that Chelsea could act to predispose children toward alcohol consumption because Chelsea product packaging and advertising suggested beer in some respects.

No quantitative data existed to refute or substantiate the predisposition claim, so its validity became a matter of opinion. Therefore, Anheuser-Busch consulted outside experts. Medical experts, religious leaders, authorities on alcoholism, and educators were involved. When their expert opinion confirmed that the "Stepping Stone" theory of Chelsea critics could be true, the required action was obvious. Those elements of the augmented product, Chelsea, which would act to precondition children had to be eliminated.

ACTIVE PARTICIPATION OF CONSUMER OPINION LEADERS

At this point, the executive might ask, "Who is running the company anyway?" Isn't the manager who invites outsiders into the decision making process abdicating his managerial responsibilities? Of course not. The consumer participants are only a sounding board, a mini-board of directors individually selected for expertise on the specific social issue identified in Step II. The corporate manager selects the outsiders, presents action plans to them, and is responsible for channeling their input in a manner which benefits the corporation. What about confidentiality? If the consumer participants exposed confidential information to the press or to competitors, wouldn't the whole screening process backfire? There was always such a risk. However, Anheuser-Busch felt the risk was outweighed by the benefit of articulate social input, and therefore selected consumer participants of demonstrated personal integrity who would respect confidentiality requests. The consumer participants included: the Director of Adolescent Medicine at a leading Virginia university, the Director of the Center for Research on Media and Children at the Wharton School of Business, members of the Virginia Nurses' Association, members of the Potomac Council of Seventh-Day Adventists and, of course, the staff of U.S. Senator Orrin Hatch. All of these individuals strictly adhered to our confidentiality requests and made significant contributions to the screening process. More specifically, each opinion leader was included in two tasks:

Articulating social issues to be dealt with

Previewing Anheuser-Busch's proposed action plan

In retrospect, the participation of outside opinion leaders was the key to successful social screening because through this process, the severest Chelsea critics became proponents of the revised product.

The Chelsea Action Plan

Based on constructive consumer input, verified by independent market research, Anheuser-Busch revised Chelsea by eliminating those elements which could act to "predispose" children while preserving the original concept of a natural, less sweet soft drink for adults. Accordingly, the alcohol was virtually removed, the foaminess was dramatically reduced, the "Not-So" Soft Drink advertising was dropped, and the bottle was changed from clear to emerald green glass. Furthermore, the Anheuser-Busch name was reduced in size on the label and positioned behind "Soft Drink Division" in order to more clearly communicate soft drink identity.

The outside participants previewed the revised product and its augmentation support and offered their public approval. Now the stage was set to complete the social screening process and inform the public of the results.

Public Communication of Screening Results

When Step I (visible corporate social commitment) is sincerely taken, the responsible manager understands that the screening process is an integral part of augmented product marketing and not a public relations tool. Therefore, rather than use advertising or a major public relations program, Anheuser-Busch management chose to conduct a national press conference to communicate the screening results. On December 12, less than two months after the screening process was initiated, a socially screened Chelsea was announced at the National Press Club in Washington, D.C. More importantly, several key outside participants in the screening process (including Senator Hatch's staff, the Virginia Nurses' Association, and the Potomac Council of Seventh-Day Adventists) attended the press conference and issued public statements commending the new product and its manufacturer.

DEFUSING A POTENTIALLY DAMAGING SITUATION

As a result, a potentially damaging situation was turned into one of those rare instances where all parties won. Chelsea critics won because they were able to change the marketing thrust of a major corporation. Anheuser-Busch won because new Chelsea more clearly fit consumer needs than the original product. The biggest winner, however, was the consumer who benefited from the exercise of democracy in the marketplace without footing the bill for governmental intervention.

The Chelsea Experience: A Summary

One of the most difficult challenges facing contemporary managers is the task of identifying those situations when the corporation's larger role as a social unit transcends short term profit motives. When such a situation does arise, responsible corporations require a process for resolving conflict. The Chelsea experience is offered as a case study of one corporation's process in action — the process of consumer participatory social screening.

Of course, the social screening process is not risk-free, nor is it appropriate in every conflict situation. Once initiated, the corporation is obligated to follow the process through. Once outside consumer opinion leader input is solicited, the corporation may forfeit the option of "doing nothing." Pursued to the extreme, the screening process could snowball management into socially positive actions that made poor business sense. In the Chelsea case, there was the possibility that the product and marketing revisions consisted of "throwing out the baby with the bath water." While it is still too early to tell if the Chelsea screening was economically successful, one point is already clear: a corporation can regulate itself on social matters if it establishes a meaningful two-way dialogue with the consumer.

Questions and Assignments

1. Critique the Chelsea incident; although the company acted quickly, could the problems have been anticipated? How valid were the arguments of the critics of Chelsea? Since Chelsea met FDA and state definitions of a soft drink, why should the company have to withdraw it?

2. Anheuser-Busch is primarily a brewer, and Chelsea was only an experimental venture. Do you believe the "social screening process" would have worked as quickly and effectively if the product had been a major new and successful beer brand?

A. H. Robins Company*

A Key West, Florida, man and his two children were awarded a $425,000 damage settlement in May 1975, as a result of legal action brought against the A. H. Robins Company, Richmond, Virginia. The man's wife had died due to complications from the use of a Dalkon intrauterine shield birth control device produced by the company. This was only 1 of the 226 cases the Robins Company stated it was defending at that time.[1] By spring 1976, the number had grown to some 533 pending civil actions alleging injuries caused by the Dalkon Shield. Customers were seeking punitive damages of $233 million and compensatory damages of $211 million. Mr. William Zimmer, the company's president and chief executive officer, informed stockholders during the 1976 annual meeting that the company had settled or disposed of another 117 cases originally seeking $75 million in damages, but which had been settled for about $2 million.[2] The company's "Message to Stockholders" in its *1975 Annual Report* stated in part:

> Consolidated net sales for the year totaled $241,060,000, an increase of 14.4 percent over the 1974 total of $210,713,000. Net earnings from 1975 operations increased 9.1 percent to $29,373,000, or $1.12 per share, before deducting after-tax charges of $2,739,000 (equal to 10 cents per share) for the settlement during 1975 of litigation, legal fees, recall of customers' inventories and other expenses related to the Dalkon Shield, an intrauterine contraceptive device which the Company marketed in prior years. Charging Dalkon Shield expenses to 1975 operations reduces the net earnings to $26,634,000, or $1.02 per share.
>
> We believe these charges should be treated under generally accepted accounting principles as a prior period adjustment in 1974, since the prob-

---

* Prepared by Professor Robert J. Litschert, Virginia Polytechnic Institute and State University. Reprinted by permission.

lem from which the charges stem originated in that year and had no relation to 1975 operations.

Under this treatment, earnings for 1974 would be restated from $26,917,000, or $1.03 per share, to $24,178,000, or $0.93 per share. However, the staff of the Securities and Exchange Commission has insisted that the charges be absorbed in 1975 operations, and as of the printing of this report the matter has not been finally resolved.

The product which allegedly caused these problems was voluntarily removed from the market in June 1974 by the Robins Company following reports of septic abortions, some of which were fatal to women wearing the intrauterine device.

Company History and Background

The A. H. Robins Company was incorporated in Virginia in 1878. Mr. Albert Hartley Robins, the company's founder, was a typical pharmacist in the tradition of the Old South. Upon discharge from the Confederate Army he opened, with great expectations, his drugstore in downtown Richmond. The business grew and prospered and when Mr. Robins' son, Claiborne Robins, became a registered pharmacist, he was handed the manufacturing end of the business and given a free rein to do what he could with it. The younger Robins' first decision was to establish a separate firm to differentiate this operation from the drugstore. At this time, the company was given the name A. H. Robins Company. After several years of just modest success, Claiborne Robins met with an untimely death and his wife, Martha Robins, elected to continue the business.

The company barely managed to survive the depression years of the 1930s under the control of Mrs. Robins. In 1933, the company employed only three people and had gross sales of $4,800. During this year, Mr. Robins' son, E. C. Robins, graduated from the Medical College of Virginia and became a registered pharmacist. He immediately borrowed $2,000 in an attempt to get the company back on its feet.

As a result of the loan and improved economic conditions, the company began to experience significant growth. By 1942, sales volume had reached $100,000. At this time, E. C. Robins began to think seriously of changing the organization from a completely salesminded operation to one which combined both research and sales. Initially, the company struggled along with a small research staff turning out only an occasional new or improved product, but with moderate success built for the future.

In 1952, the company moved into what is now a very small part of its present plant. Acquisition of the new building provided additional space for the research group. By 1955, a program of clinical research was under way and the company's first original product, Robaxin, was marketed in 1957. In 1958, a pharmacology program was initiated, and in 1960 the ground was laid for the company's current research and development group which now occupies the research center constructed in 1963. By 1965, the Robins Company was doing business in 50 states and about 55 foreign countries, with gross sales of more than $65 million.[3]

During the last decade the company has continued to expand, especially through the acquisition of other firms. For the year ending December 31, 1975, consolidated net sales were approximately $241 million, with net earnings after taxes of $26.6 million (see Exhibits 2 to 5). At the time, the company was still principally engaged in the manufacture and sale of pharmaceutical specialities promoted ethically through activities directed at physicians, dentists, and pharmacists. The principal ethical products were drugs for cough and cold ailments, antispasmodic drugs for gastrointestinal disorders, and skeletal muscle relaxants. The company distributed pharmaceutical products throughout the United States and through subsidiaries or branches, in West Germany, France, Canada, Mexico, Colombia, the United Kingdom, South Africa, Venezuela, Brazil, Australia, the Philippines, Japan, Greece, and Kenya, and through independent agents in various other countries in Latin America, Europe, the Far East, Middle East, and Africa. Sales of these ethical products accounted for 73 percent of net sales and approximately 84 percent of earnings in 1975.

Robins also manufactured through subsidiaries several brand name consumer products including Sergeant's pet care products, Chapstick lip balm, and Caron perfumes and other fragrance products. These products accounted for the remaining 27 percent of the company's net sales and 16 percent of net earnings in 1975. In the pharmaceutical industry, 105 firms had sales of over $1 million in the ethical pharmaceutical market. From this group, A. H. Robins ranked approximately 18th in sales volume.[4] Based on new prescriptions written, the company ranked fifth among U.S. pharmaceutical manufacturers and 11 of the company's products were among the most widely prescribed in the world.

Robins concentrated its basic research and development in areas in which it felt it had its greatest expertise — therapeutic agents for use in nervous system and gastrointestinal, cardiovascular, and rheumatic illnesses. Emphasis was placed on the development of new synthetic medicinal compounds and new formulations. Approximately 300 employees with fields in chemistry, pharmacology, statistics, and medicine were engaged in research and development activities. In 1975, total research and development expenditures amounted to $10.7 million, an increase of $1.1 million over 1974.

The company employed approximately 4,450 people, of which 2,300 were in facilities outside the United States.[5]

While the pharmaceutical industry has been described as a growth industry and the Robins Company has experienced substantial growth during the last two decades, it has also been plagued with problems during the 1970s. During 1973 and a portion of 1974, Robins' stock dropped from $40 to $12 per share and its price/earnings ratio dropped from 42 to 12. There were several factors which apparently contributed to the negative reaction of the public and the company's declining financial performance. Sales of a promising appetite suppressant, Pondimin, were disappointing. The Food and Drug Administration challenged the claims of a number of the company's ethical drug products. Its 90-day flea collar for pets, made from a substance akin to Nazi nerve gas, allegedly killed pets as well as fleas. But the most disastrous setback was the Dalkon Shield®, an intrauterine birth control device. The bad publicity came as a shock to management, who, as a result of their ability to develop marketing strengths, had always successfully maintained positive company and product images.[6]

Birth Control Devices

According to Dr. Sheldon Segal, medical director of the Population Council, "there is no such thing as absolute safety when it comes to contraception — you get nothing for nothing. It is not enough to look at just the risks, you must consider the benefits — the hazards that the contraceptive is protecting you from, as well as other advantages, such as convenience." [7] However, the question of the safety of modern contraceptives remains paramount in the minds of many. Family planning specialists also add that decisions as to which birth control method to use are often based on incomplete information about risks and benefits of the various methods, and are reached without taking into account factors other than safety that should influence the choice of a contraceptive.

An analysis of medical statistics suggested that although oral contraceptives and intrauterine devices could sometimes cause serious, even fatal, side effects, they nonetheless tended to be the surest methods of birth control available. While other contraceptive methods, such as the condom and the diaphragm, caused few, if any, adverse side effects, these traditional methods were more likely to result in an unwanted pregnancy than the pill or IUD. Statistics also showed that even for women receiving the best of medical care, the nine months of pregnancy, childbirth, and the postpartum period were far more dangerous to life and health than any existing contraceptive method. Family planning specialists who had analyzed the relative

EXHIBIT 1
RESULTS OF USE OF CONTRACEPTIVE DEVICES
AMONG 1 MILLION WOMEN 20 TO 34 YEARS
OLD OVER A ONE-YEAR PERIOD OF TIME

	Percentage effective preventing pregnancy	No. of deaths per million by method	No. of deaths per million by pregnancy
Pill	99.5%	13	1
IUD	97	2	7
Diaphragm	88	0	27

Source: Jane Brody, "Birth Control Devices: What Studies Show about Side Effects," *The New York Times,* March 4, 1975, p. 28.

risks and benefits of the various birth control techniques concluded that when the hazards of the various methods of birth control were weighed against the hazards of the unwanted pregnancies, the average couple was better off relying upon the pill or IUDs than upon the diaphragm, condom, foam, or rhythm methods.

Another dimension influencing relative safety was the quality of medical care a woman received. Those in the upper socioeconomic brackets had a much lower pregnancy-related death rate — approximately two thirds less than the national average of 20 per 100,000 live births. These same women were also likely to receive better medical care for contraceptive side effects.[8]

Exhibit 1 summarizes a portion of the data prepared by the Rockefeller Foundation involving 1 million women over a span of one year. The table identifies the effectiveness of the device and deaths per million women resulting both from use of the device itself and from pregnancies which in turn had resulted from the ineffectiveness of the device. On the average, the pill was found to be the most effective device for preventing unwanted pregnancies, but the study further showed that the pill's use was directly tied to the largest number of deaths. The IUD was less effective than the pill but was associated with fewer deaths overall. The diaphragm was the least effective of the three devices used, and while no deaths resulted directly from its use, a relatively large number of deaths resulted from pregnancies associated with ineffectiveness of the device. Researchers indicated that the relative safety of the diaphragm would have been higher had it been used exactly as prescribed. Correctly used, the diaphragm was thought to be about 98 percent effective; studies showed five pregnancy-related deaths per million women per year.

The Intrauterine Device

Intrauterine devices, or IUDs, are little pieces of metal or plastic in various shapes and sizes that are inserted into a woman's uterus to prevent pregnancy. Surprisingly little is known about IUDs despite the fact the device is by no means new. It is mentioned in the writings of Hippocrates and in the Jewish Talmud. One reason for the lack of knowledge may be that IUDs cannot be effectively tested on nonhuman subjects. Most drugs can be successfully tested on animals but an IUD can only be tested on women. However, two widely accepted theories as to why the device works have emerged. The first is that an IUD irritates and inflames the uterine wall, making it unreceptive to the implantation of an egg should it become fertilized. The second theory is that the continual effort of the uterus to expel the foreign object by contracting forces the egg out of the fallopian tubes before it is sufficiently developed to implant itself.

Like the pill, annoying but minor side effects are common complications of the IUD; nonetheless, as of 1975, it was used by 3 million to 5 million women. Most frequent complaints were heavy and prolonged menstrual bleeding and menstrual cramps, causing up to 20 percent of IUD users to request removal of the device within a year. More serious side effects were relatively rare. The most common serious complication associated with the use of the IUD was infection. One study revealed that pelvic infection necessitated the removal of an average of two IUDs among 100 users within two years of use. However, evidence indicated that the IUD was not so much a cause of pelvic infection as a contributor to an increase in the severity once infection arose. If treatment was delayed or inadequate, infertility could result. Another potentially dangerous side effect associated with the IUD was piercing of the uterine wall, usually at the time of insertion. Perforations occurred in about 4 in 10,000 insertions, with the risk lowest when the inserter was an experienced physician. Most perforations were of minor consequence, yet if undetected, it could mean that the IUD was not properly situated and therefore ineffective. Regardless of the type of IUD used, a pregnancy that occurred with the device in place was more likely to end in miscarriage.[9]

The Robins Company Enters the Birth Control Market

The Robins Company introduced its own version of the intrauterine device, the "Dalkon Shield," in late 1970. Its initial success was believed to be related to this country's ongoing "sexual revolution." It was advertised as the first device that could effectively be worn by a young woman who had never borne a child. The device, shaped like a crab with prongs, was difficult to expel, thereby reducing the problem of expulsion so common among young women. By the end of 1973, the shield was being used by approximately 2.2 million of the estimated 5 million American IUD users. Another 1 million shields were sold abroad.[10]

During 1973, however, the Robins Company became aware of some disquieting facts. The accidental pregnancy rate for users of the Dalkon Shield appeared to be substantially higher than earlier estimated. In addition, the company learned of 36 septic abortions among women who became pregnant while wearing the shield. Of these 36 women, 4 had died.[11] Septic abortions, which can also occur without the use of an IUD, are spontaneous abortions that cause an infection of the uterus lining which can lead to septicemia, a widespread infection of the blood system; this had been identified as the cause of death of all four women.

A spokesman for the Robins Company stated that various studies put the failure rate of the device at between 0.5 to 5.0 pregnancies for every 100 users — a figure comparable to other IUDs on the market. The spokesman also noted that the company changed the Dalkon Shield's labeling in October 1973, to add a warning about "severe sepsis with fatal outcome" associated with pregnancies that occur while the device is in place. The company also alerted the Food and Drug Administration in June 1973, to the rumors about side effects associated with the shield, and gave complete tabulated data to the agency in December. Dr. Fletcher Owen, Robins' director of medical services, reported that the company had put internal and external medical experts to work evaluating the data and was "confident" that the problem wasn't unique to the Dalkon Shield.[12]

However, as a result of the four deaths, on May 8, 1974, Robins Company sent letters to 125,000 (one third) of the physicians in the United States warning them that severe complications, including death, could occur in a small number of women becoming pregnant while wearing the company's Dalkon Shield. The letter urged doctors to remove the IUD immediately if the patient should become pregnant and if that was impossible to give "serious consideration . . . to offering the patient a therapeutic abortion." [13] The letter added that if the patient elected to continue the pregnancy, whether or not the IUD had been removed, the patient should be watched closely. The letter continued, "Furthermore, we suggest that any patient for whom you consider inserting a Dalkon Shield be advised prior to the procedure that a therapeutic abortion may be recommended in the event of an accidental pregnancy." [14]

Based on the information provided in the letter, the Planned Parenthood Federation of America instructed its 700 affiliated birth control clinics to cease prescribing the Dalkon Shield. In Washington, D.C., a Food and Drug Administration spokesman said the agency was attempting to gather data to present along with the Robins' data to two advisory panels. The panels would then recommend alternative courses of action. The spokesman stated, "we're trying to see if the problems are peculiar to the Dalkon Shield, or to all IUDs. We'll make a decision as soon as possible, but we've got to get the facts first." [15]

Action by the Food and Drug Administration

Although the Food and Drug Administration (FDA) was directly involved in the control of IUD devices once marketed, the Robins Company did not have to obtain FDA clearance before marketing its Dalkon Shield. This was because it was a medical device, not a drug, and such devices do not require FDA clearance. However, legislation had been introduced in Congress in late 1971 to require premarket approval, but it had not been passed.

On June 28, 1974, the Robins Company voluntarily removed the Dalkon Shield from the market until questions of safety could be resolved. Seven maternal deaths and ten septic abortions had then been associated with the use of the shield. Still, at this time, the FDA insisted that there was no immediate concern among women using the product, and did not recommend that it be removed as a precautionary step. A few weeks later, the agency issued a bulletin similar to Robins' original letter to physicians. However, the FDA bulletin had a far wider distribution and more emphatically stressed the need for pregnancy testing. The agency also continued to gather data about the extent of use and adverse reactions to all forms of IUDs. In addition, the bulletin asked physicians to report their experience with patient use of IUDs.[16]

On July 5, 1974, it was reported that a 1973 survey by the Health, Education, and Welfare Department's Center of Disease Control of all types of IUDs showed that the Dalkon Shield was linked to a significantly higher number of complications of pregnancy than other forms of IUDs. The study tied the Dalkon Shield to 54 percent of pregnancy complications compared to 46 percent for IUDs known as the Lippes Loop and the Saf-T-Coil. Nonetheless, Dr. Alexander Schmidt, FDA commissioner, stressed that a final decision on banning Robins' Dalkon Shield would not be made until after a review of new evidence that was being gathered from all manufacturers and sought from approximately 300,000 physicians. Several weeks prior to this statement, the two advisory panels mentioned above, after reviewing current evidence, recommended that Dr. Schmidt ban the Dalkon Shield from the market. It was speculated that this would be a serious blow to Robins since the shield was the leading seller in the field and had been adopted for use in most birth control clinics.[17]

In August 1974, after evaluating more recent data, the FDA reported a sharp increase in the number of deaths and uterine infections among women using the Dalkon Shield. An audience of 200 scientists, physicians, and industry representatives were told that the number of deaths and septic abortions associated with the use of the shield had risen to 11 and 209, respectively. The updated information gathered by the FDA's Bureau of Medical Devices, also showed that another intrauterine device, the Lippes Loop, was associated with five deaths and 21 septic abortions and another, the Saf-T-Coil, with one death and eight miscarriages, following uterine infection. The findings also revealed that between 1966 and 1974, 8.8 million IUDs had been marketed.[18]

After further investigation, in October 1974, an FDA advisory panel concluded that the Dalkon Shield didn't pose any greater risk to women than other types of IUD contraceptives. An eight-member subcommittee of the Agency's Obstetrics and Gynecology Advisory Committee, which recommends regulatory policy for IUDs, reported that it hadn't found any increased hazard from the use of the shield. "It isn't apparent from the available information that the safety and efficiency of the Dalkon Shield is significantly different from other IUDs," stated the subcommittee.[19] The panel also noted that difficulties associated with the use of IUDs appeared to be higher when they first entered the market, and then decreased with time. The Dalkon Shield was the most recent device to have been introduced, going into use in 1970. In addition, the panel noted that the liberalized abortion laws of recent years had brought more women with contraceptive problems to the attention of physicians at a time when the Dalkon Shield came into widespread use. Two thirds of the women fitted with IUDs during this period were fitted with the shield. At this point, however, the FDA didn't appear to be in any rush to recommend that the shield be placed back on the market. The FDA also planned to require that new cautionary labeling be provided with all IUDs.[20]

In December 1974, in a surprise move, the FDA ended a six-month moratorium on prescription by physicians of the Dalkon Shield. This action, however, was contrary to the recommendations of its Obstetrics and Gynecology Advisory Committee. The 18-member panel believed the moratorium should have remained in effect pending accumulation of definitive data. At a news conference, Dr. Schmidt stated that the agency's actions did not constitute an overruling of the committee's recommendations. The FDA had arranged with Robins to keep a registry of all patients using the device. The company agreed to report the number and kinds of adverse reactions, the rate at which the device was expelled by women, along with other details. Dr. Schmidt stated that the arrangement would allow for collection of the definitive data the committee called for and that he hoped manufacturers of competing devices would also agree to participate in a registry. The FDA arranged with Robins to limit distribution of Dalkon IUDs to doctors who agreed to register each patient at the time of insertion and to keep a detailed record of each patient's experience with the device in order to ensure the necessary data. At this time a joint study of the effects of IUDs was initiated by the FDA and the National Institute of Child Health and Human Development.[21]

However, after the FDA action was made public, the Planned Parenthood Association of America announced that it would continue its ban on the current model of the Shield. The ban prohibited the use of the device by its own doctors and clinics. By this time the associated deaths had increased to 14 and septic abortions had grown to 219.[22]

At least one member of the FDA advisory committee disagreed with Dr. Schmidt's explanation of the lifting of the moratorium. Protesting the FDA's action, Dr. Richard Dickey of the Louisiana State University Medical Center argued that the agency action circumvented the recommendations of the committee and might needlessly endanger many women. He believed the moratorium should remain in effect until additional data were obtained. He also felt the majority of the panel agreed with him on this issue.[23]

Reaction by the Robins Company

After clearance by the FDA, the Robins Company intended to resume marketing of the Dalkon Shield. However, a spokesman for the company stated that as a practical matter resumption probably would not occur until late 1975 so as to allow the FDA to develop new labeling guides for the product.[24] In his message to the stockholders for the year 1974, E. C. Robins, chairman of the board, summarized the company's position, "the company is of the opinion that when appropriately used with proper techniques, the shield's performance has been satisfactory." [25]

In January 1975, the company announced it would collect all unused IUDs in the United States, and fully refund its customers for the unused inventory. The announcement also indicated the company would modify the new shields. The modification would be a change in the "tail" of the Dalkon Shield. All IUDs have a tail consisting of a cord or string which facilitates their removal from the uterus. The old shield had a tail made of a woven, or multifilament string. Some medical scientists argued that it was possible for woven filament to act as a reservoir for bacteria that could infect the uterus when it swells during pregnancy and the tail is drawn into the uterus. Other IUDs, which had a nonwoven, or nonfilament tail, presumably did not harbor bacteria. Robins contended that the multifilament tail was not any more dangerous than the nonfilament tails on other IUDs, but agreed to replace the woven tail when it resumed marketing the Dalkon Shield.

Despite FDA approval to resume marketing, the U.S. Agency for International Development (AID), announced that it did not plan on continuing to supply the Dalkon Shield abroad. About 200,000 of the devices were returned to Robins by AID. A spokesman for AID also stated that due to the medical follow-ups required on the new shield, they had no plans to resume the use of the device. At this same time, the Planned Parenthood Federation of America also announced it intended to return all of its Dalkon Shields to Robins, including 96,000 meant for distribution overseas. Like AID, the Federation did not plan to use the new shield.[26]

Lawsuits

In late 1974 and early 1975, the Robins Company was inundated with lawsuits brought by customers and relatives of those using the shield. In the company's *1974 Annual Report,* E. C. Robins stated, "unfortunately, the emotionally charged atmosphere of the IUD investigation, stimulated by much publicity, which in many cases was misleading, had led to a large number of lawsuits involving the Dalkon Shield being filed against A. H. Robins." [27] The report noted that as of February 10, 1975, the company had been named defendant in 148 product liability cases which alleged various injuries due to use of the shield. The complaints, in many of the suits, sought punitive as well as compensatory damages. The report further stated the company was insured for potential liability resulting from compensatory damage awards which might be granted. However, exposure to punitive damages was not insurable in most jurisdictions.[28]

On February 6, 1975, a judgment was entered for the plaintiff in a suit filed in Sedgwick County, Kansas. The plaintiff was awarded $10,000 in compensatory damages and $75,000 in punitive damages for injuries allegedly resulting from a uterine perforation caused by a Dalkon Shield. The company planned to appeal the Kansas verdict and denied liability in the remaining liability cases.[29]

As of March 18, 1975, the company had been named defendant in 186 product liability cases involving the shield. The alleged injuries included perforations of the uterus, deaths related to septic abortions, pregnancies followed by therapeutic or spontaneous abortions, and pelvic inflammatory diseases. In its *Annual Report* to the Securities and Exchange Commission, the company stated that suits were pending in approximately 85 courts, which in the aggregate sought $110 million in compensatory and $70 million in punitive damages. Robins added that it believed the amounts claimed in many of the cases were inflated and disproportionate to the injuries alleged.

The company also noted that beginning March 1, 1975, the aggregate deductible amount for insurance coverage for Dalkon Shield related actions had been increased to $4 million for alleged injuries occurring after that date. Since it was not possible to predict the outcome of the pending suits, the company made no provisions for contingent liabilities in its balance sheet (see Exhibit 2).[30]

By the time Robins filed its Interim Report for the first three months of 1975, another 40 cases had been instituted against the company. In the report, E. C. Robins stated, "given the emotionally charged atmosphere of the FDA's IUD investigation, we anticipate that there will be still more, but it is impossible to predict with any degree of accuracy the number of additional cases, the outcome of any of these cases, or the eventual aggregate financial impact on the company." [31] Still, the company denied liability in all of the cases. The report added that the company continued to believe that when appropriately used with the proper technique, the device was a useful IUD. At that time, Robins still intended to place the shield back on the market. It was estimated that the continued suspension of sales, due to working with the FDA on the development of a registry system, would adversely affect 1975 earnings by about two cents per share.[32]

In July 1975, the company announced the adoption of an accounting procedure that would minimize the effects on current earnings of the potentially heavy expenses that might be incurred from litigation involving the Dalkon Shield. A Robins official said that they had decided to recognize the

EXHIBIT 2
A. H. ROBINS COMPANY, COMPARATIVE BALANCE SHEETS, DECEMBER 31, 1970, 1974, AND 1975

	1970	1974	1975
Current assets:			
Cash	$ 6,770,105	$ 5,004,000	$ 10,872,000
Certificates of deposit	—	10,346,000	16,497,000
Marketable securities — at cost which approximates market	3,813,924	13,878,000	14,394,000
Accounts receivable — less allowance for doubtful accounts	23,413,846	33,011,000	44,104,000
Inventories	21,767,094	49,061,000	49,906,000
Prepaid expenses	3,100,091	4,010,000	4,133,000
Total current assets	$ 58,865,060	$115,310,000	$139,906,000
Property, plant, and equipment — net	$ 21,924,959	$ 30,418,000	$ 34,640,000

continued

EXHIBIT 2 *continued*

	1970	*1974*	*1975*
Intangible and other assets:			
Excess of cost over net assets of subsidiaries acquired	25,253,876	36,315,000	42,343,000
Patents, trademarks, goodwill	2,109,164	4,586,000	3,927,000
Deferred charges	938,008	2,696,000	1,580,000
Other assets	361,804	938,000	1,148,000
Total intangible and other assets	$ 28,662,852	$ 44,535,000	$ 48,998,000
Total assets	$109,452,871	$190,263,000	$223,544,000
Current liabilities:			
Notes payable	$ 3,152,807	$ 1,784,000	$ 2,681,000
Accounts payable	5,081,687	12,096,000	21,126,000
Long-term debt payable within one year	4,119,590	750,000	750,000
Federal, foreign, and other income taxes	3,565,854	5,145,000	6,752,000
Accrued liabilities	2,415,387	6,076,000	8,210,000
Total current liabilities	$ 18,335,325	$ 25,851,000	$ 39,519,000
Long-term debt	11,600,000	5,250,000	4,500,000
Deferred income taxes	—	341,000	794,000
Deferred foreign currency exchange gains	—	1,097,000	10,000
Minority interest in foreign subsidiaries	241,300	29,000	1,446,000
Stockholders' equity:			
Capital stock:			
Preferred $1 par — authorized 10,000 shares, none issued	—	—	—
Common $1 par — authorized 40,000 shares	12,712,253	26,127,000	26,127,000
Capital surplus	347,868	693,000	693,000
Retained earnings	66,216,125	130,875,000	150,455,000
Total stockholders' equity	$ 79,276,246	$157,695,000	$177,275,000
Total liabilities and stockholders' equity	$109,452,871	$190,263,000	$223,544,000

expenses arising from the lawsuits as a retroactive charge against the earnings of the quarter in which the alleged injury occurred.[33] The earnings for the first half of 1975 did not include charges for settlement of litigation, legal fees, and other expenses involving the intrauterine device. In the Interim Report for the first six months of 1975, E. C. Robins reported that legal charges had reached a total of $1,022,000 after taxes.[34]

EXHIBIT 3
A. H. ROBINS COMPANY, STATEMENT OF CONSOLIDATED
EARNINGS, DECEMBER 31, 1970–1975

	1970	1974	1975
Income:			
Net sales	$132,551,922	$210,713,000	$241,060,000
Interest and other income	551,449	3,143,000	2,279,000
Total income	$133,103,371	$213,856,000	$243,339,000
Costs and expenses:			
Cost of sales	41,047,042	71,233,000	89,304,000
Research and development	5,881,875	9,568,000	10,690,000
Marketing, administrative and general	52,663,269	79,209,000	87,362,000
Interest	1,752,838	1,134,000	1,189,000
Litigation settlement and related expenses	—	—	5,065,000
Total costs and expenses	$101,345,024	$161,144,000	$193,610,000
Earnings before income taxes and extraordinary items	$ 31,758,347	$ 52,906,000	$ 49,729,000
Provision for income taxes	16,030,349	25,989,000	23,895,000
Earnings before extraordinary items	$ 15,727,998	$ 26,917,000	$ 25,834,000
Discontinued operations and loss on disposal	—	—	—
Net earnings	$ 15,727,998	$ 26,917,000	$ 25,834,000
Earnings per common share:			
Continuing operations	$ 1.24	$ 1.03	$ 1.02
Discontinued operations and loss on disposal	(0.05)	—	—
Net earnings	$ 1.19	$ 1.03	$ 1.02
Cash dividends	$ 0.40	$ 0.208	$ 0.20
Weighted average number of common shares outstanding	n.a.	26,126,000	26,127,000

n.a. = not available.

Dalkon Shield Removed from Product Line

Finally, in its Interim Report for the first nine months of 1975, the company announced that in August it had decided to delete the Dalkon Shield from its product line. In the report E. C. Robins verified the decision: "we had anticipated re-marketing the intrauterine contraceptive device under a patient registry system being developed by the Food and Drug Administration, but with the passing of time we couldn't foresee a date for completion

EXHIBIT 4
SELECTED NOTES TO FINANCIAL STATEMENTS, 1975

Litigation

A private action which was filed by the Portland Retail Druggists Association on August 6, 1971, as assignee of certain community pharmacies, against the company and several other pharmaceutical manufacturers, is pending in the United States District Court for the District of Oregon. The complaint demands damages for alleged violations of the antitrust laws with respect to the sale of pharmaceutical products in the Portland area. Although the outcome of this case cannot be predicted with certainty, the company does not anticipate that the ultimate disposition of the action will have a material effect on its financial position or operating results.

Another antitrust action filed by Medcor, Incorporated seeks damages in the sum of $1,000,000, plus attorneys' fees, from the company and seven other defendant pharmaceutical manufacturers. The complaint which was filed on December 8, 1975, in the United States District Court for the District of South Dakota, Western Division, alleges that the defendants conspired to prevent Medcor from competing with the defendants and to force the plaintiff out of business. Although the factual basis of the plaintiff's claim has not yet been fully developed, the company has denied liability and is not aware of any facts which might result in liability being imposed against it.

As of February 18, 1976, there were pending in various state and federal courts 467 product liability cases, in which the company has been named as a defendant and which allege various injuries arising from use of the Dalkon Shield®, an intrauterine contraceptive device formerly marketed by the company. Approximately 97 other cases involving the Dalkon Shield have been dismissed with prejudice, in most cases following settlement by the company and its insurer. As of February 18, 1976, approximately 200 Dalkon Shield claims which have not resulted in litigation were being evaluated by the company's insurer, and approximately 96 other claims have been settled or withdrawn. The pending cases (as did those dismissed) seek in some instances substantial compensatory damages and in others substantial compensatory and punitive damages. As of February 18, 1976, the company and its insurer have paid the sum of $2,014,000 in full settlement of the 97 cases and 96 claims referred to above. The major portion of the amount paid by the company was charged against the deductibles under its insurance coverage. The company believes that its potential liability for compensatory damages in the remaining cases pending as of that date and claims then under evaluation is covered by insurance except for the unused portion of the deductibles, which is relatively insignificant for policy periods before March 31, 1975 and is approximately $4,000,000 for the policy period April 1, 1975 through February 29, 1976. Exposure to punitive damages is not insurable in most jurisdictions. On February 6, 1975, in a suit originally filed in the District of Sedgwick County, Kansas, judgment was entered for the plaintiff for the sum of $10,000 as compensatory damages and $75,000 as punitive damages for injuries allegedly resulting from uterine perforation associated with the Dalkon Shield. This case is presently on appeal to the Supreme Court of the State of Kansas. The company has denied liability in the remaining Dalkon Shield product liability cases and claims. No provision has been made for contingent liabilities which may arise from these actions and claims, since it is not possible to predict their outcome.

Accounting for Litigation Settlements and Related Expenses

During the year 1975, the company incurred a charge of $5,065,000 ($2,739,000 after income tax benefit) resulting from settlement of litigation, legal fees, recall of customers' inventories and other expenses related to the Dalkon Shield. The company believes it would have been preferable under generally accepted accounting principles to accord prior period adjustment treatment to this charge which would have increased 1975 net earnings and decreased 1974 net earnings by $2,739,000 ($.10 per share). However, at the insistence of the staff of the Securities and Exchange Commission, the charge was included in earnings for the year 1975.

of the design of such a system. The additional delay which thus could have been expected, coupled with the interruption in marketing which had already extended for more than a year and the adverse publicity which had already eroded physician and patient confidence, would have made the successful reentry of the device into the market difficult, if not impossible. We concluded that this unfavorable market prospect for the Dalkon Shield did not warrant further expenditure of company funds and personnel time even though we remain firm in our belief that the device, when properly used, is a safe and effective IUD." [35] Within another month, Robins reported that it had paid $1,548,000 for the settlement of litigation, legal fees, and other expenses involved in the controversy.[36]

The Wall Street Journal in February 1976, reported that the number of civil actions alleging death and injuries had grown to 547. One hundred sixty-seven of these were pending in 48 U.S. District Courts in 28 states, with another 276 pending in state courts. The other 104 cases had been settled, presumably with payment by the company in some, if not all, of the cases. The company did not state the size of its total settlement payments, but it did reveal in 1976 that the company had incurred an aftertax charge of $2.7 million resulting from settlements and costs resulting from the IUD problem.

Assignment

1. Evaluate the actions of A. H. Robins.

EXHIBIT 5
REPORT OF INDEPENDENT CERTIFIED PUBLIC ACCOUNTANTS

To the Stockholders and Board of Directors
A. H. Robins Company, Incorporated
Richmond, Virginia

We have examined the consolidated balance sheet of A. H. Robins Company, Incorporated and subsidiaries as of December 31, 1975 and 1974 and the related statements of consolidated earnings, stockholders' equity and changes in financial position for the years then ended. Our examinations were made in accordance with generally accepted auditing standards, and accordingly included such tests of the accounting records and such other auditing procedures as we considered necessary in the circumstances.

Included in the statement of consolidated earnings for the year ended December 31, 1975 is a charge of $5,065,000 resulting from litigation settlements and related expenses (as more fully explained under Accounting for Litigation Settlements and Related Expenses in Notes to Financial Statements), which the management of A. H. Robins Company, Incorporated believes should have been recorded as a prior period adjustment. It is our opinion that it would have been preferable to accord this charge prior period adjustment treatment, which would have increased 1975 net earnings and decreased 1974 net earnings by $2,739,000 ($.10 per share).

As discussed under Litigation in Notes to Financial Statements, the company is defendant in lawsuits alleging various injuries arising from use of the company's products and claiming general and punitive damages. The ultimate outcome of the lawsuits cannot presently be determined, and no provision for any liability that may result has been made in the financial statements.

In our opinion, subject to the effects, if any, on the financial statements of the ultimate resolution of the litigation discussed in the immediately preceding paragraph, the financial statements referred to above present fairly the consolidated financial position of A. H. Robins Company. Incorporated and subsidiaries at December 31, 1975 and 1974 and the results of their operations and the changes in their financial position for the years then ended, in conformity with generally accepted accounting principles applied on a consistent basis.

A. M. Pullen & Company

Richmond, Virginia
February 18, 1976

REFERENCES

1. "Settlement of $425,000 Is Awarded in Case over Dalkon Shield," *The Wall Street Journal,* May 22, 1975, p. 12.

2. "A. H. Robins Co. Faces 533 Pending Civil Suits on Birth-Control Item," *The Wall Street Journal,* April 28, 1976, p. 10.

3. E. C. Robins, *The Story of A. H. Robins Company* (Princeton, N.J.: Princeton University Press, 1966).

4. A. H. Robins Company, *Form 10-K, Annual Report Pursuant to Section 13 or 15 (D) of the Securities Exchange Act of 1934.* Fiscal year ending December 31, 1974.

5. A. H. Robins Company, *Annual Report 1975* (Richmond, Va.: February 18, 1976).

6. "A Plague of Problems," *Forbes,* August 15, 1974, p. 35.

7. Jane E. Brody, "Birth Control Devices: What Studies Show about Side Effects," *The New York Times,* March 4, 1975, p. 28.

8. Ibid.

9. Ibid.

10. "A Plague of Problems," p. 35.

11. Ibid.

12. Barry Kramer, "Robins Warns That Its IUD May Cause Severe Complications, Including Death," *The Wall Street Journal,* May 29, 1974, p. 8.

13. Ibid.

14. Ibid.

15. Ibid.

16. "A. H. Robins Will Stop Sale of Dalkon Shield, Pending Safety Study," *The Wall Street Journal,* June 28, 1974, p. 11.

17. "Ban on Robins' IUD Becomes More Likely after New U.S. Study," *The Wall Street Journal,* July 5, 1974, p. 15.

18. "FDA Links Rise in Deaths to Birth Device," *The New York Times,* August 22, 1974, p. 17.

19. "Robins' Dalkon Shield Found No More Risky Than Other IUDs," *The Wall Street Journal,* October 14, 1974, p. 2.

20. Ibid.

21. Harold M. Schmeck, "Moratorium Is Ended by FDA on IUD Challenged over Safety," *The New York Times,* December 21, 1974, p. 25.

22. Ibid.

23. Harold M. Schmeck, "End of IUD Ban Viewed as Peril," *The New York Times,* January 7, 1975, p. 16.

24. "A. H. Robins Wins Clearance from FDA to Resume IUD Sales," *The Wall Street Journal,* December 23, 1974, p. 7.

25. E. C. Robins, *Annual Report 1974* (Richmond, Va.: February 10, 1975), p. 1.

26. "1.5 Million Is Paid to Settle Contraceptive Device Cases," *The New York Times,* October 21, 1975, p. 53.

27. Robins, *Annual Report 1974,* p. 3.

28. Ibid., p. 34.

29. Ibid.

30. A. H. Robins Company, *Form 10-K, Annual Report,* December 31, 1974, pp. 20–21.

31. E. C. Robins, *Interim Report/First 3 Months 1975,* April 25, 1975, pp. 2–3.

32. Ibid.

33. "A. H. Robins Uses Plan to Ease Effect on Net From IUD Litigation," *The Wall Street Journal,* July 18, 1975, p. 24.

34. E. C. Robins, *Interim Report/First 6 Months 1975,* July 24, 1975, p. 2.

35. E. C. Robins, *Interim Report/First 9 Months 1975,* October 27, 1975, pp. 2–3.

36. "1.5 Million Is Paid to Settle Contraceptive Device Cases," p. 53.

Economic Analyses
of Government Investments
in Commercial–Industrial Activities
(Example–A Microwave
System Case Study)*

This case study illustrates the use of Discounted Cash Flow techniques in making a sound evaluation of the economic worth of a capital investment proposal. The example concerns communications service for the Bureau of Reclamation's "North Platte–Missouri River Basin Project" and presents two alternatives for securing the communications channels associated with the Bureau's power transmission lines in that area. These alternatives are: (1) government ownership and operation of a microwave system, or (2) the purchase of commercial service from established telephone companies.

The figures used in the example are, with minor exceptions, the Department of the Interior's actual estimates for this project (as presented in June 4, 1964 hearings before the Bureau of Reclamation and Department of the Interior Power Marketing Agencies Subcommittee of the U. S. Senate Committee on Appropriations).

Comparability Adjustments

In order for the government to make a realistic economic analysis of a proposed investment, it must make the evaluation on the same basis as that which would be used by a private enterprise. In comparing a government enterprise with a private enterprise, there appear to be three major areas of difference which require adjustment:

1. Taxes which the commercial venture must pay but which the government body does not.

---

* This case is based on a report prepared by Touche Ross & Co. It is printed by permission of Dr. Dennis Mulvihill of Touche Ross, who prepared the original report in the case-history format on which this summary version is based.

2. Accounting differences resulting from variations between commercial and governmental accounting practices.

3. Methods and cost of acquiring the capital utilized by the organization.

The method suggested in this report is to impute to government the appropriate tax liabilities of a private venture, making allowance for the depreciation deductions taken by a private venture. All incremental cost reductions and expenses resulting from the investment must be incorporated in the evaluation regardless of whether or not these costs are normally identified with the proposed project under normal accounting procedures. An evaluation which does not explicitly recognize significant differences in those matters will give an erroneous financial worth to capital investments by the government sector.

Buildings, equipment, land, and other assets for proposed government projects must be purchased directly or obtained by diversion from other possible uses. To make such purchases, the government must invest cash or its equivalent. This cash or cash equivalent is derived from the private sector of our economy through taxation, government borrowing, or the creation of money. The use of capital for government projects reduces the capital available for investment in the projects of companies in private enterprise. Therefore, evaluation of proposed projects must show that the return on their investment in assets is at least equal to what these assets would earn in a private enterprise engaged in the same economic activity.

Estimated Investment Cost, Service Lives, and Other Factors

Determination must be made of the initial Capital Outlay for the microwave system, and for any subsequent investment needed. These amounts should include direct investment and all related indirect costs. It is highly important that the most accurate estimates available be used. If there is a strong likelihood that the final cost will exceed the original bid price, the best estimate of the final cost is the more relevant amount.

The initial investment figures estimated by the Department and used here are listed in Exhibit 1. All these amounts include provision for engineering, overheads and contingencies.

Subsequent Capital Outlays are determined by the economic life of the various elements of the installed system.

The lives used here are those estimated by the the Department (except that a 13-year life has been taken for electronic equipment, rather than the Department's 13.5 years). They are listed in Exhibit 2.

EXHIBIT 1

Electronics equipment (including contractor's engineering and installation)	$508,000
Power equipment	31,000
Outside plant	100,000
Right of way, buildings, path survey	39,000
	$678,000

Facilities with lives shorter than the system life will have to be replaced. The estimated cost for replacements should reflect the projected cost at the future dates. Here, the example uses the Department estimate that replacement facilities will have the same cost as the replaced items.

Salvage value, if felt to be significant, must also be estimated. The importance of this factor is diminished by the fact that the "present value" of an amount estimated to be received in the distant future may be quite small. The Department estimated no salvage for the North Platte project but, to illustrate the way it would be handled in an analysis, the example estimates salvage of $50,000 will be realized at the end of the system life.

Having determined Capital Outlays, the second step is to estimate the annual expenditures for operations, principally for maintenance. The Department's estimate was $34,000 per year; the example uses this figure. The example imputes $5,000 annually as a token amount to reflect (a) costs such as insurance and payroll fringe benefits actually applicable but not identified with the project because of the accounting system used by the government, and (b) property taxes and other state and local taxes which would be incurred by a private microwave system owner. Federal income tax effects are included, using the 48% tax rate effective in 1965. This requires computation of the depreciation deductible year by year for Federal income tax purposes. Here deductible depreciation is computed by the

EXHIBIT 2

Electronics equipment	13 years
Power equipment	20 years
Outside plant	25 years
Buildings, etc	50 years
System life	50 years

"sum of the years-digits" method, with unaccrued depreciation and salvage on retirement covered in the year of retirement. Also, the investment tax credit is reflected here at 3% of the investment amounts.

Finally, the alternative cost of this service from a commercial source must be determined. The Department estimated that the cost each year for common carrier service would be $84,000 for telephone company charges plus $8,000 of Bureau expenditures for coordination of telephone company maintenance and for administration. This $92,000 total is used here.

Discounted Cash Flow Method

The first step in the computation by the Discounted Cash Flow method is to determine the year by year differential cash flow under the alternative of a government owned and operated microwave system. These computations are shown in Exhibits 3 and 4.

Exhibit 3 shows the determination of the year by year amounts of depreciation deductible for Federal income tax purposes. Exhibit 4 shows the computation of the year by year differential cash flows. It is assumed for simplicity that none of the government capital comprising the $678,000 investment represents debt capital. This avoids the complication of computing a lower income tax arising from the deductibility of interest on debt capital. (Without this assumption, the Return on Investment would be slightly higher.)

Having the projected figures for the differential cash flows, the next step in the analysis is to compute the rate of Return on Investment for the

EXHIBIT 3
DEPRECIATION DEDUCTION FOR FEDERAL INCOME TAX PURPOSES, GOVERNMENT MICROWAVE SYSTEM
(Method: sum of the years-digits) (in thousands of dollars)

Year	Facilities with 13-year life	Facilities with 20-year life	Facilities with 25-year life	Facilities with 50-year life	Salvage at end of system life	Total
1	$ 73	$ 3	$ 8	$ 2		$ 86
2	67	3	7	2		79
3	61	3	7	2		73
4	56	3	7	2		68
5	50	2	6	1		59
6	45	2	6	1		54
7	39	2	6	1		48
8	33	2	6	1		42

Year	Facilities with 13-year life	Facilities with 20-year life	Facilities with 25-year life	Facilities with 50-year life	Salvage at end of system life	Total
9	28	2	5	1		36
10	22	2	5	1		30
11	17	1	5	1		24
12	11	1	4	1		17
13	6	1	4	1		12
14	73	1	4	1		79
15	67	1	3	1		72
16	61	1	3	1		66
17	56	1	3	1		61
18	50	0	2	1		53
19	45	0	2	1		48
20	39	0	2	1		42
21	33	3	2	1		39
22	28	3	1	1		33
23	22	3	1	1		27
24	17	3	1	1		22
25	11	2	0	1		14
26	6	2	8	1		17
27	73	2	7	1		83
28	67	2	7	1		77
29	61	2	7	1		71
30	56	2	6	1		65
31	50	1	6	1		58
32	45	1	6	1		53
33	39	1	6	1		47
34	33	1	5	1		40
35	28	1	5	1		35
36	22	1	5	0		28
37	17	1	4	0		22
38	11	0	4	0		15
39	6	0	4	0		10
40	73	0	3	0		76
41	67	3	3	0		73
42	61	3	3	0		67
43	56	3	2	0		61
44	50	3	2	0		55
45	45	2	2	0		49
46	39	2	2	0		43
47	33	2	1	0		36
48	28	2	1	0		31
49	22	2	1	0		25
50	34	9	0	0	$(50)	(7)
Total	$2,032	$93	$200	$39	$(50)	$2,314

EXHIBIT 4
COMPUTATION OF NET DIFFERENTIAL CASH FLOW ($000s)

	(1)	(2)	(3)	(4)	(5)	(6)	(7)	(8)	(9)	(10)
		Government operation			Advantage or (disadvantage) of government operation (1)-(2)-(3)-(4)	Federal income taxes or (tax credit) 48% of column (5)				Net differential cash flow (5)-(6)-(7)-(8)+(9)
Year	Telephone company service	Operating expense	Insurance and taxes other than F.I.T.	Depreciation (from Exhibit 3)			Investment credit	Investment and (salvage)	Depreciation addback	
0								678		(678)
1	92	34	5	86	(33)	(16)	(21)	—	86	90
2	92	34	5	79	(26)	(13)	—	—	79	66
3	92	34	5	73	(20)	(10)	—	—	73	63
4	92	34	5	68	(15)	(7)	—	—	68	60
5	92	34	5	59	(6)	(3)	—	—	59	56
6	92	34	5	54	(1)	(1)	—	—	54	54
7	92	34	5	48	5	2	—	—	48	51
8	92	34	5	42	11	5	—	—	42	48
9	92	34	5	36	17	8	—	—	36	45
10	92	34	5	30	23	11	—	—	30	42
11	92	34	5	24	29	14	—	—	24	39
12	92	34	5	17	36	17	—	—	17	36
13	92	34	5	12	41	20	—	508	12	(475)
14	92	34	5	79	(26)	(13)	(15)	—	79	81
15	92	34	5	72	(19)	(9)	—	—	72	62
16	92	34	5	66	(13)	(6)	—	—	66	59
17	92	34	5	61	(8)	(4)	—	—	61	57
18	92	34	5	53	0	0	—	—	53	53
19	92	34	5	48	5	2	—	—	48	51
20	92	34	5	42	11	5	—	—	42	17
21	92	34	5	39	14	7	(1)	31	39	47

22	92	34	5	33	20	9	—	—	33	44
23	92	34	5	27	26	12	—	—	27	41
24	92	34	5	22	31	15	—	—	22	38
25	92	34	5	14	39	19	(3)	100	14	(66)
26	92	34	5	17	36	17	(15)	508	17	(469)
27	92	34	5	83	(30)	(15)	—	—	83	83
28	92	34	5	77	(24)	(12)	—	—	77	65
29	92	34	5	71	(18)	(9)	—	—	71	62
30	92	34	5	65	(12)	(6)	—	—	65	59
31	92	34	5	58	(5)	(3)	—	—	58	56
32	92	34	5	53	0	0	—	—	53	53
33	92	34	5	47	6	3	—	—	47	50
34	92	34	5	40	13	6	—	—	40	47
35	92	34	5	35	18	9	—	—	35	44
36	92	34	5	28	25	12	—	—	28	41
37	92	34	5	22	31	15	—	—	22	38
38	92	34	5	15	38	18	—	—	15	35
39	92	34	5	10	43	20	—	508	10	(475)
40	92	34	5	76	(23)	(11)	(15)	31	76	48
41	92	34	5	73	(20)	(10)	(1)	—	73	64
42	92	34	5	67	(14)	(7)	—	—	67	60
43	92	34	5	61	(8)	(4)	—	—	61	57
44	92	34	5	55	(2)	(1)	—	—	55	54
45	92	34	5	49	4	2	—	—	49	51
46	92	34	5	43	10	5	—	—	43	48
47	92	34	5	36	17	8	—	—	36	45
48	92	34	5	31	22	10	—	—	31	43
49	92	34	5	25	28	13	—	—	25	40
50	92	34	5	(7)	60	29	—	(50)	(7)	74
Total	4,600	1,700	250	2,314	336	153	(71)	1,636	2,314	932

EXHIBIT 5
DISCOUNTING OF CASH FLOWS TO PRESENT WORTH

Year	Net differential cash flows	Cash flows discounted to present worth			
		At 1.7% rate		At 1.6% rate	
		Factor	Discounted amount	Factor	Discounted amount
0	$(678,000)	1.000	$(678,000)	1.000	$(678,000)
1	$ 90,000	.983	$ 88,470	.984	$ 88,560
2	66,000	.967	63,822	.969	63,954
3	63,000	.951	59,913	.953	60,039
4	60,000	.935	56,100	.938	56,280
5	56,000	.919	51,464	.924	51,744
6	54,000	.904	48,816	.909	49,086
7	51,000	.889	45,339	.895	45,645
8	48,000	.874	41,952	.881	42,288
9	45,000	.859	38,655	.867	39,015
10	42,000	.845	35,490	.853	35,826
11	39,000	.831	32,409	.840	32,760
12	36,000	.817	29,412	.827	29,772
13	(475,000)	.803	(381,425)	.814	(386,650)
14	81,000	.790	63,990	.801	64,881
15	62,000	.777	48,174	.788	48,856
16	59,000	.764	45,076	.776	45,784
17	57,000	.751	42,807	.764	43,548
18	53,000	.738	39,114	.751	39,803
19	51,000	.726	37,026	.740	37,740
20	17,000	.714	12,138	.728	12,376
21	47,000	.702	32,994	.717	33,699

22	44,000	.690	30,360	.705	31,020
23	41,000	.679	27,839	.694	28,454
24	38,000	.667	25,346	.683	25,954
25	(66,000)	.656	(43,296)	.672	(44,352)
26	(469,000)	.645	(302,505)	.662	(310,478)
27	83,000	.634	52,622	.651	54,033
28	65,000	.624	40,560	.641	41,665
29	62,000	.613	38,006	.631	39,122
30	59,000	.603	35,577	.621	36,639
31	56,000	.593	33,208	.611	34,216
32	53,000	.583	30,899	.602	31,906
33	50,000	.573	28,650	.592	29,600
34	47,000	.564	26,508	.583	27,401
35	44,000	.554	24,376	.574	25,256
36	41,000	.545	22,345	.565	23,165
37	38,000	.536	20,368	.556	21,128
38	35,000	.527	18,445	.547	19,145
39	(475,000)	.518	(246,050)	.538	(255,550)
40	48,000	.510	24,480	.530	25,440
41	64,000	.501	32,064	.522	33,408
42	60,000	.493	29,580	.513	30,780
43	57,000	.484	27,588	.505	28,785
44	54,000	.476	25,704	.497	26,838
45	51,000	.468	23,868	.490	24,990
46	48,000	.461	22,128	.482	23,136
47	45,000	.453	20,385	.474	21,330
48	43,000	.445	19,135	.467	20,081
49	40,000	.438	17,520	.459	18,360
50	74,000	.430	31,820	.452	33,448
Total	$ 932,000		$ 669,266		$ 679,926

government system. Here the principle of time value of money comes into application.

As will be seen from Exhibit 4, the total differential cash flow over the 50-year period is $932,000, which is greater than the $678,000 of government investment. If money had no time value, investment in a government microwave system would therefore be justified on economic grounds in preference to taking telephone company service, since an investment of $678,000 would decrease total government cash outflow by $254,000.

But money *does* have a time value; a government investment to be justifiable on economic grounds must earn an appropriate rate of return. Therefore, it is necessary to compute the inherent rate of return produced by this potential government investment.

This is accomplished by discounting the stream of cash flows to its present worth (applying present worth factors from tables of such factors) to determine what discount rate results in a present worth equal to the government investment. The computation for this example is shown in Exhibit 5.

Exhibit 5 represents the final computations in a trial and error process of ascertaining the two inherent discount rates which produce present worth which bracket the $678,000 amount of initial investment. Exhibit 5 shows that the discount rate is 1.6% (or, by interpolation, more precisely 1.62%). (Parenthetically, it should be noted that in this example all of the initial investment is made at the beginning of the first year. If additional *initial* investment — as differentiated from any *replacement* investment — had occurred in years subsequent to the first year, such additional initial investment would have been discounted back to year zero and added to the $678,000.)

To summarize, Exhibits 3, 4, and 5 develop, by this Discounted Cash Flow analysis, that the cash savings from a government microwave system for the North Platte project would represent a 1.6% return on the government investment in that system.

Questions and Assignments

1.   Do you agree with the assumptions underlying the calculation of the government's required return to justify this investment?

2.   Based on the factual results presented, do you think that the government should proceed with the investment?

3.   Should the government proceed with the investment anyway on a basis other than the calculation of discounted cash flows that this example illustrates? If so, what is the basis?

The Economic Case
Against Federal Bailouts
... And Who May Need Them*

With the bond market in a shambles, interest rates going through the roof, and a recession on the way, thousands of troubled, cash-poor companies — most of them small — are likely to collapse in the next few months. Economists, bankers, and policymakers are worried, however, that 1980 may become the year of the big, $100 million-plus bankruptcies and that a spate of failures by highly leveraged U.S. corporations could turn the expected mild recession into a rout.

Already, many bankruptcy experts — lawyers and investment bankers — are talking about the government as the "lender of last resort," rescuing insolvent corporations by guaranteeing loans and pumping in needed cash to prevent bankruptcy. And some even propose establishing an official bail-out agency to ensure that big troubled companies do not go broke waiting in line for Congress to hand out piecemeal aid.

Economists make a strong case, however, against awarding government aid to inefficient businesses, and they warn that eliminating failure as an option would severely disrupt the functioning of a market economy. In essence, they contend that a federal bailout program would:

- Build inefficiency, waste, and mismanagement into corporate boardrooms by removing the looming danger of bankruptcy from the system. This would lead to a decline in profit-oriented management decisions, the production of unwanted goods, and the failure to create innovative new products — all lowering the growth potential of the economy.

- Artificially raise interest rates and tighten the credit supply for companies without subsidies. Since some big troubled companies would be receiving government-guaranteed loans at less than the market rate, they would have a clear incentive to borrow far more cash than they otherwise might, and this would mean that healthy companies would be paying more than the normal market rate for a smaller pool of available funds.

- Create a bias toward big companies at the expense of smaller ones, since the latter would be excluded from the proposed bailout mechanism. This would handicap an economic system that relies on the innovations of small entrepreneurial companies.

While the public and most businessmen may look aghast at corporate failures, economists have maintained since the days of Adam Smith that business failure is essential to the smooth operation of a market economy. Indeed, the late Harvard University economist Joseph A. Schumpeter went event further, developing the idea of "creative destruction." He argued that it was only through a "cleansing" of the economy — to eliminate inefficient noninnovative producers — that a nation could reach its growth potential. To Schumpeter, bailouts of sick companies kept scarce resources from more productive uses elsewhere in the economy.

Moreover, economists today maintain, the market has already evolved a legal procedure — the nation's corporate bankruptcy laws — for ensuring a company's orderly exit from the economy. Says Edward I. Altman of New York University, one of the nation's leading experts on predicting bankruptcy: "There's a proven process known as reorganization that gives the firm time to rehabilitate itself, essentially by giving it a moratorium on its fixed debt."

Recycling.   One reason a federal bailout program seems so attractive is that many people automatically equate bankruptcy with outright liquidation and the loss of jobs. "They think of Lee Iacocca weeping while Chrysler is put on the auction block. But that's not accurate," says Jerold B. Warner of the University of Rochester. "Penn Central went through bankruptcy, and the trains still ran." Often, in fact, adds Altman, companies such as United Merchants & Manufacturers Inc. go into bankruptcy, liquidate an unprofitable division (as UM&M did with its Robert Hall retail chain), sell some money-making operations to raise cash, and emerge from reorganization a healthy entity again.

Even when a W. T. Grant Co. is liquidated, it does not mean that the physical assets suddenly vanish. Rather, says William H. Meckling, dean of

Rochester's Graduate School of Management, the goods are used by someone else or recycled elsewhere in the economy. "Even if New York City had gone bankrupt," he notes, "its buildings weren't going to disappear in the East River."

Perverse Incentives.   The danger of a federal bailout program is that it will allow W. T. Grants to continue in business, economists say. "If we subsidize inefficient companies," says Jeremy Bulow, a Stanford University economist, "we are creating perverse incentives for them to produce a lot of products we don't want in the economy." Adds Murray Weidenbaum of Washington University in St. Louis: "The possibility of bankruptcy is a necessary incentive for efficiency. I don't think big companies should be bailed out. After all, it's a profit-and-loss system."

According to Seymour Fiekowsky, the Treasury Dept.'s assistant director for business taxation, a government bailout unfairly assures companies "the use of capital at 3 to 5 percentage points below what it really does cost" and creates an incentive for them to "overuse the available flow of funds." That, in turn, puts pressure on stronger, unguaranteed companies, raising their interest rates and depleting their supply of capital. "It's a faulty bookkeeping system," he says of government-guaranteed loans, because the cost is being borne in the credit markets and passed right back to businesses and consumers. "There's no free rent. Someone pays in the end," he says.

Fiekowsky also emphasizes that government aid to ailing companies bails out their shareholders at the expense of the economy as a whole. Yet when people buy stocks or bonds, the risk of bankruptcy is already incorporated in the price. So, in a sense, a bailout creates windfall profits for shareholders and gets bad management off the hook.

Such economic arguments, however, are oversimplified, according to J. Ronald Trost, a partner in the Los Angeles law firm of Shutan & Trost. He believes the current bankruptcy system is inadequate to deal with most corporate giants, especially manufacturers whose products carry service warranties.

"Would you, if you were an airline executive, buy planes from a bankrupt company?" Trost asks. When such a company files for bankruptcy, he says, liquidation becomes a *fait accompli.*

Trost's job is to keep client companies out of Chapter 11. "There is a shock to a business that occurs just by reason of the [bankruptcy] filing," he says. "It becomes a very costly, much more difficult thing to run." And it becomes especially difficult after a bankruptcy filing to raise new capital, the primary path most companies take in order to survive the painful, often expensive reorganization process.

Such arguments can be appealing, since most companies that do go bankrupt end up in liquidation. Last year 29,500 companies filed for bankruptcy. This year, according to a bankruptcy prediction model designed by NYU's Altman, the figure could top 35,000, a record (Exhibit 1). And these numbers do not take into account the thousands of smaller businesses that simply close up shop one day and cease to exist.

Big Splashes.   But it is the possibility of big collapses that has many people calling for a federal bailout agency. If the current economic scenario develops as some economists are predicting — a severe credit crunch coupled with a deep recession — the U.S. may be in for a round of big bankruptcies this year and next. Since 1973, in the aftershock of the quadrupling of oil prices, the rate of big bankruptcies has been growing at an alarmingly rapid pace. When Altman first began making bankruptcy-prediction models in the late 1960s, the average bankrupt company had assets of $25 million. In 1977, he says, the average failing company had assets of more than $100 million. And he does not see the pattern slowing in 1980.

Altman explains that many creditors held off foreclosing on major insolvent companies in the past two years because the economy has been stronger than expected. But with a prime rate that has already hit 17¾% and with traditional commercial paper and bond markets getting tighter, many large companies could be in trouble.

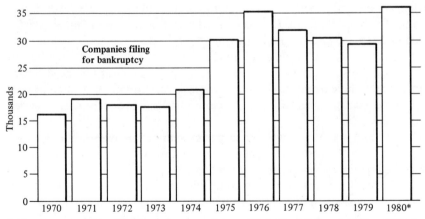

*1980 estimate from an Edward I. Altman bankruptcy prediction model using Dun & Bradstreet statistics and BW estimates

EXHIBIT 1
CORPORATE BANKRUPTCIES HEAD FOR A NEW HIGH

Corporate Reinsurance.   Says investment banker Felix G. Rohatyn, a partner at Lazard Frères & Co. and chairman of New York City's Municipal Assistance Corp.: "We're entering very dangerous times. The possibilities of major dislocations are all too real." To combat that, Rohatyn would revive the Depression-born Reconstruction Finance Corp.

He sees the new RFC as a corporate reinsurance agency, funded in part by a 1% surcharge on the profits of all businesses earning more than $1 million a year and in part by $5 billion in Treasury-purchased common stock and $10 billion in government loan guarantees. "I'm not an enormous proponent of a government bailout," he says, but after the issuing of $1.5 billion in guarantees to Chrysler Corp., "the precedent would make it difficult to deny [it to other companies] afterwards." To Rohatyn, a well-run reinsurance agency is preferable to "a number of large companies at the same time . . . stumbling around from congressional committee to congressional committee seeking a bailout."

Many government economists have serious reservations about Rohatyn's proposal. Says one high-level Treasury economist: "Once the government gets involved in doing something, it doesn't leave again." He believes, in fact, that people overstate the economic disruption that would take place if a company such as Chrysler were to go under.

Many corporate executives also oppose the Rohatyn plan. H. William Close, chairman of Springs Mills Inc., an $828 million textile manufacturer in Fort Mill, S.C., is against creating "another agency to help companies that are noncompetitive and funded by those who presumably are more efficient." Warns Richard L. Wachtell, chairman and chief executive of Chromalloy American Corp.: "I can think of nothing worse than to add a federal agency with this kind of power."

In the financial markets the question repeatedly being asked is this: "Which big industrial company or bank will be caught in a liquidity bind and face the threat of bankruptcy?" In the worst peril are capital-intensive companies that must continually borrow to finance investments already under way. Some might not be able to roll over the heavy short-term debt they arranged while the bond market was in such disarray. Also, a number of major banks have become badly overextended in recent years on the mistaken assumption that interest rates had peaked. If the Federal Reserve Board tightens money and credit further, such banks could incur huge loan losses and might even be forced to sell off their long-term bonds at discount prices, both of which would seriously impair capital.

A lot has been said about what desperate financial shape Chrysler Corp. is in. It turns out, though, that there are plenty of other big companies, including Genesco, Lockheed, and United Brands, whose financial positions appear even more vulnerable. That, at least, is the opinion of Zeta Services Inc., a financial consulting firm that has developed a computerized credit-scoring model. *Business Week* used the model to identify large companies that could be hurt most if predictions of an imminent credit crunch come true.

Essentially, the computer model chews over a company's financial data and comes up with a "Zeta score," which is a measure of the company's vulnerability to bankruptcy. Any score below zero indicates that a company may have trouble meeting its financial obligations.

Systematic Diagnosis.   This model, which has been sold to banks and institutional investors since 1977, is based on the financial data of 53 manufacturing and retailing companies that failed or were taken over by banks between 1969 and 1975. The model is a refinement of work done by Edward I. Altman, professor of finance and chairman of the MBA program at New York University.

Altman's 13-year-old version, called simply Z-analysis, appears in business school textbooks and financial journals. The proprietary Zeta version, which Altman helped develop, currently has over 20 institutional subscribers, including several major New York and Chicago banks, and covers 2,600 public companies in the data base of Compustat Services Inc., a subsidiary of Standard & Poor's Corp.

The Zeta model is basically a formula that adds up seven key financial ratios, each weighted according to its importance as an indicator of financial health — or lack of it. According to Robert G. Haldeman, president of Zeta Services, the ratio given the heaviest weight in the equation is one that measures cumulative profitability by dividing retained earnings by total assets. Two other key ratios incorporate leverage and earnings stability into the model (the latter tracks earnings variability during the past 10 years).

Other ratios in the formula include return on total assets, fixed charge coverage, and liquidity. The final variable is asset size, which obviously improves Zeta scores of bigger corporations.

The model is certainly not the last word in credit analysis. It is true that it has successfully predicted all of the major bankruptcies of the past few years, including those of United Merchants & Manufacturers, Food Fair, Allied Supermarkets, and Apeco. The problem is that the model also pointed out the serious financial vulnerability of dozens of other companies that either recovered — or at least did not go under. "Bankruptcy is a legal event," explains Altman, while the model only measures "economic events."

An otherwise failing company can, of course, be kept alive by loan guarantees from a government fearful of the consequences of a big bankruptcy, as in the cases of Lockheed and Chrysler. Such a company also can be propped up by creditors anxious to protect their investment. Itel Corp., for example, looks very troubled indeed, judging from its -1.79 Zeta score for 1978. But the company is still alive. At the moment, 100 lenders are "tugging and pulling" over whether to allow Itel to go into bankruptcy to save it by waiving loan defaults and agreeing to new credit terms, says a company executive.

Bad to Worse? While few major companies are as close to the brink as Itel, a negative Zeta score is not all that uncommon. In fact, Haldeman says that 20% of the 2,600 companies run through his service now show negative scores, including 5% of the Standard & Poor's 400. What is worse, most Zeta scores are based on 1978 data. With the huge sums of high-cost, short-term debt that companies have taken on recently, a lot of scores, when updated, could go from bad to worse.

While the model may be overzealous in predicting too many bankruptcies that never occur, it still has value as a warning of possible future dividend cuts, downgradings on debt ratings, or forced sale of assets.

The model limits its analysis to public companies and is based only on the experience of manufacturing and retailing companies. Thus it can be argued that the low Zeta scores of the highly leveraged airlines and leasing companies, which also have high cash flows, may be misleading. Further, the model is not equipped to analyze banks, many of which, including First Pennsylvania Bank, First Chicago, and Fidelity Bank, are considered to be squeezed because of their expensive short-term liabilities, poor profitability, and heavy bond portfolios.

In *Business Week*'s analysis of companies using the Zeta model, 24 major corporations were selected for having comparatively low Zeta scores. Surprisingly, Chrysler appears to be the strongest of the bunch, with a score of -1.13 for 1979. While many of the listed companies contacted by *Business Week* insist that things are really better than they look, there is no question that high leverage, poor profitability, and low liquidity leave them quite vulnerable to serious financial difficulty, particularly with a disastrous recession and credit controls possibly around the corner.

Bit of a Bind. White Motor Corp. realizes only too well the extent of its exposure. After a rough decade marred by big losses, White netted a slim $6.4 million profit from operations on $1.2 billion in sales in 1979. "We've done a hell of a lot to increase our profitability" by restructuring debt and by paring operations, says an executive. "But all the profit increases we've been able to achieve could easily be totally eliminated by the increase in interest rates." Last year, White's interest bill rose 57% to $78.3 million and could rise by a similar amount this year if the prime continues to average 16%.

There are other companies on the list whose officers deny vulnerability. Grolier Inc., the book publisher, has had a string of losing years because of misguided diversification, overexpansion, and foreign currency losses; it

EXHIBIT 2
24 COMPANIES THAT COULD HURT IN A CREDIT CRUNCH

Company	Fiscal year ending	Zeta rating* (negative score indicates vulnerability)	Comments
Grolier	12/78	−5.45	20% profit increase in 1979 should improve score slightly
Ward Foods	12/78	−5.37	$7.2 million loss in 1979 may lower score
General Host	12/78	−4.12	186% profit increase in 1979 could lift score to about −2.30
Fed-Mart	8/79	−3.95	$2.6 million loss in quarter ended 11/79
PHH Group	4/79	−2.95	27% profit increase for 12 months ended 10/79 could improve score
Lockheed	12/78	−2.91	Profits down 34% in 1979
Penn Dixie	12/78	−2.88	$2.8 million profit for 9 months ended 9/79 should improve score
Great Atlantic & Pacific Tea	2/79	−2.77	$29.7 million loss for 12 months ended 11/79
Seatrain Lines	8/79	−2.69	Profits down 65% for 12 months ended 12/79
Genesco	7/79	−2.65	$2.5 million profit — up 116% ——in quarter ended 10/79 could lift score slightly
Eastern Air Lines	12/78	−2.46	Profits down 14% in 1979
Ozark Air Lines	12/78	−2.35	$883,000 loss in 1979 vs. profit of $8.2 million in 1978

Company	Fiscal year ending	Zeta rating* (negative score indicates vulnerability)	Comments
Kay	12/78	−2.12	21% increase in profits in 1979 could improve score
LTV	12/78	−2.06	634% profit jump in 1979 (to $146.6 million) could raise score to about −1.45
White Motor	12/78	−1.95	$6.4 million profit in 1979, could raise score to about −1.65
Trans World	12/78	−1.82	90% drop in 1979 profits may lower score
Ideal Toy	1/79	−1.79	$1.5 million loss for 12 months ended 10/79
Itel	12/78	−1.79	$226 million loss for 9 months ended 9/79 may lower score
Fedders	10/78	−1.47	$36 million loss in fiscal 1979 may lower score
United Brands	6/79	−1.38	$3.9 million profit for 6 months ended 12/79 (up 95%) may lift score slightly
Pan American World Airways	12/78	−1.34	36% drop in 1979 profits could lower score slightly
Forest City Enterprises	1/79	−1.16	3% profit increase for 12 months ended 10/79
Chrysler	12/79	−1.13	Score based on balance sheet data of 9/79 and assumption of $250 million loss in 4th quarter vs. $376 million actual loss
Sambo's Restaurants	12/78	−0.54	$78 million loss for 1979 could lower score to about −2.96

* Scores were derived through a proprietary computer analysis called "Zeta," which measures the financial conditions of a company by consolidating the effect of seven important financial ratios that measure profitability, liquidity, and leverage. Because the computer model requires balance sheet data, 1978 financial results had to be used as the basis of the scores for those companies that have not yet reported 1979 data.

sports the worst score on the list. Now, with payment delinquencies rising on its credit sales and 1979 earnings of just 1.1% on sales, Chairman Robert B. Clarke says simply: "We're in a little bit of a cash bind, but nothing serious."

At Ward Foods Inc. Treasurer Martin Zoberman claims his company has licked its problems and is headed for profitability. "I don't agree with your computer," an associate fumes.

Some companies agree that they were vulnerable but say they have made improvements. General Host Corp. has had a negative Zeta score for the past 10 years and lost a total of $18.1 million between 1976 and 1978. But with earnings of $29.2 million on sales of $752 million last year, Chairman Harry J. Ashton says he is "sleeping well nights."

Genesco has been dumping unprofitable operations. James S. Gulmi, treasurer, notes that this consolidation has cut the company's cash needs. Still, the company remains highly leveraged just as retail sales dip.

Survivors?   Ideal Toy Corp., in its fiscal year ended Feb. 1, 1979, had a negative score for the first time, because of a $6 million loss on sales of $158 million. Norman Seigler, finance vice-president, blames a microprocessor operation that has recently been jettisoned.

Other executives note that, while things are bad, they have survived a lot worse. Lockheed has returned to profitability after courting disaster in 1974. Pan American World Airways Inc. also teetered on the brink of failure in 1974. With a $12.9 million loss in the last quarter, its 1979 profits fell 36%. Still, the company plans no cuts. Says an executive: "We think we're taking a very prudential approach to 1980."

Trans World Corp. is also feeling surprisingly cocky, given its −1.82 Zeta score and its $43.8 million loss in the fourth quarter of 1979. "It would take a loss of $200 million before the airline would be in serious trouble," says Frank L. Salizzoni, senior vice-president.

Not all airlines are so nonchalant. Ozark Air Lines Inc. plans no expansion this year and is trying to sell off some of its aircraft. "The belt-tightening should generate enough cash and working capital to allow us to survive in 1980 and provide for recovery in 1981," says Albert J. Rose, senior vice-president.

Parental Largesse.   Because leasing companies are leveraged to the hilt, they often wind up with low Zeta scores. PHH Group Inc., which manages large commercial auto fleets, has one of the lowest Zeta scores even though, claims Howard S. Boote Jr., vice-president for finance, "we've never had a down year." Similarly, Kay Corp. insists that high leverage is integral to its commodities operations, which have been profitable.

No matter how bad things get, some problem companies may survive, thanks to the largesse of a wealthy parent. Great Atlantic & Pacific Tea Co., with a -2.77 Zeta score, is 45%-owned by Germany's well-heeled Tengleman Group. Fed-Mart Corp., the big West Coast retail chain, is 68%-owned by Germany's Hugo Mann.

Assignment

1. Develop arguments for the bailout of large corporations with many employees — like Chrysler and Lockheed — from the viewpoint of (a) top corporate management; (b) labor union management; (c) the federal government; (d) the average consumer.

Steel Sales*

The manufacturer or builder who uses steel in his product usually obtains it from either of two different sources. If he operates on a large scale, he can purchase directly from a steel mill in carload lots. On the other hand, if his needs are more limited, if he requires a wide variety of types or sizes of steel, if he must have specialized service, or if he wants material in a hurry, he can turn to the supply division of a major steel producer or to an independent steel warehouse.

In their function as middlemen, steel warehouses purchase in large lots from the mills and maintain a variety of types and sizes of steel products to provide a reasonably effective local source of supply. They also cut steel to required shapes or sizes, deliver to the customer's door, provide credit assistance, and are a ready source of free technical advice. The independent firms compete with the warehousing divisions of the large steel producers — the main difference between them being that the independents are free to obtain their steel from numerous sources while the divisions are captive outlets.

Steel Sales Company

Steel Sales Company in the oldest steel warehouse in Clearfield. As an organization it stems from the time in 1910 when George P. Grant and Henry Cooper of Clearfield decided to form a partnership under the firm name of Grant and Cooper, Iron and Steel. The partners continued together until 1919 when Mr. Cooper sold his interest and the firm became known as Grant and Company. During the next three decades, the firm was known

---

* Prepared by Scott H. Partridge of California State University, Hayward. Permission to use granted by the author.

as Grant and Smith, Grant, Smith & Lomax, and Grant & Company, until finally incorporated as *Steel Sales Company* in 1952. The firm was the first steel warehouse to make deliveries in Clearfield by motorized truck, and was among the earliest firms to establish branch warehouses.

The Current Situation

The Cooper interests are represented on the board of directors, but are no longer active in the management of the company. As shown in Exhibit 1, the Grant family directs the firm in the persons of John J. Grant, Chairman, and his son William R. Grant, President and Treasurer. The day-to-day

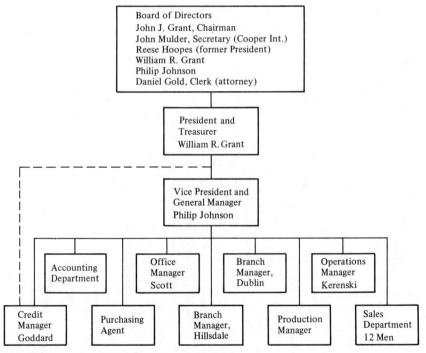

Note: The company does not have a formal table of organization.

EXHIBIT 1
STEEL SALES COMPANY
ORGANIZATION CHART

EXHIBIT 2
STEEL SALES COMPANY, CONSOLIDATED BALANCE SHEETS,
DECEMBER 31, 1957 TO 1966 INCLUSIVE (in $1,000s)

Assets	1966	1965	1964	1963	1962	1961	1960	1959	1958	1957
Current assets										
Cash in banks and on hand	158	102	108	182	258	124	160	300	484	268
Accounts receivable and notes	1,616	1,374	1,250	1,228	1,784	1,692	1,596	1,868	1,406	1,408
Inventory (at cost)	3,828	3,350	2,920	2,770	2,928	3,368	3,028	2,988	2,284	3,004
Prepaid expenses	68	68	54	68	68	84	72	68	44	34
Total current assets	5,670	4,894	4,332	4,248	5,038	5,268	4,856	5,224	4,218	4,714
Cash surrender value of life insurance	90	76	64	54	174	164	156	150	142	136
Plant and equipment (at cost less accumulated depreciation)	1,206	1,246	1,334	1,396	1,498	1,614	1,656	1,770	1,752	1,248
Total assets	6,966	6,216	5,730	5,698	6,710	7,046	6,668	7,144	6,112	6,098

Liabilities and stockholders' equity

	1966	1965	1964	1963	1962	1961	1960	1959	1958	1957
Current liabilities										
Notes payable — bank	2,182	2,332	2,006	1,828	2,424	2,440	2,256	2,672	1,600	1,350
Accounts payable	1,460	740	662	606	720	840	306	456	430	574
Employees profit sharing and retirement plans	32	32	24	10	44		106	82	112	248
Accrued expenses:										
Federal income taxes	40	140	146	168	28	50	156	118	130	374
Other taxes and expenses	160	48	180	88	162	158	152	122	142	142
Mortgage payments due within one year	44				88	88	88	88	88	62
Total current liabilities	3,918	3,292	3,018	2,700	3,466	3,576	3,064	3,538	2,502	2,750
Long-term debt										
Mortgage notes payable	20	64		180	268	356	444	532	620	462
Debenture notes payable							74	74	74	74
Total liabilities	3,938	3,356	3,018	2,880	3,734	3,932	3,582	4,144	3,196	3,286

Stockholders' equity										
Capital stock outstanding										
Preferred-$6 cumulative, without par value	266	266	266	266	266	266	142	142	142	142
Preferred-6% cumulative, par value $100	244	244	244	240	240	240	240	240	240	238
Common — par value $100	144	144	144	140	140	140	140	140	140	132
Capital surplus										
Accumulated earnings	2,372	2,208	2,060	2,160	2,082	2,214	2,312	2,226	2,142	2,048
Reserves for depreciation and contingencies					250	250	250	250	250	250
Total stockholders' equity	3,026	2,862	2,714	2,806	2,978	3,110	3,084	2,998	2,914	2,810
Total liabilities and stockholders' equity	6,964	6,218	5,732	5,686	6,712	7,042	6,666	7,142	6,110	6,096

EXHIBIT 3
STEEL SALES COMPANY, CONSOLIDATED STATEMENTS OF INCOME AND RETAINED EARNINGS, YEARS ENDED DECEMBER 31, 1957 TO 1966 INCLUSIVE (in $1,000s)

	1966	1965	1964	1963	1962	1961	1960	1959	1958	1957
Sales	12,604	11,372	9,968	9,720	10,848	9,892	12,172	11,452	11,212	13,306
Cost of goods sold	9,234	8,322	7,278	7,074	7,994	6,944	8,680	8,300	8,114	9,698
Gross profit	3,370	3,050	2,690	2,646	2,854	2,948	3,492	3,152	3,098	3,608
Deduct — operating expenses										
Warehouse	1,100	996	932	950	946	848	956	768	784	816
Delivery	462	410	354	348	362	344	350	332	304	304
Selling	414	432	426	468	530	532	572	568	542	478
Administrative	1,144	1,066	1,066	1,118	1,140	1,150	1,162	1,126	996	884
Total operating expenses	3,120	2,904	2,818	2,884	2,978	2,874	3,040	2,794	2,626	2,482
Profit (loss) from operations	250	146	(128)	(238)	(124)	74	452	358	472	1,126
Other income		44								
Total	250	190	(128)	(238)	(124)	74	452	358	472	1,126
Other charges	26	22	22	24	32	72	80	58	94	310
Net income (loss) before federal income tax	224	168	(150)	(262)	(156)	2	372	300	378	816
Federal income tax	40				28	50	154	118	162	386
Net income (loss)	184	168	(150)	(262)	(184)	(48)	218	182	216	430
Retained earnings, beginning of year	2,208	2,060	2,160	2,082	2,214	2,312	2,226	2,142	2,048	1,766
Additions and reductions:										
Federal income tax refunds				108	74					
Reserve for contingencies restored			70	250						
Dividends declared	16	16	16	16	16	60	128	92	116	138
Retained earnings, end of year	2,376	2,212	2,064	2,162	2,088	2,204	2,316	2,232	2,148	2,058

operations of the firm are managed by Philip Johnson, Vice-President and General Manager, in consultation with William Grant.

The current condition of the company as well as trends over the past ten years, are shown in Exhibits 2 and 3.

The firm has its main plant and offices in Clearfield, with smaller warehouses in two nearby cities. The company moved to its present location in 1964, and is currently using office space to near capacity and warehouse space to full capacity. All contiguous property is currently in commercial use.

William R. Grant (President and Treasurer)

Mr. Grant is a man in his late forties with a degree from an Ivy League college, and twenty-five years experience with Steel Sales. His interests in the firm center on the areas of data processing, inventory control, and new equipment purchases, although he does concern himself with the rest of company operations through Mr. Johnson. Mr. Grant commented as follows:

> The ultimate goal of the company would probably be to increase the value of the common stock. Our firm is badly undercapitalized at the present time, and we are anxious to correct the situation — the ultimate cure for the problem is, of course, to earn sufficient profits. Since we are a closely held corporation, our actions in this direction have been different over the years than they might have been in other firms. It might be better to say that our goal is to increase profits rather than the value of the stock, since most of our problems would be solved if we improved our capital position.
>
> Steel Sales currently has a market share of around 5 to 10% in the area covered by our warehouses. There are no giants in the market — the biggest firm (Ryerson) is one of twenty-two branch warehouses of a nationwide firm — and has maybe twice our volume. In the Clearfield area there are, including ourselves, only about six full-line steel warehouses. A full-line warehouse must carry a complete line of carbon steel — we not only do this, but we also carry stainless and some aluminum.
>
> We compete by offering greater service. Since there is little price competition we try to offer faster delivery whenever possible. Also, we are specialists in cut-plate, and have a reputation for offering not only a bigger and better inventory of plate, but also a higher quality job of cutting. In the case of standard steel items where no special skill in cutting or processing is required, I guess our sales efforts would depend a great deal on the friendships which our outside salesmen have developed with our customers. We have 3000 active customers — active being defined as having purchased something within the past year. Of these 3000 customers, 54

purchase over $20,000 worth of steel each year apiece, and make up 30% of our total business. This means that 1.8% of our customers make up 30% of our business. Actually, those customers making up $5,000 to $20,000 sales per year probably constitute the most important segment of our market. (Note: See Exhibit 4 for an analysis of current accounts receivable balances.)

If we wanted to increase our business by 20% next year, I'm not sure what steps we would take. Any increase in our business would have to be taken away from our competition, and I don't really know what combination of additional salesmen, promotion, equipment, etc., would be the most effective. All of these items are becoming increasingly expensive — equipment, especially, is getting more sophisticated and costly. I can remember ten years ago when it cost $7000 to set up a first-class plate burning outfit, and now we are in the process of installing a new burning machine that will cost $45,000.

There have been many changes in the steel warehouse business during the past decade. Ten or fifteen years ago, 80% of our business was "off-the-shelf" and 20% was involved with special service. This has now reversed. 80% of our business is cut-to-size now, and often marked for a specific part of a specific job, and only 20% is standard material (see Exhibit 4).

We do no formal planning. Our formal planning is held down by a lack of capital; although we do hold planning meetings on an informal basis as they are needed. In fact, no scheduled meetings are held by top management — all of our meetings are unscheduled and informal. Capital

EXHIBIT 4
STEEL SALES COMPANY, ANALYSIS OF ACCOUNTS
RECEIVABLE ON MAY 4, 1967

Ac-counts	Account balances	Group totals	Number of customers		A/R balances	
			Group %	Cum. %	Group %	Cum. %
12	Over $10,000	$481,200	1.3	1.3	30	30
24	5,000–10,000	348,000	2.6	3.9	22	52
113	1,000–5,000	461,600	12.4	16.3	29	81 [a]
770	0–1,000	308,400	83.7	100.0	19	100
919		$1,599,200	100.0	100.0	100	100

[a] 12.4% of the customers on the books on 5/4/67 made up 29% of the total accounts receivable balance; 16.3% of the customers on the books on 5/4/67 made up 81% of the total accounts receivable balance.

EXHIBIT 5
STEEL SALES COMPANY, SALES ANALYSIS BY PRODUCT
CLASS, SECOND QUARTER, 1967

Product class	Sales	Cost	Gross	%	Inventory
H.R. bars & shapes	$ 423,074	293,150	129,924	30.71	504,306
Cold finished bars	180,422	119,374	61,048	33.84	344,518
Structural shapes	234,754	166,988	67,766	28.87	220,420
Special bars	79,122	52,438	26,684	33.73	253,586
Mil-20166 bars	3,760	2,464	1,296	34.47	23,866
Total	921,132	634,414	286,718	31.13	1,346,696
H.R. & C.R. sheets	234,252	171,552	62,700	26.77	255,908
Coated sheets	228,736	197,020	31,716	13.87	187,106
Total	462,988	368,572	94,416	20.39	443,014
Plates A-7 & floor	601,596	391,492	210,104	34.92	556,508
F-M plates	128,308	78,756	49,552	38.62	202,202
Alloy plates	20,376	14,818	5,558	27.28	43,358
Total	750,280	485,066	265,214	35.35	802,068
Stainless bars	111,478	90,916	20,562	18.44	211,036
Stainless sheets	159,584	133,300	26,284	16.47	178,702
Stainless plates	12,274	8,266	4,008	32.65	26,116
Total	283,336	232,482	50,854	17.95	415,854
Non-ferrous	44,874	32,776	12,098	26.96	63,878
Miscellaneous steel	123,134	76,472	46,662	37.90	148,346
All others	42,034	31,612	10,422	24.79	61,718
Grand total	$2,677,778	1,861,394	766,384	29.16	3,281,574

expenditures are approved by myself but I, of course, seek the approval of other members of management. I have the ultimate approval, but this doesn't mean much right now because of our shortage of capital. We are currently borrowing funds from the bank against inventory and accounts receivable — money is very tight. In response to the capital shortage we are not actively diversifying. We have broadened our inventory some with the addition of aluminum sheets as an item, but that's the extent of our recent expansion.

To break into the steel warehouse business, it takes a fairly substantial investment. If this firm is a model, it would take about $1,500,000 to set up an organization that could capture 5% of this market. I know of a steel warehouse in Florida that only has $400,000 invested, but this firm acts much like a broker in many of its dealings. I suppose that if you wanted to start smaller and work up to 5% you could do it with a much smaller investment.

We buy most of our steel from Bethlehem for a number of reasons. First, Bethlehem, unlike U.S. Steel, does not have its own chain of warehouses and thus is committed to servicing the independents. This appeals to us. Secondly, Bethlehem has the closest mills, and thus the freight-in will be less than with other steel manufacturers. We also buy from Armco, Jones and Laughlin, Republic, National, Alan Wood, and U.S. Steel. U.S. Steel gives the independents preferential treatment over its own U.S. Steel Supply, so we don't mind buying from them. We like to keep friendly with all the mills — to protect our sources of supply. You never know when shortages might develop and an alternate source might be needed. Once when all the industry went on strike except Alan Wood, we were able to benefit from our years of friendly relations with them; and we got our share of their production.

In summary, we buy from producers depending on how well they perform according to the following criteria:

1. Do they have a local outlet that competes with us?

2. Does the location of the mill give them a geographical advantage that is reflected in delivery times and costs?

3. Does the producer offer financial help in the form of extended credit?

4. Are the products of high quality?

5. How good are they in providing regular and special services?

We don't apply any formal calculations in choosing suppliers, but we do have decided opinions concerning the historical value of various suppliers to us. Currently, some of our major sources are: Bethlehem, 28–34%; U.S. Steel, 16–20%; Republic, 6% (down from 10%); Alan Wood, 10% (up from 5%).

We don't buy any foreign steel even though the quality is equal to domestic, in most cases, and even though it would cost us 1½ cents less per pound. If we started to sell it instead of domestic steel, our customers would want to know. They would demand a substantial price discount, and, in addition, they would want special assurance that the steel met U.S. specifications — which it sometimes doesn't do. Also, as mentioned earlier, we feel that it is important to retain the good relations we now have with our domestic suppliers — not only to protect ourselves in case of shortages, but also for financial support from them when it might be needed. If we stocked foreign steel it would force us to set up a whole new inventory. We just haven't thought that, up until now, it is worth the risk and the trouble, even though we know that in some parts of the country nearly all warehouses are heavily involved in selling foreign steel. There are firms in the Clearfield area that handle it, and we acknowledge that this has cut into our business. Those smaller firms, which are very price conscious and less concerned with meeting specifications, tend to go to warehouses handling foreign products. We aren't willing to drop our prices to meet foreign prices, so we have lost a good share of the business we formerly did with small fabricators.

Philip Johnson (Vice-President and General Manager)

Mr. Johnson has been with Steel Sales for ten years. His background includes a degree from the state university and seven years in the military service. He came to the company as a sales trainee, and rose to become Assistant Sales Manager, Sales Manager, and eventually Vice-President and General Manager. Mr. Johnson is in charge of the operations of the firm and in this capacity, acts as a sales manager, a comptroller, and as a warehouse manager.

Mr. Johnson made the following observations concerning Steel Sales Company.

Our principal method of competing is through service. We try to offer faster delivery, of course, but more than that we try to establish a reputation for "consistent integrity." Our prices are consistent and our reputation is consistent. By having a better staff of people — both inside and outside — we try to establish personal relationships with our customers which will encourage them to do business with us. Using this philosophy we have not fared too well with smaller firms. Pricing has gotten tighter, and smaller firms are mostly concerned with the price of material. Service and integrity don't mean as much to them so they buy the cheaper foreign steel. Of course, some companies will buy American steel because they feel it's a better policy to patronize domestic manufacturers, but for many smaller firms patriotism is worth about 50 cents a hundredweight.

The most important part of the company organization is our sales staff. We have good men and we treat them well. We have a low turnover among our outside salesmen — in fact, we seldom have salesmen quit for any reason. We pay them well and we get our money's worth. Since most of their work is missionary work, we pay them mostly on salary with a small incentive payment as a spur to activity. (We don't call it a commission.) Salesmen are paid about $200 per week, plus fringe benefits plus a company car. They can use the car like it was their own; we pay for all gas and oil, and maintenance for both personal and company business. The value of the car to a salesman is about $1,500 a year plus whatever gasoline he uses for his own purposes. The salary and car are really most of a salesman's compensation. About the top incentive payment a real hot-shot salesman could hope to get if he really worked at it would be around 10% of his salary. Last year we gave a company-wide year-end bonus, but that was the first time in five years. We damn near went under about five years ago, and since that time have been reluctant to pay bonuses. The bonuses at one time got up to $800–$1200, but the latest ones were only a couple of hundred dollars.

I'm always willing to talk to a potential salesman, but I very seldom need to hire one. We don't actively recruit new salesmen. As far as sales training, I hold a sales meeting each month, and also a yearly management training program. This year, the management training will be given one full day of effort.

We judge a salesman according to how well he performs relative to an established quota. We figure a salesman's break-even point by computing the gross profit dollars that it takes to keep him out there — he has to cover his salary, car, etc. If a salesman gets over that amount he gets a commission on the gross profit. I set the quota myself, based on past experience and estimated growth in sales; the salesman is, of course, informed of the amount of the quota but does not enter into its calculation.

One of our major problems is the relationship between the sales and shipping departments. Usually what happens is that the salesman promises more than the warehouse can deliver. This is one problem, though, that we are used to and have learned to live with. My background is in sales, and as general manager I tend to go along with the salesman in any dispute. If a problem ever gets up to me, I get the principals together and we work out a reasonable solution. Our goal is to put everything on a 24-hour basis, but this is becoming increasingly difficult to do. At first, when 75% of material shipped was made up of standard sizes, almost all of it went out in 24 hours. Now that 75% is cut-to-size, delivery times are necessarily slowed down. Currently, about 45% goes out in 24 hours — with the balance, the reason why delivery can't be made in 24 hours is obvious to the customer, the salesman, and the shop, so there's no real problem. The salesman can promise delivery within 24 hours if the material is a stock size. In this case, the warehourse should be able to make delivery; if delivery isn't made within 24 hours we consider it the fault of the warehouse.

There is one basic conflict between the sales force and the warehouse that can never be solved, and that has to do with the variety in types and sizes of material we stock. We could never carry enough to satisfy the sales department and will always carry too much for the warehouse. We have tried to reach a happy balance between sales and the shop.

The sales force usually gets along well with the credit department. Five years ago we were in terrible shape with regard to the age of our receivables — so much so that we hired a full-time credit manager. At first he pussy-footed around not wanting to hurt any feelings, and the situation didn't improve any. After we made clear to him that the situation would have to improve, and after some hard and fast rules were established, there was a marked improvement. I consider that the Credit Manager has been a valuable addition to the firm. The relationship between the sales force and the Credit Manager has generally been good — the salesmen realize that he has an essential function to perform, and they try to cooperate.

Steel Sales, in spite of its emphasis on customer service, gets its share of complaints. Sometimes we will make a pricing error. Once in a great while a customer will get his feelings hurt for some reason, and I have to try to smooth things over. I had to do that just this morning. A good customer of ours wanted to take a tour through a steel mill; we contacted one of our suppliers; the supplier's representative went to see our customer and insulted him or hurt his feelings or something — now I've got to straighten things out.

Sometimes material won't perform to specifications for no reason that we can possibly know in advance or even figure out after we do know. For example, we shipped a man a piece of special alloy plate — and it broke when it fell out of a vise. We get hairline cracks in cold roll bars which can't be detected, and which cause the material to break when it shouldn't. Material will sometimes break when it should bend. When any of these things happen we just do our best to fix things up the best we can with as little trouble as possible to our customer. We stand behind our material 100% — perhaps more than the mill does. The customer knows that we will back him up as much as possible. We act right away and argue about price adjustment later. The most important thing is to keep the customer's business going; with the mill you get involved with affidavits, etc., before any adjustments are made — we simply can't afford to do that with our customers, they need the material to keep production going.

Myron Scott (Office Manager)

Myron Scott has been with Steel Sales for eleven years. His prior experience was nine years as the superintendent of a small metal-stamping firm. His remarks on Steel Sales are summarized as follows:

Steel Sales competes by offering quality custom cutting of plate and through faster delivery. We achieve faster delivery by organizing our warehouse crews in three shifts.

Skeleton — This consists of eight men who work from 7:00 A.M. to 3:00 P.M. Their job is to unload incoming shipments from freight cars and trucks. In addition, the crew processes rush orders and handles cash sales.

Full Crew — This is the largest crew — consisting of twenty men who work from 3:00 to 11:00 P.M. Their main job is to process work for shipment the next day. They cut material to size and bring together into a single bundle or pile all the various items on a single order.

Graveyard Shift — The four men in this crew work from 11:00 P.M. to 7:00 A.M., and have the responsibility for loading material prepared by the full crew onto the correct trucks.

Organization of our warehouse in this manner allows a customer to call in up until 5:00 on a business day and receive delivery of his material within 24 hours.

We rely on the judgment of our warehouse workers regarding what material should be cut from. The only area where we keep a tight control over available pieces is in stainless steel — it is kept under strict control through the use of charts showing the exact shape and dimension of each piece in stock. When an order goes down for a particular piece to be cut to order, the man in charge can see exactly what is available and thus very little is wasted.

75 to 80% of orders are shipped out within three days. Most of the material goes out in a rather routine fashion but occasionally a rush order must be given special handling. We stress to sales personnel that a rush order must truly be needed in a rush and must be designated as such. We do not want orders designated as rush orders just to impress a customer. Admittedly there are times when it does become necessary to grant some customers preferential treatment, but this only happens when the order backlog gets too big and when a big customer pushes for rapid delivery of a particular order.

Credit management was a real problem when I first came to work here. At that time, the screws were really put on slow payers and there were instances of differences of opinion and hard feelings. Now, though, the situation is fine, and the relations between the Credit Manager and the sales department are very good.

Steel Sales follows very closely rules that state that all purchasers are equal with regard to price — that is, that quantity price brackets are the same for all customers regardless of their total monthly or annual purchases. This is the law as set forth in the Robinson–Patman Act. We cannot discriminate, and we advise our customers of this; in fact, I think that Steel Sales has one of the better images with regard to compliance with the law. Since our customers realize that we must price each order individually, many of them make a special effort to combine individual steel orders into an order sufficiently large enough to warrant a lower price bracket. As to the question of whether other firms do make special price deals, I would have to answer yes. Based on invoices I have seen, some steel warehouses are billing once each month on a blanket-order basis.

We do no trading of steel or other items with other steel warehouses. If we want material we buy it and if they want material we're happy to sell it; this keeps transactions cleaner than getting involved in trades. Besides, many products that we pick up are things that we don't handle, so no trade is possible. We have established a policy of supplying our customers with all items even though we may [not] stock all of them — more so than other warehouses, and without higher prices. We are able to obtain a price break by combining orders, but the profit margins are smaller than on items that we carry in our own stock. This is really another service to the customer.

I look upon my job as more of an inside sales manager or customer relations man than an office manager. Ten years ago an inside salesman was only an order taker, now his product knowledge and personality are important. The gimmick today is the phone. A few customers will give their orders directly to salesmen, but 80 to 90% of our business comes in through the order desks.

John Goddard (Credit Manager)

John Goddard is 37 years old, married, and has three children. He has a B.S. from Northwestern University and worked as a credit manager for a number of years before coming to Steel Sales. He came to the company five years ago as Credit Manager.

As Credit Manager I have a number of sources that provide information on the past experiences other businesses have had with customers — both current and potential — and I use all of them. The principal sources are Dun and Bradstreet, The National Association of Credit Management, individual trade and bank inquiries, and information obtained by our salesmen.

Once each month I meet with the credit managers from other steel warehouses to discuss problems we all are having with particular accounts. All the credit managers know each other and there is complete confidence regarding what goes on in our meetings. In such a meeting there is always the possibility of illegal collusive action, so we try to make a special effort to stay clear of such a thing. If Smith Welding Company has a bad credit record, we cannot agree as a group not to extend additional credit, but we can agree individually. One of our competitors actually did quit sending a representative to the meetings because of fear of antitrust action.

Twice each month I'm provided with an up-to-date aged analysis of the accounts receivable. The daily cash receipts are posted to this, and it is my principal tool for keeping track of collections and the current condition of our receivables. If a customer shows up as past due on the aging, there are a number of things I can do. When an account becomes thirty days old, we will send out a statement reminding the customer of the balance owing. If this fails to bring a response, I'll follow up with a letter and then with a phone call. If the amount is still not paid I will make a visit to the customer — I spend about a day and a half each week out seeing delinquent accounts. I try to accomplish more than just collecting the money; it's also important to find out information indicating why the account is past due.

I have frequent contact with Mr. Johnson and Mr. Grant so there is no need for regularly scheduled meetings concerning the condition of the accounts receivable. We do meet twice each year to determine accounts that should be written off as bad debts.

Don Kerenski (Operations Manager)

Don has been with Steel Sales for twenty-one years. He started as a plate burner, and through the years worked as foreman on the night shift, Assistant Superintendent, Superintendent, and now, Operations Manager. He made the following comments on the work in the warehouse:

Steel Sales competes by offering service — 24-hour delivery and quality of cutting. Because our strong point is service, anything that gets in the way of serving the customer hurts us, and the two main problems we have in the warehouse directly affect how well we deliver material.

Our first big problem is that we just don't have enough space. We have increased our inventory to the point where we are losing time that shouldn't be lost. Everything is getting piled higher and closer — it never fails that if we have a stack ten feet high, we will want something on the bottom. When it takes half an hour to dig out a $10 order we just can't make any money — it takes the time of two men, one on the crane and another on the floor. We still have adequate crane capacity with five cranes operating, and we have a large enough open area for making up orders, but the storage areas are getting crammed to the point where we hardly have space to work. Crowded conditions also make it more hazardous to work. Since we became so crowded, accidents have been more frequent. I think the squeeze really began when we added aluminum sheets to our inventory. They are expensive and have to be handled carefully, so they take up a lot of space.

The second problem has to do with the workmen in the warehouse. Out of the thirty men working on the three shifts, about twenty are dependable and the rest come and go. Anybody who has worked here for ten years won't quit — will die here — but the young fellows we get don't want to work. The turnover is high among them and they do poor work while they are here. When a new man comes, I put him with an old timer for four days and then on the fifth day he makes mistakes while on his own, and we get complaints from customers that, for example, they received $11/16$ instead of ¾ inch plate. It's a real problem.

As far as the trucking end of the business, I think we have a good bunch of drivers and a lousy bunch of trucks. Occasionally we get a complaint that a driver has been fresh or has taken out somebody's gatepost, but more often we get favorable comments. We lease our trucks and breakdowns are often and service is poor — we have the mechanics from the leasing firm fix the same thing a number of times and it still won't work.

We have a union shop, but we get along well with the business agent, so it's no problem to the company — I used to be shop steward and that helps. I think that a company is smart to be on good terms with the business agent if the work force is unionized.

Assignment

1. Evaluate the current situation of Steel Sales Company; (*a*) evaluate the competitive situation of the Steel Sales Company; (*b*) comment on the activities of an independent steel warehousing operation; and (*c*) make specific recommendations on problems you perceive in the Steel Sales Company's operations.

Mid-Jersey Nursery*

Mid-Jersey Nursery (MJN) is a firm whose principal business is the whole-sale distribution of nursery products. Its clientele consists of retail nurseries, landscape contractors, and other independent wholesale distributors. Owing to the nature of their products, primary dealings occur during early spring through fall.

The MJN is proud of its propagation achievements, which allow it to grow most of its evergreens and many of the shrubs, like rhododendrons and azaleas, which it sells. It is the firm's policy to move increasingly toward propagation of nearly the entire product line. This is felt to be a key to ensuring high quality and rising profits for MJN.

The business, which is privately owned, was acquired three years ago by the present stockholders. They have continued the innovative procedures followed by their predecessors in product development. They hired the current president of the company and appointed him to the Board of Directors.

In the year ended December 31, 1980, sales of MJN totaled over $2 million. The favorable sales trend has continued into the first nine months of 1981, with sales to date of $1.9 million. The current year is expected to be the first year that the company has recognized an operating profit since its acquisition by the present owners. However, the company will probably still show a net loss due to the outstanding interest expenses arising from stockholders' loans to the company (see Exhibit 1).

Background

The MJN is one of the larger wholesale nursery firms in the area. Within a radius of about one hundred miles there are a half-dozen firms as large as

---

* Prepared by Milton Leontiades.

EXHIBIT 1
MID-JERSEY NURSERY'S INCOME STATEMENT
(dollars in thousands)

	1978	1979	1980	9 Mo 1981
Sales	$1,760	$1,875	$2,050	$1,900
Less discounts and returns	8	9	9	8
Net sales	$1,752	$1,866	$2,041	$1,892
Cost of sales	1,580	1,701	1,857	1,650
Gross profit on sales	$ 172	$ 165	$ 184	$ 242
General expenses	225	238	250	220
Net operating income	$ (53)	$ (73)	$ (66)	$ 22
Interest expense	50	50	50	50
Net income for period	$ (103)	$ (123)	$ (116)	$ (28)

or larger than MJN, plus many small nurseries and garden centers scattered throughout the region.

The competition is keen among the various nurseries. Since there is very little differentiation among the types of products sold, the emphasis by customers tends to be on the quality of products (how healthy they are and how long they last), price, and service.

The industry is currently enjoying a healthy growth trend. The area served is relatively sparsely populated for the northeastern region of the United States, but over the last few years a number of large residential developments have broken ground. Once the residential population starts to rise, it is common for new commercial and industrial firms to follow. All of these developments would create new customers for the nursery business. Moreover, there has been a trend over recent years for customers to emphasize the attractiveness of their sites and to share a common concern for the environment. This has translated into a greater number of plantings per account and a larger price tag per order. It has also attracted a number of new, generally smaller firms, into the retailing and wholesaling of trees, shrubs, flowering plants, garden supplies, and decorative accessories, as well as landscaping.

Mid-Jersey Nursery's Position

The MJN has grown along with the industry. There is, in general, stockholder satisfaction in the sales growth of the company and a feeling that profits will eventually turn around and grow more in line with sales. The present three stockholders acquired the business in the belief that, with proper management, control of costs, and an emphasis on quality, their investments would be amply rewarded. One of their first moves on assuming control was to hire Tom Harvey as president of MJN. Tom had an extensive career in the nursery business and propagation was considered a specialty of his. He had, in fact, headed the propagation department of a larger nursery prior to his accepting the presidency at MJN. Although Tom had limited administrative experience, he had run an efficient propagation department and had gained wide recognition for the hardiness, color, and long life of the plants he produced.

Until recently the stockholders had no reason to question the running of MJN. Although profits were yet to materialize, a gradual improvement was anticipated. Sales and earnings growth rates were roughly within the ballpark limits of what was expected.

There were, however, recent disturbing developments. In particular, Harry Gonzens, a major stockholder, was concerned about the abrupt departure of the head of the propagation activities for MJN. Mr. Gonzens had heard rumors of discontent among the employees generally and had questioned Tom Harvey about employee morale and especially about the abrupt departure of the head of propagation. He had received assurances that everything was progressing smoothly. A certain amount of employee grumbling was normal, Harvey said, and the propagation department was under his close supervision.

Despite these assurances, Mr. Gonzens finally decided that an outside expert should review the organization and operations of MJN. Mr. Gonzens prevailed on a long-time friend and professor connected with Cook College, the agricultural center for Rutgers University in New Jersey, to take on this assignment. The other stockholders had no objection and, indeed, welcomed an independent opinion of the condition of MJN. Although Tom Harvey continued to oppose the move, Dr. Tim Scholler of Cook College was engaged to review the situation at MJN.

Based on a briefing received from Mr. Gonzens, Dr. Scholler decided that organization and administration of the nursery were to be the first priorities of his investigation. Some of Dr. Scholler's findings were as follows.

Organization and Administration

The MJN showed signs of serious employee morale problems, which were (Dr. Scholler believed) caused by violation of the chain of command. The department heads nominally report to the general manager, who in turn reports to the president. The general manager of a nursery would normally handle the daily functions of the business. Only when a problem arose that

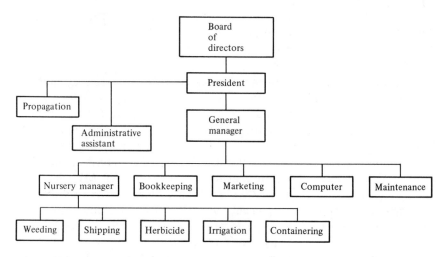

EXHIBIT 2

was outside his scope would he consult the president. However, in MJN too often the president would bypass the general manager and directly exercise his authority in minor affairs. Although Dr. Scholler had tried to interview Tom Harvey to get his side of the story, Tom refused to cooperate in the investigation. The organization chart in Exhibit 2 illustrates the present location of departmental units within the organization and the reporting responsibilities in MJN.

Tom Harvey's tendency to disregard formal and distinct lines of authority has led to considerable confusion and frustration among employees. This confusion has also resulted in communication problems among the president, the general manager, and the supervisors. Department managers feel incapable of performing effectively and suspect that Tom Harvey may not trust them or think too highly of them.

These managers, as well as the general managers, are cautious about making recommendations to the president. They feel he is skeptical of their suggestions and prefers his way of doing things. At first these employees respected Tom's expertise and hoped to build a more comfortable relationship with him over time. However, they perceived little improvement, or change, in the way the company was being administered. A recent situation described to Dr. Scholler by the general manager concerned Tom Harvey's personal supervision of the soil-mixing operation, an operation for which he was not qualified. Soil-mixing involves a technical procedure that should be handled by a field supervisor. However, Tom decided that he could do it better and tried to make a "super soil mix." The net effect of this action was a sizable loss of products because of burned roots caused by the "super mix." It had the further effect of leaving the immediate supervisor frustrated and angry.

Contributing to the growing tensions between Tom Harvey and the employees is the matter of salary levels, which are generally 10 to 15 percent lower than comparable industry averages. Raises are few and far between. Tom Harvey rarely rewards achievements by subordinates, nor does he provide incentives for superior performance. As a result many employees have become apathetic and feel dissatisfied with their jobs. In the past, supervisors or managers who terminated employment with MJN had disputes over back wages and vacation benefit adjustments. It is very difficult for employees to win such arguments without an extended and costly legal contest. So far, none of the persons who left felt it worth the trouble and expense to contest the company's severance payments.

Finally, in private discussions with Dr. Scholler, the employees of MJN expressed particular dismay over the new head of propagation, who, they felt, was not qualified for the job. The person who had been appointed was a friend of a major stockholder. Although he had previously been employed at MJN, his former position was at a much lower level. What was especially disturbing to other employees was that this new person was pushed through the hiring process, jumping over better-qualified applicants. Also, this person bypasses the general manager and reports directly to the president, unlike the other department managers. Because Tom Harvey is a director of the firm, as well as president, there is hesitancy in voicing such complaints out loud. Only after Dr. Scholler had gained their trust, and promised total confidentiality of their replies, were the employees willing to talk freely.

Inventory Control

A second area that Dr. Scholler decided to give attention to was inventory control. An inspection of MJN's records led him to believe that this function was not being properly handled and might be the source of future problems.

Inventories in the nursery business can quite easily be misrepresented on financial statements. When the physical count of inventory differs from the inventory records, a business can offer a variety of reasons, including employee theft, a disruption in the information process, or an inefficient internal control system. Inventories along with cash and accounts receivables are crucial control areas for a business. Therefore the inventory control system must be explicitly designed for accurate accounting. Safeguards to prevent misrepresentation should include prenumbered documents that acknowledge the receipt, the movement, and the shipment of goods.

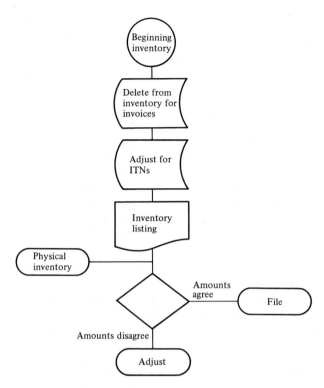

EXHIBIT 3

The MJN has had trouble keeping accurate inventory records. There are considerable differences between the physical and the perpetual inventories. These differences have been quite significant in the past (as high as 20,000 plants). The distortions in the presumed inventory of products provide unreliable data for purposes of forecasting, maintaining appropriate inventory levels, and so forth.

The present system by which the perpetual inventory is kept is diagrammed in Exhibit 3. As can be seen, beginning inventories are adjusted by invoices and inventory transaction notices (ITNs). Dr. Scholler's investigation revealed that two problem areas exist within the perpetual inventory system. The first problem occurs when an item is invoiced but not shipped. A credit memo is generated but the item is not put back into inventory. This results in items being deleted from inventory by the computer when in fact they do not leave the inventory. This problem arises from the lack of gross sales adjustment provisions in the present computer program. Therefore, once an item is invoiced, it cannot be put back into inventory without a complete deletion of that invoice and a reinvoicing of the correct order. The second problem area concerns the inventory transaction notices. These notices record any movements in inventory other than those generated by sales. The problem with ITNs is that they are often not received by the office or are inaccurately filled out. A major factor influencing ITN transactions is dead plants removed from inventory, but not accurately reported. This tends to overstate the perpetual inventory figures. A large portion of this problem arises when ITNs are written up after the fact, such as when plants are dumped in the morning and not recorded until late afternoon, or worse yet, when they are not recorded until days later, or not at all. To verify these procedural problems, Dr. Scholler observed ITNs being processed for a week's worth of dumps.

Summary and Conclusion

Dr. Scholler extended his review of these two principal areas to include checks on the physical condition of the nursery stock, and the amount of

EXHIBIT 4
MID-JERSEY NURSERY BALANCE SHEETS, 1979 AND 1980

	December 31 1979	1980
Cash	$ 1,235	$ 1,145
Accounts receivable	341,012	397,200
Notes receivable	42,000	45,000
Inventory	83,312	127,411
Total current assets	$466,559	$570,756
Machinery and equipment	142,550	160,010
Trucks and automobiles	43,020	50,250
Less: Depreciation allowances	(80,120)	(91,200)
Total fixed assets	$105,450	$109,060
Total assets	$572,009	$679,816
Accounts payable	$213,309	$240,616
Notes payable	211,200	290,100
Accrued items	27,500	29,100
Total current liabilities	$452,009	$559,816
Common stock — $1 par value (120,000 shares outstanding)	120,000	120,000
Total liabilities and equity	$572,009	$679,816

inventory on hand in relation to estimates of demand. He found both areas to be satisfactory. In addition he reviewed the balance-sheet figures of MJN for 1979 and 1980 (see Exhibit 4).

Finally, Dr. Scholler believed he had sufficient information to write his report for Mr. Gonzens and the other members of the Board of Directors. Tom Harvey, being a member of the board, would be present.

Assignments

1. Write up Dr. Scholler's report. Identify the major problem areas and recommend solutions.

2. Advise Mr. Gonzens privately of alternative approaches to implementing those parts of your report dealing with Tom Harvey.

Universal Engineers and Contractors*

Universal Engineers and Contractors (UEC) is one of the largest engineering and construction firms in the world. The company was incorporated in 1918 as a consolidation of four successful engineering and construction organizations. It began with a limited customer list and the company was highly selective in its choice of projects. Most of the people in the organization, including top management, were technically oriented. Engineering was a common background with most of the employees learning their managerial skills on the job.

In the mid-1960s UEC was acquired by a large, diversified manufacturing firm. UEC has continued to grow under the sponsorship of its larger parent. It is currently capable of bidding on the largest projects in almost any part of the world.

The consolidation of the four original firms had created a capability for UEC to perform in a wide variety of areas: power plants for utilities — both fossil fuel and nuclear — chemical plants, steel mills, manufacturing plants, plus assorted types of commercial and institutional buildings and facilities. Work has been performed in all fifty states as well as Europe, Asia, South America, Mexico, and Canada.

Power plant work, over the years, both before and after incorporation, has been the backbone of the company. To date the firm has in progress or has completed the design and construction of approximately 60 million kilowatts of electric power generating capacity for utilities. This includes more than 30 million kilowatts of nuclear power. The major part of the company's sales are generated by the engineering and construction of nu-

---

* Prepared by Milton Leontiades.

clear power plants for utility companies. UEC has a total of approximately 5,000 employees including both home-office and field-site employees.

Organizational Logic

UEC employs the project management or matrix system of organization. Each major contract is assigned to a project manager. He in turn selects people to staff the project. These persons then report to the project manager for the duration of the project, after which time they return to their respective specialty areas. In effect, each job of any significant size is a self-contained business effort that follows the steps in Exhibit 1.

As indicated in Exhibit 1, UEC is divided into four Engineering divisions (Industrial, Chemical, Power, and General Engineering) plus a Construction Division that constructs facilities engineered and designed by the four Engineering and Design divisions (as well as facilities engineered and designed by outside firms). These operating divisions are supported by Project Support Operations, Administration, Business Development and Industrial Relations. Each Engineering and Construction Division consists of several departments that report directly to their respective division vice presidents (see Exhibit 2).

Because the bulk of the work is done through the Power Division it has the most reporting units and the greatest number of employees. Its operations are representative of the project approach used by the Chemical, Industrial, General Engineering and Construction divisions, and thus we consider the Power Division as representative of the operating approach of the corporation (see Exhibit 3).

At the head of the Power Division is a vice president who is responsible for all engineering and design effort for power-plant contracts. Under him are a number of departmental heads with responsibility for different

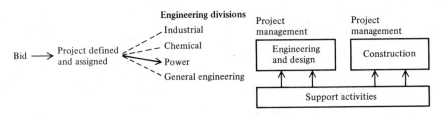

EXHIBIT 1

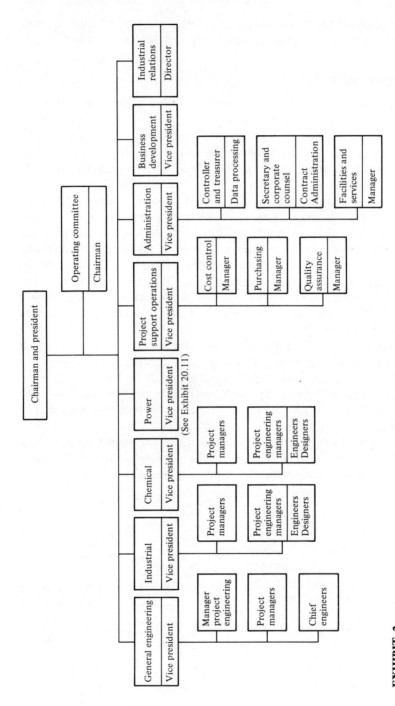

EXHIBIT 2
UNIVERSAL ENGINEERS AND CONTRACTORS: PLAN OF ORGANIZATION

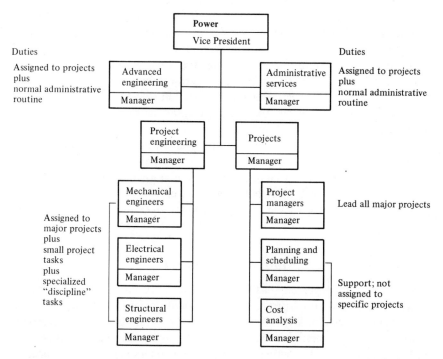

Duties

Assigned to projects
plus
normal administrative
routine

Power
Vice President

Advanced
engineering
Manager

Administrative
services
Manager

Duties

Assigned to projects
plus
normal administrative
routine

Project
engineering
Manager

Projects
Manager

Assigned to
major projects
plus
small project
tasks
plus
specialized
"discipline"
tasks

Mechanical
engineers
Manager

Electrical
engineers
Manager

Structural
engineers
Manager

Project
managers
Manager

Planning and
scheduling
Manager

Cost
analysis
Manager

Lead all major projects

Support; not
assigned to
specific projects

EXHIBIT 3
ORGANIZATION OF THE POWER DIVISION

aspects of power-plant work. The two primary individuals with direct responsibility for performing the engineering and design specifications are the project engineering manager and the projects manager. Both of these managers report directly to the vice president of power.

The project engineering manager has three departments under him divided along engineering specialties: mechanical engineering, electrical engineering, and structural engineering. The head of each of these departments has a number of engineers working in each area. Project Engineering employees maintain reporting responsibilities along "discipline" lines — i.e., mechanical, electrical, or structural engineering — except when they are assigned to a particular project, in which case they report for assignment to a project manager.

The projects manager has all project managers reporting to him as well as the support functions of Planning and Scheduling and Cost Analysis. Every job of significant size involves a project team comprised of a project manager, members from the Project Engineering Department, and the required support personnel from the two departments reporting directly to the vice president of power (namely, Administrative Services and Advanced Engineering). Planning and Scheduling and Cost Analysis personnel are not permanently assigned to a particular project but, rather, act as an advisory staff for the Projects Department, responsible for all major projects under the projects manager. Exhibit 3 indicates the nature of duties for the various units of the Power Division.

Some project tasks are comparatively small and do not require many full-time employees. This type of work is done by the applicable disciplines in the Project Engineering Department. The employees doing this work are not part of the project team but remain as employees of their respective groups. The project manager has no authority over them except to assure that the work they perform for his projects meet his requirements.

Theory of Project or Matrix Management

While matrix management has been only recently considered as a major alternative to traditional product or functional design, it has origins more than twenty years old. When America's space program began, the aerospace firms used matrix management to handle the many diverse jobs associated with a space-vehicle launching. Concentrating functional specialists around a single common task was an efficient way of organizing and managing such a complex mission. Once the individual projects were complete, the teams were disbanded.

In principle, UEC operates in much the same way. Once the company successfully bids for a major contract, a project manager is named to manage the job. He, in turn, determines the type of engineering skills required to perform the task. Next, he must identify the individuals to meet his specifications. More important, he must successfully assemble all the individuals whom he has identified for his project team and keep them for the duration of the job. There are a couple of ways he can approach this critical task of employee selection. A request may be submitted to the department managers in the Project Engineering Department asking them to furnish the necessary number of engineers and designers required for the project. The project manager will also request administrative, accounting, clerical, and secretarial help from the Administrative Services Department. Another method of staffing is to request the services of certain quality performers by name. A request can be made for particular individuals regardless of where they are working (for a "discipline" manager or for another project manager). It is up to the project manager to convince the Project

Engineering Department heads that the named individual is most needed on his project.

Application of Matrix Management in UEC

The matrix-management system is a potentially powerful method of flexible staffing and management of project-oriented businesses. It also has the potential for conflict. In UEC this potential exists between project managers and engineering and design managers. They both supervise the same personnel, and thus the employee is in the position of having two bosses: one from the project team and the other from his "discipline" department. At a given time both managers may be attempting to exercise their authority over one of the employees. New project managers, for example, are constantly attempting to steal the better performers from the older established projects and also from the engineering disciplines. Conversely, the engineering disciplines are striving to hold the more competent people.

A situation at UEC illustrates the difficulty of making matrix management work. Mr. Brickoff, a project manager, is in need of a mechanical engineer to complete the project team essential to the job requirements at a nuclear power plant. He is aware of the talents available. Since he wants the best man in that specialty, he requests Mr. Herden.

Mr. Herden is currently completing a job for his engineering boss in the Mechanical Engineering Department. Even though Herden is the only person familiar with the work he is presently performing, there is enough time for Herden to work for Brickoff and resume his present duties when he returns.

Mr. Alan Lad, Herden's engineering boss, does not want to let Herden go. "He's a good man, one of my best, and I need him right now on this job. I'll give you Miller. He's idle right now and won't hurt my department by working on that project for you," replied Lad in response to Brickoff's request.

Brickoff is not familiar with Miller's work, but knows Herden can get the job done. "I'm not going to settle for margarine, when I can get butter. Who does Lad think he is?" Brickoff responds.

And so, Lad and Brickoff are both fighting for Herden's services. Neither is inclined to give in. At this point, Brickoff can call in the next level of supervisors to reach a decision, beginning with the project engineering manager and the projects manager. If these two managers cannot agree, the question will be forced up, one level at at time, in the organization until ultimately a decision is made.

However, as Brickoff and Lad both recognize, top management strongly believes that decisions should not be forced upward. As Brickoff said, "My boss made it clear he was too busy to arbitrate my disputes." Similarly, Lad stated, "Last year the president made it very clear in memorandums to all the vice presidents that managers were expected to manage. Those who are deemed responsible for requiring their supervisors to make their decisions, by resolving disputes at higher levels, will be the ultimate losers."

With this perspective, both Lad and Brickoff are determined to defend their positions, and are equally determined to settle their argument among themselves.

Questions

1. Should the basic organizational choice of matrix management be changed?

2. Are there changes you might suggest to improve operation of the system?

3. If you were Brickoff, what might be your strategy for a solution? If you were Lad?

Northern Mammoth Equipment Company, Inc.*

On February 20, 1975, Harold Walton, office manager of Northern Mammoth Equipment Company, at the request of the board of directors, was trying to decide what should be done with respect to company sales. Mammoth's profits had been declining steadily for the last three years because, as Walton stated: "There simply isn't much construction business in the area now. We have to wait for contractors to obtain business before we can sell equipment to them."

Company Products

Northern Mammoth sold and serviced heavy equipment used in large construction projects. They handled several makes of well-known equipment. Equipment the company sold included various sizes of end-dumps, crawlers, front-end loaders, scrapers, bell-dumps, shovels, cranes, back-hoes, miners, and paving equipment. The prices for Northern Mammoth's lines of equipment ranged from $2,000 to about $130,000.

In addition to selling and servicing new equipment, Northern Mammoth sold and serviced used equipment, rented equipment, and sold parts. The sale of the new equipment and parts accounted for approximately 68 percent of the company's total sales.

History

Northern Mammoth Equipment Company was founded in 1958 in Sacramento, California, as a franchised dealer for Mammoth Equipment Com-

* Prepared by Dennis H. Tootelian, California State University, Sacramento, California, and reprinted by his permission and that of Goodyear Publishing Company.

pany, located in Cleveland, Ohio. Mammoth Equipment Company, in turn, is owned by General Equipment Company, one of the largest contractors in the world.

The board of directors for Northern Mammoth was composed of its general manager (Eugene Rayburn) and office manager (Harold Walton), two representatives of Mammoth Equipment Company, and three representatives of General Equipment Company.

Northern Mammoth maintained a relatively stable market condition within the area almost from its inception. The main reason was that it handled equipment and parts that were well accepted in the construction industry. Thus, although it still had to compete with other equipment lines, its main product was already established. Mammoth had a franchised dealer in every state, and from these outlets it also conducted foreign operations.

The Market

In northern California, the market area for Northern Mammoth, competition was very keen. Northern Mammoth competed with other companies that also sold well-known brands. For the most part these were, like Northern Mammoth, franchised dealers that had the exclusive rights to sell their respective brands. While franchise agreements placed restrictions on territorial expansion and types of products handled, no restrictions were placed on foreign operations.

Although Northern Mammoth had not made a study of its market position, the management felt that it was the second largest of its kind in northern California. It felt that Northern Mammoth's largest and most important competitor was the Caterpillar dealership located in San Francisco. As one company member put it: "We are probably the second largest dealer in northern California, but CAT is way ahead of us."

San Francisco was considered the most important market area for heavy equipment primarily because there were a large number of construction contractors located in and around the city. In general, contractors would bid for public and/or private contracts for construction projects. The winning bidder would then purchase whatever equipment and parts, etc. the firm needed from one of the dealers. Most dealers like Northern Mammoth attempted to establish good working relations with as many contractors as possible in the hope of making them "established" customers.

Organization

As of 1974, Northern Mammoth had forty-eight employees, including eight salespersons. The salespersons were located in various regions of northern California, and each maintained a small office there. For the forty-eight

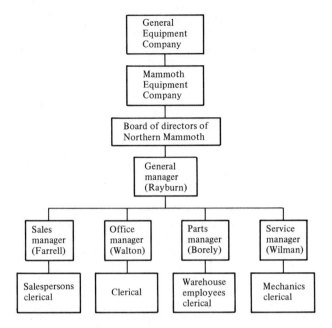

EXHIBIT 1
ORGANIZATIONAL CHART

employees there were four department managers plus a general manager who coordinated the entire operation (see Exhibit 1). The building layout of Northern Mammoth is shown in Exhibit 2. The departments were broken

Building layout

Accounting office	Parts order desk	Teletype	Billing office		Shipping room	
					Shop office	
Office manager	Cardex files		Parts manager			
Spare office	Conference room		Service manager	Stock room		Shop repair
Reception room	Sales manager	General manager	Office clerk			
	Sales office					

EXHIBIT 2
BUILDING LAYOUT

down into a sales department, service department, parts department, and an office department; there was a manager for each of these departments. With the exception of the parts manager, all the managers had been in their respective positions since the company began its operations.

SALES MANAGER

The sales manager, James Farrell, forty-eight years old, was responsible for supervising the eight salespeople. He had been in this business for almost seventeen years. Before coming to Northern Mammoth, Farrell had worked as a sales manager for a company that sold heavy equipment. That company, however, did not sell lines that competed with Northern Mammoth's.

Farrell was responsible for maintaining control over selling activities. Not only did he have to hire and fire salespersons, but he also had to approve all new and used equipment sales made for Northern Mammoth. In addition, he also handled some of the company's larger accounts.

SERVICE MANAGER

The service manager, Harold Wilman, was in charge of the service department where all repair and maintenance work was done. Although he ordinarily did not work on equipment himself, he was qualified to make repairs. Furthermore, he was directly in charge of customer relations for sales and service areas. Wilman, fifty-six years old, had been in the heavy equipment business for thirty-two years, fourteen of which were with Mammoth. Before Wilman came to work for Northern Mammoth, he had worked as a shop supervisor in the same company with Farrell.

PARTS MANAGER

The parts manager, William Borely, ordered and controlled all parts inventory, including shipping and receiving. In addition, he took care of all telephone orders for equipment for northern California. Borely, forty-one years old, had been in this field for twenty-one years and with Mammoth since 1958. Borely was a parts manager for an automobile dealership before he came to Northern Mammoth. He had worked for Northern Mammoth for four years in the parts department before becoming the parts manager in 1962.

OFFICE MANAGER

The office manager, Harold Walton, was secretary-treasurer of the company. He controlled the accounting, credit, and clerical work for the day-to-day operations. Because he had been in this field for twenty-eight years, mostly with the Mammoth company, he had been instrumental in setting company policy. In addition, he was considered by most employees of the company as the man who was most knowledgeable about the company's products. He was sixty-two years old.

GENERAL MANAGER

The general manager, Eugene Rayburn, fifty-one years old, coordinated all company operations. He was mostly concerned with establishing goodwill with clients and potential customers. Seldom did he concern himself with the day-to-day operations of the company; he left that to Walton. Rayburn had an engineering degree and twenty years' experience in the business. He was the only one of the five managers who had a college education. When Northern Mammoth was founded, Rayburn became general manager after leaving one of Mammoth's principal competitors.

Objectives

In discussing the objectives of Northern Mammoth, Walton made this comment: "Our basic policy is to make money for the stockholders." It should be noted at this point that the firm was privately owned by a small group of stockholders (headed by General Equipment Company), none of which was on the management team nor were these stockholders directly involved in the operations of the company.

Contrary to Walton's idea of the policy for Northern Mammoth, Farrell felt that the policy was service to the customers: "We do several things that are not profitable, but they give considerable assistance to our customers." Although Rayburn did not comment on this, most managers felt that he took somewhat of a middle-of-the-road course between Walton and Farrell.

A format for conducting operations was developed in 1958 when the company was formed. This format was primarily designed by Walton since he had been with Mammoth for such a long time and knew how the main office wanted operations conducted. When asked about the written policies, Walton had this to say: "That was such a long time ago that I really don't remember what they are. They are written down, and probably are around here somewhere, but I don't know where they would be."

Since each department conducted its own operations, the managers frequently met to discuss their problems on an informal and friendly basis. They had been good friends for quite some time, and there did not appear to be any real hostility among them. Although the department managers did not meet on a scheduled basis, Borely made this comment: "We bump into each other every day since we work in such close quarters. Not one day goes by that we don't discuss operations with each other." Even though Rayburn's office was in the same building, he rarely was consulted on daily matters.

Sales

The market for Northern Mammoth was, as stated before, the northern California area, extending from Eureka in the north to the Fresno and Monterey areas in the south. Although this total area had been quite busy with construction work, Walton felt that it was beginning to tail off: "We have been involved in some of the largest projects in northern California, but now there doesn't seem to be much construction taking place."

Normally, Walton and others forecast the potential demand for the area by reading about the contracts that were open for bid. From this they would try to determine who would bid for the contract and who would make the winning bid. Since many bidders were established customers of one dealer, the company could determine if it would be selling any equipment for the contract. It considered all contracts for the northern California area as potential sales.

DOMESTIC SALES

To cover this area, Northern Mammoth employed eight salespersons who had, on the average, been with Northern Mammoth for eight years. Each lived in his or her respective area and conducted business from a small regional office located in the immediate area. The regional offices for these salespersons were in Modesto, San Jose, San Francisco, Martinez, Santa Rosa, Sacramento, Yuba City, and Eureka (see Exhibit 3).

Each salesperson worked for a salary plus a commission on sales. While the salaries varied with the individual salesperson, the commissions were fixed. On new-equipment sales, the commission was 1½ percent of the *actual* sales price, and on used equipment the commission was 3 percent of the sales price. However, if there was a trade-in with the sale, the commission was reduced to compensate for any overallowance given on the equipment turned in.

In addition to the salary and commission, the salespersons were given expense accounts and the use of a rented car. The expense accounts ranged between $125 and $200 per week for meals, gas, and lodging. Except for

Eureka

Yuba City

Santa Rosa • Sacramento

Martinez

San Francisco • Modesto

San Jose

EXHIBIT 3
MARKET AREA

unusual conditions, the salespersons were not required to turn in any bills, etc., except for charging gasoline. As Mr. Walton stated: "The cost of handling all the paperwork would be higher than it's worth." On the average, a salesperson made about $18,000 each year.

The sales manager, James Farrell, and the equipment salespersons accounted for all the new and used equipment sales and rentals, and about 10 percent of the domestic parts sales. (Note: Northern Mammoth rents out both new and used equipment although this accounts for a small part of their total sales.) The remainder of the parts sales were made by the manager of the parts department either over the telephone or by mail orders.

Northern Mammoth had about three hundred steady customers who accounted for about 85 percent of the firm's sales of both equipment and parts. The orders were not definitely timed, nor were they for the same equipment or parts each time. Most customers did not stock parts and similar items since Northern Mammoth was close by and stocked parts and similar items for them. Even though orders varied considerably, sales over the years tended to remain stable except for the decline over the last three years. As Rayburn put it: "If our sales change very much on a yearly basis, the factory representatives that come by every so often want to know why." (See Exhibits 4, 5, 6, and 7.)

EXHIBIT 4
COMPARATIVE PROFIT AND LOSS STATEMENTS (in thousands)

	1974	1973	1972	1971	1970	1969	1968	1967
Sales								
Equipment								
New	2,038	2,141	2,196	2,204	2,187	2,072	1,939	1,900
Rental	406	427	438	452	463	426	378	379
Used	1,031	1,103	1,093	1,130	1,001	1,013	989	904
Service								
Customers	158	162	171	182	170	163	150	138
Other	183	199	208	216	193	180	186	192
Parts	2,013	2,092	2,111	2,187	2,081	2,000	1,893	1,630
Total	5,829	6,124	6,217	6,371	6,095	5,844	5,535	5,133
Cost of goods sold								
Equipment								
New	1,824	1,863	1,868	1,871	1,863	1,792	1,671	1,620
Rental	377	397	404	409	413	404	347	330
Used	951	1,015	997	1,063	978	998	979	900
Service	161	187	190	194	187	205	207	212
Parts	1,496	1,536	1,595	1,667	1,560	1,390	1,293	1,150
Total	4,809	4,998	5,054	5,204	5,001	4,789	4,497	4,212
Gross profit	1,020	1,126	1,163	1,167	1,094	1,055	1,038	921
Other expenses								
Wages and salaries	315	298	291	269	257	230	213	213
Other operating expenses	380	367	374	369	372	368	379	386
Fixed expenses	109	109	109	109	109	109	109	109
Total	804	774	754	742	738	707	701	608
Net profit before income tax	216	352	389	420	356	348	337	313

EXHIBIT 5
COMPARATIVE PROFIT AND LOSS STATEMENTS (percentages)

	1974	1973	1972	1971	1970	1969	1968	1967
Sales								
Equipment								
New	35.1	35.0	35.4	34.2	35.9	35.6	35.2	37.1
Rental	7.0	7.0	7.0	6.2	7.5	7.2	6.7	7.2
Used	17.6	18.3	17.5	17.0	16.5	17.3	17.8	17.5
Service								
Customers	2.6	2.5	2.7	2.4	2.8	2.5	2.7	2.7
Other	3.1	3.1	3.3	6.2	3.2	3.1	3.2	3.7
Parts	34.6	34.1	34.1	34.0	34.1	34.3	34.4	31.8
Total	100.0	100.0	100.0	100.0	100.0	100.0	100.0	100.0
Cost of goods sold								
Equipment								
New	31.4	30.5	30.1	29.2	30.5	30.1	30.0	31.8
Rental	6.5	6.5	6.5	6.4	6.8	7.0	6.3	6.5
Used	16.4	16.6	12.8	16.6	16.0	17.2	17.8	17.6
Service	2.8	3.1	3.1	3.0	3.1	3.5	3.8	4.2
Parts	25.8	25.1	25.7	25.6	25.6	24.0	23.5	22.5
Total	82.9	81.8	78.2	80.8	82.0	81.8	81.4	82.6
Gross profit	17.1	18.2	21.8	19.2	18.0	18.2	18.6	17.4
Other expenses								
Wages and salaries	5.4	4.9	4.7	4.2	4.2	4.0	3.9	4.2
Other operating expenses	6.6	6.0	6.0	5.8	6.1	6.3	6.9	7.6
Fixed expenses	1.9	1.8	1.6	1.7	1.8	1.9	2.0	2.1
Total	13.9	12.7	12.3	11.7	12.1	12.2	12.8	13.9
Net profit before income tax	3.2	5.5	9.5	7.5	5.9	6.0	5.8	3.5

EXHIBIT 6
COMPARATIVE BALANCE SHEETS (in thousands)

	1974	1973	1972	1971	1970	1969	1968	1967
Current assets								
Cash	549	567	526	575	538	498	502	478
Receivables	845	874	836	931	875	926	872	799
Inventory	1,751	1,646	1,701	1,662	1,741	1,599	1,638	1,621
Other	72	68	71	47	26	37	49	19
Total current assests	3,223	3,145	3,134	3,215	3,180	3,060	3,061	2,917
Fixed assets	82	89	96	103	110	117	124	131
Total assets	3,305	3,234	3,230	3,318	3,290	3,177	3,185	3,048
Current liabilities	678	698	702	808	825	818	831	824
Notes payable	372	372	372	372	372	372	372	372
Other liabilities	45	11	20	36	50	9	46	23
Stockholders' equity	343	343	343	343	343	343	343	343
Retained earnings	1,867	1,810	1,793	1,759	1,700	1,635	1,593	1,486
Total liabilities	3,305	3,234	3,230	3,318	3,290	3,177	3,185	3,048

Northern Mammoth Equipment Company, Inc.   517

EXHIBIT 7
COMPARATIVE BALANCE SHEETS (percentages)

	1974	1973	1972	1971	1970	1969	1968	1967
Current assets								
Cash	16.6	17.6	16.2	16.9	16.3	15.6	15.7	15.9
Receivables	25.6	26.3	26.0	27.3	26.5	28.7	27.5	26.5
Inventory	53.2	51.3	52.6	51.3	53.1	50.8	51.4	52.8
Other	2.2	2.1	2.2	1.4	.8	1.3	1.5	.6
Total current assets	97.6	97.3	97.0	96.9	96.7	96.4	96.1	95.8
Fixed assets	2.4	2.7	3.0	3.1	3.3	3.6	3.9	4.2
Total assets	100.0	100.0	100.0	100.0	100.0	100.0	100.0	100.0
Current liabilities	20.6	21.8	21.9	24.2	24.7	26.1	26.4	27.2
Notes payable	11.4	11.5	11.5	11.4	11.4	11.5	11.5	12.3
Other liabilities	1.2	—	.1	1.0	1.5	—	1.5	.6
Stockholders' equity	10.3	10.4	10.4	10.3	10.3	10.4	10.4	11.2
Retained earnings	56.5	56.3	56.1	53.1	52.1	51.9	50.2	48.7
Total liabilities	100.0	100.0	100.0	100.0	100.0	100.0	100.0	100.0

EXPORT SALES

In addition to domestic sales, Northern Mammoth exported parts and equipment to the Philippines, Indonesia, Ghana, Mexico, and Guatemala. The company did not keep records of the breakdown of domestic and foreign sales, but estimated that foreign sales accounted for about 50 percent of the company's parts sales. The amount of export sales of equipment was estimated to be about 10 percent of the total equipment sales. These sales were not solicited.

ADVERTISING

As far as other marketing aspects were concerned, Northern Mammoth did a little advertising in trade publications such as *Local Construction*. The total advertising budget ran around $18,000 annually and had not changed much over the years. When Northern Mammoth advertised its main brand, the company received a promotional allowance from the manufacturer, which was set at a maximum of $750 per year. The only other advertising that Northern Mammoth did was to buy a spot in the Yellow Pages of the telephone directory. The management as a whole felt that the main method of promoting the company's products was by personal contact with prospective contractors and with other customers who bought parts from Northern Mammoth.

PRICING

Although the company had manufacturers' suggested retail price lists, it rarely used them except as a starting point for negotiations. Sales contracts were negotiated on an individual basis, and in almost every case a discount was given on the retail price of the new equipment. In many cases, too, an overallowance was given on the equipment that was traded in, and sometimes both discounts and overallowances were given.

However, even with discounts and/or overallowances, Northern Mammoth had a policy of pricing its equipment somewhat higher than its competitors. As Farrell put it: "Our prices are a little higher because we feel that our equipment is of a better quality, and this is what we try to stress to the contractors." In this conjunction Walton added: "Our main products are sort of like the 'Cadillac' of the heavy equipment lines, and most contractors know this. We don't want to sell lower-quality lines."

DISCOUNTS AND CREDIT POLICIES

Sales discounts on new and used equipment varied in size and type with each sale. Sometimes a straight percentage was taken off the list price, or payment periods were lengthened, or both. Since each sale was negotiated independently, the discount depended on what was needed to make the sale. As for parts, no discounts were given except for export sales. In these cases, usually a 5/10/net 30 discount was offered.

As for the credit policies, contracts for new and used equipment were made for each sale. Ordinarily, either Farrell or Walton made an investigation of the credit rating of the potential buyer. Basically, Farrell or Walton checked Dun and Bradstreet reports, the retail credit associations, and the relevant banks. On some occasions the investigator analyzed the buyer's financial statements before making final decisions on granting credit for the purchase; however, there was no set policy. By being quite cautious, the company felt that it had a very low bad-debt loss, averaging approximately .9 percent of total sales, and 6.0 percent of total accounts receivable.

PROFITABILITY

The profit on new and used equipment sales was set by the terms of the negotiation and contract. For new equipment Northern Mammoth tried to make between 12 percent and 24 percent on its main lines, and between 7½ percent and 20 percent on the other lines. Furthermore, Northern Mammoth had specific mark-ups on its parts sales; the mark-ups ranged from 24 percent to 30 percent. Overall, its main line parts accounted for about 65 percent of the total parts sales while the others made up the other 35 percent. In Northern Mammoth's parts department inventory was arranged in two separate divisions, one for the firm's main line and one for the other parts.

Customer Service

Even though its prices were high, Northern Mammoth offered some services specifically designed to assist its customers. Two programs had been instituted in the last few years, the Exchange Component Program, and the Temporary Warehouse Program. Although none of the managers knew what these programs cost, they admitted that the two programs were expensive. They agreed, however, that the programs were justified.

EXCHANGE COMPONENT PROGRAM

Under the Exchange Component Program, if a customer bought a tractor or any other piece of equipment from Northern Mammoth, and the machine broke down in the field, Northern Mammoth would send a boom truck and a team of mechanics to the location to pull out the engine transmission, differential, etc., and replace it with a rebuilt one from the company's inventory. The broken part would then be returned to Northern Mammoth and repaired. The contractor only paid for parts and labor, and kept the rebuilt part that was put in by the team of mechanics. The company would then keep the repaired part. Furthermore, it should be noted that the contractor was not charged for the service call. Wilman felt that the cost to Northern Mammoth to send a boom truck and a team of mechanics out to replace a broken part cost anywhere from $25 to $100, depending on the distance and part(s) replaced.

TEMPORARY WAREHOUSE PROGRAM

The second service, the Temporary Warehouse Program, was essentially a temporary parts warehouse set up at the site of a large construction project if the contractor(s) bought some of Northern Mammoth's equipment. Ordinarily, the warehouse was something like a large trailer with one or two employees from Northern Mammoth operating it. In addition, there were usually two or three field mechanics who moved from one site to another to assist in the repair of any Northern Mammoth equipment.

Both of these services normally were run at a loss but were used to provide "a little extra" for the customers. All the managers seemed quite pleased with the two programs and considered them two of the most important actions they had initiated. As Walton explained: "These two programs are somewhat expensive to the company, but they are needed. We couldn't meet competition without them."

Purchases

Northern Mammoth bought its equipment primarily from Mammoth's plant in Cleveland, Ohio. Mammoth also had set up depot areas across the country. For northern California there were depots in Denver, Portland, Dallas, and Los Angeles. Although Northern Mammoth had made purchases from each of these, it primarily bought from Denver and Los Angeles. These depots for the most part only handled parts, although some equipment was available at times. It should also be noted that Northern Mammoth maintained its own parts warehouses at San Leandro and Arcadia, although both warehouses were quite small.

On the average Northern Mammoth tried to stick to making regular weekly orders, which averaged about $30,000 apiece. Northern Mammoth did not receive discounts on parts or equipment purchases. Although the shipping expenses from Cleveland were prepaid, the shipping expenses from the depots were not. When ordering equipment from Cleveland, Northern Mammoth usually had to wait one month. Delivery from there was most commonly by rail (piggyback). Although the company could order parts from Cleveland, this was done quite infrequently. The parts usually came from one of the depots by a special-order truck. In either case, when the shipments arrived, they were unpacked immediately and inspected for any damages, usually by a member of the parts department.

SPECIAL ORDERS

Because there are so many parts in this type of business, Northern Mammoth did not carry all the parts that were desired by its clients and ran out of parts quite frequently. In these cases they teletyped their orders to one of the depots and usually received delivery within two days. An employee in the parts department stated that the company made special orders on the average of four or five times a day, accounting for approximately 12 percent of its parts purchases. The cost of making a special purchase order like this was the cost of the teletype, a 5 percent emergency charge from the depot, and the extra freight costs since the special order was usually sent by bus or airplane. On the whole, management figured that they lost about 10 percent of their profits on a purchase order of this sort.

REGULAR ORDERING

Since Northern Mammoth did not have a purchasing department, the parts manager signed all the order forms, and he was not held to a maximum limit (dollarwise) on what he could order. Ordinarily, in fact, he was the only one who made out the purchase orders. In most cases Borely tried to order so as to maintain a stock for about ninety days. All purchases were automatically insured by an insurance policy that the company carried.

Inventory

Although sales tended to be highest between May and December, Northern Mammoth kept extra inventory on hand over and above the estimated ninety-day supply during the January to April period. On the average then they tried to maintain a parts inventory valued at approximately $800,000 and an equipment inventory of approximately $1,200,000.

Northern Mammoth carried about 15,000 different parts on hand, which were classified as "active" parts in its parts list system. The firm also handled about 5,000 parts that were "inactive" and not always carried in the supply room. Of the $800,000 in parts, approximately 10 to 15 percent were considered to be either extremely slow-moving or obsolete. Some of this inventory included specially ordered parts that were not used and could not be returned (specially ordered goods could not be returned at any time). All the extremely slow-moving and obsolete parts were kept in a loft above the actual supply room. A few of these parts were used occasionally in repairing old machines. However, since the management did not feel that it needed the extra space, no attempt had been made to dispose of these parts. Furthermore, the management did not know whether the parts could be sold.

INVENTORY CONTROL

Inventory control was handled primarily by the parts manager, but occasionally Walton assisted in this area. All inventory was kept on file by the use of a Cardex file. Each active part type, minimum and maximum quantities to keep on hand, and the actual amount on hand, were listed on a card. Although this system gave a rough idea as to how much inventory was on hand, Northern Mammoth only made one actual inventory count per year. It was estimated by Walton that it cost Northern Mammoth about $8,000 per month to maintain its inventory-control system.

PILFERAGE

Although the management did not make allowances for pilferage, the losses due to it were thought to be considerable. As one employee stated: "A lot of these parts and tools can be used on cars and other trucks. This place gets robbed of everything from neon light filaments to engine parts." Management had caught several of its mechanics stealing in the past and in most cases had fired them.

Assessment

In assessing the company over its sixteen years, Walton felt that on the whole Northern Mammoth had been fairly successful: "Sales have been somewhat steady except for 1972, 1973, and 1974. The factory representatives complain that we don't have enough penetration into different market areas, but the companies we buy from don't always have the size of equipment that the contractors need, and we do not do any product research and development ourselves."

Another member of the management team felt that Northern Mammoth could do considerably better if the factory left them alone. He stated: "They have training schools for each department, and they make us use various accounting forms that just don't fit into our operations. The representatives are always coming around and questioning us. If they would let us run the company the way we want to, we would be much better off."

Although the company had to use specified accounting procedures, other managers did not feel that the factory was being overly domineering. The general consensus was that Northern Mammoth had done reasonably well, but that the management didn't know what actions it should take to increase sales and profitability.

Assignment

1. Suggest a reorganization for Northern Mammoth Equipment. Explain each of your major organizational changes in terms of the areas of shortcoming or needed improvement that you perceive.

Building Components and Specialties*

Building Components & Specialties (BCS) is a combination sales agency, warehouse, fabricator, and wholesaler for the specialty items required in the building business in large construction. Their customers are contractors and general contractors. Their major lines are toilet partitions, hollow metal partitions, office partitions, and folding doors and walls. Some smaller lines consist of door hardware, bathroom accessories, rolling steel, and some wood specialties (for example, racquetball doors). The company employs twenty-one people and has been in existence for twenty-two years.

The building parts are manufactured by the firms they represent. Shipments are either direct to the customer's job site, if so instructed by BCS, or else directly to the BCS company for further fabrication, or installation, or storage. It will also make "take-off" bids to furnish general contractors being considered for a large contract. Blueprints from the contract being considered are secured and products that BCS supplies are "taken off," priced, and submitted to those contractors. Material is usually shipped and billed directly by the contractors to their customers. BCS is reimbursed by the contractors. Generally, about 50 percent of BCS's sales are from take-offs.

History

The company started in an office building where it existed as a sales agency for hollow metal specialty items and toilet partitions. In the back of this building was their warehouse. Also attached to this building was another shop, which they leased to a company called Partitions and Specialties. In 1960 BCS moved into the same building as Partitions and Specialties. Some

---

* Prepared by Milton Leontiades.

years later, the two companies merged and assumed the name Building Components & Specialties.

Operating Problems

In 1973–74 BCS had a serious cash-flow problem because an accountant embezzled a large sum of money and placed the corporation deeply in debt. Since that time, several key positions in the company have been filled with new personnel. Now the company finds itself in what appears to be a profitable and expanding position, but it is still faced with a high amount of debt. This debt has required a tight monitoring of expenditures and has contributed to continuing cash-flow problems.

The president of BCS, Mr. Andrew Don, finally decided to hire an outside consulting firm to review the company's operations and provide him with recommendations. His primary concern was to establish a means of projecting cash flows so he could better balance cash inflows with expenses and fixed payments and also manage his short-term borrowings more efficiently.

Consulting Firm's Preliminary Review

After an initial meeting with Mr. Don, the Acme Consulting firm did not immediately agree to a study of BCS's cash-flow situation. Mr. Max Sporer, the manager of the consulting team, felt more might be involved in a proper solution to Mr. Don's problems than could be achieved by focusing on the single aspect of cash flow. With Mr. Don's approval Mr. Sporer spent two days conducting a brief review of the major departments at BCS. He talked to each manager of the company for at least a few minutes. Based on this introductory look at the company, Mr. Sporer decided to concentrate his consulting team's attention in three areas: cash flow, organization, and internal controls.

Major Findings for a Cash-Flow Analysis

In order to begin the review of BCS's cash-flow situation, it was necessary to look at prior sales figures. From historical data, Mr. Sporer thought to develop a formula for estimating future monthly or weekly sales volumes. If sales levels could be forecast, commissions and other expenses and payments could then be estimated and deducted, and the consultants would have a basis for cost control (cash-flow analysis) rather easily implemented into the accounting system. Mr. Don supplied the consultants with a sample

EXHIBIT 1
BUDGET (OPERATING EXPENSES)

	Monthly Expenses
Payroll (tax included)	$14,135
Travel expense	400
Hauling expense	400
Officers expense	800
Truck expense	500
Advertising expense	500
Utilities	600
Telephone	1,000
Legal and professional	500
Postage	120
Office supplies	200
Estimating services	500
Repairs and maintenance	60
Interest	400
Blue Cross	150
Direct mortgage	1,800
Pioneer mortgage	575
Insurance	1,000
Real estate taxes	542
Payment on borrowings	750
Total	$25,032

of monthly expenses, as shown in Exhibit 1, exclusive of salesmen's commissions.

Unfortunately, the company was not able to furnish consistent sales data over a sufficient time period to assure a statistically high reliability in the results. However, based on lengthy discussions with Mr. Don, Mr. Sporer felt that the available data were indicative of prior trends and, for the purposes of a trial approach to the cash-flow problem, would be adequate. In order to provide a built-in check on the results, Mr. Sporer decided to use three different approaches to estimate future sales, based on data from weekly sales, billings, and from erection contracts.

WEEKLY SALES AND BILLINGS

Weekly sales figures gave the total sales for the week. There was no breakdown on the sales figures as to product type, and assembling these data from

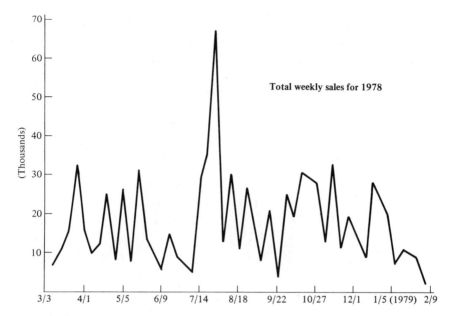

Total weekly sales for 1978

EXHIBIT 2
TOTAL WEEKLY SALES FOR 1978

invoices proved to be extremely difficult because of poor record keeping. Many of BCS's bids require little effort other than an administrative order. BCS makes the sale and notifies the appropriate manufacturer. Goods are shipped to contractors or their customers straight from the manufacturer's factory and BCS is not required to make any kind of cash outlay. Since this type of transaction avoids warehousing or inventory of goods, sales tend to coincide fairly closely with customers' billings.

On review of recorded weekly sales for 1978, the consulting team found a very erratic pattern of transactions from month to month (see Exhibit 2). With average monthly sales equal to about $26,000 and a standard deviation of $15,000, it was obvious that no simple least-squares trend line could capture the randomness of the fluctuations in weekly sales. Also, the coefficient of correlation was an extremely low .12.

Because the consulting team had only one year's history of recorded sales available, it was unable to test for seasonality of the data. However, two years' billing data were available, and since billings and recorded sales were roughly comparable, weekly billings were graphed to test for a consistent pattern of seasonality. As indicated by Exhibit 3, the data for 1977 and 1978 reflected the same manner of random fluctuations within years as

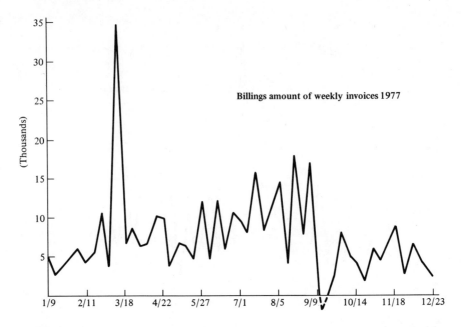

EXHIBIT 3A
BILLINGS AMOUNT AT INVOICE 1977

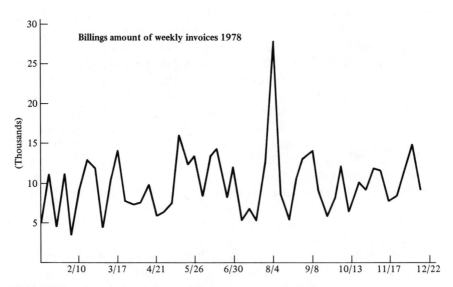

EXHIBIT 3B
BILLINGS AMOUNT OF WEEKLY INVOICES 1978

in sales, and there was no apparent similarity of seasonality trends from year to year. For example, in 1977 a sharp peak in billings occurred in March, and a sharp decline in mid-September. For 1978 only the first week in August was an abnormally high billing period, with random fluctuations for the rest of the year. From conversations with Mr. Don, it seemed that there was nothing about 1977 or 1978 to cause him to term their sales or billing patterns different from those of prior years.

ERECTION CONTRACTS

In an effort to find an alternate predictor to sales, the consulting team also looked at erection contracts. Perhaps, they speculated, the actual installation of fixtures could provide a more consistent pattern of activity. As Exhibit 4 shows, this was not the case. If anything, the variation in installations in 1977 and 1978 was more volatile than either sales or billings, and just as random.

Organization

The second consulting work team was in charge of reviewing organizational structure and internal controls. An initial step in their analysis was to develop an organizational chart (Exhibit 5) and a work-flow chart (Exhibit 6).

The organizational structure of BCS consists of six departments reporting directly to the president. The major activities under each functional department are shown along with the number of employees in Exhibit 5. A review of the responsibilities of each department follows.

SALES

The Sales Department consists of an in-office team and a road team, each with two salesmen. The president of BCS is also one of the in-office salespeople. In fact, he is by far the most productive member of the total sales force. Even though he is occupied with major operations of the business, the president accounts for 60 percent of the in-house sales volume, which itself accounts for 90 percent of the sales volume of the company.

As a former salesman and with close personal contacts among many of the company's major customers, Mr. Don finds selling a natural and enjoyable activity. However, Mr. Don is seldom able to pursue selling in a methodical, day-to-day fashion. He is continuously interrupted by emergencies requiring his attention. Consequently he is only intermittently selling. But when he is selling the sales figures for the company tend to reflect it. He is so good at sales, in fact, that other members of the sales organization tend to follow his example. When he does well, so do they.

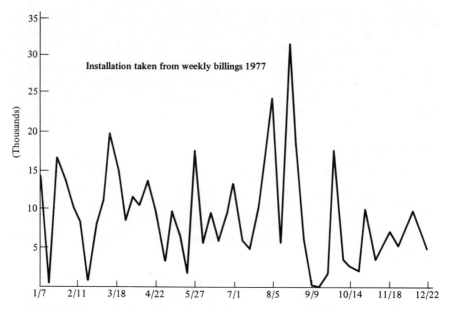

EXHIBIT 4A
INSTALLATION TAKEN FROM WEEKLY BILLINGS 1977

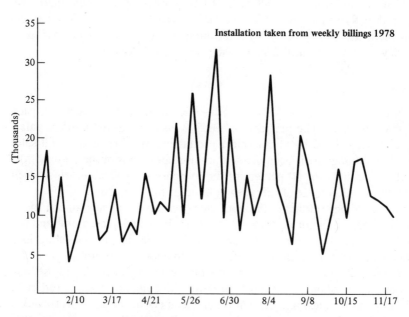

EXHIBIT 4B
INSTALLATION TAKEN FROM WEEKLY BILLINGS 1978

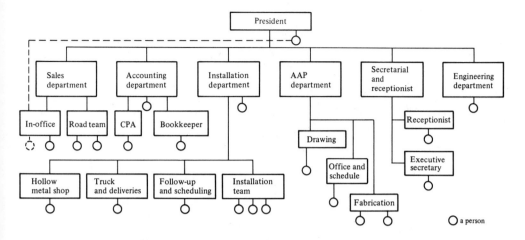

EXHIBIT 5
BCS's ORGANIZATIONAL CHART

ENGINEERING DEPARTMENT

The Engineering Department employs one man. He communicates back and forth directly with the Sales Department. He is responsible for "taking off" dimensions and specifications of jobs put out for general bid.

SECRETARIAL AND RECEPTION DEPARTMENT

The Secretarial and Reception Department helps channel the work to be processed through the company. There is a receptionist and an executive secretary. The executive secretary makes the decisions on whether to route customer orders to the AAP (see next section), or Installation Department, or to order directly from the factory of the manufacturers' products being ordered.

ASSORTED ARCHITECTURAL PRODUCTS (AAP)

If a job becomes an order and requires fabrication it is turned over to Assorted Architectural Products. The AAP Department is responsible for special fabricating work on parts shipped from factories as well as for small in-house jobs. The Drawing Unit sets up the job for approval by the customer (contractor or general contractor). The order is then scheduled for fabrication. After completion, the job is either picked up by the customer or delivered by the Truck and Deliveries Division.

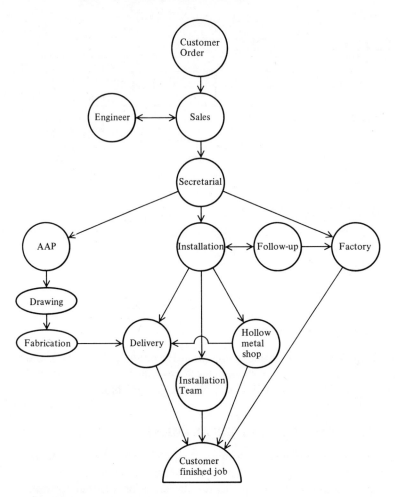

EXHIBIT 6
WORK-FLOW CHART

INSTALLATION DEPARTMENT

In the Installation Department the work is segregated into various operations as follows:

(a) *The Hollow Metal Shop:* One of the many product lines (Hollow Metal) is warehoused and modified in this shop. The work done here is either shipped to the customer through Truck and Deliveries or picked up by the customer. One man works in this shop.

(*b*) *Truck and Deliveries Division:* This unit is responsible for the shipment of products coming from AAP and the Hollow Metal Shop. Also, some minor other deliveries are made. The picking up of warehouse stock from the factory is also their responsibility.

(*c*) *Installation Team:* This unit installs the products for the customer.

These operations employ five all-purpose personnel interchangeably. In addition there is:

(*d*) *Follow-Up and Scheduling:* This activity employs one person to follow all jobs as they go through the various stages of fabrication by outside manufacturers.

These four operations of the Installation Department are controlled by one supervisor, who maintains the flow of work done by the entire department. The supervisor answers directly to the president of the company.

At present the Installation Department determines the level of work flow through the plant. That is, it can handle only a fixed flow of work with present staffing and procedures and tends normally to operate at full capacity. When large backlogs or rush orders arise, customers' deliveries are stretched out and customers' complaints increase.

ACCOUNTING DEPARTMENT

The Accounting Department has three employees. The accountant controls the Accounting Department and channels the money coming into and being paid out of BCS. The bookkeeper, who is subordinate to the accountant, posts to the general ledger, posts to subsidiary ledger cards, balances accounts, and does other work provided by the accountant. The CPA, who comes in monthly to oversee the operations of the Accounting Department, is hired to organize or set up the books, take care of unusual transactions, do quarterly reports and yearly financial statements, and the like. The CPA answers to the president, but in an informal way. His work is part of the accounting function and is prepared by the accountant.

Billing figures are supplied to the Accounting Department by the departments that complete the work in either AAP or the Installation Department. In analyzing the weekly billing statements, roughly three-fourths of the billings originate from the Installation Department and the remaining one-fourth are from the AAP Department.

Internal Control

BCS employs a manual internal control system developed by the Safeguard Business System. It is unique because it has several built-in safeguards against normal accounting errors, such as transposing numbers and erroneous entries. A clipboard is set up to hold the individual journal sheets. On top of the journal sheets are placed the accounts receivable/payable ledger cards. On top of these ledger cards are placed a page of checks, if the accounts payable account is being used. All these forms are locked into position. When a person writes on the top card, the printing is carboned through to the under sheets. This process cuts down transposition errors by two-thirds. When the summary columns on the journal are added, they can be checked right on the sheet by simply adding certain totals together and proving them with another column. At the end of the month, all totals are added, checked, and posted to their proper accounts in the general ledger. This work is done by the bookkeeper.

The trial balance for the month is made up by the accountant. Having two people work on the books acts as a safeguard over the accounts. A third check over the accounts takes place when the CPA okays the monthly balance of the books. Accounts receivables are figured by the accountant, then given to the front receptionist, who types up the invoices, mails them to the customers, and gives a copy of the invoice to both the accountant and the president. When customer payments come in the mail, they are received by the executive secretary. She makes a copy of all checks and disburses the originals to the accountant and the copies to the president. A total of accounts receivable is maintained and compared monthly by the accountant and the president. Cash receipts are handled in almost the same way.

The internal control over accounts payable is much different from accounts receivable, and must be broken down into sections. Because accounts payable originates from the receipt of goods, the best type of internal control is the segregation of the ordering, receiving, and payment functions. The company is not large enough to have separate departments for these functions, so the work is broken down as follows:

1. Stock of hollow metal, toilet partitions, and hardware is chiefly ordered by the Sales Department, received by the warehouses, and paid for by the Accounting Department. Credit limitations with the factories are set up by the president and maintained by the Accounting Department. Payment of these liabilities is authorized by the officers of the corporation.

2. Materials inventories needed for the production work done in AAP get a special consideration. Materials are ordered by jobs. The amount is figured in the pricing of the job by the salesman, broken down and ordered by the shop supervisor, and totals are reviewed and okayed by the president. The president also authorizes the payment of this liability. The actual checks are again authorized and reviewed by the officers of the corporation as a safeguard.

3. Office supplies are ordered by the executive secretary, received and inventoried by the receptionist, and paid for through the Accounting Department. A small amount of these supplies is paid for out of petty cash, which is kept by the executive secretary.

4. Truck repairs, tools, paint, small parts, and so forth are ordered by the supervisor of the Installation Department. The various persons under the supervisor receive the items and control the usage of them. Sometimes, the installation team, Hollow Metal Shop, and Truck and Deliveries Division get special permission to buy materials and necessities as they need them. When this happens, the transactions are reviewed by the installation supervisor. Payment of these liabilities is made by the Accounting Department with proper authorization and approval by the officers of the company.

5. Petty cash, a commonly abused part of internal control, is an extremely small fund controlled by a trusted employee.

Conclusion

Mr. Sporer felt he now had sufficient information to make specific recommendations to Mr. Don, president of BCS, on improving the business. Although Mr. Sporer would have liked more time to delve more deeply into some of the departments and ask additional questions of the managers, he realized that consultants seldom have unlimited time and unlimited information.

Questions

1. What do you see as major problems in the areas of (*a*) development of a cash-flow technique, (*b*) organization, and (*c*) internal controls?

2. What recommendations would you make if you were Max Sporer?

ACQUISITIONS, LIQUIDATIONS, DIVERSIFICATION, AND CHANGE

Garden State Press, Inc.*

"Basically, Ken, the key to our continued success lies not just in improving our present techniques and approaches but also in being able to convert these methods into a way of increasing sales in new geographical areas. If we sit still, we probably won't lose money — our market share attests this — but by the same token, we aren't going to improve profits with static sales."

"I agree one hundred percent with you, Joe, but to risk our present position by acquiring a troublemaker may create more headaches than it's worth. They've been losing money for the last two and one-half years, their labor staff turned over four times in sixteen months, and their reputation is rapidly deteriorating. I think Longhorn Printers would be a mistake, but I'll take the time to look into it further. They turned us down twice before while they were making money and they *have had* a number of other offers. Who knows? Maybe we could turn it around, but I have my doubts. However, I'll talk to them and get back to you as soon as possible."

Joseph R. Schwab, president and chairman of the board of Garden State Press, Inc., and Kenneth Whilt, vice-president of finance, have worked closely together since Ken's arrival four years ago and have nurtured sales growth from $14 million to an expected high by the end of the year of nearly $45 million, with projected sales through the next four years to peak at $60 million. However, Joe and Ken's interest in Longhorn Printers has had its ups and downs over the past three years. Ken's concern is that acquiring a nearly bankrupt company may strain Garden State's strong financial picture. Joe, however, believes that his strong management team could turn this operation around with increased sales and profits in future years. The difficulty is that even if Longhorn agrees to sell, it may be difficult to persuade the Board of Directors of the worth of the acquisition.

---

* Prepared by Milton Leontiades.

History and Background

Garden State Press, Inc., almost forty years old, is engaged in the graphic arts industry, including the printing of textbook covers, some periodical and catalogue printing, and commercial printing, with corporate and factory operations based in New Jersey. In addition, Garden State owns five factories in Pennsylvania as well as three subsidiaries as far away as Chicago.

The company is organized under divisional lines with the Graphics Division and the Packaging Division being the two major areas of concentration. Garden State's graphic division performs commercial printing of advertising brochures, pamphlets, direct-mail advertising, literature for pharmaceuticals, and other products. Using mostly a lithographic process, they maintain a complement of modern sheet-fed, web-fed, automatic silk-screen process, and other automatic equipment, which, together with certain production procedures and techniques developed over the years, enables them to produce consistently high-quality multicolored printing in minimum periods of time. A corporate sales group established four years ago promotes sales of commercial printing either directly with the customer or through an advertising agency. Garden State Press has 450 clients; ten are large. The loss of any one of these ten clients would not affect ongoing operations.

Supporting the primary effort of this division is Garden State's ability to produce multicolor textbook covers, which it has done effectively for thirteen years. Over this time, annual cover production has increased to the multimillion unit level, so that they are producing about one out of every four textbook covers in the country. Garden State has the facilities and capacity to produce the complete book for a publisher except that it has no equipment for binding the books.

Over the next few years the unit volume of books is expected to increase moderately with above-average gains in trade paperbound books, mail-order publications, and college and post-secondary textbooks. This increase, with Garden State's modern technological printing and composing processes, should expand Garden State's business in the publishing market.

Further, supplementing the well-rounded commercial graphics division is the so-called "free fall" advertising, which consists of printed sections in newspapers usually treated as supplements, and may or may not contain a perforated return postcard for response mailing. This technique is made possible by web-fed presses and is located solely in a subsidiary, Garden State/Lincoln Printing, Inc.

Eight years ago Garden State entered into the packaging industry with the acquisition of the Coda P. Yates Co., Inc. This division is engaged in the business of designing, manufacturing, and selling all types of set-up boxes, folding cartons, blister packaging, labeling and packaging services. These areas are tied in closely with the graphic arts departments. Overall, compe-

EXHIBIT 1
FIVE-YEAR SUMMARY OF DIVISIONAL RESULTS

Sales	Current year	Last year	Previous year	Previous year	Previous year
Graphics	86%	79%	78%	73%	74%
Packaging Division	14%	21%	22%	27%	26%

Pre-Tax Income					
Graphics Division	113%	112%	110%	99%	104%
Packaging Division	(13%)	(12%)	(10%)	1%	(4%)

tition from within this industry is keen and sales and profits have declined over the last two years, as indicated in Exhibit 1.

Garden State's over 800 employees are nonunion and have never suffered labor problems. Longevity of management, coupled with good benefits including pension and profit-sharing plans, made this an attractive and stable place of employment.

Garden State Press's Financial Condition

The Graphics Division of Garden State is profitable in all its aspects — commercial printing, publishing market, free-fall and direct-response advertising matter. This has resulted in an increase in sales of 9.3 percent over last year. The profitability of this division has apparently resulted from Garden State's effort to serve almost all markets of the graphics industry by its acquisition of subsidiaries and companies that complement the Graphics Division. For example, the purchase of Garden State/Lincoln Printing, Inc., now a subsidiary, about three years ago has opened up to Garden State Press the direct-response and free-fall advertising market, a market that has added significantly to the sales of Garden State. The year Garden State/Lincoln Printing, Inc. was acquired, total sales for Garden State increased 32.6 percent over the previous year's sales. Expected commercial printing shipments in markets served by the Graphics Division are estimated to increase in line with the industry.

Since Garden State is a growing company, it has not paid dividends on common stock for five years in order to conserve cash for internal growth through equipment acquisition and modernization of techniques and machinery. The dividend policy is also needed to maintain enough working capital to operate an expanding company.

Financial statements of Garden State's balance sheet, income, and sources and uses of funds statements are shown in Exhibits 2, 3, and 4.

EXHIBIT 2
GARDEN STATE PRESS, INC., AND SUBSIDIARIES,
CONSOLIDATED BALANCE SHEET, DECEMBER 31
(000s omitted)

Assets	*Last year*	*Current year*
Current:		
Cash	$ 1,007	$ 1,005
Receivables	7,294	7,135
Refundable federal income taxes	288	
Inventories	2,803	3,622
Prepaid expenses and other receivables	159	140
Property held for sale	147	1,372
Total current assets	$11,699	$13,274
Net property and equipment	8,222	9,397
Property held for sale	2,035	417
Goodwill	345	345
Deposits and miscellaneous	260	178
Total non-current assets	10,862	10,337
Total assets	$22,560	$23,612

Liabilities		
Current liabilities:		
Notes payable and current maturities of long-term debt	$ 962	$ 584
Accounts, etc. payable	3,416	4,332
Income taxes	78	577
Total current liabilities	4,456	5,493
Long-term debt	7,698	6,767
Deferred income taxes	738	821
Total	8,436	7,588

continued

EXHIBIT 2 *continued*

Stockholders' equity	Last year	Current year
Preferred stock (Class A and B, 6% cumulative, no par value — shares authorized, 50,000, outstanding, 804)	100	100
Common stock (no par value — shares authorized, 2,000,000, issued 849,438 and 828,104)	136	133
Additional paid-in capital	3,834	3,753
Retained earnings	5,609	6,628
Total stockholders' equity	9,679	10,615
Less treasury stock, at cost, 3,500 and 14,100 common stock	(12)	(84)
Net stockholders' equity	9,667	10,531
Total liabilities and equity	$22,560	$23,612

Note: Figures used may not be 100% accurate because of rounding.
Additional Data for Current Year:

Accumulated depreciation, including current year	$5,301,000
Depreciation and amortization expenses	799,000
Current portion of long-term debt	584,000
Total rental expense	722,000

Significant Acquisitions

ELCOMP

Acquired ten years ago by Garden State Press, Inc. Located in New Jersey, Elcomp can electronically set type for composition needs of the publishing industry for school textbooks; has contracts with many government agencies to electronically typeset several large-volume pieces; and has the capability of on-line terminals connecting the publisher to Elcomp's computer for feeding in manuscripts and editing before and during composition (although Elcomp has not yet connected up with any publishers).

CODA YATES

Acquired eight years ago by Garden State Press, Inc. Also located in New Jersey, Coda Yates is currently the packaging division of Garden State Press, Inc. It provides packaging and labeling services. Products are mainly

EXHIBIT 3
GARDEN STATE PRESS, INC., AND SUBSIDIARIES,
STATEMENT OF INCOME, FIVE-YEAR RECORD
(000s omitted)

	Previous year	Previous year	Previous year	Last year	Current year
Net sales	$22,546	$24,580	$32,591	$35,783	$39,125
Cost of sales	17,091	18,093	24,774	27,053	29,235
Selling and administrative expenses	3,971	4,846	5,652	6,534	7,355
Operating income	1,483	1,640	2,164	2,197	2,534
Other (expenses) income	171	138	(6)	(621)	(102)
Interest	154	177	502	628	637
Income taxes	737	775	771	321	745
Net income	763	826	885	625	1,051
Previous retained earnings	2,628	3,391	4,169	5,050	5,609
Preferred dividends		48	5	6	6
Retired common shares				60	26
Retained earnings	3,391	4,169	5,050	5,609	6,628
Earnings per common share	$.73	$.86	$1.00	$.74	$1.26
Weighted average number of common shares outstanding (total shares)	961,357	939,467	875,912	840,438	828,104

Note: Figures used may not be 100% accurate due to rounding.

sold to pharmaceutical companies, which use them for samples for doctors. Sometimes Garden State supplies the design for the customer's product. When this is done, the Graphics Division produces the prints to appear on the label of the product and the written inserts that go inside the product. The Packaging Division was consolidated from four facilities into one two years ago.

SPECTRUM, INC.

Acquired six years ago by Garden State; now a subsidiary located in Illinois. It produces color separations for Garden State Press, Inc. and other companies. Color separations are used in the preparation of negatives and plates for multicolor offset printing.

EXHIBIT 4
GARDEN STATE PRESS, INC., STATEMENT OF SOURCES
AND USES OF FUNDS, CURRENT YEAR
(000s omitted)

Sources

Net income		$1,051
Decreases in working capital:		
Cash	$ 2	
Receivables	159	
Refundable income taxes	288	
Prepaid expenses and other receivables	19	
Increase in other liabilities	1,415	
Total decrease in working capital		1,883
Decrease in property held for sale		1,618
Decrease in deposits and miscellaneous		82
Decrease in deferred income tax		83
Total sources of funds		4,717

Uses

Increases in working capital:		
Inventories	819	
Property held for sale	1,225	
Decrease in current liabilities	378	
Total increase in working capital		2,422
Increase in net property and equipment		1,175
Decrease in long-term debt		931
Decrease in capital stock		3
Decrease in additional paid-in capital		81
Addition to treasury stock		72
Dividends paid on preferred stock		6
Total uses of funds		4,690
Increase (decrease) in working capital		$ 27

GARDEN STATE/LINCOLN PRINTING, INC.

Acquired three years ago; a subsidiary in Illinois. All Garden State's web presses are located here and produce free-fall and direct-response advertising. Garden State consolidated their two web press facilities last year into one location in Illinois. The acquisition boosted Garden State's sales considerably.

Potential Acquisition of Longhorn Printers

Longhorn Printers, Inc., a Houston, Texas, based printer, is the oldest financial and legal printer in the growing southwest market. It can produce a large variety of briefs, financial printing, and legal documents. It has many "established" customers. Owned by a multimillionaire Texas oilman, Longhorn has suffered from apparent management negligence. Because of the president's frequent absence because of his involvement on the boards of a number of national companies, thirty vice-presidents operate their respective departments to maintain ongoing operations.

Longhorn's strength has been in their reputation for high-quality service and this quality is enhanced by an ability to handle large orders; as evidenced by a national television magazine account for which they print about 1.25 million copies a week for shipment to six states. In addition, they also have a complete mailing facility, which is of great interest to firms that have expressed interest in Longhorn.

All of Longhorn's more than 200-man labor force is unionized and has been a source of some problems over the years, with production ceasing for six months early this year due to a strike. Most of their operating equipment is old but usable, and their web-fed and sheet-fed presses allow for the production of free-fall advertising supplements. In addition, they have a bindery, typesetting equipment, hot metal composing room for financial printing, as well as a creative art department.

In recent years sales have vacillated, resulting in losing many customers due to Longhorn's weak financial position and poor performance. Longhorn has $4,379,000 in net operating loss carry-forwards available to offset future taxable income. Contributing to this loss carry-forward was the closing of Longhorn's Dallas-based plant in November of the current year.

Longhorn's current sales for the fiscal year were $10,854,000 with a pretax loss of $3,525,000. This loss greatly increased last year's pretax loss of $854,000. The loss was attributed to a strike, lack of efficient management and quality control, a high turnover of employees, and unprofitable operations of the Dallas facility that was closed November of the past current fiscal year. From the income statement for the past five years (Exhibit 5), Longhorn shows profits for the first two years but increasing losses for the last three years.

Sales growth projected for the industry next year and the following year is 11 percent and 10 percent respectively. The sales growth projected for the industry over the subsequent eight years is about 9 percent. Since Longhorn Printers, Inc. is a struggling company, it would probably only increase sales by 9 percent for the first two years after acquisition and in line with the industry growth thereafter (for comparison of Garden State with the printing industry see Exhibit 7).

EXHIBIT 5
LONGHORN PRINTERS, INC., BALANCE SHEET,
DECEMBER 31, CURRENT YEAR
(000s omitted)

Assets

Current	$1,940
Fixed *	3,100
Total assets	$5,040

Liabilities

Current liabilities	$5,053
Long-term debt	812
Total liabilities	5,865

Stockholders' equity

Capital stock	40
Retained earnings	(865)
Total stockholders' equity	(825)
Total liabilities and stockholders' equity	$5,040

* Fair market value of fixed assets: $3,326

LONGHORN PRINTERS, INC., STATEMENT OF INCOME,
FIVE-YEAR RECORD
(000s omitted)

	Previous year	Previous year	Previous year	Last year	Current year
Sales	$10,553	$11,325	$10,542	$14,271	$10,854
Profit (loss) on operations	1,196	952	(121)	(338)	(2,975)
Interest expense	242	334	481	516	550
Pretax profit (loss)	954	618	(602)	(854)	(3,525)

Based on Garden State management's belief that revenues will equal expenses in the second year if the acquisition takes place, it projects a pretax loss in the first year of acquisition of half of the current year's pretax loss

EXHIBIT 6
HORIZONTAL AND VERTICAL ANALYSIS, GARDEN STATE PRESS, INC., COMPARED WITH INDUSTRY, BALANCE SHEET
(000s omitted)

Assets	Last year	Garden State %	Industry average %	Current year	Garden State %	Industry average %	Garden State increase/decrease	Garden State increase/decrease %
Cash and equivalents	$ 1,007	4.5	7.4	$ 1,005	4.3	5.6	(2)	(.2)
Accts and notes rec.	7,294	32.3	28.6	7,135	30.2	32.5	(159)	(2.2)
Inventories	2,803	12.4	15.0	3,622	15.3	16.2	819	29.2
All other current	594	2.6	1.3	1,512	6.4	.4	918	154.5
Total current	11,699	51.9	52.3	13,274	56.2	54.6	1,575	13.5
Fixed assets	8,222	36.4	42.7	9,397	39.8	40.2	1,175	14.3
Intangibles	345	1.5		345	1.5	2.6	0	0
All other non-current	2,295	10.2	5.0	595	2.5	2.7	(1,700)	(74.1)
Total	$22,560	100.0	100.0	$23,612	100.0	100.0	1,052	4.7

Liabilities and equity

	Last year	Garden State %	Industry average %	Current year	Garden State %	Industry average %	Garden State increase/decrease	Garden State increase/decrease %
Notes payable—short-term and current maturing long-term debt	$ 962	4.3	4.6	$ 584	2.5	4.0	(378)	(39.3)
Accts and notes payable (trade)	3,416	15.1	11.5	4,332	18.3	9.7	916	26.8
Accrued expenses	78	.3	7.6	577	2.4	8.0	499	639.7
All other current	—	—	—	—	—	1.3	—	
Total current	4,456	19.8	23.7	5,493	23.3	22.9	1,037	23.3
Long-term debt	7,698	34.1	22.8	6,767	28.6	16.4	(931)	(12.1)
All other non-current	738	3.3	—	821	3.5	3.1	83	11.2
Net worth	9,667	42.9	53.4	10,531	44.6	57.6	864	8.9
Total liabilities and net worth	$22,560	100.0	100.0	$23,612	100.0	100.0	1,052	4.7

EXHIBIT 7
PRETAX INCOME ESTIMATED FOR LONGHORN,
ASSUMING ACQUISITION
(000s omitted)

Current and years ahead	Pretax income as a % of sales	Pretax income estimated
Current		($3,525)
1	(14.9%)	($1,763)
2	0	0
3	2%	281
4	3%	460
5	5%	835
6	7%	1,274
7	7%	1,389
8	7%	1,514
9	7%	1,650
10	7%	1,799

($3,525,000) and zero pretax loss in the second year. A further prediction is that by the sixth year pretax income will return to 7 percent of sales, which is average for the industry. These are believed to be conservative predictions based on Garden State's previous experience with acquiring companies. Calculations for pretax income as a percentage of sales are shown in Exhibit 6.

Conclusion

Two weeks later at an executive committee meeting, Ken brings up his discussions with Longhorn Printers. "They are definitely ready to sell and are pleased by our continued interest in them. However, they appear to be in worse shape now than they were when we spoke to them last. Refer to their current ratio and you'll see what I mean. Their sales have fallen and their management staff gives you every impression that they don't know what's going on. In their favor, however, is that they have gotten that labor problem under control and their methods and techniques, especially their web-fed presses, could be a definite asset for us in that part of the country. Even taking this into account, I still maintain that we will be buying trouble.

"As far as the cost to us is concerned, they are looking to get $1.2577 per share for the 97% shares held by their president and $1.00 per share for the remaining. There are 40,000 total outstanding shares. This, of course, is over and above the assumption of their total liabilities. As far as projected figures are concerned, we estimate the cost of acquisition (auditing fees, filing costs, etc.) to be $163,000 plus a minimum investment of $1.5 million for working capital and $300,000 spread evenly over three years starting from the date of acquisition for refurbishing of equipment and other additions. Of particular concern to their president was that he was forced to personally sign for $3 million in notes for the company, which explains why they are ready to sell. If we make the acquisition, we would project Longhorn's expenses to equal revenues after the second year with our projected total sales to meet $80,000,000 by the fourth year after acquisition. For the most part, it doesn't look like a bad deal, but it is my belief that it could cost us our shirt in the long run."

"Ken, your points are well taken," Joe remarked, "but right now I think the committee will agree that we would be wise to hire a third-party consulting firm to evaluate them more closely and objectively. I maintain we would be well served by Longhorn, and it certainly would expand our operations; but for the moment, let's look into a consulting firm."

Assignment

1.   Assume that you are the consultant hired by Garden State. What is your recommendation on the acquisition of Longhorn Printers? Support your answer.

Hershey Foods Corporation*

Hershey Foods is best known for its candy and confectionery business. The Hershey candy bar may be the most identifiable candy-bar brand to youngsters and adults alike. Headquartered in Hershey, Pennsylvania, the company in 1978 had revenues of nearly three-quarters of a billion dollars and employed approximately 8,100 people. Known as a basically conservative company, Hershey Foods didn't even advertise until 1969. However, during the last few years, Hershey has developed a more aggressive attitude, highlighted by a diversification strategy designed to lessen its dependence on the traditional chocolate and confectionery business. As part of this overall aim, the Hershey Foods Corporation acquired The Friendly Ice Cream Corp. in early 1979. This action marked a significant new direction for Hershey, in the size and type of acquisition, and provided tangible evidence of Hershey's interest in fulfilling its diversification strategy.

New Management and New Direction for Hershey Foods

Hershey's current diversification and development effort is the handiwork of Hershey's chief executive officer, William E. C. Dearden. Effective March 1, 1976, Dearden was appointed vice-chairman and chief executive officer of Hershey Foods. Simultaneously, Richard A. Zimmerman was made chief operating officer. Harold S. Mohler continued as chairman of the board and chairman of the Executive Committee.

Although these management changes signaled a significant realignment in the company's top ranks, the new members were hardly strangers to Hershey Foods. Dearden joined Hershey as assistant to the chairman of the board in 1957 and had worked his way up to group vice-president in 1971,

---

* Prepared by Milton Leontiades.

548

and to chief executive officer in 1976. Zimmerman joined Hershey in 1958 and had a similar career up the various organizational levels at Hershey. Mohler traces his association with Hershey back to 1948.

During 1976 this new management team required its senior managers to reexamine and evaluate each of the business units of Hershey. Based on an analysis of the company's strengths and weaknesses, Hershey strengthened its top-management echelons, from within and without, and developed a clear set of objectives for the company based on the overriding corporate policy of becoming a "major, diversified, international food and food-related company."

In order to implement this overall statement, Hershey mapped out four separate but related strategies:

1. To capitalize on the considerable growth potential of its existing brands and products in current markets.

2. To introduce new products in the United States market, products developed internally as well as from licensing agreements and joint ventures.

3. To expand into new markets, both international markets and new segments of existing United States markets.

4. To diversify through acquisitions and other types of alliances both in the United States and elsewhere in the world.

In a speech to the New York Society of Security Analysts, on October 25, 1978, William Dearden explained that

> the general thrust of our program is diversification. We plan to diversify our products and markets; we plan to diversify in terms of commodity usage; we plan to diversify geographically. We clearly recognize the potential benefits to our company of expanding our product lines beyond chocolate and confectionery products and reducing, as a company, our economic dependence on cocoa beans. Our strategic objectives, strategies and day-to-day programs reflect this fact.
>
> While we plan to diversify the businesses within our company, our diversification efforts will be built upon knowledge and experience in the food industry. The many years of experience in manufacturing food products and selling them through virtually all major channels of distribution are strengths upon which our future development will be based.

As implied in Dearden's comments, a strong impetus for Hershey's diversification program has been the erratic and higher prices for the cocoa used in its chocolate and confectionery business. Because cocoa is a tropical crop grown outside the United States, Hershey has very little control over

EXHIBIT 1
COCOA COSTS (PRICE PER POUND)

	1972	1973	1974	1975	1976	1977
High	$0.39	$0.95	$1.31	$0.91	$1.63	$2.60
Low	0.24	0.36	0.63	0.59	0.71	1.54
Average	$0.32	$0.64	$0.98	$0.75	$1.09	$2.22

Source: Spot price of cocoa beans delivered in New York.

its production and marketing.[1] About two-thirds of the raw crop is grown in West Africa and most of the rest is grown in Central and South America. During 1978 the company estimated that the cost of cocoa absorbed in total production costs was 20 percent higher than in 1977; and 1977 cocoa costs were roughly double those of 1976. An all-time high of $2.60 per pound was reached in September 1977. Exhibit 1 demonstrates the severe inflation in this basic ingredient.

Added to the sharp upward fluctuations in cocoa prices has been a coincidental weakening of the United States dollar relative to foreign currencies. Because the world cocoa market is a pound sterling market, as the value of the dollar weakens relative to sterling and other world currencies, the cost of cocoa beans rises for United States producers. Although Hershey is a sophisticated trader in the cocoa futures market and engages in forward purchase contracts, in order to moderate erratic future cocoa price movements, it cannot entirely escape the impact of tremendous price fluctuations.

Prompted by the uncertainty in raw commodity prices for its candy and confectionery business, and guided by a new management team, Hershey was determined to lessen its dependence on this traditional side of the business. However, Hershey is unlikely to become an aggressive conglomerate, diversifying through acquisitions at a rapid pace into many unfamiliar and unrelated markets. Hershey has stated its intention to remain in the food and food-related markets. As the chief executive officer has said, "We're not a high-flying company. We hope to be, you might say, aggressively conservative." [2]

Hershey's Operating Characteristics

MAJOR PRODUCT LINES AND PRODUCTS

Prior to the acquisition of the Friendly Ice Cream Corp., Hershey had two major product lines: (1) chocolate and confectionery products, and (2) food products and services, including pasta products and coffee services.

For 1978, chocolate and confectionery products accounted for 88 percent of sales and 94 percent of operating profits. Within the chocolate and confectionery business, however. Hershey has managed to reduce its reliance on products that are predominantly chocolate — defined as those having a 70 percent or higher chocolate content — from 84 percent of sales in 1963 to 59 percent of sales in 1978. As part of its strategy, Hershey anticipated that the trend toward products with relatively less or no chocolate content would not only continue but accelerate in the future.

Among Hershey's chocolate and confectionery products, the most popular brands include Hershey's Milk and Almond bars, Kisses, Hershey's Syrup and Cocoa, Reese's Peanut Butter Cups, and Kit Kat.

NEW PRODUCT DEVELOPMENT

The introduction of new products constitutes an important part of Hershey's corporate aim of becoming a major, diversified, international food and food-related company. In addition to new products added through acquisitions, licensing, and joint-venture arrangements, Hershey is pursuing an intensified research and development program to internally broaden its product line. Three new products were introduced in 1977: Reese's Peanut Butter Flavored Chips, Reese's Crunchy, and Hershey's Golden Almond. Additional new products were developed in 1978, and the company claims that a con-

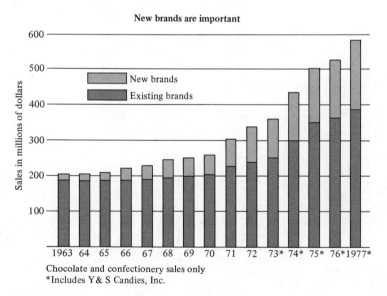

EXHIBIT 2
Source: Hershey Food Corp.'s presentation to the New York Society of Security Analysts, October 25, 1978.

siderable backlog of new products are in various stages of development and testing. The growing importance of new versus existing brands is shown clearly in Exhibit 2.

To support its emphasis on R & D activities, Hershey has committed $7.4 million for a new technical center scheduled to be completed by late 1979. This 114,000-square-foot facility will add to Hershey's R & D capability — already one of the best — in the chocolate and confectionery industry.

MARKETING AND DISTRIBUTION

Hershey uses a wide network of sales and distribution channels. The bulk of its sales go through grocery stores and grocery wholesalers, with candy distributors the next most important outlet (see Exhibit 3). Hershey's product distribution is nationwide with relatively even distribution, in relation to population, in the nation's four major geographic sectors: North (31.9%), South (24.2%), Midwest (25.9%), and West (18.0%).

The company has over 14,000 direct sales customers with no single customer accounting for as much as 5 percent of total corporate sales. The company believes its products are sold in over one million retail outlets in the United States. The physical distribution of products is handled by a network of thirty-seven warehouses throughout the United States.

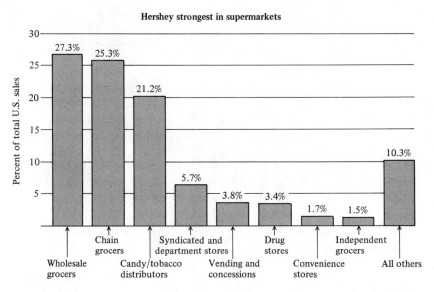

EXHIBIT 3

ADVERTISING AND PROMOTION

Advertising has increased in recent years, to reflect the company's new corporate objectives and the installation of the new management team. From a low of $1.8 million in 1974, advertising expenditures have steadily been raised, reaching $21.8 million in 1978, with management indicating even higher expenditures budgeted for 1979. As part of Hershey's marketing and advertising strategy, it has shifted its focus to adult consumers. In its Annual Report for 1978, Hershey stated that children were receiving "less than one-third of all [its] advertising impressions." Part of the impetus for this shift in advertising is due to the expected decline of the five- to 17-year age group in the 1980s — the age group with the biggest per-capita consumption of candy. An additional factor has been rising criticism from consumer groups and government: criticizing candy as "junk food" harmful to children.

FINANCIAL CONDITION

Hershey enjoys a very healthy financial condition. It has a substantial cash position as of year-end 1978. Combined with a low debt-to-equity ratio, Hershey seemed, at the end of 1978, to be in a favorable financial position to implement its strategy of diversification through acquisitions, as well as pursuing growth through internal means, licensing, and joint ventures.

HERSHEY'S ACQUISITION PROGRAM

Hershey had two principal subsidiaries up to 1979: San Giorgio Macaroni, Inc., which is a large regional producer of pasta products with major plants in Lebanon, Pennsylvania, and Louisville, Kentucky; and Corey Food Services, a Chicago-based manufacturer of coffee-brewing equipment and other appliances and provider of the nation's largest office coffee-service plan.

In recent years Hershey has made a number of acquisitions to supplement its pasta line of products as well as complement the chocolate and confectionery line. Y and S Candies, a major producer and distributor of licorice-type candies, was acquired in 1977. In 1978 the Procino-Rossi Corp. of central New York State was acquired, and Skinner Macaroni Company, a regional pasta manufacturer in Omaha, Nebraska, was acquired in early 1979.

Important as these moves were in helping Hershey achieve its objectives, they were overshadowed by the acquisition of the Friendly Ice Cream Corp. of Wilbraham, Massachusetts in 1979. It represented the largest transaction of its kind in Hershey's history. It also represented a foothold in the giant "eating away from home" food service industry. This acquisition added credibility to Hershey's defined corporate strategy of significant diversification through acquisitions.

The Friendly Ice Cream Acquisition

BACKGROUND OF FRIENDLY

Friendly operates a chain of restaurants, which serve high-quality, moderately priced menu items. It generally specializes in ice cream, sandwiches, and informal meals. From its beginnings in Springfield, Massachusetts, in 1935, Friendly has expanded to over 600 units located throughout the Northeast and in much of the Midwest.

The company is vertically integrated. Most of the food and supplies sold or used in the restaurants are shipped from Friendly's two processing and distribution facilities in its own fleet of refrigerated trucks. Friendly also maintains its own real estate, engineering, construction, carpentry, decorating, and maintenance departments. It does not franchise. There are approximately 2,700 full-time and 15,000 part-time employees.

Friendly's primary marketing strategy for the immediate future was to position itself as owner and operator of "informal restaurants," providing full service with a relaxed, informal atmosphere, and reasonable prices.

Throughout the 1950s the chain expanded slowly but steadily so that by 1960 there were fifty shops. The chain then doubled in the next five years. A more current view of Friendly's outlets by states is illustrated in Exhibit 4.

RECENT DEVELOPMENTS

Friendly was a well-established, successful regional company operating primarily in New England until the early 1970s. It then decided to expand aggressively into the Midwest. Growth in sales and number of outlets was rapid. It seemed for a while to be a classic instance of the right move at the right time. However, in fiscal 1977 (ended April 29) the company suffered a 4 percent drop in earnings. This interruption of its upward trend in earnings was variously attributed to a misreading of consumer tastes, a scarcity of good site locations, and a conservative management philosophy that avoided both advertising and long-term debt (roughly $17 million in long-term lease obligations were outstanding in fiscal 1977).

Steps were taken in the mid-1970s to modify the innate conservativeness of Friendly. Recognizing that its image was less well known in the Midwest than in the Northeast, the chief executive officer, Robert J. Gaudrault, admitted that the company had underestimated the advertising effort required for carrying the company's image into the new Midwest market. In 1976 Friendly also departed from its conservative financial practices by

EXHIBIT 4
FRIENDLY ICE CREAM CORPORATION: SHOPS BY STATE OPERATIONAL UNITS AS OF JANUARY 26, 1979

	Traditional Friendly ice cream and sandwich shops	Modified Friendly ice cream and sandwich shops	Friendly family restaurants	Friendly fast serve restaurants	SPECIAL'S fast food restaurants	Jim Dandy stores	Total
Massachusetts	155	13	3	2	1	8	182
New York	37	79	1				117
Ohio	57	9	10				76
Connecticut	61	10	1	1		2	75
New Jersey	3	45					48
Pennsylvania	33		3	1			37
Maryland	22						22
New Hampshire	8	1	2				11
Michigan	8	1	6				15
Rhode Island	5						5
Indiana	4						4
Maine	5						5
Virginia	5		1				4
Illinois	4						6
Delaware	3						3
Vermont	1		2				3
	411	158	29	4	1	10	613

Source: Hershey Foods Corporation, Annual Report, 1978.

borrowing $20 million long-term from a group of insurance companies. In the same year, the company began experimenting with an enlarged family-style restaurant, with slightly higher prices. By early 1978 twenty-four new Friendly family-type restaurants had been constructed, in addition to a refurbishing program for twenty-four existing shops in northern New York State at a cost of about $20,000 per outlet. At the same time, Friendly began experimenting (on a modest scale of 4 units) with fast-food units with limited menus, with food prepared in advance and rapid service. Looking ahead, Gaudrault saw promise in the southeastern market. But, for the remainder of 1978, the pace of Friendly's hectic expansion slowed considerably. Twenty new units were programmed for 1978 compared to seventy-five units just two years before. And despite the new departures, Friendly remained, according to Gaudrault, "still a conservative company, and growth for the sake of being the biggest just isn't us." [3]

HERSHEY'S PROPOSAL

Although Friendly's profit picture wasn't as bright in 1978 as in earlier years, the company did not lack for companies interested in acquiring its operations. During 1978 Friendly reportedly had overtures from a number of companies, including such firms as General Foods and Holiday Inns. Fearing a possible unfriendly takeover, Friendly decided to investigate the potential of a merger with Hershey, which was widely known to be looking for a food-related acquisition. Apparently attracted by Hershey's strong financial situation, and assurances from Hershey that Friendly would be allowed to run a relatively autonomous operation after the merger, Friendly accepted Hershey's cash offer of $26 a share for all of Friendly's outstanding common stock; about $6 above the prevailing market price. Recalls Gaudrault, "It seemed like the right girl was meeting the right boy. We saw that we could probably be even more successful in the future as a result of combined resources." [4]

Financial Considerations in Hershey's Acquisition of Friendly

As a result of a cash tender offer, which expired January 19, 1979, Hershey acquired substantially all of the outstanding common stock of Friendly Ice Cream Corporation. Hershey expects that Friendly will become a wholly owned subsidiary through a merger and that the total cost will approximate $164 million. Hershey borrowed $100 million under its revolving credit and term loan agreement as part of the financing for this acquisition. It currently expects to refinance $75 million of such borrowings through the issue and sale of long-term debt securities and the balance through short-term bor-

EXHIBIT 5
COMBINED OPERATING RESULTS FOR HERSHEY AND FRIENDLY

	1978	1977
Net sales	$981,251	$860,221
Income from continuing operations	$ 44,437	$ 38,413
Gain on sale of discontinued operation	—	5,300
Net income	$ 44,437	$ 43,713
Income per common share		
Continuing operations	$ 3.23	$ 2.80
Gain on sale of discontinued operation	—	.39
Net income	$ 3.23	$ 3.19

Source: Hershey Foods Corporation, Annual Report, 1978.
The pro forma amounts are based on the Company's audited results of operations for the twelve months ended December 31, 1978 and 1977, and Friendly's unaudited results of operations for the twelve months ended October 27, 1978, and October 28, 1977, respectively.

rowings. The acquisition will be accounted for as a purchase, and accordingly Friendly's results of operations will be included with Hershey's consolidated results of operations for periods subsequent to the date of acquisition. Consequently Hershey's consolidated financial statements for 1979 will include the results of operations for eleven months.

Exhibit 5 summarizes, on an unaudited pro-forma basis, the combined results of operations for 1978 and 1977 (including estimated amortization of goodwill, depreciation adjustments, and interest expense on funds expended for this acquisition) as though Friendly had been acquired on January 1, 1977 (in thousands of dollars except per-share figures).

Hershey's Initial Plans for Friendly

Since taking over Friendly, Hershey has made plans to revamp the company's Midwest shops, emphasizing booths rather than stools, and to expand its menu list to appeal to families. Hershey is also going forward with the refurbishing of the units started by Friendly. And, finally, the experiment with new drive-in restaurants called "Specials," designed to compete with other fast-food chains, is being continued by Hershey. In addition to expanding Hershey's market and product bases, Friendly might be able to take advantage of Hershey's name and its production and marketing systems. For example, Hershey, being a major supermarket distributor, may be able to sell Friendly ice cream in supermarkets.

Financial Statements of Hershey and Friendly

The financial condition of Hershey is highlighted in Exhibits 6 to 10. Relevant financial information on Friendly, prior to the merger with Hershey, is indicated by Exhibits 11 to 13.

EXHIBIT 6
CONSOLIDATED STATEMENTS OF INCOME
AND RETAINED EARNINGS
(in thousands of dollars except per share figures)

	For the years ended December 31	
	1978	1977
Net sales	$767,880	$671,227
Costs and expenses		
Cost of goods sold	519,395	453,960
Selling, administrative and general	127,494	109,585
Shipping	32,918	28,816
Depreciation	8,850	7,995
Interest income — net	(2,683)	(509)
Total costs and expenses	685,974	599,847
Income from continuing operations before taxes	81,906	71,380
Provision for federal and state income taxes	40,450	35,349
Income from continuing operations	41,456	36,031
Gain on sale of discontinued operation (less income taxes of $2,985)	—	5,300
Net income	41,456	41,331
Retained earnings at January 1	243,855	217,775
Deduct:		
Cash dividends	16,836	14,848
Cash dividends of pooled company prior to acquisition	—	403
Retained earnings at December 31	$268,475	$243,855
Income per common share		
Continuing operations	$ 3.02	$ 2.62
Gain on sale of discontinued operation	—	39
Net income	$ 3.02	$ 3.01
Cash dividends per common share	$ 1.225	$ 1.14

Source: Hershey Foods Corporation, Annual Report, 1978.

EXHIBIT 7
CONSOLIDATED BALANCE SHEETS
(in thousands of dollars)

	December 31	
Assets	*1978*	*1977*
Current assets:		
Cash	$ 7,622	$ 7,980
Commercial paper and certificates of deposit	104,134	109,258
Accounts receivable — trade (less allowances for doubtful accounts of $1,322 and $1,327)	31,787	35,756
Inventories		
Raw materials	28,071	28,136
Goods in process	6,154	6,806
Finished goods	31,386	27,008
	65,611	61,950
Other current assets	7,505	6,258
Total current assets	216,659	221,202
Property and equipment, at cost		
Land	4,226	2,773
Buildings	76,190	67,904
Equipment	184,845	160,657
	265,261	231,334
Less accumulated depreciation	94,481	88,164
	170,780	143,170
Goodwill	18,056	17,777
Other assets:		
Investments	10,295	8,095
Other assets and deferred charges	6,214	5,909
	16,509	14,004
	$422,004	$396,153

continued

EXHIBIT 7 *continued*

| | December 31 | |
Liabilities and stockholders' equity	1978	1977
Current liabilities:		
Accounts payable	$ 43,696	$ 55,650
Accrued liabilities	20,855	14,154
Income taxes payable	9,864	13,345
Total current liabilities	74,415	83,149
Long-term debt	35,540	29,440
Deferred income taxes	27,660	23,896
Stockholders' equity		
Common stock, without par value (stated value $1 per share) — authorized 20,000,000 shares; outstanding 13,745,269 and 13,730,288 shares	13,745	13,730
Additional paid-in capital	2,169	2,083
Retained earnings	268,475	243,855
Total stockholders' equity	284,389	259,668
	$422,004	$396,153

Source: Hershey Foods Corporation, Annual Report, 1978.

EXHIBIT 8
CONSOLIDATED STATEMENTS OF CHANGES
IN FINANCIAL POSITION
(in thousands of dollars)

	For the years ended December 31	
	1978	*1977*
Financial resources provided		
Continuing operations:		
Net income	$41,456	$36,031
Depreciation	8,850	7,995
Deferred income taxes	3,764	4,821
Resources provided from continuing operations	54,070	48,850
Discontinued operation:		
Gain on sale	—	5,300
Deferred income taxes	—	(2,522)
Assets sold or held for disposal	—	9,239
Resources provided from discontinued operation	—	12,017
Increase in long-term debt	7,000	—
Other	482	2,906
Total resources provided	61,552	63,773
Financial resources applied		
Capital expenditures	37,425	27,536
Cash dividends	16,836	15,251
Increase in investments	2,200	5,498
Reduction in long-term debt	900	—
Total resources applied	57,361	48,284
Increase in working capital	$ 4,191	$15,489
Increase (decrease) in working capital		
Cash	$ (358)	$ 3,152
Commercial paper and certificates of deposit	(5,124)	56,612
Receivables	(3,969)	(3,804)
Inventories	3,661	(4,354)
Other current assets	1,247	(276)
Accounts payable	11,954	(36,670)
Accrued liabilities	(6,701)	423
Income taxes payable	3,481	406
Increase in working capital	$ 4,191	$15,489

Source: Hershey Foods Corporation, Annual Report, 1978.

EXHIBIT 9
INDUSTRY SEGMENT INFORMATION
(in thousands of dollars)

	For the years ended December 31				
	1978	1977	1976 (unaudited)	1975 (unaudited)	1974 (unaudited)
Net sales:					
Chocolate and Confectionery	$678,652	$586,282	$526,822	$503,263	$438,313
Other Foods Products and Services	89,228	84,345	75,138	72,902	72,770
Total net sales	$767,880	$671,227	$601,960	$576,165	$511,083
Operating profit:					
Chocolate and Confectionery	$ 79,143	$ 69,834	$ 86,898	$ 83,551	$ 50,269
Other Food Products and Services	5,061	4,528	5,005	3,549	2,664
Total operating profit	84,204	74,362	91,903	87,100	52,933
General corporate expenses	(4,981)	(3,491)	(2,299)	(1,642)	(727)
Interest income (expense)—net	2,683	509	(357)	(1,264)	(2,279)
Income from continuing operations before taxes	$ 81,906	$ 71,380	$ 89,247	$ 84,194	$ 49,927
Identifiable assets:					
Chocolate and Confectionery	$241,070	$221,928	$222,541	$217,772	$208,504
Other Food Products and Services	50,450	47,023	44,325	44,152	45,142
Corporate	130,484	127,202	65,004	44,627	34,450
Total identifiable assets	$422,004	$396,153	$331,870	$306,551	$288,096
Depreciation:					
Chocolate and Confectionery	$ 6,574	$ 5,702	$ 5,439	$ 5,566	$ 5,538
Other Food Products and Services	1,720	1,789	1,755	1,760	2,137
Corporate	556	504	345	215	253
Total depreciation	$ 8,850	$ 7,995	$ 7,539	$ 7,541	$ 7,928

Capital expenditures:

Chocolate and Confectionery	$ 23,923	$ 22,381	$ 17,227	$ 8,489	$ 7,246
Other Food Products and Services	4,420	3,014	1,754	1,995	2,884
Corporate	9,082	2,140	1,741	58	954
Total capital expenditures	$ 37,425	$ 27,535	$ 20,722	$ 10,542	$ 11,084

Source: Hershey Foods Corporation, Annual Report, 1978.

EXHIBIT 10
FIVE-YEAR FINANCIAL SUMMARY, HERSHEY FOODS
CORPORATION AND SUBSIDIARIES
(all dollar and share figures in thousands — except market price and per share statistics)

	1978	1977	1976	1975	1974
Summary of earnings					
Continuing operations					
Net sales	$ 767,880	671,227	601,960	576,165	511,083
Cost of goods sold	$ 519,395	453,960	383,664	381,115	373,277
Operating expenses	$ 169,262	146,396	128,692	109,592	85,600
Interest expense	$ 2,620	2,422	2,240	3,126	3,710
Interest income	$ 5,303	2,931	1,883	1,862	1,431
Income taxes	$ 40,450	35,349	45,562	43,292	25,718
Income from continuing operations	$ 41,456	36,031	43,685	40,902	24,209
Income (loss) from discontinued operations	$ —	—	1,112	(1,457)	(1,608)
Gain (loss) related to disposal of discontinued operations	$ —	5,300	—	(4,898)	—
Net income	$ 41,456	41,331	44,797	34,547	22,601
Income per share of common stock					
Continuing operations	$ 3.02	2.62	3.18	2.99	1.77
Discontinued operations	$ —	—	.08	(.11)	(.12)
Gain (loss) related to disposal	$ —	.39	—	(.36)	—
Net income	$ 3.02	3.01	3.26	2.52	1.65
Dividends per — common share	$ 1.225	1.14	1.03	.85	.80
preferred share	$ —	—	—	.60	.60
Average number of common shares and equivalents outstanding during the year	13,742	13,722	13,720	13,698	13,685
Per cent of income from continuing operations to sales	5.4%	5.4%	7.3%	7.1%	4.7%

Financial statistics

Capital expenditures	$ 37,425	27,535	20,722	10,542	11,084
Depreciation[a]	$ 8,850	7,995	7,539	7,541	7,928
Advertising[a]	$ 21,847	17,637	13,330	9,499	1,814
Current assets	$ 216,659	221,202	169,872	157,579	129,226
Current liabilities	$ 74,415	83,149	47,309	53,808	59,156
Working capital	$ 142,244	138,053	122,563	103,771	70,070
Current ratio	2.9:1	2.7:1	3.6:1	2.9:1	2.2:1
Long-term debt	$ 35,540	29,440	29,440	29,856	31,730
Debt-to-equity per cent	13%	11%	13%	15%	18%
Stockholders' equity	$ 284,389	259,668	233,529	202,466	178,238

Stockholders' data

Market price of common stock — at year-end	$ 20⅝	19⅞	22⅜	18⅝	9¾
Range during year	$18½–23½	16⅝–22⅜	18½–27½	10⅛–20⅞	8½–15

Source: Hershey Foods Corporation, Annual Report, 1978.
[a] Restated to reflect continuing operations only.

EXHIBIT 11
FRIENDLY ICE CREAM CORPORATION INTERIM INCOME ACCOUNT
(dollars in thousands)

	12 months to:	3 months to:	
	1/26/79	1/26/79	1/27/78
Retail sales	$212,303	$52,116	$45,544
Net before taxes	21,880	772[a]	2,419
Income taxes	10,889	576	1,236
Net income	10,991	196	1,183
Earnings per share	$ 1.56	$ 0.03	$ 0.17

Source: Moody's OTC Industrial Manual.
[a] Reflects expenses of $2,465,000 associated with the tender offer for the company's common stock by Hershey Foods Corporation. Had these expenses not been incurred net income for the 3-month-period ending January 26, 1979, would be $1,753,000, or $0.25 per share.

EXHIBIT 12

Assets	April 28, 1978	April 29, 1977
Current assets		
Cash	$ 3,752,161	$ 2,041,076
Marketable securities, at cost which approximates market	10,562,052	—
Inventories	11,055,454	9,915,340
Prepaid expenses and other current assets	1,842,942	2,166,248
Total current assets	27,212,549	14,122,664
Investment in and advances to affiliate	695,474	763,926
Deferred income taxes	227,353	372,853
Property, plant, and equipment, at cost		
Land and land improvements	25,835,751	25,680,842
Buildings	35,992,389	33,520,714
Equipment	72,108,098	65,825,843
Leased property under capital leases	19,913,054	19,526,760
Construction in progress	3,399,602	5,713,359
	157,248,894	150,267,518
Less — accumulated depreciation and lease amortization	61,147,525	50,294,568
	96,101,369	99,972,950
	$124,236,745	$115,232,393

Liabilities and stockholders' equity

Current liabilities		
Notes payable to banks	$ —	$ 1,200,000
Current portion of long-term obligations	1,006,017	959,833
Accounts payable	7,110,103	7,927,477
Accrued salaries and wages	1,436,235	868,330
Taxes other than federal income taxes	1,499,403	1,023,889
Federal income tax	2,914,182	507,726
Other accrued liabilities	1,468,515	1,220,134
Total current liabilities	15,434,455	13,707,389
Long-term obligations, net of current portion	39,926,328	40,525,867
Commitments		
Stockholders' equity		
Common stock, $1 par value		
Authorized 15,000,000 shares, issued and		
outstanding, 7,043,379 shares in 1978		
and 7,042,259 in 1977	7,043,379	7,042,259
Paid-in capital	1,635,061	1,618,251
Retained earnings	60,197,522	52,338,627
	68,875,962	60,999,137
	$124,236,745	$115,232,393

Source: Special meeting of Friendly's shareholders, April 9, 1979.

EXHIBIT 13
SUMMARY OF OPERATIONS AND FIVE YEAR REVIEW
FRIENDLY ICE CREAM CORPORATION AND SUBSIDIARIES
(dollars in thousands)

	April 28, 1978	April 29, 1977	April 30, 1976	April 25, 1975	April 27, 1974
Retail sales	$ 200,145	$ 173,805	$ 153,985	$ 122,420	$ 90,750
Percent increase	15.2%	12.9%	25.8%	34.9%	26.4%
Cost of sales and operating expenses of shops	$ 164,167	140,336	122,281	93,101	73,225
Percent increase	17.0%	14.8%	24.6%	34.0%	28.2%
Percent of sales	82.0%	80.7%	79.4%	80.1%	80.7%
Selling and administrative expenses	$ 15,167	13,861	11,423	8,293	6,161
Percent increase	11.6%	21.3%	37.7%	34.6%	33.4%
Percent of sales	7.7%	8.0%	7.4%	6.8%	6.8%
Interest expense	$ 3,431	2,522	1,591	1,007	886
Interest income	$ 605	19	4	—	—
Other income (expense), net	$ (90)	82	73	41	16
Income before taxes	$ 17,595	17,187	18,767	15,060	10,494
Percent increase (decrease)	2.4%	(8.4)%	24.6%	43.5%	11.0%
Percent of sales	8.8%	9.9%	12.2%	12.3%	11.6%
Federal and state income taxes	$ 8,750	8,464	9,176	7,723	5,085
Net income	$ 8,815	8,723	9,591	7,337	5,409

Percent increase (decrease)	1.4%	(9.1)%	30.7%	35.6%	11.2%
Percent of sales	4.4%	5.0%	6.2%	6.0%	6.0%
Percent of average stockholders' equity	13.6%	15.3%	19.9%	18.4%	16.0%
Net income per share	$ 1.26	1.24	1.36	1.05	.77
Depreciation and amortization	$ 11,640	10,581	8,251	6,434	5,579
Cash flow (net income plus depreciation and amortization)	$ 20,485	19,304	17,842	13,771	10,988
Capital expenditures	$ 8,382	24,523	24,241	18,542	10,465
Leases capitalized	$ 386	4,314	4,538	1,779	1,829
Investment in affiliate	$ 695	764	815	857	864
Ratio of current assets to current liabilities	1.8	1.0	.5	.6	.6
Stockholders' equity	$ 68,876	60,999	52,832	43,501	36,357
Long-term debt	$ 39,926	40,526	17,108	13,275	11,997
Total assets	$ 124,237	115,232	94,505	74,397	59,004
Average shares outstanding	7,043,345	7,041,606	7,031,566	7,011,027	7,009,135
Cash dividends per share	$ .14	.10	.08	.06	.05
Number of stockholders	8,066	7,596	7,038	7,168	7,405
Number of Friendly units	603	590	536	461	407
Percent increase	2.2%	10.1%	16.3%	13.3%	12.7%
Seating capacity of units	39,112	37,454	33,343	27,891	23,971
Percent increase	4.4%	12.3%	19.5%	16.4%	13.9%

Source: Special meeting of Friendly's shareholders, April 9, 1979.

Assignments

1. Evaluate Hershey's acquisition strategy and the "fit" of Friendly as a part of this strategy.

2. Evaluate the terms of the acquisition offer and your estimate of the acquisition's contribution to Hershey's future performance and potential as a "major diversified international food and food-related company."

REFERENCES

1. Hershey Foods Corporation's *Annual Report,* 1977, p. 3.

2. "Hershey: Joining with Friendly to diversify away from chocolate," *Business Week,* January 29, 1979, p. 119.

3. "Friendly Ice Cream: Coming of Age in a Tough Market," *Dun's Review,* April 1978, p. 35.

4. "Hershey: Joining with Friendly to diversify away from chocolate," *Business Week,* January 29, 1979, p. 118.

U.S. Dredging Company*

U.S. Dredging is one of the largest publicly owned marine construction companies in the nation. Its primary business is dredging rivers and waterways. U.S. Dredging has operated for the United States, the state of New Jersey, the city of Baltimore, Maryland, and for private interests in the Delaware Valley, New York, and north Jersey areas. Typical contracts have included maintenance dredging in the Delaware River, the Christina River and Wilmington Harbor in Delaware, the Baltimore Harbor in Maryland, and the U.S. Naval Station in Mayport, Florida. The company has also performed maintenance dredging at various inlets and beaches in New Jersey for the state of New Jersey. The company uses huge silt lifters, which are specially designed and constructed for this type of work.

Dredging has never been a very popular or exciting business in terms of attracting the attention of investors. Therefore it was unusual in early 1978 when the shares of this prosaic company suddenly started to act like a glamour stock. At first the speculation was that recent legislation, which would remove the Corps of Engineers from the dredging business, was the cause of the sharp run-up in the price of the stock. At the time the Corps of Engineers accounted for roughly 60 percent of the nation's dredging and thus constituted a formidable operator in the dredging business.

However, the real reason for the higher share prices was soon traced to a takeover bid for U.S. Dredging. Another dredging company made an offer to acquire its stock. Through a brokerage agent, Xtra Dredging offered to buy all of U.S. Dredging's 386,852 shares at $30 a share on the condition that at least a majority of the shares were tendered.

The shares of U.S. Dredging had been quoted at $20 in over-the-counter trading before they began creeping upward in anticipation of the

---

* Prepared by Milton Leontiades.

release of Xtra's takeover offer. Although the offer of $30 a share represented a 50 percent increase in the price quoted only a few days before, Mr. Silter, the president of U.S. Dredging, vigorously opposed the bid, and few of the company's shares were subsequently tendered. In rejecting Xtra's offer, Mr. Silter pointed to U.S. Dredging's book value of almost $60 a

EXHIBIT 1
BALANCE SHEET

Assets

	December 31	
	1978	*1977*
Current assets:		
Cash, including time deposits of $5,974 and $1,177,986	$ 298,049	$ 1,962,568
Accounts receivable	5,279,410	5,287,689
Inventories of parts and supplies	3,695,532	3,848,939
Insurance claim receivable	6,063,330	
Recoverable federal income taxes	965,973	628,736
Other current assets	183,120	741,259
Total current assets	16,485,414	12,469,191
Investments:		
Land at cost	2,924,166	2,924,166
Stocks and municipal bonds, at cost (market value, $2,271,643 and $2,534,409)	2,662,952	2,664,727
Subsidiary company, at equity	38,686	38,469
Total investments	5,625,804	5,627,362
Property, plant and equipment, at cost:		
Floating equipment	29,908,706	32,700,146
Other equipment	1,673,789	1,538,504
Land, buildings and improvements	3,271,622	3,186,103
Construction in process	4,314,879	755,028
	39,168,996	38,179,781
Less accumulated depreciation	23,856,121	25,499,244
	15,312,875	12,680,537
Other assets:		
Noncurrent accounts receivable		564,491
Deferred litigation expenses		353,084
Other	52,461	44,486
	52,461	962,061

Liabilities and stockholders' equity

	December 31	
	1978	1977
Current liabilities:		
Notes payable, bank	$ 8,737,232	$ 3,335,712
Accounts payable	3,549,921	2,477,703
Accrued liabilities	768,592	712,289
Total current liabilities	13,055,745	6,525,704
Deferred income taxes	2,234,775	2,896,625
Stockholders' equity		
Capital shares, par value, $2.50; authorized, 1,000,000 shares; issued 386,852 shares	967,130	967,130
Additional capital	2,016,140	2,010,063
Retained earnings:		
Appropriated	367,204	367,204
Unappropriated	19,713,006	20,025,760
	23,063,480	23,370,157
Treasury shares, at cost (34,770 and 41,812 shares)	(897,446)	(1,053,335)
Total stockholders' equity	22,166,034	22,316,822
	$37,467,554	$31,739,151

Source: U.S. Dredging Company, Annual Report, 1978.

share. Furthermore, according to Mr. Silter, the book value did not adequately reflect the value of the company's extensive real estate holdings. These were carried at an original purchase basis of $2,924,166 (see Exhibit 1).

On an operating basis, U.S. Dredging had fluctuating earnings, reflecting the cyclical nature of the dredging business. In 1977 and 1978 the company showed losses from its dredging business. However, insurance proceeds, in repayment for two dredges that sank in 1978, amounted to $5.649 million. In conjunction with $1.567 million in tax-loss carryforwards, the company actually realized net income in 1978 of $1.74 a share. Moreover, in 1977 the company's operating loss of $1,190,274 was more than offset by a gain from the sale of one of the company's dredges so that, again, a loss

EXHIBIT 2
STATEMENT OF INCOME

	Years ended December 31	
	1978	1977
Operating revenue	$18,205,098	$20,442,751
Operating expenses	24,807,508	21,633,025
Operating loss	(6,602,410)	(1,190,274)
Other income, net	5,648,631	3,225,802
Income (loss) before provision for income taxes	(953,779)	2,035,528
Provision for income taxes (credit)	(1,567,000)	360,000
Net income	$ 613,221	$ 1,675,528
Earnings per capital share	$1.74	$4.84

STATEMENT OF RETAINED EARNINGS
YEARS ENDED DECEMBER 31, 1976 AND 1977

	Unappropriated	Appropriated	Total
Balance, January 1, 1977	$18,939,047	$367,204	$19,306,251
Add net income, 1977	1,675,528		1,675,528
	20,614,575	367,204	20,981,779
Deduct cash dividends, $1.70 per share	588,815		588,815
Balance, December 31, 1977	20,025,760	367,204	20,392,964
Add net income, 1978	613,221		613,221
	20,638,981	367,204	21,006,185
Deduct cash dividends, $2.65 per share	925,975		925,975
Balance, December 31, 1978	$19,713,006	$367,204	$20,080,210

Source: U.S. Dredging Company, Annual Report, 1978.

from operations was turned into an earnings gain; this time $4.84 per share (see Exhibit 2).

Xtra's offer of $30 was subsequently raised to $36 a share, and U.S. Dredging's shares responded by rising to $38. In view of Mr. Silter's belief regarding the value of his company's real estate holdings, this second offer was no more welcome than the first. In Mr. Silter's opinion, which he claimed was based on recent appraisals, U.S. Dredging's real estate holdings were worth over $105 a share at current market values. In addition, Mr. Silter stated that the company's dredging equipment represented an insured value of an additional $111 a share; making a total valuation, even disregarding the company's operating potential for profits, of $216 a share.

The sudden activity in U.S. Dredging's shares did not go unheeded in Wall Street. Twiddly Black, a brokerage firm specializing in undervalued over-the-counter stocks, had accumulated a sizable position in U.S. Dredging over the past year. Twiddly Black regularly traded U.S. Dredging's stock (in Wall Street parlance it "made a market" in the stock) and also bought shares for its own account. With a substantial number of purchased shares already in its possession, Twiddly Black stated its intention to seek control of the company at the next annual meeting.

Mr. Silter feared that Twiddly Black's offer was based on an intent to liquidate the company. Frantically searching for an alternative, Mr. Silter located a friendlier purchaser, another investment broker called Wilson W. Wilson. Wilson would continue to operate the business and made an offer of $70 per share for U.S. Dredging; $63 to be paid in cash on closing the deal and the remaining $7 a share to be paid later. A formal contract was drawn up between Wilson and U.S. Dredging and a copy sent to each of the company's shareholders.

With the proxy meeting scheduled in about a week, Mr. Silter is now anxiously awaiting the results. If Twiddly Black is successful, Mr. Silter expects it to proceed with liquidation of the company. Near-term the stock would probably drop from its current price of about $60, even though the eventual liquidation value could exceed this level by a comfortable amount. If Wilson wins the proxy contest, the shares would most likely rise to the exchange price of $70 a share. At present, both firms are believed to be interested in acquiring a 51 percent interest for operating control, with decisions on purchasing the remaining shares to be made at a later date.

The Twiddly Black Alternative — Liquidation

To obtain an approximation of the return to Twiddly Black from liquidation, it was necessary to obtain a current valuation of the company's land holdings and of the company's dredging equipment. Combined, these two estimates would indicate the real asset values supporting the stated book value of roughly $60 a share.

The company's land holdings consist of the following parcels of land in their respective locations in New Jersey:

Location	Parcel size
Florence Township	85 Acres
Logan Township	2600 Acres
Salem County	600 Acres
Atlantic City (bayfront area)	120 Acres

The estimated fair market value for each of these parcels of land has been appraised by independent professionals, with the following estimates provided:

Location	Estimated value
Florence Township	$ 900,000
Logan Township	$25,000,000
Salem County	$ 6,000,000
Atlantic City (bayfront area)	$ 1,000,000
Total estimated value	$32,900,000

In addition to the estimated fair market value, it was forecast that in an emergency sale, under a sheriff's auction, the land might be expected to bring 25 to 50 percent of its fair market value.

To determine the value of the company's dredging equipment, another independent appraisal was sought by an expert familiar with the various pieces of equipment owned by U.S. Dredging: the type and number of pieces of equipment are shown below.

Equipment type	Quantity
Cutter suction dredges	4
12-cubic yard dipper dredge	1
Clamshell dredges	3

In the opinion of this appraiser, a low-side appraisal of liquidation value of the equipment would amount to $84 million, reflecting his best estimate for each piece of equipment.

"Generally speaking, a 27 inch cutter suction dredge would bring in the range of $10–20 million, depending on the service to which it is to be used. Clamshell dredges would bring between $8–12 million. To the best of my knowledge, no new dipper dredges have been built in this country for many years. As a wild guess, I would think a 12 cubic yard dipper dredge would bring between $20–25 million," stated the appraiser.

Using the low side of the estimates, the projected liquidation value of U.S. Dredging's equipment is as follows:

Type of dredge	Quantity	Estimated liquidation value (total)
Cutter suction dredges	4	(4 × $10 million) = $40 million
12-cubic yard dipper dredge	1	(1 × $20 million) = $20 million
Clamshell dredges	3	(3 × $8 million) = $24 million
		Total estimated = 84 million liquidation value

Another more pessimistic view was offered by a second independent expert who had commented at the time of the offer by Xtra that the land owned by the company is "undeveloped industrial maritime real estate and among the most difficult kind of property to develop." Moreover, with regard to U.S. Dredging's equipment, he stated that the insured value could be significantly higher than realized liquidation prices. He indicated that the second-hand market for dredges was inactive and that orderly liquidation could take several years.

According to a Twiddly Black vice-president, his group paid "from $40 to over $60" a share on the open market in order to try to obtain control of U.S. Dredging. Assuming that Twiddly Black paid, on the average, $55 for each share of stock and acquired 51 percent of the total shares, the total cost would amount to $9,817,500. Twiddly Black believed a complete liquidation of U.S. Dredging could take five years or longer.

Wilson W. Wilson — Investment

To estimate a return on investment to Wilson W. Wilson, Inc., it is useful to determine the future outlook for the dredging industry. Value Line, a well-known investment advisory service, made this appraisal of the dredging industry:

> . . . beach nourishment and landfill are in great demand because most of the United States coastline needs restoration. This work was largely done by the U.S. Army Corps of Engineers in the past, but since Congress limited the Corps' activity, U.S. dredges can expect to be very busy in U.S. waters in the foreseeable future.

Longer term profit growth will depend importantly on federal public works appropriations. President Carter's opposition to many public works projects has cut down federal money for "new starts," . . .

During the past six years, U.S. Dredging's net income and net income per share have fluctuated erratically. This is a reflection of the cyclical nature of the business, and according to all indications such cyclicality will continue. However, it should be noted that the most recent operating losses in 1978 brought charges of "lack of management responsibility" from the vice-president of Twiddly Black. At one point during the annual meeting, Mr. Black alluded to the insurance proceeds from destroyed equipment to offset operating losses: "If it [U.S. Dredging] had not sunk two dredges it might not be open for business today." Mr. Black said later that he did not mean to imply that U.S. Dredging sank the dredges on purpose.

Net income for U.S. Dredging for the past six years is given below, as shown in the company's annual reports.

	Net income	Net income per share
1978	$ 613,221	$1.74
1977	1,675,528	4.84
1976	2,697,734	7.72
1975	785,687	2.24
1974	1,237,415	3.49
1973	750,185	2.09

Conclusion

In its defense against Xtra's and Twiddly Black's takeover offers, U.S. Dredging has spent nearly $490,000. The various activities have also distracted management from its principal duty of efficiently running the dredging business. Soon, however, control of the company should be resolved and the future direction of the firm mapped out.

Questions and Assignment

1. Develop a negotiating strategy for Twiddly Black and Wilson W. Wilson. What would you consider your "best" offer from the perspective of each of these firms?

2. What would be the "minimum" offer you would be prepared to accept if you were responsible for U.S. Dredging's decision?

The Whitley Company*

By the end of November, Al Whitley, president of the Whitley Company, had almost persuaded himself, and other shareholder members of the Whitley family, to consider selling the company to one of two firms that had made competing offers to acquire Whitley. Through the years the Whitley Company had received numerous acquisition offers. But Al Whitley had staunchly resisted takeover, and he had persuaded the majority-owning shareholders of the Whitley family that the company was best run as an independent, private firm. Although Al Whitley still held to this opinion, pressures from other family members had steadily increased. A minority of family shareholders had consistently voted at the stockholder meetings to raise Whitley's dividend payout ratio. Three of the larger shareowners of the company were over sixty-five years of age and they wished to sell their interests in order to facilitate the transfer of their estate to their heirs. Al Whitley was also concerned about the liquidity of his assets, which were mostly tied up in the business, should something happen to him. Moreover, the current offers seemed very attractive and both companies were held in high regard by Whitley and his top-management team.

The Business of the Whitley Company

The Whitley Company was started by Al Whitley's father after World War II. Benjamin Whitley had developed a modified gear drive for use in trucks, farm tractors, and construction equipment. From its modest beginnings, Benjamin Whitley managed to develop a wide range of gear drives, gears, couplings, and component parts for transmitting power, with applications to a wide number of industrial customers. In addition to the original markets, the product line had been extended to the steel, cement, paper, and

---

* Prepared by Milton Leontiades.

chemical industries. The company now produces standard products as well as specialty equipment and components. Gear sizes range from one inch to three feet in diameter, with power-transmission ratings of up to 2,000 horsepower.

The Whitley Company has enjoyed a steady expansion of business since its inception. In the three years since Al Whitley took over as president, sales have increased about 30 percent, with a corresponding although less steady improvement in earnings. The company also enjoys a strong financial position. Its debt-to-equity ratio, for instance, is a modest 6 percent, reflecting the family's conservative approach to long-term debt. Other than for exceptional investment opportunities, the firm continues to finance its expansion from internally generated funds (see Exhibits 1 and 2).

The Whitley Company has high market shares in several of its basic markets. In the cement, chemical, and paper industries, for example, its market shares range from 25 percent to 65 percent. A few of the company's products are protected by patents. But research and development is Whitley's principal strategy for staying ahead of its competition. Whereas industry spending for R&D is roughly 3 percent of sales, Whitley plows back 6.5 cents out of every sales dollar into research for improving engineering methods and design. Approximately 20 percent of Whitley's work force are engineers, and many of these have advanced degrees in mechanical and electrical engineering.

EXHIBIT 1
THE WHITLEY COMPANY
(000s omitted)

	Preceding year	Preceding year	Preceding year	Preceding year	Current year
Net sales	$39,428	$43,612	$46,019	$48,811	$51,256
Net income after taxes	$ 1,971	$ 2,316	$ 3,401	$ 2,433	$ 3,120
Per common share:					
Net income	$ 1.97	$ 2.32	$ 3.40	$ 2.43	$ 3.12
Dividends	$ .56	$ .62	$ .70	$ .70	$ .70
Stock price	$ 12–19	$ 19–24	$ 23–43	$ 21–33	$ 19–29[a]
Number of common shares	1,000	1,000	1,000	1,000	1,000

[a] Present stock price is $25.

EXHIBIT 2
THE WHITLEY COMPANY BALANCE SHEET
(000s omitted)

	Current year
Current assets	$20,100
Net property, plant and equipment	22,670
Other assets	5,730
Total assets	$48,500
Current liabilities	$10,000
Long-term debt	2,000
Common stock (1 million shares outstanding)	2,000
Additional paid-in capital	5,000
Retained earnings	26,500
Total stockholders' equity	$33,500
Total liabilities and equity	$48,500

Sedgely Automation

One of the two tender offers currently being considered by the Whitley Company was made by Sedgely Automation. A public company traded on the American Stock Exchange, Sedgely Automation had long been interested in the complementarity of Whitley's product lines with its own. Sedgely operates two major product groups in the following areas:

1. Materials handling equipment, including entire automated systems. Its systems can move finished steel, crushed stone, or cardboard boxes. The company's conveyor systems and components are especially useful in the foundry, bottling, lumber and pulp, and food processing industries. For warehouse operations, the company has designed order-picking systems that can process thousands of orders a day. Many of Sedgely's systems are custom-designed to customers' specifications.

2. Sedgely also produces construction equipment such as asphalt spreaders, concrete mixers, and large pavement rollers. This area of Sedgely's operations accounts for about 20 percent of sales. The type of equipment manufactured commonly uses mechanical drives, shaft couplings, and gears of the type produced by the Whitley Company.

Sedgely uses its own sales force to distribute products from twenty-four district sales offices nationwide. In addition, the company uses forty independent brokers to handle the less densely populated industrial centers. Together the company's own sales force plus the brokers-distributors cover the entire United States, including Alaska and Hawaii, and most of southern Canada. In comparison, Whitley's distribution system depends on four regional warehousing operations, and ten district sales offices in the United States. Whitley conducts business abroad with eight sales representatives who cover Europe and most of South America. All of Whitley's marketing and sales activities are centrally administered by a department headed by the vice-president of marketing. Organized by function, Whitley believes in a strong central structure to control its wide-flung operations.

Both Sedgely and Whitley have a diversified customer list. No single customer account is responsible for as much as 5 percent of sales in either company. Thus both firms are protected by fluctuations in the fortunes of individual customers. However, Sedgely and Whitley tend to be sensitive to general economic conditions. Recessions typically affect the capital goods sectors where the principal customers of both companies do business.

Sedgely operates three plants in California, Illinois, and Pennsylvania. Its work force is unionized but labor negotiations have always been settled without a strike. Each of the two major product divisions of Sedgely maintain their own R&D and marketing departments. Both division managers run fairly autonomous operations with only financial, long-range planning, and coordinating staff functions performed at the corporate level.

EXHIBIT 3
SEDGELY AUTOMATION
(000s omitted)

	Preceding year	Preceding year	Preceding year	Preceding year	Current year
Net sales	$114,500	$131,400	$148,900	$159,000	$176,300
Net income after taxes	$ 2,975	$ 3,190	$ 3,880	$ 4,302	$ 4,720
Per common share:					
Net income	$ 3.72	$ 3.99	$ 4.85	$ 5.38	$ 5.90
Dividends	$ 1.00	$ 1.05	$ 1.15	$ 1.20	$ 1.25
Stock price	$ 19–29	$ 25–33	$ 31–41	$ 39–49	$ 47–59a
Number of common shares	800	800	800	800	800

a Present stock price is $53.

EXHIBIT 4
SEDGELY AUTOMATION BALANCE SHEET
(000s omitted)

	Current year
Cash	$ 4,200
Accounts receivable	10,800
Inventories	32,000
Total current assets	$47,000
Net property, plant and equipment	36,300
Other assets	2,800
Total assets	$86,100
Current liabilities	$10,500
Long-term debt	5,500
Common stock (800,000 shares outstanding)	8,000
Capital surplus	8,100
Retained earnings	54,000
Total liabilities and equity	$86,100

SEDGELY'S TERMS

Sedgely has made an offer to acquire Whitley and operate it as a separate division. Al Whitley would be retained as president of the new division and also made a member of Sedgely's Executive Committee, which determines long-range policy and strategy for the enterprise. The Whitley Company would be operated as a separate business with no changes in personnel or policies.

Sedgely would acquire 500,000 shares of Whitley in a tax-free exchange of 1 share of Sedgely for each 2.08 shares of Whitley. The remaining common stock of Whitley would be purchased for cash at $57 per share. Sedgely's stock is traded currently at $53 per common share. The range of share prices from 1976 to 1981, plus other financial information on Sedgely, is indicated in Exhibits 3 and 4.

Able Electrical Company

Able Electrical is the other company that wishes to acquire Whitley. Able is a fast-growing public company that has achieved much of its recent growth by acquiring companies related to its principal business of engineered electromechanical equipment and components. Such systems are designed for continuous process lines in automated plants such as automobile factories, steel foundries, and food processors, as well as a number of other special-purpose applications demanding precise, synchronized systems. Original equipment (OEM) accounts for 85 percent of total sales, with the remainder coming from component parts and service. About two hundred engineers and graduate engineers are employed on a wide range of theoretical and applied development programs. It is Able's policy to spend 5 to 6 percent of sales on R&D work. Able holds a number of important patents, which protect its system designs in many industry applications. Able employs sales representatives in fourteen foreign countries, including most of Europe, Australia, and the northern half of Africa. It exports to these countries from its United States plants and has licensed selected manufacturers abroad to produce its proprietary systems. In the United States the company's technically trained salespeople sell and service the systems, which Able installs. Able considers one of its major advantages to be the technical background of its sales force and its policy of prompt attention to customer complaints and requests for assistance.

Able operates eight manufacturing plants around the country. Six of these facilities were the result of Able's active diversification program. Able has concentrated on acquiring small specialty manufacturers with good technical capabilities and industrial customers concentrated in its particular region of the country. In the last five years Able's sales have increased about 30 percent annually. Roughly half of this growth could be attributed to acquisitions made during this period.

Able's interest in the Whitley Company is based on the potential for integration of Whitley's equipment into some of Able's systems. Able has a concept of a line of automated continuous process systems that would significantly improve on existing systems. The new system would use advanced electronic controls and measurement devices (on which Able has done considerable research). It would also require heavy mechanical drives, drive couplings and gears, all of high quality, which Whitley could provide. Able's management is very excited about the potential merger leading to a complete new generation of continuous-flow systems. Because of its emphasis on proprietary, custom-engineered processes, Able believes the combination of its advanced electronic and electrical know-how with Whitley's quality mechanical components would allow it to leapfrog the competition.

After acquisition, Whitley would be merged with Able's existing organization. As a hierarchically structured organization, Able believes in strong central direction by top management. Al Whitley would be made an executive vice-president of Able with positions on two of Able's top-management committees. Whitley's plants would continue to operate under their present managers but these managers would report to the vice-president of manufacturing operations for Able. A number of Whitley's top engineers would be assigned to the corporate R&D staff at Able's headquarters in Oakland, California. They would be responsible for assisting in the development of the new continuous-process system. Other top officers of the Whitley Company would be absorbed into the Able organization, although not all of their duties could be clearly defined in advance.

Able employs around 3,000 employees, of whom 1,800 are production and maintenance workers. These employees are unionized and during a forty-five-day strike last year they kept four of Able's plants closed down. They were ultimately successful in negotiating a substantial pay raise with new fringe benefits in the areas of pensions, medical assistance, and insurance benefits. Employees' salaries are now roughly 25 percent above those of the Whitley Company before consideration of incentive and bonus payments under Whitley's compensation system.

ABLE'S TERMS

Able proposed to offer Whitley's stockholders .41 shares of Able's common stock for each share of Whitley common stock; plus $1,000 of a new issue of convertible debentures, paying 9.5 percent interest, for every 100 Whitley shares. Each $1,000 debenture would be convertible into ten shares of common stock of Able. See Exhibit 5 and 6 for details on Able's financial position.

EXHIBIT 5
ABLE ELECTRICAL COMPANY
(000s omitted)

	Preceding year	Preceding year	Preceding year	Preceding year	Current year
Net sales	$93,790	$121,000	$159,300	$210,500	$272,160
Net income after taxes	5,400	6,150	8,906	11,400	$ 13,608
Per common share:					
Net income	3.38	3.51	4.69	5.43	$ 5.67
Dividends	.85	.90	.90	.95	.95
Stock price	22–47	36–53	42–59	47–61	$ 51–71 [a]
Number of common shares	1,600	1,750	1,900	2,100	2,400

[a] Present stock price is $68.

EXHIBIT 6
ABLE ELECTRICAL COMPANY BALANCE SHEET
(000s omitted)

	Current year
Cash and marketable securities	$ 1,025
Accounts receivable	61,475
Inventories	96,500
Total current assets	$159,000
Net property, plant and equipment	87,600
Other assets	6,700
Total assets	$253,300
Current liabilities	$110,000
Deferred liabilities	10,000
Long-term debt	82,000
$2.75 convertible preferred stock (1,000 shares outstanding)	1,000
Common stock (2,400,000 shares outstanding)	7,200
Capital surplus	11,100
Retained earnings	32,000
Total liabilities and equity	$253,300

The Whitley Company's Reaction

It has been several weeks since Sedgely Automation and Able Electrical Company have made known their interest in acquiring Whitley. Al Whitley has so far deferred a decision in order to evaluate both offers adequately and to sound out other shareholders and family members. Eleven family shareholders have significant common stock holdings in the Whitley Company. Al Whitley is the largest single shareholder with 150,000 shares; another 45,000 shares each are owned by two brothers, Ralph and Jason Whitley. In total, 59 percent of the company is closely held. Most of these shares were acquired many years ago at prices considerably below the current market value. In considering the tax impact of a cash offer, Al Whitley has estimated that capital gains taxes would average between $8 to $10 per share.

In discussing the merits of the competing proposals with his senior managers, Al Whitley came away with mixed emotions and conflicting arguments. One part of management seemed impressed with Able's demonstrated ability to manage a diversified company. They were excited by the prospect of working jointly to develop a new engineered continuous-process system.

Also, they were impressed with the Able people they had met. They had talked very knowledgeably about financial and accounting techniques of acquisition, which all seemed esoteric to Whitley's management.

On the other hand, some of Whitley's managers were in favor of Sedgely Automation precisely because its image was more like their own. It was growing, but not explosively and not by acquiring other companies. The people managing Sedgely seemed to know where they wanted to go and had a thorough plan for growth for the next five years. Although not as exciting a company as Able, Sedgely also enjoyed a good reputation in its field.

Ultimately it was Al Whitley's decision. He was confident he could convince the majority shareholders to go along with his recommendation, as well as keep the trust of his managers and employees. In the end he would weigh all the arguments and decide which of the two offers came closest to satisfying the needs of Whitley's various interest groups.

Assignment

1. If you were Al Whitley, which offer would you choose? Develop separately (*a*) the financial aspects and (*b*) the nonfinancial aspects of each proposal.

DEVELOPMENT OF BUSINESS PLANS

Recreational Equipment, Inc.*

The Problem

Recreational Equipment, Inc. (R.E.I.) is a supplier of recreational supplies and services through a cooperative membership form of organization. Although the business has shown a steady growth in membership since its organization in 1938, it has recently been unable to maintain its position relative to such major competitors as Eddie Bauer and L. L. Bean. This erosion in competitive standing is due to several operational problems. Significant among these are the lack of an information system necessary to provide the marketing and financial data for effective decision making. R.E.I. is also facing a period of decreasing employee morale and extensive internal adjustments.

In order to address its problems, R.E.I. feels it imperative to formalize the planning of operations. A first priority is the establishment of a framework for controlling and monitoring progress toward the established objectives within a business plan. By reviewing and modifying the components of the plan, the company can set its priorities and implement action in a controlled sequence.

The first cut of a formal business plan will be reviewed and modified to conform to the actual results of 1977. After review and modification, R.E.I. expects that the plan will formally be reviewed and adopted by the Board. Implementation is expected to have begun by February of 1978.

R.E.I.'s History

The R.E.I. story began in the 1930's when climbing hardware was not available in this country. A few close friends decided to pool their resources

---

* This case is based on a consulting engagement supervised by Harvey Braun, partner of management services for the international CPA firm of Touche Ross & Co. Permission to use granted by R.E.I. and Touche Ross & Co.

and purchase mountaineering equipment directly from Europe. Soon the demand from other Pacific Northwest climbers created such a large volume that it became apparent that a better business organization had to be established.

The first meeting of Recreational Equipment Cooperative was held on June 23, 1938, and on July 21, by-laws were adopted and a Board of Trustees was formed which elected Lloyd Anderson, General Manager and Treasurer.

At first the Co-op used shelf space in a grocery store, later in a gas station, and offered six items in its first mimeographed price list. In May of 1944, arrangements were made for a small space in an office on the second floor at 523 Pike Street in downtown Seattle. This location was to become the Co-op's first store. The first printed catalogue was published in 1948 and offered over 200 items.

Members who had moved out of the Seattle area continued to buy from the Co-op and by 1953 the amount of business through the mail had grown to such an extent that a mail order department had to be established at the downtown store. Increased retail store business had necessitated several expansion remodelings and the hiring of the first full-time help in 1954.

Jim Whittaker, the present General Manager of Recreational Equipment, Inc., who joined the staff in 1955, was appointed Equipment Coordinator for the American Mt. Everest Expedition in 1961. R.E.I. was the major outfitter for this expedition and Co-op equipment proven on the slopes of Mt. Everest put Jim on the summit on May 1, 1963.

Some years before, the Co-op had printed its first ski catalogue, making it a truly year-round outdoor sports equipment center. Since then, the steadily increasing ski business has made R.E.I. one of the nation's largest ski dealers. 1968 marked the beginning of R.E.I.'s manufacturing of its own products by the acquisition of THAW. In 1975, 1976, and 1977, additional retail stores were opened in Berkeley (California), Portland (Oregon), and Carson (Los Angeles, California) to serve areas with high membership concentrations. 1977 marked another big change when corporate headquarters and the distribution center moved to a 115,370 square foot facility in the Seattle suburb of Tukwila.

Over the years Co-op sales have shown a steady growth. Membership has increased from the original 23 in 1938 to 2,000 in 1948, 12,000 in 1958, 80,000 in 1968 and to an amazing 660,000 in 1977. The original price list of six items has grown to two annual catalogues.

Despite rising costs, the Co-op has consistently tried to give its customers the best possible merchandise at the lowest prices and has never failed to pay its members a dividend. R.E.I. continues to offer the finest selection of camping, skiing and mountaineering equipment and its stores are staffed with experts in all areas of outdoor recreation.

Management Philosophy

BROAD

It is the desire of R.E.I. to provide the quality and range of services and products that will result in sales sufficient to provide Co-op member dividends, support growth and expansion, and to provide both extremely competitive compensation and a healthy working environment for our employees.

DETAILED

R.E.I. will provide products and services only for those activities which are primarily individual and noncompetitive in nature. The emphasis will be on muscle-powered activities which are nonmotorized and which involve the enjoyment of the outdoors in its natural state.

R.E.I. will carry the best quality products available with prices set as low as possible. The payment of yearly dividends will be a continuing aim of the business. Prime consideration will be given to safety as a factor in design and construction of merchandise or in planning services. Since R.E.I.'s genesis was as a climber's equipment supplier, this historic connection with mountains remains central to R.E.I.'s operations.

The manufacturing of merchandise will not be R.E.I.'s primary function. R.E.I. will manufacture products when quality and assortments are thus augmented, or when substantial savings to members result, or when the product is otherwise unavailable.

Membership in R.E.I. will remain open to all. Facilities will be expanded only when such action will better serve the needs of the existing membership.

Organizational Structure

R.E.I. is committed to the cooperative organizational form as the best means for providing goods and services to its members consistent with its organizational objectives. The needs of individual workers of R.E.I. are of paramount consideration in the evaluation of the continuing relationship between the individual and R.E.I. In recognition of this, R.E.I. will attempt to provide every employee the opportunity to demonstrate his or her skills and abilities. To further this objective the company will internalize growth opportunities and promote those employees demonstrating the skills and abilities required for advancement whenever possible. Exhibit 1 provides the current organization chart for R.E.I.

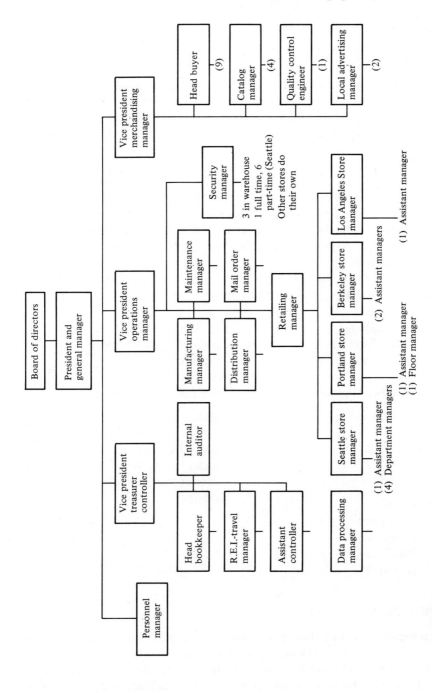

EXHIBIT 1
CURRENT ORGANIZATION

The Market

COMPETITION

Two of the major competitors for R.E.I. are L. L. Bean and Eddie Bauer. These two firms have significantly increased their market positions during the last two years. L. L. Bean has expanded by aggressively broadening its lines and a soft goods catalogue campaign, and Bauer has expanded through increased retail outlets.

R.E.I. recognizes that these rapid expansions have shifted its position in the market. It acknowledges that it must become more aggressive to maintain market position. R.E.I. intends to do this through increased catalogue mailings and the opening of additional retail outlets at the rate of at least one each year from 1979 through 1982. R.E.I. also intends to analyze in more depth the responsiveness of members and customers to its greater competitive efforts.

R.E.I. has identified the following as its competitors and will attempt to monitor its product and price mix against theirs:

Alpine Designs	Loe Alpine Systems
Sierra Designs	Co-op Wilderness Supply
Eastern Mountain Sports	Trail Tech
Ski Hut	Altra, Inc.
Houlibar Mountain	Snow Lion
Northface	Alpine Products
Camp 7	Hine Snowbridge
Class 5	Parker Distributors
Gerry	Gander Mountain
Eddie Bauer	Norm Thompson (soft goods)
Frostline	Herters
L. L. Bean	
Camptrails	
Pacific Ascent	
Jans Sport	

CUSTOMERS

In recognition of the short-term nature of demand during the last three years, and the apparent changing of the national and regional demographic profiles, R.E.I. acknowledges the need for a more detailed evaluation of members' and customers' demands. In order to anticipate changing demand patterns and product mix requirements, it will, therefore, formalize and isolate demand analysis requirements. It must also anticipate when and how the results of the planned analysis will be computed and how the data will be applied in order to be of use.

As an illustration, within the company's retail expansion plans, the following factors are recognized as being of significant weight in the evaluation of additional store sites:

Site Criteria

1. Transportation
2. Labor supply
3. Room for expansion
4. Community attitude
5. Opportunity for combining or exploiting existing distribution systems
6. Nearness to supply
7. Local suppliers
8. Adequacy of transportation facilities and cost
9. Pleasant living conditions
10. Nearness to market
11. Membership density
12. Universities and higher education facilities
13. Opportunity for effective advertising
14. Topography of site
15. Power supply
16. Ability to retain present management personnel
17. Area labor-management relations
18. Fuel cost
19. Labor rates
20. Tax structure
21. Schools (elementary and high)
22. Availability of skilled and experienced management personnel
23. Competition
24. Community property offers
25. Communications
26. Climate
27. Favorable experience of similar retailers
28. Property costs
29. Local government and taxation policies

INDUSTRY AND MARKETPLACE CONDITIONS

R.E.I. expects that 1978 will be a good year. Economic predictions for 1978 indicate real economic growth of 4.5% for the national economy. The company anticipates that its dollar sales will increase at least 15%. It also anticipates that inflation will account for between 6.3 and 7.0% of this growth. Because of this, R.E.I. expects real growth in dollar sales of at least 8%.

In 1978 the primary demand emphasis is expected to be in softwear and clothing as the short-term demands resulting from recreational camping declines. Casual recreational wear (clothing and foot) should be major movers. Increased rainfall in the West may result in some increase in wilderness recreation activities but no quantum jump is anticipated for camping hardware. The focus of the market analysis will, therefore, concentrate in the softwear lines while attempting to maintain controlled growth in the recreational hardware.

The Planning Process: Procedures and Assumptions

I. Corporate level (president and department/division managers)

    A. Each department or division head should review the present five-year objectives of the company and submit to the President:

        1. Suggestions for improving or modifying these objectives.

        2. Specific objectives the company should achieve during the next 12 months.

    B. Using the above information and input from the corporate auditor, the President will modify the five-year objectives as appropriate and develop the specific objectives he believes the company should achieve during the next year.

II. Business level (department/division)

    A. Each department and division manager will develop the specific objectives that he feels must be achieved in his department to enable the company to meet the objectives as modified by the President for the coming year.

    B. This can be best achieved by:

        1. Listing the things he wants to accomplish during the year.

        2. Listing the major problems he would like to overcome.

        3. Listing the opportunities he would like to exploit.

        4. Taking each of the items on these lists and phrasing it as an objective. (Adequate definition of an objective is the first step toward attaining it.)

        5. Evaluating each of these objectives in light of their practicability, importance to stated corporate objectives, and contribution to profit.

6. Listing the objectives in the order of his priorities.

7. Determining which ones can and should be accomplished during the planning timeframes.

C. The manager and President will then review the resulting list of objectives, and determine which will receive corporate priorities.

III. Business level (department/division)

A. Each department and division manager will then take one objective at a time and list the things that must be done to accomplish it. That is, he will:

1. List all practical alternatives.

2. Choose the best approach.

3. Arrange this approach in a logical sequence of steps to be followed.

B. The manager will next outline how each of these steps will be accomplished.

C. The manager will determine the resource requirements necessary to carry out each objective. He will:

1. Set up a planning worksheet for each objective.

2. List each step on the worksheet and determine to the best of his ability:
   a. Personnel, financial, equipment, material, facility, policy and procedural requirements.
   b. Assignment of responsibility.
   c. Target dates.

D. The manager will determine the coordination with other departments necessary to carry out his plan. This will require him to:

1. Review the planning steps for each objective and list the information or action needed from other departments to insure successful achievement.

2. List the information that other departments will have to receive from his group to keep well informed.

E. The manager will discuss the information and assistance he needs from other departments with each manager concerned, outlining his specific requirements and fully explaining the reasons for them.

F. The manager will modify his objectives and plans to take into account the needs of other departments.

    G. Finally, he will submit his detail plans to the President for approval.

IV. Corporate level (president)

    A. The President will review, reconcile, consolidate, and approve the plans of the department and division managers.

    B. He will incorporate all these plans into the long-range business plan and use this as a control measure and as an input concerning individual managers' progress.

    C. He will hold a meeting at which each division head will present his portion of the business plan.

Key Strengths and Areas for Evaluation

ORGANIZATIONAL

Strengths

Organization staffed by enthusiasts who use the products

Employees are committed to the organization and its "guiding philosophy"

Management's motivation for change is internalized

Organization is receptive to change for improvement

Areas to be addressed

Significant lack of non-R.E.I. retail experience at bottom and middle management levels

Definitive marketing plans

Definitive growth plans

Organizational training programs

CONTROLLER'S DIVISION

Strengths

Employee attitudes

Familiarity with current task assignments

Functional DP systems (memberships, dividends, mail order and warehouse inventories)

Areas to be addressed

Cash flow planning

System's ability to provide cost of goods sold

Ability to identify shrinkage

Functional merchandising purchase order and inventory control systems

Financial operations procedures manual

Vertical growth potential in division employee base (learning curve and educational prerequisites)

Long-range planning

Ability to identify product contribution

MERCHANDISING DIVISION

Strengths

Commitment to philosophy

Employee attitude

Areas to be addressed

Buyer training program

Marketing plan and associated analytical data

Control of product line

Means of measuring product line contribution

Long-range planning

OPERATIONS DIVISION

Strengths

Management attention to detail and willingness to address operational problems

Employee attitude

Organized for potential growth within current physical plants

Attention to the detail and requirements necessary for planning

Areas to be addressed

Accessibility to retail locations

Manufacturing production scheduling and control capabilities

Standard retail operating procedures

Balance concerning R.E.I. production demands

Retail inventory control and ability to identify sales and shrinkage by item

Retail training program

Long-range planning

Corporate Overview and Operational Objectives

BOARD OF DIRECTORS

Formalize the role of the Board of Directors as monitoring the progress of R.E.I. in the achievement of established goals and objectives and adherence to established policies. Develop Seattle financial community representation on Board (4 members by 1980). Reduce Board of Directors meetings to once each quarter. Hold committee meetings not more frequently than once each month. Formalize role of relationships between R.E.I. and subsidiaries.

BUSINESS PLAN

Develop five-year business plan by end of the first quarter 1978. Obtain approval of Board of Directors for business plan. Implement plan and monitor progress toward stated objectives.

OPERATIONAL OBJECTIVES

1. To increase dollar sales by not less than a 15% annual compounded growth rate.
2. To return a Co-op member dividend of approximately 10% per year.
3. To maintain a return on investment of greater than the industry average of 25% for the planning period.
4. To define operational information requirements and develop the financial and merchandising systems necessary to provide the data to assist in the management decision-making processes.
5. To train merchandising and retail store employees in order to increase job knowledge and productivity and to provide the retail sales employees with the skills that should result in increased dollar sales per employee.

Assignment

1. Assume you are the consultant in charge of evaluating R.E.I.'s approach to formal planning. Evaluate and critique the procedures and assumptions used by R.E.I.

Strategic Management the Monsanto Way*

It has become increasingly obvious that few companies can continue to provide goods and services in the same way as in the past, and remain economically viable. New government regulation of products and product usage, competitive serving of identical market needs, and increased competition from new companies make it clear that we must focus more attention on factors formerly regarded as extraneous to our job of managing the organization.

We must pay more attention to socio-political trends or suffer costly surprises. A well-directed study of underlying trends might make us recognize that many of the events which have surprised us in the past — and seemed to be discontinuities — might well have been anticipated. More importantly, concerned businesses can influence such trends if they are recognized, and their possible consequences anticipated.

Whether or not business can substantially influence such trends, however, it must accord them explicit treatment in planning. Business has had to internalize so many externalities in recent years, that it is clear management must think in terms of positioning businesses in the total environment — competitive, economic, and socio-political. Such positioning is the real essence of business strategy and the continuing determination and re-determination of such a position is strategic planning.

Strategic planning requires information on matters both internal and external to the business. Positions that cannot be supported by the resources of the organization — or that will not be allowed by society, or business competitors — are not valid. Furthermore, strategic plans must be supported by sound operational plans, and the coordinated and focused efforts of individual members of the organization to succeed.

---

* From the article by Ralph L. Neubert, Director of Strategic Planning, Monsanto Company, in *Planning Review,* January 1980. Reprinted by permission.

In short, strategic planning has to be an integral part of the management system. We in Monsanto have moved toward development of a management system incorporating explicit business strategies as guidance for major resource allocation decisions and operational plans, as well as for performance goals for individual members of the organization.

First, some background. Exhibit 1 is a simplified diagram outlining the function of management in strategy formulation and implementation. It shows that proper implementation of business strategies requires both optimum operational effectiveness and a continuing strategy review used for new strategy or improved implementation, as appropriate. That is to say, business strategy development — as well as its implementation — is a continuous, iterative process.

Exhibit 2 shows the system as part of a larger, diversified organization, with the role of corporate, or central, management added to the schema. This is a general system applicable to almost any decentralized corporation.

The two-headed arrows in the diagram demonstrate that optimizing the corporate portfolio is dependent on optimal individual business strategy and a major determinant of strategy. This mutual dependence also applies to the corporate role of adding new businesses. The bottom line is that both optimal operational effectiveness in individual businesses and optimal corporate portfolio management are necessary to maximize long-term corporate performance.

With this general schematic as background, we can more closely examine the Monsanto system for integrating strategic planning into business management.

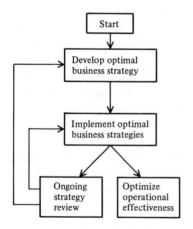

EXHIBIT 1
STRATEGIC MANAGEMENT

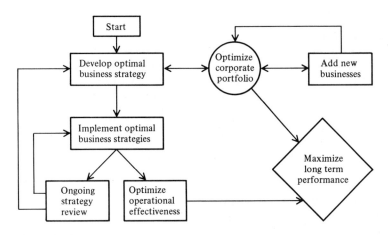

EXHIBIT 2
STRATEGIC MANAGEMENT IN A DECENTRALIZED CORPORATION

For many years, we in Monsanto tried to think about our businesses in terms of the present on one hand, and the future on the other. Our long-range plans were not accorded very high credibility; however, they were the sole expression of the future of individual businesses made explicit and recorded. You didn't have to be in the organization very long before you recognized that management devoted primary attention to the on-line aspects of business — the management of present business — and delegated formulation of so-called long-range plans to subordinate staffs. Once a year, we manfully faced the onerous task of preparing our five-year plan. We went about this task as expeditiously as possible so that we could get this silly planning out of the way and get back to the more important task of running the business.

Perhaps most important, as we ran the business, we made little if any distinction between operational, organizational, and strategic decisions. We directed about the same degree of analysis and attention to all three.

Several attempts were made to put a strategic plan together at the corporate level, but these proved to be little more than intellectual exercises and failed to gain support of Monsanto management. There was no conspicuous commitment to these plans by top management. At lower organizational levels, the plans were perceived as too esoteric and general to provide guidance for divisional or product-group management.

Considering this history of planning in Monsanto, it seemed important to stress two fundamental concepts necessary for an effective, functional planning and management system (see Exhibit 3). These seem quite

EXHIBIT 3
FUNDAMENTAL CONCEPTS

Long-range planning cannot be viewed as a distinct, separate management function. That is, current management of a business cannot be separated from the management of its future — what we do today clearly influences what we *may* do tomorrow.

We can distinguish between directional (strategic) and operational decisions in the management of a business — even if not perfectly.

---

straight-forward — almost trite — today and were, I believe, sufficiently self-evident to win early acceptance for our efforts.

We coupled these two concepts in our presentations because we felt it essential to offer a different, practical system for categorizing decisions other than by time. We especially wanted management to recognize the difference between directional (strategic) and operational decisions, a difference important to the management of any business and not just a large decentralized organization, such as Monsanto. (The successful entrepreneur in a small business makes this distinction, possibly subconsciously. It is only a professional manager whose personal commitment to the long term success of the business may be limited who can be comfortable in allowing this distinction to blur.)

The explicit basis of the Monsanto system is shown in Exhibit 4. Experienced business managers know quite well that there is not a *clear* line of demarcation between directional and operational management. We cannot sort things into two nice, neat cubbyholes and achieve a clean division of labor among managements. Even if it were possible, such a sorting would be inappropriate. Corporate management, bearing the ultimate responsibility for the conduct of business, will pragmatically delegate different degrees of management freedom to subordinate managers in accord with many business variables, including that of the specific managers in place at the time. The basis of our system is not a formula and cannot be treated as such. It must

EXHIBIT 4
BASIS OF MONSANTO SYSTEM

Distinguish between directional and operational decisions to permit:

Centrally controlled directional (strategic) management

Fully decentralized operational management

---

be clearly recognized and respected as a general guideline, however, if our style of management is to function effectively, with corporate and operating management working as a team.

Before going into the functioning of the Monsanto system, let us review some points — some philosophy, if you will — necessary to its success.

Planning is a part of the management process. Effective management systems must strongly discourage attempts to treat planning for the future as a separate exercise from management of the present business.

There are different general types of decisions in management. Russel Ackoff's categorization is as good as any. He distinguishes between strategic, tactical, and organizational decisions. In any event, there is a logical division of labor among managements of a large corporation predicated on differences in the types of decisions being made.

Central directional decision-making can encourage decentralized operational decision-making. This is not done easily, but it is practical. With such a division of labor, however, it is necessary to ensure a coordinated effort in total management.

Coordination of directional and operational decision-making is essential. This may seem like circular logic, but making the distinction creates the need to assure coordination.

When we thought in terms of positioning Monsanto's various businesses relative to our customers, competitors, and society as a whole, we recognized that organizational units developed to administer our businesses were not particularly appropriate for the purpose of strategic management. We coined the name "Strategic Planning Unit" to help emphasize departure from the structure of organizational units — the basis for all earlier planning systems — and to show the focus of the new system would be on strategy.

In our system, a strategic planning unit is a unit of the corporation for which a discrete strategy can be written. It is also a unit that warrants visibility at the corporate level, due to the level of sales, potential profit, complex nature, or other similar reasons. Some of our strategic planning units cover single products; others handle an entire division.

We do not attempt to structure our strategic planning units for permanency. We believe that changes in either business environment or internal developments can — sometimes must — cause us to change our strategic planning unit structure to avoid problems caused by a structure differing from that actually used for management of our businesses.

Compared to some better known systems, our strategic planning units are more similar to the strategy centers described by A. D. Little than they are to General Electric's strategic business units, but they clearly differ from either of these.

We believe that considerable effort must be directed toward development of appropriate structures for strategy units. The structure and array of these units must be recognized as key elements of corporate strategy — not merely organizational decisions. We have found, incidentally, that Monsanto can be meaningfully described by about 50 strategic planning units.

The development of concept and design of a "Business Direction Paper" was the real key to establishing our new system and the initial strategic planning unit structure defined the units for which business direction papers would be required.

A business direction paper at Monsanto (Exhibit 5) is a brief, two to four page statement prepared by operating management responsible for the specific strategic planning unit. Preparation and presentation of the document provides a clear opportunity for unit management to contribute knowledge and expertise to the directional decision process for the unit. This contribution is important in terms of both the validity of decision and the commitment to its implementation. The paper provides a summary of the unit's strategy.

Note in Exhibit 5 the emphasis on positioning. Our intent is to have the document represent a candid perspective of unit operating management with much heavier external orientation than that contained in earlier Monsanto business plans. Unit management reviews the paper with corporate management to establish a true corporate consensus on the points addressed. Not surprisingly, initial reviews of business direction papers require a focus on point one, the current position of the business. We encourage this since it really is difficult to achieve agreement on where you're going, until you're pretty well agreed on where you are.

The preparation of these documents is not easy; to provide the needed information in a maximum of four pages requires personal effort by the top person in the management of that particular unit.

EXHIBIT 5
BUSINESS DIRECTION PAPER CONTENT

Our position in this business today.

Position we might realistically expect to achieve in the future.

General course of action recommended to achieve this future position.

Indices appropriate for measurement of this business and our progress.

It is important that unit management — faced with the prospect of preparing another new document or another review for corporate management — fully understand the need for the effort. It is, of course, essential that the Chief Executive Officer makes it clear he fully supports the new initiative, but it is also important that the preparers understand the potential value of the new effort in functional terms, particularly with respect to its impact on their jobs. In our case, we sold the idea of a business direction paper by emphasizing its function:

> From the point of view of corporate management, the business direction paper better ensures that delegated management of particular activities is consistent with corporate policy and makes optimum use of corporate resources for enhancement of shareholders' equity.

> From the perspective of operating management, corporate consensus on the directional management of the business ensures timely, favorable action by corporate management on requests for resources needed to manage the unit in accord with agreed business strategy.

Stated candidly, operating managements were persuaded that the business direction paper — and the approval process — would give them clearer license to run the business and minimize corporate involvement in operational decisions.

I have dwelt on the role of the business direction paper because it is the principal tool we use for designating strategic decisions for units and for achieving integration of strategic planning into our management system. We have made the business direction papers the cornerstone on which to build our system of strategic management.

Review of the business direction paper with the CEO allows operating management to explain the positioning of each unit in the socio-political, economic and competitive environment in which it operates. Candid exchanges with the CEO and his advisors at these reviews develop a genuine corporate consensus on the business direction for the unit. The perceptions of top corporate management concerning the environment in which each unit operates, and the trends in those environments, are important to these reviews. Serious differences in perceptions or optimum corporate portfolio considerations can make substantial revisions necessary before submitted papers are approved.

The CEO's approval of a business direction paper constitutes creation of a standing order for the management of the strategic planning unit. This remains in effect unless — and until — a revision is proposed and approved. Approval indicates that the paper is consistent with the strategic goals of the corporation.

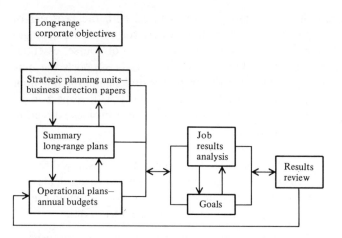

EXHIBIT 6
MONSANTO'S PLANNING/MANAGEMENT SYSTEM

Exhibit 6 is a comprehensive schematic of the Monsanto Planning/ Management System. Note in Exhibit 6 the placement of the business direction paper, which we have described as being the cornerstone of our system. Note also all of the familiar words: Corporate Objectives, Long-Range Plans, Budgets, Goals, and so forth.

It may be helpful to analyze the illustration piece by piece, beginning with the business decision paper (Exhibit 7). The dotted line through the box and the indication of "corporate" and "operating" management indicates that this is the document on which a consensus between the two groups is achieved. It is the interface between directional and operational management for each strategic planning unit.

Exhibit 8 shows the relationship between long-range corporate objectives and business direction papers. Many companies do not have explicit corporate objectives; among those who do, there is a great deal of variance in the degree of definition. Monsanto has had explicit corporate objectives for only a few years. As a matter of fact, in our old corporate management guide there was a tab titled, "Corporate Objectives," followed by a page with only the four words: "To be issued later."

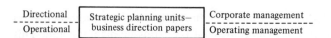

EXHIBIT 7
DIRECTIONAL/OPERATIONAL INTERFACE

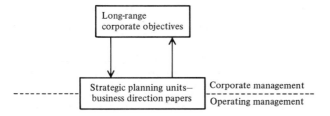

EXHIBIT 8
OBJECTIVES/DIRECTIONS RELATIONSHIP

Almost all organizations have objectives, but in many cases, they are not made fully explicit. Our concept of a management system requires that these objectives be recognized as corporate strategy, and be made fully explicit, to provide broad, general guidance for strategic, organizational, and operational decision-making throughout the corporation. We think corporate management has an obligation to state these objectives and to make changes to them when change is appropriate.

Meaningful organizational objectives can only be achieved through negotiating a consensus of influential participants in the organization. This may be a time-consuming, often frustrating chore even with the whole-hearted support of the chief executive officer.

We chose to structure our major corporate objectives under three umbrella statements, shown in Exhibit 9. There are a number of more specific statements under each of the three umbrellas, but none is specific to only one of Monsanto's businesses. The full set of corporate objectives is contained in a small, pocket-sized book distributed to approximately 15,000

Shareowner objective
We will manage Monsanto to optimize shareowner values through consistently superior long-term performance in growth of earnings per share and return on equity.

Social responsibility objective
We will conduct our business at all times in an ethical, lawful, and socially responsible manner.

Employee relations objective
We will provide a climate in which our employees can realize their full potential, and in which employment with Monsanto can be a rewarding experience for the individual as well as for the company.

EXHIBIT 9
MONSANTO CORPORATE OBJECTIVES

management people worldwide. The objectives are also displayed in our board room to provide a constant reminder of the basic corporate strategy they express.

Planning staffs assist line management in meeting all objectives and certain other staff departments provide key support for line management in specific objectives. For the first, the controller and financial organization; for the second, a social responsibility committee, environmental policy staff, and public affairs staff; and, for the third, the personnel department staff.

Moving away from the corporate end of the management system, Exhibit 10 shows an additional item in the area of operations. Summary long-range plans are issued annually to reflect up-to-date estimates by operating management or the costs and consequences of implementing the approved business direction paper — of carrying out their standing orders. Summary long-range plans are prepared for corporate management and informally reviewed with them to ensure maximum awareness of operational decisions and actions taken or soon required to move in the approved business direction.

Issuance and review of summary long-range plans provide an opportunity for annual reinforcement of the business strategy consensus established by the business direction paper. The procedure may, of course, provide cause for changes in business direction papers — but most changes of these papers do not originate from this annual exercise.

Exhibit 11 shows the position of operational plans and annual budgets in the planning/management system. There are a variety of operational plans — including long- and short-range marketing, product, function, production, and R & D plans — which may be appropriate for a strategic planning unit. Operational plans should exist to the extent needed for proper conduct of the business by the current managers in place. There is no rigid

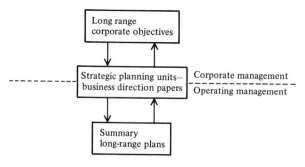

EXHIBIT 10
SUMMARY PLANS ADDED TO SCHEMA

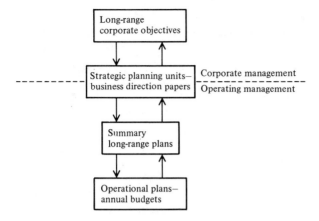

EXHIBIT 11
BUDGET RELATIONSHIP TO SCHEMA

corporate requirement in this regard, but we have encouraged explicit tactical planning by our six principal operating companies, and each now has its own system for this.

Profit budgets, on the other hand, are prepared in a specified format. Since they are the annual plans for income results and resource allocation, they are necessary for control of the business. They are, however, more than just an instrument of control. Budgets are recognized as part of the total planning management system and as shorter term expressions of the resource allocation necessary to achieve approved business positionings.

Use of the budget as a key document in the planning/management system requires that it be expressed in accord with the strategic planning unit array in addition to fitting the organization of profit centers. This expression of the budget helps achieve better recognition of the integration needed between directional and operational plans. More importantly, regrouping permits the focus of resources on business strategy implementation, as well as on achievement of the year's profit budget.

In a purely mechanical sense, the integration between budgets and summary long-range plans is accomplished by making the budget numbers one of the columns in the statistical presentation of the summary long-range plan for each unit.

Our management by results program coordinates individual, personal commitments with the plans of the organization as shown in Exhibit 6. A job results analysis (JRA) is prepared annually for approximately 15,000 employees, ranging from the Chief Executive Officer to plant foreman. (The word "results" is one which some might translate into "goals," but there are important differences between the two at Monsanto. Results are the expression of longer term achievements expected, while goals are shorter term and frequently are milestones toward the accomplishment of results.)

The interaction between "JRA" and "Goals" is obvious. Goals are generally established for a small number — maybe five or six — of the results described in the job result analysis. The selection of results and the goals attendant to them is clearly key to the implementation of plans for the unit. Individual employees and their unit managers must establish those results most critical for success of the business and agree on realistic goals.

Results reviews are conducted quarterly, and adjustment of goals is permitted if there are significant unanticipated changes in internal or external premises. The reviews provide feedback to both goals statements and operational plans — and through these plans to the next issue of the summary long-range plan for the unit. Results achieved or events of sufficient significance might, of course, be reflected in a revised business direction paper before the next annual issue of summary long-range plans.

We feel that an effective, functioning system for management by results — or by objectives, if you prefer — is essential to the management of the significantly differentiated individual business strategies appropriate for a corporation such as Monsanto.

Goals for individuals — as well as operational plans, business direction papers, and long-range corporate objectives — must be kept up-to-date at all times. Each must be revised as soon as revision is desirable to improve performance; they are "on-line" documents and, as such, differ significantly from annual summary long-range plans and budgets. To draw an analogy, summary long-range plans and budgets are snapshots, while "on-line" management of the business is a motion picture.

There are many sub-elements of the Monsanto management system not discussed here. Many of these relate to the organizational dynamics of the corporation and include the important relationships among line and staff groups. Some concern allocation of resources between the strategic planning units or business development activities, such as product research and development, new ventures, and acquisitions. The important thing about these other elements is that they are all tied into the basic framework described. All are part of the fabric of the planning management system described in this article.

Like any living system, the management system at Monsanto develops and evolves on a constant basis. This development must be closely controlled to ensure that the basic concepts of the system are not compromised, and that we do not build in excessive constraints. It is easy to over-institutionalize a system of management — to build form without substance and to generate more and more paperwork — but such developments would defeat the advantage inherent in the simple and uncomplicated logic, structure, and function of the system.

My experience with the irresistible growth of bureaucracies leads me to believe that there is a 50-50 chance we can stretch the life-cycle of this system to 10 or 15 years before considering a new start — and creating a new system to correct aberrations that have slipped into this one. By then, new management tools and techniques will have been perfected, a new generation of managers will be in the saddle, and perhaps a different style of strategic planning and management will be appropriate.

Questions and Assignments

1. Identify the major parts of Monsanto's process.

2. Contrast Monsanto's approach to the traditional annual planning cycle described in Chapter 12. In what respects does it differ? In what respects is it similar?

Norton's Top-Down, Bottom-Up Planning Process*

Eight years ago when I examined the corporate planning process at the Norton Company, I had one major complaint — the wrong people were doing the job. Possibly no one else sees the same problem, but ever since then, I have asked managers in other companies how their planning is organized and how it operates. At this point, I must conclude there are some very well-known companies that have ineffective systems, for the same reason that I felt ours was ineffective then.

So, what is my message? My message is simply this — in three parts:

A corporate planning process of some kind is essential to any and all businesses;

Top management cannot delegate the corporate planning process;

Managers of the individual business units in the corporate portfolio should have incentives appropriate to their specific task.

With reasonable assurance that everyone agrees a planning process is essential, I will move to the second part of my triad and describe how we maintain at the Norton Company the kind of top management involvement I consider essential to an effective, ongoing process.

Three Key Questions

Even though the organizational structure required to get the job done will vary with the size and complexity of the business, in every case, top line and staff managers must be personally involved in developing corporate strate-

---

* From the article by Robert Cushman, Chairman of the Board and Chief Executive Officer of the Norton Company, in *Planning Review,* November 1979. Reprinted by permission.

gies and plans. They cannot delegate to a group of individuals in a department called Corporate Planning because they cannot delegate answering three key questions:

Where and what are we now?

Where do we go and what do we want to become?

How can we best get there?

In addition, they cannot or should not delegate the second and ongoing job of determining the character and content of the corporation's portfolio of business investments.

There's a fairly obvious reason for this. The degree of success in the execution of a corporate strategic plan will be in direct proportion to the degree of dedication to it. Dedication to it depends on the degree of involvement in its creation. This means planners cannot go around talking to division managers and staff departments like R&D, product planning and sales, then put their own corporate plan ideas down in big, black, well-tabbed binders and make a major presentation to senior management. Corporate planners must insist that they work with top management — not for it — in this vital function.

Prior to World War II, there were relatively few large diversified companies. General Electric was an exception. Single or limited line companies were and still are headed by individuals who grew up with their products, understood the manufacturing, and knew the marketplace. In fact, I believe America's greatest companies succeeded because one man or a small group of individuals with strong convictions made things happen. They had vision and used intuition in varying degrees — and they did their own planning. It would not have occurred to them to delegate to anyone else the task of planning the future direction of their company.

Today, in the larger diversified organizations, it is obviously necessary to delegate to others many vital functions. But overall corporate strategic thinking always should involve top management. It is, in fact, up to the chief executive officer (CEO) to involve the board of directors to the extent that they agree and are committed to the company's plans and objectives.

The same is true of each division or strategic business unit (SBU). The division's manager and its top management must be involved in developing divisional strategic plans and objectives.

The total planning process involves many activities that I will not describe. I will not cover our annual financial planning cycle, our material or human resource planning, our acquisition and merger activities or our research and internal development process.

I will describe what I consider to be the heart of our total process — the portfolio management concept. It is by working with various portfolio charts such as growth/market share matrices that we answer these key questions:

What are we now?

What are we trying to become?

Can and how will we get there? (i.e., strategically not tactically)

The portfolio management concept is based on the fact that every business is really made up of many businesses when properly dissected into discrete product/market segments. To understand the competitive position of an individual unit, one needs to know its position in its industry's life cycle, its rate of growth and its market share as related to that growth (Exhibit 1). Then, using the Experience Curve Theory together with an evaluation of future trends and available resources, one can predict a particular unit's likely financial return (Exhibit 2).

Each SBU at Norton is responsible for developing its own overall strategy and the various segments within it.

Monitoring Committee

Six and a half years ago, we formed a top management committee whose function is to continuously assess the company's various businesses, to de-

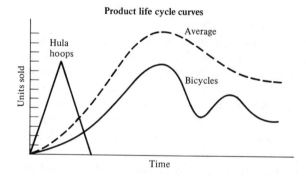

EXHIBIT 1
PRODUCT LIFE CYCLE CURVES

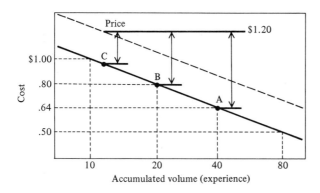

EXHIBIT 2
EXPERIENCE CURVE

velop and monitor the company's portfolio, and to consider possible goals and objectives.

At the moment the committee is composed of the chairman and CEO, the president and chief operating officer, the executive vice president of finance, the corporate controller, the corporate development vice president, and ten key operating officers.

Each SBU is asked to prepare a detailed strategy for each major segment of its operations and come before the committee, normally every 24 months. This is required for two reasons. Management wants to ascertain the viability of the unit's strategies unto themselves, but also to be certain they are still in harmony with overall corporate objectives and strategy.

The meetings open with a review of the corporate portfolio and the position of the SBU to be discussed within it.

Exhibit 3 shows the strategic business units classified by market share strategy on the left, and by the organizational groups in the three columns labeled Abrasive Operations, Diversified Products, and Christensen. Note that an SBU may be a particular business in a country, region, or worldwide or it may be our operations in a particular country. In the strategy reviews, SBUs are always analyzed in further detail by whatever segmentation is appropriate.

The chart in Exhibit 4 illustrates how Norton ranks SBU's by Return on Net Assets — or RONA — showing clearly the relative position of the business being reviewed. Similar rankings are used for Return on Sales and Asset Turnover.

EXHIBIT 3
NORTON COMPANY PORTFOLIO BROKEN OUT BY SBUs
(Figures = 1977 sales — $ million)

Market share strategy	Total sales $ million	Abrasive operations	Sales	Diversified products	Sales	Christensen	Sales
Build	xxx	Country A Business a Business b	xxx xxx xxx	Country H — Bus. r Region J — Bus. r — Bus. s — Bus. t — Bus. u	xxx xxx xxx xxx xxx	Business w Business x	xxx xxx
Build/maintain	xxx	Business c Country B — Bus. d Country C Region D — Bus. d	xxx xxx xxx xxx				
Maintain	xxx	Region D — Bus. g Country H — Bus. g Region D — Bus. h Country H — Bus. h	xxx xxx xxx	Country H — Bus. v Business W	xxx xxx	Business Region D — Bus. aa Country H — Bus. aa	xxx xxx
Maintain/harvest	xxx	Business p Business g	xxx xxx	Region D — Bus. v	xxx		
Harvest							
Total	$848		xxx		xxx		xxx

Norton Company portfolio
ranking by RONA (Return on Net Assets)

		Average 1966-1977	1976	1977
1. Business	a	xx%	xx%	xx%
2.	b			
3.	c			
4.	d			
5.	e			
6.	f			
7.	g			
8.	h			
24.	x	xx	xx	xx
Norton average (Operations)				
25.	y	xx	xx	xx
26.	z			
27.	aa			
28.	bb			
29.	cc			
30.	dd			
40.	hh	xx	xx	xx

EXHIBIT 4
NORTON RONA RANKINGS

Exhibit 5 shows how the company compares the recent actual RONA for each unit to its long-range RONA objective, while Exhibit 6 shows a ranking of the "PAR" * RONA results indicated by the PIMS Model for each unit.

In Exhibit 7, we show the company portfolio on a "Balloon Chart" or "Growth — Market Share Matrix." On this matrix, the vertical axis is the market growth rate in real terms, while the horizontal axis is relative market share. The balloon (or circle) sizes are proportional to sales, and the balloons are coded by market share strategy. (The information on this chart has been disguised somewhat, but the actual Norton portfolio has a similar appearance.)

---

* The PIMS (Profit Impact of Marketing Strategies) Model is developed and operated by The Strategic Planning Institute, Cambridge, MA, using information from member companies. "PAR" RONA is the expected return on net assets indicated by the model for the particular business given the characteristics of its market, competition, technology, and cost structure.

Norton Company portfolio
RONA comparison: 1981-83 objectives vs. 1977 actual

		Actual 1977	Objective 1981-83	Objective higher/ (lower)
1. Business	a	xx%	xx%	xx%
2.	b			
3.	c			
4.	d			
5.	e			
22.	v	xx	xx	xx

Norton average (Operations)

23.	w	xx	xx	xx
40.	hh	xx	xx	xx

EXHIBIT 5
RONA COMPARISON TO 1980–81 OBJECTIVES

Norton Company portfolio
ranking by PIMS "PAR" RONA — Regular model

		PIMS "PAR" RONA 1974-76 average after tax
1. Business	a	xx%
2.	b	
3.	c	
4.	d	
5.	e	
20.	t	xx
PIMS average (All companies)		11%
21.	u	xx
40.	jj	xx

EXHIBIT 6
NORTON "PAR" RONA RANKINGS

Norton Company portfolio
Balloon areas proportional to sales

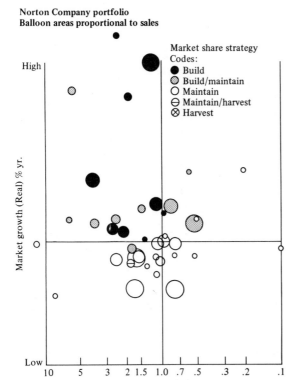

EXHIBIT 7
COMPARISON OF RELATIVE MARKET SHARES

Exhibit 8 is an example of a particular business in a region showing the breakdown of this business by market.

The balloon chart (Exhibit 9) shows the same business segmented by country.

The chart in Exhibit 10 illustrates our test of cash generation versus market share strategy. The matrix includes cash generation in the vertical direction and market share strategy in the horizontal direction. The shaded-coding indicates which locations in the matrix are either acceptable, unacceptable, or questionable. Past and expected future locations of businesses and appropriate segments are plotted as shown by the examples (a) and (b). Note that example (b) has been in an unacceptable location but is expected to move to an acceptable location.

Norton Company

Test: cash generation
vs.
market share strategy

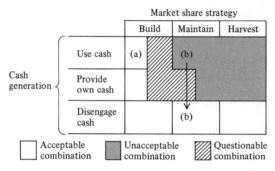

Market share strategy

		Build	Maintain	Harvest
Cash generation	Use cash	(a)	(b)	
	Provide own cash			
	Disengage cash		(b)	

☐ Acceptable combination   ■ Unacceptable combination   ▨ Questionable combination

Funds generated/(consumed) - average/yr.

Business	Market share strategy	Actual last 5 Yrs. $000	% to N.A.	Expected next 5 Yrs. $000	% to N.A.
(a)	Build	(200)	(8)%	(100)	(2)%
(b)	Maintain	(150)	(5)%	200	5 %

EXHIBIT 8
BUSINESS IDENTIFIED BY MARKET

Exhibit 11 is a test of sales growth rate versus market growth rate versus market share strategy. Let's look at example (c) — the third column of figures.

The market share strategy is M or Maintain (Line B2). The expected market growth rate including inflation is eight percent annually (Line B5) — three percent real growth plus five percent inflation.

Our expected sales growth is 12 percent annually (Line B6) — significantly higher than the market growth rate. Therefore, the expected sales growth rate is not consistent with the market share strategy (Line B8).

Top-Down, Bottom-Up Orientation

Each of these charts may produce a great deal of useful discussion, and questions such as:

What are the contributions of that unit in the overall scheme of things?

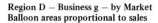

Region D — Business g — by Market
Balloon areas proportional to sales

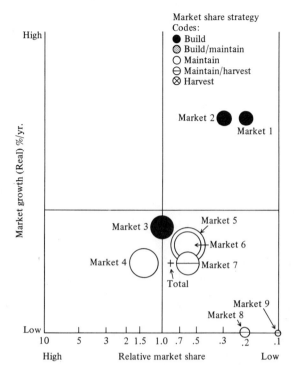

**EXHIBIT 9
BUSINESS IDENTIFIED BY COUNTRY**

Does it help balance or add stability to the total?

Does it increase or decrease the cyclical nature of our abrasive business?

To what extent does it relate to other Norton technologies, processes or distribution?

Does it hurt or improve our image in the investment community?

Since committee members receive all material in advance of the meeting, there is no formal presentation. Discussion, and probing questions start immediately and normally follow a pattern which includes:

Facts as presented, trends and assumptions;

Region D – Business g – by Country
Balloon areas proportional to sales

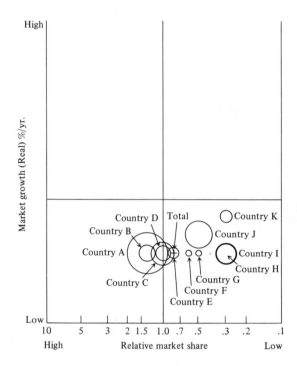

EXHIBIT 10
CASH GENERATION VS. MARKET SHARE TEST

The mission and mode of operation in terms of build, maintain, or harvest;

Current appropriateness of strategy;

Reasons for changes since last review;

An analysis of the PIMS data obtained from the Strategic Planning Institute, which provides a feel for what each unit should expect in profitability compared to similar businesses, what results might be expected from certain strategic changes, and a number of other "what if" questions;

Relationship to other Norton businesses; and

Fit with corporate portfolio.

Norton Company.

Test: sales growth rate vs. market growth rate
vs. market share strategy

	Percent Per Year Businesses		
	(a)	(b)	(c)
A. Last 4 Years			
1. Sales Growth	15%	7%	10%
B. Next 5 Years			
2. Market Share Strategy	B	M	M
3. Real Market Growth	10%	3%	3%
4. Price Increase Rate	6%	5%	5%
5. Market Growth Incl. Inflation (3 & 4)	16%	8%	8%
6. Expected Sales Growth	20%	7%	12%
7. Growth: Partic. Incr./ (Decr.) (6-5)	4%	(1)%	4%
8. Participation Change (7) Consistent with Market Share Strategy (2)? (Yes, No, or ?)	Yes	Yes	No

EXHIBIT 11
SALES GROWTH VS. MARKET GROWTH TEST

While there are a large number of separate strategic and sub-strategic business units, they are currently grouped to enable the committee to reveiw about 40. We meet about 25 times per year for two to five hours per session. An SBU which has a problem may ask or be asked to meet more frequently. The committee may also meet to discuss an acquisition candidate. It meets annually to update our ongoing five-year financial model, a major progress check on our planning. When appropriate, it meets to review a collection of broad corporate strategy statements which are communicated to our employees in several different ways.

While this committee is obviously very powerful, it takes no votes as such, and approves neither capital expenditures nor budgets. In no way does it replace the company's executive committee.

In fact, it has no chairman. The job of moderator or facilitator is always assigned to a committee member whose own responsibilities do not include the business unit being discussed.

The committee is a sounding board, a diverse top management group that probes, critiques, and advises in matters relating to the company's portfolio of businesses and its future. But its most important function is to keep senior managers focused on corporate direction rather than just on areas of personal accountability. It provides the top-down direction necessary for effective management, while maintaining bottom-up involvement.

Management's commitment to the process indicates its importance to all. And because managing a portfolio is dynamic, it is a never ending involvement.

Finally, Appropriate Incentives

We all realize that managing and maintaining a healthy cash business is quite different from managing a high growth star — and that managing a high growth business in an emerging new industry is yet another job. So, we look for individuals suited to each task.

Whatever the business, though, it is important that each manager and his subordinates be challenged and made to realize that each assignment is vital to improving the total corporate portfolio.

To make that challenge credible we have developed over 50 different incentive plans, tailor-made to match each specific situation. It is not a difficult task. Once the basic formula is established, different goals and objectives are weighted differently. For example, gaining market share, and extensive investments in research may be more important than current profit margins in a high growth industry. But good asset management, such as low inventory to sales ratios, low manufacturing costs, and high productivity are more important to maintaining the cash generator. So, our managers' incomes are related directly to specific results.

I said before I was sure we could agree on the importance of a strategic planning process. I believe that without top management's continuing involvement in the process, it is unlikely to be effective. In backing up my belief, I have described how one medium-to-large sized company insures the necessary involvement among a broad range of people.

There are undoubtedly other methods of managing a multiproduct, multinational business; blind obedience to any one theory is dangerous. But the portfolio management technique has been found to be useful at the Norton Company as a way

To manage

To control an increasingly diversified company

To assure that capital appropriations are not considered in isolation but in comparison with the needs of other units

To assure working toward a balance of cash generation and growth opportunities

To highlight divestment of units when appropriate.

We do not consider our planning to be nearly as sophisticated as those in operation at companies like General Electric and Texas Instruments. While it is constantly becoming more sophisticated, it is probably appropriate to a company of our size and complexity at this time.

We feel there are benefits to keeping such functions simple, because we can be sure a maximum number of employees understand the process and feel involved in what the company is now and what it is trying to become.

Questions and Assignments

1. List the different types of techniques used by Norton in evaluating its various businesses. How was each used by Norton? How does each complement or support the other?

2. Cushman did not attempt to cover other aspects of Norton's total approach, like "our annual financial cycle, our material or human resource plan, our acquisition and merger activities and internal development process." How would these other processes fit in with the "heart" of Norton's total process?

Index to Authors and Companies

Index to Subjects